EDUCATION IN ANCIENT ROME

From the elder Cato to the younger Pliny

Fig. 1 *A Roman boy, with papyrus roll and book box.*

EDUCATION IN ANCIENT ROME

From the elder Cato to the
younger Pliny

STANLEY F. BONNER

Methuen & Co Ltd

First published in 1977 by Methuen & Co Ltd
11 New Fetter Lane, London EC4P 4EE

© 1977 Stanley F. Bonner

Photoset in English Times by Red Lion Setters, Holborn, London
Printed in Great Britain at the
University Printing House, Cambridge

ISBN (hardback) 0 416 79710 5
ISBN (paperback) 0 416 85710 8

Contents

List of illustrations

Note: The diagram of an abacus on p. 184 based on a miniature abacus once preserved at Augsburg, of which Markus Welser's illustration (1682) is reproduced in Alfred Nagl's authoritative study, 'Die Rechentafel der Alten', p. 17. It represents a type, of which very similar examples exist in Paris and Rome. See further c. xiii, notes 107 and 109.

Acknowledgements

The author and publishers would like to thank the following for permission to reproduce the illustrations which appear in this book:

Berlin Staatsmuseen for nos. 10 and 16.
British Broadcasting Corporation (with thanks to Mr Robert Erskine) and National Trust for no. 1
British Library for nos. 20, 21, 22 and 23
Trustees of the British Museum for nos. 5, 14 and 15
Cairo Museum for no. 4
Deutsches Archäologisches Institut, Rome, for nos. 7 and 8
Foto Aldo Reale for nos. 24 and 25
Institut francais d'Archéologie Orientale, Cairo, for nos. 18 and 19
Musée du Louvre for nos. 2 and 13
Paul Monroe Slide Collection for no. 12
Rheinisches Landesmuseum, Trier, for no. 9

Preface

I hope that the present book, by bringing the picture of Roman education into a clearer light, may show that this is not merely a subject of antiquarian or specialised academic interest, but one which has in several ways a continuing relevance far beyond ancient Rome, and is not without significance today. It is concerned with human relationships, with perseverance amid difficulties, with the home as well as the school, and with those changes in society which affect both home and school. The very word 'education' sprang originally from the Roman home, for the Latin *educatio* referred not to schooling and intellectual progress but to the physical rearing of the child and his or her training in behaviour. A person who was *bene educatus* was not necessarily one who was 'well-educated' in our sense — he would be termed *eruditus* — but one who was 'well brought up'. It would be true to say that the best Roman parents and teachers were as much concerned about character and conduct as they were about the acquisition of culture. But as social standards gradually deteriorated the effects were felt in home and school alike.

As to intellectual training, it has often been observed that the Romans, rather unenterprisingly, were content to model their basic curriculum and their teaching methods as closely as possible on those of the Greeks. Yet, as both Greeks and Romans were teaching at each stage in Rome, it could also be claimed that this gave a certain cohesion to the course. Primary teaching, even if in parts somewhat painfully thorough, was basically sound and often produced good results. At the ensuing stages, as both languages continued to be taught together, Virgil took his place alongside Homer and Cicero beside Demosthenes; so the young student had the best of both worlds before him. We may indeed regret that, although facilities for a wider education were available and were by no means neglected, the standard school curriculum in our period should have become so strictly confined to 'grammar' (that is, grammar and literature) and rhetoric, the art of public speaking. Even so, the value of these subjects continued to be accepted for centuries after Roman times, and formed two of the three components of the mediaeval Trivium. The treatment of them remained remarkably consistent down the ages, and still made its influence felt in the schools of Elizabethan days and long afterwards.

The evidence on which the book is based has been drawn wherever possible, and in the vast majority of instances, from the period under review, and especially from Quintilian. But sometimes, where the writers of my period offered only a shadowy outline, I have thought it reasonable, in view of the constancy of ancient educational tradition, to develop the details by a limited use of later evidence, and thus to restore the picture. The work itself is the result of many years of thought and preparation, and I trust that it will be found to contain not merely a synthesis of what was already known but also original contributions which may be of service to future scholars in further extending the frontiers of knowledge.

My particular thanks are extended to Emeritus Professor Eric Laughton, until recently Professor of Latin at the University of Sheffield, who not only read the whole of the text but discussed it personally with me, and made valuable suggestions for amendments and improvements which I was happy to accept. I was also gratified that Emeritus Professor David Daube, formerly Regius Professor of Civil Law in the University of Oxford, and now of the University of California School of Law, readily consented to read my concluding chapter and again, as in an earlier book, gave me the benefit of his expert knowledge. My warmest thanks are again due to him for his helpful advice.

As regards the acquisition of suitable illustrations for the book, I would like to record my appreciation of the assistance of those who, both at home and abroad, have answered my inquiries and supplied my needs. In particular, the Director of the British School at Rome, Dr. David Whitehouse, together with Professor A.D. Trendall and Mr. Frank Sear, went to considerable trouble in helping me to secure photographs which I was finding it hard to obtain. I am also indebted to the Research Committee of the University of Liverpool for a grant towards the cost of illustrative material.

Stanley F. Bonner
University of Liverpool

PART ONE

The Historical Background

CHAPTER I

Early Roman upbringing

In seeking to form some impression of what Roman family life was like and how children were brought up in the days before the second Punic War, it is best to look first at the Sabines, the near neighbours of the Romans, with whom they then had much in common. Both were agricultural communities, and historically they were closely connected. There is good reason to believe that from the regal period onwards, despite intermittent border warfare, there was a continuing Sabine element in the Roman population.[1] But after their final defeat by M.' Curius Dentatus in 290 B.C. much of their homeland was parcelled out in small farming plots, and many from Rome itself and the surrounding districts went to live and work in the Sabine country, following the same way of life and developing the same characteristics.[2] Here, in the hilly terrain north-east of Rome towards the Apennines, they found conditions in many places much harder than in Latium, and, according to the early annalist Fabius Pictor, it was only when the Romans conquered the Sabines that they began to realize how prosperous they were themselves.[3]

In one of his celebrated 'national' odes, Horace expressed his belief that this environment, and the toil therein involved, helped to create qualities of character which were often deplorably lacking in his own time.[4] Extolling those who had vanquished Pyrrhus, Hannibal and Antiochus, the most formidable enemies of Rome, he describes their early life in picturesque lines, which recall the Sabine country known to him so well. They were, he says, 'farmer-soldiers' sturdy sons, trained to turn the soil with Sabine mattock, and to carry in the hewn logs at a strict mother's command, when the sun was shifting the shadows on the mountain sides and bringing the weary oxen relief from the yoke'. At first sight, this scene — a worthy subject for a landscape-painter — may seem to be simply a poet's romantic idealization of the past, and it was indeed a favourite rhetorical commonplace to lavish praise on 'the men from the plough' (*illi ab aratro*), who had left their small farms to serve, and sometimes to save, the State, and had then returned to the land.[5] Such had been Cincinnatus, such was Curius Dentatus, who, after celebrating a triumph over Pyrrhus, was content to return to his Sabine farm of seven *iugera* (about four and a half acres), though a grateful Senate offered him fifty.[6] Posterity made something of a legend of the poverty and integrity of national heroes such as Curius and his contemporary Caius Fabricius, and it was easy and natural in a later age of growing extravagance and moral decline to represent the old agricultural life as the mother of all the virtues.[7] But Horace's picture is demonstrably close to recorded fact. No better illustration of the passage could be found than the early labours and subsequent career of Marcus Cato, the censor. Born in 234 B.C., he had inherited from his ancestors the small estate in the Sabine country where, in his own words, he 'spent all the period of youth in a thrifty, rough, laborious life, cultivating the land, turning up the rocks and stones of the Sabine soil, and planting the seed'.[8] This he continued to do until the age of seventeen, when he first saw military service in the Hannibalic War. He distinguished himself at the battle of the Metaurus in 207, and in later life still bore the scars of wounds he had received.[9] What is more, after his consulship, he showed remarkable resource and initiative in Greece, reconnoitring the enemy position one moonless night on the heights above Thermopylae; and he claimed that he had contributed in no small measure to the ensuing victory over Antiochus.[10] This was in 191 B.C., but after that date the Romans began to engage in further expansion abroad. Through foreign conquests and foreign trade they brought in the wealth which gradually transformed their way of life and made possible for many the enjoyment of leisure and urban luxury. The Sabines, however, (who in 268 B.C. had been granted full Roman citizenship) were not so affected by change, and retained for centuries their original characteristics, as many later writers testify.

From the nature of their lives and environment, the Sabines had always been a hardy, self-disciplined people; 'austere', 'dour', 'rigorous' are some of the epithets which Roman writers constantly applied to them.[11] A good illustration of Sabine upbringing is the early experience of Marcus Terentius Varro, who was born at Reate in 116 B.C. and lived to be nearly ninety. He tells how, as a lad, he had but a single toga and tunic, sandals, but no leg-coverings, no saddle for his horse, and rarely the pleasure of a proper bath.[12] The morality of the Sabines was also widely admired, and was almost proverbial. Cicero called them 'excellent people', and Livy said that no race had been more free from contaminating influences.[13] The Sabine women were respected for their fidelity and trustworthiness, long after moral laxity had become prevalent at Rome.[14] But the agricultural writer Columella makes no distinction when he refers to 'the ancient practice of the Sabine and Roman mistresses of the household' in earlier days.[15] In both communities, the husband and wife shared their responsibilities as partners, the man looking after his interests out of doors, the woman taking charge of the home. 'The utmost respect', he says, 'was paid to the matrons, as a result of harmony combined with diligence; the woman was stirred by a laudable desire to emulate her husband, and was zealous to increase and improve his substance by her prudence', for 'both worked together to the common advantage'.[16] The strictness with which children were brought up was much the same, whether Sabine or Roman. Horace makes it clear that the Sabine mother expected her sons to obey her behests without question, and, if we wish to see the old family discipline at its sternest, we may recall the example of one of the most famous Roman patriarchs, whose ancestors had, in fact, originally come from the Sabine land.[17] Here is Cicero's description of Appius Claudius Caecus, the builder of the Appian Way, in his closing years: 'He kept control over his five sturdy sons, his four daughters, all that great household and all those dependants, though he was both old and blind; for he did not idly succumb to old age, but kept his mind as taut as a well-strung bow. He wielded not merely authority, but absolute command (*imperium*) over his family; his slaves feared him, his children venerated him, all loved him; in that household ancestral custom and discipline held sway.'[18]

The question does arise, nevertheless, whether the ordinary Roman paterfamilias, even in the third century B.C., was quite so rigorous a disciplinarian as old Appius Claudius Caecus, or whether, as one might naturally expect, there were at all times varieties of individual temperament. In this connection, it is important to draw a distinction between the power of coercion and punishment which the father could, when he deemed necessary, exercise over his dependants, with the full sanction of the law (*patria potestas*), and the extent to which he actually exercised — or, indeed, needed to exercise — that power in the ordinary course of daily life. The rights of the father, as regards treatment of his children, had been accepted in practice even before they were enshrined in the Twelve Tables; they remained unparalleled throughout antiquity, and the jurist Gaius could still write: 'The power which we have over our children is peculiar to Roman citizens and is found in no other nation.'[19] The father could not only expose a child at birth; he could repudiate an erring son and dismiss him to servile labour, or order him to be flogged, or imprisoned, or even put to death,[20] and all these things did, on occasion, happen. Viewed in itself, the picture does, indeed, seem extremely dark and forbidding, but it does not accurately represent the normal Roman character. In the first place, the examples of drastic punishment (nearly all in Republican times) mostly stem from some grave misdemeanour, such as flagrant disobedience to the express order of a father holding command in war,[21] or a revolutionary attempt to seize political power, or a plot against the life of the father himself,[22] or some other act calculated to bring the family name into disgrace.[23]

Secondly, in normal circumstances the erring son was not condemned without trial; but it was a family trial in a 'domestic court', [24] where the father himself became a judge, whose decision (though he might risk the displeasure of the censors)[25] was final. Thirdly, and most important, there was the force of public opinion to be considered, and public opinion grew increasingly hostile to excessive severity.[26] Even the early Romans were not an inhuman people, and not insensitive to the claims of natural affection. The passage of time had a mellowing effect, and although some of the Greeks considered the whole system of paternal power tyrannous, the historian Dionysius was much impressed by it, and praised its dignity and effectiveness as contrasted with the mild and lax attitude of his own countrymen.[27] It was probably the Greeks who, by their questioning and arguments, did most to raise doubts as to the extent to which the legal powers of the father should reasonably be allowed to operate in practice, and we shall later see that this was one of the most popular types of debate in the Roman schools of declamation. [28] But the general effect of paternal authority throughout the Republican period was not that it exercised a cruelly repressive influence in daily life, but that it created an atmosphere in which the children grew up with a deep respect for their parents, and, until the decline set in, took it for granted, and without resentment, that they should do as they were told. Even under the Empire, the philosopher Seneca declared that nothing could be more laudable than that a son should be able to say: 'I obeyed my parents, I deferred to their authority, whether it was fairly or unfairly and harshly exercised; I showed myself compliant and submissive, and in one thing only was I stubborn, in not allowing myself to be surpassed by them in kindness done.'[29] This was of the very essence of Roman *pietas*, and truly reflects the spirit of the sons and daughters of the old Republic.

This attitude of respect for parental authority found its counterpart in the deference which was shown generally to older people in early Roman society. This may best be illustrated by putting together a few scattered observations made by later writers whose primary interest was antiquarian, or whose context suggests that they were not merely praising the past. For instance, it was accepted as a natural token of respect to rise and offer one's seat at the arrival of an older person, or, generally, to yield place to him.[30] Younger men regarded it as a privilege to escort their elders to the Senate House, where they would wait at the doors and then accompany them home.[31] At festal gatherings, preliminary inquiry was made as to who the guests were likely to be, in order that the younger might not take their places before their seniors; and there was reluctance to leave before the elders had risen.[32] If a party of three should be walking along the street, the oldest man would be given the middle place in the group; if there were two only, the younger man would take the outer, more exposed position.[33] Children noticed these things, and put them into practice themselves.[34] But the important point was that the elders merited these attentions not only in view of their position or experience, but by reason of their own conduct; serious in outlook, dignified in manner, and sensitive to any breach of decorum, they were conscious of the importance of their personal example. They benefited from a wider extension of parental respect, in that older citizens were regarded as the common parents of the community.[35]

There was also a certain orderliness about Roman family life, which resulted partly from their inherent national character, and partly from the conditions imposed by their agricultural work. There was nothing haphazard about the farmer's life. As Virgil well knew, he constantly needed to plan ahead, and there were many tasks which had to be done at their proper season. Surviving rustic calendars, inscribed on stone, give the details for each month.[36] So long as peace prevailed, the Roman family remained united, devoting its energies to the common task. As the busy months came and went, practical parents found that a few extra pairs of hands were not to be despised, and so the older boys helped on the land, whilst their sisters helped in the home. The girls learnt to spin and weave, for the mistress of the household made the clothing for the family herself, and did not, as yet, delegate the duty to a farm-bailiff's wife. Wool-making was an activity in which the womenfolk took great pride, as many a Roman epitaph shows,[37] and so symbolized devotion to the home that, in the Roman marriage ceremony, a spindle and distaff were carried by the bride.[38] It was in this domestic art that, even in the sophisticated days of the early Empire, Augustus had his daughter and grand-daughters trained.[39] So too Varro, who likewise valued the old domestic traditions, urged that every young girl should be taught embroidery.[40] Meanwhile, although the girls, too, in some areas, helped in tending the flocks,[41] the boys spent most of their time out of doors, much of it in preparing the soil and attending to the animals and the crops. At harvest-time, they shared the labours of father and kinsfolk, and with them enjoyed the hilarities of harvest-home.[42] After that, they took part in the grape-harvesting, an occasion to which they doubtless (like young Marcus Aurelius) looked forward most of all.[43]

When, in the late afternoon or early evening, the family assembled for the main meal of the day, the children sometimes had their own tables, placed near the couches on which their elders reclined, or sat at the foot of the lowest couch.[44] Conditions were anything but luxurious, their couches being plain, with roughly-carved rustic headpieces, and their tableware, like their household goods, of common earthenware. Nor was the accommodation lavish; even in the second century B.C., there were sixteen members of the Aelian family living under a single roof.[45] After the preliminary course, it was the boys and girls who made the formal

offering to the gods whose images were set near the hearth, and only
when they reported them propitious did the meal proceed;[46] and in
early days the children themselves served at table.[47] By comparison
with the sumptuous banquets of later times, when imported delicacies
abounded and armies of gastronomic experts ministered to fastidious
palates, the early Roman fare must have been simple indeed. But even
plain-living country folk would doubtless, like Horace's friend Ofellus,
have produced a more respectable repast for birthdays, or festival days,
or for the visits of their friends.[48] Not only at meals, but at all times,
these early Romans were generally believed to have been, like Cato,
particularly careful of what they said and did in the presence of their
children.[49] This was not so much a matter of policy as of natural
instinct, which the Romans called *verecundia*, an inherent sense of
propriety. It was a fast-disappearing virtue in the days when Juvenal had
to urge that 'the greatest reverence is due to a child'.[50] Finally, even in
a rather stern and rigorous society, the spontaneous affection of children
for their parents must have been much as Lucretius and Virgil described
it,[51] and the lives of the young ones were, as always, brightened by
their toys, their games, and their pets.[52]

But the peaceful pursuit of agriculture and the orderly life of the
household had always been liable to sudden interruption when the entire
community was thrown into consternation by the report of an enemy
attack, or dismayed by the news that their men must leave for a war with
neighbouring tribes, or further afield. It was with this likelihood in mind
that boys were trained by their elders in activities which developed their
fighting powers, their physical skill and agility. Horsemanship, hunting,
archery, javelin-throwing, swimming, boxing and racing are the forms of
exercise which Virgil attributes to the youths of legendary times.[53]
When they came of age for military service, there was the more
professional training of the camp, and, even then, much was to be
learned in the hard school of experience in the field. But their discipline
stood them in good stead, and it is not surprising that Sallust, noting how
often a small band of Romans had routed larger enemy forces and
stormed fortified towns, remarked with pride: 'To men such as these, no
toil was unfamiliar, no position rough or difficult, no armed foe
formidable; their courage conquered all obstacles. But their greatest
competition for glory was amongst themselves; each rushed to be the first
to strike the foe, to climb the wall, to be conspicuous in action'.[54] This
passage, which is markedly rhetorical in style, might easily be dismissed
as a declamatory commonplace, heightened with patriotic praise. Yet, in
fact, writing a century earlier, Polybius, a historian not given to
rhetorical exaggeration, confirms the truth of what Sallust says.
Speaking of the incentives and rewards given to young soldiers, he shows
himself equally impressed.[55]

But the ambitions of young Romans were not confined to achieving distinction in the field; those of them who came from the select circle of leading families, which had become accustomed to the holding of public office, looked forward keenly to emulating the fame of their forefathers. It is again Polybius who speaks of the effect upon the young of the Roman practice of cherishing in their homes, and bringing forth on special public occasions, the life-like waxen images which represented the features, and briefly recorded the services, of their illustrious forbears.[56] At the funeral of a great man, he tells us, it was not only the oration, delivered by the son, in praise of the virtues and achievements of the deceased, which moved the youthful onlookers. It was also the public procession to the Forum of men who actually wore these masks, and were dressed in all the regalia which each past representative of the family had been entitled to wear. 'There could be no more ennobling spectacle', says the historian, 'for a young man who aspires to fame and virtue; for who would not be inspired by the sight of the images of men renowned for their excellence, assembled together and as if alive and breathing?' These manifestations of public pride, the oration and the procession, made young men determined 'to endure every suffering for the commonwealth'. Fabius Maximus and the great Scipio Africanus himself were only two of those who declared that the sight of such *imagines* had fired them with a determination to perform some comparable service themselves.[57] This same consciousness of the importance not only of maintaining the family honour but of adding further lustre to it is still to be seen in the details of the last of the Scipionic epitaphs at the end of the second century B.C.[58]

In a society such as that of the third century, in which concentration on agricultural pursuits was always liable to be disturbed by service in war, it is understandable that intellectual training played only a minor part, though, as we shall see, it was by no means entirely lacking. But if we now move on a little in time, we may picture a son's education, both physical and intellectual, by a father who, in the eyes of many, exemplified the best qualities of the old Roman character.

CHAPTER II

Education within the family

(I) Parents and relatives

Thanks to Plutarch's admirable biography of the elder Cato, we are enabled to obtain a series of most interesting glimpses into the training which that remarkable, if rather formidable, personality gave his son.[1] First, we see him hurrying away from the Senate House so as to be certain of being back at home when the child was bathed and put to bed; for only important public business would cause him to forego this pleasure. Then we see him teaching the child to read and write, despite the fact that he led an exceptionally active public life, and had in his house an accomplished slave, who could easily have performed this service for him. 'I do not think it fitting', Cato once remarked, 'that my son should be rebuked or have his ears pulled by a slave, if he should be slow to learn, or that he should be beholden to a slave for so important a thing as his education'. So he takes the trouble to write out, in large and extremely legible letters, stories from the early history of Rome, so that the boy may become familiar from the outset with the ancient traditions of his country. The scene changes, the boy is older, and we see them swimming in the Tiber on a gusty day or camping out together, whether in the heat of summer or in winter frost. This was part of Cato's hardening process, and with it went lessons in riding, in boxing, in throwing the javelin, and in the manipulation of weapons. Then the pair are home again, and in the evening, maybe, by the light of oil-lamps, they turn over together the basic documents of the Roman Law, certainly the Twelve Tables, and perhaps the recent Commentary of Aelius Sextus upon them, the father answering the boy's questions and giving him the benefit of his own knowledge and long experience.

Cato had acquired his own legal knowledge early in life, and had placed it freely at the disposal of other farmers in his neighbourhood, whom he would meet in the early morning in the market-places, to learn of their problems. He had thus won a reputation as an advocate, and the experience stood him in good stead when he entered public life in Rome.[2] He became quite the most litigious of his contemporaries, for he brought innumerable prosecutions, right up to the end of his life, and was frequently prosecuted by his enemies in consequence.[3] But he was the finest orator of his day, cogent in argument and trenchant and terse in style. 'Grasp your subject, the words will follow' (*rem tene, verba sequentur*) was the celebrated advice which he passed on to his son.[4] Blunt and outspoken, he could not only impress his listeners with his pithy wisdom, but also delight them with his apt comparisons and the tang of his pungent wit.[5]

So Marcus Cato, in true Roman fashion, sought to mould his son to his own image. Remarkably versatile himself (he even composed an encyclopaedia at some later date, and addressed it to 'son Marcus'),[6] he was an expert guide, as farmer, soldier, lawyer, orator and statesman.[7] But Nature does not always comply with Man's insistent demand for a replica of himself. Marcus Cato Licinianus, though he readily faced up to the rigorous course of training imposed upon him, had not his father's strength and stamina, and Cato was eventually compelled to relax somewhat for the boy the severity of his own mode of life. For the hardships of military campaigning he was not physically well fitted. Not that he lacked courage, for at least on one occasion, in his early twenties, he earned his father's commendation for his bravery in the field at the battle of Pydna.[8] But his real bent was towards the law, and here his father's teaching fell on particularly fertile ground. Young Cato became a distinguished jurist, and author of a work in fifteen books on the rules of law, which was held in esteem long after his own day.[9] Fate did not, however, grant him a long life, for he died at the age of forty in the year of his praetorship. His father lived on a little longer, and died at the ripe age of eighty-five.[10]

The education which Cato gave his son, though based on traditional Roman values, was really an education *par excellence*, for, even in the upper classes of society, a father who was in a position to give his son so much devoted and thoroughgoing attention, and was, at the same time, so admirably qualified an instructor as Cato, would have been the exception rather than the rule. Certainly, Roman historians accepted that, long before Cato's day, the father's influence was paramount; so Valerius Maximus makes an impassioned rhetorical address to the dictator of 431 B.C. on behalf of the son 'whom you had trained as a boy in letters and as a youth in arms',[11] and Livy imagines a retiring military tribune in 396 B.C. offering in his place his son, his 'effigy and likeness', a young man 'trained by my own discipline'.[12] Pliny, too, looked back to the good old Republican days when senators used to initiate their sons, after their first military service, into the methods of senatorial procedure, explaining to them what privileges a senator possessed, when he should speak and for how long, how he should distinguish between conflicting motions, how move an amendment. Herein, he remarks, 'every father was his son's instructor, or if he had no father, the oldest senator acting on his behalf'.[13] Such was the traditional ideal; but, as we shall see, circumstances could often arise which would prevent its realization in practice.

There is some contemporary evidence to show that, in substance, the kind of training which Cato gave his son must have been fairly normal in the upper classes at Rome in the early years of the second century, though it now also becomes clear that the father did not take on all the teaching himself. A scene in the *Mostellaria* of Plautus[14] (who died in 184 B.C., the year of Cato's censorship) contains allusions to upbringing and education which are markedly Roman, even though the plot of the play is derived from a Greek model. It is that in which a young man, Philolaches, soliloquizes on parental training, and ruefully recalls — being now love-stricken and dissolute — the virtues of his earlier years. Parents, he says, 'teach their children letters, law and the principles of justice' and, in order to make them an example to others, spare neither trouble nor expense — which shows that extraneous teaching assistance was also employed. Speaking of his moral and physical training, Philolaches says: 'Not one of the young men was more energetic than myself ... in thrift and toughness, I was an example to the rest', and the words which he uses (*industrior, parsimonia, duritia*) are exactly those which Cato himself used to describe his own early life. The various forms of exercise in which Philolaches says he excelled, though there are Greek elements among them, also include the riding and weapon practice in which Cato trained his son. Finally, he adds, when the time comes for the sons to depart for military service, parents appoint a kinsman to accompany them and give them the support they need; and this, as we know from other sources, was certainly an old Roman custom.[15]

In one important respect, however, even by the standards of his own lifetime, Cato's programme was deficient, for it contained no provision for the study of Greek, which he had not the least desire to encourage. But interest in the Greek language and literature was developing rapidly among the upper classes in his day, and more modern families would have wished to see it included in the education of the young. As expert tuition, by men whose native language was Greek, became more and more available, the sons of parents who were keen on a literary education pursued their studies 'at the father's behest', or 'with the father's eager encouragement', but not necessarily under his personal tuition. This was true of the son of M. Fulvius Nobilior,[16] who was the patron of Ennius, and, later, the orator Crassus, according to Cicero, recalled his father's keenness (*studium*) in promoting his boyhood education.[17] Cicero uses the same expression of his own father, but Cicero had many other teachers;[18] and whilst Atticus' father, a lover of literature, gave his son the best possible education, it included sending him to school.[19]

From other aspects, too, whilst the custom of the father teaching the son was characteristically Roman, it would be a mistake to assume, as is not infrequently done, that Cato's example may be taken as a standard pattern. In the first place, Cato Licinianus was an only child, and, even allowing for a high infant mortality rate in Roman times, such a situation must have been rather unusual. The family of the Domitii was regarded as quite exceptional because it had a succession of only sons,[20] but much more typical of the old Republic was that of the Metelli. When in 221 B.C. Caecilius Metellus pronounced the customary eulogy at his father's funeral, he listed the ten ambitions which his father had had the good fortune to fulfil, one of which was 'to leave many children'.[21] Another descendant, who won the surname of Macedonicus (consul in 143 B.C.), was likewise accounted blessed in his family of four sons, three of them ex-consuls, and three married daughters. This was the Metellus whose oration (as censor, 131 B.C.) on the subject of raising a family (*de prole augenda*) Augustus more than a century later read out approvingly to the Senate.[22] Clearly, the preoccupation of the heads of such families with the ever-increasing business of the State would not have been compatible with constant personal attention to the education of their children.

Fig. 2 *Four scenes of childhood, from a Roman sarcophagus of the time of Hadrian.*

There is a further consideration. When Cato Licinianus was born (*c.*192 B.C.), his father was already forty-two years old, and the boy's education between, say, 187 and 177 B.C. would have taken place when the father was between forty-seven and fifty-seven, and thus beyond the age of military service. In most families, of whatever class, the children would have been born long before that time of life, and the father, as they grew up, would often be absent from home for long periods, especially as the Roman dominion was extending overseas. We may take, in illustration, the example of one of Cato's own contemporaries, a centurion who had served under him, and whom he had promoted in Spain. This is how Livy makes the man speak when, in 171 B.C., in his late forties, he had served in no less than twenty-two campaigns: 'I, Spurius Ligustinus, of the Crustumine tribe, am of Sabine stock. My father left me an acre of land and a little cottage, in which I was born and brought up, and I live there to this day. When I came of age, my father gave me his niece in marriage, who brought as her dowry nothing but her free birth, her good name, and a fertility which would have graced a wealthy home. We have six sons, and two daughters, both now married. Four sons are of age, two still boys. I entered the army in the consulship of P. Sulpicius and C. Aurelius' (that is, 200 B.C.).[23] It is obvious that such a parent, with the best will in the world, could not possibly have emulated Cato's example.

Then again, since Cato took complete charge of his son's education and the standard age at which primary education was begun in antiquity was seven, it is commonly said that up to that age the child remained with the womenfolk, and that thereafter his father became his constant companion and teacher. This was not always necessarily so. Let us consider one of the most well-known and widely-quoted passages on early Roman education, from the *Dialogue on Oratory* ascribed to Tacitus.[24] There, one of the interlocutors, Messalla, giving reasons for the decline of oratory, sharply contrasts the strictness and care of parents in the upbringing of children under the Republic (which he regarded as a kind of Golden Age) with the laxity and negligence of his contemporaries. But from the very outset, it is to the mother that he gives especial praise, for 'it was her particular pride to look after her home and devote herself to her children'. He does not claim that she always did so single-handed, for she might rely on the assistance of an older kinswoman whom she could trust implicitly to keep them in order from hour to hour, whether at their work or play. Again, the picture here is not that of the education of a single child, for, in Messalla's words, 'the entire offspring of the same family' was thus brought up together. There is mention, too, of serious studies as well as games, and, though their nature is not clarified, one would suppose that they included not only reading and writing, but such favourite children's activities as drawing, painting and modelling.[25] Although the emphasis is on discipline and moral training, the mother is said to have urged them to the study of the liberal arts, and to have guided them towards the kind of career for which they seemed best adapted. It is not necessarily implied that she taught them herself, though many Roman mothers could at least have taught their children to read and write, but her interest and influence clearly extend well beyond the early years of childhood; and it is noticeable that, in this context, no specific mention is made of the father.

This, then, was a quite different pattern from that of Cato and his son, and, as we may now see, there was sometimes a particular reason for it. The interesting fact is that the three women whom Messalla here selects as examples of excellent mothers, namely, Cornelia, mother of the Gracchi, Aurelia, mother of Julius Caesar, and Atia, mother of Octavian, were all left widows with young families. Let us consider their circumstances individually. Cornelia, the daughter of the great Scipio Africanus, had married T. Sempronius Gracchus, a man some thirty years older than herself, and by him she had no less than twelve children, six boys and six girls, born alternately.[26] But Gracchus died in 153 B.C. or thereabouts, leaving her with a large family, the youngest of whom, Caius, was in his cradle. Fate dealt her a succession of further blows, for illness and death repeatedly intervened, and she was only able to rear three of her children to maturity — a girl, Sempronia, who not long after the father's death married the younger Scipio, and two boys, Tiberius (who was nine or ten when he lost his father) and Gaius. To their education she devoted herself with scrupulous care; she found the best available tutors for them, but also exercised a profound influence herself, for she was a well-educated woman, excellent in speech and conversation, and of great strength of character.[27]

Of Aurelia and Atia much less is known. Aurelia lost her husband, C. Iulius Caesar, in the Marian massacres of 87 B.C., when her son Julius was barely thirteen years of age. A strict and careful woman, she took the father's place,[28] and encouraged his studies under a good tutor.[29] Atia, who was Caesar's niece, was left a widow in 58 B.C., when Octavian and his sister were young children, though, happily for her and for them, not for long. We shall meet the family again later.[30] We know, too, of other widowed mothers who did everything possible for their sons and helped to establish them in life. The mother of Sertorius, a woman from the Sabine country, lost her husband some time after 120 B.C., when her son was young. Through her, he was enabled to take up a legal and oratorical career at Rome, until military and administrative service abroad proved a more powerful, and ultimately fatal, magnet.[31] Again, towards the middle of the first century A.D. after the senator Iulius Graecinus was put to death, his child, Agricola, was reared with the utmost care by his mother, Iulia Procilla, whom Tacitus calls 'a woman of exceptional virtue'. From their home at Forum Iulii (Fréjus), she placed him in a good school at nearby Marseilles, and continued to guide and supervise his studies throughout boyhood and youth.[32]

But it was not always the bereaved mother on whom the full responsibility fell. Other members of the family might take charge of the children, and the pattern of their early life be changed. Here we have to take examples from imperial times, and deduce that, as Roman traditions were so consistent, what happened then must, in all likelihood, have happened long before. In the first place, especially if the marriage of the parents had taken place at an early age (as it quite often did), the grandparents might be not merely alive, but still in the prime of life. It was the natural result of *patria potestas* that, when the father died, the sons still remained subject to the control of the father's father. But grandparents on either side might educate the children. When Agrippa, who was married to Augustus' daughter Julia, died in 12 B.C. leaving a very young family of five children, it was Augustus himself who taught his grandsons to read and write, to imitate his own handwriting, and also to use abbreviations (*notae*).[33] In A.D. 14, the year in which Augustus died, a little boy of five, the future emperor Vespasian, was being brought up under the care of his paternal grandmother, Tertulla, to whom he was greatly attached.[34] Sometimes, too, it was the untimely death of the mother rather than the father which caused a child to be transferred to his grandparent's care, as happened with Quintilian's younger son for the short space of his remaining life after the young mother's death.[35] Even though these examples are taken from rather exalted circles, family affections were, and are, much the same, irrespective of social status, whether the child is destined for the purple or the plough.

Grandparents, then, might play an important part; but the pattern could be different again, for very frequently, for various reasons, children were brought up and educated in the home of an uncle or aunt. The paternal uncle evidently often performed his duties, particularly as a guardian, with considerable severity of control, for the expression 'don't play the uncle with me' became proverbial.[36] But kindly affection was by no means always lacking, and sometimes children were transferred temporarily to an uncle's charge whilst the father was still alive, for reasons of family convenience. Cicero and his brother Quintus were sent to Rome as children, where they were educated together with their young cousins.[37] Much later, in 54 B.C., when Quintus was serving on Caesar's staff in Gaul, Cicero actively participated in the education of young Quintus, his nephew, as well as of his own son Marcus. But it is significant that he could only do so when at leisure away from the city, for 'in Rome, one does not have a chance to breathe'. Both boys also had tutors, but Cicero was not always satisfied, and supplemented their tuition, even going so far as to compose for Marcus the rhetorical textbook, in question and answer form, called the *Partitiones Oratoriae*.[38] A further interesting case of transference (this time through family bereavement) was that of the younger Cato (great-grandson of the Censor), who in childhood lost first his father, then his mother, and was then educated in the home of Livius Drusus, his mother's brother, together with his sister, Porcia, and two other children, Caepio and Servilia, of his mother's second marriage.[39] Another example is that of Nero and Drusus, the eldest of the children of Germanicus and Agrippina, whom Tiberius placed in their uncle's charge, to be brought up along with their cousins, after the father's death in A.D. 19, when they were aged about fourteen and twelve respectively.[40] In Pliny's circle, too, we find nephews and nieces welcomed with kindly care. Pliny himself, when his father died, was placed in the charge of his extremely learned uncle, who became his adoptive father, and of another guardian of high integrity, Verginius Rufus. Similarly, Calpurnia, who became his third wife, had lost her mother, and then her father, in childhood, and was brought up with exemplary care by her aunt, Calpurnia Hispulla, who, in Pliny's words, 'not only showed her an aunt's affection, but supplied the love of the father whom she had lost'.[41] Very different was young Nero's aunt, Lepida, for when the child's father died (he was then three years old), and his mother was driven into exile, she merely placed him in the charge of two totally unsuitable 'pedagogues'.[42] Again, to diversify the picture still further, a widowed mother might remarry, or a bereaved father take a second wife, not always with happy consequences for the children; or children might be placed with guardians.[43] Finally, already in the late Republic, we find an occasional indication of the consequences to children of divorce.[44] Examples such as these could be multiplied and diversified, so various were, and are, the vicissitudes of human relationships; but at least they serve to show that there were many exceptions to the much-emphasized pattern of 'education by the father', and 'education within the family' would be a truer description of the practice of the age.

Let us now return to the family whose life had not been disrupted by bereavement, and where the father was able to take an active part in the training of his children. An important aspect of this training — whether or not it was accompanied by more formal education — consisted in the advice given by the father to the son, known generally as 'paternal precepts' (*praecepta paterna*), on a wide range of subjects, practical, political, social and moral. A father who was himself experienced in public affairs, and who hoped that his son would follow in his footsteps, might begin to advise him at a quite early age, and would certainly do so in the years immediately preceding the youth's assumption of the toga of manhood. So Cicero, whilst urging his son Marcus to aim high, forewarned him of the pitfalls which might lie in his path; Marcus was not more than eleven years old at the time, and his father admitted that 'he is rather young as yet for such precepts'.[45] Long before Cicero's day, the younger Scipio, thanks to his father, received an excellent academic education, but said that he had learned more from such 'domestic precepts', combined with subsequent experience, than from any books which he had read.[46] The context in these instances is political, but very often the advice concerned practical subjects which the young man would need to know, and on which valuable hints could be given, usually in succinct and sententious form. The elder Cato included in the encyclopaedia composed for his son in adult life precepts on subjects as diverse as agriculture, warfare, medicine and oratory. But even in boyhood, Licinianus must have heard from his father's lips many of the precepts on farm management which are found in Cato's surviving treatise on agriculture. Closely associated with these would be exhortations to industry and thrift. Cato himself was the author of such remarks as 'by doing nothing men learn to do ill', 'buy not what you need, but what is essential; what you do not need is dear at a penny', and it was he who coined an observation closely akin to the saying 'it is better to wear out than to rust out'.[47] Horace, in an admirable sketch of the hard-headed, practical Romans of earlier times, describes how they took pleasure in 'listening to their seniors and telling their juniors how to increase their substance and avoid ruinous loss';[48] and one of the foremost precepts which Horace himself received as a boy from his father, the owner of a small farm, was that he should live frugally and not squander his inheritance.[49]

There are times when scenes in Roman Comedy depict father-son relationships very much as they must have been in real life. In the *Trinummus* of Plautus, a stern, old-fashioned father, Philto, warns his son Lysiteles not to consort with people of low character, who disgrace ancestral custom (*mores maiorum*). 'Live as I live', he says, in staccato imperatives, 'by the good old standards; what I enjoin upon you, that see that you do'. 'But, father', protests the virtuous youth, 'from my earliest days I have always been entirely subservient (*servivi servitutem!*) to your commands and precepts'.[50] Such precepts were often reinforced by drawing attention to examples of individuals whose lives were good or ill. In the *Adelphi* of Terence, Demea, a countryman with strict ideas of discipline, as yet ignorant of the misdemeanours of his son, prides himself on the efficacy of his home-training. 'In short', he observes with satisfaction, 'I tell him to look into the mirror of other people's lives, and to take from others a model for himself. "Do this", I say, "Avoid that" ... "This is praiseworthy" ... "That is reprehensible".'[51] Exactly so, when Horace was a boy, his father, being anxious that his son should preserve the way of life handed down from old times, used to point out, as they walked the city streets together, living examples of men whose qualities he should imitate, or whose vices he should avoid.[52] In the *Self-Tormentor* of Terence, Chremes reminds his son that it is in order to deter young men from loose living that fathers 'provide a scanty allowance'.[53] This, too, must have been fairly characteristic of Republican Rome. In Terence's own day, Polybius noted the Roman exactitude in money matters, and their keenness to obtain interest on their capital, and Cicero generalized later on 'the parsimony of fathers'.[54] Rarely, in real life, would a Roman have been found so completely generous and open-handed as Micio in the *Adelphi*. In this play, which is a study in two radically opposed systems of upbringing, he exemplifies the indulgent father (*lenis pater*), whilst his brother Demea is typical of the harsh parent (*durus pater*). The development of the plot shows that neither system has produced satisfactory results, and the moral presumably is that both extremes are best avoided.[55] This accorded, in fact, with the official Roman view. The only people who could interfere in any way with the freedom of Roman parents to treat their children as they pleased were the censors, and we are told that one of the powers which the censors possessed was to stigmatize those who were either excessively severe, or excessively indulgent, in the upbringing of their sons.[56]

Such were the general conditions of home-training and education in the later Republic, so far as the members of the family itself were concerned. During this period, the practical Roman training, which Cato, in the old national tradition, had encouraged, was ever more widely supplemented by instruction in the language, literature, oratory and, to some extent, philosophy of Greece. In such learning, Roman families were rarely self-sufficient, and — to introduce their children to this new and exciting world of unfailing interest — those parents who had the requisite contacts brought in tutors from far afield.

CHAPTER III

Education within the family

(II) Private tutors from distant lands

In the beginning, teachers of Greek who were introduced into Roman families came from cities of Italy in which Greek was spoken, not yet from Greece itself. One of the earliest known tutors was Livius Andronicus, who, we are told, 'was given his freedom, in recognition of his intellectual ability, by Livius Salinator, whose children he taught'.[1] There is some uncertainty as to which Livius Salinator this was, particularly as St Jerome, who gives this notice, puts the *floruit* of Andronicus as late as 187 B.C., following the dating of Accius. This dating, however, which creates many difficulties, is not generally accepted; and if the strongly attested opinion that Andronicus produced the first Latin play in 240 B.C. is true (and Atticus, Cicero and Varro all vouched for it), then his activity must have fallen in the third century rather than the second; one of the children whom he taught would most likely have been the Livius Salinator who was born *c.* 254 B.C., and was twice consul (in 219 and 207 B.C.).[2] At all events, Andronicus' origin was connected with the Greek-speaking city of Tarentum, and Suetonius describes him as 'half-Greek'.[3] But he taught in both Greek and Latin; in Greek, he was perhaps the first of a long line of tutors who read Homer with their pupils in Rome, and this teaching he supplemented with one of his own compositions in Latin, a translation of the *Odyssey* into Saturnian verse. The surviving fragments show that this was a pioneer work of little literary merit,[4] yet, remarkably, it remained a standard textbook in Roman schools right down to Horace's day, by which time it had a decidedly odd and archaic flavour.[5] In his own age, Andronicus won considerable public recognition. In 207 B.C. he was commissioned (probably not for the first time) to compose a State Hymn, and shortly afterwards the guild of writers and actors, with which he was intimately associated (for he acted in his own plays) was allowed in his honour to use as its official meeting-place the temple of Minerva on the Aventine.[6] Livius Andronicus, then, was not only a tutor but an original, if primitive, literary artist. But in 204 B.C., shortly before his death, there arrived in Rome another, far more gifted poet, who, like

Andronicus, maintained himself by acting as a tutor to Roman families, but as a creative writer far outshone his predecessor, and won lasting fame as one of the great founders of Latin literature.

Ennius, who is also described by Suetonius as 'half-Greek' because of his place of origin, was a citizen of Rudiae in Calabria, and spoke both Greek and Latin, as well as the local dialect, Oscan.[7] He served as a centurion in the second Punic War, and was brought to Rome by the elder Cato.[8] There he became well-known to leading families, and particularly to Scipio Africanus and to Marcus Fulvius Nobilior, whom he accompanied on his Aetolian expedition in 189.[9] It was the son of Fulvius who obtained the Roman citizenship for him in 184, an honour of which he was immensely proud.[10] Ennius was a man of versatile genius, but his work as a tutor must have ranked in his own esteem much lower than his literary production, which included many tragedies, based particularly on Euripides, and his historical epic in hexameters, the *Annals*. But even though his teaching in Latin was confined to readings from his own compositions, Ennius must have been an inspiring tutor for any young Roman. Despite his excessive fondness for alliteration and the heaviness of his verse, he had a splendidly sturdy vigour of expression; he had also a great reverence for Homer, whose Latin spiritual descendant he believed himself to be,[11] and a real feeling for the pathos of Euripides, as the more emotional passages of his fragmentary tragedies show.[12]

Livius Andronicus and Ennius, then, had this in common, that they were both creative writers as well as teachers; they began at Rome what had also existed at Alexandria, namely the tradition of scholar-poets engaged in both original composition and instruction of the young, a tradition which later included such conspicuous figures as Valerius Cato at the close of the Republic, and Ausonius of Bordeaux towards the end of the Empire. Yet only a minority of tutors, or of public teachers, in literature, can have risen to this level — the majority were better at interpreting what other poets had written than at writing poetry themselves. In another respect, too, Livius and Ennius must be regarded as rather exceptional among the early literary tutors, for, as they originated from Italy itself, they are likely to have been more Romanized than most. In Ennius' time, especially after the end of the Second Punic War and the ensuing conquest of Greece, such tutors came from further and further afield, from the mainland of Greece, and the islands, and from the Greek-speaking cities of Asia Minor. Although, as later examples prove, such immigrants quickly adapted themselves to their new surroundings, and sometimes became quite expert in the Latin language, it was the Greek language and literature which they were primarily engaged to teach.

Suetonius says of Livius and Ennius that they taught not only 'at

home' (*domi*) but also 'abroad' (*foris*). By this it seems most likely that
he means that they not only acted as resident tutors for a period with a
particular family, but also, from time to time, became visiting tutors to
others.[13] The nature of our information on the activities of tutors at
Rome (which must have been widespread at all periods) is such that we
usually hear only about those who were connected with, and resided
with, leading families, whereas the visiting, or peripatetic, tutor is a
much more shadowy figure. We meet examples, at a rather humble level,
in Petronius,[14] and one might deduce that the tutor depicted in a
wall painting from Herculaneum (evidently a philosopher, as he carries a
staff) was a visitor, as otherwise he would hardly have needed to bring his
portable book-box (*capsa*) with him (see Fig. 6).[15] Even as late as the
fifth century A.D., in Constantinople, at a time when teachers had long
been publicly appointed by the municipality or the State, special mention
is made of those who were 'accustomed to conduct their classes in
numerous private houses',[16] and this practice could also have been
common at Rome.

Although language and literature remained favourite studies for which
tutors were engaged, we are able to trace, within Ennius' lifetime, the
presence of teachers in other subjects too, in Rome. Ennius died in 169
B.C., and before that date two young Romans were being provided with
educational advantages which any of their contemporaries might well
have envied. They were the two sons of Aemilius Paullus (consul 182
B.C.) by his first marriage, that is, the sons who (being adopted into
different families after his divorce) became known as Fabius Maximus
Aemilianus (born *c.*186) and Scipio Aemilianus (the younger Scipio,
born *c.*185).[17] For them their father, a most ardent Philhellene, spared
no trouble and expense in acquiring a whole staff of tutors from Greece.
These included not only men whose interests were intellectual (teachers
of literature, rhetoric, and philosophy), but also those whose abilities
were artistic (modellers and painters), and those whose concern was with
field-sports (hunting-masters and trainers of horses and dogs).[18] Some
of these tutors may also have begun to instruct the two younger sons of
Aemilius by his second marriage, but they, as we shall see, did not
survive to maturity. It was perhaps partly for their benefit that, in 168
B.C., after his resounding victory over Perseus of Macedon at Pydna,
their father asked the Athenians to provide their most esteemed
philosopher 'to educate his children'. He also required a first-rate artist
to paint pictures for his forthcoming triumphal procession at Rome, and
the Athenians pleased him by sending Metrodorus, who fulfilled both
requirements.[19]

But the time of triumph was also a time of tragedy for Aemilius, for
only five days before it, the elder of the two sons by his second marriage
died at the age of fourteen, and only three days after it he lost the other

boy, who was only twelve.[20] Thus an ironical Fate struck a cruel blow in the very hour of transcendent success, for Aemilius was devoted to his children. So far from merely delegating the education of his four sons to the tutors whom he had chosen with care, he took the deepest personal interest in their progress, and, whenever his public commitments allowed, he would be present himself at their studies and exercises.[21] The two older boys, Fabius and Scipio, had also been with him at Pydna, and after the spoils had been collected, he gave them the opportunity of selecting for themselves whatever books they liked from the library of Perseus.[22] But he had not allowed them, for all his love of Greece, to receive an exclusively Greek education; he had himself prepared them for Roman public life by initiating them into what Plutarch calls 'the native, ancestral discipline which he had himself received', that is, in their own national history, statecraft, and law.

The period which followed the end of the third Macedonian War was one of great significance in the history of education at Rome. Thousands of prisoners were brought across the Adriatic, many of whom must have found employment as 'pedagogues' or tutors in Roman families, thereby greatly extending the knowledge of Greek. There were also the hostages exacted from states which might be inclined to resist Roman supremacy, such as the thousand hostages sent over from Achaia and distributed among Italian cities. Among these was the future historian, Polybius, who had the good fortune to be known already to Aemilius Paullus, and who became the close friend of his sons, especially Scipio. It was they who prevailed upon their father to allow Polybius to remain in Rome.[23] Their companionship began with the loan of books and discussion about them, and Polybius tells how he offered to help Scipio in his studies, an offer which was readily accepted.[24] He was invited to take up residence in Aemilius' house, and became Scipio's counsellor and friend. It was in the course of a conversation with Scipio that Polybius remarked that 'a whole tribe' of Greek teachers had recently flocked to Rome. Apart from this, interest in Greek studies was further stimulated by Greek scholars of free birth, who arrived on embassies from time to time, and among whom none were more influential in the field of language, literature and philosophy than the Stoics. One of these ambassadors was the Stoic grammarian, Crates of Mallos, who came on an embassy from Pergamum at about the time of Ennius' death. His visit was longer than intended, for he had the misfortune to break a leg by falling into the opening of a sewer, but utilized the period of his convalescence by giving lectures. These must have been concerned mainly with Homer, and not only aroused general interest, but also introduced to the Romans the methods of the experts of Alexandria and Pergamum in the preparation and interpretation of literary texts; thus Crates was considered by some to have laid the foundations of Roman scholarship.[25]

Another such embassy was that which arrived from Athens in 155 B.C., and included the Stoic, Diogenes of Babylon, an important theorist in language and style, as well as two other celebrated philosophers, Critolaus the Peripatetic and Carneades the Academic, whose enthusiastic reception is described by Plutarch.[26] The circle which gathered around the younger Scipio himself, to which Terence had belonged, became a major centre of Greek studies,[27] and it was joined by another Stoic philosopher, Panaetius of Rhodes, the pupil of Diogenes of Babylon, who came to reside with Scipio and lived in close intimacy with him and his friend Laelius. Finally, it was in this period, too, about the middle of the century, that Cornelia, the mother of the Gracchi, secured

Figs 3, 4 and 5 *Greek terracottas depicting 'pedagogue' and child.*

Fig. 4

the finest available tutors from Greece for her sons, and welcomed in her home Diophanes, a political refugee from Mitylene and a most able speaker, as tutor in rhetoric to Tiberius, and Blossius of Cumae as his adviser in philosophy.[28] From then on, Hellenism continued to flourish at Rome, with profound effects upon its education, its literature, and its thought.

From the evidence which concerns the last half-century or so of the Republic, we learn rather more about the background, personalities and activities of some at least of the men who acted as tutors in leading families. Some of them had redeemed an unpromising start in life or had recovered from adverse circumstances. One such scholar was the

Fig. 5

'grammarian' Alexander of Miletus (a pupil of Crates), whose vast and varied learning entitled him to the name 'Polyhistor'. He had been captured in war, and then put up for sale as a 'pedagogue' to children; he had been purchased by a Cornelius Lentulus, by whom he was most likely employed as a tutor. He became the author of 'books beyond number', and in 81 B.C., or thereabouts, was granted Roman citizenship by Sulla.[29] An even more remarkable example was that of Antonius Gnipho, who became a tutor in the home of Julius Caesar when Caesar was a boy (*c.*89 B.C.). Though of free birth, he had been exposed as a child by his parents somewhere in Gaul, but by good fortune had been rescued and later given his freedom by his foster-parent. He somehow acquired an education, became skilled in both Greek and Latin, and owed his acceptance as tutor to a combination of intellectual ability and charm of manner. He subsequently made a reputation as a teacher. It is interesting to note that his published work took the form of a treatise on the Latin language and (probably) a commentary on the *Annals* of Ennius.[30] The sparse fragments of his work show that he was one of the first to apply to Latin the principles of analogy in determining the correct form of words — that is, the practice of rational deduction from existing forms in other similar words rather than of deference to common usage ('anomaly'). This reminds us that Caesar himself, who was a great stickler for purity of language, composed, whilst being transported to his province across the Alps (probably in 54 B.C.), a work entitled *On Analogy*.[31] Although this may have been more immediately due to Cicero's recent pronouncements in his *De Oratore*, it seems not unlikely that, during that arduous journey, as Caesar turned his thoughts from military conquest to linguistic studies, his powerful and retentive mind may have recalled some of the teaching of his old tutor in his boyhood days. Antonius Gnipho became not only a teacher of language and literature, but also of rhetoric, and many distinguished Romans regularly attended his declamations. But perhaps the greatest compliment ever paid to him was the presence on several occasions in his audience of no less a person than Cicero; and this was as late as 66 B.C., when Cicero was forty years of age, praetor, and at the height of his oratorical renown.[32] Cicero had himself, in more youthful days, learnt a great deal from his tutors, as will subsequently be seen.[33]

During this period of the later Republic, there is clear evidence that not only the sons but also the daughters of the upper classes benefited from the higher education which tutors could provide. Pompey the Great, for instance, had two sons, Gnaeus and Sextus, and also a daughter, Pompeia, by his third wife Mucia. The sons were taught (*c*.65 B.C.) by a Greek scholar named Aristodemus of Nysa (in Caria), who subsequently returned to his native city to teach, and numbered the geographer Strabo among his pupils;[34] but Pompeia also was taught by a tutor, for when Pompey returned from the East in 61, it was he who selected a passage of Homer for her to read aloud to her father.[35] Not long after this, Pompey divorced Mucia for infidelity during his absence, and married Caesar's daughter Julia. But Pompey's marriages seem to have been under an unlucky star, for in 54 B.C. Julia died in childbirth. He then married a girl so much younger than himself that people said that he was 'old enough to be her father'. This was Cornelia, a consul's daughter, who, says Plutarch, 'was well versed in literature, in playing the lyre, and in geometry, and had been accustomed to listen with profit to philosophical discourses'.[36] Clearly, she too must have had her private tutors, and the education of girls to a high standard was by now by no means uncommon. Plutarch's wry comment on this subject is rather amusing; after praising Cornelia's accomplishments and beauty, the approving sage adds: 'and besides this, she had a nature which was free from that unpleasant officiousness which such accomplishments are apt to impart to young women'! From the late Republic onwards, there is considerable evidence that girls were often well read, especially in poetry, both Greek and Latin, and merited the compliment of being called *docta puella*. For example, Catullus tells how appreciative of a poem on Cybele, which his friend, Caecilius of Novum Comum, had begun, was a learned young lady of their acquaintance,[37] and this was in all likelihood a quite erudite and allusive composition in the typical neo-Alexandrian manner. Admirable short elegies by the poetess, Sulpicia, survive in the Tibullus collection,[38] and Ovid recommends girls to become familiar with a whole range of Greek lyric and elegiac poetry from Sappho and Anacreon to Callimachus and Philetas, as well as with Menander, and the poets of Augustan Rome.[39] Clearly, all this would presuppose a considerable degree of home tuition.

We should really know very little of the relations of tutors with parents and children in the Roman households of the Republic had it not been for the preservation of the correspondence of Cicero. It so happened that the orator and his brother, Quintus, had sons who were very much of an age, young Quintus Cicero being born in 67 B.C. and Cicero's son, Marcus, in 65. When, therefore, some ten years later, Cicero's brother went to Sardinia as Pompey's legate (56 B.C.), and afterwards to Gaul as legate to Caesar (54 B.C.), it was natural that the two boys should be educated together at the orator's house in Rome. Cicero was keenly interested in the progress of both of them, but, living as he did a full and busy life, he was glad to secure the assistance of a tutor. He made a good choice when he engaged Tyrannio (the elder of the two scholars of that name), and in the spring of 56 was able to report to Quintus in these words: 'Your excellent boy, Quintus, is receiving an admirable education; I note his progress all the more, now that Tyrannio is teaching in my house'.[40] Tyrannio had owed his presence in Rome to a mischance which turned out to be a blessing in disguise. He had been a teacher at Amisus, on the shores of the Black Sea, where he had made a reputation, and he had travelled as far as Rhodes to hear the lectures of Dionysius Thrax, the author of the earliest Greek grammar. But in 70 B.C., when Amisus was captured by Lucullus, he was taken prisoner, and might have expected to spend the rest of his life in slavery.[41] The Roman commander, however, was himself a man of culture, and much interested in the Greek civilization, so much so that, being an aristocrat of immense wealth, he had formed his own private libraries, which he generously allowed other readers to use freely. Greek scholars were delighted to resort to these libraries and the adjoining study-rooms at Lucullus' house, and to discourse as they walked around the colonnades. The place became for them a little Greece in Rome, and Lucullus himself, when free, would readily join in their discussions.[42] So Tyrannio was lucky, for Lucullus took particular note of him, and gave him into the keeping of his legate Murena. He was, however, displeased when Murena proceeded formally to manumit him, as though he were an ordinary slave. [43] Once in Rome, Tyrannio prospered exceedingly; in due course, he became wealthy, acquired a large library, and published a variety of learned works.[44] He became an authority on geography (Strabo was one of his pupils),[45] and on Homeric metre and Greek accentuation;[46]

he also devoted particular attention to examining and arranging the manuscripts of Aristotle and Theophrastus, which Sulla had brought over in 86 B.C. from Greece, where they had formed part of the library of Apellicon.[47] Tyrannio was a thorough-going bibliophile. Cicero treated him as a friend, and made good use of his services, not only in the education of young Quintus and Marcus, but also in the organization and classification of the library in his villa at Antium. Cicero was delighted with the improvements which Tyrannio made, and in the early summer of 56 B.C. he wrote enthusiastically about them to his friend Atticus. 'It will be extremely nice if you will come over', he says, 'you will find Tyrannio's classification of my books marvellous'.[48] He

Fig. 6 *A private tutor at Herculaneum, from a nineteenth-century engraving of a painting no longer extant.*

requests Atticus to supply him with a couple of library-slaves to help in gluing together damaged pages, and to send parchment to make the title-slips, and a little later reports: 'since Tyrannio arranged the books for me, my house seems to have acquired a soul'.[49] More than two years later, in the autumn of 54, Quintus Cicero, then in Gaul, wrote to his brother asking him to supplement his (Quintus') Greek library, and also to exchange some of his books and to purchase further Latin texts. Cicero promised to instruct his freedman, Chrysippus, to see to this, but also added: 'I'll have a word with Tyrannio'.[50] But it is probable that

Tyrannio did not remain for very long exclusively in Cicero's service, for he was much in demand, and also much devoted to his scholarly work. Soon, therefore, we find other tutors in charge of the education of young Quintus and Marcus.

The lessons of Tyrannio were probably confined to grammar and literature, these being his special province, but by the autumn of 54 the older boy, Quintus, was already thirteen years of age, and was beginning a course on rhetoric. Cicero writes to his brother, praising his nephew's diligence, and assuring him of his personal interest in the boy's education and his confidence in its successful outcome. Soon we learn that Quintus, 'our Cicero', as the orator fondly calls him, 'is most enthusiastic about his rhetoric-master, Paeonius, an extremely experienced and sound teacher', and that, although Paeonius uses modern declamatory methods rather different from Cicero's own, the orator is satisfied, for Quintus is taking the course with enjoyment.[51] Meantime, the younger boy, Marcus, was still needing further instruction in grammar and literature, and Cicero had no hesitation in engaging for this purpose a learned freedman of Atticus, named M. Pomponius Dionysius, who remained in his service for several years. Dionysius had already helped Tyrannio with Cicero's library at Antium, and Cicero had formed a high opinion of his scholarship. He himself found the man a mine of information, and they had spent whole days together 'devouring literature', as he put it.[52] This was in 56/55 B.C., and in the summer of 54 Cicero had written to Atticus, asking him to urge Dionysius to come over as soon as possible, 'so that he may teach my boy Cicero, and also me myself'.[53] A few years later, in 51/50 B.C., when Cicero became governor of Cilicia, Dionysius accompanied him, and continued to act as tutor to both boys. Cicero himself constantly found him of value, and whenever, in the course of his correspondence with Atticus, some geographical or linguistic query arose, it was to Dionysius that he would turn for an expert opinion.[54] But, as the boys grew older, they became less easy to teach. Quintus, who was by now sixteen, was proving headstrong and difficult to manage, and Marcus was inclined to be lazy; as Cicero remarked, applying Isocrates' well-known metaphor, one of them needed the bridle and the other the spur. In Cilicia, there was friction between Dionysius and his pupils, and the tutor frequently lost his temper with them. Cicero, nevertheless, took his part, and wrote to Atticus: 'for myself, I am very fond of Dionysius; the boys say he rages like a madman, but you couldn't find a more honourable person, or one more devoted to yourself and to me'.[55] When they all returned to Italy, towards the end of 50 B.C., Cicero again made appreciative reference to the tutor's character and services.[56]

But within a few weeks of their return the good relations between Cicero and Dionysius were completely changed. Some time after landing in Italy, the tutor had made off to Rome, where he remained for more than two months. Meantime, the Civil War had broken out, and Cicero's own position was precarious and his movements were uncertain. At Formiae, he took immediate steps to recall Dionysius, without effect, and was plainly offended at what he now regarded as the ingratitude of the man whom he had patronized, praised and recommended.[57] By 22 February 49, the tone of his references to the tutor was one of considerable asperity — 'an absolute chatterbox, not a bit suited to teaching'![58] When, a few days' later, probably at Atticus' instigation, Dionysius had an interview with Cicero at Formiae, matters came to a head. The tutor explained that he was obliged to stay at Rome because he had to collect several outstanding debts, and had other money shortly becoming due to him; he could not, therefore, agree to place himself unreservedly at Cicero's disposal. Cicero then dismissed him as an ingrate, but, despite his previous disparaging remarks about Dionysius' teaching abilities, he now acknowledged to Atticus that he was reluctant to lose the tutor's services.[59] But for some time he continued to show himself remarkably bitter and resentful — probably because he expected too much, and was, in any case, particularly touchy at this highly critical time. Whatever the rights and wrongs of the case, Atticus, who did his best to mediate, expressed the opinion that Cicero was judging too harshly.[60] Eventually, it seems, the quarrel was made up,[61] but the episode is not without interest, for it suggests that sometimes, in return for patronage, even an independent scholar (and Dionysius was, in any case, Atticus' freedman, not Cicero's) might be expected to remain at beck and call. It is quite possible that Dionysius, and other tutors, liked to keep a number of contacts and find other ways of improving their financial position, rather than devote themselves exclusively to one family. But there were many less deserving tutors than Dionysius, and also many good ones who were less handsomely treated by their patrons.

With the advent of the imperial system and the Augustan peace, both the available supply of tutors and the demand for their services greatly increased; but, in varying circumstances, appointments might prove fortunate or unfortunate, whether for the patron, or the tutor, or both. One of the happiest relationships was that formed by another Dionysius, a Greek scholar who arrived from Halicarnassus soon after Actium, with the family of the Metilii. He soon became *persona grata* at Rome, being a whole-hearted supporter of the new regime,[62] and his valuable historical work, *Antiquities of Rome*, together with his critical essays on the Greek orators and on Thucydides, show the width of his interests and the quality of his scholarly judgment. There was also a genuine earnestness about his moral outlook (in which he was not unlike Livy), as may be seen, for instance, in his recommendation of the study of Isocrates' speeches for their inculcation of the most desirable virtues.[63]

He was also a sensitive critic of Greek literature and the subtle variations of its style, and it was to his young pupil, Metilius Rufus, to whom he gave daily lessons, that he presented as a birthday gift on reaching manhood an admirable example of his own research, the treatise *On the Arrangement of Words*.[64] Clearly, the Metilii (and maybe other families, too) were most fortunate in their choice.

Very different had been the experience of Cicero's friend, Atticus. He had engaged one of his freedmen, Q. Caecilius Epirota, to teach his young daughter, Attica, who was already married to Agrippa, but Caccilius was suspected of betraying the trust reposed in him, and was dismissed. He was a scholar-poet of the Alexandrian school (the 'neoterics'), and was an intimate friend of Cornelius Gallus, until the latter's disgrace and death in 26 B.C., after which he opened a school. But, although he was highly regarded in his own circle, his moral reputation and his assocation with Gallus did him no good, and the number of those who attended was limited. Nevertheless, Caecilius deserves to be remembered for one innovation which he made: he was the first to introduce the reading of Virgil and other recent poets into his curriculum, thus preparing the way for that predominance which Virgil has never lost.[65]

The gradual deterioration of standards of behaviour in the schools themselves, which will be described later,[66] soon began to cause anxious parents to look more frequently for reputable tutors whom they could employ in their homes; and among the many who, for various reasons, were attracted to this kind of life, there was keen competition to secure posts with families of social distinction and of wealth. Initial contacts could be made by attending morning levées, but heads of families were cautious, and did not readily accept a stranger, who might well be also a foreigner, into their midst without first having examined his credentials. The prospective patron would first elicit in the course of conversation the kind of knowledge and qualifications which the applicant possessed, and would then take his time in making discreet inquiries of any who knew of the man's character and previous life. If he was satisfied, there would be an interview to arrange the terms of service and the fee.[67] A qualified and conscientious tutor might reasonably expect not only his keep, but some kind of regular recompense and occasional gifts in kind, in token of appreciation. A really first-rate man, who had already made something of a name, would require a high payment,[68] but everything depended on the integrity and generosity of the patron, and there were at all times those who, whatever their capabilities, were disappointed in the high hopes which they had entertained. Well-to-do people could also be mean and niggardly, and one late writer has recorded a number of instances, both Greek and Roman, of teachers whose services were inadequately recognized. One of those mentioned is Ennius, to whom Fulvius Nobilior was said to have given merely a single cloak out of the spoils of his Aetolian campaign.[69] The worst offenders were some of the vulgar rich, whom Lucian satirizes, and in whose homes a 'grammarian', rhetorician, or philosopher might be treated as a mere hireling and subjected to many humiliating indignities. At its best, nevertheless, as in the younger Pliny's circle, private tuition could be satisfying and rewarding, both to the tutor and to the children whom he taught.[70]

Finally, from Augustus onwards, the tutorial system was encouraged at the very highest level, in the form of state appointments of teachers for the children of the imperial family. Naturally, those who benefited from such appointments — such as Verrius Flaccus, the distinguished 'grammarian', Seneca the philosopher, and Quintilian the rhetorician — were relatively few and extremely select; but it is at this level that we see how wide the range of possible subjects could be. An interesting example is that of the future emperor, Titus, who was educated together with the ill-fated Britannicus by the same tutors.[71] Titus was a quite gifted boy; not only was he skilful in arms and horsemanship, but he became a fluent speaker, and was so good at poetic composition that he could even extemporize in verse. Moreover, he had some musical ability, and both sang and played the harp agreeably. He was so adept at shorthand that he could compete in speed with his own amanuenses, yet he was also quite expert in handwriting; so effectively, in fact, could he imitate other people's writing that he used jestingly to say that he could have become a first-rate forger![72] All this implies that Titus had quite a number of tutors. Later, the system of imperial tutorships reached its zenith in the remarkably wide education of the young Marcus Aurelius;[73] but this is beyond our period. It is now time to descend from this exalted level and these highly sophisticated days to a much earlier age, and to consider the much more humble arrangements made by ordinary families for the guidance and elementary instruction of their children, whether at home or at school.

CHAPTER IV

Primary schools and 'pedagogues'

Viewed against the background of Roman family life as a whole, the accession of tutors, such as those whom we have described, would appear to have been something of a luxury, and the children who benefited from such teaching generally belonged to the more favoured classes of society. Moreover, as this kind of tuition was provided by scholars, who had a particular interest in such subjects as language and literature, rhetoric, or philosophy, it was an intellectual and cultural education, and it would presuppose a basis of elementary knowledge, which might also be imparted within the home. But this more practical instruction at a lower level was in much wider demand, for, whatever the family circumstances, it was generally appreciated that children needed to be taught to read and write, to count, weigh, measure and calculate. For this purpose, parents who had not the time, the inclination or, sometimes, the ability to teach them themselves, and who lacked any suitable assistance, would send their children to a primary school.

The origins and early development of primary schools at Rome form a subject of interesting speculation, but not one on which it is possible to be at all dogmatic. The historians Livy and Dionysius, who are probably following a common source, mention quite incidentally that there were primary schools in the Forum at the time of the rape of Verginia in the mid-fifth century B.C.[1] Livy, too, has a picturesque reference to 'the schools humming with the voices of pupils' when Camillus entered Tusculum in 381 B.C.[2] But we cannot be at all sure that either of these writers had any substantial evidence which would have proved what they say. Plutarch, however, is more explicit. In a section of that curious collection of miscellaneous queries entitled *Roman Questions*, he states that in the very earliest times teaching was regarded as a service, and an honourable one, 'for people taught their friends and relatives only'. He then adds that 'it was not until late that they began to teach for money, and the first to open a (primary) school was Spurius Carvilius, the freedman of that Carvilius who was the first to divorce his wife'.[3] In another section, he says that it was Spurius Carvilius who first introduced the letter G into the Latin alphabet, and that this, too, was a late development.[4]

It is curious, in the first place, that Plutarch should elsewhere say that the Spurius Carvilius who 'was the first to divorce his wife' did so in the 230th year of the City, that is, 524 B.C., in the time of Tarquinius Superbus.[5] The reason which he gives for the divorce was the inability of Carvilius' wife to bear him the children he desired, and this was undoubtedly true. But two important witnesses, Dionysius and Aulus Gellius, who had looked into the history of this interesting, and obviously unusual, case, both aver that the man concerned was Spurius Carvilius Maximus Ruga, who was consul in 234 B.C., and again in 228 B.C., and this is the identification which scholars generally accept.[6] In this case, it was not the first divorce at Rome, even though it was loosely thus described, for there appears to have been a provision on divorce in the Twelve Tables, and one recorded instance dates from 307/306 B.C.[7] But the Carvilian divorce was exceptional because of its grounds, for the wife had committed no matrimonial offence, and Carvilius claimed that he had sworn before the censors that he had married for the purpose of begetting children. Therefore, it is reasonable to suppose that Gellius, who had looked up the account in a work of the Republican jurist Servius Sulpicius, *On Dowries*, was on the right lines when he reported that this was the first divorce which led to a legal enactment to protect the wife's interests by enabling her to recover her dowry.[8] Plutarch, then, expressed himself rather carelessly in this matter, but he may well be relaying a true tradition that the freedman of this Carvilius was the first to open a *fee-paying* school quite late in the third century B.C. If, as seems most likely, this practice soon became normal, then certain passages of Plautus, even though derived from Greek originals, gain added point in that they were also appropriate to contemporary Rome. Love-affairs are of the very essence of Plautine Comedy, and we find that they are sometimes described in terms which are clearly designed to recall school life. The art of love is an 'alphabet', or a 'lesson' which has to be learnt; the place where one learns is a 'school', the mistress is a 'teacher', and, if she is a professional, she has to be paid a 'tuition fee' by her 'pupil'.[9] So, in the *Mercator*, old Demipho has fallen in love with a girl whom his son has brought back from Rhodes. He is suddenly rejuvenated, and feels like a seven-year-old (the age at which schooling usually began). 'I've begun to go back to elementary school today', he confides to his friend, Lysimachus, 'I know three letters already'. 'Which three?' inquires the other; 'A-M-O', replies the old man with a chuckle. There may have been something similar in the original Greek,[10] but Plautus is clearly recalling the teaching of the alphabet in Latin. Who, then, were the teachers? To answer this, we must look more closely into the organization of Roman family life.

Throughout the ages, not all the children who clustered around the brightly-gleaming Roman hearth and played games together in the wintertime were the freeborn sons and daughters of the household. There was usually among them at least one slave-child, who was the offspring either of slaves of the family, living together in the loose association known as *contubernium*, or of a slave-woman of the family by some citizen of free birth. The young freeborn sons were known as the 'infant masters' (*infantes domini*) but the slave-child was called *verna*, or *vernula*, that is, 'homeborn' or 'native', to distinguish him from slaves of foreign origin or otherwise acquired,[11] and from him we derive our word 'vernacular'. Juvenal, picturing the country cottage of earlier times, imagines a scene in which 'four infants were playing together, one home-slave and three little masters', who are later joined by the older boys, returning to supper after labouring on the land.[12] It was a recognized sign of a prosperous family that it had several of these home-born slaves,[13] and in the large households of the city they became quite numerous. From early times they had acquired a special place in the affections of the Roman family. The elder Cato's wife was probably following an old custom in nurturing such slave-children at her own breast, and they continued, long afterwards, to be known as 'foster-brothers' (*collactanei*).[14] They were often well looked after, and developed into lively and cheerful creatures — Horace found their company amusing on his Sabine farm.[15] Under the Empire, they were frequently petted and spoiled by indulgence and gifts; as a result, their liveliness turned into sauciness and impudence.[16] But in Republican Rome we may be sure that they were expected to conform to the discipline of the rest of the household.

The custom of bringing up the *vernae* together with the freeborn children survived throughout the period of the Roman Empire;[17] it was known already in Homeric times and was Asiatic in origin,[18] but the words *verna, vernula*, have been thought to be derived from the Etruscan language.[19] It is intrinsically probable that the Etruscans should have adopted such a practice, for they are said to have treated their household slaves with humanity.[20] Moreover, there are one or two recorded instances which strongly support this belief. Tradition had it that, at the time of the Etruscan domination of Rome in the sixth century B.C., the elder Tarquin and his wife Tanaquil not only brought up but educated the young Servius Tullius along with their own sons, and Servius was by origin a *verna*.[21] That letters were taught as early as the sixth century B.C. is proved by the ivory writing tablet from Marsigliana d'Albegna,[22] as well as other model alphabets (one accompanied by a syllabary) which survive from that period.[23] Then again, Livy, describing the adventure of a Roman soldier who, in 310 B.C., penetrated the Ciminian forest in disguise, says that he knew Etruscan because he had been brought up at Caere with guest-friends of his parents, and that he was accompanied on the expedition by a slave 'who had been nurtured with him and knew the same language'.[24]

It does not necessarily follow, of course, that the home-born slave was always taught to read and write. Very often he was put to learn some manual craft, but he comes into the picture of Roman education for two reasons. First, when quite young, he might become one of the attendant slaves (*pedisequi*) who accompanied their young master to school; in Juvenal, it is he who carries the boy's book-box for him (*capsarius*).[25] When he was older, and the sons of the house had children of their own, he was the natural person to whom to entrust them when the parents were busy or away from home. He became their *custos*, or guardian, and, as he was also responsible for conducting them to and from school, he served in the same capacity as the Greek child-attendant, or 'pedagogue'. In fact, the terms *custos* and *paedagogus* were interchangeable, and the Latin word remained in common use long after Greek slaves had arrived in great numbers and largely taken over such duties.[26] As a 'pedagogue', he might well remain with his young charge during lessons, and acquire useful knowledge himself. The classic example of this was Remmius Palaemon, who began life as a home-born slave at Vicetia (Vicenza), and, after learning the craft of weaving, accompanied the son of the house to and from school; by staying during the lessons, he became so proficient himself that, as a freedman, he eventually set up as a teacher and was soon one of the most well-known grammarians in Rome.[27]

This was no doubt exceptional, and most would reach only an elementary level;[28] but there was a further means by which the home-born slave might be brought into the field of education. Any slave acquired a higher value if he became literate. Cato had a system whereby he bought up slaves, had them taught by a slave-teacher and then sold them at an enhanced price; but sometimes he allowed the teacher to benefit from his work by crediting him with the amount of the increase in value, and retained the newly-literate slave on his staff.[29] His slave, Chilo, who, says Plutarch, 'taught many other children'[30] but was not allowed to teach Cato's son, was evidently a valued member of the household, and may have taught not only slaves but the children of Cato's neighbours, who had no literate slave-teacher of their own, but would presumably have made some kind of recompense to Cato. This may, perhaps, have been the earliest form of the Roman 'school' before Carvilius. A century later, the financier Crassus kept a large establishment of valuable slaves, including readers and amanuenses, whose education he had not only supervised, but had taken part in himself.[31] Atticus, too, had a large number of copyists, all of them 'highly literate boys' (*pueri litteratissimi*), not one of whom had not been born and trained in his household.[32] If any slave who could read and write should chance to be sold when the rest of his former master's estate was auctioned, he was described in the sale catalogue as *litterator*,[33] and the interesting point is that this was the term which, in addition to *ludi magister*, long remained in use to describe the Roman primary schoolmaster.[34] Of the numerous literate slaves who were taught in the home, or were self-taught, or who changed hands in the commercial world, many would eventually secure their freedom, and it was largely due to them that primary education spread, when they found their occupation as masters in their own schools. But essentially their proficiency would be in their native Latin. Some, no doubt, had at least a smattering of Greek,[35] but Rome's foreign conquests introduced many whose native language was Greek, which was much in demand, and they brought the Greek methods of training with them. It is necessary, therefore, to consider the personality and the work of the Greek-speaking *paedagogus*, first in Greece itself.

The education of the Greek boy in letters, music and physical accomplishments usually necessitated daily journeys between his home and the various teaching establishments, whether school, palaestra or gymnasium. In order, therefore, to protect him from danger, both physical and moral, he was placed in the care of a trusted slave of the household, who conducted him to and fro, and was known as his *paidagogos*.[36] But the 'pedagogue', as we may call him, was attached not so much to the individual child as to the family, and could become responsible for the safety and welfare of more than one boy, and, with the assistance of nurse or handmaid, girls as well.[37] The boys came under his authority from a very early age, as soon as they left the care of mothers and nurses, not only out of doors but within the home. It was he who helped the parents to instil into the children what was right and what was wrong, and all the details of proper behaviour. He could not only reprimand, but also mete out corporal punishment when necessary,[38] for the misbehaviour of his young charges could be held to reflect upon himself.[39] Plato remarked that boys were often 'very difficult to cope with', and fully approved of strict control.[40] The authority of the 'pedagogue' was thus not confined to early boyhood, but lasted until the young man achieved his independence,[41] and the exercise of it was usually entrusted to one of the older servants. Among well-regulated families, as on the stage in Greek tragedy,[42] the 'pedagogue' was a respected figure. Occasionally, it is true, an unsatisfactory choice might be made, as when Alcibiades was placed in the care of an aged and infirm 'pedagogue', a Thracian called Zopyros.[43] But generally the 'pedagogue' (though he did sometimes have a rather foreign accent)[44] appears to have been a sturdy fellow, as he needed to be, and, though prone to err on the side of severity rather than leniency, often concealed a kind heart under a rough exterior. Greek terracottas depict him as an oldish man, stockily built, heavily bearded, and with rather unprepossessing features; sometimes he rests his right hand on the little boy's head as they stand together[45] (cf. Fig. 4) and sometimes tweaks his ear, as Cato's slave, Chilo, used to do, when he has done something wrong.[46]

It was natural for parents who had an intelligent 'pedagogue' to expect that he would not only conduct the children to and from school, but also see that they learnt their lessons properly. He might well remain present at these himself (as did Palaemon in Roman times), and on returning home would test the children and make them repeat to him what they were supposed to know by heart. The more literate he was himself the better, but, in general, he was primarily engaged to supervise rather than to teach, and often, in both Greek and Roman times, the 'pedagogue' was clearly differentiated from the 'teacher' or 'master' (*didaskalos, praeceptor, magister*).[47] Nevertheless it did also happen, certainly in the Hellenistic period, and probably earlier, that he was able to give primary instruction himself. So, again, terracottas sometimes depict him seated, with a tablet on his knees, and teaching the young boy, who stands beside him, to read or write (cf. Fig. 2). This is also well illustrated by a scene in Plautus' play, the *Bacchides*, where the educational references, with their Greek setting, clearly suggest that Plautus is faithfully reflecting the original play (the *Double Deceiver*) by Menander.[48] Here one of the characters, Lydus (whose name facilitates a pun on the Latin *ludus*)[49] is not only an attendant but a 'pedagogue' in the modern sense, for he gives tuition to Pistoclerus, the unruly son of Philoxenus; and his remarks in the course of conversation make it clear that it was quite normal for his out-of-doors supervision to be combined with elementary teaching in the home.[50]

What is more, it could happen, even if perhaps somewhat exceptionally, that a Greek family might be lucky enough to secure the services of a man who was far superior in knowledge to the ordinary educated slave, but who had fallen on bad times and was placed at the mercy of fortune. In the fourth century B.C., according to one of his biographers,[51] the philosopher, Diogenes of Sinope ('Diogenes the Cynic'), having been captured by pirates and sold as a slave, was purchased by a Corinthian called Xeniades — a man of wealth, it should be noted — to whose sons he then became not only an escort but an instructor. This is how his life with his master's sons is described:

After their other studies (i.e. their primary education), he taught them to ride, to shoot with the bow, to sling stones and to hurl javelins. Later, when they reached the wrestling-school, he would not permit the instructor to give them full athletic training, but only so much as would heighten their complexion and keep them in good condition. The boys used to get by heart many passages from poets, historians and the writings of Diogenes himself; and he would practise them in all the quick ways to cultivating a good memory. In the house, too, he taught them to wait upon themselves, and to be content with plain fare and with water to drink. He used to make them crop their hair close, and leave it unadorned, and to go lightly-clad, barefoot, silent, and not looking about them in the streets. He would also take them out hunting. They, for their part, had a great regard for Diogenes, and made requests of their parents in his favour.

It is evident, therefore, that, in Greece, the person chosen to supervise the young might be of very varying quality; he might have no pretensions to knowledge, or he might be capable of giving primary instruction, or he might, at times, be one who, like Diogenes, had every right to be thought of as a qualified tutor. From this Greek background, we may now return to Rome.

There is good reason to believe that the Greek 'pedagogue' would have become known to the Romans in the course of the third century B.C.: the war against Pyrrhus had brought them into closer contact with the Greek cities of southern Italy, such as Tarentum; much of the first Punic War was fought in Sicily; and in the second Punic War a three-year campaign culminated in the capture of Syracuse (214-211 B.C.). Moreover, when, as early as 217, the extremely cautious commander, Fabius Maximus, constantly followed Hannibal around, avoiding a pitched battle, his troops already scornfully referred to him as 'Hannibal's pedagogue'.[52] This rather suggests that it would be unwise to accept the view that the Romans made their first acquaintance with the *paedagogus* when he appeared as a character in Roman adaptations of New Comedy.[53] At least some of the leading families must have acquired such assistants in Plautus' day. But it would be mainly in the second century, and especially after the end of the third Macedonian War in 168 B.C., that they became really numerous at Rome. The names of 'pedagogues' in inscriptions are almost entirely Greek.[54]

It may perhaps seem rather surprising that Roman parents should have become so readily accustomed to entrust their children to slaves who were not born within the household, but were of foreign origin and might, at first, not even speak the same language. But there were several reasons why they found such an arrangement acceptable. In the first place, the Greeks had a long tradition of child-protection, and the Greeks at Rome, as a rule, seem to have performed this essential duty well. Such protection became increasingly necessary in the last half-century or so of the Republic, with all the turbulence and strife caused by embittered political factions, when the streets were frequently the scene of disorder and bloodshed, and the home itself was not secure. It is a writer of this period who imagines a master of the house, whose life is endangered when intruders break in, call out to the Greek slave-attendant: 'Hide the children, protect them, see that you bring them safely to manhood'.[55] In the proscriptions of the time of Sulla, and again in those which followed Caesar's murder, the orphaned children of rich parents were often in imminent danger. One such child, in 43 B.C., was going to school with his 'pedagogue' when they were suddenly attacked; the slave flung his arms around the boy, and held on to him, but without avail, and both were killed together.[56] 'Pedagogues', like nurses, were often remembered with affection, as Cicero says, in later years;[57] their services were frequently recognized by manumission, and numerous inscriptions exist from funerary monuments, which testify to their loyalty and devotion.[58] Augustus honoured his former 'pedagogue', the freedman Sphaerus, with a public funeral.[59] There were, of course, cases in which a 'pedagogue' might come under suspicion,[60] but the penalty for any kind of serious misconduct was severe,[61] and, in one instance, when a 'pedagogue' allowed a young girl to be seduced, the father, a Roman knight, with all the ruthless severity of early Rome, put them both to death.[62] But usually the 'protector' merited the trust reposed in him. Horace's father, who took no chances but personally conducted his son to and from school, was evidently an exceptionally conscientious parent.

It seems to be widely believed that the 'pedagogue' did not take any part in Roman family life until the children were of the age of seven, or thereabouts, and ready to go to school. This, however, was not always so, for he could appear upon the scene in the days of their infancy, at any rate in the imperial period. Martial addresses his former 'pedagogue', Charidemus, as one who rocked his cradle as a child.[63] In fact, our word 'educate' finds its origin here. It is derived from a verb which, in Latin, had a mainly physical connotation; for *educare* meant 'to rear', and was applied not only to the parents themselves but, increasingly, to others who tended a child in its earliest years. A foster-parent who rescued and brought up an exposed child was called his *educator*, but this term was also commonly used of persons of servile origin, to whom the responsibility of rearing was, especially under the Empire, so often entrusted.[64] The nurse (who might sometimes be called *educatrix*)[65] was not in sole charge, but was assisted by one of the older, trusted slaves, who was properly described as an *educator*, being a sort of foster-parent, but who was known in family language as the child's *papas*.[66] He helped the nurse to prepare the food and drink, and was sometimes called *nutricius* or *nutritor*, a 'nourisher', as in Greek, *tropheus*.[67] Nurses, incidentally, had the alarmingly unhygienic habit of first chewing the food into small morsels themselves and then popping them into the baby's mouth![68] But preliminary testing of the drink often became a very necessary precaution under the Empire, not so much lest it be too hot, but lest it be poisoned. Jealous wives might be tempted to use this method of getting rid of the children of concubines; but the child might lose its life, as Britannicus very nearly did, through the treachery of the 'nourishers' themselves.[69] Sometimes, the old servant who performed these duties may have been one who was no longer sufficiently active to go around as an escort, but often the one function would be followed by the other, so that the 'nourisher' became a 'pedagogue'. Thus the terms became almost interchangeable, and whereas Tacitus describes Anicetus as the *educator* of Nero's boyhood, Suetonius calls him his *paedagogus*,[70] and, as early as the elder Seneca, those who test the food and drink are referred to as the 'pedagogues'.[71]

A further reason why Roman parents came to rely more and more upon Greek 'pedagogues' was that the Greek ideals of children's behaviour, deportment, and dress, as seen, for instance, in Plato and Aristophanes, were very similar to, though quite unconnected with, the old Roman tradition. When these writers speak of the importance of children maintaining a respectful silence in the presence of their elders, of rising at their entrance and showing other courtesies, of paying proper attention to hair, dress and shoes, their standards are exactly those which would have been approved by the best parents of Republican Rome.[72] Thus the 'pedagogue' took over from the parents the general training in manners, and inculcated the traditional proprieties of behaviour in the home and out of doors. Table manners were considered important, and, at midday meals with their 'pedagogues',[73] children were told not to grab for their food, and not to reach with the open hand, but to take it more elegantly, using thumb and one finger, or, at most, two.[74] Some 'pedagogues' also had a rooted objection to children sitting with their legs crossed.[75] The good 'pedagogue' insisted that children out of doors should proceed quietly to their destination without taking notice of all that was going on around them in the streets. Whereas the modern child is often told to hold his head up, the Greek or Roman boy was told to walk with head slightly bowed, and to keep his eyes on the path ahead.[76] Naturally, children became restive and obstinate at times under such constant supervision and direction, and the 'pedagogue' was, after all, only a slave in status. So there were sometimes 'scenes', and the attendant scolded the child severely,[77] or rapped him with his knuckles, or boxed his ears. Many 'pedagogues', in both Greece and Rome, ruled by fear,[78] and the less educated they were themselves, the more likely they were to impose their will by force. Very different was Sarpedon, the 'pedagogue' of the younger Cato. Even as a child, Cato was of a very independent nature, and would not simply do what he was told without demanding to know the reason for it. But Sarpedon did not use a heavy hand; instead, he patiently explained, and was so successfully persuasive that Cato became very obedient to him.[79] It was this kind of approach

Fig. 7 *Philocalus, primary schoolmaster at Capua. The inscription above mentions that he also 'faithfully wrote out wills'.*

that caused the good 'pedagogue' to be regarded as an authoritative 'adviser', or *monitor*, a word which, often applied to the philosopher (who, says Seneca, is 'the pedagogue of the human race'), was thus drawn more closely into the terminology of education.[80]

Escorting the young on all manner of journeys was a very important part of a 'pedagogue's duties; the words of Ruth to Naomi, 'whither thou goest, I will go', might have been his permanent motto. When a boy made a social visit (*salutatio*), or went along to the baths or the theatre, his attendant-companion (*comes*) went with him.[81] Augustus instituted the practice of allocating a separate section of theatre-seats for boys, and another close at hand for their 'pedagogues'.[82] But the most frequent journeys were those made between home and school; originally, there was only the primary school, but these were soon followed by the school of 'grammar' and the school of rhetoric, which together formed the standard pattern of Roman education. To these might be added, as in Greece, the music school, for, although music did not play so fundamental a part in Roman education as in Greek, and the Romans were not so impressed with its influence in the formation of character as were the Greeks,[83] it was far from being neglected [84] as an accomplishment. Boys and girls learned not only to sing in chorus for special religious occasions, but also to perform individually, and to accompany themselves on stringed instruments.[85] Much of this might be learnt within the home, but we know from Horace, Columella, and Seneca, that music schools became a regular feature of Roman life.[86] Dancing, too, which was anathema to the more staid Romans (at least, as regards adults)[87] was learnt by children in school as early as the second century B.C. In a speech of 129 B.C., the younger Scipio expressed his surprise and displeasure at finding a dancing-school (*ludus saltatorius*) attended by more than fifty boys and girls of noble birth, where a boy of twelve was dancing with castanets.[88] He says, too, that boys and girls went to the actors' school (*ludus histrionum*) to learn to sing and to play such stringed instruments as the *sambuca* (an Asiatic harp, mentioned as early as Plautus)[89] and the *psalterium*. Learning to play the *cithara* became especially popular.[90] Here, too, then, the 'pedagogue' would be in attendance, just as he was in Greece,[91] and the same was true as the children played games and took their exercise. Not until the young man took the toga of manhood did he become finally free of such supervision, and feel (like Martial) that he could, at last, really have his fling.[92] Thus the system, for all its value to the very young, was vastly over-restrictive, and it was when the restraint was finally removed that, as the Romans themselves found, the trouble often began.

There was, however, one further advantage, which should not be overlooked; for the 'pedagogue' was the person from whom the Roman boy or girl first began to understand, and to speak, Greek. As the presence of Greeks, and the use of Greek, became so prevalent in Rome that Juvenal called it 'a Greek city',[93] Roman children grew up bi-lingual; and conversation in Greek, even a little before Latin (which would come naturally) was encouraged by those who felt, as did Quintilian, that knowledge of Greek literature was indispensable for the proper appreciation of Latin writers.[94] To be termed 'skilled in both languages' was a compliment desired by any well-educated man. Here, however, much depended on the selection of the 'pedagogue'; if wisely chosen, he would be one who spoke good Greek, not some low-class person (like the ex-muleteer, placed in charge of the future emperor Claudius),[95] whose language might exercise a bad influence and produce faults difficult to eradicate later on. But if the 'pedagogue' was not only well-spoken but, to a degree, educated, there was no reason why he should not be encouraged to teach the elements of Greek more formally. Sarpedon, who is described by Plutarch as 'accomplished' (the same word which he uses of Cato's slave, Chilo), may well have taught the younger Cato Greek. Quintilian, too, speaks not only of children 'conversing' in Greek, but of 'learning' it, and says that 'pedagogues' in his day were only too anxious to be allowed to teach, even though they may have been insufficiently qualified to do so properly. But if they were 'thoroughly educated' (*plane eruditi*) themselves, he had no objection.[96]

When, as often happened, a 'pedagogue' was eventually granted his freedom, he might well look round for a paid position[97] in which he could continue to exercise some authority and utilize his previous experience, preferably in a static rather than a peripatetic situation. This he might find, in the imperial period, in one of the large training-establishments, called *paedagogia*, which existed not only in wealthy households (as they had done in those of Atticus and Crassus) but also in the imperial palace. These were quite thriving and well-organized institutions, the purpose of which was to satisfy the enormous demand for properly trained young slaves, needed for a wide range of domestic duties within the larger households.[98] These boys, who were between the ages of twelve and nineteen, were called *paedagogiani*, and their teachers, who were nearly always freedmen, 'pedagogues of the slave-staff' (*paedagogi puerorum*). Many of the boys became pages, waiters at table or cup-bearers, specialists in the preparation of food or hairdressers, and were trained not only to perform their various duties but to be fastidious in dress and deportment. But there were also those who would become stenographers, secretaries, bookkeepers, or stewards with financial responsibility. Consequently, they needed to be good at writing and calculation, and the *paedagogium* became quite a busy hive of primary education in its own special quarters. Some of those who received their elementary education in such surroundings may, on achieving freedom later in life, have put it to good use by organizing a school of their own.

Thus, apart from members of the family, it was the slave, or freedman, rather than the freeborn citizen, who did most to lay the foundations of education for Roman children. In fact, as a result of the lowly origin and social position of such teachers, citizens of free birth who found their occupation in conducting primary schools were looked upon with disdain.[99] Their remuneration, as we shall see, was minimal, and they rated far below the 'grammarian' and rhetorician. Very little is recorded of the lives of these teachers of the youngest children. Of their pupils, many, having learnt to read and write, to count and calculate, went out into the world; but some were more fortunate and found a new and wider interest in the studies of the 'grammar' school.

CHAPTER V

Schools of Grammar and Literature

Many of the educated Greeks, of varying background and social status, who arrived in Rome from the mid-second century B.C. onwards must have been as surprised as was Polybius to find that there was no officially established system of education, such as existed in so many of the Greek cities.[1] They missed the highly organized communities of the Greek gymnasia, equipped either at public expense or by private benefaction with a very efficient professional staff, and crowded with boys and youths in their various age-groups, all imbued with the Greek love of physical perfection and prowess, stimulated by constant competition, and urged on to the highest endeavours by the hope of one day achieving the coveted distinction of a victory in the national games. But athleticism, though predominant, was not exclusive of other interests, for there were also in many places competitions and prizes in such subjects as reading, writing, recitation, singing and lyre-playing, and rewards for general knowledge, and good behaviour. There might also be lectures by visiting scholars, and a gymnasium-library in which to browse.[2] It was very different in Republican Rome, where the Campus Martius was the training-ground, and the exercises most favoured were those which were directly related to future military needs. But even in Greece, in the Hellenistic period, the more advanced teaching arrangements, in grammar and literature, and in rhetoric, were still largely a matter of private enterprise, and schoolmasters fixed the best fee they could get. At Rome, too, there was nothing to deter a teacher from opening his own school, if he thought he could make it pay, and this was a step which some of the better-qualified newcomers, who might have served for a time as private tutors, thought it worth their while to take.

In the previous chapters, we have sought to draw a distinction between the 'pedagogue', who, if capable of teaching, would, in most cases, not aspire to anything beyond an elementary level, and the tutor (*praeceptor*) who had some particular expertise. Whereas the 'pedagogue' would usually have served for a long period before he gained his freedom, a man of superior abilities, if he happened to be of slave origin, or reduced to slavery by circumstances, might expect to secure manumission much more quickly. Such generous recognition of talent was by no means uncommon at Rome. Terence, for instance, owed both his education and his freedom to the Roman senator, Terentius Lucanus.[3] And some tutors were, as we have seen, freeborn citizens of distant states. Thus the tutor might well be the sort of person who would collect a library of his own, become familiar with the higher learning in his subject, and perhaps publish his own works. Such men, as Quintilian says, often wished to do more than private tuition, in a milieu in which they might easily be mistaken for mere 'pedagogues'; they were more ambitious, felt that they deserved a wider audience, and therefore decided to try their luck in opening a school.[4] There were others, too, besides Greek tutors from abroad, who had similar ideas and the necessary learning; they were men, whether slave or free, from the towns of Italy or Cisalpine Gaul, who, sometimes after having had teaching experience, decided to start a school in Rome. Those whose services were most in demand were the teachers whom, for want of a better term, we have to call 'grammarians', whilst recognizing that this gives a quite inadequate definition of their work; for, although they had more and more to say about grammar, the real centre of interest of *grammatici*, in both Greece and Rome, had always been literature, and their main field of study was poetry. To understand how the term *grammaticus* originated, and developed in meaning, it is necessary, as so often, to return to Greece.

In classical Greece, the teacher of reading and writing, who was called *grammatistes* because he started with the letters of the alphabet (*grammata*), made it an important part of his work to familiarize his pupils with the writings of the poets, especially Homer, and not only made them learn much poetry by heart but stressed the moral lessons which it conveyed.[5] One who was a good student at this level was said to be *grammatikos*, which at that time was an adjective, and simply meant 'literate', as opposed to *agrammatos*, 'unlettered'.[6] But in the post-classical period, in the much more exalted circles of librarians and scholars, most particularly at Alexandria, the classification, textual correction and elucidation of collected works soon resulted in a vast extension of literary erudition. The works of the poets were examined with particular care (some of the leading Alexandrians, like Apollonius Rhodius and Callimachus, being poets themselves), and none more so than Homer; for Zenodotus, Aristophanes of Byzantium, and Aristarchus, each of whom became head of the Alexandrian library, laid the foundations of Homeric scholarship.[7] But the problem was — how should a scholar with such specialized interests and expertise be designated? Eratosthenes, a man of encyclopaedic knowledge, called himself *philologus*, 'a lover of learning' (for the word then meant infinitely more than the modern 'philologist'), but this was a very wide term, embracing much more than the study of literary works.[8] Much more favoured was the word *kritikos*, our 'critic', for the learned scholar had to be a 'judge' (*krites*) of literature. Polybius made no distinction between a 'critic' and a 'grammarian',[9] but Crates, the first head of the library at Pergamum, and his pupil, Tauriscus, insisted on being described as 'critics', and the term always had a very reputable connotation.[10] But being a 'judge', though it certainly included assessment of literary quality, was particularly associated in Hellenistic times with decision on the authenticity of lines, passages, or whole works, doubtfully attributed to the authors studied; and not every student of literature could claim so special a skill. Consequently, the most generally accepted term, from the third century B.C. onwards, came to be *grammatikos*, which meant a 'man of letters' in the wider sense, or 'literary scholar'. But even in antiquity it was a matter of inquiry among the learned as to who was first granted this title.[11] For our purpose, the important point is that much of the scholarship which emanated from such great centres as Alexandria and Pergamum filtered down into the schools, with the result that a schoolmaster, who knew much more than the ordinary primary teacher, became distinguished as a *grammatikos*, and thus instituted a higher, or, as we should say, secondary level of education. But the same term had now to be applied both to the professional scholar, who might not take any pupils, and the master of a secondary school. It is now necessary to see how it came about that this appellation, which originally was especially associated with literature, came increasingly to include the study of formal grammar, and so gave us our 'grammarian'.

So long as there was no literary teaching in the Greek schools to a standard beyond that of the *grammatistes*, grammar was not yet a subject in the curriculum. Indeed, in classical Greece, it was not yet properly formulated; but a beginning had been made by the early sophists, such as Protagoras and Prodicus, and in the *Cratylus* of Plato there is not only speculation about the origins of language, but discussion of the phonetic value of the letters, an awareness of their classification, and some indication of grammatical categories (nouns, verbs and genders).[12] But it was the scholars of the Stoic school, from Chrysippus onwards, who did most among philosophers to further the study of grammar.[13] The earliest formal grammatical scheme which we possess (though, regrettably, only in the barest outline)[14] is that of Diogenes of Babylon, pupil of Chrysippus and head of the Stoic school, who visited Rome on the embassy of 155 B.C. His work began with a classification of the letters of the alphabet on phonetic lines, proceeded to distinguish and illustrate the parts of speech (five in his, the orthodox Stoic, view), and then enumerated the virtues of style (headed by the all-important 'correct Greek'), and condemned the vices of barbarism and solecism. Meanwhile, the Alexandrians themselves had not been idle in

Fig. 8 *Epaphroditus of Chaeronea, Greek 'grammarian'. He taught at Rome from the time of Nero to that of Trajan.*

this branch of knowledge, but had gradually evolved their own system. It is under the name of Dionysius Thrax, a pupil of Aristarchus, who taught in Rhodes *c.* 100 B.C., that the earliest manual of Greek grammar has come down;[15] it had an astonishingly prolonged influence, acquired an immense accretion of ancient scholia, and was still in use at the Renaissance and long afterwards. Here we have a succinct and methodical treatment of letters, syllabic quantity, and eight parts of speech — the same number as that recognized by Aristarchus.[16] The authenticity of the work has been sometimes challenged, but by no means disproved.

Once evolved, the basic classifications which constituted formal grammar could, whatever the differences of individual opinion, be set forth, as in Dionysius Thrax, in fairly modest compass. But when decisions had to be made as to what was the correct Greek in particular word-forms, and whether it was legitimate to use this or that parallel in declension or conjugation, a wide field of acrimonious discussion was opened up, which resulted in considerable extensions to the manuals of grammar. Aristophanes and Aristarchus had developed the principle, and the prerequisites, of analogy, or 'likeness', and applied their doctrine (which, of course, formed the very basis of all that was 'regular' in grammar) in cases of doubt; their opponents, on the other hand, refused to be thus bound, but maintained that wide allowances must be made for anomaly, and (especially if they were Stoics) claimed that usage was the only true criterion. The dispute was particularly associated with the names of Aristarchus and Crates, but lasted long after their day, both in Greek and in Latin.[17] Etymology, too, which had long been a subject of learned speculation, especially among Stoics, was brought into this all-pervading problem of correctness. Consequently, the situation arose in which the *grammatikos* found himself obliged to give his pupils a preliminary course in grammar, in the fullest sense, as well as to lecture on the poets. Not only would he need to refer back to this material in his commentary, but he also had in mind the progress of his pupils into rhetorical studies, and, for rhetoricians too, the first essential was correct speech. It so happens that this change of balance in the work of the *grammatikos* can be well illustrated, in Greek, from a little-known but very important teacher of the late Republic whose name was Asclepiades.

Asclepiades was born at Myrlea in Bithynia, probably towards the end of the second century B.C.[18] He acquired a great knowledge of the history of his own country, one of his major works being a *History of Bithynia* in ten volumes; but he also travelled widely, and was teaching at Rome in the time of Pompey the Great. How long he stayed we do not know, but he then transferred his activities to southern Spain, where he sojourned and taught among the Turdetani in the province of Baetica. He produced an account of the tribes in that area, which was later used by the geographer Strabo. He was also the author of a very substantial *Grammar*, of biographies of grammarians, of a separate work on orthography, and of commentaries on Homer and Theocritus, which are referred to by ancient scholiasts. He was far from being an isolated figure, for the expression 'the followers of Asclepiades', used in the second century A.D. by Sextus Empiricus,[19] shows that he must have numbered among his pupils some who became professional 'grammarians' themselves. Sextus was the author of the essay *Against the Grammarians*, a rather clever and amusing satire of their teaching and pretensions. The importance of this essay for our purpose lies not so much in the shrewd, though often sophistical, arguments by which he seeks to deflate them, as in the fact that he systematically follows their plan of work, and gives summaries of its content, section by section. The authorities whom he uses, and sometimes quotes, were all very much earlier than his own day, and date back to the late Republic. One of his major sources was undoubtedly the *Grammar* of Asclepiades, and it is particularly noteworthy that the main structure of his essay closely corresponds to the divisions of the subject which he himself quotes from Asclepiades.[20] The first part, which he calls the 'technical', or systematic part, is concerned with grammar, and deals with letters, syllables, parts of speech, parsing and scansion, spelling, correct Greek (with analogy, barbarisms, and solecisms) and etymology. The second part, called 'historical', deals with mythology, and the third part, sometimes called the 'specialized part' because it is concerned with authors rather than general principles or background material, is devoted to the reading and exposition of writers, especially poets. Thus it is evident that, in Greek, before the end of the Republic, Grammar had been raised to become an integral part of the scholarly equipment and the teaching programme of the *grammatikos*, and, in the opinion of some, stood on a par with Literature. Individual interests differed; some became absorbed in language, others were more attracted by mythology, and others were most concerned with the exposition of the poets themselves. The best teachers strove to maintain a balance, though the increase of specialized knowledge in all departments made this no easy task. If we turn now to Latin, we may see that, from the mid-second century B.C. onwards, events had begun to move in the same direction as in Greece, and by the first century A.D. remarkably parallel developments had taken place.

For the early history of Latin 'grammatical' scholarship, considerable interest attaches to the opening chapters of an essay of Suetonius, which came to light in the fifteenth century in the monastery of Hersfeld. The codex of which it formed part also contained the hitherto unknown minor works of Tacitus, and it was the discovery of the new Tacitus which was hailed with particular enthusiasm. Suetonius' work, written in the early second century A.D., perhaps before the more famous *Lives of the Caesars*, is entitled *De Grammaticis et Rhetoribus*, and originally formed part of a whole series of biographies, including poets, historians and orators.[21] The twenty-four chapters on the 'grammarians' have survived intact (though the surviving copies of the lost original codex still present textual problems); but only six chapters remain of the section on the rhetoricians, the rest being represented merely by an index of names.[22] This unpretentious little work, of which St Jerome made use in compiling his *Chronicle*, begins by discussing the introduction of 'grammatical' studies at Rome, and then surveys the lives of the most distinguished schoolmasters over a period of two centuries, briefly recording their origins, their experiences, their interests, their achievements and their failures. Enlivened as it is with occasional anecdotes in the true Suetonian manner, it makes a valuable little 'Who Was Who' of Roman education.

According to Suetonius (who in his introduction is most probably following Varro),[23] serious interest in literary scholarship was first aroused in Rome by the lectures of Crates, the librarian of Pergamum. These were pretty certainly concerned with Homer,[24] and they gave some of his listeners the idea of acquiring a wider publicity for the works of their own national poets by public readings, to which they might add their own commentaries. To do this, they, like the scholars of Alexandria and Pergamum, had to perform the necessary editorial work in preparing the texts. So Q. Octavius Lampadio dealt with the *Punic War* of Naevius, which he divided into seven books, and he must have written out other poets, too, for, in the second century A.D., any manuscript in the hand of Lampadio was a rare and prized possession.[25] Similarly, Q. Vargunteius gave public readings of the *Annals* of Ennius, which drew large audiences. Later, the *Satires* of Lucilius became more widely known through readings given by his friends, Laelius Archelaus and Vettius Philocomus. But this was only a beginning, and Suetonius rightly draws a distinction between these early pioneers of literary scholarship and the far more wide-ranging and detailed studies of Aelius Stilo and his son-in-law, Servius Clodius, both professional scholars and both Roman knights. Aelius, as we shall see, had contact with Alexandrian methods of text-correction, and it is worth remembering not only that Aristarchus had many pupils, but that, after the great 'scattering' (*diaspora*) of scholars who fled from that city in the mid-second century under Ptolemy VIII, men who had been trained there made its scholarly work known in many parts of the Mediterranean world. Later, Strabo says that in his day there were many Alexandrian scholars in Rome.[26]

Aelius' full name was L. Aelius Stilo Praeconinus, the name Stilo being given him because he was a 'penman' (from *stilus*) who wrote speeches for his friends among the nobility, and Praeconinus because his father had been the public herald (*praeco*) of Lanuvium.[27] Aelius was extremely learned in the antiquities of Rome, and produced a commentary on the almost unintelligible Salian Hymns. He had a strong interest in rare and obsolete words (glossography), but made very fanciful use of etymology in some of his notes on meanings and derivations. But his most valuable contribution to scholarship was his critical work on the plays of Plautus. Varro, who was his pupil (privately, for Aelius did not teach in school) transmitted his somewhat over-enthusiastic remark that 'if the Muses had spoken Latin, they would have spoken in the language of Plautus'.[28] In works performed for the stage, whether comedy or tragedy, there was particular need for an authoritative recension, as so many alterations and interpolations had been made over the years by those who had acted in them. There is definite evidence from a late source that Aelius made use in his textual work of the critical signs of Aristarchus, as also did Valerius Probus under the Empire.[29] These signs had been devised by the Alexandrians as a neat method of indicating their opinions to those who used their recensions, and we have the list as used by Aristarchus. If, in particular, he thought a line, or passage, spurious, or unworthy of the author's normal standard, he put a short horizontal line, an *obelos*, in the margin to indicate it. There were also, for instance, the asterisk (·✕·), to mark verses wrongly repeated elsewhere, the *antisigma* (Ɔ), to mark verses in the wrong order, the *antisigma* with a point (Ɔ̇), to mark doubt as to which of two similar passages was genuine, and many others. Aelius inherited this system. Now it is known that in 100 B.C. Aelius accompanied his friend, Metellus Numidicus, into exile, and that part of the exile was spent in Rhodes, where Metellus listened to the lectures of distinguished scholars. It is, therefore, a fair supposition that he and Aelius took the opportunity of hearing Dionysius Thrax.[30] In that case, Aelius may well have learnt from him the use of Aristarchus' signs, and later introduced them into his Latin texts. Servius Clodius may also have followed suit; he, too, had a special interest in Plautus, and Cicero, who knew him, observed that he could declare without difficulty: 'This is a verse of Plautus, that is not' — so trained an ear had he for discerning the idiosyncrasies of the genuine Plautine style.[31] Both Aelius and Servius went beyond the correction of individual texts; they also sorted out from the mass of plays which had come down under the name of Plautus those which they considered were definitely genuine, and each formed his own Index. Aelius accepted only twenty-five plays as genuine, but quite a number of other Latin 'grammarians', such as Volcacius Sedigitus and Aurelius Opillus, also produced their own lists at this early period, all of which were later taken into consideration by Varro.[32]

Thus the early Roman scholars were particularly interested in the Latin poets, and, like their predecessors in Alexandria and Pergamum, were much concerned with questions of authenticity and with the accurate transmission and elucidation of their texts. But in order to carry out this work of 'correction' to their own satisfaction, they needed to examine their own language more closely, to reduce it to some sort of system, which they could use as their standard, and to determine what was correct Latin and what was not. When any branch of knowledge was systematized, it could be presented in the form of a compact manual (in Greek, *techne*, in Latin, *ars*),[33] and Cicero includes grammar among those studies which had been thus formalized (*conclusa artibus*).[34] This must have happened in Latin as early as the time of Sulla, for the author of the rhetorical treatise addressed to Herennius (itself a manual) mentions that he intends to compose a textbook (*ars*) of grammar.[35] What is more, such a textbook, even in the Ciceronian Age, would have contained not only a structural analysis of the language, but also the further extension, which we have mentioned in Greek, into the determination of correctness. Not only does the author referred to make mention of barbarisms and solecisms, but Cicero, too, speaks of 'the precepts of correct Latinity, which are communicated in the education of children'.[36] Undoubtedly, great contributions to every branch of grammatical scholarship were made by Varro, whose voluminous works (including the partially extant treatise *On the Latin Language*) were a mine of information for later grammarians. It is a matter of chance that the earliest Latin Grammar, of which some sort of reconstruction can be made, is that of Palaemon in the first century A.D., for this became a standard textbook.[37] But, in the over-all view, the important point is that, by the first century A.D., the balance of Grammar and Literature in the 'grammarian's' curriculum was very much the same in Latin as it had become in Greek. Seneca, speaking of Latin, gives the same threefold division of work which we have met in Asclepiades, into linguistic study (*cura sermonis*), mythology, and the exposition of the poets (including metrics).[38] But the general view was that which is presented in Quintilian, that there were two major parts of the subject, Grammar and Literature, though Quintilian, who did not give mythology so great a prominence, was aware that this was a telescoping of the three-part system, which we found in Asclepiades.[39]

As earlier in Greece, the question must already have arisen before Cicero's day as to what appellation should be given to a scholar who possessed this kind of knowledge. It was obviously quite unsatisfactory to term him *litterator*, which would equate him with the Greek *grammatistes*, and imply too elementary a standard. In fact, there is, in our period, only one certain example in which a 'grammarian' is termed *litterator*, and that is almost certainly sarcastic.[40] It was much more complimentary to call him *litteratus*, a 'man of letters', but this did not quite suggest the requisite degree of special expertise.[41] The best solution seemed to be to Latinize the Greek terms, and to call him *criticus* or *grammaticus*; the former, however, was rather too closely associated with textual and literary criticism, and, though accepted, [42] was much more rarely used than *grammaticus*, which became the standard word. But, as in Greek, it had to serve a double purpose, and was equally applicable, for instance, to Varro, who did not keep a school, and to Orbilius, who did. Greek influence is also seen in the fact that by Cicero's time, the word *schola* had been introduced to describe the school of higher standard, and from then on was regularly applied to that of the 'grammarian', the rhetorician, or the philosopher. The Greek word *schole* originally meant leisure, then the occupation of leisure in learned discussion or lectures, then a group to whom, or a place in which, such lectures were given; hence, through Latin, the old English spelling 'scole'. The native Latin word for 'school' was *ludus*, but this now remained particularly associated with the primary school (*ludus litterarius*, or 'school of letters'), as the expression *ludi magister* ('primary teacher') shows.[43] It has always been something of a puzzle as to why the Roman word *ludus*, which meant 'play', should have come to be used

Fig. 9 *Ave magister! A reading-session disturbed. A relief from Neumagen, third century A.D.*

to mean a 'school'. Ancient etymologists were very fond of explaining that word-meanings could be derived from contrary ideas; and Aelius Stilo probably first suggested, and Quintilian and the lexicographer Festus accepted, that a school was called *ludus* because it was the very opposite of a place of play.[44] According to Festus, the word was chosen lest a less attractive term might discourage children from attending.[45] Sir Walter Scott, with dry humour, makes Erasmus Holiday, the schoolmaster in *Kenilworth*, quote this hoary old derivation, and remark 'that he was inclined to think that he bore the name of Holiday *quasi lucus a non lucendo*, because he gave such few holidays in his school'.[46] This derivation, nevertheless, is exceedingly dubious; certainly, the notion of contrast lies behind the usage, but it is a contrast of a different kind. Perhaps a new explanation may commend itself, namely, that the word *ludus*, which came to be applied to various kinds of training-establishment (reading and writing, music, dancing, acting[47] — even a rhetoric school could still be called a *ludus dicendi*)[48] originally existed in a military context; the training exercises of young recruits were called 'play', or just a 'game', in contrast to the stern reality of battle. The most ancient form of organized youthful training, revived by Augustus and described by Virgil, was called *lusus Troiae*, 'The Game of Troy',[49] and Virgil makes Ascanius say that in sport (*ludo*) he 'aroused the mimicry of war' (*belli simulacra*).[50] Furthermore, the words *proludere* and *prolusio* (which Cicero jestingly uses as a play on *ludus*, 'school')[51] retained a particularly military connotation, that is, preliminary practice for battle.[52] Hence, a group of young soldiers organized for such practice would be called a *ludus*, and the same term would be used of a building designed for such preliminary exercises, as in the 'gladiatorial school'. Thus, metaphorically, a critic of declamation remarks that 'the rhetoric school (*scholam*) had always been considered a *ludus* ('training-ground'), and the Forum an arena'.[53] It is easy to understand, therefore, how, in early times, a group of young boys, gathered now for elementary mental training as well as physical exercises, should have acquired the name of *ludus*. Finally, to return to the immediate subject, a further indication of the higher standing which the *grammaticus* enjoyed may be seen in the fact that, in the imperial period, he, like other teachers of the 'liberal arts', was commonly described as *professor*, a term of which the use was expressly denied to teachers of the primary grade.[54]

The increasing accumulation of knowledge which took place in the late Republic and early Empire, and which affected first scholarship and then the teaching-programme, was also reflected in certain distinctions which came to be applied within the profession itself. Under the Republic, it seems to have been quite usual for the same person to teach both Latin and Greek; but gradually, as inscriptions show, there came about a separation, and the *grammaticus Graecus*[55] was distinguished from the *grammaticus Latinus*,[56] each of them keeping to his own province. Under the Empire, there would be more Greeks teaching only Greek, and more Romans who specialized in Latin. On the other hand, there are also inscriptions in which there is no specification beyond 'grammarian',[57] and there must still have been many who taught both languages. Suetonius, of course, deals only with the most distinguished teachers (*clari professores*), but what does not seem to be generally realized is that he gives a rather one-sided picture. He directs his attention to those who, in scholarship or in teaching, gave valuable service to Latin studies, whether or not they taught Greek as well. Hence he says nothing of those who were primarily, or exclusively, Greek teachers, such as Tyrannio and Asclepiades. Noteworthy, too, is his omission of Epaphroditus of Chaeronea, an important scholar, who taught for very many years at Rome in the latter part of the first century A.D., the basis of whose surviving portrait-statue carries the inscription *grammaticus Graecus* (cf. Fig. 8).[58] We could well have done with the same kind of record for Greek which Suetonius has given, mainly, for Latin. Much relevant information was pretty certainly contained in the work of Hermippus of Berytus, entitled *On slaves who won distinction in learning*, which is not extant. As it is, although Suetonius tells us that 'grammatical' studies were already flourishing in the provinces, especially Gallia Togata, early in the first century B.C., he does not inform us whether any of the Greek scholars, who were in Rome before that time, had transferred from private tuition and opened schools in Greek. But it is interesting to learn from him that even under the Republic, there were, at times, more than twenty well-attended 'grammar-schools' in Rome.[59]

In some of these schools, at least an introductory course on rhetoric was given, in Latin, to follow the main teaching on grammar and literature; the same remained true under the Empire, though by then the two professions had become more sharply distinct, and this was really, as Quintilian complained, an encroachment.[60] Becoming involved in rhetoric meant dealing with prose and with prose authors, but the generally accepted view was that the *grammatici* were, in Cicero's words, 'interpreters of the poets', and that 'a thorough treatment of the poets' was their primary duty.[61] There can be no doubt that, as scholars, and as teachers of grammar, the *grammatici* were indeed familiar with prose authors, and could not afford to neglect them. But, as may be seen from Quintilian,[62] when they expounded a text in class, and illustrated it with wide-ranging and detailed comments, it was a text in verse, and not in prose; for poetry always remained their main concern.

It is a remarkable fact that even the more successful *grammatici*, who arrived from places often far distant from Rome, were usually either former slaves, who had acquired their freedom, or else, if freeborn, had risen from humble origins and often from conditions of exceptional hardship. Of the 'grammarians' mentioned by Suetonius, most were freedmen, though a few were of free birth. The elder Seneca remarked that, under the Republic, all the finest disciplines were in the hands of freedmen;[63] under the Empire, this generalization would have needed to be modified, as both 'grammar' and rhetoric gained ground and attracted also men of free birth. Of 'grammarians' mentioned by Suetonius, some who were, or claimed to be, freeborn, had been the victims of adverse circumstances in very early life. Orbilius, who taught Horace, had lost both parents on a single day, murdered by the treacherous act of their personal enemies; left destitute, he became an attendant (*apparitor*) to the local magistrates in Beneventum, a lowly office usually performed by slaves. Nevertheless he studied hard as a boy in his spare time, and laid the foundations for his work in later life.[64] His younger contemporary, Valerius Cato, also fared ill in youth; he, too, according to his own account, was an orphan, and was robbed of his patrimony in the disturbances of the Sullan era, but rose by his own efforts to make a name at Rome.[65] As we have seen, Antonius Gnipho, the teacher of Caesar, had been exposed as a child, but was reared and educated by his rescuer. Another exposed child of free birth was C. Melissus, who came from Spoletium in Umbria; when his parents quarrelled, he was left to fend for himself, but, like Gnipho, was brought up and educated by some unnamed benefactor, who then presented him as a gift to Maecenas. He lived on friendly terms with Maecenas, was manumitted, and won the favour of Augustus.[66] Sometimes, a slave-child owed his education to the fact that he happened to be in the household of a *grammaticus*, who thought him worth teaching. Scribonius Aphrodisius, who made a name as a teacher under Augustus, had been the slave and pupil of Orbilius, until he was purchased and given his freedom by Scribonia, the former wife of Octavian.[67] Similarly, Julius Modestus, who became a scholar, followed in the footsteps of his patron, the 'grammarian' Hyginus.[68] The Greek Epaphroditus was a slave (perhaps a foundling) in the house of a grammarian called Archias at Alexandria. He was then acquired by M. Mettius, the Prefect of Egypt, as a tutor for his son, was manumitted, and, as M. Mettius Epaphroditus taught and worked as a scholar with conspicuous success in Rome.[69] Thus these future teachers might have been self-taught, or they might have benefited from an act of generosity, or they might have been educated with a view to enhancing their market-value, for, even at the *grammaticus* level, commercialization often played a part.

As early as the beginning of the first century B.C., a slave, who had the distinction of mind and the acquired learning to render him valuable as a teacher or a literary collaborator, might be put up for auction and sold to the highest bidder. The highest price ever paid in Roman times was reported to have been given for a certain Daphnis; he was apparently educated by the poet Accius, who sold him for 700,000 sesterces to M. Scaurus, leader of the Senate, who later transferred him for the same sum to the wealthy patron of letters, Q. Lutatius Catulus. Catulus generously manumitted him, and he became Q. Lutatius Daphnis.[70] Sometimes a *grammaticus* was hired by contract to teach, and a surprising indication of the rapid growth of demand for secondary education may be seen in the report that a very wealthy Roman knight, Aeficius Calvinus, hired L. Apuleius to teach, at an annual fee of 400,000 sesterces; evidently, there were so many pupils that Calvinus could more than recoup his outlay from the proceeds of fees paid by parents. This, however, may not have been at Rome, but in some provincial centre, where the best teachers were not so easy to obtain.[71]

Only a tiny fraction of the history of the commercial transactions involving teachers has survived, but there is one story which has a particular interest. In the time of Sulla (*c.* 83 B.C.), a youth called Eros, subsequently Staberius Eros, was one of a crowd of slaves who were herded together, like so many cattle, on a transport-ship, plying between Antioch and Italy. With him were two companions, one of them Syrus, later Publilius Syrus, who made his name as a writer of mimes, and many of whose lines came to be learnt by heart in Roman schools; the other was a Manilius, quite possibly an ancestor of the writer on astronomy. When they reached Italy, their feet were marked with white chalk to denote their foreign origin, and they were set up along with others on a high sale-platform known as a *catasta*. How Manilius fared we do not know, but Syrus and Eros were lucky. Syrus was bought by a freedman, whose patron he impressed by his lively intelligence and wit, and soon won his freedom. Eros also found a master who recognized his ability and freed him. He formed a school, and even during the horrors of the Sullan proscriptions, a time of the most brutal carnage, he continued, it was said, to teach the sons of the proscribed without accepting a fee — a good deed in a naughty world. Later, Staberius included both Brutus and Cassius among his pupils.[72] His published work was also important, and was known to and valued by that omnivorous reader, the elder Pliny, who calls him 'the founder of Latin grammar'. This was probably a reference to his studies in analogy.[73] Staberius also copied out in his own hand texts of classical writers, some of which survived, and were highly esteemed, centuries later.[74] His career epitomizes the extraordinary tenacity, courage in adversity and devotion to learning displayed by so many of these teachers of the Republican period.

Those who, from their varied origins and experiences, had somehow acquired a good knowledge of language and literature, did not necessarily take up teaching at once; circumstances sometimes led them into quite different fields of activity, perhaps for many years, and then only in later life did they open a school. This was so with Orbilius; after a period of service with the magistrates in Beneventum, he entered the Army and was sent to Macedonia, where he rose to become a kind of adjutant, or head of a legionary bureau (*cornicularius*), and later transferred from this administrative work to join the cavalry. Only after this military service did he resume his studies, and begin what was to be a long teaching career, first at Beneventum and then in Rome. But few could have seen more of the world than Pompeius Lenaeus, who began life as a slave, was rescued either from kidnappers or some form of bondage, and, after an adventurous boyhood, managed to obtain a good education and purchased his freedom. His literary and linguistic ability made him a useful member of Pompey's staff, and, in a secretarial capacity, he accompanied that roving commander on nearly all his expeditions. In the year 63 B.C., when Orbilius began teaching in Rome, Lenaeus was, on Pompey's behalf, investigating the contents of the library of the defeated Mithridates in Pontus; in a bookcase there, that monarch's collection of medical treatises came to light, and Lenaeus was instructed by Pompey to translate them into Latin, which he did. Lenaeus became a recognized authority on pharmacology (there were many herbs in Pontus), and his works were among those used later by the elder Pliny. He remained passionately loyal to the family of Pompey throughout his life, and was so incensed by an insulting remark made about his hero by the historian Sallust that he retaliated with an extremely abusive satire on Sallust's own personal life, as well as his historical work. It was in the district of Rome known as the *Carinae*, a fashionable locality, where Pompey's house had been, that he finally settled down to teach (*c.*35 B.C.) for the remainder of his life. Altogether it was quite a remarkable career after a singularly unpromising beginning.[75] Probably many other grammarians, too, had tried their hands at a variety of occupations before opening a school. In the early Empire, Crassicius, a freedman from Tarentum, had been connected with the stage, and assisted the writers of mimes; Pomponius Marcellus

Fig.10 *'Work hard, boy, lest you be thrashed'. A salutary warning, or an imposition; written by the master and copied four times by the boy.*

had originally been a boxer (an art which he may have found useful in dealing with unruly pupils) and the celebrated Remmius Palaemon had been trained as a weaver.[76] It is a pity that more of them did not publish their memoirs, which would probably have taken us into some of the more interesting byways of Roman social life. To judge from Suetonius' record, it would seem that men of free birth probably only took up teaching when there was no better option open to them. Varerius Probus, who spent his early life at Berytus in Syria in the first century A.D., had made repeated attempts to obtain a post of centurion before he finally devoted himself to scholarship and teaching. He evidently had sufficient means to be able to content himself with a few pupils at a time, whom he taught privately. He was a true scholar in the tradition of Aristarchus and Aelius; he did a great deal to rescue texts of early Latin literature from threatened oblivion, and produced critical recensions not only of Terence but also of Lucretius, Horace and Virgil, marking his texts with the critical signs of Aristarchus. His was one of the most distinguished names in Latin scholarship.[77]

Though of less enduring fame than Probus, quite a number of those whose lives Suetonius records were *grammatici* in the sense of 'literary scholars' as well as 'teachers'. It is a remarkable fact that, although their native language was quite often Greek, they were counted among the leading authorities on the Latin language and literature, and the antiquities of Rome. They covered a wide range of interests. Some, like Antonius Gnipho, Staberius Eros and Palaemon, were primarily linguistic scholars; others concerned themselves with literary investigation, and some, like Aurelius Opillus and Ateius Praetextatus, who called himself Philologus (following Eratosthenes), were all-round antiquarians. Sometimes these varied activities were combined. Opillus, a freedman, who at various times taught philosophy, rhetoric and 'grammar', and finally closed his school to accompany Rutilius Rufus into exile in 92 B.C., was a voluminous writer, and ranged over a wide field of miscellaneous erudition; he also contributed particularly to the study of Plautus.[78] Pompilius Andronicus produced a critical study of the *Annals* of Ennius,[79] and Curtius Nicias, who hailed from the island of Cos, wrote books on Lucilius, which gained subsequent recognition. [80] Valerius Cato and Pompeius Lenaeus also had a special interest in Lucilius; but Cato, besides writing grammatical treatises, also composed poems in the Alexandrian manner, gained high repute as a teacher of young poets, and was accepted as a leading figure of the neoteric school.[81] A further interesting illustration of the connection between contemporary poetry and the *grammatici* may be seen in the fact that the mythological poem entitled *Smyrna*, written by Catullus' friend, Helvius Cinna, which took nine years to compose, was so full of learned allusions, and even obscurities, that the grammarian Crassicius made a name by producing a commentary on it.[82] Some of the *grammatici*, however, even in Horace's day, were still admirers of the older literature, and obstinately opposed to acceptance of the new.

Although Horace disdained their company,[83] the respect in which the most learned *grammatici* were held is clearly illustrated both by the friendships which they made, and by the fact that cultured Romans, interested in literature, history or antiquities, often turned to them for help and advice. Cicero acknowledged his friend Curtius Nicias as an authority on Homer, 'a second Aristarchus', and he is probably the Nicias whose name often occurs in the Homeric scholia in connection with matters of punctuation. The orator also consulted him on questions of correct Latinity.[84] Ateius Philologus, a native of Athens, became the friend and adviser of both Asinius Pollio and Sallust, and composed for the latter's use a compendium of Roman history.[85] Caecilius Epirota, who was closely concerned with the neoteric school of poetry, was an intimate friend of Cornelius Gallus.[86] At the highest level, a 'grammarian' might become accepted in court circles, and hope to win the Emperor's patronage. So Iulius Hyginus, a freedman of Augustus, was appointed by him as head of the fine Palatine Library, and not only continued to teach many pupils, but made several important contributions to scholarship, including a commentary on Virgil.[87] Similarly, C. Melissus became friendly with Augustus, and was placed in charge of the library in the *porticus Octaviae*.[88] It was even possible to go higher than this, for Dionysius of Alexandria, who was in Rome from the time of Nero to that of Trajan, not only became chief librarian, but was appointed to imperial secretaryships, most influential posts.[89]

It is understandable, therefore, that any 'grammarian' who aspired to make a name would strive to improve his social connections. Again and again, Suetonius notes that celebrated *grammatici* taught not merely 'many pupils', but 'many pupils of high birth'.[90] It was also true, at all times, that a teacher's standing and prospects could be enhanced by the known fact that some of his pupils had achieved distinction in life and occupied important positions.[91] A very good example of a successful schoolmaster was the father of the poet Statius. His school at Naples was attended by boys of good birth (*generosa pubes*) not only from the immediate surroundings, but from a wide area of southern Italy. When he later transferred to Rome, it was to teach the 'future leaders' there, and his pupils included those who became provincial governors, magistrates, members of the priesthoods, and officers in the Army. He himself came from a family which had once been well-to-do, but had been reduced to straitened circumstances;[92] and it may be noted that, in the later Empire, too, many more of the teachers were men of good birth themselves.[93] But all this represents only the more attractive side of the picture; for Suetonius clearly shows that, even for 'grammarians' who made a name, there were many pitfalls on life's road. For the rank and file of the profession, on whom Fortune did not smile, and who found no helping hand, the going was hard; and some, like the future emperor, Pertinax, gave up because teaching did not pay.[94] The most that those who persevered under difficulties could hope for was that their boys would do well at the next stage of their education, and win some recognition for their teachers when they reached the rhetoric school.

CHAPTER VI

The rhetoric schools and their critics

The art of rhetoric, the creation of the Greeks, was late in gaining acceptance at Rome. Certainly, in the centuries which preceded its introduction, there must always have been men who surpassed the rest in readiness of speech (*facundia*), and who were chosen to represent them, for 'spokesman' was what *orator* originally meant. But there is no evidence that they were trained to do so. In a community which had seen so much political strife and so many hard-fought causes, there would always have been those who could sway their fellow-citizens by speeches which bore the stamp of their own personality.[1] The manner of speech of Fabius Maximus Cunctator, says Plutarch, accorded closely with his life, 'for there was in it no embellishment, none of the superficial charm of the forensic orator, but the expression of his own thoughts, which took an individual and highly sententious form, and carried weight'.[2] Tribunician oratory, on the other hand, must often have been far more vehement and impassioned. But, whatever the circumstances, these early orators had what Quintilian calls a 'natural eloquence', which owed nothing to preparatory exercises and the study of textbook rules.[3]

From a tantalisingly brief fragment of Ennius, of which we do not know the context, but which reads 'some will take up rhetoric',[4] it would seem that already before 169 B.C., the date of his death, it was possible to obtain instruction in the subject. If so, the teachers at that time, as long afterwards, would have been exclusively Greeks, and many more of them must have become available after the defeat of Macedon in 168. There is, however, as yet nothing to show that their teaching was organized in the form of schools, and, in default of such evidence, we must suppose that rhetorical studies were pursued under the guidance of a private tutor at home, as later by Tiberius and Caius Gracchus.[5] But by 161 B.C. the influence of such teachers had developed so much that it became a matter of official concern, and in that year, by decree of the senate, both rhetoricians and philosophers were suddenly expelled from Rome.[6] Unlike the later edict of the censors of 92 B.C., by which the organized teaching of the 'Latin rhetoricians' was suppressed, the decree makes no special mention of schools. As to the motives which lay behind the decree, it would hardly be likely to have been simply due to conservative reaction against Greeks as such, on the ground that, as foreigners, they represented an alien tradition. This prejudice did undoubtedly exist, but the fact remains that the teachers of grammar and literature were also Greeks, and there was never apparently any suggestion that they should be expelled from Rome. It is more probable that it was anxiety about the possible effects of their teaching which led to their dismissal. These fluent Greeks had an argument for everything; they were too ingenious to be trusted. Cato remarked of the philosopher Carneades that, once one had listened to him, it was impossible to tell what was true and what was not.[7] Rhetoricians had always been notorious for 'making the worse appear the better cause', as Plato said, and it may well be that Cato, and others like him, felt apprehensive about the effects of Greek plausibility on Roman audiences and their decisions. In the course of time Roman listeners did become suspicious of orators who were thought to be using some kind of Greek craft (*artificium*) to persuade them, and this was why M. Antonius deliberately disclaimed any knowledge of Greek studies, and, by so doing, made himself more acceptable as a speaker.[8] Nevertheless, ambitious young men did not look at the matter in this way. Their enthusiasm, as Cicero says,[9] had been kindled by listening to the Greeks, and they became the more keen to bring in professional rhetoricians to teach them the art. So, despite the opposition of the Senate in 161, rhetorical instruction soon came to be in increasing demand.

For most young men, although training in the deliberative branch of oratory could be useful for those who in the future would need to urge, in the Senate or before an assembly of the people, the advisability or inadvisability of measures affecting the State, judicial oratory was the most immediate field, and offered the most attractive rewards. Those rewards were not necessarily financial in the first instance, for the *Lex Cincia* of 204 B.C. had forbidden advocates to accept fees, though its provisions were often evaded. Rather, the young advocate looked first to making his name known by an initial success, and then to acquiring a stock of goodwill (*gratia*) by his services to his clients; most of all, he aspired to win public recognition, which could subsequently prove of great value in entering on a political career. Of the two great departments of legal activity, the civil and the criminal, it was the latter which appealed most strongly to the ambitious young orator. Although there was always an immense amount of private litigation, and advocates were very much in demand, pleading before a single judge afforded a very limited scope for eloquence. Even addressing a panel of judges, as in the centumviral court, on a matter of civil law, was not particularly rewarding, and it is said that none of the Republican orators made anything of a reputation in it.[10] In the innumerable quarrel-producing grievances of daily life, the result was mainly of concern to the litigants themselves rather than to the general public. But in criminal cases it was different; here there was much greater scope and widespread interest, especially if the defendant should happen to be a man of wealth or political standing.[11]

Political prosecutions were among the most notoriously recurrent features of Roman public life in the last century and a half of the Republic. To the aspiring young advocate, prosecution — even if he appeared only as a junior counsel (*subscriptor*) — was much more attractive than defence. The younger Scipio, when Polybius first met him at the age of eighteen, felt himself to be quite exceptional in not appearing in the lawcourts like his contemporaries; but Polybius praised him for this, 'for the others could only win praise by injuring one of their fellow-citizens, this being the usual consequence of prosecutions'.[12] This was in 167 B.C., but less than twenty years later, in 149, the *Lex Calpurnia* established the first permanent court (*quaestio perpetua*) for the trial of cases of alleged extortion; the consequence was that, as the expansion of Roman dominion offered quick avenues to wealth through provincial exploitation, the number of such criminal trials began to rise sharply. In 137, the introduction of voting by secret ballot in criminal trials held before an assembly of the people (*iudicia populi*) also increased the number of cases and the demand for advocates. These were the two developments which provided scope for the oratory of C. Carbo, the most eminent advocate of his day.[13]

In the last half-century or so of the Republic, not only political corruption, but assassinations, poisonings and all kinds of violence became so rife[14] that the opportunities for able young men to take part in criminal proceedings were immense; and this was particularly true after the reorganization of the criminal courts by Sulla. There was no state prosecutor at Rome, and the field was wide open to private individuals, provided that they could get themselves officially accepted as prosecutors in particular cases. Crassus, Lucullus, Appius Clodius Pulcher, Julius Caesar, Caelius Rufus and Sempronius Atratinus all began their careers in this way.[15] There were also, naturally, opportunities to make a name in defence, and the custom developed of employing several advocates, who divided the case between them. Normally, it should be observed, the fact that a young man began by prosecuting did not mean that he continued to maintain this role in his subsequent career. There were still certain ethics in advocacy, at any rate in the best society. Cicero's view was that defence was a most honourable role but that prosecution was sometimes both praiseworthy and necessary in the public interest; but to be frequently engaged in it was most reprehensible. Prosecution, in any case, should only be undertaken when it was to the public advantage, and a justifiable reputation might be made by coming to the aid of the oppressed; but retaliating against a wrong done to oneself or a member of one's family was also to be regarded as a just cause.[16]

During the lifetimes of two of the greatest Republican orators, L. Licinius Crassus (140-91 B.C), and M. Antonius (143-87 B.C.), grandfather of the triumvir, there became available in Rome not only an ample supply of teachers of rhetoric, but also a number of established schools.[17] Until nearly the end of that period, these were in the hands of Greeks, who inherited the tradition that instruction in public speaking could be reduced to a system, and the necessary precepts learned by heart and applied in practice. Their teaching was based on the textbooks, or 'craft-manuals' (*technai*), compiled by the 'technographers' for the use of students. Such handbooks had been produced in Greek for generations, beginning long before Aristotle, who had made a collection of those which survived in his own time.[18] During the Hellenistic period, and especially after Hermagoras, the most influential theorist of his day (mid-second century B.C.) and fragments of whose work survive,[19] these manuals became quite stereotyped in form. They classified the branches of oratory (judicial, deliberative and epideictic), and gave rules for the treatment of each type, paying by far the fullest attention to the judicial branch. They distinguished the parts of oratory (invention of material, arrangement, style, memory-training and delivery), and discussed each in turn the necessary sections of a speech, (basically) introduction, statement of the case, proofs and refutations, and peroration. Each section was equipped with its appropriate precepts, but Hermagoras set the pattern for his successors by concentrating on the clarification of the central issue involved in different types of cases, and supplying standard arguments which should be used either in accusation or defence. The question might be one of establishing fact, especially when evidence was largely circumstantial ('Did the defendant commit the act, or not?'), or one of definition ('What precisely constitutes the particular offence?'), or one of the justification, or palliation, of an admitted act ('Does the defendant deserve to be penalized?'),[20] or (mainly in Greek cases) one of the competence of the court. Cicero acknowledged that these lines of approach were useful, but found Hermagoras deficient in his treatment of style — so much so that orators trained exclusively on his system were undistinguished and arid.[21] Other rhetoricians did pay much more attention to style, at least to the tropes and figures, drawing upon the classical Greek orators or poets for illustrations of them. But from Hermagoras onwards there was a certain family likeness about these manuals of rhetoric, though, naturally, individual authors liked to introduce their own modifications of the divisions and subdivisions, and to refine on the work of their predecessors. It was not, it seems, until early in the first century B.C. that such textbooks began to be produced in Latin. Cicero's own treatise *On Invention* (limited to this particular part of oratory) was a work of his early youth, which he subsequently disparaged. There are, however, as is well known, many similarities between it and the anonymous treatise addressed, probably *c.*86-82, to a certain Herennius (*Rhetorica ad Herennium*). This is a valuable and more comprehensive work, in which the illustrations are often illuminating, not least in the very full treatment of the figures of speech. But both treatises owe their basic doctrines to the Greeks.

Although rhetoricians were paid to teach such material, it would, of course, have been quite fallacious for anyone to suppose, at any period, that simple adherence to their precepts would, of itself, produce a good orator. In fact, the more eminent a Roman orator became, by virtue of wider personal study, practice and experience in various kinds of public speaking, the more likely he was to stress the inadequacy of the textbooks, as compared with the kinds of skill which he found to be necessary in the arena of real-life debate. This was the attitude of Crassus, Antonius, and other interlocutors in Cicero's full-scale dialogue *De Oratore*, which purports to represent a discussion of 91 B.C., when Cicero was a boy of fifteen, though not actually composed until very much later, in 55. By that time, Cicero himself had long realized the shortcomings of his early work *On Invention*, and desired to replace it by a much more cultured and liberal treatment of the whole subject of oratory,[22] which would not only be graced by the artistically developed views of his most distinguished predecessors, but would also, in many ways, reflect his own mature judgment and the sources of his own success. In this dialogue, the interlocutors, being themselves men of exceptional oratorical ability and great practical experience (for several of them had held the highest offices of state) are naturally represented as critical of the professional rhetoricians, who spent their lives in schools, hammering the principles of speech-construction into their young pupils. They are habitually disparaging in their references to 'those fellows' (*isti*), their handbooks, and their concentration on the sections of speeches.[23] It was in character for them, as Romans of high standing, to look down on those who taught for fees, and, as men of culture, to deplore the dogmatic and unimaginative methods of contemporary teachers. Yet there is a certain illogicality in their position, for, when they come to expound their own views on oratory, we find that they themselves accept the traditional divisions of Greek rhetoric, and take for granted many of the traditional precepts. But, in so doing, they like to claim that whatever they take over is 'obvious' and 'natural', and depress its importance in comparison with their own mature observations. It is quite evident (though they did not like advertising the fact) that they, like Cicero himself, had made a close study of Greek rhetoric in their youth. It is understandable that they should criticize Greek rhetoricians as having no practical experience of Roman political debates or of advocacy in the Roman courts, and as men who 'teach other people what they have not tried themselves'.[24] Yet it still remains significant that Crassus, after giving what is tantamount to a resumé of standard rhetorical doctrines, admits that he had learnt them, and derived some benefit from them, when young. 'If', he says, 'I were to say that such precepts had no value, I should be lying'.[25] For a modern reader, this certainly takes some of the sting out of the rather facile, uncomplimentary remarks about rhetoricians in the dialogue.

The orator Antonius was particularly well qualified to assess the value of rhetorical textbooks, for he had examined a very large number of them himself, from Aristotle's collection down to his own time.[26] His detailed criticisms of the precepts are good, since he had applied them and modified them in his own experience. He accepted that the fivefold division of oratory, into invention, arrangement, style, memory and delivery, was 'obvious';[27] he also accepted that the division of a speech into sections, whether four, five or six, was 'in the very nature of oratory', and these sections were 'neatly set out' in the handbooks.[28] He agreed that the introduction should have the threefold aim of arousing the listeners' attention, informing them of the facts, and winning their favour; but in practice, he found, people were usually attentive and aware of the facts, at the beginning anyway, and it was later on in the speech that it became more difficult, and more necessary, to keep them so. Certainly, Antonius accepted that the introduction should aim principally at securing good-will, but, in practice, the orator needed to use conciliation elsewhere, too, and not merely in the introduction. Antonius did not approve of the implication of the handbooks that the introduction should be prepared first. On the contrary, he knew that the impression created by it was so important that it was better to take time in deciding what were the strongest lines of argument to take in the case as a whole, and then to compose the introduction last, when one knew exactly how the case was to be developed.[29] As to the presentation of the facts (the 'narrative'), Antonius agreed that it should be clear and convincing — as should other parts of the speech — but rejected the rhetoricians' rule that it should be brief, for brevity could create obscurity. But one did not always need to make such a statement, for one might use the opponent's statement and set about refuting it.[30] Antonius accepts the threefold classification of the types of issue (fact, definition, quality), and had himself published some observations on the subject.[31] His chief complaint here is that when teachers of rhetoric have shown how to elicit the fundamental question, the gist of the matter in each case, they restrict it too much by treating it in relation to the persons and circumstances of that particular case, instead of broadening the whole matter into a question of general principle; and the same general principle might underlie quite a number of cases.[32] Finally, Antonius stresses the importance of using emotional appeal in reinforcing argument, or in digression, and not reserving it so particularly, as rhetoricians tended to do, for the peroration.[33] Such were the orator's criticisms on the structural development of speeches; basically, what he required was a more free and liberal manipulation of the rules. This is understandable, but what is much more surprising is that Crassus, Antonius' contemporary, should have not merely criticized rhetoricians, but actually used his official position to suspend the activities of a rhetoric school, in which the subject was being taught in Latin.

It was during Cicero's boyhood, about the year 94 B.C., that a certain Plotius Gallus opened his school.[34] His exclusive use of Latin in teaching rhetoric was an innovation, and he soon attracted numbers of pupils. These did not, however, include Cicero, who was advised to attend Greek teachers instead. Evidently Plotius was either associated with, or followed by, other rhetoricians who were, unlike himself, too obscure to be remembered, but the activities of these self-styled 'Latin rhetoricians' were very soon abruptly curtailed. In a censorial edict of 92 B.C. (preserved by Suetonius), Crassus and his colleague, Domitius Ahenobarbus, summarily ordered them to close the school. The reasons given were that they were introducing a new style of teaching, which did not conform to traditional Roman standards, and that their students were merely wasting their time. In the *De Oratore* of Cicero, Crassus is made to accept personal responsibility for the edict, to explain his motives, and defend his action.[35] In closing what he called a 'school of indecorum' (*ludus impudentiae*), he had been concerned to check a modern trend which he felt might spread and be entirely detrimental to good oratory. No suggestion is made in the ancient records that Crassus acted for other than academic reasons; but modern scholars have given considerable support to the idea that the action was politically motivated. They regard it as a partisan measure taken by one of the *optimates* to repress teachers who belonged to the lower orders of society, and were connected with the democratic cause.[36] There are, however, reasons for scepticism about this argument.

In the first place, it is pointed out that Plotius was, according to Cicero, a close friend of Marius, who admired his talents.[37] It is then deduced that Plotius, who bore a plebeian name (he was pretty certainly a freedman) belonged to the democratic party, and would be likely to be a supporter of Marius, who was a self-made man. Crassus, on the other hand, moved among the aristocracy, and, being at enmity (so it is said)

with Marius,[38] could have determined to use his power to silence
Marius' adherent. Here the fact seems to be quite overlooked that, not
long before the edict, Crassus' own daughter had married Marius'
son.[39] It is further argued that Crassus was an ardent admirer of Greek
culture, and that the study of Greek literature and thought had long been
the privilege of the aristocracy. Therefore, it is claimed, he must have
wished to keep the teaching of rhetoric in the hands of the Greeks,
whereas Marius, a man of no culture, who was ignorant of Greek and
proud of it, welcomed the use of the vernacular in his friend's new
establishment. This is fallacious reasoning, for it assumes that Crassus'
attitude to contemporary Greek teachers of rhetoric was quite as
approving as his attitude to classical Greek culture. It was nothing of the
kind. In the *De Oratore*, these modern Greek rhetoricians receive, at
most, the lukewarm praise of being more tolerable than their new
counterparts in Latin.[40] That there may have been an element of social
prejudice in Crassus' motivation is not to be denied. The elder Seneca, a
member of a wealthy equestrian family, shows this kind of attitude when
he remarks that, until Rubellius Blandus became the first Roman knight
to open a rhetoric school, the teaching remained in the hands of
freedmen, so that, paradoxically, 'it was a base occupation to teach what
it was honourable to learn'.[41] But that is no reason why one particular
freedman should have been singled out for such drastic treatment by
Crassus.

It is fairly certain that, in his rhetoric school, Plotius Gallus adopted a
long-established Greek custom of making his students rehearse aloud
practice-speeches on subjects parallel to those which occurred in the
law-courts and public assemblies; for Quintilian mentions his name in
this connection.[42] The purpose of such rehearsals was to develop not
merely firmness of voice, but, most especially, good modulation, for
various passages might need to be rendered in an indignant, or an
argumentative, or a conversational tone.[43] This was sensible; but very
closely associated with the rhetoricians in this matter were the
professional voice-trainers (*phonasci*), who, whilst they had exercises to
develop the range and stability of the voice (and of these later medical
writers approved),[44] were also most particularly concerned to build up
its loudness and power.[45] It was they who also trained the tragic
actors,[46] and we may recall how Aeschines, an orator who had been a
tragic actor, was repeatedly ridiculed by Demosthenes for his cultivation
of a loud tone.[47] Now we know that Plotius Gallus was the author of a
work on the subject of gesture,[48] which, in rhetoric, was closely
associated with voice-production. What is more, in a fragment of
Varro's *Satires*, we find a character derisively described as one who 'had
bawled like an ox-driver (*bubulcitarat*) in the school of Plotius the
rhetorician'.[49] Plotius, therefore, if not actually a voice-trainer

himself, must have been making an unwise use of their methods. Such vocal exercise was known in Greek as *anaphonesis*, or 'voice-raising', and that is undoubtedly the word which was Latinized as *declamatio*, 'declamation'.[50] Originally, this term referred simply to the voice-training process, but before the end of the Republic, it was extended to mean the rhetorical practice-speech itself. Then, in Latin, any kind of rhetorical speech on a stock theme came to be termed a 'declamation', whether it was delivered in loud tones or not, and the speakers were called 'declaimers'.

Roman orators of the old school, like Crassus and Antonius, did not like public speakers who shouted; habitual vociferation was ungentlemanly. In Cicero's *De Oratore*, Antonius, distinguishing three types of students of oratory, classifies them thus: first, in the highest class, is the genuinely gifted person, who must also be a good man (*vir bonus*), and who may become an ornament to the State; secondly, there is the mediocre student, who should not be discouraged, but, if found unsuitable, should be relegated to some other profession; thirdly, in the lowest grade, is he who 'bawls beyond all decent propriety and beyond his own power'.[51] Similarly, Crassus, whilst approving in principle of practice-speeches, if they were closely related to real life, severely criticized would-be orators who misused them. 'Most students', he commented, 'merely use the practice to exercise their voice in an unwise manner, to develop their power of utterance, to whip up their speed of delivery, and to revel in a spate of words'.[52] High-speed delivery was a feature of contemporary Asiatic oratory,[53] and volubility was notoriously a Greek characteristic.[54] Some Greek teachers must also have encouraged vehemence, for Cicero himself, who went to them, regretted the over-straining of his voice (*contentio vocis*), and subsequently had to correct it.[55] But loudness of tone must have been a particularly Roman fault at this period. Yet surely, one might think, no Roman official would close a rhetoric school simply because its students shouted? That is so, but this was not the only consideration. We must remember that these students would go directly as advocates into the Roman courts. Even as late as 56 B.C., Plotius Gallus, to whom Caelius Rufus alluded in sarcastic terms, was evidently still helping young advocates to prepare their court-speeches.[56] Now there is a further fragment of Varro, in which a character, punning on the name Gallus (very much in Varro's manner) asks someone if he means 'this *gallus* (cock), who arouses a tribe of brawlers'.[57] The term 'brawler' (*rabula*) was extremely disparaging, and was applied to a lawyer who was not only loud-voiced but coarse and aggressive. Cicero not only makes Crassus speak contemptuously of such people, but himself speaks in the same breath of 'the brawling advocate from the Forum' and 'the declaimer from the schoolroom', contrasting them both with the truly cultured orator.[58] Evidently, then, among the crowd of students (*concursus*) who flocked to Plotius Gallus' school, there were many — and they not necessarily of plebeian origin — who developed these undesirable characteristics. Such men, especially if — as would often happen — they appeared as prosecutors, could do a great deal of damage to innocent people by their blustering and bullying methods. Surely, then, we may here have the key to the situation — Crassus was determined to put a stop to the recruitment of young advocates who could become a dangerous element in the Roman courts, and who would be likely to become all the more numerous if they could learn their trade in Latin.

After Plotius Gallus, the list of those who subsequently taught rhetoric in the late Republic, as given by Suetonius, is, to say the least, unimpressive, and certainly includes men very different from the distinguished and high-minded interlocutors in Cicero's *De Oratore*. They were either of low origin, or of low character, though they must have had some ability to have raised themselves to prominence. Next in the review is a man whose exact name is problematical, but who is commonly referred to as L. Voltacilius Plotus.[59] He was a freedman, of whom it was said that he had risen from a degrading slave-occupation, having been originally a chained door-keeper; but he somehow found the means of educating himself, and, in a favourite Suetonian phrase, was 'set free on account of his talent'. For a time, he appears to have engaged in legal work, and, on at least one occasion, assisted his patron as a supporter in prosecution. When, later, he opened a school of rhetoric, he included Pompey among his pupils. The career of the next teacher, M. Epidius,[60] has a more suspicious look about it, for although he lived to teach Marcus Antonius and Octavian (and, according to a late source, Virgil)[61] he had at one time been denounced as a calumniator. Following Epidius, we have Sextus Clodius, a native of Sicily, who taught rhetoric in both Latin and Greek, 'a man of bad eyesight and sharp tongue', who became a crony of Antonius.[62] These two, according to Cicero, were hardened topers, who practised declamation not to sharpen their intellect but to evaporate their wine. Cicero's scathing attack shows how incensed the orator was that Antony should have made Clodius a grant of 2000 acres of land at Leontini, an outrageous 'fee' for one who taught nothing but folly.[63] Finally, to complete Suetonius' portrait gallery, we may add the name of Timagenes, who came from Alexandria, and was brought to Rome as a prisoner of war by Gabinius in 55 B.C. For some time, he followed slave occupations, first as a cook, then as a litter-bearer. Then, after his manumission, he opened a school of rhetoric, and became a notoriously powerful declaimer. He enjoyed the favour of Pollio, and even Augustus, but he was an irascible, quarrelsome fellow, sour, sardonic, and excessively outspoken. Augustus showed remarkable tolerance, but finally dismissed him for his derogatory comments on the imperial family.[64]

If the practice of declamation had remained what it was originally intended to be, that is, simply a method of improving delivery, it would never have incurred the censures of its many subsequent critics. But already under the Republic there were rhetoric-teachers with vocal power and fluency who utilized it, even if only within the school, to draw attention to themselves, and to win the bubble reputation bestowed by an often ill-judged acclaim. What is more, the style of these declaimers was often that which was generally known from its place of origin as 'Asianist', and which manifested itself in grandiose diction and resounding phrases. Plutarch remarks that Marcus Antonius had all the faults of the bombastic Asianist style.[65] It was this kind of oratory which caused Virgil to desert the 'nation of schoolmen', with their gross turgidity and high-sounding words, signifying nothing (*inanes*), for the calmer and more pleasant haven of philosophy.[66] Yet the notoriety of these men, who used declamation to seek the limelight (hence their prominence in Suetonius), should not be allowed to mislead us and obscure the fact that there were also rhetoricians who made a sensible use of it, and put it in its proper place. Also, especially under the Republic, there were conscientious teachers who considered it their main duty to explain and illustrate the rules of rhetoric, and to avoid stylistic excesses. For example, Octavian, after leaving Epidius, thought it worth-while to continue his studies with Apollodorus, who incidentally came from Pergamum, and, being probably therefore Stoic-influenced, may well have contributed to his subsequent aversion to the Asianist style.[67] Finally, whilst the aberrations of some of its practitioners were causing school-rhetoric to become dissociated from practical oratory, there was one powerful influence which had been working in the opposite direction, towards a far more balanced and liberal concept of oratorical training, and that was the influence of Cicero.

CHAPTER VII

Cicero and the ideal of oratorical education

At one of the most important points in his whole career, just before taking on the prosecution of Verres, Cicero had to address a Roman court in a preliminary process (*divinatio*), in order to prove that he was a more suitable person to conduct the case than his opponent, the Sicilian freedman's son, Caecilius. One of the arguments which he then used in his own favour was that he had received an education far superior to that of his rival. He was, he claimed, equipped with all the oratorical skill necessary for dealing with a matter of such widespread public concern, and that skill was based on studies ardently pursued since boyhood, most particularly in the literatures of Greece and Rome.[1] Beyond doubt, the linguistic and literary teaching of the *grammaticus* would have won Cicero's warm approval; but, within this field, he made certain interesting distinctions, both between language and literature and between Latin literature and Greek. His literary criticism in the *Brutus* shows that he regarded the correct use of the Latin language as a fundamental requirement for the orator,[2] and he frequently praised those who spoke properly (*recte*), even flawlessly (*emendate*), and who showed taste and discrimination (*elegantia*) in their diction. This quality, however, was not always necessarily derived from study, for it might be the result of good home environment and family tradition, and some spoke well without much acquaintance with literature.[3] But literary culture did show up in a man's style, and there were degrees of literary culture.[4] The study of Latin literature alone would only take a man a certain way;[5] it was Greek which made all the difference, though one should not despise Latin in enthusiasm for Greek.[6] An orator's training in Greek was often worthy of special comment,[7] but to be 'learned in literature, both Greek and Latin' was to earn particular praise.[8]

The love of literature in mature years often owed its origin to the reading of the poets in early life, whether in private tuition or at school. One who inspired Cicero in his boyhood had been the poet Archias, who had come to Rome from Antioch as a young man, and, in 102 B.C., had been welcomed into the home of the Luculli. In the ensuing years,

Archias, who had already made a reputation in the cities of Magna Graecia not only as a poet but as a gifted improviser, became *persona grata* to several leading families in Rome.[9] When, many years later, in 62 B.C., Archias was charged with having illegally assumed the Roman citizenship, Cicero came to his defence with a charming and eloquent little speech, in which he combined praise of Archias, and acknowledgement of his personal indebtedness to him, with a glowing panegyric on literature in general and poetry in particular. Even though Archias' services to him may perhaps be somewhat exaggerated, it is evident that poetry was Cicero's first love, and he was already composing in boyhood.[10] Posterity never found in Cicero the poet anything like the inspiration of Cicero the orator,[11] but Roman audiences appreciated his many apt quotations from the early Latin poets,[12] and he himself, throughout his life, found in Greek and Latin literature a solace in times of trouble and a source of perennial refreshment and delight.

Hand in hand with poetry and music in the educational curriculum of classical Greece went the four 'mathematical disciplines' of arithmetic, geometry, astronomy and musical theory. Throughout Hellenistic and Roman times these four subjects held together,[13] and they were included in Varro's encyclopaedia of the liberal arts, entitled *Disciplinae*. But at Rome, although they could be started at the secondary stage, they took only a subordinate position in the standard curriculum, which concentrated on grammar and literature. The *grammaticus*, apart from explaining astronomical references in the poets, did not teach them himself.[14] Boys who needed, or who were interested in, mathematics and music would have to attend specialist teachers, usually Greeks, and, even though one such teacher might offer more than one subject,[15] this would involve an additional fee. But this does not mean that these subjects were neglected. Cicero, indeed, regarded them as forming an integral part of boyhood training (*puerilis doctrina*),[16] and had certainly acquired a knowledge of them himself.

For very many years there lived in the house of Cicero a blind scholar named Diodotus, a philosopher of the Stoic school. Cicero tells us that he began to learn from Diodotus in boyhood;[17] and so, too, later, did P. Crassus, the triumvir's son.[18] Diodotus, despite his disability, was a skilled musician, and continued to play stringed instruments, but, what was more remarkable, he also gave lessons in geometry, instructing his pupils verbally on the points from and to which they should draw their lines.[19] They would have used the sand-table form of abacus, and we may well imagine that Diodotus would not only explain but also test his pupils by the favourite method of question and answer. The philosopher was also a keen teacher of dialectic, but what is significant is that Cicero was still studying not only this but 'other subjects' too with him in 84 B.C., when he was twenty-two years of age.[20] Then again, Cicero's interest in astronomy also showed itself in his production, when quite a young man, of the first Latin verse translation (the greater part of which is extant) of the astronomical poem of Aratus.[21]

Cicero may not have been altogether exceptional. It is true that only rarely do we hear of Romans who acquired high expertise in mathematical subjects, as did Sextus Pompeius, uncle of Pompey the Great, in geometry,[22] and Sulpicius Gallus (cos.166), the first Roman to predict an eclipse of the moon, in astronomy.[23] But it is quite possible that interest among young Romans was wider than the rather limited evidence suggests. Pompey's young wife had, as we have seen, studied geometry.[24] One would hardly have suspected, moreover, had it not been for a chance remark of his biographer, that Virgil had studied not only medicine but 'especially mathematics'.[25] Similarly, the architect Vitruvius was familiar with all the mathematical disciplines, and mentions his teachers in astronomy.[26] Under the Empire, there were established schools of geometry,[27] which would pretty certainly be run by Greeks, with Euclid as their text. The term 'geometry' might also include arithmetic, but practical arithmetic, at the level of everyday usage, was the special province of the *calculator*.

Most Romans, whilst aware of the high attainments of the Greeks in the mathematical disciplines, took a distinctly utilitarian view of them. Geometry and arithmetic seem to have been most in favour, closely followed by astronomy; musical theory probably least. Geometry was considered mainly useful for the correct determination of the areas of estates, and the works of the Roman land-surveyors show how they applied it to this purpose.[28] Cicero regretted this limitation, though Seneca was content to accept it.[29] The Romans would also have agreed with Polybius on the need for geometry in certain military calculations, and especially in camp-measurement. Practical astronomical observation was an obvious necessity for understanding the calendar, for navigation, and for farming, and, as Polybius said, it had a military application in forecasting the hours of light and darkness, which affected the planning of an army's movements.[30] But the fundamental question was — how far could mathematical studies be justified as part of the training of the orator?[31] Here, it is doubtful whether Cicero would have laid much stress on Quintilian's claim that arithmetic and geometry were necessary because the orator might have to deal with law-suits involving numerical calculations or boundary-disputes.[32] Such cases did undoubtedly occur, but they must have formed only a minority. Rather, he would more readily have accepted the argument put forward by Quintilian, and by Isocrates long before, that the mathematical disciplines were a valuable form of mental training, from which the student derived the habit of clear and orderly thinking, and of concentration, and that they could have a beneficial effect in quite different fields.[33] But Cicero's own view was not restricted to practical values. For him, all such studies were liberal arts, and he saw in them part of that general culture (*humanitas*), towards which boys should be guided; they were conducive to the good life and he would have regarded them as worthy of further study beyond boyhood. Herein Cicero was taking a quite Platonic view, which he likewise attributes to Crassus.[34] But the Roman schools of 'grammar' and rhetoric, which held the field, had no such exalted concept. Consequently, it was eventually left, in the main, to the philosophers (though not all philosophers were agreed) to foster them as preparatory studies, for with philosophy they had more in common. It was chiefly through philosophical interest that the four mathematical disciplines ultimately became standardized as the mediaeval *quadrivium*. [35]

We come now to Cicero's views on the teaching of rhetoric, the most important subject in Roman education. As regards the construction of speeches, Cicero had been brought up on the traditional text-book classifications of the types of issue, the treatment section by section of the speech-divisions, and the standard arguments and commonplaces, which were associated particularly, though by no means exclusively, with the name of Hermagoras. In later life, although he was inclined to dismiss his youthful *De Inventione*, and replaced it with a far more broad and liberal treatment of the whole subject of oratory, this did not mean that he had condemned the substance of a long-established system, merely that he found it inadequate. Even in the *De Oratore*, he admitted that he 'did not despise' the doctrines of the Greeks,[36] and his criticism of Hermagoras in the *Brutus*, written in 46 B.C., shows what his verdict really was. Although Hermagoras was arid in exposition, he found him useful and effective, for he showed the student the lines on which he must proceed in the various types of case, and he put into his hands the necessary arguments, all ready to be hurled, like spears equipped with their thongs.[37] Cicero must have felt the stock divisions and precepts to be useful, at least as a beginning, for he utilized them himself in the text-book entitled *Partitiones Oratoriae*, which he composed for his son Marcus. His own speeches, which have often been rhetorically analysed, show much correspondence with theory, but also considerable divergencies, which resulted from experience and the practical conditions of pleading.[38] In maturity, Cicero, like any good orator, refused to be bound by a rigid system, and he would have agreed with most of the modifications which Antonius had found to be necessary. But it was, in the first instance, in the province of style, where his own supreme mastery lay, that he took a much more comprehensive view than the average rhetorician, and here he had much to say that was both stimulating and instructive.

The authors of rhetorical textbooks had long been familiar with the standard threefold classification of style into Plain, Middle and Grand, which has widely (though not universally) been considered to derive from Aristotle's pupil, Theophrastus.[39] Greek rhetoricians would draw illustrations of each type from passages of standard prose authors, most particularly the orators. In Latin, the author of the treatise *Ad Herennium* claimed originality in composing his own examples, instead of merely selecting them from previous writers.[40] Cicero himself brought the three styles into relation with the three functions of the orator, recommending use of the easy, conversational Plain Style to instruct, the pleasant, smoothly-flowing Middle Style to charm, and the striking, impressive Grand Style to stir.[41] But in his later years, as may be seen in the *Orator*, the doctrine of the three styles, and the choice of a suitable model, or models, had become part and parcel of a controversy between Cicero and the so-called 'Atticists'.[42] This school, in which Cicero's rival, Calvus, was prominent, was dedicated to a straight-forward, correct, and unadorned style, for which its supporters selected Lysias as their model, and eschewed all artificiality, affectation, and high-flown expression, such as characterized their opponents, the 'Asianists'.[43] It was against Asianism that they had reacted — and not without good reason — but in the opinion of Cicero (who had himself not escaped adverse criticism), they had reacted too far. He fully acknowledged the merits of Lysias, a consummate artist in his own field, who achieved an enviable grace and simplicity, and a naturalness of style which was hard to emulate; but he had only a limited range. To claim him as the only true representative of classical Attic oratory was to take far too narrow a view. For Cicero, the orator must be master of all three styles,[44] and herein, Demosthenes was unsurpassed.[45] This view was later wholeheartedly endorsed by the Greek critic, Dionysius, whose essay on the style of Demosthenes admirably illustrates it by examples and comparisons. There is one difference of approach, however, which should not be overlooked. Cicero calls up the panoply of styles in order to combat the narrow 'Atticists', and only incidentally does he censure Asianism, mainly on the grounds of sing-song delivery and faulty rhythm.[46] In the *Brutus*, he is far from uncomplimentary to Asiatic orators;[47] after all, he had studied in Asia himself. But for Dionysius it is the Asianist style which is the real menace, and he is implacably opposed to it from the outset.[48] Cicero's involvement in the controversy tends to put the essential issue out of focus, for whereas the Atticists never had more than a very limited following, the Asianist style was lasting and pervasive, and found a new channel in the declamations of the Empire. Next to Demosthenes, Cicero also admired Aeschines, his rival, particularly the speech against Ctesiphon, which he translated into Latin along with Demosthenes' masterpiece, *De Corona*.[49] In Latin, likewise, Cicero selected the best wherever he found it. He recommended the speeches of Caius Cracchus as particularly instructive and inspiring.[50] Important political speeches, he thought, should be closely studied, and passages of them even learnt by heart; in his own boyhood, the peroration of a speech of C. Galba was regularly memorized,[51] and he himself took the speech of Crassus on the law of Caepio as his model masterpiece in Latin.[52] Finally, Cicero was able to point to his own speeches as illustrating command of all three types of style, and modern studies have fully justified his claim.

As regards the essential virtues of a good style, Cicero accepted the judgment of Theophrastus that they were purity, lucidity, appropriateness and ornament;[53] to these four the Stoics had added brevity.[54] He was also familiar with the Theophrastean criticism of style according to diction, composition and figures,[55] but here there was a marked difference of emphasis between his own treatment and that of the rhetorical textbooks of his day. If we may take the fourth book of the treatise *Ad Herennium* as typical, the rhetoricians devoted by far the greatest part of their exposition to an exhaustive list of the figures, each of them equipped with its definition and illustration. But the treatment of composition was very meagre. All that the author of the *Ad Herennium* has to offer here is a few comments on such rather obvious faults as excessive hiatus and repetition of similar-sounding words and endings.[56] On periodic structure and prose rhythm he is silent, and Cicero says that this subject was not included in the regular curriculum.[57] Cicero himself, whilst by no means neglecting the figures,[58] which, indeed, abound in his speeches, paid detailed attention to composition, which takes a prominent place in his treatise on the perfect orator.

It is quite clear, both from chapters in Aristotle's *Rhetoric* and from Cicero's references to Aristotle, Theophrastus and Theodectes,[59] that it was mainly the Peripatetic school which had provided the starting-point for his own researches, though he was fully aware of, and gave full credit for, the great contribution of Isocrates in the development of rhythmical and artistic prose.[60] The most characteristic feature of Isocrates, which, though overdone, had much influence on his pupils and on subsequent orators, was his avoidance of hiatus;[61] but he also achieved — thanks largely to his predecessor, Gorgias — a skilful symmetry, a careful balance of parallel or contrasting clauses which, though it could quickly become tedious, gave a certain formal beauty to his style.[62] In the earlier speeches of Cicero, particularly, there is much evidence of this kind of neatness (*concinnitas*).[63] But Aristotle and Theophrastus, whilst agreeing with Isocrates that prose should be rhythmical without becoming metrical,[64] had analysed more closely the types of rhythm which were desirable, or less acceptable, in prose. Aristotle had pointed out the importance of the opening and closing cadences in the sentence, and it was particularly to the latter, the *clausula*, that Cicero devoted meticulous attention; though this is not to say that he advocated consistent patterns and then followed them religiously in practice.[65] But he also discussed the pervasive rhythm of the period, the extent to which rhythm was desirable in different kinds of prose, and the achievement of variety, particularly in the interweaving of shorter, or very short, sections.[66] Naturally, he would not have expected schoolboys to grasp all the detail of so complex a study, but he was setting up an ideal for all who aspired to become orators, and he would have wished them to be at least aware of the subject at an early stage, as did Quintilian, and later to take it into fuller account.

A further important difference between the outlook of Cicero and that of the professional rhetoricians was that the latter concentrated on the use of reasoned argument; they tended to confine the subject of emotional appeal to the peroration, and they paid little attention to the giving of pleasure and the adroit resort to wit. Cicero would have acknowledged that emotional appeal and command of wit were qualities difficult to achieve, and still more difficult to instil by teaching; their successful use depended so much on personality and natural gift. But he had a high regard for Aristotle's treatment of the psychological approaches by which the emotions of an audience might be aroused,[67] and he would have thought that wit and humour, a field in which, from the broad jest to the many subtle grades of irony, he was himself a master, could at least be illustrated by examples. The many types of humour, whether derived from the immediate subject or from verbal play, had been studied and classified in detail, again notably by the Peripatetice, and Cicero devoted a long passage of his *De Oratore* to examples from Roman oratory.[68] But perhaps his most practical advice was that in which he recommended the occasional use of digression as a means of either entertaining or arousing an audience. He was adept at this, as the many examples in his speeches show, using the digressive anecdote to amuse, the digressive description to please, the digressive eulogy, satire or invective to stir the feelings.[69] As a teacher, Cicero would have brought the whole subject to life.

As a young man, Cicero had supplemented his studies of rhetorical theory with daily exercises in what subsequently was called declamation, that is, he rehearsed aloud, often in the company of friends, practice-cases (*causae*, later *controversiae*), presenting the arguments now for, now against.[70] He claimed that he kept up this habit longer than any of his contemporaries,[71] but, as he grew more interested in philosophy and became less satisfied with the methods of the rhetorical schools, he preferred to develop a form of practice which, in 54 B.C., he termed 'more generalized', because it was based on debating the general question (*thesis*) rather than the particular case (*hypothesis*).[72] Herein, like Crassus, he was much influenced by the contemporary Peripatetic and Academic schools;[73] they inherited the old practice of Aristotle and Theophrastus, who had taught their students to amplify themes rhetorically, both for and against, whether on natural science, or ethics, or politics, or other subjects.[74] Both philosophers published many books of *theses*.[75] But general questions, though of a more restricted kind, were also of concern to orators and rhetoricians, and the subject was to some extent disputed territory between them and the philosophers.[76] Cicero must have been aware that, in preliminary rhetorical studies, one of the most important exercises was the *thesis*, in which boys were expected to present the case, for and against taking part in politics, or for and against marriage, and other general topics.[77] In one of Cicero's philosophical dialogues, the young orator Cotta is asked, apropos of arguing *pro* and *contra,* to show 'that facility of discourse which, inherited from your rhetorical exercises, the Academy has amplified'.[78] But it was at the advanced level of rhetoric that Cicero wished to see the use of the general question extended. Not that it had been neglected even here. In law-suits where the issue was one of determining the facts, pre-Ciceronian orators had found it useful to have learnt up beforehand certain commonplaces (*loci*), which, because they might need to be argued either way, were really *theses*. Examples are: 'Should witnesses be trusted, or not?', 'Is evidence given under torture reliable, or not?', 'Is rumour admissible as evidence, or not?' Such general questions as these were recommended for previous preparation by Antonius,[79] and Cicero's older rival, Hortensius, actually published his versions of them.[80] The arguments for and against are set forth in some detail in the treatise *Ad Herennium*, and were evidently standardized in rhetorical teaching.[81]

But the general question could be more than an incidental aid to the advocate; it could form the sum and substance of his entire case. There was a very interesting example (which, incidentally, shows the modernity of ancient Greek), in one of the lost speeches of Lysias, where the charge was one of having procured an abortion, and the whole oration centred round the question whether the foetus should be regarded as a human being or not, and whether or not women should be held accountable for its destruction.[82] In the rhetoric schools, which concentrated on eliciting the central issue in any given case (*krinomenon*), the line between the particular and the general question was very narrow indeed. For instance, in the favourite school-exercise on the trial of Orestes, one might posit the issue in the form: 'Should *Orestes* be condemned for killing his mother, since she had slain his father?'; but one has only to alter this to: 'Should *anyone*, who slays his own mother, be condemned?' for the whole matter to be widened into a general question.[83] In deliberative oratory, especially, transfer from the particular to the general was easy and natural; for example, in a debate whether or not the Romans should agree to an exchange of prisoners, the whole matter might be raised to a question of general policy regarding prisoners of war.[84] There is some evidence that Greek rhetoricians, despite the adverse criticisms of Antonius in the *De Oratore* (which are rather suspect), had been quite aware of the immanence of the general in the particular.[85] But Cicero prided himself on his special skill in this kind of transference,[86] and it is understandable that he should have wished to widen the whole treatment of general questions, partly because they offered so interesting a range of cultured debate, and partly because an orator could never be quite sure when he might need to shift the whole issue to a matter of principle.

Rhetorical theory and practice, however, good though it might be, was most fruitful if it could be matched with experience of the actual conditions of public oratory. Under the Republic, there flourished an excellent system, approved, without doubt, by Cicero, by which a young man, whether he had completed his rhetorical studies or not, was given a year's active preparation for entry into public life. This was in effect a sort of apprenticeship, and was known as *tirocinium fori*, or 'recruitment to the Forum'.[87] It was suited to two of the three careers open to a young Roman of good family, that of an orator and that of a professional lawyer, for these two had something in common. If he chose to become a soldier, the training was different, but the arrangement was similar, and was known as *tirocinium militiae*, or 'recruitment to military life'. This period began when, at the discretion of the father, the youth who had hitherto worn the boyhood toga bordered with purple (*toga praetexta*) was permitted, as the time seemed ripe, to adopt the pure white toga of manhood (*toga virilis, toga pura*), which symbolized his acceptance into full adult life. The age at which this was done varied both according to the parental wish and according to the practice of different periods. It appears to have been originally at the completion of the seventeenth year, but in the later Republic the toga of manhood was usually assumed earlier than this; with Cicero, as with his son and nephew, it would seem to have been at the age of sixteen, with Virgil and Octavian at fifteen.[88] Although there were always exceptions, the age tended to be lowered, rather than raised, with the passage of time. The occasion itself was one in which the family took some pride — it was a sort of 'coming of age' — and after the *toga praetexta* and the ornament (*bulla*), which had hung around the boy's neck, were dedicated to the household gods in a private ceremony at the home, the young man, now in adult dress (*vesticeps*), was escorted to the Forum amid the congratulations of relatives and friends. A favourite date for this occasion was the festival of the *Liberalia*, on the seventeenth of March. If the young man had in mind a military life, he would naturally spend the ensuing period in weapon-training and soldierly exercises, before being attached to a military formation, where he would learn the duties of an officer.[89] If his aspiration was towards oratory or the law, he would not, during this year, neglect his physical exercises on the Campus Martius,[90] which he might need in a subsequent period of military service, but he would be mainly concerned with his chosen profession. It was here that much depended upon family influence and connections. The most favoured youths were those whose fathers could place them under the direct personal supervision of some distinguished orator or lawyer whom they knew. Thus for training in oratory, the young Caelius Rufus, on assuming the toga of manhood, had been placed by his father in the care of Cicero,[91] and Cicero himself, for legal studies, had at a similar age been attached to Mucius Scaevola Augur.[92]

Besides receiving guidance and tuition, the young 'recruit' would naturally be concerned with the selection of a model, or models, whom he most desired to imitate. Usually, he found a single orator — often, naturally, the man to whom he was personally attached — whom he regarded as his ideal, whose every word, whose every movement, he observed,[93] and whose manner he strove to reproduce in his own speeches — for continuing practice remained quite indispensable. There could, however, be disadvantages in the widely recommended and often adopted practice of imitating a single model. There was always the risk that the young student would fail to match the original;[94] or he might merely succeed in copying those features which were easiest to reproduce.[95] The great advantage of this year of recruitment (which was much admired, as typical of the Republic, by Quintilian and Tacitus),[96] was that, in legal oratory, young men were watching a live performance, in which there were to be seen the matching of wits of the rival advocates in close altercation, the examination of witnesses, the reaction of judge or jury, and the quick appreciation of the audience as some good point was scored. Similarly, in deliberative oratory, they were listening to speeches on the most immediate issues of the day,[97] with the swaying by an experienced orator of the feelings of a volatile, and sometimes hostile, multitude. In both spheres, there was so much to be learnt about the handling of the issue, the use of flattery, emotional appeal, or wit, the variations of tone, and appropriate and effective gesture.

One might well have thought that the education so far described would have provided a very satisfactory training for the future orator. But Cicero did not think so. Following the ideals expressed by Crassus in the *De Oratore*, he expected the student, now in his late teens and no longer attending the rhetoric-school,[98] to acquire a wider culture by the study of philosophy, history and law. Cicero's own interest in philosophy had begun unusually early, and had continued, and increased, during maturity. As a boy, he had heard the lectures of the Epicurean, Phaedrus, to whom he also listened, many years later, in Athens.[99] His tutor, Diodotus, taught him the doctrines of Stoicism, and in 88 B.C., at the age of eighteen, he found the lectures of Philo of Larissa, the head of the New Academy, who was on a visit to Rome, a source of particular inspiration.[100] It is also very probable that Cicero had learnt something of the outlook and methods of the Peripatetic school from the learned Staseas of Naples, of whom Crassus thought highly, and who had resided since 91 B.C. at the home of M. Pupius Piso, with whom Cicero practised declamation.[101] Thus by the time he was twenty Cicero would have become familiar with the teaching of all four of the main philosophical schools. It was not until he was approaching thirty, between 79 and 77 B.C., that he was able to make an extended tour abroad, and to continue his study of philosophy, as well as rhetoric, at Athens and Rhodes.[102] But, before the end of the Republic, it was the fashion for young Romans who had sufficient financial provision to complete their education in philosophy and rhetoric with a fairly lengthy study period in Greece, usually in their late teens or early twenties.[103] It is important, however, to realize that they were a particularly favoured minority, and Cicero observes that Roman advocates as a general rule had not enjoyed the opportunities for acquiring so liberal an education.[104]

In relating philosophical studies to the needs of the orator, Cicero expressed a high opinion of the value of dialectic. It taught the student to define his terms, to distinguish the genus from the species, and to relate the parts to the whole and to one another; thus it was useful for any kind of systematization.[105] It also provided a training in close reasoning, and could be regarded as the counterpart of rhetoric, which encouraged copious expression; in the famous illustration of Zeno, the founder of Stoicism, the one was the closed fist, the other the open palm.[106] In Cicero's view, dialectic was indispensable for the orator, who would often need to challenge his opponent's interpretation of the law, or clear up some ambiguity in it, as he himself had done in his defence of Caecina.[107] It also trained the future advocate to be mentally alert, and to detect any self-contradiction or false hypothesis on the part of an adversary. But, excellent though it was in itself, dialectic could become impracticable when taught by some of those who specialized in it (*dialectici*), particularly among the Stoics, owing to their pedantic distinctions and their excessive zeal for chasing every possible ambiguity.[108] In fact, the pupils of the Soitcs, though expert in disputation, were often too arid and argumentative to become effective public speakers. Cicero often criticized Stoic orators, with the notable exception of the younger Cato, who won his unqualified praise.[109] Although he must have found the instruction of Diodotus of some value, it was the Academic teaching of dialectic which he recommended most highly to his son.[110] But, in general, among the philosophical schools, he expressed the strongest preference for the Peripatetics, who succeeded in combining philosophical reasoning with a pleasing and copious eloquence.

No less important to the orator was that part of the philosophical territory which formed the province of ethics. In every branch of his art, whether he was delivering a panegyric or an invective, or urging or deprecating some political measure, or justifying a client's action, or establishing or defaming a man's character, or maintaining the principle of equity — in all this, the orator had to have moral arguments at his command. He must be prepared to speak on virtue and vice, on right and wrong; he must, as the occasion demands, have something to say on piety and patriotism, on duty neglected or fulfilled, on the manifold effects of human emotions.[111] It was, indeed, possible to become too facile in introducing these philosophical commonplaces (which were also practised in the rhetorical schools), to become familiar with all the stock arguments, and to slide deftly into them as the occasion arose. But the true orator, who should be, as the elder Cato said, a good man skilled in speech, would be expressing thereby his own personal convictions and character. Finally, beyond the province of ethics, observations on religion and on the workings of Providence in the affairs of men might, upon occasion, inspire the orator to loftier and more magnificent utterance.[112] Cicero, in his defence of Milo, rose to the heights of dramatic eloquence when he spoke of the unseen power which guides human destinies, and which had brought the nefarious Clodius to his end near the shrine of the very goddess whose mysteries he had once profaned.[113]

For Cicero, Greek philosophy was no mere intellectual study, but a genuine source of solace and guidance, especially in his last years, after the death of his daughter Tullia; and he did a great service to his fellow-countrymen in presenting so much of it in Latin dress. He claimed that in his own speeches there were abundant philosophical reflections, and a fair number of examples have been collected.[114] He was, however, more than a little over-enthusiastic about his indebtedness as an orator to philosophy, as opposed to rhetoric, when he declared that he owed more to 'the spacious grounds of the Academy' than to 'the workshops of the rhetoricians'.[115] The 'spacious grounds' were intended to suggest the cultured, leisurely discussions of the intellectual Roman gentleman, the disinterested pursuit of knowledge. But the rhetorical 'workshop' (*officina*, a term which Cicero used even of the school of Isocrates),[116] rather implied artifice and mass-production. And Cicero would not have liked anyone to think that he could possibly have been manufactured.

The general Roman attitude towards philosophy, however, was that expressed by Antonius, namely, that it was acceptable if kept within limits; it was summed up in a favourite quotation, a line from a play of Ennius, which ran: 'We must philosophize a bit, but we don't like a lot of it'.[117] Most of Cicero's contemporaries would have given a warmer welcome to that part of his programme which appealed to their national pride, and they would have needed less convincing that the orator must be familiar with the law, the antiquities, and the history of Rome. As a boy, Cicero had been brought up on the old tradition which required schoolchildren to learn the Twelve Tables by heart and to recite them.[118] But here, again, he had been in a more fortunate position than most, for, as he grew more interested in the subject, he was able to consult the greatest living authority on Roman antiquities, himself the author of a commentary on the Tables, the erudite Aelius Stilo, at whose house he became a frequent visitor.[119] In his late teens, in his study of the law as it existed in his day, he had access to the best possible sources of knowledge, and long remembered the answers of old Scaevola the Augur to those who came to consult him.[120] This was in 89 B.C., when Cicero was seventeen, but when Scaevola died, not long afterwards, he was able to transfer to Scaevola Pontifex, also an eminent jurist, and continue his studies.[121] The speeches which he subsequently made in civil cases all testify to his confident handling of quite complex questions, and, in time, experience and application taught him enough to enable him to set about composing a treatise on the classification of the civil law.[122]

But at heart Cicero was always an orator rather than a lawyer, and, like most orators, he held the view that, in the hierarchy of professions, oratory took precedence over jurisprudence.[123] It is an indication of the high respect accorded in antiquity to mastery of the spoken word that orators were able to regard themselves as rather superior people, who could have become lawyers if they wished, whereas lawyers were to be regarded as men who would have become orators if they could. Since the elder Cato's day the two careers had become more distinct. Jurisconsults, though they were sometimes able speakers,[124] were essentially scholars who developed their own expertise, which they handed down to sons or sons-in-law, and formed their own select community. When they taught invited pupils privately in their own homes (in Republican times),[125] or answered inquirers, they charged no fee. Thus, as a jurist could be consulted beforehand, the question arose whether the advocate himself really needed a thorough grounding in law, and to this question very different answers were given.

Cicero, like Crassus before him and Quintilian afterwards, had no doubt that such knowledge was essential.[126] Antonius, however, took the opposite standpoint. He claimed that he had never had any proper legal training, but had learnt by experience; law was a subject on which the experts themselves often differed, and if, on analysing a case, one needed advice on the legal position, one could always consult a jurist, or look up the textbooks.[127] What the orator really needed was common sense in the selection and arrangement of his arguments. Quintilian would have thought this very dangerous doctrine, for experience had taught him that the advocate might have to tackle impromptu some legal point which arose in the course of the case itself.[128] Cicero praises orators with good legal knowledge,[129] but, in practice, the amount of law which advocates had mastered probably varied greatly with individuals.

In Cicero's view, however, as in that of Crassus, the orator was not merely a person who was regularly engaged in civil and criminal processes; he should also aspire to be something of a statesman, capable of giving advice over a wide area of public policy. He should be familiar with traditional custom, as well as with contemporary political questions, and be able to draw upon a wide knowledge of the past.[130] Thus Cicero emphasized the value of the study of history, for 'to be ignorant of what happened before you were born is to remain always a child'.[131] It was a view which would have appealed to Roman audiences, and it had a more practical application on that account; for shrewd speakers knew that a timely reference to a historical precedent (whether or not it was exactly analogous at the time), a passing allusion to the great men of the past to reinforce an argument or adorn a commonplace, was often a useful implement of persuasion. Such historical examples and allusions are common in Cicero's speeches, and have often been collected, classified and studied.[132] But, quite apart from utilitarian motives, Cicero's resumé of the characteristics of many Greek and Roman historians, his welcome of the chronological work composed by his friend Atticus (*Liber Annalis*), and his own unfulfilled desire to write historical works himself, all show the genuineness of his interest in this field.[133]

Such was the wide range of culture which Cicero thought the orator should, ideally, possess. Before his own day, Crassus had come nearest to achieving it,[134] and Cicero could also claim that his own liberal education had enabled him to surpass his contemporaries.[135] For those who aspired to such an education, and could afford to pursue their studies, there was no shortage of teachers who could help them on their way. But it is noticeable that Cicero's programme extended well beyond the age of normal schooling, and required continued assiduity on the part of those who had already reached their late teens. This was just the time of life at which the more fortunate among them would be thinking of a period of study abroad.

CHAPTER VIII

The Roman student abroad

Long before the end of the Republic, it often happened that Romans with intellectual interests, when on official service abroad, would take the opportunity of visiting one or other of the main centres of learning, in order to listen to their leading scholars, and perhaps to join in friendly discussion with them.[1] Athens, Rhodes and various cities of Asia Minor welcomed such visits, which could give rise to a stimulating exchange of ideas, and sometimes led to an invitation to join a Roman retinue or to teach in Rome. Athens and the philosophical lectures and discussions of a flourishing New Academy proved a particular attraction. It was there that Metellus Numidicus had listened to the aged Carneades, its founder, and here Crassus, returning from his quaestorship in Macedonia in 110 B.C., met several of his pupils, as well as philosophers of other schools, and read the *Gorgias* of Plato with Charmadas.[2] Some years later, in 102, Antonius, visiting Athens on the way to Cilicia as pro-praetor (and accompanied, incidentally, by Cicero's uncle, Lucius) heard these same philosophers, and also the rhetoricians, including Menedemus, who later became his guest at Rome.[3] He also called at Rhodes. Such contacts opened the way for young Romans to enjoy a more extended period of study abroad. Usually, they would be younger than Cicero had been in 79-77 B.C., or than Julius Caesar was when, in 75, or thereabouts, he set out to study rhetoric with Molo at Rhodes.[4] Both Brutus and Cassius later studied in Greece, Cassius at Rhodes[5] and Brutus at Athens. Brutus became devoted to his teachers, especially Aristus, brother of Antiochus, of the Academy, and the orator Pammenes, with whom he read the whole of Demosthenes' speeches. Empylus, a Rhodian rhetorician, also became his close friend.[6] Then, at the very end of the Republic, we find Horace, who would be about twenty, 'seeking for truth amid the groves of the Academy',[7] and he was followed there, under the Empire, by Ovid,[8] and, later, Lucan.[9] By Ovid's day, it would seem, Athens was beginning to lose its monopoly as the centre of study *par excellence* for young Romans, for Strabo tells us that many parents were then sending their sons to Marseilles, a city which was not only an ancient seat of learning but also much respected for its good morals.[10] But, before that time, particular interest attaches to a small group of students who were together at Athens in 45 B.C. It included not only Valerius Messala Corvinus, who became a distinguished statesman, orator, scholar and patron of literature under Augustus, and Calpurnius Bibulus, son of Brutus' wife, Porcia, by her first marriage, and grandson of the younger Cato, but also Cicero's son, Marcus.[11] It is due to his appearance in Cicero's correspondence that we know at least something about student life at Athens at that time.

We last met Marcus in the year 49 B.C., when, a few months after the outbreak of the Civil War, Cicero dismissed the tutor who had been in charge of him and his cousin, Quintus. It was just about this time that Cicero wrote to Atticus, giving his views about the character and upbringing of the two boys.[12] About Quintus, he had serious misgivings; Quintus' father, he says, had always indulged him, and although he was not untruthful, or grasping, or disloyal to friends, his upbringing had perhaps made him self-assertive, arrogant and aggressive. Such defects, however, he was prepared to tolerate, 'with young men as they are today'; but he wished to make it clear that the worse features of the lad's character were a source of distress to him, for he had not condoned them, and would have eradicated them had he been allowed. His own son, Marcus, however, was easily controlled and was as tractable as he could wish. At that time Marcus was about sixteen, and his father gave him the toga of manhood. Soon afterwards he joined the army of Pompey, and was given nominal charge of a squadron of cavalry; he may not have seen much active service, but he won high praise for the aptitude he showed in all his military exercises.[13] After the disaster of Pharsalus he wished to change sides and serve Caesar's cause in Spain, but Cicero was adamant in his opposition to this course.[14] Nor did he grant Marcus' wish to set up his own house in Rome. In April 45 B.C. he sent him to study philosophy and rhetoric at Athens. He particularly wished Marcus to study under Cratippus, the Peripatetic philosopher, of whom he had the highest opinion. At no time do Cicero's affection for and generosity towards his son appear more clearly than in his arrangements for the young man's university studies. It may well be that after the death of his daughter Tullia in February 45 — a crushing blow to him — Marcus meant more to him than ever. His domestic affairs, too, in these last years of his life, were far from happy, for he had divorced his wife, Terentia, and embarked on a second marriage with a very young woman, which did not prove successful.[15] When Marcus was preparing to leave for Athens in the spring of 45, Cicero made generous provision for his equipment and journey (though he drew the line at paying for a private carriage in Athens), and gave him a remarkably lavish allowance.[16] His arrangements for the payment of this through his friend, the banker Atticus, are an interesting example of the financial methods of the time. Cicero was in receipt of rents from flats which he owned in Rome; they had originally come to him as part of Terentia's dowry, and this part he retained after the divorce for the maintenance and education of their son. Atticus was to receive the amount of this income (80,000 sesterces annually) from Cicero's freedman, Eros, who collected the rents, and it was then transferred to a certain Xenon in Athens, with whom Atticus had dealings, for payment to Marcus. But as, in the first instance, Xenon owed Atticus money, Atticus arranged for him to liquidate this debt by direct transfer to Marcus.[17] There are frequent references in correspondence between Cicero and Atticus in the years 45/44 to the making of payments to Marcus, and it is evident that there was an element of understandable pride in Cicero's munificence; for he repeatedly insists to Atticus that his son must not be allowed to fall short in any way of a style of living which was consistent with his own standing, and which fully matched that of Marcus' fellow-students. Herein, even with the best intentions, Cicero was sowing the seeds of future trouble for both himself and his all-too-prodigal son.

It was not very long before the wise and thrifty Atticus was writing to Marcus about the expenses he was incurring, and also to Cicero to suggest that he was treating his son too handsomely.[18] Cicero himself subsequently began to have some misgivings, but he placed Atticus in a difficult position by claiming that any restriction on funds might so limit Marcus' way of life as to reflect on his own (Cicero's) dignity and social standing.[19] Whether he really felt this, or whether he was using the argument as an excuse for continuing his paternal indulgence, it is hard to say. 'It would be discreditable to me', he writes as early as August 45, 'that he should run short in this, his first year, *whatever he is like*. Later, we shall restrict him more carefully'.[20] Marcus himself had an eye to the main chance, and was careful to send home letters couched in his most classical style, and doubtless presenting his activities in the most favourable light. It was on receipt of one of these letters, in mid-April 44, that Cicero seized the opportunity of pointing out to Atticus that so stylish a composition could only be evidence of progress in studies, and urged him to continue to see that Marcus was well supplied with funds.[21] Atticus acquiesced and wrote to Xenon. Xenon, who, as the man on the spot, was in a better position than anyone to know where the money was going, was now becoming very tardy in payment. By mid-June, Marcus had written to Tiro complaining that he had received nothing since the beginning of April, and Cicero, on learning this, wrote instructing Atticus to see that the full allowance for Marcus' second year, which began on that date, should be paid to him.[22] But Atticus himself seems to have had some difficulty at this time in securing the full amount of the rent-income, and Xenon remained so dilatory that even as late as 8 July Marcus wrote complaining to his father that he was only being paid in niggardly fashion, in very small instalments.[23] Meantime, the picture of Marcus' activities in Athens was becoming clearer in Rome, and, although reassuring news arrived from time to time, there was throughout that summer an undercurrent of anxiety and unwilling suspicion in Cicero's mind. Eventually, the disclosure of the true facts drove him to a sharp and angry intervention.

The first disquieting hints reached him at the beginning of May in a letter from one of Marcus' tutors, Leonides, to Atticus, forwarded by Atticus to Cicero. In this, the tutor had remarked that Marcus' conduct was good 'for the time being', a phrase which was no comfort to Cicero, and suggested, as he saw, apprehension rather than confidence. He felt that he had to act, and wrote to another tutor, Herodes, calling for a detailed report. He also had in mind to 'make a trip' (*excurrere*) to Greece, to 'drop in on his studies';[24] but he did not do so, and was only too willing to be reassured, towards the end of that month, that all was well, in a letter received from Trebonius. Trebonius, making his way to his province in Asia Minor after his part in the murder of Caesar, had stopped at Athens, where he met Marcus. He was quite effusive in his praise of the young man, who was 'devoted to the highest studies', and enjoyed 'the highest repute for discreet conduct'; no one could be more popular, or more studious. Indeed, Marcus had suggested that he would like to accompany Trebonius for a short stay in Asia, and Trebonius had invited him with enthusiasm; they would take Cratippus along with them, so that Cicero should not think that Marcus was merely taking a holiday from his studies.[25] One suspects that either Marcus had prepared the ground very well for his visitor, or Trebonius found his company so congenial that he thought it worth a fulsome and flattering letter. By mid-June, further affectionate and stylish letters from Marcus, a glowing report from Herodes, and a visit from Marcus' fellow-student, Messalla, encouraged Cicero to further indulgence, though Leonides had only said that all was well 'up to now'. 'I readily allow myself even to be hoodwinked' writes Cicero to Atticus, 'and am only too willing to show myself credulous'.[26] But not for long; for, later that summer, he received information that one of Marcus' rhetoric-masters, a certain Gorgias (whose treatise on figures of speech partially survives in the Latin translation of Rutilius Lupus), had been leading Marcus into dissipation. Cicero was furious on learning about drinking-parties and pleasure-seeking, and wrote angrily and abruptly to Marcus, ordering him to dismiss Gorgias at once.[27] Plutarch was able to read letters written by Cicero in Greek at this time, in one of which he severely castigated Gorgias as a worthless and licentious fellow.[28] His reaction to his son's aberrations was very different now from that benevolent indulgence towards young pleasure-seekers which he had once advocated in his defence of Caelius; having been something of a Micio, he now became for the time, at least, a Chremes. But Cicero did not harbour ill-feelings; Marcus at once dismissed Gorgias in accordance with Cicero's peremptory behest, wrote home to apologize, and, it seems, remained on the same terms of mutual affection with his father as before.

For a time, Marcus was undoubtedly crestfallen, and perhaps genuinely repentant. Some time later, he was delighted to receive a reassuring letter from Tiro (which took six weeks to reach him), in which Tiro accepted Marcus' regrets for his conduct, and promised to be 'the trumpeter of his repute'. 'The errors of my youth', he writes in reply, 'have caused me so much pain and torment that not only does my mind recoil from what I have done, but even my ears shrink from the very mention of it'. He proceeds to write enthusiastically of his friendship with Cratippus, who spends whole days with him, and often in the evenings drops his austere philosophical manner and, at dinner with him, delights the company with his geniality and wit. He is also on excellent terms with his fellow-student, Bruttius, for whom he has rented a house next door 'alleviating his poverty from my own narrow resources'. He practises declamation daily, and is sorry to lose Gorgias on that account. Finally, he calmly makes the request that Eros will send him a secretary with all speed — a Greek, if possible — 'for it would save me a lot of trouble in writing out lecture-notes'![29] But the end of these halcyon days was soon at hand, for about September 44, Brutus arrived in Athens, made friends with the Roman students there, and recruited them into his service. So Marcus left his studies and found himself once more in command of a squadron of cavalry.[30]

Altogether, it is difficult to form a fair estimate of Marcus. Posterity undoubtedly saw the worst side of his character, and often contrasted him with his father. The chief charge against him was that he was habitually drunk,[31] and the elder Seneca caustically remarked that 'he had none of his father's qualities except his affability'.[32] On the other hand, Brutus thought well of him,[33] and Octavian, having pardoned Marcus for joining Sextus Pompey against him after Philippi, gave him a consulship in 30 B.C., and a proconsular command in Syria afterwards.[34] History has perhaps been rather unfair in writing Marcus off as a mere prodigal. Weak, idle and extravagant he certainly was, though he was generous and, in youth at least, his amiability and lively company seem to have won him many friends. He had also been, as we saw, no mean performer in military exercises.[35] Despite his disreputable episodes, he may not have been quite so devoid of merit as his detractors would have us believe.[36]

In view of Marcus' record, it is a curious irony that some of the best indications of the continuing survival of traditional standards of behaviour are to be found in the treatise *On Moral Duties* (*De Officiis*), which Cicero composed and addressed to Marcus whilst he was a student at Athens. It is a very high-minded essay, developing the doctrines of the Stoic philosophers, Panaetius, Hecato and Posidonius (all of them from Rhodes), with purely Roman observations and illustrations, drawn from Cicero's own wide knowledge and experience. Subsequently, it became one of the very first Latin classics ever to be printed.[37] Basically, it is concerned with the cardinal virtues, but it also throws occasional shafts of light on the important matter of public interest in the early promise shown by young men, especially if they came from distinguished families, and of public opinion on the kind of youthful behaviour which deserved to win commendation. Cicero reminded Marcus of the responsibility which he had inherited in the following words: 'If anyone in early youth is in a position to make his name known, because repute has either descended to him from his father — as, I think, my dear Cicero, has happened in your case — or has been acquired by chance and some lucky turn of events, he becomes the cynosure of all eyes; people inquire about his conduct and his way of life, and he moves, as it were, in a glare of publicity, so that nothing he either says or does can remain in the dark'.[38] But, continues Cicero, young men of humble parentage should also aim high and work hard, for people were interested in them, too, and looked favourably upon their youthful efforts and promise.[39] Later in the work, he again reminds Marcus that people confidently expected that he would emulate his father's industry, and carve for himself a similar career and fame. Moreover, he adds, Marcus had a duty to prove himself worthy of his teacher, Cratippus, and of Athens, the seat of learning to which he had been sent to acquire a store of sound knowledge. When so much had been done to open the way for him, he must not fail to play his part.[40] What Cicero himself, perhaps, did not adequately realize was how difficult it was for any young man to follow in the footsteps of a famous father. It was all very well to point out that the sons of the famous often followed their fathers in their choice of a career, and sometimes strove to add further lustre in a different sphere (whilst those of undistinguished ancestry were more likely to strike out on a path of their own),[41] but it could also happen, as the elder Seneca said of Pollio's son, Asinius Gallus, that 'the greatness of the father overwhelmed the son'.[42]

When we look further into the *De Officiis* for indications of the qualities of youthful deportment and behaviour which were still appreciated in the most respectable Roman society, we find that (apart from military achievement, which always took pride of place) 'the best recommendation a young man can have for popular esteem is his self-restraint, his affectionate regard for his parents, and his generous goodwill towards his kin'. Next to this, Cicero adds, popular approval is most readily won if young men become attached to those who have already won renown for their wisdom and patriotism in affairs of State;

for 'if they are frequently seen in their company, they create a popular impression that they themselves will become like those whom they have chosen to imitate'.[43] Also, people very much appreciate a courteous mode of address, and, of course, oratorical ability; and if a young man's oratory shows dignity and restraint (*gravitas, modestia*), nothing excites greater admiration.[44] But even if a young man does not possess such gifts, he can still win respect for his other qualities — his just dealings and good faith, his generosity and his temperance.[45]

This was not mere philosophical moralizing, for frequently in his speeches Cicero had reason to draw attention to such qualities in the early life of his clients, as, for example, the devotion of Plancius to his father, and the admirable behaviour of the young Murena.[46] Much depended, as always, on the parents themselves and the tradition of their families. Perhaps no better example could be selected than that of Octavian. From his earliest years, says Nicolaus of Damascus,[47] he was brought up with care by his mother, Atia, and his step-father, Lucius Philippus, who inquired daily of his teachers regarding his activities, his progress, and his friends. His great-uncle, Julius Caesar, also kept a friendly eye upon him, had the highest hopes for him, and may well have helped to guide the course of his studies. After his assumption of the toga of manhood, Octavian was frequently seen in public in Caesar's company, and through him met many leading figures of the day. But even then, his family insisted that he should not associate with any contemporary of dubious character, that he should not remain at banquets after nightfall, and that he should not join such festivities before the tenth hour except at the homes of Caesar, Philippus, and his brother-in-law, Marcellus. It was when Octavian was eighteen years of age, and was studying rhetoric at Apollonia with Apollodorus of Pergamum, whom he had brought with him from Rome, that he received the news of Caesar's murder,[48] which brought him directly into the arena of political conflict.

CHAPTER IX

Education in a decadent society

When Octavian's victory at Actium had brought to an end the long turmoil of the civil wars, and the Augustan peace ensued, Rome became not only more resplendent with her many new marble buildings, but a much more cosmopolitan city than before.[1] Many scholars and teachers were among those who now flocked to it from all parts of the Mediterranean world.[2] Their presence, together with the increased availability of books in the new public libraries, combined to make it one of the leading centres of learning. Until 38 B.C., when Asinius Pollio established the first public library in Rome,[3] books had existed only in private collections, such as those of Lucullus and Cicero, but under Augustus (who carried out a plan envisaged by Julius Caesar)[4] the splendid Greek and Latin libraries adjoining the temple of Apollo on the Palatine, and that at the Colonnade of Octavia, provided ample resources for study and research.[5] But many who had leisure had little interest in learning. In a general atmosphere of prosperity and expansion, the building trade was a hive of industry, engaged not only on public works, but on the construction and decoration of luxurious private villas for the rich, whether in the country or at attractive spots on the coast. The chariot-races in the Circus, the gladiatorial shows, the stage productions, and the baths were more lavish and magnificent than ever, whilst unimpeded sea-transport and the increase of foreign trade brought in luxury goods from far afield. Jewellery, furnishings and furniture, purple dyes, perfumes, exotic foods, spices, silk sent from Cos or along the caravan routes from the Seres of the Far East — all this, and much more, could now tempt those who had money to spend it.[6] The result was that such words as thrift and industry were often qualified by the epithet *antiqua* — 'old-fashioned' — and it was mostly in places well removed from the capital that the stricter way of life survived. Tacitus spoke of 'an Italy still austere and tenacious of ancient custom' in Nero's day,[7] and noted that the emperor Vespasian (who was a native of the Sabine country) was an outstanding example of old-style parsimony.[8]

There was also a considerable shift in the distribution of wealth. The *nouveau riche* (*novicius dives*) became a familiar figure in Roman society.[9] Many of these newcomers to affluence were ostentatious freedman, who either attempted to disguise the fact that their culture was rudimentary by acquiring libraries and having a scholar or two to dance attendance,[10] or else confidently asserted that anything beyond a primary education was a waste of time. 'I never learnt geometry or literary criticism', says one such character in Petronius' novel, 'or any such wretched stuff, but I know my capital letters, I can say my percentage tables, I know my weights and measures, and how to divide up money ... you will soon find that your father wasted his fees, even though you are a rhetoric-scholar'.[11] This represents the kind of education which boys of the poorer classes — unless their fathers had higher ambitions for them — usually received, but among the middle and upper classes grammar, literature and rhetoric continued to provide a generally respected training. Many, however, who received such an education must have been exasperated, as was Martial, to find its rewards so meagre compared with the wealth that a low-born, ill-educated person might acquire by a stroke of luck.[12]

But education was not only a matter of academic training; it was also a matter of home upbringing, and was affected by contemporary standards of behaviour. Under the Empire, conditions of family life were, in general, nothing like so stable as they had been under the Republic. Quite apart from the fact that concubinage was common, and so many remained unmarried, or childless, that serious civil disabilities were imposed on them in Augustan legislation, adultery and seduction were so rife that Augustus enacted a law under which the penalties were severe.[13] Divorce, which had been so rare in the earlier Republic, but had become more common later, was now far more frequent. Here Augustus does not seem to have done more than to insist on certain forms of procedure, and to regulate the legal arrangements for the return, in whole or in part, of the dowry.[14] On the other hand, the considerable privileges accorded to parents with three children (*ius trium liberorum*) must have helped to encourage and consolidate family life.[15] We cannot, however, form any clear idea of the proportion in the community of such close-knit families as those described in the last poem of Propertius and the letters of Pliny. The mass of evidence on moral decline is only partially counterbalanced by indications, particularly in inscriptions, which testify to a better state of affairs.[16] But in the study of education, we can at least make an assessment of some of the worse trends of the time, and of the attempts which were made to correct them.

In writers of the imperial period, Roman youth is not infrequently censured for its idleness, effeminacy and extravagance, and it is significant that among its severest critics are Spaniards of the old school, such as the Senecas, Columella, and, to some degree, Quintilian. The elder Seneca expresses the utmost contempt — the young men of his day are languorous, they cultivate the smoothness of their skin, arrange their hair in waves, adopt cajoling feminine tones, and dance and sing voluptuously — evidently, after the fashion of the Greek artists of the stage, the 'pantomimes'.[17] Columella, writing under Nero, contrasts with the sturdiness of earlier generations, who worked on the land, the degeneracy of an urbanized community, in which over-indulgence in food and wine, gaming and sleep, is followed by ill-health, and young men's bodies become enervated and flabby.[18] Quintilian, too, noted the idle lounging at the baths, and the distracting round of pleasures which consumed so much of the time needed by a young orator for study.[19] Such was the decadence of youth, in the eyes of its critics; but this was only the least attractive side of the picture.

The surest indication that these highly disparaging observations were by no means universally true lies in the evidence for the continuing popularity of those vigorous and competitive exercises for which the Campus Martius provided so admirable a setting. The geographer Strabo was greatly impressed by the Campus and its activities; he speaks of the vast extent of its greensward, the multitude of athletes engaged in equestrian exercises, chariot races, ball games and wrestling, all against the scenic background of the hills beyond, sloping down to the Tiber.[20] For Horace, it is the 'sunny Campus', in which the youth, once free of the control of his 'pedagogue', takes delight.[21] In three of the *Odes*, horsemanship and swimming take pride of place among exercises, but there are also wrestling, boxing, weapon-training and contests with the javelin and discus.[22] Horace clearly valued most highly those activities which had some military bearing,[23] and he also approved of hunting, which had long been a popular Roman sport.[24] On the other hand, he, too, acknowledged that there were those who shirked such exercises, who could only muster up sufficient energy to trundle a Greek hoop, or wasted their time at dice.[25] There was a serious danger of youth becoming too soft, and there was every need to encourage a more virile training.

Horace's attitude is of particular interest in view of the determination of Augustus to encourage those physical exercises which had military value,[26] and his institution, to this end, of those associations of young men of the upper classes which came to be known as 'youth clubs' (*collegia iuvenum*). These, as numerous inscriptions testify, proved most popular, and long continued to flourish both in Italy and the provinces.[27] They were originally a pre-military organization,[28] the Roman equivalent of the ephebic colleges of Hellenistic Greece, but appear often to have developed later into fashionable sporting clubs. In Rome their members exercised, especially on horseback, in the Campus and frequently held competitive games. They were divided into sections of younger and older boys; the former took part in the tournament known as the 'game of Troy' (*lusus Troiae*),[29] which was revived by Augustus, and the latter in *ludi servirales*. They had their own well-equipped headquarters, and were often seen on parades. Considerable success, therefore, must have attended this movement to bring back boys and youths to the more virile and invigorating exercises of the Republic.

When, however, young men had grown up idle and undisciplined, it was often due not merely to the influence of contemporary society, but also to the lack of proper parental control at a much earlier age. Livy complained that parental authority was already much diminished in his day,[30] and it is clear that, especially among wealthy families, the strict upbringing of Republican times had given place to the opposite extreme of parental indulgence. Both Seneca and Quintilian warn of the folly of 'molly-coddling' (*mollis educatio*), and the latter has an eloquent little declamation on the subject. 'Would that we did not ourselves ruin our children's characters', he laments, 'from their very infancy we spoil them with our petting, and this soft upbringing, which we call fondness, saps all the vigour of mind and body. What will the child who crawls about on purple not crave when he grows up?'.[31] Children, he says, are not brought up to be self-reliant, but are constantly carried around in litters, and, as toddlers, hold the hand of an attendant on each side. Seneca, too, in one of his essays warns how children should *not* be trained, and throws some interesting sidelights on their behaviour in his day. The spoilt child, he observes, soon finds that he can get what he wants by pestering and crying. He is brought up on delicate foods and loaded with gifts, especially if he is an only child, and money is lavished on his dress. When he mingles with his playmates, and has to compete, he is either dejected or resentful if he loses, or, if he wins, becomes boastful and conceited, especially as there is usually someone around to flatter him. Such an upbringing, noted Seneca, augured ill for the future, for 'the child who has never been refused anything, whose tears an anxious mother has always wiped away, and who has learnt to vent his annoyance on his pedagogue, will not stand up to hard knocks'.[32] When children were treated so indulgently by their parents, it is understandable that the nurses and 'pedagogues', with whom they were left for much of the time, should have found them hard to control, and they evidently sometimes had difficulty in keeping their own tempers. Hence Seneca's advice that those selected to take charge should be of an imperturbable disposition; but that they often were not so is suggested by Nero's remark about Thrasea that he had 'the gloomy expression of a pedagogue'.[33]

There were, however, even more serious matters than indulgence, in which parents were often to blame. Both Seneca and Quintilian stressed the need for care in the selection of nurses and 'pedagogues', who might influence the children for good or ill.[34] In the *Dialogue on Oratory*, Messalla, tracing the decline of eloquence in part to the deterioration in home-upbringing, criticizes the negligence of parents in this respect. They allowed some foreign-born serving-girl (usually a Greek) to have charge of the children in her own cramped quarters, and used as 'pedagogue' some slave who could not profitably be employed in any other capacity.[35] Delegation of parental responsibility was one of the most common features of life under the Empire. The young sons and daughters of the household were still brought up together with the slave-children in the earliest stages, but less regularly now was the mother herself, or an elderly relative, present to supervise them. The attendant slaves, unless carefully chosen, were capable of all kinds of vulgarity. 'No one in the entire household', says Messalla, 'cares a scrap how he speaks or behaves in the presence of the young master'. The parents themselves, asserts Messalla, are also much to blame, for they often have no standards of modesty, and Quintilian and Juvenal thought the same.[36] Children are thus allowed to become pert and impudent, and grow up with no respect for themselves or anyone else. It is clear, too, that much of the harm was done by permitting children to be present from quite early years at convivial parties which ran late into the night.

Nevertheless, although more children were either pampered or neglected under the Empire than under the Republic, this was certainly not the only pattern, and perhaps not even the most prevalent pattern, of family life. There were also many parents, especially among the less wealthy classes, who, though fond of their children, would not allow them to have all their own way. There was often a strong economic motive, which led them to urge their sons to study hard, with a view to securing a profitable vocation later. There is a well-known passage of Petronius' novel in which Echion, the old-clothes dealer, invites the rhetorician, Agamemnon, to his humble abode, and tells him about his little son, who, he hopes, will do better than he has himself.[37] 'He already knows his four-times-division table', says Echion proudly, 'and, in his spare time, he never lifts his head from his tablet. He's a gifted boy, and has good stuff in him' (aptly put, in view of the parent's occupation). We learn that the lad is also 'very fond of painting', and that 'he is digging himself into his Greek, and is taking well to his Latin'; Echion has managed to find a couple of quite undistinguished tutors to visit the house from time to time, one of whom comes in on holidays, and neither of whom, evidently, costs very much. With unfailing insistence he reminds the boy of the importance of study, 'Primigenius', he says, 'take my word for it, whatever you learn, you learn for yourself. Look at Philero the advocate — if he hadn't worked, he would be facing starvation today. Why, not so very long ago, he was hawking around goods for sale on his shoulder, and now he's almost a match for Norbanus. Education is a treasure-house, and a special skill never lets you down'.

Usually, it is the father who supplies the incentive. Seneca, at much the same period, speaks of fathers who order their sons to be aroused from sleep, so that they may be at their studies early, and even on holidays do not allow them to be idle, whereas the mothers wish to shelter them, and cannot bear to see them so hard pressed.[38] Much later, Juvenal pictures the insistent parent arousing his son 'after midnight' (which is Juvenal's way of saying 'very early'), and calling: 'Here, lad, take your writing-tablets, start scribbling, keep alert, prepare your cases, and read through the red-titled laws of our forefathers'.[39] There is evidence, too, that some fathers, desiring their sons to excel quickly, made excessive demands on them, with the result that they could not cope with the work, became dejected, and ceased to respond to instruction.[40] It is particularly noticeable that advocacy stands high in the esteem of such parents as a promising vocation. Despite official restrictions, advocates often did very well for themselves.[41] The commonest avenue to advocacy was the rhetoric school, and that is why, as we may now see, the influence of parents soon became a source of pressure on the schools.

Despite the limitation of the scope of free speech, and what Maternus in the *Dialogue on Oratory* calls the 'pacification' of eloquence under the imperial system,[42] the Romans never lost their old desire to shine in oratory. The opinion of parents, reported by Agamemnon in Petronius, that there was 'no finer gift than eloquence'[43] finds its parallel in Juvenal's picture of the young boy beginning school after the holidays, fired with the determination to become a second Demosthenes or Cicero.[44] But although orators now rarely had opportunities to sway public opinion on great national issues, as they had done in the past, a great deal of legal activity still continued unimpeded; the building of new fora, and the successful careers of Seneca and Pliny at the bar are clear evidence of it.[45] Parents, therefore, still had their eyes on the Forum. But, as the rhetorician Agamemnon pointed out, they now wanted quick results, and were apt to push their callow and ill-prepared sons far too soon into the arena of public life.[46] In their ambition and over-haste, they had no patience with a controlled and graded system of education, which required time and steady development, but expected a short cut to be made to the ultimate objective. Consequently, only the independent and strong-minded teachers — and there were few enough of them — would hold to their convictions and not bow to the popular demand. For parents and pupils alike, rhetoric, which culminated in declamation, was the stage to be reached as soon as possible. One result of this was that many of the *grammatici* were tempted to curtail the amount of reading done in their literature course,[47] and (at any rate in Latin) took over as many as possible of the preliminary exercises in rhetoric, which strictly belonged to the higher level, so that a boy would be ready to declaim at once as soon as he reached the rhetoric school.[48] Another regrettable feature, which resulted from this compression of studies at the secondary level, was a curtailment in general education. The more urgently a teacher felt the need to prepare his boys to demonstrate their ability in declamation, the less ready he was to recommend the study of subjects of less immediate relevance, such as arithmetic, geometry, musical theory and astronomy, which had formed a part of liberal education in Cicero's day, and which Quintilian still advocated.[49] Finally, it was in part due to changed social conditions, and in part also to the false standards of parents and the follies of teachers, that declamation itself, the introduction to advocacy, lost, in many quarters, much of its old effectiveness as a method of training.

In the late Republic, declamation was already coming to the fore as a school exercise, but when adults made use of it they did so in a private house, either to give themselves practice, or, like Cicero, to run an occasional small seminar for a few student-friends.[50] From the time of Augustus onwards, it not only gained an enhanced position in the school curriculum, but also became much more of a public affair, a form of social activity, and a highly intellectual pastime, which both helped to fill the gap left in practical oratory and attracted all kinds of listeners. 'Admitting the public' became a current phrase,[51] and some teachers of declamation, like Albucius, opened their school to all and sundry on several days each year. Then there were occasions, which provided so much of the material for the elder Seneca's reminiscences, when the audience was largely composed of rival declaimers, and a hired hall was used for the purpose. Declamation thus became a kind of exhibition, with a marked competitive element, made more interesting by subsequent debate and mutual criticism.

Parents, who noted how greatly admired the popular declaimers were, naturally wished their sons to excel in this kind of exercise. The boys themselves listened to their master's declamations in school, and sought to emulate him. Even more than Quintus Cicero had done,[52] they enjoyed making speeches on subjects which now often had exciting and bizarre themes. One result of the greatly increased vogue of declamation was that preparation for speaking in the lawcourts was done very largely within the walls of the rhetoric school, and was much less often supplemented by the system of personal attachment to an experienced orator,[53] which had prevailed under the Republic. The boys themselves not only wished to concentrate on declamation, but made it clear what sort of themes they most enjoyed. Thus teachers began to take the line of least resistance, fearing, as the rhetorician Agamemnon said, that otherwise they would be 'left deserted in their schools'.[54] So they played up to their class and indulged its whims, for, said Agamemnon, 'unless the teacher of eloquence, like a fisherman, puts the kind of bait on his hook which he knows the little fish will bite, he will sit dawdling on his rock without the hope of a catch'. Some teachers went further, according to Messalla, and made a point of pandering to their young men by chatting with them in the classroom about their outside interests — horses, gladiators, stage-shows — and even secured their pupils 'not by the strictness of their training, or by proof of their talent, but by touting at morning levées and using the allurements of flattery'.[55]

The classroom behaviour of boys and youths, when rhetorical exercises were being declaimed, too often illustrated the effects of an indulgent, or careless and undisciplined, home upbringing. Certain days were regularly set aside for boys to declaim their speeches before the rest of the class.[56] Instead of listening quietly, the others demonstrated their appreciation in the most vociferous manner. Leaning forwards in their seats, they were ready to spring to their feet, or even dash forward in their enthusiasm, loudly applauding as each sentence fell from the speaker's lips.[57] Applause being the accepted criterion of success, they developed a mutual service in this respect, and signified approbation in order to receive it in turn. If, at the end, the master's praise was somewhat cool, and did not come up to their expectations, they were liable to conceive a resentment against him. This was the more easily fostered, as it was the custom for the master to give his criticisms publicly before the class. 'They listen to instruction more readily than they take criticism', remarks Quintilian, 'and the more spirited ones, especially with present-day manners, even become angry when admonished and offer a sulky resistance'.[58] But the ordinary class-demonstration, however conducted, was not the end of the matter. Parents, says Quintilian, 'counted rather than weighed' their sons' declamations, and they were also present on special occasions to hear for themselves. This was an invitation to the boys to show off. Hence the 'senseless delight of ignorant parents' of which he complains.[59] The boys, he says, learnt to despise hard work, became brazenly self-assured, and made their faults worse by constantly repeating them. Such were the conditions which teachers like Quintilian sought to combat as best they could; but the underlying cause lay in the fact that many of these boys came from homes where they had been either spoiled, or ill-controlled, or encouraged by over-ambitious parents to a premature exhibition of their abilities.

Nothing could be more admirable in this connection than Quintilian's advice on the conduct of a rhetoric school.[60] His first concern is that the teacher should preserve those of tender years from bad influences, and by his authority deter the more unruly boys from licence. He should adopt the attitude of a parent towards his pupils, and consider that he has taken over the position of those who entrust their children to him. He should display neither a morose austerity nor an easy-going familiarity, lest the one breed dislike and the other contempt. He should have much to say about what is honourable and good; the more frequently he admonishes, the less often he will have to chastise. He should be not at all prone to fly into a temper, nor yet turn a blind eye to what should be corrected. He should be straightforward in instruction, patiently perform his task, and make steady, but not excessive demands on his class.

The trouble was, however, that, in an age of general moral laxity, many of the schools in Rome failed to maintain anything like so high a standard as this. Not only were the boys ill-behaved, and a bad influence upon newcomers, but sometimes the teachers themselves were morally disreputable.[61] The more people talked about conditions in the bad schools, the more difficult it became for even the good ones to command confidence, so that, probably long before Quintilian's day, the general comment had spread around that 'morals are corrupted in schools'.[62] Consequently, many parents who were concerned for their children's welfare were reluctant to send them to school, or, at least, kept them at home as long as possible, and arranged for the best private tuition they could afford. This is why Quintilian found it necessary not only to stress the importance of finding teachers of good character, but also to discuss, at some length, the relative value of home and school education. But, even though Quintilian himself taught for many years with conspicuous distinction, his example, and that of others with high standards, could not entirely dispel the widespread doubts of parents. Even after Quintilian's day, Marcus Aurelius noted that his own great-grandfather (Catilius Severus, who held high office under Hadrian) had passed on the advice that the schools should be entirely avoided, that the employment of good tutors at home was far better, and that no expense should be spared in acquiring them.[63] This was all very well, of course, for well-to-do families, but not everyone could afford it. Moreover, as Quintilian says, the really good teachers liked to have a larger audience, and to form their own schools, rather than commit themselves to a single household, where they might be regarded as mere 'pedagogues'.[64] But, when the subject was looked into more closely, there was more to it than this, and Quintilian adduces some very pertinent arguments to show why parents should think twice before deciding to rely entirely on home tuition.

As to the moral question, Quintilian's view, based on wide knowledge, was that although there had been many examples, both in homes and in schools, of bad reputation, there had also been many examples, in both spheres, of good repute most religiously maintained.[65] He uses the word *sanctissime*, and the term *sanctus* often recurs in this connection. It was used by Cicero of Dionysius[66] (when he was in Cicero's good books); it is, like *castus*, a standard term in Quintilian and Pliny, and both words occur in inscriptions regarding 'pedagogues' and teachers who had given devoted service.[67] The equivalent term of praise for a boy is that he is *modestus*, 'well-behaved', and it is interesting to note Quintilian's observation that natural disposition (*indoles*), as well as the manner of home-upbringing, played a part in this. If a boy was by nature perverse, and lacked proper supervision and direction in early years, he could come to as much harm among bad slaves at home as among licentious boys of free birth at school. There was also the possible chance that the tutor would prove untrustworthy.[68] In his view, given a good natural disposition, and proper parental care, a boy would benefit most from being sent to a good school, where the teacher was of exemplary character and his standards of discipline firm.

Moreover, Quintilian observed, there was misapprehension among parents about the academic advantages of home tuition.[69] Parents might think it a good thing to secure a private tutor, who could devote all his time to his pupil, whereas in a large school he would not receive this individual attention. Quintilian admitted that numbers did present a problem, though there were some teachers who deserved a large attendance, and the best advice he had to offer here was that parents should establish a friendly relationship with the teacher; for, if their sons showed any promise, it would redound to his own credit if he brought them on, and he would be inspired by a personal interest as well as a sense of duty. In home tuition, on the other hand, there was the disadvantage that the use of the teacher's time was uneconomical; he would be certain to find that he had insufficient work to keep him busy all day, for the boy had to be allowed time to do his own reading, to memorize his work, and to write out exercises. Much of the instruction, whether grammatical or rhetorical, was of such a nature that it could be imparted to a large class with no more effort, and to better purpose, than to a single pupil. On the other hand, he had to admit that there was less time in school for personal explanation and correction of individual errors. There were, however, compensating advantages. First and foremost, the boy who intended to become an orator must not have grown accustomed to a sheltered life, but must become used to society and publicity from an early age. Secondly, school friendships were of inestimable value, and school life generated the feeling that one belonged to a society, and developed a community spirit. Thirdly, at school, a boy would benefit from seeing what the master approved in his school-fellows' work, he would learn from their mistakes as well as his own, and would note how idleness was censured and industry praised. Most important, he would be stimulated by competition, whereas 'the boy who cannot compare himself with anyone else inevitably thinks he is better than he is'. Quintilian was entirely convinced of the value of competition, which, from his own experience, he asserted was a more powerful incentive to the future orator than the exhortations of teachers, the attentiveness of 'pedagogues', or the prayerful hopes of parents. He added, however, a note of warning — that the teacher should not push his younger pupils too hard, or overload them, or expect them to match his own standards at an early age; it was better to encourage them to emulate the best boy in the class, and to surpass him if they could.

Finally, in the teaching of declamation, on which all the schools concentrated, he noted how absurd, and, indeed, inhibiting, it was for a tutor at home to have to rouse himself to eloquence before a single pupil; for declamation, in his view, the classroom was indispensable.[70]

Quintilian evidently expected that in the well-to-do class, for which he was mainly writing, primary education would still be given within the home. It is only when he begins to discuss children who are of an age to attend a grammar school that he introduces the question of the relative merits of home and school instruction. But in the circle of Quintilian's pupil, the younger Pliny, it seems to have been quite common for boys, and normal for girls, to continue their education at home with tutors at the grammar and literature stage. It is evident that such relationships could be entirely happy. In one of his letters, Pliny pays a rather touching tribute to the young daughter of his friend, Fundanus, consul in A.D. 107, and himself a well-educated man.[71] At the age of thirteen, the girl, who was already betrothed, had fallen ill and died (by a singular chance, the actual urn and epitaph were recovered from the family tomb).[72] Pliny not only describes the girl's charming demeanour, whether grave or gay, and her natural demonstrations of affection for her father and his friends, but also mentions her fondness for her nurses, 'pedagogues' and tutors, and her care and expression in reading. The real problem arose when the boys were ready to take up rhetoric (which was rarely relevant for girls), and it was here that Pliny was able to be of service to his friends. There is a good illustration of this in the letter which he writes to Corellia Hispulla, the now widowed daughter of the consular, Corellius Rufus, whom Pliny had held in the highest esteem.[73] Her husband's father had also been a man of great distinction, and both her husband and his brother might have hoped for high office had they lived; Pliny, therefore, was most ready to do all he could to further the education of Corellia's son. He had every hope that the boy would grow up worthy of his family, provided that the rest of his training was of a high order; but everything depended on the quality of the person from whom he received it. 'Up to now', he writes, 'being only a boy, he has been kept within your own establishment, and has had tutors at home, where there is little, or, I should say, no temptation for him to err. But now his studies must be extended beyond those confines, and we must look around for a Latin rhetorician, of whose school the discipline and restraint, and, above all, the moral purity, are beyond question'. He therefore recommends a man for whom he has a personal predilection — based, however, on a quite dispassionate judgment — namely, Julius Genitor, who is 'a man of flawless character and serious disposition, even a little rough and austere, as seen in the light of this licentious age'. His eloquence (which, we may notice, Pliny places second to character) is widely attested. Pliny will stand guarantor, for 'your son will hear nothing from this man, save what will benefit him, he will learn nothing that he would better not have known, and he will be reminded as often by his teacher as by you and me, of the responsibility he has — no light one — to maintain his ancestors' repute, and of the high honour of the name he bears'. The ideals of the old Republic at its best could hardly have surpassed these of Pliny, and, for this stage of education, Quintilian could not have wished for a more practical application of his own advice. Just as he had asserted that, if schools were good for studies but bad for morals, he would consider virtuous living preferable even to the highest oratorical ability,[74] so Pliny recommends a teacher from whom the youth will learn 'good conduct first, then eloquence, for eloquence without good conduct is ill-acquired'.

Another letter of Pliny shows how much he enjoyed going round the rhetoric schools in order to find a suitable teacher, and oblige a friend.[75] Junius Mauricus, a senator recently returned from exile, had asked him to perform this service for the sons of a brother who had died; for Mauricus had the greatest affection for his bereaved nephews. Pliny was only too pleased to 'go back to school', for he remembered his schooldays as the happiest period of his life. He was suitably flattered when he entered one crowded schoolroom, and the hubbub of voices was immediately stilled — he took it not only as a mark of respect to himself, but also as a promising indication of a proper standard of behaviour. He proposed to make a tour of all the rhetoric schools, and submit a detailed report on each. He was aware that, in presenting a single recommendation, he would have to make an invidious distinction between teachers, but he was as ready to risk the displeasure of unsuccessful aspirants as he would have been if the boys had been his own. On another occasion,[76] he recalls with pride and pleasure his early association with his own former pupil and friend, Ummidius Quadratus, a young man who, now in his mid-twenties, had made a name for himself as both lawyer and orator, and subsequently reached the consulship. Quadratus had been brought up in boyhood and youth in the house of his grandmother Ummidia Quadrate, a lively old lady, who, in her seventies, still retained her enjoyment of the pleasures of her youth, whether it was a little 'flutter' at backgammon, or a stage-show put on by her own household troupe of actors and ballet-dancers. On such occasions — so she confided to Pliny, whom she had invited to supervise Quadratus' legal and oratorical studies — she had always told the boy to 'go away and study', and he, says Pliny, always deferred most respectfully to her wishes. Pliny was more than delighted when Quadratus, who regarded him as his guide and model, proved an excellent orator, and his audiences commented that he was clearly following in his master's footsteps. A similar relationship had existed between Pliny and another young man, whose death he elsewhere deplores,[77] named Junius Avitus. Avitus had looked up to him as both moral guide and teacher, but in this connection Pliny makes the significant remark that such respect was now rare among the young. 'How few of them', he asks, 'being junior, defer to another's age or authority? They have instant wisdom, instantly know everything, respect no one, imitate no one, and are models unto themselves'.[78]

Nothing redounds more to the credit of Pliny than the generosity and public-spiritedness which he showed in helping to provide educational facilities for the sons of his fellow-countrymen at Como. In a letter to Tacitus,[79] he tells how a number of parents had attended his morning levée, one of whom had brought along his young son. In conversation with the boy, Pliny learnt that he and others were going to school in Milan (most likely a rhetoric school), the reason being that there were no teachers available in Como. On the spur of the moment, he suggested that parents should themselves contribute to a fund to hire their own teachers, so that the boys could study in their own home town; 'for where', he asked, 'could they dwell more agreeably than in their own birthplace, or be trained to more respectable habits than under the eyes of their parents, or be kept with less expense than at home?' He urged that all the money at present required by the boys for travelling, for accommodation in Milan, and for all the other things they had to pay for away from home, would be much better used for the remuneration of teachers locally. He himself, though childless, then generously offered to contribute one third of whatever sum they might raise between them, and to help to secure teachers from Rome for the benefit of those families which had subscribed. It was with this in mind that he wrote to Tacitus, on the parents' behalf, for recommendations, being careful, however, not to commit himself to acceptance beforehand, for the parents themselves must make the final choice. But he was confident that Tacitus, whose reputation attracted many scholars and students to his company, would be able to suggest the names of some of whom he might approach. Pliny's move was an excellent example of that enlightened attitude to education which became so manifest under Nerva and Trajan.[80]

Finally, there was no class of people who did more to combat the evils of the age than the philosophers. Of these, none were more influential than the Stoics, whose discipline and high principles, frugality of life, and courage in face of adversity appealed to what had always been best in the Roman character. But their influence was personal rather than organized, and they were often welcomed as friends and advisers in the homes of educated people, who, in the vicissitudes of life and the dangers of a dissolute and politically treacherous society, or in personal bereavement, turned to them for sympathy and guidance.[81] Philosophers exercised an influence both within the home as tutors to the children, and in public by their lectures, which appealed to those who took a more serious view of life and reacted against the evils, especially the luxury, of the day. Seneca tells how the diatribes of the Stoic Attalus on this subject caused him to change his way of life, and his father has recorded an eloquent passage from Fabianus, who turned his declamatory skill to moral themes.[82] Persius the satirist, at the age of sixteen, came strongly under the influence of the Stoic Cornutus, to whom, as a close and trusted friend, he expressed his deep gratitude for wise guidance at the branching of the ways to good or ill.[83] Agricola, brought up at Fréjus by a mother of exceptional goodness, became so interested in philosophy at Marseilles that he would have devoted himself to the study of it, had she not deterred him.[84] The influence of the Stoics on educational thought, especially through Seneca, may be seen in the works of Montaigne and Rousseau.[85]

But, for our present purpose, no better summary of philosophical education at its best could be found than the admirable, Stoic-influenced essay *On the Education of Children* which, though not generally accepted as genuine, has come down under the name of Plutarch, and became widely known at the Renaissance.[86] A bare outline of its contents will serve to substantiate much that has been said in this chapter. The author (who is concerned only with free-born children) begins by observing that, although natural ability, constant study and practice are all essential for the best results, much can be done to enhance even a limited ability by steady application. After the mother has reared her child herself, great care must be taken in the selection of nurses and 'pedagogues', and it is asking for trouble to employ unsuitable slaves. Teachers must be of unimpeachable character and sound experience, and it is folly to engage those whose services are cheap (though the author admits that the children of the poor are in a difficult position). Ill-trained boys soon develop the characteristic vices of youth, for some take up with flatterers and parasites, whilst others purchase freedom for courtesans, or become gluttons, or go to rack and ruin through gambling, revelry, and worse. As to academic training, he warns against extempore declamations, and considers that a general education is desirable; but it should lead up to philosophy, for philosophy teaches the great moral virtues, honour and justice, reverence for the gods, respect for parents and elders, obedience to the laws and to those in authority, love for friends, purity in relations with women, affection for children, and forbearance with slaves; it teaches, too, that one should not be over-elated by success or unduly downcast by misfortune, and that one should be neither dissolute nor bad-tempered. In addition to moral training, physical education must not be neglected, though it should be of a military kind, not merely the cultivation of physique. As to methods of training, parents and teachers should use praise and encouragement, and misdemeanours should be corrected by rebuke rather than by blows.

Children should not be over-worked, for relaxation is essential. Parents should constantly check their children's progress in studies, and especially encourage memory-training. The cardinal rules of conduct to be instilled are that the children should not steal, that they should not fly into a temper, that they should learn to control their tongues, and, above all, that they should speak the truth. Finally, the father should be especially vigilant during the period of adolescence, should take a line between excessive strictness and excessive indulgence, and should not comment on any and every fault; but, in serious offences, he must not fail to threaten, or entreat, or explain the consequences, or point out good and ill by examples. He must see that the youth does not fall into bad company, whether of strangers or schoolfellows, and, above all, he must set a proper example himself. Such, without its enlivening similes and illustrations, is the substance of this valuable little essay, which, although written primarily for Greeks, has also much relevance for Rome.

PART TWO

Conditions of Teaching

CHAPTER X

The problem of accommodation

There is scarcely any part of the study of Roman education in which precise information is so difficult to obtain as that which concerns the localities and premises in which teaching took place. From Hellenistic Greece there is more evidence, for archaeological excavation has not only brought to light the remains of gymnasia and palaestrae, but has secured therefrom a rich harvest of inscriptions of educational interest;[1] though, even in Greece, we do not always know exactly in which part of the buildings lessons or lectures were held.[2] In Greece, too, we hear of teachers who had the use of temples,[3] particularly those dedicated to the Muses, and designated by the title 'Museum';[4] and, in late antiquity, an eminent public teacher of rhetoric, such as Libanius, might be provided with a lecture-room in the council-house itself.[5] But even in Greece there were very many teachers who were not officially appointed, or attached to gymnasia, and who had to find the best accommodation they could; and, though we are ill-informed as to its nature, it is unlikely that it was often in buildings designed for educational purposes.[6] This is even more true of Rome, where the State took practically no interest in financing public education until Vespasian made a start by instituting official appointments in rhetoric.[7] The teacher usually had to depend upon his fees for a livelihood; consequently, the environment in which he worked might vary very much according to his personal circumstances, and the amount he could manage to pay for a hired room. At the very lowest level, he might not be able to afford rented accommodation at all, and might have to teach when and where he could in the open air; and this was also true of Greece. If he had suitable living-accommodation, the teacher might use it for the purposes of his school, either permanently, or at least as a first step. The disadvantage of this arrangement was that it usually imposed too much restriction on the size of the class, and teachers for whom it was imperative to expand their school had to look round for premises which they might hire. From the point of view of attracting public interest and becoming known, the best proposition was to secure accommodation in or near the Forum, or one of the *fora*, where people most congregated; but this brought the teacher, who was often lamentably impecunious, into competition with the shop-keepers and the business community, and he might be driven to look for less expensive, and therefore inferior, premises. It was only if he was fortunate enough to secure a public appointment that he could expect to be provided by others with accommodation worthy of his work. Thus the teaching scene at Rome, as elsewhere, was one of very considerable variety; but, even though the evidence is limited, it may be possible to clarify, to some degree, the different settings in which the teacher held his class.

To begin at the most humble level, it is perhaps insufficiently realized that the Mediterranean climate permitted a much wider use of open-air teaching than is possible in more northerly latitudes. Not that such teaching was in any way organized — it had a certain primitive simplicity about it, and all that the teacher needed was a seat, or bench, a few children and a book. As he was not elevated in a schoolmaster's chair (*cathedra*), he was known to the Greeks as a 'ground-teacher' (*chamaididaskalos*). In late glossaries, this term is equated with *ludi magister*,[8] and it is thus evident that his teaching was confined to an elementary stage. Since so many Roman children were taught to read and write at home, either by their parents or by their 'pedagogue', and many others went to organized primary schools, his pupils would be drawn from the poorest classes, and his recompense would be meagre indeed. But he needed to make some sort of a living, and could not, therefore, afford to select a secluded spot; rather, he had to set up 'school' where he could be seen to be teaching, in the hope of attracting more pupils. Thus he became a familiar sight in the city streets, despite the crowds and the noise; for, as Dio Chrysostom tells us, 'the teachers of letters sit in the streets with their pupils, and nothing prevents the pursuit of teaching and learning, even in so dense a throng'.[9] The extent to which such teaching was possible, however, must have depended on the width of the streets, which at Rome were often notoriously narrow.[10] But it was possible for the teacher to take up his position in the space, or 'square', where three or four streets met, that is, at a *trivium* or *quadrivium*, and this must have happened commonly in many parts of the Mediterranean world. The story was often told how the exiled tyrant of Syracuse, Dionysius, was reduced to the lowliest of occupations, that of a primary teacher, at Corinth, and Justinus says that 'he taught at the meeting of the ways' (*docebat in trivio*).[11] Quintilian, too, at Rome, speaks disparagingly of what he calls *trivialis scientia*, that is knowledge acquired, as we might say, 'at the street-corner', and equates it with the *ludus litterarius*.[12] There is an interesting allusion to this kind of teaching-scene in the last poem of Horace's first book of *Epistles*.[13] Here he addresses his book, as it is about to be published, as though it were a home-born slave (*verna*), handsome and smart, but anxious to escape from his master and exploit his charms in the wider world.

Horace, half-jesting, half-serious, forecasts a chequered career for him, and prophesies that in the end, in faltering old age, he will be reduced to providing elementary lessons (that is, first steps in reading) for boys *extremis in vicis*. This phrase, as the scholiast Porphyrio and some of the early editors saw, was intended to mean 'at the ends of the streets', that is, at the *trivium* or *quadrivium*, and recalls a scene which Horace himself must often have witnessed in his walks in Rome.[14] Evidently, he regards it as a dismal fate for his book, to be put, when old and worn, to such a use, and the *trivium* was, indeed, a far from salubrious setting. It was a place of noise and bustle, where friends met and gossiped, and rowdies argued and exchanged abuse; it was frequented by quacks peddling their wares, parasites angling for an invitation, vagabonds, fortune-tellers, and itinerant musicians.[15] Here the child bent his head over his book, and the street-teacher patiently guided him, only too pleased when, as the morning sun grew warmer, a few casual strollers stopped to take an interest, and asked him who wrote the book which was being read.

Sometimes, too, the teacher would collect his little troop in one of the public arcades (*porticus*), which abounded in the city. Here (Fig.11) we may actually see the scene as it was, depicted in one of the wall-paintings of Pompeii.[16] This formed part of a series which illustrated life in the forum there, and shows a boy who had misbehaved being hoisted by two of his schoolfellows for a thrashing; also in the picture are three other children, sitting demurely on a bench, their reading-books on their knees, and behind them are shown the columns which formed part of the forum-colonnade. Further in the background are passers-by, two of whom have stopped to see what the children are reading, and peer around a column, looking down over their books. The portion of the Forum here represented is thought to have been near the temple of Apollo,[17] and this would accord with other evidence of teaching activities (though not necessarily in the open air) in the vicinity of temples. At Athens, the primary school at which Atrometus, the father of Aeschines, either taught or was employed, was near a shrine,[18] and, at Rome, the 'grammarian' Lenaeus had a school near the temple of Tellus.[19] In another Pompeian wall-painting of the same series (which includes pictures of the most varied activities of the Forum — the citizens who stroll about, or stop to read an advertisement, the vendors of shoes, or cloth, or food, the artist who sits making a sketch, and so on) the street-teacher may again be seen, seated on a bench in front of a column, his book open on his knees, whilst a young boy gazes up with an inquiring look.[20] Such, at Rome too, was education at its lowliest level, simple and natural, merely a tiny facet of everyday life amid the pride and splendour of the imperial city.

Even elementary teachers, however, though they ranked lowest in the

Fig.11 *School scene in the Forum at Pompeii: a thrashing in the*
catomus ('over the shoulders') position.

academic hierarchy, must usually have aspired to something better than
street-teaching, and looked for more regular accommodation. So, too,
did the 'grammarians' and rhetoricians, but in this group there were also
those who did not need, or did not desire, to look for hired premises, but
preferred to gather their pupils in their own homes. Antonius Gnipho
taught both 'grammar' and rhetoric in his own house,[21] and, just as
Aelius Stilo was visited by a small and select group of students (which
included Cicero and Varro),[22] so his spiritual descendant, Valerius
Probus, conducted an informal seminar in the afternoons, reclining
comfortably, like some old-style Oxbridge don, as he discoursed.[23]
Few 'grammarians' were fortunate enough to possess a private villa, like
Valerius Cato, but such villas must quite often have provided pleasant
and tranquil surroundings for those engaged as private tutors to the sons
and daughters of wealthy families. It was in the *atrium* of a villa on the
Palatine that Verrius Flaccus, when officially appointed as tutor to
Augustus' grandchildren, conducted his class, but, although he was
permitted to bring with him his existing pupils, he was not allowed to
augment their number.[24] Furthermore, the architects who designed
Roman villas did not fail to provide for their clients' enjoyment of
studious pursuits and leisured conversation. For this purpose, the villa was
often equipped, already in Cicero's day,[25] with an *exedra*, or
'sitting-out place', usually a rectangular room which was entered from
the peristyle, and gave a view across the garden-court. It served the same
purpose as a spacious modern garden-chalet, but it was a much more

solid and permanent structure, and, as we know from examples at Pompeii, its walls were often luxuriously decorated and its floor artistically designed in mosaic.[26] Interesting evidence of its occasional use as a schoolroom has been recovered from Pompeii, where among the comments scribbled on the walls and columns of the *exedra* of the villa of Albucius Celsus (better known as the 'House of the Silver Wedding'), occurs the ominous warning: 'If Cicero pains you, you'll take a beating'![27]

Most teachers at Rome, however, did not enjoy so pleasant a retreat, but had to descend to the arena of public teaching amid the crowds and clatter of the city. How they sought to establish themselves is best seen from two examples of late antiquity, which must have had many parallels in previous centuries. The first is St Augustine, who tells us that when he first arrived in Rome to teach rhetoric, he began by gathering together in his home those acquaintances who might help to recommend him and make his presence as a teacher known.[28] The other is Libanius, who, in A.D. 354, returned to his native Antioch from Constantinople, where he had held an official position, but, finding himself now without a corresponding post, became, for a time, an independent teacher. He had then fifteen pupils, most of whom he had brought with him, and these he taught in his own house. He was, however, extremely despondent, until an old man advised him that he would never make headway unless he set up school in some more public place. He saw the wisdom of this, and took over premises from a shopkeeper on the fringe of the forum; 'the position', he says in his autobiography, 'did me some good, for the number of my pupils was more than doubled'.[29] Let us, therefore, turn from his experience to the scene at Rome, and see what there is likely to have been there in the way of rented accommodation.

It is generally considered that Roman teachers would, likewise, normally rent a shop and convert it to school use.[30] This was doubtless sometimes done, but the evidence is hardly sufficient to permit one to generalize. For instance, Livy, in his account of the rape of Verginia, is in agreement with Dionysius that the early elementary schools were at that time in the Forum,[31] and he is commonly thought to have added the information that they were 'in shops' (*in tabernis*); but in fact modern editors prefer the alternative reading *in tabernaculis*, 'in booths'. It would seem much more likely (if schools did, in fact, exist so early) that such make-shift structures, covered merely with tent-cloth, which were used long afterwards by hucksters in the Agora at Athens, and elsewhere,[32] were the original school accommodation, than that any of the very limited number of shops in the Roman Forum at that time[33] should have been given over to educational purposes. Then again, the existence of a school, in imperial times, in a shop in Caesar's Forum has been deduced from *graffiti* found on the outside wall of the Basilica of the Bankers and on the nearby pilasters.[34] Certainly, these scribblings contain the opening line of the *Aeneid*, and the first two words of the second book, and even the *Mantua me genuit* of Virgil's epitaph; but these represent only a fraction of the extremely miscellaneous material there inscribed, and we cannot be certain that it is the work of schoolboys.[35] A more significant indication may be derived from the excavation of a house at Pompeii (the 'House of Potitus'), the front portion of which was used as a shop, whilst an interior balcony immediately behind and above accommodated, it is claimed, at one time, a small school. This is deduced partly from a section of the surrounding frieze, which represented philosophers in discussion (perhaps the 'Garden of Epicurus'), and partly from *graffiti* which read 'Take a beating' (*vapula*) and 'I've taken three beatings' (*III vapulo*).[36] It may be of interest to bring this into relationship with rather similar premises, closely connected with shops, which we think were adapted to teaching purposes at Rome.

It is recorded by Suetonius that the grammarian Crassicius, before his published work brought him fame and many pupils of noble birth, gave his lessons in a *pergula*.[37] This was evidently not an isolated instance, for in the third century it was claimed that Julius Saturninus, the rival-emperor to Probus, must have been a good orator because he had studied rhetoric in Africa and 'had attended the *pergulae* of the masters at Rome'.[38] This clearly suggests that such premises were then commonly used for educational purposes. But what exactly in this connection (which has, of course, nothing to do with the *pergula* of viticulture) did the word mean? Being derived from *pergere*, 'to go forward', it was certainly an extension to a building — but what kind of extension? Writers on Roman education have long thought of it as a shop with an extended front, which encroached upon the street.[39] They thus relate it to the kind of open-air teaching which we have discussed, and sometimes claim that the *pergula* was curtained off from the street for privacy.[40] Now it is certainly true that shopkeepers in Rome — such as wine-sellers, pastry-cooks, barbers — did often extend their activities forwards into the streets, rather in the way that some greengrocers do today. As a result, the congestion in narrow streets became a nuisance, and in A.D. 92 Domitian prohibited the practice by law.[41] But, whether or not such make-shift extensions were ever given the name of *pergulae*, there are two reasons for reconsidering this explanation. In the first place, the *pergula*, in some contexts, was demonstrably not on the ground floor at all. Suetonius says that when Octavian and Agrippa went to consult an astrologer at Apollonia, they *ascended* to his *pergula*.[42] In other references, especially in connection with the studios or display rooms of painters, the location is not described specifically,[43] but one legal enactment provides for a claim of damages if a picture, or painted shield, should have 'fallen out' (*excidisse*) from the *pergula* on to the head of an unfortunate passer-by; this at least suggests a higher level.[44] Secondly, the *pergula*, though often mentioned in connection with shops, must have been quite distinct from a shop,[45] since it could be rented, either separately, or with the shop itself. In the great tenement-blocks (*insulae*), the ground floor was often occupied by shops, and advertisements relating to such premises at Pompeii read: SHOPS: *PERGULAE*: APARTMENTS; and: SHOPS, TOGETHER WITH THEIR *PERGULAE*.[46] It has been suggested therefore that, in such cases, the *pergula* was the room, or loft, immediately above the shop, where the shopkeeper and his family often lived; indications of such rooms are identifiable in the *insulae*, and above the shops which formed the front of the House of the Faun at Pompeii.[47] This interpretation seems to point in the right direction, but, if true, the usage can only be a development of the original meaning, for the etymology of the word clearly suggests an extension beyond the original building line.[48] A late glossary[49] gives as the Greek equivalent of *pergula* both *probole*, 'a forward extension', and *hyperoon*, 'an upper room', and these two interpretations may, in fact, be reconciled. Tenement blocks in the wider streets were often fronted with arcades; it was therefore quite practicable to extend the room above the shop fowards over the arcade, and this is probably what a *pergula* strictly meant.[50] But such loggias could also be constructed in much more distinguished settings than those of the *insulae*, and may at one time have adorned the Forum itself.

There is a story told by the elder Pliny[51] that, during the second Punic War, a certain Fulvius, one of the bankers in the Forum, committed the indiscretion of looking forth from his *pergula*, wearing a chaplet of roses on his head in broad daylight (evidently after an all-night carousal) and that this so outraged the Roman sense of wartime decorum that he was tried, convicted and jailed for the rest of the war! Pliny's use of the expression 'looked forth' (*prospexisse*) rather suggests that his loggia was higher than ground level, and it was, in fact, pretty certainly built over an arcade. Arcades and shops — a common feature of fora — had existed in the Roman Forum from the time of the elder Tarquin,[52] and the bankers' shops there are frequently mentioned.[53] But, under the Empire, the vast increase of public building beyond the main Forum must have provided not only more colonnades, but also, in some settings, *pergulae* above them, which could be publicly rented.

Let us now briefly consider the history of a structure very similar indeed to the *pergula*, known as a *maenianum*, or 'balcony-room'. Balconies became a very popular feature of Roman private houses under the Empire, and were frequently constructed without the aid of a supporting colonnade, as, for instance, in the 'House of the Hanging Balcony' at Pompeii.[54] But earlier, and in public buildings, the *maenianum* was built over an arcade. The name was derived from a certain Maenius, who had devised this particular form of architecture in order to improve the facilities for viewing the gladiatorial games in the Forum. To this end, he extended the length of the supporting beams so that they went beyond the line of the columns beneath, and this extra projection seems to have been the main structural difference between the *maenianum* and the *pergula*.[55] A number of *maeniana* side by side could form a long covered gallery. In Cicero's day, that part of the south side of the Forum where the 'Old Shops' had been, and where later stood the Basilica Julia, was still known as the 'Old Maeniana'.[56] Later Vitruvius, in his designs for fora, proposed that 'bankers' shops should be sited in the arcades, and balcony-rooms on the floors above, being rightly thus placed for convenience and public revenue'.[57] The reference to public revenue is interesting, for a late legal enactment also allows that *pergulae* 'in public places' may be used free of rent by teachers of painting.[58] But we may draw even closer than this to our subject. There was, in the imperial period, at Augustodonum in central France (the modern Autun), a celebrated school, which is claimed to have been the oldest educational establishment in Gaul after Marseilles; and its name was *Maeniana*, 'The Balconies'.[59] It was a prominent building in the centre of the town, and it certainly was connected with a colonnade, for Eumenius, who, as the newly-appointed head of the school at the end of the third century A.D., generously devoted his salary to restoring it, says that this was where the famous map, to which we shall refer later, was painted.[60] Considering, therefore, the enormous extent of the colonnades in imperial Rome, it seems highly probable that any available rooms immediately above them, whether *pergulae* or *maeniana*, were, as Vitruvius suggests, officially rented to, or, sometimes, placed at the disposal of, approved persons for teaching purposes and that this is what was meant by 'the *pergulae* of the masters'. Finally, one last scene, to complete our investigation. In one of the so-called 'School Colloquies' (*Colloquia scholastica*), dating from the early third century, which, being set out in both Greek and Latin, a word or phrase at a time, have survived among the Latin Glossaries, a young boy describes his journey to school in these words: 'with my pedagogue following me, I went straight along the arcade which leads to the school ... when I reached the stairway, I climbed the steps ...'.[61] Thus we may suggest that educational activities must often have been pursued at a rather more elevated and attractive level than is usually supposed. We may observe, too, that superstructures of the kind described would be the least likely to survive the destructive process of the centuries, which may be one reason why remains identifiable as schoolrooms have so rarely been found at Rome.

There were also other kinds of extension to public buildings in the city

LABORA ASELLE QVOMODOEGO LABORAVI
ETPRODERITTIBI

Fig.12 *LABORA, ASELLE, SICUT EGO LABORA VI, ET PRODERIT*
TIBI — 'Toil on, ass, as I have toiled, and much will it profit
you!': a school graffito from a paedagogium *on the Palatine.*

where teachers of literature, rhetoric, and philosophy would congregate,
and where lectures and readings must often have been given. In
Hellenistic Greece, as the gymnasia began to be more adapted to
intellectual studies as well as physical activities, it was not uncommon for
one or more *exedrae* to be constructed, quite spacious rooms, sometimes
rectangular, sometimes semicircular (*hemicyclia*), built outwards from a
colonnade. It was probably in the *exedra* of the gymnasium at Priene that
lessons were given, and there a whole wall is covered with the signatures
of students, who must have climbed on one another's shoulders to record
their presence at the school for the interest of posterity.[62] At Athens, it
was in an *exedra* of the Academy that the philosopher, Carneades, gave
his lectures.[63] At Rome, Vitruvius recommended that such *exedrae*
should be built out from three sides of the colonnades of palaestrae, and
that they should have seats, 'so that philosophers, rhetoricians, and
others with intellectual interests may sit and discuss'.[64] But particularly
fine public *exedrae* were also a feature of the imperial fora, notably that
Trajan, where the large absidal recesses at each end could well have been
used for declamations and recitations.[65] As late as the sixth century
A.D., recitals of Virgil and other poets were still being held 'in the Forum
of Trajan',[66] and in the fifth-century Constantinople the *exedrae* on the
north side of the Capitol were officially placed at the disposal of
publicly-appointed grammarians, rhetoricians, and others.[67] It has
therefore been quite reasonably argued that the *locale* of the so-called
'school of Trajan' (*schola Traiani*) could have been the *exedra* adjoining
Trajan's market.[68]

The fact that 'grammarians' often gave public readings from the poets,
or recited their own compositions, and rhetoricians made their

declamatory display-speeches a public affair, meant that they regularly needed some kind of 'theatre' in which to perform. Large rooms in private houses could be used or hired, and adapted to this purpose. For poetic recitations, not only were benches brought in, but the seating was built up in tiers (*anabathra*), so as to provide a rough approximation to a theatre;[69] and the same was very probably done for declamations. At

Fig.13 *Caricature of a school (terracotta): a donkey with his class of young 'monkeys'.*

least, Albucius addressed large audiences in his house, and a wealthy sophist might even have a proper miniature theatre constructed in his own home.[70] When, therefore, under the Empire, Rome was increasingly adorned with fine new buildings, and the State gave some encouragement to the arts, it was natural that important poetic and oratorical competitions and displays should take place in properly-constituted public theatres.[71] But it was not until Hadrian set up his

Athenaeum that, so far as we know, a public building was specifically designed and reserved for such occasions.[72] Unfortunately, we do not know where it was situated, but we learn that it had a theatrical form, for its tiers of seats were divided into the familiar 'wedges' (*cunei*);[73] and there is evidence of its use not only for recitations and declamations,[74] but also for general teaching purposes, for it was a veritable 'school of the liberal arts' (*ludus ingenuarum artium*).[75] Naturally, however, it would only be the most distinguished grammarians and rhetoricians, who held public appointments, who were privileged to lecture there. But we must now return from these rather exalted surroundings to the ordinary schoolroom, in which the teacher plied his daily task.

CHAPTER XI

Equipment: organization: discipline

School work in ancient times began at a very early hour. Rather in the way that the old English grammar schools might be instructed by statute to commence 'at sixe of the clocke', or at six in summer and seven in winter,[1] Roman schoolmasters, by a generally accepted tradition, awaited their pupils at the crack of dawn. Martial says that even before cock-crow boys were on their way to school, and would stop on the way to break their fast at a baker's shop.[2] On dark winter mornings, the 'pedagogue' would guide his young charge's steps by the light of a lamp, and would sometimes carry a child on his shoulder (cf. Fig. 3). On arrival, boys who took a pride in their personal appearance would, after depositing their cloaks, make themselves neat and tidy in an anteroom (*proscholium*) before entering the schoolroom.[3] Conspicuous in the room sat the master in his high-backed chair (*cathedra*), which the Greeks called his 'throne', placed, as it was, on a dais (*pulpitum*);[4] beneath his feet was a footstool (cf. Fig. 7). Clad in a Greek mantle[5] or Roman *toga*, he had his cylindrical book-box, containing his papyrus rolls, beside him, rather as Orbilius was represented in his statue at Beneventum.[6] Equipped with the menacing ferule as his 'sceptre', he was monarch of all he surveyed. Well beneath his eye, his pupils pushed to gain their rightful places on their backless benches,[7] for only, perhaps, in select schools, or those held in private houses, did they themselves enjoy the comfort of round-backed chairs[8] (cf. Fig. 9). Sometimes they would form a semicircle round the master, and this is perhaps why the Greeks referred to 'those around so-and-so', when they spoke of a teacher's group. Horace says that his father was present '*around* all my teachers',[9] and Martial speaks of a *circulus*.[10] Most remarkable was the complete absence of desks, but even this deficiency still existed quite as late as Elizabethan times in England, for we read in an old school-statute: 'if they wish to write, let them use their knees for a table'.[11] When the lesson began, it could still be barely light, and Juvenal, in a well-known passage, describes how, at the grammar-school, 'Horace was all discoloured, and the soot clung to the blackened Virgil'.[12] Whether he was referring to the soiling of the texts of the poets,[13] or of busts of them in the schoolroom[14] (common in Greek gymnasia, but at Rome more usually found in libraries[15]), or even of paintings of them on the walls[16] (such decorations suffered badly from smoke[17]), it is no longer possible to determine. Suffice it to say that the flickering light of oil-lamps and the whiff of their fumes were familiar to Roman boys in their early lucubrations on dark and dismal days. But in the fresh air of a spring or summer morning, at an hour when the city was as yet barely awake, conditions must have been much more pleasant.

For the study of literary texts, the papyrus roll was in general use, but it was by no means as easy to handle as a modern book.[18] Although each end was firmly attached to a roller, it might be very many feet in length, and the reader had to be careful not to open it too far at a time, for papyrus was easily damaged, especially by tearing. It was necessary to unroll it section by section with the right hand, and fold it over with the left as one proceeded (cf. Fig. 9). The writing itself was neatly disposed in columns, but any consultation of parallel passages by reference back or forward must have been a slow and rather cumbersome business. Even more awkward was the copying out of passages, when both hands were already needed to keep the roll open at the proper place, and there was no desk on which to set it. This, in addition to the shortage of texts, may have been one reason why dictation by the master was so common. But the papyrus roll was in itself fairly compact, and light, and a number of them could easily be carried around, each in its parchment wrapper, and furnished with a ticket (*syllabus*) which indicated the contents.

Exercises were written on wooden tablets, often oblong in shape, the interior surfaces of which, within the surrounding rim, were coated with wax, which was often artificially darkened so that the writing would show up (cf. Fig. 20). The letters were incised with the sharp *stilus*, usually made of metal or wood, but sometimes of bone, or even ivory, the reverse end of which was beaten or fashioned flat, so that it could be drawn across the wax for purposes of erasure (cf. Fig. 14). Thus the phrase 'to turn the *stilus*'[19] was a way of saying 'to erase'. Sometimes the surface of the tablet might be left unwaxed, and the wood itself, which might be of a light colour or could be whitened (cf. Fig. 10) was left as a writing-area, and pen and ink were used. School tablets, whether waxed or not, were not only used singly, but were made up in twos, threes, and more (diptychs, triptychs and polyptychs) of identical size; these had holes drilled through one side, and could be set one above the other and fastened together (cf. Fig. 16). But although tablets were as common as slates used to be in more modern times (and some very good examples have survived from antiquity), most of the fragments of school-work which have been recovered, and which originate from Greek schools in Egypt, are written on papyrus. Papyrus was also in general use in Roman schools, but boys were not always able to afford to buy fresh sheets, and Martial mentions school-work done on the reverse side of pieces already used.[20]

Writing implements were carried around in a small case, known as a *theca* (cf. Fig. 9). The pen (*calamus*) took its name from the fact that it was originally shaped from a reed, but, although this remained common, bronze pens were also made (cf. Fig. 14); in either case, the nib was split. On papyrus, erasures could easily be made with a small sponge. The ink itself could be made either from the natural juice of the cuttlefish, or

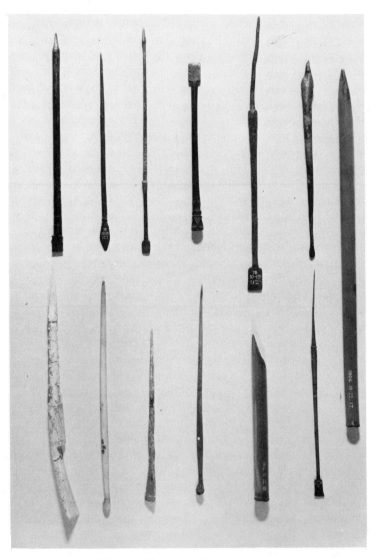

Fig.14   *Roman stili and pens.*

from an artificial compound in solid form, which could be powdered and mixed with water. The elder Pliny, an indefatigable collector of facts of all kinds, offers the interesting tit-bit of information that if an infusion of wormwood is mixed with the ink, the mice will not eat the writing![21] As to inkpots, several examples of Roman date are preserved in the British Museum, one of which, made of metal, still has its hinged and decorated lid intact (cf. Fig. 15).

But pen and ink were not only used on wood or papyrus. Before the first century A.D. references in Horace show that parchment was in general public use for the preliminary drafts of written work, such as poems,[22] and subsequently parchment exercise-books (*membranae*) came into use in schools. These were in the codex form, which, as literary texts were more and more transferred to parchment, became the forerunner of the modern book. We are told by Quintilian that note-taking with pen and ink on parchment was slower than with a *stilus* on wax, as the writer had constantly to be reaching out to the inkpot, and that erasure was also less easy. On the other hand, he says, writing on parchment could be read more easily than notes scratched on a wax surface, and imposed less strain on the eyes. Boys were advised by him to keep occasional pages blank, for the insertion, or addition at the end, of further material as required.[23] But it should be added that Quintilian dealt with a rather well-to-do clientele, and we may be pretty sure that not every Roman schoolboy could have afforded the luxury of a parchment exercise-book.

Apart from reading and writing materials, very little is known about teaching equipment, and aids which nowadays would be considered indispensable were either lacking or inadequate. There was as yet no use of blackboard and chalk, and when demonstration was essential, as in a writing lesson, the master would have to attend to each pupil individually. There may, however, have been a rather primitive approximation to it, for passages for copying — as for example, from Homer — might be written out in ink in large letters on a board (sometimes whitened for the purpose), and part of one such board, preserved in the British Museum (though later than our period) still has the iron handle at the top, by which it once hung from a nail on the schoolroom wall.[24] In connection with the study of Homer, from the point of view of illustration, an interesting problem has long centred around the famous 'Iliad Tablet' (*Tabula Iliaca*) in the Capitoline Museum at Rome, which is one of several such 'pictorial chronicles' recovered from time to time.[25] It is made of marble, and, although the left-hand section is lost, it depicted, in remarkable small compass, and originally with colouring, scenes in relief illustrating famous episodes from the whole of the *Iliad*, book by book. Along the top frieze, a series of scenes (only the first is missing) illustrates the story of the first book —

Chryses' prayer to Apollo, the ensuing pestilence, the Achaian chiefs in council, with Achilles drawing his sword and being restrained by Athena, the restoration of Chryseis, and Thetis' appeal to Zeus to avenge her son. Down the lost left-hand side, eleven reliefs depicted scenes from the second to the twelfth book, and, on the remaining portion may be seen, running upwards, illustrations in twelve reliefs for the latter half of the poem. There is a central portion of the *tabula* devoted to pictures of the sack of Troy, inspired by Stesichorus, and the base contains material for illustration of the Epic Cycle. That the whole tablet was intended not merely as an artistic composition, but for practical instruction, is clear not only from the epitome of the poem inscribed on the vertical pilasters dividing the series of reliefs, but also from the inscription, inviting the observer to 'learn the exposition of Homer, so that you may attain to the limit of all knowledge'. Several scholars have therefore considered that the tablet must once have found a place in an ancient schoolroom,[26] but serious misgivings have been expressed about this view. The detail, it is pointed out, is so microscopic that it could not be seen to advantage by a class at any distance (the whole tablet was not very much more than ten inches square), and it would be too heavy to be handed round conveniently from pupil to pupil.[27] If, on the other hand, as some have thought more likely, these decorative *aides-memoires* were in private possession,[28] they could have been found useful by tutors, such as Dionysius, in their daily lessons on Homer. It must be admitted that there is no certainty about this, but, even in default of such compact illustrations, any schoolboy could have seen the battles of the *Iliad*, the adventures of the *Odyssey*, and many a story from mythology, depicted with much more ample scope in the wall-paintings of public porticos and promenades.[29] He had only to walk around the city to bring his studies to life.

The side wall of a colonnade also offered an excellent opportunity for the painting of maps, quite the most famous of which was the world map which adorned the Porticus Vipsania, originally designed by Agrippa (who also wrote geographical commentaries), and brought to completion about 7 B.C. by Augustus.[30] Often, one imagines, would a small group of schoolboys have been seen studying its wealth of detail, relating its information to their reading, and finding it of absorbing interest. Only much later, in the third century, do we learn of a school which itself enjoyed the luxury of a similar map; this was in the colonnade of the *Maeniana* at Autun. It was provided, says Eumenius, 'for the instruction of the boys so that they could more clearly grasp what they found difficult to visualize when listening to their teachers; for here were to be seen all the place-names and the distances, the source and the course of each river, the winding coast-lines, and the circumambient Ocean'.[31] But there were also at Rome, from the beginning of the imperial period, and probably before, small portable maps in private possession. In a poem of Propertius, a young woman feels constrained to follow her soldier-husband's distant wanderings by studying her painted map (*tabula*).[32] It is more than likely, too, that military commanders proceeding to the provinces also carried with them, as a later military writer recommends,[33] illustrated route-maps, forerunners of the Antonine itineraries and the still extant Peutinger Table, which, though mediaeval and curiously elongated (21 ft long by 1 ft wide), derives from a much more ancient source.[34] World maps in miniature also existed, for Suetonius mentions one, on parchment, which a senator carried around with him under Domitian, and Florus, probably under Hadrian, compares his comprehensive compendium of Roman history to the geographer's representation of the world in a small picture.[35] Strabo, who was born *c.* 64 B.C., and contributes so much to knowledge of ancient geography, speaks of the geographer's map as full of detail, including seas, harbours, isthmuses, capes, tribes and sites of cities; and Vitruvius, in whom the Greek word *chorographia* is already Latinized, draws attention to 'the sources of rivers, painted on maps of the world'.[36] Geographical digressions were much in favour with both historians and poets, and there are some good examples in Lucan,[37] such as his account of the tribes of Gaul, and, especially, that of the rivers which flow from the Apennines, which reads like a geography lesson in verse. Admittedly, such information may have been derived from reading, and from geographical manuals which were current[38] (there is one extant by Pomponius Mela), but consultation might also have been made of maps. The Romans, then, certainly did not lack interest in geography; Seneca, Lucan, and their contemporaries, for instance, were greatly attracted by the perennial mystery of the source of the Nile,[39] which was not solved until the explorations of the nineteenth century. As regards the schools, despite the lack of direct evidence, it is hard to believe that the *grammatici*, all of whom were concerned to explain place-names in their texts, and some of whom passed as proficient geographers in their day, would not have been able to produce some kind of map from time to time to hand around their class. But this is not to deny that their knowledge (though soon to be greatly improved by Ptolemy) was often quite inaccurate, and their visualization of landscapes, apart from areas they had visited, could be more than somewhat hazy.

The size of what might be termed a 'school' varied greatly; sometimes there was a mere handful of pupils, sometimes (so far as later evidence permits us to deduce) a few, or several, scores; but, even in flourishing schools, numbers never remotely resembled the modern multitudes. At the lowest end of the scale, poor Munna, says Martial,[40] having been accustomed to teach only two, now has a third, and thus can claim the *ius trium liberorum!* The jest is reminiscent of a witticism of Diogenes the Cynic, who, entering a Greek schoolroom in which the statues of the Muses (presumably nine) outnumbered the boys, remarked to the teacher: 'With divine help, you have plenty of pupils'.[41] But even in a well-established school, numbers were apt to dwindle in times of civil disturbance, and the experience of Libanius, who found that in such a period his attendance dropped to twelve, and then to seven, must often have been known long before in Republican Rome.[42] Numbers in grammar schools might sometimes remain small, either because parents would entrust to the teacher only their older boys, as with Caecilius Epirota, or because the teacher himself, like Valerius Probus, could

Fig.15 *A selection of inkpots of Roman date.*

afford to keep his school select.[43] Quintilian, on the other hand, repeatedly refers to the 'crowd' (*turba*) or 'large concourse' (*frequentia*) of pupils in the grammar and rhetoric schools.[44] But such expressions cannot be evaluated in anything like modern terms; when Libanius had something over eighty students in rhetoric at Constantinople, he accounted himself a great success, and at Antioch he thought that he was beginning to do reasonably well when he had around half that number.[45] It is surprising, then, to find that, in Spain, the elder Seneca apparently attended a school (grade unspecified) of more than two hundred pupils.[46] At Rome, the only teacher of whom we may be fairly certain that his school matched this size was the *grammaticus*, Palaemon, and he was quite exceptional. Palaemon was a notoriously enterprising businessman[47] and, whilst teaching groups himself, may well have 'farmed out' a good deal of the necessary work to others. Whatever the size of school, a considerable amount of personal tuition was expected, and there was often sufficient work for more than one teacher in the same establishment. Sometimes two teachers went into partnership; in the *Digest*, a case is recorded from the Augustan jurist, Alfenus Varus, of two grammarians who agreed by contract to share the work and the remuneration.[48] Much later, the emperor Pertinax, who had at one time taught grammar, but gave it up because he found it did not pay, continued to entertain an old friend, Valerianus, who had taught with him.[49] Even in Cicero's day, the 'under-master' (*hypodidascalus*) was a familiar figure, seated on a cushioned stool near the master, but was probably ill-paid, like the *subdoctor* of the grammar schools in later antiquity.[50] In Quintilian's time, the Greek rhetoric schools had their assistant teachers (*adiutores*), who took reading-courses in prose literature before the students went on to the master himself for declamation, and Libanius himself had at least four assistants at one time.[51] At Rome, Petronius refers to an assistant in a rhetoric school called an *antescolanus*, though whether he was a teacher in his own right, or a senior pupil allowed to take some lessons, is not quite clear.[52] But this evidence of the employment of further staff (who, of course, until such time as official appointments were made, had to be paid by the master) does raise the question as to how their teaching was conducted, in view of the limited facilities of school-accommodation.

Juvenal is clearly thinking of a single large class when he speaks of 'so many boys', who have to be closely watched by the *grammaticus*, and of the *classis numerosa* of the rhetorician.[53] For full-scale lectures, or declamations, this would be understandable, but the impression which we gain from later antiquity is that sometimes several group-activities were going on, under different teachers, at the same time in the same room. At an elementary level, we find the small boys (*pusilli*) being tested on their letters and syllables by an older pupil, or the under-master, whilst there are two groups to whom passages of literature are being explained.[54] Much depended on the type of work being done, but even the main rhetoric-school at Antioch in Libanius' day only had one large room, and as he had four or five 'symmories', or sections, which would number about ten each, the groups were probably divided off from each other by curtains or screens.[55] At Rome, even the Centumviral Court, held in the Julian basilica, was divided into four separate panels, which functioned at the same time, and were merely curtained off from each other, with the result that a loud-voiced orator, or a burst of applause, could easily be heard in the adjoining section.[56] A rather similar situation may, therefore, at times have existed in the schools.

But there is also considerable evidence of an orderly arrangement of pupils within the class, the main determining factor being that of individual acumen and progress (*profectus*). Young boys attending their first lessons on literary passages would simply be divided into two groups, the slower and the quicker,[57] but, as their education proceeded, and especially in the grammar and rhetoric schools, they had each their own place in class, according to achievement. There was keen competition for the honour of being top of the class (*ducere ordinem*, or *classem*). The traditional procedure in the rhetoric schools of Quintilian's youth was for the class-order to be established monthly. Each boy was placed according to the master's assessment of his abilities, and, for the rest of the month, each declaimed according to his position in class. Commendation was eagerly sought, and high places were only retained by effort, for by the month's end a determined rival might have forged ahead.[58] The grammarian Verrius Flaccus made a name for himself by his competitive system, and by his generous gift of a prize — some fine, or rare, old book — to the winner, for an essay on a set subject.[59]

Fig.16 *Waxed writing-tablets, strung together*

It might well be assumed, as Quintilian offers no evidence on this point, that there was nothing which corresponded to an 'examination'; but there was, in fact, something which came rather close to it. In Hellenistic Greece, teachers were expected — and, indeed, sometimes specifically required by local regulation — to present a public 'display' (*apodeixis*) of their pupils' achievements; and this meant not only athletic prowess, but also, in such places as Teos, Priene and Miletus, ability in literature and music. The occasion was a public one, and prizes were awarded, sometimes not only to the successful competitors, but to their teachers as well.[60] Now something like this system — though less organized — is likely to have become accepted at Rome in the imperial period, for there is evidence that it was known earlier than this in the West. Sertorius, when in Spain, devised an ingenious method of retaining the allegiance of local chieftains by providing their sons, the future leaders, with a free education at the large city of Osca. He engaged teachers of both Greek and Latin for them, and treated them entirely as young Romans, for, says Plutarch, 'their parents were marvellously pleased when they saw their sons, dressed in embroidered togas, going to the schools in very orderly manner, and Sertorius paying their fees and *often holding test-displays, and awarding prizes to the deserving*, and bestowing on them the golden necklaces, which the Romans call *bullae*'.[61] The implied presence of the parents is an interesting feature of this account, for Plutarch tells us elsewhere[62] that when Cicero was very young, his distinction at school was so outstanding that the parents of the other boys came along to admire his brilliance, and sometimes, if churlish, to reprimand their own sons for their inferior performance. Cicero's friend Atticus, we are told, also stimulated keen competition among his schoolfellows by his excellent reading.[63]

In educational contexts, the use of the word *pueri* is so ubiquitous that one might naturally assume that all Roman classes were composed exclusively of boys. Quintilian, particularly, at all three stages of education, constantly speaks of boys, but this is understandable, as he is concerned throughout with the training of the orator. But the most exactly contemporary evidence of Martial shows that, at the primary stage at least, both boys and girls might be present in the same school; for he addresses an 'accursed schoolmaster', whose shouting disturbs his early morning sleep, as 'a fellow hated by boys and girls alike'.[64] Some primary schools, therefore, though not necessarily all, must have been mixed. But the question which has given rise to some difference of opinion is whether co-education existed in the grammar schools.[65] Here, it is irrelevant to cite evidence that, under the Empire, girls often received an education quite beyond the primary stage; for anything which could be taught in a grammar school could have been taught equally well by tutors in the home. Ovid's claim that Menander 'is read by boys and girls' is too loosely expressed to be used as evidence of co-education in grammar schools.[66] Juvenal, indeed, although he knew (and disliked) women who were learned in both grammar and rhetoric, depicted the grammar school, in his seventh satire, as one in which the pupils were boys. It is again Martial whose words may be held to point to the presence of both boys and girls in the same grammar school. Three of his epigrams require to be considered closely together.[67] In the first, he mentions a complaint that his verses are too wanton (*parum severos*), and 'not such as a master would read aloud in school' (*nec quos praelegat in schola magister*). In the second, he congratulates Cosconius on writing highly proper verses, 'which deserve to be read by boys and girls'. In the third, which is most immediately relevant, he imagines one of the Muses advising him not to give up writing epigrams, and not to compose tragedy or epic instead, 'so that the blustering schoolmaster may read you aloud (*praelegat*) in hoarse tones, and the grown girl and the good lad may hate you'. Tragedy and epic, the Muse adds, may be left to over-serious and over-austere writers to compose (*nimiumque severi*). Now there are three references in these passages which point unmistakably to the grammar school, and are not compatible with the view, sometimes expressed, that a primary school is meant. First, Martial twice uses the term *praelegere*, and this word occurs particularly — and perhaps exclusively — in grammar-school contexts, referring to the preliminary reading aloud of poetry by the master. Secondly, he uses the term *schola*, not *ludus*, and this is a word used especially of grammar and rhetoric schools. Thirdly, he speaks of the moral quality of texts used in schools, especially tragedy and epic, and it is when Quintilian discusses the grammar-school curriculum that he is most concerned with moral values, and recommends the uplifting power of epic and the value of tragedy.[68] Finally, it would be pedantic to object that the boy and the girl are not necessarily in the same class; if they were not, the already hoarse schoolmaster would be duplicating his work. We must, therefore, it seems, accept that, in Martial's day, there did exist grammar schools, as well as primary schools, in which boys and girls were taught together. But we may discern an interesting limitation in what Martial says, for he has perhaps chosen his words rather carefully. Apart from his references to the moral quality of the literature read, he speaks of the *bonus puer*, the well-behaved boy, and he must therefore be thinking of schools in which the standards were good. Then he speaks of the *grandis virgo*, the big girl, which means that she would be well into her teens, and this may perhaps suggest that parents who had provided a private tutor for their daughters for some years, would sometimes send them to a good grammar school to complete their education.

Such indications as we have regarding the age at which pupils transferred from one kind of school to another suggest that there was some elasticity in both the arrangements for acceptance and the duration of the course. We may say that, in general, a boy would certainly have reached the school of the *grammaticus* by the age of twelve; this was the age at which Persius, of whose earlier education at Volaterrae nothing is known, joined the classes of Palaemon,[69] and at which another young boy died when he had just come to Rome from Reggio to study poetry.[70] But Quintilian considered that it was time for a boy to transfer to the 'grammarian' as soon as he had acquired proficiency in reading and writing, and, as he thought that a start could be made well before the normal age of seven, there must have been many in his day who reached the grammar school by the time they were eleven, and possibly a few even earlier.[71] We shall later meet a boy who won a public competition with improvised Greek verses on a mythological subject at the age of eleven and a half, but he was doubtless a prodigy.[72] Similarly, according to Quintilian, ability rather than age was the best criterion for transference to the rhetorician,[73] and, even though many 'grammarians' were encroaching on the rhetoric programme,[74] boys would normally have joined the school of rhetoric by the age of fifteen. By the time Persius was sixteen, when he became devoted to the philosopher, Cornutus, he had already studied for a period with the rhetorician, Verginius Flavus.[75] At sixteen, he took the toga of manhood,[76] and this proof that he was still wearing the *toga praetexta* at the rhetoric school tallies with the evidence of Quintilian, and later antiquity, that many of those in the rhetorician's classes were still boys.[77] As the course proceeded, they would become *adulescentuli* or *iuvenes*, and stay until they were around eighteen (or, in later antiquity, even twenty).[78] But the segregation of the younger from the older boys, which Quintilian recommended, was still practised a century later in the schoolroom of Proclus of Naucratis at Athens, of whom Philostratus was a pupil;[79] for he tells us that the boys sat together, and the youths by themselves, with the 'pedagogues' in the middle. Finally, those who decided to transfer to philosophy would be most likely to do so, like Persius and the philosophy students whom Plutarch counselled on behaviour at lectures,[80] when they had just assumed the toga of manhood.

The arrangement of the various activities which made up the school day was by no means uniform at every level of study, or at all times and places. The evidence is very scattered, but the limited amount which survives from our period may be shaped at least into tentative patterns by a judicious use of later information. At the primary stage, classes were held in both the mornings and the afternoons, and those who lived within reasonable distance of the school would usually return home for lunch around midday.[81] As so early a start was made to the day's work, there was plenty of time to allow for various forms of physical exercise, but these periods could be fitted in at different hours. Evidence which reflects Greek practice shows that both young beginners and those who were more advanced in the study of literature and music would first attend lessons and then take their exercise — such as riding or javelin practice, followed by a visit to the *palaestra* — during the morning. This would be followed by a quick bath and midday lunch, after which there were further lessons in school, probably throughout the afternoon.[82] But in Roman writers the morning hours as a whole[83] are associated with school-work, and the sequence given in the 'School Colloquies' was probably normal. Here the boy remains at school until midday, but, having done so much in the morning, returns only for a lesson in the afternoon, after which he proceeds to enjoy his visit to the baths.[84] But, in this pattern, one would assume that there would have been some kind of morning-break as well. Boys who lived at a distance from school brought their lunch with them, and it is in connection with this that the elder Pliny relates a remarkable and delightful story about a boy and a dolphin.[85] The boy lived near Baiae, in the time of Augustus, but his school (a primary school) was at Puteoli (Pozzuoli), and his way lay past the Lucrine Lake, where, one day, as he loitered around noon (evidently he was excused morning school) he made friends with a dolphin by feeding it with morsels of bread, part of his lunch. This he often repeated, so that the dolphin not only regularly responded when he called it, but allowed him to mount its back, and would carry him across the bay to school. This, we are told, went on for several years, the dolphin providing transport both ways, until at last — unhappy sequel — the boy fell ill and died and the dolphin, after repeatedly waiting in vain at the accustomed place, 'like a mourner', itself died, 'undoubtedly of grief'! A little embroidery to the tale, perhaps, but all staunch supporters of that highly intelligent creature, the dolphin, will be pleased to know that Pliny had seen the story written down by the three Augustans, Maecenas, Fabianus and Alfius Flavus, 'and many others'. At least it proves that in the Naples area (where the Greek pattern would be followed), there were lessons in the afternoon.

At the higher stages of study, there is considerable evidence from the fourth century that, in normal practice, teaching was confined to the forenoon. Ausonius speaks of the *grammaticus* spending six hours of the day at school (that is, six Roman hours, of varying length according to the time of year), and six at home.[86] St Augustine says of his period of rhetoric-teaching that 'students take up the hours before noon',[87] and several passages in Libanius show that teachers in Antioch usually expected to be free by that hour.[88] But there were frequent exceptions to this arrangement, which must also have been true of our period. Much depended on the size of the school, and even though most of the formal teaching was done in the morning, the need to follow this up with individual attention and exercise-correction could keep a teacher busy, as it did with Libanius, until dusk.[89] Sometimes, too, a declamation by the master would take place in the afternoon. Certainly those who, in our period, taught both 'grammar' and rhetoric as separate subjects would be actively engaged in both parts of the day. Under the Republic,

Aristodemus of Nysa taught rhetoric in the mornings and 'grammar' in the afternoons, and, in the first century, a certain Princeps sometimes discoursed on literature in the mornings and then, having had his *cathedra* and dais removed, delivered a declamation in the afternoon.[90] Finally, at the grammar-school stage, boys who were studying other subjects as well as grammar and literature required time to attend different masters. Whilst the *grammaticus* himself might be available throughout the day, he did not need every boy to be present all the time, and thus Quintilian recommended that periods when any boy could be released might with advantage be used by him for his wider education.[91] In general, it would be true to say that, at all periods, most of the formal teaching was done in the morning hours, but that the teacher could only hope for leisure for his own studies and compositions if his school was of modest size. Nor did the boys necessarily have the rest of the day free after leaving school, for, although teachers do not seem to have set regular written work to be done at home, they might well expect a passage to be learnt for recitation the following morning; and even if they did not, keen parents and 'pedagogues' would often make children repeat what they had learnt during the day, and were not satisfied until they were up to standard — so this was a kind of retrospective homework.[92]

After every eight days, the market-day (*nundinae*) brought a short respite to teachers and pupils in the primary and, probably grammar schools;[93] in the rhetoric schools, too, formal teaching is likely to have been suspended, but a display-declamation might be held instead.[94] There were three main holidays in the year, two of which, the *Saturnalia*,[95] from 17 to 23 December and the *Quinquatrus*,[96] from 19 to 23 March, had originally been restricted to a single day, but were gradually extended to seven and five days respectively. These periods of freedom were meagre, but they were all the more appreciated for that, especially the *Saturnalia* which, like our Christmas, was celebrated with gaiety and exchange of presents. The longest holiday by far was that of the summer, though its exact extent cannot now be ascertained. Martial makes it clear that it ended on the Ides (15th) of October,[97] which corresponded with what was, certainly in later times, the conclusion of the grape-harvesting holiday (*feriae vindemiales*);[98] but whether the school vacation began in June or July must remain uncertain. Martial speaks of a primary teacher still at work with his class in the dog-days of late July, but his protest may be directed against some over-zealous teacher, for this period would be within the general harvest-holiday (*feriae messivae*), which (again in late antiquity) ran from 24 June to 1 August. The likelihood is that not much was done in the schools at Rome after the end of June, though, as poets could be heard reciting in the month of August, rhetoricians may have declaimed as well.[99] In fourth-century Antioch, likewise, classes were suspended from mid-summer to autumn.[100] Apart from these longer holidays, the imperial period saw considerable additions to the number of festive days in the calendar; but this does not necessarily mean that all the schools took advantage of them and were closed — at least, in Libanius' day the rhetoricians often continued to teach on days on which they would have been justified in joining in the general cessation of work.[101]

Conduct in school, as we have seen from Pliny and Quintilian, varied greatly. The 'School Colloquies' again, though later than our period, give a good idea of what the Roman classroom must have been like at all times in such schools as maintained a high standard of decorum. The behaviour of the young scholar is quite genteel, his relations with his schoolfellows friendly, his attitude to his teachers respectful. Evidently he comes from a good home, and has been well trained by his 'pedagogue'. He takes a pride in his cleanliness and general appearance, and goes to school looking tidy (*mundus*), 'as befits a boy of free birth'.[102] On the way, he exchanges polite greetings with acquaintances; on entering the schoolroom, he bids the master 'good morning' (*ave, magister*), and his greeting is acknowledged (*ave, discipule*). He greets his schoolfellows, this being good policy 'lest they disparage you', signs the attendance list, and stands listening attentively as the master corrects a schoolfellow's pronunciation, 'since we make progress by observing what is criticized in others, and thus gain confidence'.[103] When the morning's work is over, and he is dismissed, he politely bids the master good day, and returns home to lunch. These descriptions, though doubtless written with an eye to magisterial approval, show very clearly both the naturalness and the shrewdness of a young boy, and they represent the kind of attitude towards school and teachers which Quintilian most liked to see. If, he says, boys feel that their teachers are like parents to them, 'they will gladly listen to them, trust what they say, and desire to be like them; they will come to school cheerful and keen, will not be annoyed when corrected, will rejoice when praised, and will try to win affection by their devotion to study'.[104] The methods used by such teachers — their combination of gentleness and firmness with the very young, their encouragement by competition and reward, their readiness to answer questions and explain, and their concern to elicit the best of which each boy was capable — developed an excellent teacher-pupil relationship, and produced the best results. Cicero reminded his listeners of the grateful memories which educated men had of their former teachers, and Seneca was conscious of the debt which was often owed to them.[105] It is true that he remarked that there was a tendency in later life to forget their services,[106] but inscriptions set up by former pupils, as well as by wives, friends and freedmen, show that they were often remembered with gratitude.[107] Life-long friendships, too, often began in school, as between Atticus and Cicero and other contemporaries, and, probably, Ovid and Tuticanus;[108] Octavian and Agrippa first met in a rhetoric school at Rome.[109] Even allowing, therefore, for a certain natural nostalgia in later life, the schooldays of those who were lucky enough to find kindly, intelligent and understanding teachers must have been reasonably happy.

Often enough, however, boys did not much like their school-work. Persius hated having to produce, as an exercise, 'the magniloquent speech of Cato at the point of death', and discovered an ingenious means of avoiding it; a little temporary eye-trouble was created by a judicious infusion of a few drops of olive oil. This was a good excuse for claiming that he could not see to read, and hence could not learn up and declaim his work.[110] Some boys were idle and inattentive, and quietly whiled away the time by sketching on their waxed tablets, sometimes, perhaps, risking a caricature of the master.[111] Erasure was quick, but misuse of writing-tablets invited chastisement, if discovered, as Lucian found when he scraped off some of the wax for his favourite pastime of modelling.[112] The sharp *stilus* was also a very convenient instrument for producing more permanent inscriptions. Not being able, like the schoolboys of old Eton, to apply their diligence to a little surreptitious wood-carving, and to leave the record of their names on their desks for the edification of posterity, their ancient counterparts, when the master was away, or his back turned, found ample scope on the school walls, as at Priene. *Graffiti* from Pompeii testify to boredom with school lessons,[113] and someone at Rome made a sketch of a heavily laden donkey, (Fig.12), with the caption: 'Toil on, ass, as I have done, and much will it profit you' (*labora, aselle, sicut ego laboravi, et proderit tibi*).[114] The author of it would have been delighted if he could have seen a terracotta relief which takes the form of a caricature of a school-scene, for there sits the master, upright in his high-backed chair, below him his pupils, all symmetrical with their *abaci* on their knees, but the master's head is a donkey's and the boys have the heads of young monkeys![115] (Fig.13). Doubtless, there were circumstances in which both features would have been entirely apt.

History has recorded but a fraction of the unofficial activities of schoolboys, but we know something of their misdemeanours and unruliness. Pilfering occurred as early as the time of the elder Cato, when a boy might find that someone had stolen his *stilus* or his little purse.[116] But Martial's chief objection to schools was the intolerable noise both masters and pupils made, which was worst of all when it disturbed his morning sleep.[117] In an ill-controlled school, talking in class was common, and the master's stentorian calls for silence[118] increased in volume as the buzz of youthful chatter was added to the competition from the street. Even a classroom of beginners could become a bedlam, as an epigram in the post-classical *Latin Anthology* describes: 'The ignorant Calculo has taken on youngsters of tender years, and makes them learn their first little letters, but when he fails to intimidate his pupils and takes no steps to check their behaviour with his ferule, the boys fling aside their tablets and play Floral Games, and he is now rightly termed master of a *ludus*'.[119] The pun on the two meanings of *ludus*, 'game' and 'school' is neat enough, and must often have been made, but the reference to the 'Floral Games' is perhaps not so innocent as it sounds, for this public event was notoriously immoral. Even in Varro's time, there was occasionally a 'black sheep' who had to be expelled, for in a work on education, now, alas, fragmentary, that author likens such boys to the 'rejects' (*reiculae*), which the shepherd has to remove, 'for often a single wanton and dirty boy defiles the flock'.[120] Matters became much worse under the Empire, as the elder Seneca and Juvenal knew.[121]

There were times, too, when boys became aggressive, and a private altercation might lead to fighting, as when Cassius punched Faustus Sulla, the dictator's son, for praising his father's proscriptions and saying he would follow his example in due course.[122] Outside school, boys had their own gangs in times of political disturbance, and, during the Civil War, the young 'Pompeians' lined up to do battle with the young 'Caesarians' in the streets.[123] Even in the rhetoric schools, in Juvenal's day, irate students were sometimes known to strike their masters, and disorderly conduct persisted in late antiquity.[124] One might have expected that in the philosophy schools, even under the Empire, orderliness and serious concentration would have prevailed, but Plutarch's essay on students attending philosophy lectures shows that this was not necessarily so. They were not dangerously aggressive, but either excessively uninhibited or bored. Some, he says, interrupted with commendatory exclamations at anything of which they approved, whilst others wore a supercilious expression, as though they could have done better themselves. Some listened with an inscrutable impassivity; others nodded as though they understood, to conceal their lack of comprehension. Others raised objections, or plied the lecturer with unnecessary and irrelevant questions to draw attention to their acuteness. Some grinned when the subject was serious. Some frowned, some looked sour, some had a roving eye, some twisted uncomfortably in their seats, some whispered, and some yawned sleepily.[125] Altogether, an admirable subject for a caricature!

At the lower levels, it was not so much the mischievousness or apathy, as the sheer dullness of his dim-witted pupils which tested the master's patience. Much depended on his own temperament, but Cicero observed that 'the more clever and talented a man is, the more short-tempered he becomes in teaching, and the heavier weather he makes of it, for he suffers torments when he sees that what he has himself grasped so quickly is so slowly apprehended'.[126] Thus the irritable schoolmaster became a byword, and Seneca noted the paradox that 'the most ill-tempered schoolmaster teaches that the temper must be controlled'. [127] Long afterwards, Ausonius, who had himself found teaching no easy task, advised his young grandson, on beginning school, not to be deterred by the 'domineering voice' and the 'ferocious expression' of the 'testy master'.[128] When work or behaviour was bad, the teacher would certainly issue sharp rebukes and stern warnings; but if these were of no avail, he could have resort to a varied selection of weapons of punishment which make even a Dickensian schoolmaster seem an amateur.

Throughout antiquity, from the time of Socrates to that of St Augustine and beyond, across the whole Mediterranean world, from Egypt to Bordeaux and from Carthage to Antioch, corporal punishment was a constant feature of school life. Even though prominent individuals, from time to time protested against it in the strongest terms, it was never widely condemned by public opinion. The instruments of chastisement were formidable indeed. Commonest, and least damaging by comparison with the rest, was the ferule (*ferula*), which corresponded roughly with the cane. Cut from the stalk of the giant fennel (*narthex*), it was light and easy to manipulate, but might have in it a few nasty knots.[129] Ovid knew how small boys held out their 'tender hands' to receive its 'cruel blows', and later writers mention palms so swollen that children could scarcely hold their books.[130] It was small wonder that, long before Shakespeare described the schoolboy as 'creeping like a snail unwillingly to school', the apprehensive pupils, as Lucian says, made their way there 'with a sulky expression', and sometimes 'emerged in tears'.[131] Juvenal remembered how, even at the rhetoric school, he flinched and withdrew his hand as the ferule cut through the air.[132] Far worse, and generally reserved for the most serious offences, was the *scutica*, or whip, which was not merely a single strap, but in Martial's words, 'tufted with thongs of Scythian leather'.[133] Similarly, there were some teachers who relied on the use of a dried eel-skin;[134] and at Alexandria a grammarian called Dionysius acquired the permanent nickname of 'Leather-arm' (Scytobrachion) from his addiction to the whip. Lastly, and quite ghastly in their effect, there were the rods (*virgae*), formed of a bundle of pliant withies. For such whipping or flogging, the boy was made to strip down to his loin-cloth, and was hoisted up by two of his schoolfellows one of whom, turning his back, took the culprit's arms over his shoulders and grasped his wrists firmly, whilst the other lifted him up by the ankles. Back and buttocks were thus conveniently exposed. This was known as the *catomus*, being the Greek expression for the 'over the shoulders' position. There is a very good depiction of it in the famous school-fresco from Pompeii (Fig.11), but earlier Cicero[135] envisages a similar scene, where the look-out boy warns of the master's unexpected return, and dire consequences are foreseen if order is not quickly restored. Most notorious for his heavy-handed methods was Orbilius, of whom Horace had rueful memories, and he immortalized with the single epithet, *plagosus* ('the Whacker').[136]

Whatever justification the schoolmasters of antiquity might have claimed for the use of corporal punishment in cases of sheer idleness or serious misbehaviour, those who resorted to it simply as a means of driving their pupils to study harder, to memorize accurately, and to read impeccably, laid themselves open to serious criticism. Varro's verdict was that 'fear, undue nervousness and all mental disturbance are utterly alien to true learning, whereas pleasure is an urge to progress'.[137] Seneca, too, would have entirely repudiated the methods of the 'pedagogue' in Plautus, who talked of thrashing a boy if he made a mistake in a single syllable. 'Which kind of teacher', he asks, 'is more worthy of liberal studies — he who flays his pupils if their memory lapses, or if an insufficiently quick eye makes them falter in reading, or he who prefers to correct and teach by admonishing and encouraging a sense of pride?'[138] Quintilian, too, was firmly opposed to corporal punishment on principle: he regarded it as degrading, and suited only to slaves, and said that although children, like slaves, became hardened to it, the method, apart from other dangers, raised further problems when it failed to produce any result among older boys. He preferred to rely on reproof and the constant supervision and pressure of a good 'pedagogue'.[139] The author of the treatise attributed to Plutarch took the same view.[140] Nevertheless, Ausonius, the kindliest of men, who won the respect of the younger boys without severity, admitted that he had a hard task to control the 'young colts' around the age of puberty by these methods: and, looking back over a long teaching career, he was not particularly satisfied with the results of his mild attempts to curb the 'headstrong youth'.[141]

Moreover, there were many parents who took corporal punishment in school for granted, and some even encouraged it, for, like Metrotime, the mother of the lazy, good-for-nothing Cottalus in Herondas' mime, they objected to paying school fees to no purpose.[142] The parent of a stupid child at Oxyrhynchus, who had decided to withdraw him from school, wrote to the master: 'Chastise him; for ever since he left his father, he has had no other beatings, and he likes getting a few — his back has got accustomed to them, and needs its daily dose'![143] Even St Augustine's self-sacrificing parents merely smiled when he complained of painful punishments, and he tells us that most parents readily accepted such methods as a means of deterring boys from counter-atractions. [144]

Whatever views may be taken about corporal punishment as a necessary, or, at least, ultimate sanction, one cannot but deplore the general callousness of ancient attitudes to it. But the fact remains that, in antiquity, there was an additional reason for its use which does not exist today. From the point of view of conscientious parents, the fee-paying system was an acceptable one, and it gave them the opportunity of selecting the best school they could afford. But when parents were not conscientious, they could simply claim that their boys (who might be ill-controlled and in the hands of an inferior 'pedagogue') had not been taught properly, and refuse to pay the fees; and short of going to law, there was no third authority between teacher and parent who could intervene. Consequently, to protect their own livelihood, teachers were the more tempted to adopt severe methods, and to make sure that, willy-nilly, the boys learned what they were told. If we further examine the fee-paying system, as it existed in those days, we shall see that the teachers, excessively repressive though many of them were, deserved some sympathy.

CHAPTER XII

The hazards of a fee-paying system: municipal and State appointments

For the vast majority of teachers in our period, the main and often the sole source of remuneration was the fee (*merces*) which pupils, or more usually their parents, agreed to pay for their instruction. If, in general practice, this fee had been payable in advance, teachers would have been in a much stronger position, and parents would have had to take the risk that the standard of teaching might not come up to their expectations. So Aristotle remarked that the sophists of his day often met with subsequent recrimination because the quality of their instruction did not match their original promises, and was an inadequate return for the money paid.[1] In Roman times, however, parents were rarely prepared to take any such risk; only a much sought-after sophist or rhetorician could afford to demand an initial payment in advance,[2] and for most teachers — who were only too glad to accept all the pupils they could — the settlement of their fee was retrospective. All that was done at the outset was that the parent, when introducing his son, made an agreement (most probably merely a verbal 'stipulation')[3] with the teacher regarding the amount of the fee which he would pay, and the times — whether monthly or annually — at which it would become due. Very rarely was mutual confidence so great that a teacher, like Antonius Gnipho, could feel no need to stipulate a fee, and could rely on the generosity of his patrons.[4] But the system of retrospective payment, though it must often have worked satisfactorily, undoubtedly left loopholes for all kinds of knavery, and could place a teacher's livelihood in jeopardy. The easiest excuse for avoidance of payment when the time came was the allegation that the pupil had made insufficient progress, and that the teacher must therefore be to blame.[5] In that case, it might be very difficult to convince the parent that his boy was a dullard and unable to master the subject, or that the parent himself, or the pedagogue, had failed to see to it that the boy was kept to his studies. So whilst parents blamed, or professed to blame, the teachers, angry and disillusioned teachers, like Orbilius, blamed the parents.[6] On the other hand, even when parents had excellent intentions, they might sometimes find that their own economic difficulties were such that, perhaps a year after their original commitment was made, they were unable to honour their obligations.[7] It was then for the teacher to decide whether he would continue to teach the boy on trust, and this he often did. Dismissing a non-paying pupil from the school was a measure which the teacher was reluctant to adopt, for this simply meant playing into the hands of his rivals, who would be only too ready to take a chance and augment their class.[8] On the other hand, when pupils paid regularly, there was sometimes a temptation for a teacher to spin out his course with a view to ensuring the continuation of his fees — a procedure adopted by some rhetoric teachers in Quintilian's day, and much despised by him.[9] The possibility of avoidance of payment must at all times have been a source of anxiety to teachers, whom Ovid describes as 'a tribe generally defrauded of their income',[10] and of whom Juvenal says that many lived to regret their vain and unprofitable chair.[11]

Recourse could be had, nevertheless, to legal remedies, and claims for the recovery of fees could be made not only by grammarians, rhetoricians, and teachers of geometry, who were accounted 'professors of the liberal arts', but also by teachers of the elements, of shorthand or of calculation. In the provinces such cases were brought before the provincial governor, and were treated as judicial inquiries outside the ordinary processes (*cognitiones extra ordinem*).[12] At Rome, too, no ordinary action lay for the recovery of remuneration, and Juvenal was evidently using quite accurate terminology when he said that the grammarian's fee was 'rarely paid without the judicial inquiry of a tribune' (*rara tamen merces sine cognitione tribuni*), even though he probably overstated the position.[13] Little is known of the jurisdiction of tribunes under the Empire (apart from intercession), but they appear to have retained some minor administrative functions.[14] Juvenal likewise refers to rhetoricians as having to leave the mock-legal declamations of the school in order to engage in real litigation for the recovery of their fees.[15] Although arrangements for annual payment were quite normal from early times to the end of the Empire, some teachers could not afford to wait so long, or take so heavy a risk, and required their fees to be paid monthly. The primary teacher, particularly, as at Venusia in Horace's day, would most probably have needed his fee monthly.[16] Also, the philosopher in Lucian's *Hermotimus* threatens to sue for a fee due at the end of the previous month,[17] and all the allocations of maximum fees for various kinds of teacher made in the Edict of Diocletian (A.D. 301) are calculated on a monthly basis. Both annual and monthly remuneration must have been common at all times, and the arrangement would be a matter of negotiation at the outset. But although, in the late Empire, defaulting became a positive plague, and unscrupulous students at that time made wholesale migrations to another teacher just before their annual payment was due,[18] there can have been nothing quite so bad in our period. With a retrospective system there was always an element of risk, but there were pupils of all kinds, good, bad and indifferent. The Cynic philosopher, Bion of Borysthenes, wittily summed up the situation when he compared them with the three ages in Hesiod — the gold, the silver and the bronze; the golden pupils paid and learned, the silver paid and did not learn, and the bronze learned and did not pay![19]

Even when payment was regularly made, it was not always made in full, for the parental fee often went through other hands before it reached the teacher, and there were thus small percentage-commissions to be deducted. In wealthy families, financial disbursements were controlled by the household steward (*dispensator*), who expected to retain something for his services; but whatever the family status, the person most to be reckoned with was the 'pedagogue', and he, too, claimed his commission.[20] As we know from later evidence, the 'pedagogue' was in a strong position in this respect, for, as he constantly attended the pupil, and often supervised his studies at home, he could report either favourably or unfavourably on the teacher. A thoroughly disgruntled 'pedagogue' might even persuade the parents that the boy should be transferred elsewhere, whilst one who was well satisfied might do the teacher a good turn by speaking well of his school.[21] From time to time, however, the teacher might look forward to an extra recompense to set against these discounts, for it was a long-established tradition that at certain festivals pupils should bring presents to the teacher. Although each individual contribution might be small, and be made either in cash or in kind, the sum total of such gifts was not to be despised, and brought some pleasurable consolation in what was often a dreary economic struggle.

One of the most important occasions in the Roman school year was the nineteenth day of March, for this was a day of celebration in honour of Minerva, the patroness of learning and the arts. It was called the *Quinquatrus*, because it was the fifth day after the Ides of March, and it was probably selected as Minerva's day because it was the 'birthday' or anniversary of the founding of her temple. On this occasion, as on other festival days, the schoolroom was decked with flowers, there was a procession to the goddess' temple, and those who, like the schoolmasters, considered themselves under the special protection of Minerva, made offerings to secure her favour.[22] Although it was the first day of what became a five-day holiday, it was regarded as the most auspicious day on which to enrol pupils for the new school year, which would begin on 24 March; for the Roman year originally began in March, and long after 153 B.C., when the consuls began to take up office on the first of January, the schools maintained their old tradition, and it was in March that the fees for the previous year's teaching became due.[23] But, apart from this, it had always been customary for the pupils to bring their master a gift (*minervale munus*, or *minerval*) on Minerva's day, whether they were beginners in his school or continuing under his tuition. In country districts, and probably generally in early times, the gift was made in kind. In his work *On Farming*, Varro makes one of his characters, Axius, ask another, Merula, for instruction in the rearing and feeding of fowl, hares and fish (*villatica pastio*), and, using the language of the schools, he says: 'Take me on, please, as your pupil'. To this, Merula replies: 'Certainly, as soon as you promise me a *minerval*, I will begin', and it appears from the rest of the conversation that the *minerval* will take the form of a goose or a peacock.[24] Similarly, a glossographer's explanation of the term *nefrenditium* shows that such gifts in country districts took the form of younglings from the farm. The word *nefrendes* meant 'non-chewing', and was particularly applied to the young of animals;[25] so, we are told,[26] 'the *nefrenditium* is an annual tribute, which, at a fixed time, country folk are wont to bring to their masters, *or pupils to their teachers*, provided that it consists of meat, such as a piglet'. A letter partially preserved in a Greek papyrus of the second century A.D. gives instructions for pigeons and other small fowl to be sent to a teacher, and further delicacies to be sent 'to the teacher of my daughter, so that he may be diligent with her'.[27] In city-life, too, payments were sometimes made in kind (as with advocates' fees), but the gratuities paid to teachers at the *Quinquatrus* and other festivals could also be given in cash, for Tertullian speaks of these as occasions when teachers of all grades 'tot up their receipts'. When a new pupil was enrolled on 19th March, the teacher was expected to make a small token contribution (*stips*) to Minerva's temple, to ensure the goddess' favour towards the boy's studies.[28] The other most notable days for the teacher were the *Saturnalia* on 17 December, and New Year's Day, when he received the *strenae calendariae*, or New Year's gifts, but by Tertullian's time, and possibly already in our period, there were also several others. Such gifts must have been very welcome accessions to an income which was often meagre.

Very sparse information survives from our period of the actual amounts paid in fees to teachers of the various grades. Of one thing we may be quite certain, and that is that the primary teacher (*ludi magister*) fared far worse than the grammarian and the rhetorician. This was a permanent feature of Roman life, and is nowhere more clearly demonstrated than in the Edict of Diocletian, where the ratio of the maximum fees payable to the three grades of teacher is 5 : 4 : 1.[29] A well-known passage of Horace[30] tells us that at Venusia the boys took their payment to the primary teacher on the Ides of each month, but the textual variants do not permit us to decide with certainty what the actual amount was. According to one reading (*octonis referentes Idibus aera*), the payment was made in each of eight months — that is, in all but the long summer vacation — but *aera* simply means 'cash', and does not specify the sum. According to the other reading, more widely accepted (*octonos referentes Idibus aeris*), the payment was eight *asses*, or half a *denarius* for each pupil per month. If we assume that, in any case, there were hardly more than eight months of actual teaching, this would give only four *denarii* a year for each pupil (reckoning sixteen *asses* to the *denarius*); in which case, a teacher would have had to have a very large school, and regular payments, to make as much as an ordinary workman, paid at the rate of a *denarius* a day. Even though the tariff quoted, being that of a country town, may have been less than at Rome, it remains very doubtful whether a primary teacher could have made a living wage without finding other means of supplementing his income. This must have been often done, and an interesting example survives in the inscription on the funeral monument in the Naples Museum of Furius Philocalus, a *ludi magister* of Capua, probably of the Augustan period, where we are told that he also 'faithfully wrote out wills'.[31] Also, it is very probable that such teachers made use of the long summer holiday to earn the necessary extra money by giving lessons as visiting tutors, like those employed by Echion in Petronius. Their general economic position can only be described as deplorable. Yet this sad state of affairs was by no means confined to antiquity. There is a remarkably close parallel in Sir Walter Scott's description of Dominie Sampson in *Guy Mannering* (ch.2):

> He sought to assist his parents by teaching a school, and soon had plenty of scholars, but very few fees. In fact, he taught the sons of farmers for what they chose to give him, and the poor for nothing; and, to the shame of the former be it spoken, the pedagogue's gains never equalled those of a skilful ploughman. He wrote, however, a good hand, and added something to his pittance by copying accounts and writing letters for Ellangowan.

The assessment of the grammarian's fee depends on the interpretation of a rather puzzling, and much-discussed, line at the end of Juvenal's seventh satire.[32] After drawing the most dismal picture of the grammarian's life, and the intolerable demands made upon him, the satirist imagines someone telling the teacher to be satisfied, after all this, with a miserable sum: 'then, when the year rolls round, take the amount of gold which the people demand for a successful contestant'. The gold referred to is clearly the coin known as the *aureus*, worth twenty-five *denarii*, or 100 sesterces; an indication of a more modern valuation would be the fact that in the late nineteenth century, when gold sovereigns were still in general circulation, an *aureus* was estimated to have been worth rather more than a sovereign.[33] But the question is — what kind of contestant, and what amount, is meant? The scholiast took the reference to be to a successful actor in the theatre, and pointed out that a reward of not more than five golden coins (*aurei*) was normally paid to him.[34] The amount is right, but the setting imagined is not the theatre. Nor are the editors justified who take the reference to be to a payment made to a successful charioteer, for charioteers won huge prizes, far more than a *grammaticus* could dream of collecting.[35] Undoubtedly, Juvenal has in mind a gladiatorial contest, and it may be observed that elsewhere in the same satire, he uses the same source of metaphor when he advises the ill-paid rhetorician to 'give himself a discharge' (*ergo sibi dabit ipse rudem*).[36] A close parallel is the remark of Suetonius about the habit of the emperor Claudius (who took a morbid interest in gladiatorial shows) of 'counting out aloud on the fingers of his left hand, like the common people, the gold pieces paid to the victors'.[37] Fronto, too, uses the expression 'at the demand of the people' (*populo postulante*) of rewards demanded for winning gladiators.[38] The passage of Suetonius, it has been observed,[39] indicates a reward of not more than five *aurei*, and there is some confirmation of this in a Spanish inscription of *c.* A.D. 177, which gives full details of gladiatorial arrangements.[40] There we find a clause which enables the winning gladiator to claim, as of right, one-fifth (if a slave), or a quarter (if a free volunteer) of the sum which the giver of the games (*editor*) paid to the trainer (*lanista*) when purchasing him. For the lowest grade of gladiators (*gregarii*), the minimum price was 1000 and the maximum 2000 sesterces. The winner, therefore, might secure anything from 200 to 500 sesterces, i.e. from two to five *aurei*. It may well be, therefore, that before this became a legal stipulation, this kind of prize-money had been demanded by popular acclaim. At least, these parallels put us on the right lines regarding the amount which Juvenal had in mind; but the next stage of the deduction requires care.

It is rather too readily assumed that the passage therefore means that the grammarian received as much as five *aurei*, that is 125 *denarii* or 500 *sesterces* as a year's pay *for each pupil*.[41] Now if this were true, it would be surprising that Juvenal should think it — as he obviously does — a despicable amount, for two reasons. First, we know that the Greek sophist, Proclus of Naucratis, who was in a far better position than most grammarians, was wont to accept pupils for a single advance payment of 100 *drachmae*, which would amount to seventy-five *denarii*, or three *aurei*, apiece, and for this they could attend as long as they liked.[42] Secondly, the fourth-century grammarian, Palladas of Alexandria, who bitterly complained of his poverty, thought himself lucky if he obtained a single gold coin from a pupil for a year's tuition.[43] By this, he meant a *solidus*, a gold coin which replaced the *aureus* after Constantine, and a scholium on line 241 of Juvenal says that the grammarian received only one *solidus* (i.e. per pupil) per annum.[44] How, then, are we to reconcile these varying amounts?

The fact may well be that when Juvenal implies that the teacher found himself with only a few gold pieces at the end of the year — no more than a successful gladiator's reward for a single contest — he was thinking of his total receipts (by the most pessimistic calculation) before any steps were taken to claim arrears. The context shows that this is the meagre recompense with which he is presented after fulfilling his duties and supervising the class *as a whole*, and he is indignant that people should expect him to be satisfied with this. Juvenal is not therefore alluding specifically to the amount of the individual fee;[45] nevertheless, if, as he says, only a small minority paid up on time, it would be easily understandable that only from two to five pupils out of the whole class paid an *aureus* apiece when it was due. It is quite conceivable, therefore, that one *aureus* was the grammarian's annual fee, at its lowest level, in Juvenal's day; but, as we shall later see, there were those who must have been able to charge much more than this.

Although the general conditions of payment left so much to be desired, the financial success or failure of the *grammaticus* also depended to some extent on his personality, his ability and his initiative. Antonius Gnipho succeeded not only because he was an extremely good scholar, but because people liked his friendly and agreeable manner;[46] but he was also fortunate in dealing with parents who were appreciative and honest enough to make good recompense for his services. Orbilius, on the other hand, however justified his grievances, was a dour and quarrelsome fellow,[47] and in the end failed dismally. Different again was Pompilius Andronicus, a Syrian and a confirmed Epicurean, who was considered too indolent to run a school efficiently, and soon lost ground to his competitors, who included not only Gnipho but also men of inferior scholarship.[48] He retired prematurely to Cumae, to a life of utter indigence, only temporarily relieved by the sale of a scholarly little work on Ennius. For, it may be noted, there was at all times a certain market for learned publications, and also for school text-books, from which some grammarians may have derived a supplementary income. But in teaching, as in all else, even conspicuous success did not afford any permanent security, unless the gifts bestowed by capricious Fortune were husbanded with care. The career of Valerius Cato was an example and a warning.[49] For a time, perhaps many years, he was in great demand as a teacher, since he had not only a gift for poetic composition, but the ability to impart his skill. He had many pupils of good family, and ranked high among poets of the 'new', or Alexandrian, school; he may well have been on familiar terms with Catullus and his friends, and was hailed by the younger set as 'the Latin Siren, who alone reads and makes poets'. He acquired a handsome villa at Tusculum, and lived the life of a gentleman; but he must have extended his enjoyments, or his hospitality, beyond his means, for suddenly, to the surprise of some of his younger friends, like the heartless jester Furius Bibaculus, he had to surrender his villa to a creditor, and was reduced to living in his old age in a miserable hovel, unable to afford anything but the most humble fare. In times when the individual was left to fend for himself, and the State took no heed for the welfare of the old and the retired, teachers, who quite often lived to an advanced age, had good reason to dread the approach of their declining years. Some, like Oppius Chares, went on teaching until they could barely walk or see,[50] and the once-notorious Orbilius, now old and penurious, occupied the sort of garret which Juvenal so well describes, 'under the tiles'.[51] There, the man who had taught Horace lived on to be nearly a hundred, his memory almost gone. Sometimes it is hard to divine why a grammarian should have failed, and it is surprising that Hyginus, who had not only had many pupils, but was officially appointed by Augustus as head of the Palatine Library, should have had to rely for his support on a consular friend of Ovid in his later years.[52]

Nevertheless, gloomy though these reports of the remuneration of the *grammaticus* are, there was also a brighter side to the picture, for there were some who made a very good living out of teaching. Whilst Pompeius Lenaeus' school was merely sufficient to maintain him (*schola se sustentavit*),[53] Curtius Nicias managed to live in considerable comfort, and Cicero commented on the fastidiousness of his tastes.[54] Verrius Flaccus, too, was already a very successful teacher when Augustus invited him to take his grandchildren as pupils, and to bring over his entire school to the Palatine at an annual salary of 100,000 *sesterces*, which would amount to 100 *aurei*.[55] But quite the most extraordinary success, under Tiberius, Claudius and Nero, was that of Remmius Palaemon, whose enterprise and wealth were phenomenal. He was undoubtedly a man of great business acumen, and he may well have amassed capital before he built up his exceptionally large school, which alone, according to Suetonius, brought him an income of 400,000 *sesterces* a year.[56] At the same time, he did not rely merely on teaching, but also drew large profits from his business interests. He had been trained originally as a weaver, and put his knowledge and his capital to good use by running a clothing factory! Juvenal may well be alluding to this (though scholars do not observe the point) when, overlooking the undoubted wealth of Palaemon, he commiserates with him on having to bargain and accept deductions from his fee, 'like a hawker peddling winter matting and white blankets', and having to work longer hours than 'the workman who teaches how to card wool with slanting iron comb'.[57] Nor was this the only sphere of interest of Palaemon's fertile financial brain. He also bought, for 600,000 *sesterces*, a vineyard in the area of Nomentum, some ten miles out of Rome, and engaged an exceptionally successful vine-cultivator named Sthenelus to re-dig and re-plant it, with the result that it became quite staggeringly productive; within eight years Palaemon could sell the entire vintage, as it hung there for inspection, for 400,000 *sesterces*. This extraordinary success (which, says the elder Pliny, was attributed by the local people to Palaemon's great learning!) had the effect of inducing Seneca, most parsimonious of plutocrats, who envied and detested Palaemon, to buy the vineyard from him at four times the price he paid for it![58] Considering that Palaemon was chiefly remembered (apart from his boastfulness and extreme vulgarity) as the author of a standard Latin grammar, his record is quite the most astonishing in the history of classical scholarship. At much the same time, too, the Greek grammarian, Epaphroditus of Chaeroneia, was active in Rome; he, also, amassed wealth, which enabled him to spend lavishly on books, for when he died in the time of Nero, he owned two houses in the city and left a fine library.[59] He appears to be the only ancient grammarian whose portrait still survives (Fig. 8).[60] Evidently, then, Juvenal's mournful diatribe on the miseries of the *grammaticus* should be somewhat counterbalanced by these occasional glimpses of high success.

The incomes of teachers of rhetoric, like those of the grammarians, might also show great disparities, but the demand for the subject was so great, and the opportunities which it created for advancement in public life so varied, that the rhetorician ran less risk than the grammarian of being reduced to the poverty line, and, though he might have bad times, stood a better chance of achieving prosperity. People expected to pay him more than the grammarian for his services,[61] and if, like the Asiatic Heraclides of Temnos, whom Cicero derided, he could attract wealthy pupils, he could charge high fees.[62] Also, as Philostratus noted from experience, arrogant young men, who had great ambitions, were usually the most reliable in the matter of payment.[63] Sometimes, however, it was good policy to begin by taking a low fee, in order to obtain more pupils and build up the school, and even in Isocrates' day this was a common practice among rhetoricians.[64] When the elder Seneca mentions that some people complained because Clodius Sabinus, who taught declamation in both Greek and Latin, accepted 'puny fees' (*pusillas mercedes*), the explanation probably is that the objectors were rival teachers, who resented what we call 'undercutting'.[65] But even the acquisition of a large clientele did not necessarily spell prosperity, though Juvenal is probably painting the picture at its blackest when he says that the rhetorician had to go to law to obtain the price of a corn-ticket;[66] for the *tessera frumentaria*, which was distributed monthly and entitled

the holder to five *modii* of grain,[67] would in his day have been worth
only about twenty *sesterces*.[68] Libanius, however, was probably stating
what was generally true at all times when he remarked that work-people
were often mistaken in assuming that teachers of rhetoric must be
wealthy because they had so many pupils,[69] since many of them did not
bring in regular fees — either the parents found that they could not
afford to pay (and he says he often taught their sons for nothing) or else
the young men squandered their allowances, when away from home.[70]
His view was that fees could not be relied upon as a major source of
income, and that those teachers were in the best position who had
inherited wealth or property to begin with; influence also played a part in
securing pupils.[71] But the most promising feature of rhetoric-teaching,
and especially public declamation, from a material standpoint, was that
it could be a very useful stepping-stone to something higher. Suetonius
says that there was so much enthusiasm for declamation that teachers of
it abounded and some rose from the lowliest estate to senatorial rank and
the highest positions.[72] One example was that of Junius Otho, who
began his career as a primary teacher, transferred to rhetoric, and
became a senator through the influence of Sejanus.[73] Juvenal's neat
comment is well known: 'if Fortune wills, you, a consul, will become a
rhetorician; again, if she so wills, you, a rhetorician, will become a
consul'.[74] In fact, under Trajan, Valerius Licinianus, a senator and
former praetor, when banished for an intrigue with a Vestal Virgin, took
up rhetoric-teaching in Sicily, and began his first declamation with the
expostulation: 'What games you play, Fortune! You make professors out
of senators, and senators out of professors!'[75] Quintilian, on the other
hand, received consular honours under Domitian, and possessed wide
estates. In Juvenal's view, he was one of the lucky ones; Juvenal does not
mention that he was also State-appointed and salaried, but it is of interest
to note that he does not attribute Quintilian's wealth to his fees. He
merely observes that parents are mean when it comes to paying for a
son's education, and even a plutocrat who lavishes money on his new
villa begrudges Quintilian his 2000 *sesterces* (that is, 20 *aurei*).[76] This
was, in fact, far more than most less distinguished rhetoricians could
have hoped to charge, and probably represents payments for the whole
course rather than, as is usually supposed, a single year. But the best
evidence for the value of rhetoric as an avenue to wealth, position, and
fame is to be found in the careers of the famous Greek Sophists. These
men, who became extremely prominent from the late first century
onwards, were mainly rhetoricians with a flair for declamation; they
were surrounded by admiring pupils, and used much the same kind of
subjects as are found in the elder Seneca and Quintilian. But they were
also public figures, and accorded the highest dignities in their native
cities, most notably in Asia Minor. They often represented their

communities on embassies, and included Rome in their wide travels,[77] as did Isaeus in the time of Juvenal and Pliny.[78] They could either charge a high fee, or afford to be generous, as they pleased;[79] often they had inherited money or land from their families, and many became public benefactors. But these eminent Sophists were a race apart, and, although they raised still further the esteem in which declamation was held, their incomes far exceeded those of the average rhetorician at Rome.

On the whole, then, the fee-paying system, with all its uncertainties and the fierce competition which it engendered, was a far from satisfactory one, especially if the teacher had no other source of income. This remained true long after our period, for there were always teachers who either preferred to operate independently, or were not in a position to secure a public appointment. But the system of public appointments, which gave the teacher a fixed salary, and did not necessarily, or usually, preclude his claim to fees, was already developing strongly in cities and towns throughout the Roman Empire. This municipal system of education which, though it never entirely ousted independent teaching, became increasingly predominant, was no new thing, but had, in some ways, a sort of prototype in Hellenistic Greece. From the third century B.C. onwards, we find examples of the payment of regular salaries to public teachers from the donation of some benefactor, whether a munificent foreign potentate or a wealthy, public-spirited citizen. When the donation was a substantial one, such as that of King Eumenes of Pergamum to the people of Rhodes in 160 B.C., or those of Eudemus at Miletus and Polythrus at Teos nearly half a century earlier, a fund could be established, and the teachers were paid from the interest accruing on the capital sum. The important and enlightening inscriptions concerning the gifts of Eudemus and Polythrus contain full instructions regarding the administration of the fund, the notification of vacancies, and the interview and selection of applicants. The regulations also fixed the amounts of the annual, or monthly, payments which teachers were to receive.[80] Naturally they included specialists in various forms of physical training, and in music, but they provided also for teachers of reading and writing. This last form of instruction represented only an elementary level, but we sometimes find in other inscriptions that more advanced teaching was made available, by private generosity, for the older boys in the Greek gymnasia, and also for anyone else who happened to be interested. The curriculum of the Greek colleges, though concentrating mainly upon physical accomplishments, included, in the later Hellenistic period, a certain amount of more advanced study, under the direction not merely of visiting lecturers, but also sometimes of a more regular staff.[81] At Eretria, Priene, and elsewhere, the inscriptions commemorate the bounty of the local 'gymnasiarch', who voluntarily

defrayed the cost of providing teachers, e.g. a specialist in the study of
Homer, a grammarian or a rhetorician.[82] Very numerous gifts indeed
were made in the Greek cities for a wide variety of purposes, including
the repair of the gymnasia, or the provision of schoolrooms, or baths, or
other necessities such as oil for the athletes. These gifts did not always
stem, however, from a single benefactor, for the principle of combined
effort, in the form of subscriptions from a number of contributors, was
also well known.[83] Pliny's combination at Como of personal
munificence with a limited public subscription for the provision of
teachers, was entirely in accord with the Greek spirit, and may well have
been tried elsewhere before his day.

It is interesting to note Pliny's remark that there were 'many places in
which teachers are publicly engaged',[84] for municipal pride and rivalry
with other cities had long since encouraged the formation of teaching-
staffs, who were publicly appointed and paid, either from special
endowments or from the general city funds. As early as the time of
Augustus, Marseilles, a city which had inherited the best traditions of
Greek culture, and even became a serious rival to Athens as a centre of
higher education for the Roman youth, employed rhetoricians and
philosophers, who were either paid from public funds or supported by
private subsidy.[85] It is of interest to note that physicians, too, were
publicly salaried at Marseilles, for again and again in legislative contexts
we find them ranged with the 'professors of the liberal arts', both being
recognized as performing a similar public service and entitled to similar
privileges.[86] There was frequent movement of rhetoricians between
Rome and Marseilles, as the reminiscences of the elder Seneca indicate;
Volcacius Moschus, pupil of Apollodorus of Pergamum, taught rhetoric
there when banished from Rome in 20 B.C., and the declaimers Pacatus
and Agroitas were also connected with the city.[87] Later, the young
Agricola found its teachers of philosophy inspiring.[88] Although not all
teachers were necessarily publicly appointed, interest in higher education, especially rhetoric, became widespread in Gaul, and 'Gallic
eloquence' was proverbial for centuries.[89] The school at Autun was
already in existence before A.D. 23,[90] and many other cities produced
distinguished orators. Three of the most eminent teachers of rhetoric,
listed by Suetonius as earlier than Quintilian, hailed from Gaul, though
little is known beyond their names. L. Statius Ursulus of Toulouse, and
Sextus Iulius Gabinianus taught there with great renown, and P. Clodius
Quirinalis of Arles 'with conspicuous distinction' at Rome.[91] Three
Gallic orators of whom Quintilian makes special mention were Iulius
Africanus, Domitius Afer (a native of Nîmes) and Iulius Florus.[92] At
Lyons, Caligula instituted a contest in oratory which brought honour to
the victors and unusual ignominy to the vanquished.[93] Again, at least
two, and probably three, of the interlocutors in the *Dialogue on Oratory*

were of Gallic origin — certainly Marcus Aper and Iulius Secundus, and probably also Maternus.[94] From Gaul, the interest spread to Britain, where Agricola encouraged the higher education of the sons of British chieftains, with the result that 'those who of late abjured the Latin language now conceived a longing for eloquence'.[95] Juvenal's remark that 'even distant Thyle is talking about hiring a rhetorician', though couched in a characteristic hyperbole, shows how widespread public appointments had become in his day.[96] Long before, a similar system must have existed in Spain, where higher education had flourished from the late Republic onwards. Spain was a fertile field of orators, poets and scholars, and contributed to Rome not only the elder Seneca and many of the declaimers whom he knew,[97] but the philosopher Seneca, Lucan (whose maternal grandfather, Acilius Lucanus, was a noted orator),[98] Mela, Columella, Martial and Quintilian. Inscriptions testify to its teachers of grammar and rhetoric,[99] and one informs us that even the small township of Tritium Magallum employed a 'Latin grammarian' who was accorded a public salary.[100] Teachers of high merit were also, in various cities of the Empire, often honoured with statues, or elected as decurions, by their appreciative fellow-citizens.[101] In general, during our period, and beyond it in the time of the Antonines, the municipalities enjoyed a considerable measure of prosperity, and the magistracies were coveted positions (*honores*), usually held by the wealthiest citizens, who were prepared to contribute a great deal in the interests of either public welfare or ostentation, and were also often lavish with city funds. The decline of the later Empire had not yet set in when adverse economic conditions, increasing control and taxation by the central government, and the compulsory maintenance of an extensive imperial bureaucracy vastly reduced their financial resources.[102] Then, as we know from Libanius,[103] teachers' salaries sometimes suffered in consequence; but that is a later story.

Public appointments in teaching were made by the local council, which had the permission of the central government to pay salaries for this purpose. The candidates elected were described as 'approved by decree of the decurions',[104] though the actual task of selection appears to have been delegated to a smaller body, a board of electors formed to make recommendations, and consisting of a number of the most distinguished citizens.[105] In assessing the qualifications of candidates, the local authorities were repeatedly instructed by the central government to satisfy themselves both as to the moral character of the applicants and their ability in their subject.[106] Fluency of expression, which was expected of the rhetorician, could easily be tested by a display speech,[107] and open competitions of rival candidates could arouse much public interest and acclamation. The art of the *grammaticus* was less flamboyant, and there appears to be no direct evidence of the way in which a decision was reached. Skill in literary interpretation was the main requirement, and we may surmise that the knowledge of candidates was tested on the kind of linguistic and literary questions which abound in the pages of Aulus Gellius. It was always open to the council to fill the post by invitation, and personal recommendation must often have played a considerable part in decisions to appoint. Pliny makes the significant remark that he rejected the method of establishing a fund himself without involving the parents, lest at some subsequent date elections might be vitiated by canvassing (*ambitus*), which, he says, frequently occurred in public appointments.[108] Whilst this is an indication that often all was not fair and above board, it also shows that teachers themselves regarded the honour of nomination and the acquisition of a regular salary as a very desirable advancement from independent teaching. At least, the official teacher, as he might still claim his fees, had two strings to his bow; and, so long as he did not prove lazy, or incompetent, or begrudge instruction, he was securely installed.[109]

In addition to this, before the end of our period, those engaged in higher education by official appointment also benefited from a whole series of concessions which gave them exemption from taxes and from civic duties of various kinds in their cities. Such duties might be both time-consuming and expensive, and even wealthy sophists, who did so much for their communities, sometimes had to claim their immunity as teachers. The early stages of the development of these exemptions can no longer be traced, but they originated in the following way. In 23 B.C., Augustus, who had been gravely ill, was restored to health by his physician, Antonius Musa, a freedman, and in gratitude granted not only Musa himself, but all medical practitioners at the time and in the future, immunity from civic obligations.[110] But physicians were often teachers of their subject,[111] and even before that time were classed together with those engaged in higher education. Julius Caesar had granted the Roman citizenship to all who practised medicine at Rome, and also to all teachers of the liberal arts, so that those who were there might more readily stay and that others from further afield might be induced to join them.[112] Again, in A.D. 6, when famine caused Augustus to expel foreigners from Rome, he made a special exception of physicians and teachers.[113] It was only natural, therefore, that teachers should now have begun to hope, if not to press their claim, for civic immunities. Whether any concessions in this direction were in fact made under the Julio-Claudian dynasty, we do not know,[114] but certainly from the Flavians onwards, partial (and some think complete) exemption was officially granted. At the very least, a Pergamene inscription of A.D. 74, emanating from Vespasian himself, makes it clear that physicians, grammarians and rhetoricians were not to be called upon to provide accommodation when billets were required (as for visiting magistrates, or for troops), and were also to enjoy freedom from taxes.[115] The fullest list of specific exemptions was found by ancient lawyers in a letter of Antoninus Pius, who stated that the privileges named were those which Hadrian had confirmed as already existing — in other words, the list goes back at least to Trajan.[116] Some of the exemptions which it includes are particularly appropriate to Greek cities, such as exemption from acting as gymnasium-director (*gymnasiarch*), or inspector of weights and measures (*agoranomos*); others are of a more general application, such as exemption from priestly duties, from billeting, from supervisory duties in the distribution of grain and oil, from jury-service, ambassadorial duties, and military service.[117] Not only physicians, grammarians and rhetoricians, but also philosophers are here named as privileged, and the case of the philosopher Archippus, referred by Pliny to Trajan, shows that he claimed official exemption, as a philosopher, from jury-service.[118] Whether Vespasian and Domitian, who both found reason to expel philosophers from Rome, had yet included them in their list is disputed, and they did not fare so consistently well under some later emperors as did the other groups;[119] but the general position is that, well before the end of our period, those engaged in higher education on an official basis were relieved very considerably from public duties, though it is only fair to add that those who, like the sophists, had wealth, often showed a very patriotic spirit. The danger was, however, that too extensive a use might be made of these opportunities for exemption from public service, with the result that the burden fell more heavily on the rest of the community and the cities suffered some loss; it was for this reason that Antoninus Pius strictly limited the numbers of each of the privileged groups according to the size and importance of the cities, which he classified.[120] He also precluded exemption for those teaching in cities other than their own, unless they were men of exceptional distinction.[121] Finally, at the lower end of the scale, the primary teacher rarely benefited from any such concessions, though he was usually too poor to make much contribution in any case. In later enactments, he is specifically denied any claim to exemption, though the proviso is added that such teachers should not be burdened beyond their slender means.[122] The general principle underlying the granting of exemptions was that their recipients should already be performing a service valuable to their city; medicine and *litterae humaniores* were accepted as a valid qualification, whereas, illogical though it may seem, primary teaching was not. Only rarely is a special concession to *ludi magistri* recorded, as in an inscription of the time of Hadrian containing regulations for a small community engaged in copper-mining at a place called Vipasca in southern Portugal, which states that they are to be exempt from any taxes and duties imposed by the controller of the mines.[123]

It was likewise characteristic of the Roman official attitude to education that when, very late in the day, State professorships, with a salary paid direct from the treasury, were first instituted, and imperial gifts and honours were lavished upon outstanding individuals, the people who benefited were a very select few of the rhetoricians, and (eventually) philosophers, who were considered the cream of the profession. From the time of Augustus onwards, the Roman emperors, who, whatever their character, were often men of considerable culture themselves, had done a certain amount which helped the cause of education indirectly, especially in the provision of public libraries[124] and the institution of literary competitions from time to time at great public games.[125] They also occasionally created lucrative posts for distinguished men as tutors to the imperial family. Augustus granted Verrius Flaccus payment of 100,000 *sesterces* per annum to take over the instruction of his grand-children, and Seneca, Nero's tutor, prospered exceedingly until his former pupil turned against him and brought about his downfall.[126] But there were no permanent State-paid teaching posts at Rome until Vespasian established imperial chairs in Greek and Latin rhetoric.[127] The salary, again, was 100,000 *sesterces* per annum, and it is some indication of status that this was the amount paid, in the following century, to imperial procurators of various kinds, who were designated *centenarii.*[128] There were only two such posts in rhetoric, and we do not know who was appointed to the Greek chair; but it is not likely to have fallen into abeyance even after Vespasian, for when, under Marcus Aurelius, the sophist Adrian of Tyre was promoted to it from his chair of rhetoric at Athens, it was still recognized as the appointment *par excellence* in the subject and was generally called 'the higher chair'.[129] The honour of the Latin appointment was conferred by Vespasian on Quintilian, who had come to Rome from Spain with Galba,[130] and who held the post for twenty years.[131] Quintilian was one of the few intellectuals who continued to prosper, at least materially, under Domitian, to whose two great-nephews he later became tutor;[132] but domestically he suffered cruel blows in the loss of both his wife and two young and very promising sons.[133] It was in his retirement, about A.D. 96, after a career which had embraced both advocacy and teaching, that he completed, by sustained and painful effort, the masterly treatise in twelve books on *The Training of the Orator*, which remained influential for centuries, and which tells us more than any other single work about the Roman educational curriculum.

Otherwise, the increasing tyranny and repression of Domitian's reign proved particularly perilous to philosophers and rhetoricians, who were most easily suspected of using their public utterances to foment opposition to the ruler. Philosophers suffered severely. Arulenus Rusticus and Herennius Senecio paid with their lives for their openly expressed admiration of Paetus Thrasea and Helvidius Priscus,[134] philosophers who had been put to death for their outspoken criticism of the imperial régime under Nero and Vespasian respectively. Many others either perished or were driven into exile.[135] Rhetoricians, too, whose traditional stock-in-trade regularly included declamations on the subject of tyranny, might find the sentiments which they expressed in a rhetorical exercise reported by informers and used to bring about their downfall. Just as Secundus Carrinas had lost his life on this account under Tiberius,[136] so did Maternus under Domitian.[137] But after the assassination of Domitian, the brief reign of Nerva and the accession of Trajan brought new hopes of a brighter future to those engaged in higher education. In his fulsome panegyric of Trajan, composed in A.D. 100, Pliny lauds the new emperor as one who has honoured rhetoricians and philosophers, and revived the spirit of those who fostered interest in higher studies.[138] The praise was probably well deserved, for, although Trajan was a military leader rather than an intellectual, he was a close friend of Dio Chrysostom, and thought so well of the sophist Polemo that he allowed him free travel to all parts.[139] But it was the accession of Hadrian in 117 which brought to the throne a true intellectual, who, although he spent years at a time in travelling around the Empire and taking a personal interest in public welfare, was never more happy than when he was in the company of grammarians, rhetoricians and philosophers. As a scholar and poet himself, he enjoyed teasing them with his questions, but he also bestowed honours and gifts upon them,[140] and his foundation of the Athenaeum gave the most distinguished of them a fine centre for publicity. Philostratus mentions some of his benefactions,[141] but none was more indicative of his genuine philanthropy than his granting of pensions to those who, through age or infirmity, were forced to continue teaching when no longer able to give of their best.[142] It was probably to enlist the sympathy of Hadrian, at his accession, that Juvenal wrote his seventh satire, welcoming his interest, as Pliny had welcomed Trajan, and announcing that 'the hopes and prospects of learning depend upon the Emperor alone'.[143]

PART THREE

The Standard Teaching Programme

CHAPTER XIII

Primary education:
reading, writing and reckoning

The circumstances under which Roman children learned to read and write, and the extent of the linguistic knowledge which they acquired at an early age, varied considerably according to their family background. Many received their lessons at home, when the father, mother or other relative had the leisure and ability to teach them, or when, as often happened, their 'pedagogue' was competent to do so. Others, whose home circumstances were less favourable, were sent to school. The chief difference, so far as we can judge, seems to have been that those who went to the primary schools concentrated mainly on reading and writing in Latin, as these schools had to cater for the ordinary working population, whereas those who were taught at home were often able also to acquire greater proficiency in Greek. Instruction was based on a logical and orderly progression from letters to syllables, from syllables to words, and from words to sentences and short continuous passages. It was the same in both languages, as may be seen from a comparison of the brief descriptions given in Greek by Dionysius of Halicarnassus and in Latin by Manilius at much the same period.[1] Quintilian's account of primary education, which was later used and adapted by St Jerome,[2] is also applicable to both languages. The system was Greek in origin, and, as the Greek teachers kept to the same general pattern wherever they went, the Romans followed suit. The richest source of illustrative material is in Greek, mostly in the form of alphabets, syllabaries and other exercises, written by schoolchildren themselves on waxed or wooden tablets, on papyrus, or, in the poorest circles, on potsherds, which have been recovered from Graeco-Roman Egypt.[3] But quite the most interesting document for our purpose is a Cairo papyrus of the third century B.C., published by O. Guéraud and P. Jouget in 1938. It is a manual designed for the use of primary teachers (published under the rather misleading title of *Un Livre d'Ecolier*), which, though not completely preserved, gives an admirable picture of the graduated process of learning.[4]

Any wanderer in the streets of Rome, who happened to be in the vicinity of a primary school, would soon be made aware of the fact by the discordant concord of young voices, raised in a kind of sing-song as they repeated together, with varying degrees of gusto, the words which their teacher uttered. Just as, until the time of Cicero's youth, boys learned and recited the Twelve Tables as 'an obligatory chant', so St Augustine, recalling his early arithmetic lessons, remembered the 'hateful sing-song' of 'one and one makes two, two and two makes four'.[5] The same method was used in teaching the names of the letters in alphabetical order, and this was probably why, in classical Greece, the alphabet was set in a metrical form.[6] In the last days of the Empire, St Jerome still recommended that a young girl should be taught her letters in a kind of *canticum*.[7] But this memorizing by ear naturally had to be combined with visual images of the letters themselves; teachers therefore wrote each letter on the children's tablets, named it and then explained its sound.[8] They might then test their pupils' understanding by asking them to identify the letters in a written word, such as 'Socrates'.[9] There was, however, some discrepancy in practice according as teachers believed that the appeal to the ear, or the appeal to the eye, should come first. Many contemporaries of Quintilian made their pupils learn the alphabet parrot-fashion first, but he himself protested that this was unsatisfactory, and urged, with justice, that the teaching of the shapes should receive priority.[10] He would perhaps have agreed with the remark of Horace that 'what enters through the ears stirs the mind less vividly than what is presented to the trusty eyes',[11] and he approved of the practice of giving children sets of letters cut out in ivory; these were also available more cheaply in box-wood.[12] We see from St Jerome that the child (1) learned to recognize each letter and name it, (2) learned to chant the names in the correct order and place the letters in series, (3) learned to single out any required letter when they were all jumbled up together. The value of teaching children to learn by play was fully accepted in both Greece and Rome. So, too, was the desirability of encouraging young children by giving them tasty rewards for success; Horace speaks of 'coaxing teachers', who give their pupils little pastries (which might be made in the shapes of the letters) to get them to learn their alphabet.[13] The value of group-teaching, which encouraged competition, and stimulated the desire to excel, was also recognized.[14]

Whether or not children had previously had movable letters to play with, they had to be taught to form them in writing, and here the usual method was for the teacher to make a faint outline of each letter in turn on their tablets.[15] Quintilian calls these 'pre-formed letters',[16] but the Greeks termed them 'hypograms', or 'under-writings', because the child had to work over them and bring them out more boldly. Naturally, he often found difficulty at first in manipulating the stilus and following the outline accurately, so the teacher would place his hand over the

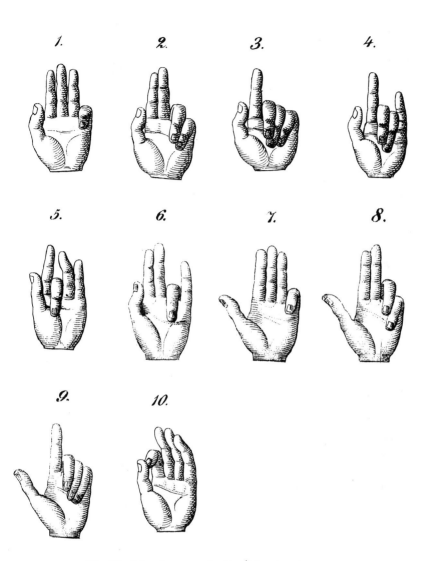

Fig.17 *Numbers symbolized by the fingers.*

child's hand and guide him.[17] The next stage was for the child to emphasize the tracing unaided, and then, as he gained confidence, he would make separate letters of his own to match the models provided. Quintilian also mentions a further, and probably supplementary, method, which was in use in his day.[18] This seems to have been a sort of half-way house between personally-guided writing and freehand. The shapes of the letters were deeply incised on a wooden board, but *not* on a waxed tablet, as is sometimes stated (the word *tabula* has both meanings), and the idea was that, in following these deep grooves, the child's stilus could not go astray. He was not actually, it would seem, making his own letters, but the movements of the hand, made repeatedly and with increasing speed and facility, gave him the 'feel' of each letter, and a sense of the varying directions and pressures involved. Transferring to his waxed tablet, he could then try forming letters for himself. Even when he could do so without assistance, he still had to put in plenty of practice, and he would make a whole row of each letter in turn — examples of this (in ink on papyrus) from the first century A.D. have survived.[19] He would also write out the alphabet continuously, not only in the correct order, but also in reverse.[20] Sometimes the letters were made to run horizontally across the tablet or page, but it was also a favourite practice to set them down vertically and in columns. Sometimes the letters were coupled, the first being set in line with the last, the second in line with the last but one, and so on ('boustrophedon' style), ending with the middle letters (M and N of the Greek alphabet) together.[21] All these variations served to impress on the memory the position of each letter in the series. In writing, the capitals were naturally taught first, the cursives very soon afterwards; so the elder Cato, as we saw, taught his son with large letters, and a semi-literate person in Petronius proudly claims to know his 'lapidary letters', that is, the capitals, as used in inscriptions.[22] As a letter might also be used as a form of abbreviation or a symbol, and was then termed a *nota*, it was immediately after learning the alphabet that Roman children became familiar with such abbreviations as P for Publius, Q for Quintus, T for Titus, and so on. In the rather charming classifications of late antiquity, [23] the 'abecedarians' (*abecedarii*) graduated to become 'notarians' (*notarii*), and then 'syllabarians' (*syllabarii*), so to syllables we now proceed.

As might have been expected, the syllables were treated in a very orderly fashion. Each of the consonants in turn was combined with all the vowels (seven iñ Greek, five in Latin), that is, in Greek *ba, bĕ, bē, bi, bŏ, bu, bō*, followed by *ga, ge*, and so onwards. Here Quintilian had no objection to the usual procedure, which was to make the children learn and chant each set before they were written down.[24] The name of each consonant and vowel were called out, then the resulting syllable, thus *'beta, alpha, ba', 'beta ei bĕ', 'beta eta, bē'*, and so on. We know that this practice existed in classical Greece, because in a play of Callias the members of the chorus came on to the stage singing these combinations in turn after the fashion of schoolchildren learning their syllables.[25] At the point where the Guéraud-Jouget papyrus first becomes legible, the writer has just arrived at the tail-end of the list, finishing with *psa* to *psō*. What is more interesting is that we may see the whole list, with the changing consonants running horizontally and the changing vowels running vertically, in a papyrus written by a schoolboy, a certain Apollonius, son of Glaucias, in the early second century B.C.[26] There is also similar papyrus and ostracon evidence from the imperial period. The next stage was to add a further consonant to make a three-letter syllable, this consonant remaining unchanged throughout; for instance, *n* was added, giving the series *ban, bĕn, bēn, bin*, etc.; examples of several others are found, but this is the choice in the Guéraud-Jouget papyrus (Fig. 18) and elsewhere.[27] Sometimes the series is formed with the initial and terminal consonant identical, that is *bab, beb*, etc., followed by *gag, geg*, and so on.[28] Quintilian required that *all* syllables should be thoroughly learned by heart, but it may be doubted whether many teachers regarded this extremely long and tedious process as necessary. As it was, children could very easily become muddled as they wended their way through the maze of syllables, and it was easy to drop out a whole section. Rather interesting is the example of a boy who, having very nicely worked his way through the series *bal, bel* ... as far as *tal, tel* ... forgets his guiding principle for a moment and proceeds to write *phan, phen* ... instead of *phal, phel* ...; but he soon recovers and ends up successfully with the correct termination.[29] Some children found the more extended syllables hard, forgot letters here and there, and had to be patiently guided back to what they had previously learned.[30]

After the syllables, with as many permutations as the teacher deemed necessary, had been written, pronounced, and learnt, came, at last, real words, but only words of a single syllable at first. The list of these was limited in scope, but it might contain a few that were quite rare; for example, a reader of Greek might go a long way before he met *knax* ('milk'), *klanx* ('din'), or *stranx* ('trickle'). But the reason for including such examples was clearly that they gave practice in pronouncing sounds which a child might find difficult.[31] In fact, out of eighteen words left in the Guéraud-Jouget manual, no less than eight, that is, nearly a half, end in *x*. The teacher, of course, made his own selection, but it is noticeable that the twenty-four examples in the well-known Bouriant papyrus[32] (a schoolboy's exercise-book of the fourth century A.D.) include *aix* ('goat'), *Thrax* ('Thracian'), *lynx*, and the very rare *rhōx* ('breach'). There were children in antiquity, as in modern times, who had trouble with the letter R, to which they gave the lisping L-sound,[33] but in Greek there were also some rather awkward combinations of consonants, such as syllables beginning with *kn*, or *kt*, and, particularly, combinations of aspirated consonants, such as *kh*, followed by *th*, e.g. *khthon* ('earth'). It was for the purpose of improving enunciation that Greek teachers made their children repeat lines of meaningless doggerel, formed by juxtaposition of words (some of them archaic) in the most tongue-twisting combinations.[34] Each line was, in fact, a jumble including every letter of the alphabet, and may have been tried out even at the earliest stage; but the result was formidable, and, anglicized, ran something like this:

KNAXBIKHTHYPTESPHLEGMODROPS
BEDYZAPSKHTHONPLEKTRONSPHINX

Children must have felt a sense of achievement when they mastered these, and they probably enjoyed emitting such barbarous sounds. These Greek tongue-twisters first appear on a school papyrus in the first century A.D.,[35] and the Romans must have known these or similar ones, as Quintilian mentions them; but when they were originally invented is not known.

Once the young learners were able to cope with monosyllabic words, the way was open for them to tackle words of two, three or more syllables. Here the general practice was to give them proper names, for the most part, rather than common nouns, at any rate in the first instance. Teachers, being methodical, liked to bring together these names in homogeneous groups; sometimes they gave personal names of two syllables, then of three, four and five; and in the imperial period they became increasingly fond of setting them in alphabetical order. All this the children wrote down on their tablets, ostraca, or papyri; for just as proper names are listed in the Guéraud-Jouget manual, so they are also found in the remains of the work of schoolboys in the imperial period. The manual begins with names of gods and goddesses, followed by

Fig.18 *Part of a teaching manual, showing layout of syllables from a papyrus of the third century B.C.*

Fig.19 *Part of the same manual, showing division of words into syllables.*

names of rivers;[36] similarly, lists of divinities are found on later ostraca.[37] It proceeds to names of famous persons in Greek mythology and history; a very similar, and much longer, list recurs in the Bouriant papyrus. There is, however, one noticeable difference, for whereas in the latter the names of these persons are written out in the normal way, in the former they are divided into their component syllables, a space with two points intervening, thus: AI:AS; I:A:SON; HIP:PO:ME:DON; AR:KE:SI:LA:OS (Fig. 19).[38] But, naturally, proper names were only a beginning, and were followed by numerous common nouns. Extension of vocabulary was always a major objective, and Varro remarked that 'parents send their children to school to learn how to write words which they do not know'.[39] Here again, classification of words in homogeneous groups was much favoured. We must remember at this point that many children were learning not only a Latin, but also a Greek vocabulary. It is therefore extremely probable that their tablets and papyri had very much the appearance of the pages of *hermeneumata* (interpretations) which are printed in the collection of Latin glossaries, where the Greek word and its Latin equivalent, or the Latin word and its Greek equivalent, are placed side by side. Here, too, the categories are very interesting — they include not only the names of divinities, but numerous words denoting parts of the body, words connected with the schoolroom, warfare, the weather, navigation, agriculture, lists of fishes, trees, vegetables, birds, beasts, and so *ad infinitum*.[40] The connection of glossography with the schoolroom becomes more noticeable at the grammar-school stage, where rare or obsolete words occurring in early literary texts required explanation. But Quintilian wished to have such words introduced even at this early point in the primary course to save teachers time later on.[41] This may have been possible with keen and very intelligent children, but one may suspect that teachers in less exalted circles, whose pupils found it difficult enough to spell out the words of everyday life, may have regarded it as somewhat premature.

Only when children had had plenty of practice in writing down and reading individual words were they allowed to proceed to the next stage, which was the reading of sentences, followed by short continuous passages, at first in verse. But they could not immediately be introduced to even an easy text as it stood, for the simple reason that, in antiquity, the words themselves were not separated. The letters ran on continuously along the line, and the reader had to become accustomed to distinguishing them for himself, and observing where one word ended and the next began. This must have presented at first a formidable obstacle, and even children learning to read in their own language needed some initial help. In Greek, it was more necessary still. The lines with which they began, therefore, still had the syllables spaced out, and the teacher explained, or marked, the end of each word. In the Guéraud-Jouget papyrus, a short passage of Euripides, *Phoenissae*, is marked out syllable by syllable, with double points, and divided into half-lines.[42] In later Homeric papyri, too, we find examples, even at the grammar-school stage, where the words are marked off.[43] A text of easy poetry was usually chosen first,[44] and the child was made to read slowly. Any mistakes in pronunciation were corrected by the teacher, and only by degrees was the speed increased.[45] Even for an adult who became literate, reading at first sight was regarded as something of an achievement.[46] If, as often happened, there were insufficient texts for the class, the pupils would each read in turn from the master's copy, coming up to him one at a time. Sometimes, on the sarcophagi of children who died young, there are depicted scenes from their early education, and one of the positions occasionally found in the reading lesson is rather interesting. Here the child himself, as he stands in front of the seated teacher, does not face him, but has his back turned, and, as he holds up the text at eye-level, the teacher looks down at it over his shoulder.[47] In one scene, the child has memorized his work and is seen reciting it to his father (Fig.2). Alternatively, the relevant text might either have to be copied out, or taken down by dictation, but this could only be done when adequate proficiency in writing had been acquired. To writing, then, we may next turn, for the two activities were, naturally, closely interrelated.

There was a strong inclination among teachers at all times in antiquity to ensure that the earliest lessons in both reading and writing should have not only a practical but also a moral value. The lines which were set for practice in writing were specially selected because they contained some useful observation on life or conduct, some exhortation or warning, which might with advantage be remembered in later years. Experience proved that the best lines for the purpose were those which expressed their point succinctly, in a single sentence, or, better still, in a single line. Such were the moral 'maxims' (*gnomai, sententiae*) which abounded in Greek didactic and dramatic poetry, and were popular at all times in Greek teaching.[48] Verse maxims were particularly easy to memorize, and ready-made collections, drawn, for instance, from such writers as Hesiod, Theognis, Epicharmus, and, most particularly, Euripides and Menander, were in circulation in Hellenistic times.[49] These two authors served the purpose admirably, for their plays provided a wealth of succinct reflections on human life. In fact, so alike were they in this respect, that sometimes one cannot be sure whether a particular line was written by the one or the other. The famous example quoted by St Paul, 'evil communications corrupt good manners', is found ascribed to both authors, and appears in a fragment of an anthology as early as the third century B.C.[50] Such quotations might form part of a selection of short passages, compiled for pleasant and profitable reading, or might merely be listed, one after the other, sometimes in alphabetical order, to form a 'gnomology'. A particularly good example of this is the collection of single iambic lines which has come down under the name of Menander,[51] though it doubtless includes a good deal of extraneous material, and such lines were also easy to adapt or imitate. More than a score of maxims are written out in the Bouriant papyrus, in alphabetical order according to the initial letter.[52] There were also many such single-line maxims available in Latin, and the collection drawn from the mimes of Publilius Syrus is again in alphabetical order. Quintilian, too, makes mention of verses containing some moral lesson, and set for practice in writing.[53] Maxims in two verses also became popular, and particularly celebrated, from the third century onwards, were the so-called 'Distichs of Cato'.

Surviving examples from Greek schoolrooms show that the teacher wrote out the maxim in his own hand at the top of the page as a model, known in Latin as the *praescriptum*; the pupil then wrote his own copy, or several copies, beneath. Attention was paid to neatness of presentation, as well as correctness in spelling, and lines might be ruled out beforehand, so that the letters could be kept straight and of even height. Of particular interest is a waxed tablet in the British Museum on which the teacher of Greek has written, on ruled lines, two verses, one by Menander, beneath which, also between ruled lines, the pupil has written two copies himself. As it happens, the teacher made a slip in the final syllable of the second line, and this is faithfully copied without question by the boy (Fig. 20).[54] In surviving exercises from Greek schools, the teacher, when not dissatisfied with a pupil's progress, has added encouragingly at the end of the words *philoponei*, or *philoponei graphon* — 'Work hard', 'Work hard at your writing'.[55] An unsatisfactory pupil might be made to write out several lines, either as a salutary warning or as a punishment — a forerunner of the 'imposition'. On one Greek tablet there appears, written first by the master and then copied several times by the pupil, the ominous reminder: 'Work hard, boy, lest you be thrashed' (Fig.10.[56] These maxims had also to be learned by heart, and it is not surprising that pupils acquired a very considerable stock of them, and that authors in later life sometimes recalled a *sententia* which took them back to the lessons of the primary school.[57]

At this point, then, we may glance through the 'Menander' collection, and select examples to illustrate the kind of precept with which the teacher sought to shape the young child's mind. There are observations on the value of education, of course, such as: 'Men's culture is a prize that none may steal', 'Their education men can never lose', or 'By education all are civilized', together with incentives to industry and exhortations to avoid idleness: 'Work hard, and you will win fair livelihood', 'Though rich, if you are idle, you'll be poor'. Emphasis is laid on prudence and foresight: 'Take counsel first in every enterprise', and the young are especially advised to seek guidance from their elders: 'When young, to older folk give willing ear', 'From a wise man you should good counsel take'.[58] Parents should be honoured, and — a very frequent and favourite theme — friendships should be valued: 'Honour your parents and treat well your friends', 'There's no possession finer than a friend', 'Regard your friends' misfortunes as your own', but it must be remembered that 'Time will test friendships as the fire tests gold' and 'Bad friends an evil harvest do create'.[59] It is important to speak the truth, for 'Deception is the greatest curse of man', and 'No liar undetected is for long'. One should not prattle foolishly, and silence is often golden: 'Better is silence than unseemly speech', for 'The tongue of many evils is the cause'. All forms of self-esteem are to be condemned: 'Many will hate you if you love yourself', 'Esteem yourself too much, you'll win no friends'.[60] Unselfishness and self-control are to be commended — 'Life is not living for yourself alone', ''Tis good to master temper and desire'. Anger is a bad thing, for 'No one in angry mood may safely plan'; so is self-indulgence: 'Never to pleasure make yourself a slave', 'Shun pleasure which brings pain as aftermath', and running into debt: 'Debt maketh slaves of freeborn citizens'.[61] Life has its blessings: 'Health and good sense are blessings in this life', but 'No man alive in all things happy is', 'No single mortal life is free from pain'.[62] Often these maxims take the form of a simple statement or exhortation, but sometimes they derive added effect from neat antithesis: 'Favours received recall, those done

Fig.20 *'From a wise man see you accept advice;*
Place not a thoughtless trust in all your friends.'
Iambic verses, repeated twice from the master's fair copy on ruled
lines. The first is from Menander, and maybe the second also.

forget', or word-play: 'Life is no life without a livelihood', or exclamation: 'How futile knowledge is without good sense', 'How sweet is beauty with chaste mind allied', 'How gracious, if humane, can humans be!'[63]

In Latin, similarly, the teacher could extract many lines of pithy wisdom from early Roman plays, both comedy and tragedy. In both substance and form, some of the verses of Ennius, whether or not adapted from Euripides, show their kinship with the Greek examples, and were much used in schools.[64] Here we find such lines as 'Ill-wishers raise up disrepute, well-wishers fame'; 'A friend at need is seen a friend indeed'; 'Good deeds misplaced, methinks, are deeds ill-done'.[65] Terence, too, like Menander, offered many excellent *sententiae*, and, from the Augustan age onwards, it was yet another stage-writer, Publilius Syrus, whose lines were collected to supplement the earlier sources, at a time when the aphorism was more than ever in vogue.[66]

The writing and learning of maxims was not confined to lines of verse, for there was also an abundance of similar material in prose. The 'sayings of famous men', which Quintilian recommends for primary study,[67] had long before his day been collected; they were known as *apophthegmata*, and often found their way into anthologies. In Greek, the succinct comments on human life and conduct made by the Seven

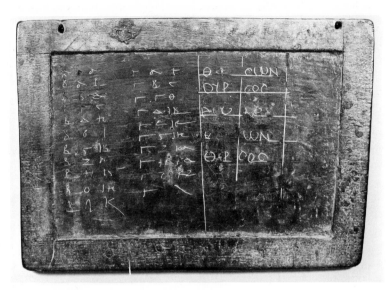

Fig.21 *Multiplication table and spelling exercise; this and the previous tablet are a pair.*

Wise Men and by the philosophers had long been a popular source for copy-book maxims,[68] and were sometimes given a Latin form. Seneca, in a letter devoted to the use of philosophical precepts, remarks that one could find much of their vaunted wisdom simply by entering a primary school and glancing at the models set for copying (*in puerili praescripto*). [69] Among the numerous authors of such sayings, one of those selected for school use was Diogenes the Cynic, whose brief, caustic (and sometimes vulgar) repartees were much appreciated in antiquity. These usually took the form of: 'Diogenes, being asked ... replied', or 'Diogenes, seeing ... remarked', and so are really a brief form of the instructive anecdote known as a *chreia*. The close association of maxim and anecdote is seen in Seneca's remark that both were given to boys to learn by heart, and we find examples from Diogenes in the Bouriant papyrus.[70] In Latin, the elder Cato, whose own celebrated pithy remarks were long remembered and even included in translation in Greek anthologies,[71] had also, in his old age, made a practice of putting together notable sayings from both Greek and Latin sources. The collection was in circulation in Cicero's day,[72] and it is more than likely that schoolmasters made some use of it. We shall meet both maxims and anecdotes again when we reach the earliest exercises in rhetoric.

As proficiency in writing developed, it became less necessary for the teacher to provide a model on each tablet, and passages of several lines, particularly of poetry, could be taken down by the boys either by copying or by dictation. Sometimes there would only be one text, or anthology, circulating round the class, and each boy would be allotted a passage to transcribe. Writing, learning by heart, and reciting now went together. Each boy brought up his copy to the master for correction and explanation of the contents; he was then allowed time to learn it, and later came up to recite it.[73] Alternatively, the master could dictate a passage to the class, and the same procedure would be followed. Dictation was especially associated with primary schools (though also used at higher levels), but, with beginners, it had its disadvantages. Sometimes a boy failed to hear a word properly, or could not spell it, or the master's enunciation was not as clear as it should have been, and not all teachers were conscientious in correcting errors. It is often the mistakes which, along with other criteria, indicate to papyrologists that they have before them a schoolroom exercise.[74] Sometimes the very nature of the errors is such that they seem to presuppose dictation and the misinterpretation of sound. This has been deduced, for instance, in a passage of Euripides (again, from the *Phoenissae*), inaccurately reproduced on a British Museum ostracon of the second century B.C.[75] Passages of the classical poets, both Greek and Latin, were selected as most worth the effort of writing out and learning, but, after the end of the Republic, some teachers evidently became much less selective, and pressed into service contemporary verse, which might, or might not, have merit. Hence Horace's scornful remark: 'Would you prefer your poetry to be dictated in the wretched primary schools? Not I.'[76] Persius, too, shows his contempt for modern poetasters who pride themselves on having provided dictation material for 'a hundred curly-headed boys'.[77]

Dictation, however, was not always deemed the best procedure, for the ultimate purpose of studying selections from poetry was to profit by learning them. There was, therefore, a third method, derived from classical Greece, by which the intermediate stage of writing was eliminated altogether, and this was for the boy simply to repeat his lines after the master, who took them a word at a time, so that gradually the pupil had them by heart. The Greeks called this process *apostomatizein*, [78] or oral repetition. Horace refers to this when he compares the habit of a flatterer of repeating each word as it falls from his patron's lips, to that of a boy repeating his teacher's words.[79] But, whatever the method used, the greatest importance was attached in antiquity to memorizing, and Quintilian observed that this kind of aptitude, when seen at a very early age, was one of the best criteria in estimating future ability.[80]

So far, in describing the kind of literary material used for reading, writing and memorizing, we have mentioned only lines, short passages and selections, but the question now arises whether children after this stage began to have access to some reading-book of a more homogeneous nature for continuous work. Quintilian does not enlighten us here, but later evidence strongly suggests that books of collected fables must have been familiar in the primary schools. In the volume of Latin glossaries which includes the 'School Colloquies', and which throws so much light on primary teaching (words and expressions being set down in both Latin and Greek), we read the following: 'At this point, then, I will begin to write fables of Aesop, and will provide an illustration, for it is from him that the pictures are drawn; these fables are very necessary for the practical conduct of our lives, so I will begin with the fable about the stag'.[81] It is of particular interest to note here that the text of Aesop is used in connection with coloured illustrations, either accompanying each fable, or, perhaps, in a separate form.[82] Children would already have heard some of the fables, as told by their nurses, at a very early age,[83] and now they could read them and write them out for themselves. A further pointer in this direction, though again later than our period, is seen in the waxed tablets of school origin known as the Assendelft Tablets (in Leiden), which contain several of the fables of Babrius, either in verse or in prose form.[84] What makes the early study of fables even more likely is the fact that, when boys reached the 'grammar' school, one of the very earliest types of preliminary rhetorical exercise which they were taught to compose was that based upon the fable.[85] Whether, in Greek, boys at the primary stage acquired sufficient knowledge to begin to read Homer, as Greek boys did, is very doubtful, for, at Rome, Homer is associated with the 'grammar' school.

But surely, it may be thought, if boys and girls were expected to do a good deal of their primary work in Greek as well as in Latin, they must at some stage have been given instruction in grammar? This was indeed so, and children had to begin their grammar before they reached the 'grammar' school. Dionysius, thinking of Greek boys learning their own language, says that even when they were dealing only with individual words, before they reached continuous reading and writing, they were taught to recognize what was a noun, and what was a verb, what the inflections were, and the differences of accent and quantity.[86] If this was necessary for Greek boys learning their own language, then, *a fortiori*, it must have been even more necessary for Roman boys learning Greek. Quintilian expects children to begin by picking up simple conversational Greek at home,[87] but this was not sufficient for understanding literary texts, unless the 'pedagogue', or the schoolmaster, taught the case endings, verbal forms, tenses, rules of agreement and so on in more systematic fashion. Quintilian says that he assumes that declensions and conjugations will have formed part of primary school teaching.[88] In fact, it is not easy to differentiate between the knowledge acquired by the time a pupil had reached the top class of a primary school and that acquired in the lowest class of the 'grammar' school, for it is likely that primary teaching overlapped secondary, just as secondary teaching overlapped rhetoric.

When the syllabus of the primary school is described in sequence, the whole seems simply a matter of logical and orderly progress. But we have to remember that, in most schoolrooms, the organization of this programme was not so straightforward as it may appear, for there were boys of different ages and abilities attending at the same time. Some were absolute beginners, some had attended for quite a time, and some were in

Fig.22 *Part of a schoolboy's exercise-book, listing the letters by their phonetic values.*

Fig.23 *Part of the same exercise-book, showing a list of cases in Greek.*

the final stages. Consequently, there had to be several divisions of work, and the various activities went on in the same room at the same time. The pattern would not necessarily be the same everywhere, but the description of a school scene in the Latin glossaries, though later than our period, will afford a widely applicable illustration.[89] First thing in the morning, some of the boys are engaged in a writing and reading lesson. Each one in turn, in his seat, copies on his tablet lines, for which the master has supplied the model. On completion, each takes his copy to the master, who corrects it, and makes him read it. This done, each in turn learns a vocabulary list, which he then repeats to the master. Whilst others are thus occupied, some of the boys test each other's ability at taking down and reading back a dictation, after arguing with each other as to who shall begin. Whilst all this is going on, the master has arranged for the very young boys to be taught and tested. They stand in two groups, one, in charge of an older boy, repeating to him their letters and syllables, the other, in charge of the undermaster, repeating word-lists, after which its members sit and copy out lines of verse. Then the master himself gives a dictation to the boys in the top class. They are allowed a little time to study the word-lists (probably available in dictionary-form) and grammatical text-book, which circulate in class. Then each proceeds to the master, listens to his explanation of the subject-matter, and reads the passage to him, after which he is tested with a series of questions on the parts of speech and the declensions. By the time the whole school has carried out these various activities, the hubbub at last subsides, and the boys go off to lunch.

At the same time that Roman children were learning to read and write, they also began to acquire a rudimentary knowledge of the third of the 'three Rs', arithmetic.[90] With the aid of Greek sources, it is possible to discern the stages at which this elementary instruction was interwoven in the programme. As with the letters, it began with practical demonstration and beginners learnt to count on their fingers and with the pebbles (*calculi*),[91] which they would later use in conjunction with the reckoning-board (*abacus*); they would also be attracted and encouraged by play-methods such as Plato and Quintilian approved.[92] They would then learn their simple additions, and later their multiplications, in the form of a chant, as with the alphabet, but they would also have to recognize and write the symbols by which these numerals were signified. These symbols were themselves letters of the alphabet. In Latin, they were limited to V,X, L, C, D and M, together with the required number of Is. This was clear enough, but also rather clumsy by comparison with Greek, because Greek never needed to use a whole conglomeration of letters to represent a number. The Greeks used all the twenty-four letters of their alphabet, together with three additional signs, and evolved a very neat system by which they could represent any number up to 99 with only two letters, and any number up to 999 with only three. A horizontal bar about the letter (often omitted in practice) indicated that it was being used as a number. Thus *alpha* stood for one, *beta* for two, and so on up to *theta* for nine and *iota* for ten, an extra sign being introduced for six. Then followed *iota alpha* for eleven up to *iota theta* for nineteen, then *kappa, kappa alpha*, on the same principle. (On the Greek abacus, there were distinctive signs for five, ten, fifty, a hundred, etc). In Greek, if we judge from the Guéraud-Jouget manual, and a later school-papyrus,[93] this numeration system was introduced immediately after the syllables were learnt, but other Greek evidence shows that it could accompany the teaching of the letters.[94] In Latin, where only a few letters were used, it would probably be taught when the letters were treated as abbreviations. Next came the writing down of simple additions. This stage is omitted in the Guéraud-Jouget manual, but a late Greek school-papyrus shows that it could be done at the time when the boy was learning single words, for, at two points, we find such words, divided into their syllables, on the left, and, on the right, simple sums such as six (and) one (makes) seven, six (and) two (makes) eight.[95] But a boy might also have reached his multiplication table by this stage. We referred earlier to a waxed tablet in the British Museum, of the second century A.D., on which the boy had copied two lines, one by Menander, from the master's model. It is one of a pair of tablets,[96] and the other is equally interesting (Figs. 20 and 21). Here, on the left hand side, written in a mature hand, is a multiplication table in Greek, representing 'once one is one', 'twice one is two', 'twice two is four' up to 'twice ten is twenty', followed, in the next column, by 'thrice one is three', 'thrice two is six', up to 'thrice ten is thirty'. On the right hand side, written in a childish hand, are disyllabic words beginning with theta (of which *thyrsos* caused trouble and is repeated), and these words have their syllables divided by a vertical line. It looks very much, therefore, as though the teacher wrote out the multiplication table for the boy to memorize at the same period of study that the boy was practising the writing of words. In the Guéraud-Jouget manual, it is not until after the presentation of continuous reading passages that a multiplication table is set out, but it is a rather more advanced one, for it gives not only the squares of the units (i.e., up to nine times nine), but higher multiples as well.[97] Naturally, the aptitudes of individual children would differ, and the system could not be rigid, but the evidence does show that reading, writing and simple arithmetic went closely together, and this must have been equally true in Latin.

Just as subtraction would be taught together with addition, so with multiplication would go division. Echion, in Petronius, is proud that his little boy can already divide by four,[98] and the progression would have continued to the higher units. But division was not confined to whole numbers; it led on to fractions, and this meant, to a very large extent, duodecimal fractions. In Greek, immediately following the squared numbers in the Guéraud-Jouget manual, we have a list of the symbols used to express fractions of the drachma, and, as there were six obols to a drachma, and each obol was worth eight *chalci*, the main sub-divisions of the drachma down to one forty-eighth are given.[99] In a papyrus of the first century B.C. we again find a table of squared numbers up to ten, followed this time by fractions of the drachma, and additions thereof, such as 'one-quarter and one-twelfth make one-third'.[100] This is

Fig.24 *Roman sarcophagus of the Flavian period, showing a slave reckoning up his master's bequests on an abacus.*

Fig.25 *Detail of the abacus.*

immediately relevant to the Roman duodecimal system used in subdividing money, weights, and measures, for not only the *as*, but the pound weight and the foot were divided into twelve *unciae*; from *uncia* both *ounce* and *inch* are derived. There is a well-known passage in Horace in which an arithmetic lesson is described as follows:[101]

> *Teacher*: Now let the son of Albinus tell me — if one-twelfth (*uncia*)
>   is taken from five-twelfths (*quincunx*), what is left over?
>   You might have told me by now.
> *Pupil*:   One third (*triens*).
> *Teacher*: Good — you'll be able to look after your money.
>   Suppose that one-twelfth is added instead — what does it
>   come to?
> *Pupil*:   One half.

The understanding of such fractions would be greatly facilitated by the daily handling of small coins, but the system was also frequently applied to large amounts, particularly in the apportioning of inheritances. The estate as a whole was treated as though it were one *as*, and the proportions allocated as parts of the *as*, so, unless the entire estate went to one person (*ex asse*), an heir might be granted any number of twelfths from eleven down to one. He might become, say, heir to the *quincunx*, or heir to the *triens*, and, if he inherited only a twenty-fourth, he was 'heir to the half-ounce' (*ex semuncia*).

On the other hand, the decimal system was also necessary, particularly in working out percentages to calculate interest. The slave in Petronius, who is described as able to read at sight, can also divide by ten,[102] and this would be the first step to division by a hundred. So the semi-literate character who claims to know his large letters declares that he can divide money, or weights, by a hundred,[103] in which case his arithmetic must have far outstripped his reading and writing. Such division meant applying the decimal system to the duodecimal, which was awkward, because, the 'remainder', whether *denarii* or *asses* or *unciae*, had first to be reduced to fractions which were duodecimal. The *uncia* itself was reducible to most minute subdivisions, so it is not surprising that Horace says that Roman boys were involved in 'long calculations' in order to 'divide the *as* into a hundred parts'.[104]

We come next to the use of the *abacus*, or wooden reckoning-board with raised edges. Its appearance may best be illustrated by the sculpture on a marble sarcophagus, of the Flavian period, in the Capitoline Museum (Figs. 24 and 25).[105] Here a slave-accountant is shown taking down his dying master's bequests, seeing that their total keeps within the estate, and he is working with pebbles (*calculi*), which are round and flat. These were set in position, supplemented, or removed, as required. A person who was expert in this field was termed a *calculator*, and, so far from being identical with the ordinary primary schoolmaster, he seems to have been something of a specialist who might, like the shorthand teacher, be a rival to him in collecting pupils.[106] We do not, therefore, know at what stage boys, having no doubt received some initial instruction in the use of the *abacus* from the primary teacher, transferred to the *calculator* for more complicated work.

In attempting the difficult task of explaining briefly how the Roman abacus worked — or may have worked, for one cannot be dogmatic without definitive evidence — it is best to begin with a type which not only survives, but shows clear evidence as to how it worked. There are in existence at least three examples — one each in Paris and Rome, and one (thought to be a late copy) in the British Museum — of *abaci* which, apart from small divergencies of detail, belong to the same class. They are not of the type shown on the sarcophagus, but are of the 'bead-frame' variety. They are made of metal, and small enough to be held in the palm of the hand, and are worked by moving small knobs in a series of slots.[107] The device is very neat and compact; here is a diagram, the small letters at the top being added for facility of reference:

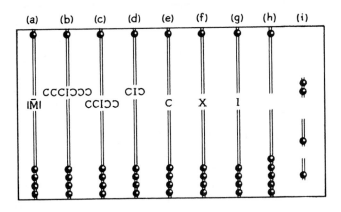

The symbols in the centre of the diagram, from column (g) to column (a), in that order, represent units, tens, hundreds, thousands, ten thousands, hundred thousands, and millions; columns (h) and (i) may be disregarded for the moment, as they represent fractions. Below the centre-numerals, the slots are longer, and each bead represents a unit of the denomination indicated immediately above. Above the centre symbols each bead represents five times the unit designated immediately below. This is an extremely convenient arrangement, and was used to avoid the unnecessary confusion which might arise if all the beads were single units and brought together within a single slot, making nine in each case; four beads can be taken in by the eye at a glance, whereas the larger the number of them together, the more the risk of error. The diagram shows the beads in a position prior to operation; in the working of it, the required number of beads are moved along the slot towards the centre-line, upwards for the units, downwards for the five-multiples. Any number from 1 to 9,999,999 can now be represented. When fractions were involved, lines (h) and (i) came into play (the position of these two being sometimes reversed), but here there was an important difference. The system here was a duodecimal one; the beads under (h) represented *unciae*, or twelfths. Since, therefore, it was necessary to be able to indicate up to eleven-twelfths, the top bead here has six times the value of those in the slot below, and there are five beads, instead of four, in the lower section. The smaller fractions under (i) are also duodecimal. Whether they are disposed in three separate grooves or in a single groove (originally, with different colorations) they represent one twenty-fourth, one forty-eighth, and two seventy-secondths, as the symbols, whether still legible or reported, indicate. Only a single amount could be shown at a time, and this was also true of the board and *calculi* type, for archaeological evidence shows that this was commonly used in conjunction with writing tablets. An illustration on the Darius vase (an Apulian vase of *c.*300 B.C.), showing the treasurer of the Persian king receiving tribute, and a very similar illustration on a Roman engraved seal, showing a *calculator* at work, both represent the operator holding a writing tablet, with figures inscribed on it, in his left hand, whilst he places the *calculi* on the abacus (a 'table-model') with his right.[108] He would need to suspend operations from time to time to take notes.

On the reckoning-board depicted on the sarcophagus, there is nothing to indicate how the lines were drawn, though lines, or grooves, there would certainly have been. If then, we make the assumption that the layout corresponded to that of the miniature variety, we may suppose that the lines ran vertical to the user, that the counters were placed on the lines, and that there was a transverse line to divide the five-multiples from the single denominations. We may now attempt a reconstruction of the processes of addition and subtraction, remembering that the operator had a supply of spare pebbles, which he could add or remove as required. Let us suppose that he has to add 967 to 1274.

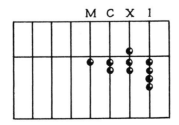

Having made a note of the two amounts, he starts with a clear board, and then places pebbles on the appropriate lines to represent the higher of the two amounts; the relevant section of his board then appears as in the diagram on page 185 above. He has first to add seven to the units-line; he does not need, however, to put down seven pebbles, for he knows that he can take a five out of it, so he keeps two pebbles back, whilst placing one on the upper section of the units line. When he brings up the two pebbles to the existing four in the lower section, he sees that this makes six, and so he removes five of them, leaving only one below the centre-line and, in lieu, places a pebble on the upper section. But he now has two five-multiples there; this makes a ten, so he removes them and, in lieu, adds one to the lower section of the tens line. On this line, he now has to add six (i.e. six tens) but he sees that he can take a five out of this six, so he places only one on the lower section of the line, thus leaving four there, and adds a pebble above. This, however leaves two multiples on the tens line (each worth fifty units), so he removes them, and adds one pebble in lieu to the lower section of the hundreds line, leaving three there. He now has to add nine to that line; seeing that he can take a five out of this, he places a pebble on the upper section. When he now brings up the remaining four to the existing three in the lower section, he sees that he can take a five out of this seven; so he leaves only two pebbles there, and adds another to the upper section. But he now has two pebbles there (worth 500 each), so he removes them, and adds one to the lower section of the thousands line. His board now looks like this:

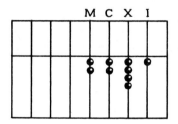

The result, 2241, would have been achieved by a good pupil in a fairly short space of time.

Next, suppose that he has to subtract 967 from 1274. In this case, he has to subtract seven from the units line, where there are only four pebbles, so he removes one from the lower section of the tens line, and adds three to his units. As this brings the units up to seven, he leaves only two there and adds one above in the multiple section. He now has to take six from the tens, which is the number already there, so this line is cleared. He must next take nine from the hundreds, so he removes the one pebble on the thousands line and adds one to the hundreds on the lower section. His board now presents 307, which he writes down.

The processes of multiplication and division were more complex, especially if the multiplicator or divisor were large. Multiplication could be effected by repeated additions, and this might be somewhat simplified by the doubling method. That is, for example, if an amount had to be multiplied by nine, it could first be doubled by addition, the resulting amount would then be doubled again, and then the further result doubled, making eight times, and finally the original amount would be added. Division, likewise, could be effected by repeated subtractions, though the process would be long and tedious. But, as the multiplication table would have been memorized, it seems unlikely that such roundabout methods would have been necessary.

One must add, however, that it cannot be confidently asserted that the layout of the Roman reckoning board corresponded so closely to that of the miniature type in metal. Indeed, some may perhaps believe that these miniatures are not genuinely Roman, but are a mediaeval or later invention; but this has not been the general opinion.[109] As to form, the nearest parallels appear to be oriental. The Chinese *suan-pan*, a bead frame type with transverse string, is similar in operation, but has an extra bead above and below on each vertical line.[110] It is also possible to argue that the board was not divided into an upper and lower section, but that the five-multiples were interposed between the units, tens, hundreds and thousands, and that the intervening spaces between the lines were brought into use. Thus the former might be on the lines and the latter in the spaces, or vice-versa. This would have the effect of widening the operation area, and it could be contended that the lines, on and between which the counters are placed, ran horizontally across the board, and that the symbols of the denominations were set vertically, the highest at the top. These things can neither be proved nor disproved. But whatever the exact form, the principle of working in five-multiples would have been basic, and these are, in fact, marked on the Salamis abacus from ancient Greece.[111]

Finally, mention should be made of a remarkably highly-developed system of counting, and of indicating numbers to others, which did not require an instrument or writing, but simply the use of the fingers.[112] When Quintilian remarked that 'a knowledge of numbers is necessary for an orator, even if he has only an elementary education', because calculations are so often necessary in legal cases, he adds that the speaker should also be able to represent accurately on his fingers any number that he may mention in words — evidently, as an ocular demonstration to reinforce his point.[113] This use of the fingers (and thumbs) by adults is attested long before Quintilian's time, and Ovid speaks of 'the fingers on which we are wont to count' and on which men anxiously 'tot up their income'.[114] Similarly, in the game of *morra*, which Cicero calls 'flash-fingers' (*micare digitis*), a number was momentarily indicated by finger-symbolism, and the opponent had to identify or repeat it.[115] The ancients were extremely adept at thus indicating numbers, an art which they may have originally acquired from Eastern trading, and there must have been a system of representation which was widely understood. We begin to gain an insight into it from Juvenal's remark that a centenarian like Nestor 'already counts his years on his right hand', which indicates that units and tens must have been calculated on the left hand, and hundreds on the right.[116] There is evidence of this sort of system elsewhere, and, particularly, a number of metal discs of the imperial period survive, on which the position of the fingers is shown on one side and the corresponding figure, in Roman numerals, on the other.[117] Further interesting, and similar, illustrations are appended to the Regensburg manuscript of the Venerable Bede's *De Temporum Ratione*, which includes an account of the various positions (Fig. 17).[118] Thus the units are indicated by the depression, or partial depression, of one or more fingers of the left hand. In representing the tens, the thumb was brought into play — for instance, thirty was expressed by bringing the tip of the forefinger and the tip of the thumb together in a circle. Similar operations with the right hand expressed the hundreds and thousands, and, beyond ten thousand, different positions of one hand or the other on breast or hip were used. We are told that beginners, at whatever age, found the system difficult at first, but became used to it with practice,[119] and there is every likelihood that a start, at least, was made in school.

Such was primary education in the 'three Rs' in Roman times. It was done systematically, and step by step, for, as Varro, quoting Ariston, remarked: 'it is important how a child begins to be formed in the earliest stage, for on that depends the way he will turn out'.[120] There was nothing about it which was not designed to meet the practical needs of life, and, in reading and writing, it managed to combine a moral element as well. For many Roman citizens, it was the only education which they ever received, but it served them well in everyday life, and it counted for something in the Army, for in the legions those who were competent in reading and writing, or in arithmetic and shorthand, were classed apart.[121] But it also paved the way for those who now proceeded to the more scholarly instruction of the 'grammar' school.

CHAPTER XIV

The Grammatical syllabus

(I) The elements of metre and the parts of speech

The teaching of grammar, with which the secondary stage of education began, laid the foundations both for the subsequent study of the poets and for the training of the future orator.[1] It may be seen to have fallen into two major parts.[2] The first part was mainly formal, and was concerned with classification of the letters, the scansion of verse, the parts of speech, and declension and conjugation.[3] The second part dealt with correctness in speech and in writing, beginning, on the negative side, with examples of the barbarisms and solecisms which must be avoided, and proceeding, on the positive side, to the establishment of criteria by which one should decide what is correct in doubtful cases. The first part was essential in both Greek and Latin, but the second part, with which Quintilian himself deals at considerable length, must have been, in practice, preponderantly concerned with Latin; for it was of overriding importance that the boy should learn to speak his own language correctly.

Just as the primary course had begun with the letters of the alphabet, so did the ensuing course under the 'grammarian', but there was now a difference of treatment. At the primary stage, it had been sufficient to train the child's observation, memory and imitative capacity; he learned to recognize the shapes of the letters, knew their names, practised forming them in writing, and could pronounce them as they occurred in syllables and words. At the secondary stage, he was introduced to a closer study of their phonetic values, and became familiar with their standard classification.[4] The teacher began by distinguishing vowels from consonants, and, in Latin, made special reference to consonantal *i* and consonantal *u*.[5] In Greek, it was shown that two of the seven vowels were naturally long, two naturally short, and three could be either long or short; these (a, ι and υ) were termed 'dichronous', or 'double-timed'. In Latin, all five vowels had this common nature. Next came the possible combinations of vowels in diphthongs, and then the analysis of the consonants. These were divided into the 'semi-vowels' (which, owing to their continuing sound, we call continuants) and 'mutes' (which we call plosives). Boys were taught to distinguish between consonants which gave only a 'half-sound' (as opposed to the full sound of vowels), such as the lingering *l*, the murmuring *m*, the whirring *r*, and the sibilant *s*, and those which, though not quite soundless, produced, as it were, merely a 'sputter' by themselves, namely *b, g, d, k, p, t,* and, in Latin, also *c*. In Greek, the existence of aspirated consonants led to a further classification.[6] Here the plosives were subdivided according to the degree of roughness or smoothness created in their articulation by the intensity or gentleness of the emission of breath. Thus the Greek φ (*p-h*, pronounced as in *shepherd*, not as in *photo*), χ (*k-h*), and θ (*t-h*), were classed as rough, κ, π and τ as smooth, and β, γ, and δ as 'intermediate', a term which has given rise to some discussion, and may perhaps imply recognition of the distinction between voiced and unvoiced plosives.

At this stage, the main object was to teach the classification, particularly with the future needs of correct pronunciation, spelling and verse-scansion in mind. In connection with the last-named, the grouping of *l, m, n* and *r* (the term 'liquids' was already in use) and the recognition of certain letters as double-consonants (ζ being equated with σδ, ξ with κσ, and ψ with πσ) were of obvious relevance. The method of teaching is well illustrated by one of a series of tablets from Graeco-Roman Egypt of the third century A.D. (forming a school book) in the British Museum (Fig. 22), in which all the letters of the alphabet are listed, vertically, in order, and to each is attached a label, such as 'long', 'short', 'double-timed', 'rough', 'smooth', 'intermediate', 'liquid', the terminology being almost exactly identical with that of Dionysius Thrax.[7]

At this point, it may be of interest to add that the Roman schoolboy had a means of memorizing the distinction between continuants and plosives which was not available to his counterpart in Greece. In Greek, there was no consistent identity between the names of the letters and the sounds which they represented; for example, *alpha, beta, gamma*, were not the same as the sounds which they conveyed. But in Latin, when the naming of the letters was finally standardized (probably by Varro), there was a much closer relationship between the name and the sound. Not only did the Latin vowels take their names from their own sound when pronounced long, but the distinction between continuants and plosives was also reflected in their names. It was felt that continuants needed a vowel *preceding* them to make a complete sound, and this vowel was taken to be best represented as *e*; so *f, l, m, n, r* and *s* were called *ef, el, em, en, er* and *es* (*x*, being a double letter, equivalent to *cs* or *gs*, was called, rather differently, *ix*). Plosives, on the other hand, required a *following* vowel to make up a full sound, and so *b, c, d, g, p* and *t* were called *be, ce, de, ge, pe* and *te*. Three of the plosives were rather exceptional, namely *h* and *k*, which were called *ha* and *ka*, and *q*, which was called *cu*. Thus, if a Roman boy wished to decide to which of the two groups a consonant belonged, he had only to reflect for a moment on its name — if the name *began* with a vowel, he would class it as a 'semi-vowel', but if the name *ended* with a vowel, it was a 'mute'.[8] The system also shows, incidentally, how we owe our own names for most of the letters to the Romans. Finally, as the Roman alphabet originally ended in *x*, the letters which we call *wi* and *zed*, after they were added for the better representation of words derived from Greek (e.g. *zephyrus*), were regularly known as the 'Greek' or 'foreign' letters.[9] *Y* was simply the Greek capital Υ, and as the Romans could do no better than call it the 'Greek *u*', this terminology still survives, for example in the French *y grec*.

There were other interesting matters connected with the alphabet, which Quintilian would have liked the grammarian's pupils to know. He was evidently familiar with Varro's lost treatise *On the Antiquity of the Letters*, and, like Varro, raised the question whether *h*, *k*, and *q* were really needed, or even *x*, which had sometimes been rejected.[10] Then there was the opposite question, whether Latin required extra letters, to represent the *w*-sound, as in *seruus, uulgus* (i.e. the digamma), or the sound intermediate between *u* and *i*, heard, for instance, in the middle syllable of *optimus*, for which the emperor Claudius introduced (with only temporary success) one of his new letters.[11] Teachers probably did mention these points. Quintilian would then have gone on to discuss examples of vowel-weakening and consonantal change, which reflect the interests of the scholar.[12] But it is doubtful whether the average teacher had much time or inclination to pursue such paths of philological study in class. He had a great deal of ground yet to cover, and, in all likelihood, now proceeded to the next part of his subject.

Just as at the primary stage, the treatment of the letters was followed by the study of syllables. This was primarily directed to the scansion of verse, and included the precepts with which schoolboys in all ages have become familiar. They were taught that a short syllable was equivalent to one 'time' and a long syllable to two 'times'.[13] Examples were given of syllables containing a vowel long by nature, or a diphthong, and of short-vowelled syllables made long by position when the vowel was followed by two or more consonants, or a double consonant, such as *x* or *z*.[14] Next came the rule for the 'common' syllables, that is, short-vowelled syllables which might either remain short or be lengthened, when the following consonants were a combination of a plosive, or *f*, with a liquid, *r* or *l*, as in *Cy̆clops* or *Cȳclops, pătris* or *pātris*. In Greek, this might also happen when the second consonant was *m* or *n*. Mention was also made of various exceptions, such as those arising from irrational lengthening, or shortening in hiatus.[15]

The hexameter was the metre selected and the illustrations were drawn from Homer and Virgil, with whom the reading course would begin. In dividing the line up into feet, the teacher would emphasize the verse-ictus by drumming with his fingers or stamping with his foot;[16] he would indicate elisions, and would mark the caesura. He would present the verse-line in the way that a late grammarian does with *Arma virumque cano* ..., which, for scansional purposes, takes the odd appearance of *Armavi rumqueca notro*...[17] But here the question arose — and Quintilian clearly thought it of importance — as to the exact point at which a syllable should be marked off; should a boy divide *virum* into *vi-rum* or *vir-um*, and *cano* into *ca-no* or *can-o*? This whole matter of what is termed 'syllabification' was discussed more fully later as part of the teaching of spelling, but the gist of it was given at this point.[18] The general rule was that division should be made after a vowel or diphthong, except in words with a prepositional prefix, which was kept separate. Modern studies have shown that in both Greek and Latin inscriptions, when there was only room for part of a word at the end of a line, there was a very considerable degree of consistency in observing this rule.[19] But there was one important proviso, given by the later Latin grammarians but pretty certainly accepted in our period, that no syllable should begin with any combination of consonants which could not in themselves form the beginning of a Latin word.[20] Even here, however, there appears to have been some dispute as to whether the letter *s*, when followed by one or more consonants, should be attached to the preceding syllable or not.[21] Double consonants, of course, were always divided, because they could not begin a word.

At this point, some teachers may have gone on to discuss the iambic trimeter, which was also of basic importance. Some influential theorists, indeed, including Varro and Caesius Bassus, argued that, with one or two exceptions, all other metres were derived, by addition, subtraction, substitution or transposition, from the hexameter or the trimeter.[22] Horace's description of the iambic line reads almost like a poeticized version of a schoolroom lesson: 'A long syllable following a short is called an iambus, a quick-moving foot ... in order to reach the ears with more slowness and weight, it admitted the steady spondee to share its ancient rights ... but without being so obliging as to yield up the second and fourth place',[23] or, he might have added, the sixth. Further metrical instruction must have followed later, for by the time boys began to read the poets, Quintilian expected them to identify the metrical feet in the various types of verse.[24] But he also required them to parse, so the next topic was the very important one of the parts of speech, which formed the hard core of grammatical teaching.

There was not, during our period, any general agreement regarding the classification of the parts of speech, and teaching, therefore, could not have been entirely uniform. There had existed, from Hellenistic times, two main schools of thought, that of grammarians who followed the Alexandrian tradition, and that of philosophers, among whom the Stoics were the most authoritative. In the Alexandrian scheme, which, transmitted evidently by Aristarchus,[25] is set forth in the manual of his pupil Dionysius Thrax, there are eight parts, as follows: (1) Noun, (2) Verb, (3) Participle, (4) Article, (5) Pronoun, (6) Preposition, (7) Adverb, (8) Conjunction. The apparent omission of the Adjective is due to the fact that this was never given separate status in antiquity, but was classified as a form of the Noun, with which it was especially associated. In Latin, this system, with one modification, formed the basis of the *Grammar* of Remmius Palaemon, which was a standard textbook by the time of Juvenal.[26] Here, as Latin has no Article, this part disappears, but the Interjection is included, so the number remains at eight.[27] In Greek, the methodical manual of Dionysius Thrax, despite its amazingly long survival in the schools, has, as a teaching instrument, some serious deficiencies, and would require a good deal of supplementation. For instance, when dealing with prepositions, the author lists eighteen of them, and divides them into monosyllabic and dissyllabic, but says not a word about the cases which they may govern![28] In Latin, the treatment of the preposition in Palaemon's work was much more satisfactory.[29] Unfortunately, although this textbook became an important source for later grammarians, there is only a very limited amount which can now be confidently attributed to it.[30]

A different form of classification, which is of Greek origin and easily reconcilable with the Alexandrian system, appears in three places in Varro's *De Lingua Latina*.[31] Here the basic division is between types of word which are 'declinable' and those which are not. His word 'declinable' covers changes in word-termination both in declension of nouns and conjugation of verbs, and also changes made by degrees of comparison in adverbs. As 'indeclinable', he merely instances such words as *vix* and *mox*, but obviously conjunctions and prepositions would fall within this group. His declinable words fall into four classes, as follows: (1) words which have case-inflections, but no tense-forms (his instances, *docilis facilis*, are adjectives, but nouns and pronouns, of course, meet these requirements), (2) words which have tense-forms, but no case-inflections (*docet, facit*, i.e. verbs), (3) words which have both case-inflections and tense-forms (*docens, faciens*, i.e. participles), and (4) words which have neither (he instances *docte, facete*, i.e. adverbs admitting degrees of comparison).

The Stoics, from Chrysippus onwards, went their own way. Their classification did not remain entirely static, but they made less major categories than the Alexandrians, despite the fact that they introduced one curious distinction, which remained characteristic of their doctrine, in maintaining that the common noun and the proper noun were separate parts of speech. Their standard classification as given by Diogenes of Babylon (second century B.C.) was fivefold:[32] (1) common noun,

(2) proper noun, (3) verb, (4) conjunction, (5) article and pronoun, classed together as 'joints' (*arthra*). Under this scheme, participles went along with nouns, adverbs with verbs (though Diogenes' pupil, Antipater of Tarsus, made them a separate category), and prepositions with conjunctions. In the long run, however, although the Stoics made important contributions to grammatical studies, it was the eight-part classification which prevailed.

Teaching began with the noun. Here the listing of the cases was quite different from that of modern times. The standard order, as given by Dionysius Thrax and seen in school-exercises, was nominative, genitive, dative, accusative, vocative, though it is not certain that the Stoics included the vocative in their list.[33] The nominative was the 'upright' case, the rest 'oblique'. In this and all other respects it was the Greeks who invented the terminology of grammar, and the Romans translated it as faithfully as they could. Their rendering, however, of the Greek name for the fourth case as *accusativus* was notably infelicitous.[34] In Latin, a name had also to be invented for the ablative, which was at first called 'the sixth case', or 'the Latin case', before it settled down as *ablativus*;[35] but the Romans were by no means agreed that the term satisfactorily covered all the various ways in which the case was used, and even considered the need for a seventh case.[36]

In dealing with the noun, the determination of gender was of primary importance.[37] If the meaning of a word gave no sure indication of its gender, how was a boy to decide whether it was masculine, feminine or neuter? Dionysius Thrax (at the end of his section on the letters) gives the rule that masculine nouns end in the consonants ν, ξ, ρ, s, or ψ, feminine nouns in the vowels a (long or short), η and ω, though they might also end in these same consonants, (giving eight possibilities in all), and neuter nouns ended either in the vowels a, ι, υ or the consonants ν, ρ, s. A similar approach, applied to Latin, is found in some of the late grammarians. This method, though it had its value, had also (like any other method of determination) its limitations, in that there was overlapping, and several letters appeared in more than one gender. The development of the process of analogy (a subject of fundamental importance, which will be discussed later)[38] drew attention rather to the final syllable than the final letter. But the terminations in themselves were often not a safe guide; for instance, Latin words ending in -*us*, though predominantly masculine, were sometimes feminine or neuter. There was, however, a third method applicable only to Latin, which was mentioned by Varro and Quintilian, and would be known in the Roman schools.[39] It consisted in one simple rule: if you wish to know the correct gender of a noun, consider the form which it takes in the diminutive, which will end in *us, a* or *um*, and will thus give the answer. For example, a 'small branch' is *ramusculus*, so *ramus* is masculine, a 'small tree' is *arbuscula,* so *arbor* is feminine, a 'small gift' is *munusculum,* so *munus* is neuter, and so on. Even the diligent Latin grammarians could not find many exceptions to this rule — such as the instance that 'a small frog' was *ranunculus,* but *rana* was feminine. Admittedly, some nouns, notably abstracts, did not form diminutives, though those in *-io* often did, as *quaestio, quaestiuncula, ratio, ratiuncula.* But, even allowing for this, the method of determination would have been useful to Roman boys, for diminutives were not only numerous, but of the very essence of colloquial speech, and would be, therefore, usually familiar to them.

Apart from his notes on gender, Dionysius Thrax includes brief sections on number and case, but the substance of his treatment of the noun is mainly concerned with the classification of its types and forms. But the most surprising omission is the total lack of any information on declension. Evidently the three declensions of the Greek noun (the third of which has to carry a large variety of types anyway) had not yet been formally classified. But this does not mean that individual patterns had not been recognized, in view of the progress of studies in analogy. The 'canons of the nouns' (i.e. paradigms), of which Apollonius Dyscolus speaks in the second century,[40] must have become quite familiar within our period, though it is curious that the supplements to Dionysius Thrax do not give any examples of them. But there is a good illustration of the teaching of declension in a school-exercise on waxed tablets from Graeco-Roman Egypt, in which an adjective together with a noun in each of the three genders is set out in full.[41]

In Latin, we are on firmer ground, for already, before the end of the Republic, the way towards a classification of the five declensions had been well prepared by an ingenious method known to, and perhaps devised by, Varro.[42] In studying the Latin noun, Varro focused his attention on the terminal letter of the ablative, the purely Latin case, and noted how the five vowels recurred in that position. Taking them in order, he was able to distinguish between nouns which ended in the ablative with A (type *terra*), with E (type *lance*), with I (type *clavi*), with O (type *caelo*), or with U (type *versu*). Eventually, by a slight rearrangement, the A-terminations became the first declension, the O-terminations the second, the E and I-terminations the third, and the U-terminations the fourth. Varro does not appear to have taken the quantity of the final E into consideration; if he had distinguished the long from the short E, he would have been able to identify the fifth declension as well. But Latin grammar was certainly taking shape.

There was, however, one perennial problem which arose in Latin, and this concerned the declension of Greek nouns (especially proper names) which had been taken over — should they be declined throughout as though they were still Greek, or should their forms be thoroughly

Latinized? Or should either the Greek or the Latin termination be accepted in various cases? Should the accusative of *Hector*, for instance, be *Hectorem* or *Hectora*? On such questions, opinions varied, and room was left for compromise.[43]

Turning next to the treatment by Dionysius Thrax of the verb, we find it more satisfactory than his account of the noun, in that he not only has sections on voice, mood, number, person and tense, but also includes classifications of the regular conjugations, in which the *tertia* essential groupings are already clearly defined.[44] He first deals with verbs ending in ω, and subdivides them into the uncontracted and the contracted, or, as he calls them, the 'barytone' (where the final ω is unaccented) and the 'circumflexed'. With the former, he takes consonant-stems first, and distinguishes five types according as the final ω is preceded by (1)π, β, φ, or $\pi\tau$ (2)γ, κ, χ or $\kappa\tau$ (3)$\sigma\sigma$ or ζ (4)δ, θ, or τ, and (5)λ, μ, ν or ρ, which is fairly close to the division in modern grammars into labials, palatals, dentals, and liquids and nasals. The vowel-stem, which is taken first in modern grammars, he mentions next. The contracted verbs are next exemplified by three types, and finally the verbs in $\mu\iota$ by four types. Beyond this he does not go, and says nothing about the formation of tenses, the use of the augment, the two forms of aorist, or reduplication in the perfect, but the Stoics had systematized the tenses, and schoolboys must have learnt these things. School tablets of imperial date afford a few interesting examples of boys who mastered their Greek verbs, like one who wrote out all the forms of the optative of *niko*, and another who conscientiously listed his verbs according to the case which they governed;[45] but there were some who floundered, like the confused boy who wrote out the aorist passive of *grapho* beginning *egegraphthen*.[46] But, at any period, the manual of Dionysius Thrax must have needed a great deal of supplementation here by teachers, as the later addition of a very full paradigm of *tupto* shows.[47]

Irregular verbs in both Greek and Latin must have been a constant source of joy to anomalists, but in Latin it was again Varro who succeeded in establishing a working system for the conjugation of regular verbs.[48] He was aware that analogy was not a satisfactory method if applied to the first person singular of the present indicative; for example, *dolo* and *colo* might look entirely comparable, but one had only to go a step further, and the second person *dolas, colis*, showed that they did not belong together. But comparison of the second person singular was a very useful test indeed, and it enabled Varro to classify separately verbs in which it ended in *-as*, verbs in which it ended in *-es*, and verbs in which it ended in (short) *-is*. His examples were *meo, meas, neo nes*, and *ruo ruis*. Whether he also distinguished the long *-is* terminations is not quite certain.[49] Later grammarians often took our third and fourth conjugations together, as parts of a third conjugation (*tertia correpta* and *tertia producta*). By the end of the Republic, then, if not before, the lines for teaching the Latin regular verb were already firmly laid.

Speaking generally of the declension of nouns, Varro remarked that 'when you have learned the method of declining one noun, you can apply it to an indefinite number of nouns', and added that a newcomer who joined a large household of slaves, being once told what the names of all of them were, in the nominative case, was able to use those names correctly in the oblique cases as well.[50] In the same way, children would, in the first place, pick up the various inflections by ear; only when they began to receive grammar lessons would they see how they could be set out in standard patterns. Varro also observed how very orderly in lay-out were the regular declensions and conjugations in Latin. In presenting the paradigm of the adjective *albus*, he set the six cases out horizontally (*ordo transversus*), though not in the modern order, and the three genders vertically (*ordo derectus*), singular and plural, producing a square of six words by six. This kind of tabulation he called a *forma*, or *formula*, and he compared the appearance to that of the pieces on a gaming-board.[51] Similarly, with the indicative of regular verbs, he set out horizontally the tense-forms, again six of them, in two triads, according as the action was 'incomplete' (imperfect, present, future), or 'complete' (pluperfect, perfect, future perfect).[52] By setting out vertically the first, second and third persons, singular and plural, he would again have made a square of six words by six. Varro even composed a work entitled *On the Patterns of Verbs*.[53] Greek, on the other hand, with its five cases and its addition of dual forms, was much less amenable to geometrical design.

Quintilian considered that learning the regular declensions and conjugations (including, of course, voices and moods) was 'almost elementary-school work', though his 'almost' suggests that it might need continuing at the grammar school.[54] At this stage, he himself expected that pupils would be dealing with features which did not show conformity with the general rules, such as verbs which were defective, or changed entirely in the perfect tense, or had an impersonal use, and participles which, though passive in form, were active in meaning, such as *pransus*.[55] There were plenty of irregularities to discuss in Latin, and even more in Greek. But Quintilian did insist on the importance of this initial grammatical training, and strongly criticized contemporary teachers who sought to curtail it.[56]

Such, then, was the content of the first part of the course in grammar, much of which could be learnt by rule of thumb. In the second part, to which we may now turn, it was by no means so easy for the teacher to be factual and dogmatic, for in pronunciation, spelling and the determination of correct word-forms, fashions changed, standards and opinions differed, and there was constant room for debate.

CHAPTER XV

The Grammatical syllabus (*continued*)

(II) Correctness in speech and writing

From the time of the early Greek sophists, Protagoras and Prodicus, the teaching of the correct use of language had been regarded as an indispensable part of education.[1] It had strong support from the philosophers, for both Peripatetics and Stoics were agreed in recognizing pure Greek (*Hellenismos*) to be the very fountain-head of good style.[2] In the Hellenistic period, the need for concentration on this aspect of speech and writing became very much more pressing. Although there always remained the fact that Greek was spoken in different dialects, and what was good Greek in one might not be good Greek in another,[3] yet, as a result of the wider mingling of peoples after the conquests of Alexander, it was felt that the language itself was in danger of becoming debased by an admixture of foreign elements. Thus faults of expression, known as 'barbarisms' and 'solecisms' were more closely analysed, and classified in detail. Under Stoic influence, it became accepted that a barbarism was a fault in the use of a single word, and a solecism was one arising in words in conjunction, that is, an error of syntax.[4] In Greek, the brief resumé of a grammatical manual of the Stoic Diogenes of Babylon shows that he defined them both, and evidently discussed them with examples.[5] In Latin, material illustrating the rules of correctness was being used in grammatical teaching in the late Republic, for the author of the *Rhetorica ad Herennium* proposed to publish a manual of grammar, in which barbarisms would be discussed, and Cicero spoke of 'the precepts of Latinity, which are communicated in the education of boys'.[6] The subject involved not only diction and grammatical construction, but pronunciation and spelling, in all of which the teacher concentrated in the first instance on explaining types of error. The study of correctness in word-forms, particularly in connection with declension, was a more technical matter, and involved understanding of the various criteria which might be applied. This, and the discussion of alternative possibilities in spelling, formed the more advanced part of the course. A beginning, then, was made with barbarisms.

The first and most obvious type of barbarism consisted in the use of a word or words belonging to a foreign language, which, not having won general acceptance, sounded strange to Roman ears, or looked strange to Roman eyes.[7] Here the difficulty was that the Latin language, like any other, did not remain static, but was constantly acquiring and adopting new words, not only from Greek, but also from other countries with which the Romans were regularly brought into contact by trade, military service and travel. For instance, although Roman visitors to Gaul heard there many words which were quite unfamiliar to them,[8] some words of Gallic origin were in common use at Rome. The names of several types of wheeled vehicles, which the Gauls supplied to Rome (such as *raeda, essedum, petorritum*), acquired, as it were, the Roman citizenship.[9] But when Catullus spoke of a wagon-box as a *ploxenum*, he was using a little-known word from the Po Valley, which might well have been classed as a barbarism.[10] It depended whether one considered a word to be 'accepted' (*receptum*) or not, and this meant accepted at Rome, which set the standard for Latin as did Athens for Greek. But the term 'barbarism' was a strong expression, and implied something like 'outlandish', and there were many words in use in Italy, especially in country districts, which, if heard in Rome, might have been more mildly criticized as 'rustic'.[11] Between 'rusticity' and 'barbarism' it was not always easy to draw the line.

Much more common than such oddities of diction were faults connected with spelling and pronunciation. In Quintilian's day, there existed published collections of standard errors, to which inexperienced teachers might turn for their examples, though Quintilian thought that a teacher of any merit would supplement them with his own.[12] In the treatment of errors of spelling, it was the common practice to classify them by that curious mathematical formula which we find in a number of contexts in grammatical teaching, that is, according as they arose from addition, subtraction, substitution, or transposition, of letters or syllables.[13] It is rather as though, in English, one should classify such common misspellings as 'beautifull', 'accomodation', 'bicicle', and 'sieze' on that basis. The procedure was rather typical of the analytical mind of the ancient grammarian.

Particularly important were errors of pronunciation. Here bad habits of speech, which it was the duty of the grammarian to correct, often arose from the upbringing, or environment, of his pupils. Whether for good or ill, the influence of the family on young children was strong, and errors acquired by imitation of the mother or father might have been derived by them from their own parents, especially in families where there was no tradition of culture. Cicero remarked that 'it is of great importance whom each child listens to daily at home, and with whom he speaks from boyhood', and made Crassus praise the pure speech of Laelia, observing that 'that must have been how her father, and her ancestors spoke';[14] but parents often did not set so good an example. Cicero also makes particular mention in this connection of the 'pedagogues' — who, as we have seen, were often of Greek origin. The problem of checking the possible bad influence of both 'pedagogues' and nurses, and of the slave-children who grew up within the family, was one which much concerned Quintilian,[15] as it did others of his generation. There was the further disadvantage that even children accustomed to speak Greek properly from an early age might transfer to their Latin some of the characteristics of a foreign tongue.[16]

There was in Roman times a classification of the study of pronunciation, already found in Varro, into (1) vowel-quantity, (2) accent, and (3) aspiration.[17] This lies at the base of the treatment of barbarism in pronunciation as we see it in Quintilian and later grammarians,[18] and shows that the teacher would have selected examples to indicate that mistakes occurred because a speaker pronounced a vowel short instead of long, or vice versa, or misplaced the accent, or wrongly omitted or added the aspirate. With regard to the first of these topics, the chief trouble which schoolmasters foresaw was that boys would soon be reading poetry, in which there was no guarantee that the writer would always observe the quantity established in normal usage. The correct sound was long in the middle syllable of *illius, unius*, but could be found short in verse, and conversely, the first syllable of *Italia*, which was short, had to be lengthened to suit the hexameter.[19] Such divergencies, when they occurred in the poets, would have to be excused on the grounds of poetic licence, and were euphemistically labelled as 'metaplasms', or 'adaptations'. The main thing was that boys should not be misled into imitating them in their everyday speech.

On errors arising from incorrect accentuation, Quintilian is disappointingly brief, and his remarks are not always easy to evaluate.[20] We have to accept the fact that, like the Latin grammarians in general, he speaks of the Latin accent in terms of acute, grave and circumflex, which imply variations of pitch, whereas there are strong arguments in favour of the view that the Latin accent was predominantly one of stress. Even though stress and pitch are not entirely mutually exclusive, it remains something of a puzzle as to whether there really were words in Latin which were pronounced with the rising-falling tone signified by a circumflex accent (e.g. *Rôma, mêta*).[21] It may be considered that Roman grammarians, knowing no other treatment of accentuation except that which they inherited from the Greeks, simply misapplied it to Latin.[22] Whatever the truth in this long-debated question, the grammarian gave his pupils what we call the 'Penultimate Law', that is that, in polysyllables, if the penultimate is long it bears the accent, but if it is short the accent is on the antepenultimate. Quintilian's examples of error, which all involve proper names, exemplify accentuation of the wrong syllable. What is interesting is that the incorrect accentuation is clearly caused by imitation of Greek. For example, in Greek, *Kámillos* had an acute accent on the first syllable, but in Latin the (stress) accent was on the penultimate, *Camíllus*, and anyone who said *Cámillus* was committing a barbarism. Similarly, in Greek, *Kéthegos* had an acute accent on the first syllable, but in Latin, it was accented *Cethégus* (though Quintilian calls the accent here a circumflex). These are Roman names, but it was with the Greek names that the difficulty more often arose. Here Quintilian says that, whereas in his own youth he was advised by scholars to pronounce *Atreus* with the accent on the first syllable (which would be the normal Latin stress), people were now making the mistake of adopting the Greek accentuation, and saying *Atreús*, as also with similar types of name. In short, it does seem that the constant use of Greek in conversation, and the presence of so many Greeks in Rome, was having a bad effect on the pronunciation of Latin. Apart from this, the teacher would mention the fact that in some cases the natural word-accent was shifted by the addition of an enclytic, so that, for instance, whereas one would normally say *vírum*, the addition of *que* would cause one to say *virúmque*. He would also, like Quintilian, make the further point that the exigencies of metre caused alterations of accent in words involving plosive-liquid combinations, such as *vólucres*. Normally, Quintilian says, one would pronounce this with the accent on the first syllable, but at the end of a hexameter, such as *pictaeque volúcres*, the accent would be placed on the second.[23]

Considerable attention was paid to the use and misuse of the aspirate. The most obvious fault here was the careless dropping of an initial *h*, and certainly grammarians would have been as annoyed as they were in St Augustine's day at those who said *omines* instead of *homines*.[24] The opposite fault, that of adding an aspirate where it was totally out of place, as in Arrius' *hinsidias* ('hambush') for *insidias* in Catullus' famous poem, was probably far less common. But most cases were not quite so clear-cut, for not only did habits of speech change but there were words about which the grammarians themselves were in dispute. For instance, the choice between *harena* and *arena* was not immediately obvious, and, in the last resort, the grammarian had to rely on his own ideas of etymology. At this stage, then, he would probably simply tell his pupils what, in his view, was right and what was wrong.

One problem, however, is specially mentioned by Quintilian in connection with barbarism, and this arose in connection with the aspiration of consonants.[25] Aspirated consonants were not native to Latin, and for a considerable time the Romans were not particularly concerned to represent faithfully the Greek sounds of θ, ϕ, and X in the Latinized forms of Greek names and loan-words. But from the latter part of the second century onwards, more attention began to be paid in educated circles to the correct enunciation of these sounds, though, even in Quintilian's day, an ignorant person might still pronounce *Amphion* as *Ampion*.[26] Towards the end of the Republic, mainly under Greek influence, the movement towards consonantal aspiration had gone so far as to affect not only words thought, rightly or wrongly, to be derived from Greek, but also words known to be of Latin origin. But authorities differed as to how far this should be allowed to go. Cicero, the orator, judged by ear, and tells us how he eventually came to accept *triumphus* for *triumpus*, and *pulcher* for *pulcer*, though he objected to saying *sepulchrum* for *sepulcrum*.[27] Varro, the antiquarian, favoured more strongly the ancient forms.[28] But Cicero would certainly not have been persuaded to speak, like some of his contemporaries, of *chorona*, or *lachrima*, still less of *praecho*, or *chenturio*. Thus Roman schoolboys needed to be advised not only how they should reproduce aspirated consonants in reading Greek aloud, but to what extent they should use them in reading Latin.

From barbarism, the teacher now proceeded to solecism, which resulted when words were wrongly used in conjunction, as when the gender of an adjective did not agree with that of its noun, or there was some other syntactical error.[29] Interesting evidence has survived of Cicero's concern over such matters, and shows that he was as strict with himself as he was with his son Marcus. Marcus once wrote to his father, saying, 'I have despatched two letters', and used the expression *direxi litteras duas*, which a modern schoolboy (probably rightly) might think good enough Latin to pass O-level. But he was forthwith reprimanded by Cicero senior for bad Latinity, for *duas litteras* could only mean 'two letters of the alphabet'; when *litterae* referred to correspondence, it was used only in the plural form, and with words which had a different meaning in the plural from the singular (e.g. *castrum, castra*), or existed only as a plural (e.g. *nuptiae*), the distributive numeral was used, and what Marcus should have written was *binas litteras*.[30] But even Cicero himself occasionally had some troubled moments in connection with possible solecisms. On one occasion, he had written, in a letter to Atticus, *in Piraea* for 'to the Piraeus' and evidently Atticus had queried it.[31] Cicero was concerned about having used the preposition *in*. Its correctness depended on the decision whether 'Piraeus' was the name of a town or not; if it was, he had been guilty of a solecism; if not, his Latin was impeccable. So he consulted the learned tutor, Dionysius, and his friend Nicias (the grammarian Curtius Nicias) and they said they did not think it was a town. Not content with this assurance, Cicero made some investigations of his own, and his procedure is interesting because it is exactly what a *grammaticus* would normally have done. He looked up some authorities. First, he found that the early comedy-writer, Caecilius, had written *in Piraeum*; but this was not a satisfactory guarantee, for Caecilius was known to be a 'bad Latinist'. Much more convincing was Terence, who had written not only *coimus in Piraeum*, but also *e Sunio* (though there was a settlement on Cape Sunium);[32] and Terence's Latin he accepted as beyond reproach. Even so, Cicero concludes: 'You are a scholar (*grammaticus es*), and if you will solve this problem for me, you will save me a deal of trouble'. If, then, such matters of detail in expression could be taken so seriously even in private correspondence, one may well imagine the care bestowed upon them by professional teachers.

There are one or two very close parallels to this instance from Cicero in Quintilian's discussion of solecisms, in which he certainly had school-teaching in mind. In his day, grammarians applied to solecisms the same classification which they applied to barbarisms, that is, they analysed them according as they arose from faulty addition, or subtraction, or transposition, or substitution. One of Quintilian's examples of faulty additions is *in Alexandriam* for 'to Alexandria', and of faulty subtractions *Aegypto* for *ex Aegypto*.[33] The use of *enim* or *autem* to begin a sentence is an example of faulty transposition; *igitur* in that position was possible, though very little favoured by Cicero. The greatest number of solecisms, however, could, under this system, have been classified as due to wrong substitution. It was not merely the use of a wrong part of speech (e.g. noun instead of verb), but occurred frequently when a wrong voice, mood, tense, person, case, number or gender was used. Solecisms could occur in any of the parts of speech.[34] For instance, there might be incorrect use of adverbs of place. In Latin, it was correct to use *intro* only if movement was implied, and *intus* if it was not, whereas in English 'inside' serves both purposes. To say *eo intus*, 'I go inside' was a solecism for *eo intro*, and so was *intro sum*, 'I am inside' for *intus sum*. This is from Quintilian, but the interesting point is that this very example was given by Lucilius, and the treatment of solecisms by the Roman grammarians must have stemmed very largely from the examples given by the satirist long before.[35] Not only did Lucilius speak of 'the hundred varieties of solecism and their names', but he actually gave examples of them, as we know from the late grammarian Pompeius, who possessed a text of Lucilius in full.[36] The whole subject of solecism, on which there is also a good deal of information in Greek (particularly in Lucian and Sextus Empiricus)[37] should incline us to reconsider the position of syntax in ancient grammatical teaching. It is commonly said that, in Greek, systematic treatment of syntax, being totally lacking in Dionysius Thrax, is first found in Apollonius Dyscolus (second century), and that, in Latin, it is not found until Priscian. Of *positive* teaching of rules that may be true, but surely the scores of examples of different kinds of solecism given by the grammarians throughout our period must have covered, in a *negative* (but not ineffective) way, a wide area of the subject. Whenever a mistake was made, it broke some rule of sequence or agreement, and the pupil, therefore, had to be told what the rule was which was broken. Moreover, the poets, from Homer onwards, frequently did not observe the rules — for instance, Homer uses a plural instead of a singular verb after a neuter plural,[38] and both Chrysippus and Zoilus found 'solecisms' in him.[39] Consequently, even though teachers said that one should call such cases 'figures' (*schemata*),[40] they must thereby have drawn attention to many of the standard rules.

Up to this point, the *grammaticus* had concentrated on illustrating many types of definite error in speech or writing. The purpose of the next part of his course was to explain to his pupils the kinds of test, or criteria, which they might apply in order to determine what was correct in doubtful cases, where alternative word-forms, or forms of declension or conjugation, existed. One of the most important tests was that of analogy, but, having shown what analogy meant, the teacher had to indicate how far one should be prepared to go in utilizing it, especially if it conflicted with other criteria, such as usage. Here the difficulty was that the whole subject of the application of analogy in arriving at 'correct' forms had been, from the second century onwards, first in Greek and then in Latin, an area of considerable dissension; the *grammaticus*, who might himself hold strong views one way or another, had to give his pupils the best guidance he could without involving them too much in the jungle of scholarly controversy.[41]

The formulation of the doctrine of analogy was the work of the great scholars of Alexandria.[42] It was not at first a controversial subject, but an attempt to systematize the Greek language, so far as possible, by establishing that there were certain patterns of inflection, arrived at by grouping and comparing many words which behaved alike. 'Likeness' and 'regularity' were the key-words of the analogists, and formed the very foundation of what we call the regular declensions and conjugations.[43] But there was a good deal left over, and it was often necessary to decide whether a word should be referred to one pattern or another. In order to make a workable system, it was necessary to draw up a list of pre-conditions for comparability, for it was no use attempting to relate words to a particular category unless they bore certain marked features of similarity at the outset. Even then, it was often a case of trial and error. Aristophanes of Byzantium, according to a late authority,[44] maintained that the following controlling factors, or prerequisites, must be present before any two Greek nouns could be compared: they must be (1) of the same gender, (2) of the same case, (3) have the same termination (an important feature in all subsequent discussion, though some later grammarians found it insufficient), (4) have the same number of syllables (this requirement was later often dropped), and (5) bear the same accent. If all these prerequisites were present in the two compared examples, e.g. two nouns in the nominative case, and one of them formed its genitive in a certain way, then it could be deduced that the other should also form its genitive in the same way, and they should decline alike throughout. Subsequent theorists had to modify and extend their prerequisites[45] (e.g. that compared words must belong to the same species), but the underlying basis of the whole process was a conviction that language maintained a sort of mathematical correspondence of parts, which was what the word analogy meant.

Theorists of the Stoic school had, on the other hand, always taken a radically different view of language, which they regarded as a natural growth, not as something which could be shown to conform to an artificial scheme of analysis. They pointed to irregularities in declension, conjugation and word behaviour generally, which, they argued, were so numerous as to undermine the validity of analogy as a determinant in doubtful cases. One must take language as one found it, and usage was the best criterion. It was this approach which led to the long-remembered dispute between Crates of Mallos, an ardent disciple of the Porch, and Aristarchus, the leading light of Alexandria,[46] but controversy long persisted, and found its way into Latin grammatical studies. Latin responded, on the whole, very much better than Greek to the application of system, and Antonius Gnipho, Staberius Eros (author of a work on *proportio*, a Latin term which meant the same as *analogia*), and Julius Caesar were all leading analogists — though with differing degrees of judgment. Varro, whilst recognizing the force of many anomalist objections, was convinced that analogy, applied within carefully prescribed conditions, was of fundamental value as a criterion in Latin,[47] and it is from Latin that our examples will be taken.

One of the most celebrated examples with which anomalists plagued their opponents, was that of *lupus*, 'wolf', and *lepus*, 'hare', for these two nominatives were so similar that they seemed likely to fulfil any prerequisite which the analogists could devise — yet *lupus* formed its genitive *lupi* and *lepus* formed it *leporis* — how then could one say that analogy was a valid criterion? The hard-pressed analogist came up with the reply that the two words were not really comparable at the outset, for they did not exactly correspond in gender; whereas *lupus* was undoubtedly a male wolf, *lepus* might be either a male or female hare — grammatically speaking, the word was epicene. But even this awkward point was combated, for it was discovered, on investigation, that some early Latin writers had occasionally used *lupus* when they meant 'she-wolf' so this word, too, was epicene, and the two were comparable after all![48] It was really a triumph for the anomalists, but only when the declensions were sorted out did *lepus* eventually escape from the uncomfortable proximity of *lupus*, which was safely boxed up in the second declension, whilst *lepus* found more congenial quarters in the third. But there were many masculine nouns ending in -*us* which looked alike in the nominative but declined differently, such as *fusus*, genitive *fusi*, and *lusus*, genitive *lusus*.[49] Similarly, there was the anomaly of *dies* and *quies*, which looked as though they were born for one another, yet *dies* formed its genitive *diei*, and *quies* gave *quietis*. Even when the regular declensions were determined, there remained a very considerable number of words in which the forms were debatable. For example, whilst *domus* might be declined throughout on the analogy of *anus* and *manus*, there was strong authority for the forms *domo, domos*, and *domorum*.[50] One might argue that the genitive of *senatus* should be *senatūs*, or that it should be *senati*, for both forms were found.[51] The principle of analogy might likewise be applied — and contested — in the conjugation of verbs.

There was, however, one aspect of the subject which sharpened controversy. If both of two alternative forms could be shown to be sanctioned by usage, decision was a matter of personal choice, and there was no need for acrimony. But there were some scholars who were so devoted to analogy (which, in Quintilian's phrase, they regarded as 'sent down from Heaven' for the regulation of language)[52] that they proposed to bring into circulation forms which had little sanction in usage, or even went directly against it, but which they claimed as grammatically proper. For instance, although in analogy it was usual to start from the form of the nominative case, which was called the 'first position', it was also perfectly legitimate to start from an oblique case, and then consider the nominative in relation to it.[53] But some analogists went so far as to propose to alter an established nominative form to bring it into accord with the genitive, and argued that one should say *ebor* and *robor*, not *ebur* and *robur*, because the genitives were *eboris, roboris*, and in cases like *sulpur, sulpuris*, and *guttur, gutturis*, the vowel remained consistent. Antonius Gnipho was not much better, and, as Quintilian saw, showed equal ignorance of morphology when he argued that, accepting *ebur* and *robur*, one should decline *eburis* and *roburis*.[54] Such arbitrary procedures naturally aroused opposition, and only served to strengthen the hands of those who regarded usage as the ultimate sanction. Cicero, unlike Caesar, had given his powerful support to usage (*consuetudo*),[55] and Quintilian declared that it was 'the most certain law of speech'.[56] In his view, as in Varro's, analogy was not a law in itself, but a useful principle which often, in fact, accorded with and derived strength from usage. But it should not be pressed too far, for 'it is one thing to speak grammatically, and another thing to speak Latin'.[57] In the schoolroom, then, teaching of this part of the subject would vary according to the views of the schoolmaster, but the material for lessons would be such as we find in Quintilian. An important earlier contribution to the study of debatable word-forms was the *Dubius Sermo* of the elder Pliny.[58]

Usage was obviously a major criterion, but it was not something static, and there was the problem of defining it. There was good usage and bad usage, present usage and past usage, and each teacher had to explain what he meant by the term, and exactly what his attitude was. If the term implied contemporary habits of speech, then any good scholar or teacher would have had to admit that there were many improper features in current practice.[59] Caesar was praised in his day because he made a moderate use of analogy to remove faulty and corrupt tendencies, and his own prose style was a model of correctness.[60] The grammarian Sisenna, on the other hand, was more of an extremist, and in emending common usage tried to introduce new forms which never won general acceptance.[61] The best solution was to define usage, as did Quintilian, [62] as the consensus of educated people as expressed in their speech, and with this view Cicero would have concurred. But, although this was a sound basis in general, even educated people did not always speak uniformly. For example, there were variant genitive plural terminations in -*orum* and -*um*: should one say *deorum* or *deum*? Cicero thought either permissible, but, whereas the analogists wished to make -*orum* the rule for all second declension nouns, he, like the anomalists, insisted that such established forms as *triumvirum, sestertium, nummum* could not be jettisoned.[63] There was similar controversy over such syncopated verbal forms as -*asse* for -*avisse*, -*isse* for -*ivisse*, in the perfect infinitive, and -*ere* for -*erunt* in the perfect indicative.[64] Here again, the analogists wished to insist on the full form, but Cicero and Quintilian agreed that such shortenings had the sanction of usage, and might be supported on grounds of euphony.[65]

In the prevailing uncertainty, it seemed best to establish a further criterion in authority (*auctoritas*), to which, said the grammarians, everyone turns in the last resort when all else fails.[66] But the question was — whose authority? It had to be literary authority, and inevitably meant, to a considerable degree, reference back to the past. But how far back into the past should one go? And could any great writer, poet or prose author, be called in evidence? It depended on how much of an archaist one was prepared to be. Cicero, as we saw, thought highly of the Latin of Terence, and so did Caesar.[67] But not everyone would have gone so far as to add 'antiquity' (*vetustas*) in general to the list of accepted criteria, as does Quintilian.[68] Indeed, even the most eminent prose writers had not been immune from criticism. There were Greek grammarians who found fault with the language of Thucydides, Plato and Demosthenes,[69] and, in Latin, even Cicero was attacked by such critics as Asinius Gallus and Largius Licinus.[70] The best judges were more balanced and discriminating. Cicero himself referred back to orators such as Scipio and Laelius because theirs was an age of 'good usage' (*bona consuetudo*), and Quintilian took as models not only Cicero but many other Republican and Augustan orators, without, however, unreservedly accepting their evidence.[71] But he was never more pleased than when he could show that an expression of his, which was criticized, had not only the authority of good prose writers but was also supported by analogy.[72] We may deduce, in short, that all these varying interpretations of Latinity must have found their way into the teaching in schools, and, in fact, the main criteria are already found in Varro.[73]

Finally, there was one test of correctness, namely etymology, which was ranked by Quintilian together with analogy, because both were based on rational deduction (*ratio*) rather than on some external standard. But it deserves to be mentioned last because it was, in practice, often the least reliable of all the criteria which were proposed. In itself, the study of word-derivation was a subject well calculated to arouse the interest of schoolboys, and there were many words of which the source was not in doubt. Quintilian wished the discussion of the origins of proper names (so often derived from occupation, or appearance) to be introduced at a much earlier stage, and now to be extended to those of localities, races and cities.[74] A great deal of work had been done in the whole field of etymology, in Greek by both Alexandrians and Stoics, and in Latin, especially, by Varro.[75] Roman grammarians had begun by using it to determine the origin and meaning of words found in early Latin, and had then extended it to words in common use. But in actual fact the results did not anything like match the efforts expended. Even Varro was pretty well as often wrong as he was right. The methods which were commonly applied, though sometimes successful, often led to serious aberrations. Once more we meet the theory (probably of Alexandrian origin) that words changed by the addition, subtraction, substitution or transposition of letters, or, further, by the addition, loss, lengthening or shortening of syllables.[76] This certainly gave plenty of scope for experimentation. It could give the right result, as when *meridies*, 'midday', was derived from *medidies*, a form which Varro verified on an old sundial, and *bruma*, 'mid-winter', was derived from the superlative of *brevis*, originally *brevima*, meaning the shortest day.[77] But it could be quite misleading, as when *volpes*, 'fox', was derived from *volipes*, 'flying-foot', and *lepus*, 'hare', from *levipes*, 'light-o'-foot'.[78] The Stoics, on the other hand, favoured a different approach, and associated word-derivation with underlying or related ideas.[79] This could lead to all kinds of false associations, as that *foedus*, 'treaty' was connected with *foedus*, 'foul', from the sacrifice of a pig, whereas Varro rightly associated it with words denoting trust (*fidus, fides*).[80] The Stoic notion of derivation from opposites, as of *lucus*, 'grove', from the absence of light (*a non lucendo*), could lead to fantastic results. As a criterion of correctness, etymology, when well based, could have a practical application in the field of spelling. For example, Varro's idea that decision whether or not to use an initial aspirate should be based on the presence or absence of an initial *f* (slightly aspirated) in the Sabine or Faliscan dialect form, was scientific and constructive. Hence *fasena, faedus, fordeum* and *fircus* were held to justify the spellings *harena, haedus, hordeum* and *hircus*.[81] But, in general, scholars looked to Greek as the source of Latin words, and, not knowing anything about a common ancestry, spoke of what we would call 'cognate' as 'derived'.

The last topic discussed by Quintilian (though included earlier by Sextus Empiricus) is that of orthography. This was a subject to which Lucilius had devoted his ninth book, and which remained of primary importance to grammarians. Among those who wrote special treatises on it were Verrius Flaccus and Cornutus, whose works are lost, and Terentius Scaurus and Velius Longus, whose accounts, from around the end of our period, still survive.[82] Quintilian begins with certain matters of practical convenience in writing and spelling, which were designed to prevent possible confusion.[83] Of particular relevance here is his remark that an apex-mark was generally placed over the terminal vowel in first declension nouns in the ablative case, to distinguish it from the nominative form. This would certainly have been a help to boys in reading aloud, for such aids to pronunciation were all too few in ancient texts. The same principle of differentiation was also applied to spelling, when there might be confusion — better, he says, to write *exspecto*, than *expecto*, because *expecto* suggested a different meaning (presumably 'comb out'). Many differentiated by variant spelling when a word had two quite different usages, and wrote, for instance, *cum* for the preposition, but *quom* in introducing subordinate clauses. Sometimes it was not grammatical reasoning but euphony which suggested a preference between variants, and this led to approval of the assimilation of prepositions, as in *optinuit* for *obtinuit*, *immunis* for *inmunis*. It is interesting to find this matter already discussed in Lucilius.[84] The division of syllables was also more fully treated at this stage.

After this, Quintilian proceeds to discuss the question of changing fashions in spelling, and looks at some old controversies. One of the most well-known arguments, which continued to echo down the centuries, stemmed from the dispute between Accius and Lucilius on the use of the diphthong *ei* to represent the long *i*-sound.[85] Accius, anxious to represent graphically the difference between a long and a short vowel, proposed, as a general rule, to write the short vowel singly and the long vowel double, so that *pacem*, for instance, would become *paacem*, and his temporary success may be seen in inscriptions of his time. But he felt himself precluded from writing a double *i* (possibly because the symbol II was in common use as a form of E)[86] and, instead, extended to overall use the diphthong *ei*, which had long been current and represented the old pronunciation in many words — e.g. *deivos* for *divus, deico* for *dico*. Lucilius thought this reform too sweeping, and proposed certain limitations on the scheme. In the nominative plurals of the second declension, he fully agreed in writing, e.g. *puerei* for *pueri*, but refused to allow it in the genitive singular, which must remain *pueri*. On historical grounds (whether or not Lucilius considered them), this was at least reasonable, for the nominative plural termination had originally been a diphthong, though perhaps no longer pronounced differently from *i*, whereas the genitive singular termination had always been a pure *i*; but on practical grounds the distinction introduced an awkward complication. Lucilius also accepted *ei* in the dative of the third declension, as *furei* for *furi*, and, quite apart from terminations, wrote e.g. *meille, meillia, meiles*, for *mille, milia, miles*; but the absurdity of the distinction became patent when he proposed that the singular for 'javelin' should be *pilum*, and the plural *peila* (more javelins, more letters!). Varro, whilst criticizing Lucilius, compromised by keeping *ei* in second declension nominative plurals, but rejecting it in the genitive singular;[87] but many ignored the distinction, and were satisifed with *i*. From the standpoint of the teacher, the practical relevance of the topic, apart from its academic interest, lay in the fact that his boys would constantly be meeting these old *ei* spellings in their texts of early Latin poets.

A further important point of discussion was a reform, attributed to Caesar, which concerned the middle vowel in words such as *optimus* and *maximus*.[88] The earlier practice had been to write such words as *optumus, maxumus*, but, before the end of the second century B.C., spelling had begun to fluctuate between *u* and *i*, and inscriptional evidence shows both *infimo* and *infumum*. In pronunciation, as grammarians repeatedly tell us, the sound was an intermediate one between *u* and *i*, and it may have approximated to German short *ü*.[89] But already, in Cicero's day, the *u*-spelling, though archaizers still adhered to it, was regarded in progressive circles as too 'rustic', and the *i*-spelling gradually began to supersede it. This affected a wide range of words, in which, before labials, the vowel had this intermediate quality, notably superlative adjectives, which began to change from *-umus* to *-imus* (e.g. *facillumus/facillimus*), and adverbs likewise. Even when the syllable concerned was accented, as in e.g. *manubiae/manibiae, surrupuit/surripuit*, the move was towards the *i*-spelling, and Brutus, Messalla, Agrippa and Augustus even went so far as to write *simus* for *sumus*, though without permanent effect.[90] No new ruling, however enthusiastically adopted, could carry all before it, and in some words the spelling remained optional, whilst occasionally (as in *documentum*) the old habit prevailed. There was also an intermediate vowel-sound between *i* and *e*, in which the old spelling with *e* was superseded by that with *i*, as in *sibe, quase*; but here, too, tradition sometimes died hard, and not everyone accepted *heri* against *here*.[91]

There were many other topics of orthography which aroused discussion, of which only brief mention can be made here. The termination *ai* for *ae* in the genitive of first declension nouns was already antiquated, but required comment.[92] There was the question of the adoption of *e* in place of the earlier *o* in words such as *advorsus adversus, vortex vertex*, where already the younger Scipio favoured the modernization.[93] There was the question of the duplication of certain consonants, notably *s*, which led, in Cicero's day, to spellings such as *caussae*.[94] There was trouble over the consonantal *i* (*aio* or *aiio*?) and consonantal *u* (*seruos* or *seruus*?) and much else. In fact, as Sextus Empiricus remarked,[95] the whole subject of spelling was one on which the grammarians were everlastingly at loggerheads, and we may be sure that their arguments were familiar in the schools. Fortunately for them (and for us), Latin was not a language in which, as so often in English, the spelling and the pronunciation differed.[96] But it is high time to emerge from the tangled undergrowth of grammatical disputes, and to climb to the more pleasant uplands of poetry.

CHAPTER XVI

Study of the poets

(I) Reading aloud and reciting

At the primary level of education, as we saw, pupils had made their first acquaintance with some of the Greek and Latin poets by copying out and learning by heart selected passages of limited extent. Now, with the *grammaticus*, they began continuous study, usually of full texts, and their lessons included not only reading aloud and memorizing, but also the detailed exposition of the master. Naturally, with this degree of thoroughness, only a limited number of texts could be covered in the available time, but later, when the boy proceeded to the rhetoric school, though he now concentrated more particularly on the prose writers, he was still expected to continue to read the poets, but without receiving more than general guidance from his teacher. There was also a difference of approach at the 'grammar' and at the rhetoric stage. At the former, the purpose was to read the greatest poets (or, at least, considerable portions of their work) for the inspiring and elevating effect which their subjects, their thoughts and their expression had upon the young mind.[1] At the latter, the poets, like the orators and historians, were perused with the objective of eliciting and imitating those features of style and treatment which were likely to be useful to the future orator[2] — though this did not by any means preclude continuing appreciation of poetic quality for its own sake. At each stage, both Greek and Latin poets were studied, but, although there is considerable firm evidence for the basic content for the 'grammar' school course in both languages, we have nothing like so detailed a picture as that given for the rhetoric stage in Quintilian's tenth book. But, for Greek authors, it may sometimes be helpful to take account of the degree of interest shown in particular writers, or works, by teachers and other educated readers elsewhere, particularly as indicated by the statistics of papyrus texts from Graeco-Roman Egypt.[3] But it is recognized that these may become subject to modification as further discoveries are made.

The first step is certain. Whether their master taught both languages or only Greek, the poet whom boys began to study first and foremost was Homer. Horace says that, at Rome, it was his good fortune 'to be taught how much the wrath of Achilles harmed the Greeks', and Petronius, Quintilian and Pliny are all unequivocal about Homer's priority.[4] Homer, 'the educator of the Greeks',[5] was regarded by Quintilian, as by them, as the fountain-head of wisdom,[6] and took precedence irrespective of time and place. In the 'grammar' school of the poet Statius' father at Naples, he heads the list of authors read, and Statius also tells of the boy Glaucias, who died very young, but who had won admiration for his recitals of 'the toils of Troy and the mishaps of Ulysses' slow return'.[7] It was the same in late antiquity, when the epigrammatist Pallades of Alexandria referred to his teaching of 'the wrath of Achilles' as his most characteristic task.[8] But, although both the *Iliad* and the *Odyssey* were familiar texts in schools, it may be doubted whether there was usually time to peruse them both completely in class; and in that case, as the evidence of Greek papyri suggests, the *Iliad* may have been more favoured than the *Odyssey*,[9] but, as in both it was usual to begin at the beginning, boys may have become more widely familiar with the earlier than with the later books.

Once boys were initiated in Homer, it was not long before, in the Latin class, their attention was directed to Virgil, and, first and foremost, the *Aeneid*. Long before the Augustan age, Roman schoolmasters, following in the footsteps of the Greeks, had begun with epic, and even very early poems, written in the archaic Saturnian verse, Livius Andronicus' translation of the *Odyssey* and Naevius' *Punic War*, remained in use in the schools right down to the time of Horace — even though the former was primitive and practically devoid of poetic merit (Cicero called it a 'work of Daedalus'), and the latter, though more attractive, still had only the qualities, in Cicero's view, of the early Greek sculptor, Myron.[10] But it was the *Annals* of Ennius which always commanded the greatest admiration and respect as the national epic, and it was not until the appearance of the *Aeneid* that it was superseded in the schools.[11] Here, at last, in the *Aeneid*, was a work which really invited comparison with both the *Odyssey* and the *Iliad*; and at almost exactly the time that Caecilius Epirota was introducing the *Eclogues* and the *Georgics* to his classes (after the death of Cornelius Gallus in 26 B.C.), Propertius was able to announce that 'something greater than the *Iliad* is coming to birth'.[12] When the *Aeneid* was published after the poet's death in 19 B.C., without his final revision, it immediately began to attract the attention of the *grammatici*, who examined it in the closest detail both in their published works and in their lectures. Although some carping critics among them (the so-called 'detractors of Virgil') took a pedantic pleasure in finding faults,[13] they were far outnumbered by his staunch champions; Virgil became the Latin school-text *par excellence*, and remained so through the centuries. Already in the first century A.D., the assessment of the degree of Virgil's success in 'borrowing', or echoing, lines and passages from Homer, the Greek tragedians, and earlier Latin poets, such as Ennius and Lucretius, was a favourite occupation of the *grammatici*, and was still a major interest of the *savants* whose discussions Macrobius reports in late antiquity.[14] When it came to weighing the merits of Homer and Virgil in the critical scales, learned ladies of Juvenal's day, to his professed disgust, were more eloquent than the 'grammarians' themselves.[15] The schools undoubtedly did a great deal to ensure the immortality of Virgil's works, and no part of them was more widely known (or, probably, more intensively studied in class) than the early books of the *Aeneid*. Dozens of *graffiti* from Pompeii and elsewhere record the writers' familiarity with the openings of the first and second books, *Arma virumque cano* and *Conticuere omnes* (even though they sometimes misspelt it *Contiquere!*),[16] and Ovid says that no part of the whole poem was more widely read than the love-story of Dido and Aeneas. [17] It was still much the same in St Augustine's day, for he tells how, at the 'grammar' school, he was made to learn Virgil's descriptions of the sack of Troy, the wanderings of Aeneas, and Dido's tragic death.[18]

After epic, Quintilian mentions tragedy (meaning both Greek and Roman), but his remark 'tragedies are beneficial', though subsequently augmented by an enthusiastic recommendation of early Roman drama, is disappointingly brief,[19] and leaves us in the dark regarding the extent to which the plays of the three long-accepted masters, Aeschylus, Sophocles and Europides, were read and commented upon in the Greek 'grammar' schools of Rome. Also, it so happens that they are not mentioned in Statius' list of the poets read in his father's school. Yet it is most unlikely that the Greek *grammaticus* at Rome would not have included, at the very least, a few plays of Euripides in his programme. Euripides was the most widely read of the three tragic poets, as is proved by the fact that the papyrus fragments of his plays (including many that are no longer extant) greatly outnumber those of Aeschylus and Sophocles.[20] In Roman times, quotation from Euripides is common, and at all periods his tragedies provided models for the Roman dramatists — to take only one example, Ennius, Ovid and Seneca all wrote a *Medea*. We should naturally expect this to have stimulated interest in the originals. At the primary stage of education, Euripides was introduced in the form of maxims and short passages from anthologies, and much later, at the rhetoric stage, he was recommended as by far the most useful of the three dramatists for the student of oratory.[21] It is not likely, therefore, that he was neglected at the intermediate stage, when his literary qualities could already begin to be appreciated. Also, for a Roman boy, he was, in general, the easiest of the three to read. Exactly which plays were most studied of the standard collection, which became equipped with scholia, we do not know; but the choice may have included some plays which are less read nowadays, for the *Phoenissae* and the *Orestes* are particularly prominent in the papyrus statistics. After Euripides, it would seem that Sophocles rather than Aeschylus would have been the next favourite, for Quintilian says it was a standard subject of debate as to whether Sophocles or Euripides was the better poet.

In Latin, Ennius, Pacuvius and Accius were thought of as the nearest equivalents to the three masters of classical Greek tragedy,[22] and there is no doubt that their plays were regularly studied in 'grammar' schools, especially under the Republic.[23] Although, under the Empire, Accius and Pacuvius took some hard knocks,[24] Quintilian found much merit in early Roman drama, which in archaizing circles obtained a new lease of life. Cicero, too, had been very fond of quoting from early Roman tragedy, as is particularly evident in the *Tusculan Disputations*. At one point in that work he remarks: 'but we, doubtless taking our cue from the Greeks, read and learn these things from boyhood, and consider them a liberal education and training'.[25] It may be, moreover, that he did not intend this observation to apply only to Latin plays, for, immediately before, he had himself translated into Latin verse a couple of quite long passages from Greek, one from the *Trachiniae* of Sophocles and the other from the lost *Prometheus Unbound* of Aeschylus. As to those teachers in the imperial period who reacted against early Roman tragedy, they may well have preferred Varius' *Thyestes* and Ovid's *Medea*, both of which won high renown.[26]

Tragedy, especially in view of the common basis in legend, combined very well with epic as a subject for reading and exposition in class, and Martial refers to these two genres as typical of the schoolmaster's work.[27] Both were high-minded and inspiring, and both could be used for serious lessons on human conduct and emotions. Comedy, however, which in the schools meant New Comedy and its Latin derivatives (for Aristophanes had not yet come fully into his own), was on a quite different footing, with its recurrent love affairs and its altogether lower moral tone. In Greek, the prime favourite was Menander, and the only question among teachers seems to have been, not whether, but when his plays should be introduced. Certainly, at the primary stage, all were agreed that he provided, like Euripides, wise maxims in abundance for copying and learning by heart. Some teachers, as is evident from both Statius and Ausonius, accustomed their pupils to read aloud from him on entering the 'grammar' school, for his name is linked with that of Homer.[28] Ovid, too, said that Menander was read by boys and girls alike, though he does not explicitly say that they did so in school.[29] Quintilian, however, had serious doubts, and would not have any comedy read in full until the morals of pupils were thought to be 'secure', even though he himself had the highest regard for Menander's works.[30] He did recommend, however, that, before complete plays were read, young boys should attend a professional comedy-actor, who would select the most suitable passages for expressive reading, especially as Comedy had so many virtues of narrative, characterization, and emotional expression.[31] At the rhetoric stage, he had no reservations, and found that Menander's plays, which always entailed stock characters, and sometimes legal situations, were particularly useful for students of declamation.[32] Thus we cannot say to what extent the 'grammarians' at Rome shared his moral qualms, but the probability is that, even if the advantages were felt to outweigh the disadvantages, comedy still took second place to epic and tragedy, and was more commonly read with older boys. Among Latin comedy writers, Plautus and Caecilius, Terence and Afranius were all highly rated,[33] but in the schools it was Terence who finally emerged as the Roman Menander. His purity of style was praised by Cicero and Caesar, his characterization by Varro, and his art by the Augustan critics in general.[34] In later antiquity, teachers had the advantage of being able to read him with the commentaries of Aemilius Asper and Donatus. Nor do they appear to have been unduly deterred by considerations of morality in Comedy, for St Jerome, St Augustine, and the pupils of a 'grammarian' friend of Sidonius were all set to read the *Eunuchus* in school.[35]

Quintilian, however, made a similarly cautious approach to lyric poetry, for, at the 'grammar' school stage, he required a selection to be made not only of the authors but within their works.[36] On the other hand, the Greek lyric poets certainly held a prominent place in the school of Statius' father at Naples, where not only Pindar, Stesichorus, Alcman, Sappho, Ibycus 'and the rest' appeared on the reading-list, but even Corinna, who was not one of the original 'canon' of nine, was included.[37] As has often been observed, however, this school was in a Greek-speaking area; also, the range may reflect the personal interest of the elder Statius, a successful composer himself, in the variety of lyric metres. But, even though it may be hazardous to transfer the list to the programme of the Greek *grammaticus* in Rome, Pindar, at least, was greatly admired, and accepted as quite pre-eminent.[38] Petronius even uses the expression 'Pindar and the nine lyric poets'.[39] Several references to Greek lyric writers in the Augustan poets show that their texts must have been at least available for study,[40] and Seneca's evidence shows that they were sometimes learnt by heart for recitals.[41] In school, it is probable that they were not read consistently, but, as Quintilian advocated, in selections. In Latin, the *Odes* of Horace held the same high place as the poems of Pindar in Greek. Quintilian thought him 'pretty well the only one of our lyric poets worth reading', and in the schools, the 'well-modulated poems of Horace', as Ausonius called them, could not possibly have been ignored.[42] Much less attention (to judge from Quintilian) was paid to Catullus, for personal love-poetry was not generally favoured at this stage, and the hendecasyllabic metre was associated with light, if not lascivious, verse.[43] But there were some circles, as we may now see, in which it is not likely that he was entirely neglected. For Catullus' longer poems take us back to his Alexandrian models, and Alexandria was the spiritual home of so many of the *grammatici* that they would naturally have had a warm corner in their hearts for its scholar-poets and their Roman successors.

Quintilian was also very reluctant to include elegiac poetry at this stage, though he qualified his views by adding 'at any rate, love-elegy', and had less objection to its being read by older boys. This was probably a fairly usual attitude, but it did not mean that elegiac poets were excluded by all *grammatici*. In Greek, Callimachus, who was generally accepted as *princeps* in this field,[44] was read in the school of the elder Statius, and, in late antiquity, Palladas of Alexandria says that he taught Callimachus, as well as Homer and Pindar.[45] To judge from the numerous papyrus fragments, the most widely read work would have been the learned and allusive narrative elegy, the *Aetia*, on which Epaphroditus wrote a commentary at Rome.[46] This brings us immediately, of course, to the Alexandrian movement at Rome, and it is noteworthy that at least three of the Roman *grammatici* of the late Republic and the Augustan period had close association with the neoteric poets. Valerius Cato was prominent in this circle, Crassicius owed his reputation to a commentary on the miniature epic, *Smyrna*, which Catullus' friend Cinna had taken nine years to write, and Caecilius Epirota was the first to read not only Virgil but 'other recent poets' with his pupils — that is, he began a new fashion. [47] As Caecilius had been a very close friend of Cornelius Gallus, who had himself been influenced by the Greek poet Parthenius, it seems that we are here in the very heart of neoteric territory, and that the way was thus opened for at least a limited acceptance, in due course, of the Roman elegiac quartet, Gallus, Tibullus, Propertius and Ovid. But two points should be stressed. First, Caecilius only taught 'youths' (*adulescentes*), and his school was a small one. Secondly, both his pupils and those of Valerius Cato were particularly interested in the art of poetic composition — evidently, much more so than in literature as an approach to rhetoric — and Caecilius was termed 'the nurse of tender bards'.[48] Thus it seems likely that, when the neoteric poets were studied in 'grammar' schools, it was mainly by a rather select reading group of older boys, who aspired to become poets themselves. But in the more traditional genres of epic and tragedy, the modernist teachers found, in the imperial period, a wider scope. Lucan's name, within a decade of his death, was linked with that of Virgil,[49] and, even though his epic on the Civil War was more particularly valuable for students of rhetoric,[50] Suetonius tells us that Lucan's poems were soon being read in 'grammar' schools.[51] Statius, too, claimed that his *Thebaid* was becoming familiar to young readers, and Martial implies that recent tragedies could be brought into the 'grammarian's' programme.[52]

The *grammaticus*, then, beyond Homer and Virgil, may have felt free to exercise some liberty of choice, but it should not be supposed that the reading of the Roman boy was entirely confined to the authors expounded in class. With beginners, especially, class-teaching was thorough and rather slow, but, as time passed, boys would become able to read more quickly by themselves, even if such reading had to be done at home. Quintilian, discussing private tutors, argued that even they had to allow time for private study, and added: 'not every kind of reading on all occasions requires someone to precede and interpret — otherwise, when would a boy find time to become familiar with so many authors?'[53] It has to be remembered, in this connection, that the young Roman, unlike his Greek counterpart, was studying two languages, not one, and attending school-classes in both; thus it could well be that he would need to read at home some of the Greek texts which a Greek boy would have had the opportunity of studying in class. For example, in the teaching curriculum of Greek-speaking areas, Hesiod appears to have featured regularly, along with Homer; but the only reference to a Roman boy of 'grammar' school age being recommended to study and learn him (or, at least, the *Works and Days*) occurs in a letter of Cicero, who urges the young Lepta to do this, and means, evidently, in his own time.[54]

So far we have only spoken of poets, for Cicero and Quintilian make it quite clear that it was the 'grammarian's' proper function to read and expound them. This is generally accepted, but there have been differences of opinion on the question whether the *grammaticus* also commented upon prose authors in his school. In Greek, the definition of 'grammar' by Dionysius Thrax as 'a working knowledge of the writings of poets and prose-writers' might, at first sight, seem to point in this direction, but it is not so. Certainly, the 'grammarian' could not possibly have fulfilled his task of teaching proper grammatical usage without being thoroughly familiar with the texts of the standard prose writers, and he would also frequently refer to them in his classroom commentaries on the poets. He might publish his notes on them, as did Asconius on the speeches of Cicero. But that does not mean that he also expounded prose-texts in class. Sextus Empiricus, who examines this definition, makes this distinction when he says that the 'grammarian' *interprets* the writings of poets such as Homer, Hesiod, Pindar, Euripides, and Menander, but *pursues the study of* prose writers such as Herodotus, Thucydides and Plato, 'as his own personal task' (*idion*).[55] Sextus himself constantly speaks of both poets and prose-writers as the 'grammarian's' area of study, especially in connection with grammar in the narrower sense, but when he comes to discuss the treatment of authors, he at once makes it clear that poetry is the 'grammarian's' pride, and all his quotations are taken from Homer and Euripides.[56]

Such was the Greek tradition, and, at Rome, too, all the authors recommended in Quintilian's reading-list at the 'grammar' school stage are poets, whether Greek or Latin. Elsewhere, too, he makes it clear that elucidation of the poets is the 'grammarian's' business, while the prose authors are the field of the rhetorician; similarly, Martial associates Virgil with the *grammaticus* and Cicero with the *rhetor*.[57] When Cicero himself speaks of schoolboys learning his speeches by heart, he must mean in connection with their rhetorical studies.[58] Admittedly, at Rome, the position is made, at first sight, more complicated by the fact that some of the Republican 'grammarians' also taught rhetoric, and many Latin teachers under the Empire who were, strictly, *grammatici* invaded the province of rhetoric.[59] But they did so by taking over the preliminary written exercises, and, in order to teach these, they did not need to give a line by line exposition of prose texts, as they did with the poets. The standard rhetorical method was for the teacher to select passages of prose authors as models for each type of exercise, and also to compose versions himself, for his pupils to learn by heart.[60] Naturally, it was a good thing for these young students also to do some reading in prose, and that is why Quintilian advises that 'beginners' (i.e., in rhetoric) should read particularly Cicero and Livy, as being easier than Sallust, for the improvement of their style.[61] Even in the Greek rhetoric schools, the rhetorician often did not have time to expound prose texts himself, and left it to his assistants,[62] and Quintilian nowhere suggests that the Latin *grammatici* made a practice of this. They, in modern terms, expounded the poets thoroughly as 'prescribed texts', but, when they taught rhetorical exercises, expected their pupils to study selected prose themselves to improve their 'prose composition'. Nor should we be misled by the association of the words *historia, historiae* with the 'grammarian's' teaching, for they refer not to history as we understand it, but to the myths.[63] Certainly, in their wide range of personal knowledge, the *grammatici* included the historians, but there is no evidence in our period that they expounded them in class.

Whatever the text selected for study in class, the 'grammarian' would not have been likely to plunge immediately *in medias res* without first having given his boys some information about the author and his work. Quintilian does not enlighten us here, but it has been well argued that the kind of scheme which later scholars applied in the introductions to their published commentaries was a traditional one, derived ultimately from one of the great seats of learning, and long used in classroom teaching.[64] This scheme is seen, for instance, in the prefaces of Donatus and Servius to their commentaries on Virgil, and that of Eustathius on Homer. Something similar existed in prose, as in the introduction to Syrianus' commentary on Hermogenes. First, then, the teacher would say something about the poet's life. Even though, with Homer, he could only give varying opinions as to just when the poet lived, and mention the cities which claimed the honour of being his birthplace, with Virgil he would have much fuller information. For Euripides, there was the biography of Satyrus; a fair amount was known about Terence, and a great deal more about Horace. Next came a few words about the title of the work to be read — why it was chosen and how it was appropriate — and then something about the background and characteristics of the literary genre to which it belonged, the metre in which it was written, and the general style in which it was couched. The poet's purpose in writing might also need a few sentences — one might say that Virgil's purpose in the *Aeneid* was to emulate Homer and to honour the lineage of Augustus.[65] Sometimes, too, there was a question as to the number of books, their arrangement, or their genuineness. With plays, the *hypotheses* available since Alexandrian times provided an introduction to the plot. These prefatory remarks completed, the *grammaticus* would proceed to his first major task and primary duty, that of teaching his boys to read the text effectively aloud.

The art of reading aloud and reciting from memory was much prized in antiquity, and the *grammatici* were recognized exponents of it. One 'grammarian's' epitaph calls attention to the fact that he was not only a reader (*lector*), but 'one of those who gave pleasure by the purity of their enunciation'.[66] But with a class of young boys, fresh from primary school, there was much to be done. Some, who had natural ability and had been well taught, would already be showing signs of promise, and could recite selected passages well; but some still would find it difficult to sort out the words from a continuous line of script, and might have to mark them off for themselves. The *grammaticus* would only draw attention to occasional places in the text, where there might be pitfalls for the unwary; particularly if the letters could be run together in two different ways, one of which made sense and the other nonsense. For example, in Greek capitals, *estinaxios* might be rightly divided to give *estin axios*, 'he is worthy', or wrongly to give *esti naxios*, 'he is a Naxian'.[67] A famous instance in Latin was Virgil's line ending *conspicitur sus*, 'a sow is espied', where, as a late grammarian observed 'a boy might go astray' and read *conspicit ursus*, 'the bear espies'.[68] Such cases, which would not be very common, had to be marked by a dividing comma, or *diastole*. Otherwise, the teacher concentrated on the three aspects of reading aloud which Dionysius Thrax had set forth, namely, punctuation, accentuation, and expression.

It is a rather surprising fact that even the ancient Greeks, for all their inventiveness, never succeeded in devising a really satisfactory system of punctuation. One of their most obvious deficiencies was the complete lack of a question-mark; if there was doubt, the teacher had to point out that the sentence should be taken as a question. Nor was the exclamation-mark yet available.[69] The use of the *paragraphos*, a short horizontal line placed in the margin, and commonly found in papyri, was convenient enough as a metrical sign to denote the end of a strophe or antistrophe, but it was less satisfactory as a way of denoting the end of a sentence. It was always possible to leave a short space in the text, but a dot, or 'point' (*punctum*) was obviously the simplest solution. Here, however, the ancients complicated matters by using different positions of the dot, in relation to the final letter, to indicate both the sentence-end and a shorter pause, equivalent to our comma. One method, explained by a late Latin grammarian,[70] was to place the dot opposite the top of the final letter to indicate a 'full stop', opposite the base of it to indicate a short pause, and beside the middle of it to indicate a pause of intermediary length. Whether this was the method of Dionysius Thrax, or even Aristophanes of Byzantium earlier, is debated, but it certainly did not become a generally accepted system.[71] To make matters worse, in order to clarify pauses within the sentence, Nicanor, in the time of Hadrian, used no less than seven positions of the dot, together with another sign called the *hypodiastole*, (which was something like our comma), and gained himself the nickname of the 'Dotter' (Stigmatias). The Homeric scholia, like Dionysius Thrax, use the terms *stigme* and *hypostigme* for the equivalent of our full stop and comma, but they also frequently refer to the need for a 'short pause', and we do not know if, or how, this was meant to be indicated in the text. The practice of the papyri suggests that there was considerable diversity in methods of punctuation, and that no agreed common practice was evolved. Even in the texts which were in general circulation, signs appear to have been only sporadically introduced, and the reader added them himself for his own convenience. [72] So the *grammaticus* had first to punctuate his own manuscript, and then hand it round, or communicate the details, to his class. This explains why the late grammarian Pompeius thought it advisable to include in the preface to his work a section on punctuating a text.[73]

It is in Greek, from the Homeric scholia, that the best ideas may be gained of the treatment of matters of punctuation. Whilst it is true that many of these notes are derived from writers of the second century A.D., notably Nicanor,[74] and that experts frequently disagreed about individual passages, there was a good deal of accepted convention (*synetheia*), and the general principles were as relevant to schoolboys as to scholars. Such frequently recurring admonitions as 'allow a full pause at the end of the line, for the sense is complete',[75] or 'This must be connected with what follows'[76] must often have been on the lips of schoolmasters. Very frequently, instructions were given where to place the equivalent of a comma, and where a full stop; also in the placing of shorter pauses, though these were not necessarily marked in the text. The primary necessity was, in the words of Ausonius to his young grandson on correct reading, 'to enhance the sense' (*distinctio sensum auget*), and scholiasts frequently note that punctuation 'makes the meaning clearer'.[77] Usually, specific reasons for the punctuation would be given. Boys were also told to make a brief pause, for instance, between two or more co-ordinated sentences connected by 'and' or 'but', and immediately before a relative, or temporal, or final, or explanatory clause, and immediately after the protasis (or each protasis) of a conditional.[78] A parenthesis, or an appositional phrase, or two adjectives qualifying a single noun, required to be similarly observed,[79] and any conceivable ambiguity must be avoided.[80] All this was very much in the province of grammar, but the pause might also be introduced for rhetorical, or dramatic, effect, though the two reasons might easily become merged. For example, it was usual to advise that a short pause should be made after addressing someone in the vocative case,[81] for the vocative was a detached item in the structure of the sentence. But it also carried rhetorical force, especially when Homeric heroes upbraided one another in a whole series of vocatives, each of which had to be given its full staccato force.[82] Such brief pauses, as Ausonius remarked, add vigour to the speech (*dant intervalla vigorem*).

An interesting, but tantalizingly brief, demonstration of the use of the pause in Latin reading is given in an analysis by Quintilian of the opening lines of the *Aeneid*.[83] After *Arma virumque cano*, he says, allow a momentary suspension, but no more, since *virum* has yet to be explained by the succeeding *qui*-clause; then, after *Troiae qui primus ab oris*, make a further brief pause, followed by *Italiam*, the destination. The words *fato profugus* are really parenthetic, so a slight suspension immediately before and after should mark them off; after which we proceed *Lavinaque venit litora*. Here it is necessary to make a longer pause, in order to take breath — evidently, the pause which would be marked by some with a 'middle dot' — and then one may proceed. At this point, however, Quintilian's detailed exposition breaks off, except for the comment that only after *altae moenia Romae*, the conclusion of the passage, will a long pause be made. This is exactly the kind of method which must have been used in teaching generations of boys to read their Virgil.

Next came a subject of vital importance for all good reading, that of correct accentuation. It is unlikely that the Greek texts in general circulation were more than scantily supplied with accent-marks, even if they were present at all. Even in Homeric papyri of the early imperial period, they appear to have been usually added by a second hand, though the lyric poets, to judge from the Bacchylides papyrus, might sometimes be much more fully marked.[84] But, as regards Homer, numerous observations on accentuation had been made by Aristarchus, and it is also interesting to find, among the names of authorities mentioned from time to time in the scholia, two well-known Republican teachers whom we have already met, Tyrannio (the elder) and 'Nicias', who is most probably Cicero's friend, Nicias of Cos.[85] The teacher would use his own discretion as to the accents which he considered it necessary to mark, remembering that many of Homer's words, and word-forms, would be quite obsolete and unfamiliar to his boys. Also included under the general heading of 'prosody' were two other important aspects of reading, namely, quantity and breathings. In Greek, only those vowels which might be either long or short were marked, and more particularly in cases where confusion might arise, because, in words of similar appearance, the vowel was, in the one, long, and in the other short.[86] Breathings also needed to be marked, especially when a word meant one thing with a rough breathing and something quite different with a smooth breathing, as in *hoios*, 'such as', and *oios*, 'alone', or *hauton*, 'himself' and *auton*, 'him'.[87]

But, important though correct punctuation and accentuation were, the real essence of reading aloud lay in expression, in entering into the spirit of the passage, or, as the Greeks said, the 'acting' of it. In order to teach this, one could only use the method of personal demonstration.[88] It was, in the first place, necessary to have a sense of appropriateness, and the teacher had to explain what was meant by this very general term — appropriate to what? Dionysius Thrax here contented himself merely with observing that reading aloud must suit the type of literature which is being read, the literary genre; tragedy requires to be read in heroic tones, comedy in those of everyday life, elegy in a high tone, clear and sweet, epic with manly vigour.[89] But, although there was a measure of truth in this, such generalizations by category were obviously far too wide to be of much practical help. As Horace remarked, 'sometimes comedy, too, raises its voice, and angry Chremes storms in blustering tones, but the Telephus and Peleus of tragedy grieve in the language of ordinary life'.[90] Much more applicable to directions on reading aloud were the other aspects of appropriateness which are discussed by Aristotle and Horace regarding style, namely, appropriateness to the character represented and to the emotions involved.[91] So the scholiasts note when a particular line or passage is in keeping with the speaker's character or mood and needs to be read 'ethically';[92] and their marginal notes advising the reader to communicate the various emotions by adaptations of tone or speed must be very similar to the comments of the schoolmaster in class.

Cicero has an interesting chapter in which he quotes several passages from early Roman Tragedy, and observes how the voice and delivery must match the very varied feelings expressed.[93] The plays of Ennius, Pacuvius and Accius abounded in scenes of strong emotion, and these were the very plays which boys were called upon to read aloud in school. A few illustrations, based on Cicero, will give some idea of the different emotional situations which needed to be convincingly reproduced. A recurrent feature of these early tragedies was the speech of a person so distraught that he or she knows not where to turn. Such situations frequently stress the dilemma of the speaker, and naturally find expression in rhetorical questions. The famous 'dilemma' speeches of Medea, of Caius Gracchus, of the deserted Ariadne in Catullus are all of this type.[94] Very similar, in Ennius, is the lament of the distracted Andromache, when Hector has been slain and Troy is in flames.[95] Then there were scenes of bitter and intense hatred, of dire quarrels between brothers, such as Atreus and Thyestes, and Ennius again gives the words of Atreus as he plots his terrible revenge.[96] Sometimes, too, it was not so much vehemence as agitation and terror which required to be reproduced, as in Ennius' depiction of the frenzy of Alcmaeon, who had slain his own mother, Eriphila, and was pursued and driven mad by her avenging shade.[97] Such were some of the more powerful scenes of early Roman tragedy, rugged in style yet vivid in imagination, which must have been read aloud by schoolboys and would leave a lasting impression in their minds.

Whilst the *grammaticus* kept the teaching of epic and tragedy in his own hands, he would also allow his boys to attend the lessons of a professional comedy actor (*comoedus*), who was often accepted as a teacher (*magister*) and would use selected passages of comedy — especially Menander and Terence — as his text.[98] Such men had great experience in pronunciation and effective delivery; Pliny, for instance, warmly praises his personal reader, Zosimus, as having all the qualifications of a *comoedus*.[99] They were chosen in preference to tragic actors because they were much more natural in tone, and did not, like actors in tragedy, seek to impress by powerful vociferation.[100] The lines which they spoke were in the language of everyday life, but they were not mere conversational prose, and could be gracefully enhanced by appropriate tones, facial expression and gesture.[101] Quintilian did not, however, wish such teachers to go so far as training boys to act the parts. Nor would he encourage them to over-do facial expression and gesture, or to seek to reproduce a woman's voice, or to imitate the quavering tones of the aged; and he particularly objected to the 'lilting' delivery so fashionable on the stage.[102] Rather, he had his eye on oratorical values, and urged the comedy actor to select passages suited to this end. He should teach 'how narrative should be delivered, how advice should be tendered with authority, how rapid vehemence should reflect rising anger, how to adapt the tone when appealing for pity'.[103] There were all kinds of voice-modulations (*flexus*) which might be called into play, and in Donatus' commentary on Terence there are numerous notes which tell how lines should be spoken — softly or loudly, calmly or excitedly, slowly or quickly, ironically, indignantly, wearily, sympathetically, or with an air of surprise.[104] The comedy actor could also help greatly in training boys to overcome speech-difficulties, such as lisping, or inability to enunciate *r* or *l*, and he would criticize any unevenness or monotony in expression. He would insist that letters and syllables should not be blurred in slovenly fashion, and, especially, that the voice should not trail away at the end of a sentence.[105] Nor would he allow a boy, when reciting, to keep his eyes lowered. Also needing correction were faults all too easily acquired in a degenerate society, such as speaking in an effeminate fashion, or using affected mannerisms, such as an artificial resonance of voice.[106] When all this teaching fell on fruitful ground, excellent results might be obtained even with quite young boys. So Cornelius Nepos wrote concerning Atticus: 'He had as a boy, in addition to his capacity for learning, a most agreeable quality of expression and voice, so that he not only quickly learned the passages which were set, but also recited them admirably'.[107] Quintilian, too, recalled how his young son, who died in his tenth year, already possessed all the incidental advantages for good reading, 'a pleasantness and clarity of voice, a sweetness of speech, and perfect correctness in pronouncing every letter in Greek and Latin, as though either was his native tongue'.[108] But these were boys of more than average gifts.

The reading-lesson of the *grammaticus* was known, in Latin, as a *praelectio*, or 'preliminary reading', because the most essential feature of it was the demonstration by the master himself, before the pupil made his own attempt. Although, especially if the class were large, this demonstration might have to be given to the boys as a whole, who would then imitate in chorus,[109] it was not originally designed as a class-lesson at all, but as a form of personal guidance given to each boy in turn. So Quintilian speaks of 'going ahead of individuals as they read', and it is clear, too, that, one after the other, boys left their seats and came and stood before the master.[110] It was fully realized in antiquity that pupils had different degrees of ability and comprehension, and instruction was varied accordingly. Above all, as Quintilian says, it was essential that the boy should understand not only the general sense of what he was to read, but the meaning of each word and phrase. He needed his teacher not only to 'go ahead' of him, but also to 'interpret',[111] and he both asked questions and was questioned in turn, to ensure that he fully understood. When he found the order of the words, or the exact sense, obscure, the master patiently recast and paraphrased, saying 'the order is this' or 'the sense is this' — expressions which occur again and again in the ancient commentators and scholiasts, at points where they felt that even adult readers might need help.[112] Once the passage was clearly understood, the master could proceed to read it continuously, and the boy noted where he paused, where he adapted his speed of delivery, and how he modulated his voice, bringing out of the text not only a clear pattern of thought, but also the warmth of feeling which the poet intended to convey. Then the boy himself read the passage back, and the master corrected his pronunciation, his delivery, his interpretation, point by point. He could then commit it to memory, and recite it when required. But, of course, it was more especially with beginners, or less gifted pupils, that this amount of personal preparation was needed; as time went on, individuals would be called upon to stand and read,[113] and the *praelectio* became more of a class lesson. But, before that stage was reached, some teachers put a great deal more into it, as we now may see.

CHAPTER XVII

Study of the poets
(*continued*)

(II) From reading to commentary

Those leading scholars who, like Varro, defined the various duties of the 'grammarian' in the treatment of authors, or, like Dionysius Thrax, divided his subject into its component parts, produced a brief classification, in which reading (*anagnosis, lectio*) stood first, and was separated from exposition (*exegesis, enarratio*), which came next.[1] But in actual teaching practice there was no such sharp distinction between them, for the one merged into the other. When giving individual tuition in reading, more especially to the younger boys in his school, the *grammaticus* constantly had to provide, or elicit, a 'construe', in order to ensure proper understanding. Likewise, he had constantly to draw attention to syllabic quantity, in order to ensure proper pronunciation. Consequently, at this stage, most teachers felt that they might as well use this opportunity to find out how their pupils had assimilated the 'technical' part of the course by making them parse and scan.[2] Both processes were known as 'partition' (*merismos, partitio*), because, whether one analysed the sentence and classified each word grammatically, or distinguished the metrical feet, one had to divide the line into several sections.[3] The practice was undoubtedly an old one, going back at least to the time of the late Republic, and Quintilian approved of it, provided that it played only a subsidiary role. The general method (though carried to excessive lengths) may be seen in the handbook of Priscian, called *Partitiones*, published in the sixth century A.D. Here the author takes the opening line of each book of the *Aeneid*, and, proceeding by the favourite method of question and answer, requires boys both to scan and to classify grammatically, and discourses at great length, word by word.[4] Obviously, Quintilian, whilst approving of the general approach, would have deprecated, even disdained, such expansion of what he considered a subsidiary matter (*illa minora*). On this scale, the 'grammarian's' lessons would have become exceedingly dull, and the amount of reading covered would have been drastically reduced. Instead, Quintilian wished to take matters further at this stage, and encourage boys to detect forms of words and expression which contravened the rules of correctness which they had been taught, always provided that it was explained that they were allowable by poetic license, and often due to the exigencies of metre. The teacher, he added, certainly should not use them to censure, and diminish confidence in, the poets, but should call them 'remouldings' and 'reshapings'. The purpose of all this, as Quintilian observed, was to recall the technical rules, (*artificialia*), that is, the strictly grammatical part of the course.[5]

It frequently happened, however, especially when reading Homer or early Latin poetry, that a boy found, in his preliminary reading, that some of the words did not appear to make sense in the meanings he normally attached to them, and that others were completely unfamiliar. So he asked his teacher to 'interpret', and the teacher explained the different meanings which a word might have in different contexts, and substituted for the rare or obsolete word (the 'gloss') a modern synonym.[6] As Quintilian accepted that such matters arose even in the preliminary stages (*prima rudimenta*), it is evident that the *praelectio* could begin to include some of the ingredients of a commentary. We have also, again from the sixth century A.D., a Greek treatise entitled *Epimerismoi*, which covers the first book of the *Iliad* line by line, and contains not only a great deal of grammatical analysis (though not in dialogue form), but glosses and etymologies as well.[7] All that has been mentioned so far, however, produced only a rather pedestrian type of exegesis, and it seems to be with a sigh of relief that Quintilian, at this point, turns from linguistic to more literary topics, to which he urges the *grammaticus* to attend 'with greater care', that is, in his commentary proper.[8]

It is a matter of great regret that we no longer possess in more than fragmentary form any ancient commentary on a Greek or Latin poet from the period under review, for those of Servius on Virgil and of Donatus on Terence, though partly derivative, are fourth-century work. Nevertheless, a few brief comments on the kind of notes which Servius gives on the first book of the *Aeneid* may serve to suggest at least the general flavour of ancient teaching, for the connection of his commentary with the schools is generally accepted.[9] Here, line by line parsing and scansion are a thing of the past; otherwise, the constituent elements of the *praelectio* are still there, but only when there is something unusual, or of interest, which seems to deserve a note. In the second line, for instance, Servius notes the scansion of *Italiam* with a long *i*, and observes that the word is used here without a preposition. 'Lavinian shores' needs a comment to show why Lavinium was so called and where it was. Many individual word-meanings and usages are discussed with parallels from Virgil himself and other authors. The scansion of *unīus* and *leniit* is worth a note, and a line ending *hominumque locorumque* is hypermetric.[10] *Gaza* is a gloss, being a Persian word for 'treasure'.[11] Etymology often comes in, sometimes erroneously, as to explain *Parcae*, 'the Fates' as 'the unsparing ones', from *parco* (typical of derivations by contrast), whereas they were originally 'birth-goddesses', *Paricae*, from *pario*, but sometimes rightly, as when *Vesta*, the hearth-goddess, is connected with *Hestia*, and *Trinacria*, Sicily, is derived from the Greek word for 'of three promontories'.[12] Notes on spelling are given, for instance, on *relliquiae, the(n)saurus*, and the forms *repostum, compostus* are noted as syncope.[13] The material is, as in any commentary, very miscellaneous; but there is one strikingly recurrent feature, which Dionysius Thrax associated especially with exegesis, and which always remained grammarian's work,[14] and that is the very frequent reference to the various turns of expression known as 'tropes'.

The Greek word *tropos*, when applied to style, meant a different 'way' of saying something, a turn of expression which involved a transference from a commonly accepted norm of meaning or usage. There was a good deal of rather arid controversy in antiquity, particularly between 'grammarians' and philosophers, as to what should be labelled a 'trope' and what should be designated a 'figure'. Theorists could not agree among themselves about the criteria which should determine the classification, the major and minor divisions, or the numbers. Some wished to confine tropes to single words, others to include words in conjunction; some wished to make a distinction between turns which merely arose from the necessity to express the meaning, and those which added positive ornament to style.[15] Moreover, both tropes and figures could occur in either verse or prose, and, as either the 'grammarian' or the rhetorician might draw attention to them, there was some confusion as to who should teach what. But there was at least a measure of agreement that there were a dozen or so tropes which were more particularly 'poetical', and were therefore very much the 'grammarian's' concern, though he might lay claim to some of the figures as well.[16] The actual listing, with definitions, of tropes and figures might be found in either a 'grammatical' or a rhetorical textbook,[17] but in practice the teaching of the basic, or ordinary, tropes was conventionally associated with the reading of the poets, most especially Homer and Virgil, and it is from them that the illustrative examples were taken. So we have, in Greek, *inter alia*, a little treatise doubtfully ascribed to the Augustan grammarian, Tryphon of Alexandria,[18] and a fuller treatment in the essay *On the Life and Poetry of Homer*, which has survived among the works of Plutarch. In Latin, many of the illustrations in the eighth book of Quintilian are taken from Virgil, and ample material of every kind has been assembled from the commentary of Servius.[19]

Quite the most important and striking of the tropes was Metaphor, (*metaphora, translatio*) which, as its name implied, was a 'carrying over' of a word from one sphere of existence or activity to another. The ancients were well aware of the distinction which could be imparted to style by metaphor, and of the vivid impression which, when imaginatively used, it could create upon the mind; they also recognized that its use must not overstep the bounds of propriety and discretion. In teaching, the first need was, of course, to draw attention to the sphere from which a particular metaphor was transferred, and to remark upon its relevance and aptness. The sources of metaphor were much more limited in antiquity than they have since become, and some types, such as those from navigation, from agriculture, from war, from medicine, from various trades — to name only a few — would frequently recur. But the *grammatici*, like the philosophers whom they followed, had a very analytical approach to metaphor, and sought to formulate a neat scheme of classification into which all types could be fitted.

According to this scheme, all metaphors could be divided into four major categories, which were based on the criterion whether the source from which they were derived, and the context to which they were applied, was animate or inanimate.[20] When Homer called Agamemnon the *'shepherd'* of the hosts', he was transferring the description of a living person in one kind of society to a living person in another; the same was true when a Latin poet spoke of a charioteer as a 'steersman' (*gubernator*) guiding his steeds.[21] Secondly, the transference might be from the inanimate to the inanimate, as when Virgil said of Aeneas that 'he gave the *reins* to his fleet', or applied the same metaphor to anger given full vent, or fire raging uncontrolled, or young vine-shoots allowed unimpeded growth.[22] The third type was that in which the transference was from the animate to the inanimate. Aristotle made special mention of this, noting how effective it was when Homer described the boulder which Sisyphus had pushed almost to the top of the hill, only to find that it rolled down again, as 'the *shameless* stone'. Equally striking was Homer's description of the spears aimed at Ajax, which fell short and stuck in the ground as '*longing to taste* his flesh'.[23] Virgil, too, boldly and successfully took the risk of referring to a river in spate as 'Araxes, *scorning* the bridge'.[24] Finally, there was transference from the inanimate to the animate, when a living person was described by a term normally applied to an object; a well-known example was Homer's description of Achilles as 'the *bulwark* of the Achaeans'.

One might have thought that this was carrying analysis far enough, but apparently ancient theorists were not satisfied unless they subdivided further, and elicited subordinate species as well as major types. Thus it was argued that the term 'animate' included both rational beings and irrational creatures, and this involved more subdivision.[25] Again, it was thought (and here Aristotle certainly led the way) that the degree of logical equivalence between the factors which made up the metaphor should be noted. Was it 'analogous' or not? When old age was described as the 'sunset' of life, the relationship between age and the full span of life was parallel to the relationship between the sunset period and the day as a whole. Equally exact was Pericles' metaphor when, speaking of young men who died in war, he said 'the springtime has perished from the year'.[26] But the relationship might not be so closely equivalent, and might have to be distinguished as that of a part to a whole, or species to genus.[27] It is not surprising that Quintilian should imply that boys were apt to be confused when required to detect these doctrinal refinements. But, in spite of this excessive scholasticism, there was some good teaching on metaphor,[28] as when it was shown to contribute to vividness, or warning was given that it must not be too prolonged, or mixed, or over-bold, or trivial, or sordid. It was observed, too, that some metaphors were not felt to be such because they had become part of common parlance. What seems to have been less commented upon was the quality of mind reflected in a fine metaphor, the power to capture a likeness on the instant and to communicate it in a word.

Closely associated with metaphor were certain tropes which, though they quite lacked the imaginative range and appeal of metaphor, involved the same general idea of transference, or some form of contiguity in expression. When, for instance, one spoke of 'the *lip* of a cup' or 'the *shoulder* of a mountain', it was regarded not so much as a metaphor as a misuse of terms, and was known as Catachresis (*abusio*).[29] Sometimes there were no other words which would express the meaning, but poets much favoured the device even when alternatives did exist. Stoic interest in the exact, or 'proper' use of words no doubt influenced the *grammatici* in their readiness to detect examples of Catachresis in their texts, and led to some rather futile and pedantic observations.[30] The same idea of contiguity underlay the trope of Metonymy, or 'different naming', the most frequent examples of which consisted in the favourite poetical habit of referring to a thing by the name of the god who had a special interest in it. So Virgil's description of corn spoiled by water as 'Ceres corrupted by the waves', and the common use of Mars, Vulcan and Neptune for war, fire and sea, were readily accepted, but duly marked as tropes.[31] It was possible to extend the use wherever there was some sort of mental connection, but even Quintilian thought it daring when Virgil said 'Ucalegon is afire next door', meaning, of course, his house.[32] Then again, in poetry, there was the favourite device of referring to a person by a patronymic, or some other substitution of terms which would add a touch of variety or distinction; this, too had its label, and was termed Antonomasia.[33] Finally in the same kind of category, there was the trope called Synecdoche, examplified when a word was strictly applicable only to a part of something, but was used to signify the whole of it, or vice versa. Common examples were *puppis*, strictly 'poop', for 'ship', *tectum*, 'roof', for 'dwelling', *mucro*, 'sword-point', for 'sword'. Sometimes there might be a transference from genus to species, or vice versa, as when poets used the word *quadrupes* for 'horse', or spoke of 'gold' or 'bronze' when they meant objects of gold or bronze.[34] Synecdoche, like other tropes, also existed in the language of ordinary life, simply because people do not always trouble to be particularly accurate in their use of words, but it called for comment by the *grammaticus* because it frequently occurred in poetry, and was sometimes boldly used. Virgil for instance, used the picturesque expression, *'vina coronant'*, 'they crown the wine', meaning that they wreathed with garlands the goblets containing the wine, and Servius duly noted the Synecdoche, the part for the whole.[35] But the 'grammarians' were sometimes quite absurdly fussy about identifying cases of this trope, especially when they included as examples such famous Homeric epithets as 'rosy-fingered dawn' and 'white-armed Hera', on the ground that dawn as a whole was rosy, not merely its rays, and the rest of Hera was presumably white, as well as her arms![36]

Apart from metaphor, which finds itself here in very much inferior company, these tropes are rather pedestrian, and anything but exciting to the critic or student of literature; but a much more interesting trope is Onomatopoeia. Literally, this meant the invention of a word, and could be applied to various forms of neologism, such as those formed by analogy from existing words, or original compound adjectives (a device much favoured by Pacuvius), or skilful adaptations from the Greek. But the most common application of the term in antiquity, as today, was to describe words either coined or utilized to reproduce some particular sound.[37] To the ancient *grammaticus*, the most admirable examples of onomatopoeia were those which he encountered in Homer, especially words which the poet had invented — or apparently invented — to represent the splash and roar of the sea, or the clangour of armed combat. The Greeks themselves, being accustomed to hear Homer recited, took the greatest delight in these strange words which often brought back so effectively the sound which Homer wished to convey. They heard the hiss and boom of the sea in *polyphloisboio thalassēs*, its roar in such words as *bremetai* and *smaragei*, the suck of the retreating waters in *rhochthei*, the loud murmur of onward-sweeping waves in *mormurei*,[38] the furious rush of the gale in his 'blustering winds' (*byktaōn anemōn*). They listened intently, and knew the difference when Homer spoke of a *bombos*, 'boom', a *doupos*, 'thud', a *kanachē*, 'clash' or 'clang'.[39] They saw, and heard, the armed warrior hit the dust in the line: 'Down with a *thud* he fell, and his armour *clattered* about him'.[40] They could hear the wolves, after their carnage, *'lapping* the dark water with their thin tongues'.[41] And how they must have loved that single word which Homer used when he told how Odysseus plunged the red-hot stake into the eye of the Cyclops, and the eye *'sizzled'* in its socket![42] Many a schoolboy must have been thrilled by the effects which the inimitable poet could produce by onomatopoeia.

Often, however, the trope was contained not in a single word, but in several, though some theorists then classed it as a figure, as, for example, Periphrasis. This was a device very commonly used by poets, and frequently noted by ancient commentators. Particularly favoured by the epic poets from Homer onwards were periphrases which described in picturesque form the time of day, and could have been expressed more prosaically in a word or two. Homer's recurrent formula for 'at dawn' was 'when the early rosy-fingered dawn appeared'; his 'at midday' was 'when the sun bestrode mid-heaven'.[43] Virgil, too, used various periphrases for dawn,[44] his 'after midday' was 'dawn with her rosy chariots had now passed the middle of the sky in her heavenly course',[45] and his late evening was 'the time when the first sleep comes to weary mortals, and, by the god's blessing, steals most deliciously upon them'.[46] Ancient critics fully approved of such periphrases, in which they recognized the grandeur of epic. Sometimes, however, they noted, the poet used a periphrasis to avoid a term which would be too trivial or commonplace, or vulgar, as when Virgil spoke of 'the offspring of a bristly boar', or 'the white bird, hated by the long snakes' instead of merely 'a pig' or 'a stork'.[47] This, of course, was a convention very much used by poets of the Alexandrian school. Equally conventional were those circumlocutions which were used, especially in epic, to elevate the personality of a god or hero, such as Homer's 'the strength of Poseidon', 'the might of Heracles', in place of the simple name.[48] Virgil's 'the father of gods and king of men' was similarly noted by Servius as a periphrasis for Jupiter, though Quintilian preferred to regard it as antonomasia. Servius frequently comments approvingly on such periphrases as 'hollowed rock' for 'cave', or 'hollowed barque' for 'ship', and Quintilian would readily have accepted his observation that 'poets love to use circumlocutions for things which require only a single word'.[49]

Sometimes, though less commonly, it was not the superfluity of words but their disturbed order which called for remark. When several words were thrown out of their natural sequence (whether through the exigencies of verse-composition, or to secure a more artistic effect), the trope was termed Hyperbaton.[50] An unusually disjointed word-order, criticized by Quintilian, is seen in Virgil's line: *saxa vocant Itali mediis quae in flucibus Aras*, which became a stock example of the trope.[51] When, as often happened, only two words appeared in a reversed order (e.g., a preposition following, instead of preceding, its noun), the trope was labelled Anastrophe. Then again, without any unnecessary expansion or unnatural sequence, the words might contain within themselves an element of exaggeration, and gave rise to the trope Hyperbole.[52] It was natural to accept and admire the hyperbole when Homer described the rock which the Cyclops hurled as a mountain-peak, and to note with approval Virgil's more discreetly expressed imitation, [53] but, once the principle was accepted, many less extravagant examples, such as 'whiter than snow', 'as fast as the winds', were duly pointed out as hyperbole.[54] Also, by that curiously logical approach so characteristic of ancient *grammatici*, it was felt that not only exaggeration, but excessive understatement should be classified under the same heading.[55] Writers of the imperial period were not given to understatement, but at least it was useful to point out to young pupils the dangers of exaggeration in an age in which transgressions against credibility and good taste were so common as to give rise to constant criticism of the vice of *cacozelia*, or 'perverse enthusiasm'.

Finally, there was one trope which could affect not merely a few words, but a considerable passage, or even an entire poem, namely, Allegory.[56] Metaphor could be so sustained that the reader's mind was, as it were, continuously transferred to a particular sphere of thought, whilst he still remained aware that the poet was merely using this elevated form of expression to convey a different basic meaning. The Greek *allegoria* implied saying one thing and meaning another, a sort of extended *double-entendre*. When, for instance, Virgil, at the end of the second *Georgic* wrote: 'But in our *course* we have covered a huge *field*, and it is time to *unyoke the necks* of our *steaming steeds*', he was speaking allegorically, but everyone could see what he meant.[57] More extended allegory was illustrated by Quintilian from the fourteenth ode of Horace's first book, where the poet speaks throughout of a ship, but really means the 'ship of state'.[58] The presence of sustained metaphor was a clear enough pointer to allegory, but a writer did not necessarily have to use metaphor in order to say one thing and mean another. Virgil, in the *Eclogues*, sometimes made his pastoral characters speak in a way which was undoubtedly intended to recall the real events of contemporary life, in which the poet himself played a part. Quintilian observed that, in a passage of the ninth *Eclogue*, Virgil used Menalcas as a pseudonym for himself.[59] But the fact that the poet evidently used allegory tempted some readers to look for further allegory, and to equate pastoral characters with real people, sometimes with awkward consequences. Servius, introducing the first Eclogue, made the rather lame proposition that 'we must take Virgil to be meant beneath the mask of Tityrus — not, however, everywhere, but where reason requires it'. Similarly, in the fifth Eclogue, he notes that whereas some take the lamented Daphnis to be simply the shepherd, others see in the poem an allegory on the death and deification of Caesar.[60] In Virgil, there was at least a prima facie case, but by far the most assiduous allegory-hunters in antiquity were the philosophical interpreters of Homer, and the 'grammarians' whom they influenced. For them, it was not enough simply to let Homer tell his own story; he must be shown to have intended to convey some particular doctrine, or to have been familiar with some particular concept of the universe. But even in strictly 'grammatical' teaching, Allegory produced a numerous offspring, for it was the mother not only of Enigma but of Irony, Sarcasm, and their sister-tropes — for logic demanded that if it was 'allegory' to say one thing and mean another, it must surely also be 'allegory' when one said the opposite of what one really meant.[61]

Such were the main tropes which formed the basic stock-in-trade of the *grammaticus*. Far more numerous — though the border-line often fluctuated — were the figures, both those of 'speech' and those of 'thought'. Almost any figure might occur from time to time in poetry, and would be commented on by the teacher,[62] but the richest harvest was drawn by the rhetorician, especially from oratorical prose. There was, however, one figure which had a particularly close association with poetry, for, of all the features of poetic style, none was used with greater beauty and effectiveness than the Simile. Quintilian discussed this in close connection with the virtue of vividness in style, and Tryphon, who was also greatly impressed by the vividness of Homer's similes, dealt with it at some length.[63] These were much more pervasive than his metaphors, and the scholiasts, too, point out that 'there are many similes in Homer, each one appropriate', and 'Homer always distinguishes himself by his comparisons'.[64] In the classification of similes, it was unusual to separate the brief, passing 'image' (*eikon, imago*), such as Homer's description of the Cyclops' club, 'like the mast of a twenty-oared ship', from the more fully extended 'comparison' (*parabole, similitudo*), which often began 'even as when ...', and could be developed in several lines.[65] Similes could also be classified according to subject, and there is a rather amusingly thorough list of this kind in the treatise *On the Life and Poetry of Homer*. The author gives examples of Homeric similes drawn from all kinds of living creatures (bees, wasps, grasshoppers, cranes, hawks, eagles, snakes, hares, dogs, wolves, boars, leopards, lions, horses), from human beings (e.g. reapers), and from the elements, especially the sea. It is interesting to notice that he, like other ancient critics, was conscious of the degree of 'elaboration' which might distinguish a simile. Speaking of a well-known example in the second book of the *Iliad*, in which Homer compares the shout of the Argives to the dashing of a wave against a high crag on the sea-shore, he thus explains the effectiveness of each detail:[66] 'It is clear that the poet has used exaggeration and amplification, for he was not satisfied to liken the shout to the sound of a wave, but compared it to a wave driven

against a steep shore, where, being hurled into the air, it makes a louder
roar; and he speaks not merely of a wave, but of one stirred up by the
south wind, which most of all disturbs the waters, and of one which
breaks on a jutting rocky headland, which stretches out into the sea, and
is washed on all sides, where there is incessant surf, from whatever
direction the blasts of the winds fall upon it'. A similar awareness of the
extent of elaboration is seen in the remarks of scholiasts on two passages
of the twelfth book of the *Iliad*, where the comparison of stones hurled at
the enemy to a snow-storm appears first in a brief form, and later with
full elaboration of detail. Here the scholiast remarks: 'The poet seems to
be outdoing himself in his comparison ... now he works up the image and
makes it more magnificent.'[67]

When we turn from these Greek critics of Homer to the comments of
Servius on the similes in Virgil, we find a much more sober appreciation
of the poet's merits, and an altogether more rationalistic approach to the
subject. In longer similes, Servius is mainly concerned with the content to
which the individual details of the comparison are 'apposite' (*congrua*) to
the situation which they are supposed to parallel. Here, he is evidently
much influenced by the fact that many pedantic critics before him had
insisted that each and every aspect of a simile must exactly correspond to
the existing situation. Not that he himself takes such a view; but the idea
of 'congruity' dominates his thinking. For example, in the first book of
the *Aeneid*, when Virgil describes Dido, in all her queenly beauty,
approaching the temple, accompanied by a large retinue of courtiers, he
compares her with Diana surrounded by her mountain-nymphs as she
leads the dances beside Eurotas or on Mount Cynthus. The simile was
based on the lines of Homer on Nausicaa, and was sharply criticized by
Probus.[68] 'Many critics censure this comparison', says Servius, 'being
unaware that exemplifications, parallels, and comparisons are not always
entirely apposite throughout; sometimes they are wholly, sometimes only
partly so'; and he adds that the leading of the dance by Diana is not
relevant to the comparison.[69] He gives full approval to the famous
simile in the same book, in which the workers building Carthage are
compared to the busy bees, because 'there is nothing otiose in this
comparison'.[70] Macrobius thought that it surpassed Homer.[71] In an
equally fine simile in the twelfth book, where the defenders of a
beleaguered city are compared to bees which a shepherd smokes out of a
rock, he finds each detail entirely apposite.[72] Among the comparisons
noted as 'quite apt' is that in the fourth book in which the love-stricken
Dido is likened to a hind, smitten by the hunter's arrow; also that in the
ninth book, where the silent advance of Turnus' army is likened to the
onward sweep of Nile or Ganges.[73] But one has the impression that
Servius is never more satisfied than when each detail of the simile fits into
place, though sometimes modern editors also debate whether the

explanation should complete the pattern.[74] Appreciation of similes depended greatly on the quality of mind of the critic; but it was at least to the credit of ancient *grammatici*, both Greek and Roman, that they did encourage their pupils to analyse and find the sources of beauty and effectiveness, and were not satisfied with a superficial expression of admiration.

One of the most important duties of the *grammaticus* in commenting on the poets was that of explaining to his pupils the numerous allusions to people, places, and events, which occurred from time to time in the text. Sometimes he could do so in a few words, but often there was more to be said, for there might be a 'story' involved. This was termed a *historia*, whether it was a matter of fact, or, as far more frequently happened, of fiction. The range of reference here was extremely wide, and the teacher needed to give information of the most diverse nature, now on gods, or heroes, or legendary, or genuinely historical figures, now on cities, tribes, mountains, rivers, promontories, now on ancient customs and religious observances, now on the association of gods and goddesses with mortals, now, maybe, on some miraculous birth, or marvellous transformation, or strange death. Some attempt was made, as by Asclepiades of Myrlea, to classify this material by applying the stock divisions of narrative into what was true, what was false, and what was plausible, and by distinguishing stories according to their concern with persons, places or times.[75] But such distinctions were rather academic, and, in practice, most of the 'grammarian's' comments were in some way connected with mythology.[76] Teachers of literature, said Tertullian, were obliged to discourse on the pagan gods, and to explain the names given to them, their genealogies, the tales told about them, and the honours bestowed upon them.[77] Any educated Roman boy, Cicero remarks, would know the story of Latona giving birth to Apollo and Diana at Delos.[78] Many of the myths would become familiar visually from works of art and various forms of decoration,[79] and the more of them one knew, the more readily would one understand the allusions to them in the poets. Also, such knowledge would soon prove useful in a different way, for among the earliest preliminary exercises in rhetorical composition, begun at the 'grammar' school, were short narrative essays on mythological themes.[80] In themselves, when told simply as stories, as Ovid told them, the myths were a delight, and, doubtless, a refreshing change from grammar. But, unfortunately, in the hands of scholars, the subject had become very complicated. As Servius observed, myths very often appeared in variant forms.[81] There was an extensive literature on them, especially in Greek, and the teacher would often have to mention how authorities differed, and which one he followed, and why. To take a single example, Aesculapius, who became the god of medicine, was killed, it was said, by lightning, and it was natural to ask why so great a benefactor should have been thus struck down by Zeus.[82] Sextus Empiricus cites no less than half a dozen authorities, each of whom gave a different explanation.[83] Thus these *historiae* came to occupy so prominent a place, first in the studies and then in the teaching of the *grammaticus*, that several critics, including Quintilian, thought that they were being given quite disproportionate, and sometimes futile, attention.[84] There was a further consequence, which does not seem to have been adequately stressed. Published commentaries, as Quintilian said, were apt to become swamped with mythology, but in the schoolroom it was obviously undesirable to have to discourse at length on each allusion as it arose. Many teachers, therefore, lightened this material by transferring much of it to separate lectures, or even a separate course, on mythology.

At the outset, without doubt, it was essential for boys to become familiar with the names and relationships of the gods and heroes involved in the story of Troy. Here it seems to have been usual to give preliminary instruction, which was followed up by a sort of catechism, of which Epictetus gives us a specimen:[85] 'Who was Hector's father?' — 'Priam'; 'Who were his brothers?' — 'Alexander and Deiphobus'; 'Who was his mother?' — 'Hecuba'; 'From which writer have I taken the story?' — 'From Homer, but I think Hellanicus and others also tell it'. Interestingly, too, a similar catechism survives on a Greek school papyrus of the fifth century A.D., where we read: 'Which gods aided the barbarians?' — 'Ares, Aphrodite, Apollo, Artemis, Leto, Scamandros'; 'Who was the king of the Trojans?' — 'Priam'; 'Who was their commander?' — 'Hector'; 'Who were their advisers?' — 'Polydamas and Agenor'; 'Who their soothsayers?' — 'Helenus and Cassandra, children of Priam'; 'Who their heralds?' — 'Idaeus and Eumedes, Dolon's father, and perhaps Dolon himself'. This must have been done at a quite early stage, for on the reverse there is written a fragment of the *Grammar* of Dionysius Thrax.[86]

In the notes given, whilst reading the text, on the characters who appeared in the story, or on persons to whom a passing allusion was made, genealogy was a recurrent feature.[87] In the *Iliad*, for example, the scholiast can tell his readers (quite unnecessarily) who were the mother and father of Thersites, and in the *Aeneid*, Servius explains (necessarily) the reference to the 'house of Assaracus' by recording that Assaracus was the father of Capys, who was the father of Anchises, who was the father of Aeneas.[88] But mythological relationships were a tangled skein which made the family tree of the Caesars look like child's play, and the *grammaticus* was expected to know all the answers — or, at least, where to find them. It was also necessary to explain why certain gods were given particular epithets, such as 'Sminthian'[89] Apollo, or what were the great achievements of their lives, such as the exploits of

Hercules. Legendary heroes were often reputed to have founded cities; so Servius, commenting on Virgil, tells how Antenor came to found Patavium (Padua), and how Diomedes founded many cities, including Beneventum, in southern Italy.[90] Here again, as Servius tells us, there was quite a literature on the subject of founders and a great deal of dispute.[91] To add to the problems, it was often not merely a question of eponymous heroes and aetiological myths, but a matter of derivation of place-names by etymology, and etymology could be one of the most fanciful of scholarly pursuits.[92] When there was no 'topical history' attached to a place, it was enough to explain where it was, or that there were two or more places of the same name. But if a teacher wished to be thorough, he could use a particular opportunity, as scholiasts sometimes do, to mention all the rivers in a particular area together, rather as Lucan digresses to list those which flowed from the Apennines.[93] But there were always problems; everyone knew that the Nile had seven mouths, but even scholars were not sure whether the same was true of the Timavus or the Ganges.[94] Finally, as Latin investigations were added to Greek, the field of knowledge widened further, and to the Trojan legend and the Theban legend was added the story of Rome's early history and its kings, until, as in the pageant unfolded by Anchises in the sixth book of the *Aeneid*, mythology merged into history.

There is no better evidence of the importance attached to mythology than that which the classification of the 'grammarian's' fields of interest provides. For Quintilian, there are only two major divisions — Grammar, and Exposition of the Poets. But already, under the Republic, the system of Asclepiades was based on a threefold division, Grammar, Mythology (with history) and Exegesis. Sextus Empiricus[95] follows the same scheme, and it reappears in Ausonius.[96] It is seen in Seneca's observation that the *grammaticus* moves from Grammar to Mythology, and from Mythology to Exegesis, and its presence has not been properly commented upon, but is still there, when Juvenal says that the 'grammarian' is expected 'to be faultless in language, to study the myths, and to know all the authors'.[97] Nor does this triple division refer only to the knowledge required by the *grammaticus* himself. It must also have affected his teaching, for, in one passage, Quintilian himself speaks of a whole class listening whilst the teacher 'discusses the use of language, explains problems, sets forth myths, and expounds works of poetry'.[98] Clearly, then, there must have been separate lectures devoted to mythology, whether preliminary, concurrent, or supplementary, as well as the normal practice of commenting more briefly on such matters in the explanation of the text. Quintilian was not alone in thinking that far too much time was spent on the ramifications of mythology.[99]

The 'problems' (*quaestiones*), which Quintilian here mentions, are a good example of such separate treatment. They were innumerable, but the record which we have shows that they included both genuine literary questions, especially concerning the Homeric poems and the *Aeneid*, and more recondite inquiries, including a good deal which was trivial or pedantic. Subjects most likely to have been lectured upon in schools would be, for example, which city was Homer's birthplace, whether Homer or Hesiod was the earlier, whether the *Iliad* or the *Odyssey* was written first, whether both poems were by the same author, and what was the course of Odysseus' wanderings — within the Mediterranean or beyond?[100] In Latin, one such problem, on which Ateius Philologus composed a treatise, concerned the question of whether it was really Dido whom Aeneas loved; for we know that Varro also discussed this, and held that it was not Dido but her sister, Anna, who became enamoured of Aeneas.[101] Many of the problems involved investigation into antiquities, or language, as may be seen from Plutarch and Aulus Gellius. But there was also no limit to the ingenuity of inquirers who, from casual acquaintances at the baths or dinner-parties to emperors like Tiberius and Hadrian, amused themselves by testing the detailed knowledge of scholars.[102] There were questions of identification — 'Who was Anchises' nurse?', 'Who was really the mother of Aeneas?', 'Who was Hecuba's mother?', 'Who was the stepmother of Anchemolus, and where did she come from?' (This worthy appears just once in Virgil, entering his stepmother's bed-chamber).[103] Then there were questions of age, which were supposed to have been elicited by diligent study, such as 'How old were Achilles and Patroclus?' 'What was the relative age of Hecuba and Helen?', 'How long did Acestes live?'. Then there were such apparently mischievous inquiries as: 'How many rowers had Odysseus?', 'What was Achilles' name among the maidens?', 'What song did the Sirens sing?'. Nevertheless, it should not be too readily assumed that it was usually impossible to find an answer. From Hellenistic times there were scholars who were called 'propounders' of problems, but there were also those known as 'solvers'.[104] The *grammatici* frequently tested one another, and Valerius Cato was one of those who were reputedly very good at finding the answers.[105] In the examples given, Anchises' nurse was Tisiphone, Anchemolus' stepmother was Casperia, Achilles' name was Pyrrha.[106] Such things mattered little, but often the queries involved a debate which was worthwhile. But it is time to return to the commentary proper.

The aspects of study so far considered —grammar and metre, glosses and etymologies, tropes and figures, myths and problems — remained the most permanently characteristic features of literary exposition at the secondary level. But the *grammatici* were by no means the only people who had an interest in, and a use for, poetry; there were others whose mentality and approach were radically different, and from whose powerful influence they could not remain entirely immune. Poetry was an open field for philosophers and rhetoricians as well as 'grammarians', and, as Seneca says in a most instructive passage,[107] 'in the same meadow, the ox looks for grass, the dog for the hare, the stork for the lizard'. Seneca is not here primarily speaking of teaching, but what he says admirably illustrates the difference of attitude of the strict 'grammarian' and the philosopher. He observes that when the *grammaticus* reads Virgil's expression on the swift flight of time (*fugit irreparabile tempus*), he is not prompted to any reflections on the need for a sense of urgency in human life; instead, he is interested in the use of the verb *fugit*, and cites a parallel example from the same book.[108] Here the poet says that the best time of life 'flies' first, and associates the idea with the stealthy approach of old age and death. Yet, says Seneca, the 'grammarian' is still not disposed to draw salutary lessons, as would a philosopher, on the importance of effort and devotion to study and self-improvement. Instead, he notes how like Virgil it is to associate old age with ill-health, and cites another passage in which he applies the same epithet, 'gloomy' (*tristis*) to it.[109] For, above all, the 'grammarian' is interested in the use of words. He picks up a line of Ennius, where the expression *opis pretium* occurs in the sense of 'recompense for service', whereas the current phrase was *operae pretium*, and notes that in old writers, the word *ops* meant not only 'help' but 'effort'. Then he finds a passage in which Ennius uses the expression 'the gate of Heaven', and argues that this must have been the source of a parallel use in Virgil, but that Ennius himself had taken it from Homer. Seneca then sums up by remarking that 'all philosophical study and reading should be directed to the object of attaining a happy life, and we should not be hunting up archaisms, neologisms, daring metaphors, and figures of speech, which will not help us at all, but looking for valuable precepts and lofty and inspiring utterances, which may in due course be translated into action'.[110] This was a typically philosophical view, and it had a long history behind it in Greek, especially in connection with the study of Homer; but the *grammatici* themselves were not all so free from moralizing as Seneca would have us believe.

The Cynics and the Stoics, particularly, from the days of Antisthenes and Chrysippus, had much favoured the moralizing interpretation of Homer,[111] and the same kind of approach was made to the tragic poets. One of the most instructive essays in this connection is that of Plutarch, entitled *How a Young Person should study Poetry*. Here, for instance, when reviewing the quarrel-scene between Achilles and Agamemnon, the author intersperses moral judgments step by step. Agamemnon dismisses the priest, Chryses, 'harshly', says Homer, thus indicating his own disapproval. Disaster follows. Achilles rightly advises consulting a seer. But when Calchas expresses his fear of the king's anger, Achilles swears that no man shall lay a hand on him, not even Agamemnon himself — not rightly, says Plutarch, for he shows contempt for his leader. Soon, Achilles' anger blazes up; he draws his sword and threatens to kill the king — 'not rightly', says the moralist, 'either for honour or expediency'. Then, mollified by Athena, he relents and puts back his sword — rightly and honourably, subduing his anger and listening to the voice of reason. Even so Achilles bitterly abuses Agamemnon — vehement words, which could do no good. Yet Agamemnon, thinks Plutarch, even though he had made a fool of himself before the assembled troops, behaved in a kingly and dignified manner in relinquishing Chryseis, for whom he deeply cared, without further untoward act, whereas Achilles, when deprived in turn of Briseis, burst into tears and sat aloof from his comrades. Thus, where the literary critic would admire the vividness and immediacy of this quickly-moving drama, the moralist soberly weighs each act and word, and finds a lesson in each successive scene.[112] It is not surprising, then, that this kind of interpretation should have left its mark on the Homeric scholia, and there are many notes which begin: 'The poet teaches that ...', or 'The passage is instructive, because ...'.[113] In fact, quite often the reader feels that the scholiast has been looking out for any possible peg on which to hang a moral observation, and will even force the text to elicit it, whether it be to inculcate some lesson of piety and reverence for the gods, or to praise respect for the aged, for parents, for benefactors, or the patient acceptance of hardship, or gentleness and restraint in conduct and the dangers of arrogance.

There were, however, as the philosophers themselves fully realized, some difficult problems here, and it was only at a later stage, in the event that boys should attend a philosopher's lectures, that they could be fully and properly resolved. So Lucian makes the philosopher, Menippus, declare that when, in boyhood, he learnt from Homer and Hesiod not only about the wars and quarrels of gods and heroes, but about their adulterous amours, assaults, abductions, and much else, he thought these things must be permissible, only to find to his perplexity, when older, that they were the very acts which the laws forbade.[114] Plutarch seeks to supply the answer. The young, he says, need guidance (*paedagogia*) in such matters, as in all else, and it is best to explain that poetry, like painting, is an imitative art, and that it reflects the bad as well as the good. They must be brought to see that those who behave sinfully, or utter wicked or fallacious sentiments, are to be discredited, and it is best of all to show, wherever possible, that the poet *intended* them to be discredited.[115] For example, in the famous story in the *Odyssey* of the ingenious device by which Hephaestus exposed the adulterous lovers, Ares and Aphrodite, the gods said to each other: 'evil deeds do not prosper', for by poetic justice, the swift Ares was caught by the lame Hephaestus, and paid him the penalty.[116] Thus Homer himself showed his disapproval of such conduct. This is how Plutarch wished it to be presented. 'If', he says, 'the description and portrayal of bad actions represents, as it should, the disgrace and injury resulting to the doers thereof, it benefits instead of harming the listeners'.[117] Again, if, as often happened in the dramatic poets, a character should express, quite unequivocally, sentiments of which the moralist disapproved, there were several possible alternatives. The best procedure was to find, if possible, some other passage in the same poet, in which a directly opposite sentiment, or, at least, a counterbalancing opinion, was expressed, and to praise its superior wisdom. If, as rarely happened, the poet proved entirely consistent, passages should be sought from other writers of acknowledged repute, which would restore the balance to the better side. If even this failed, it might be possible to reinterpret the statement in its context, or to draw an argument from parallels which showed the significance of particular words, in fact to take a leaf out of the 'grammarian's' book.[118] But, naturally, the *grammaticus* himself, with so much else to comment upon, had not the time to discourse at great length, like the professional philosopher, on the moral lessons of poetry.

In Roman studies, a very good example of appreciation of Homer for what he had to teach about human life and behaviour is seen in one of the epistles of Horace, in which he tells how he has been re-reading the poet. He observes that the *Iliad* is a tale of the folly of kings, through which their peoples suffer, for wiser counsels do not prevail, and, on both sides, evil passions are released by war. The *Odyssey*, on the other hand, in Horace's view, has many positive moral virtues to teach, especially in the character of Odysseus, who is a model of prudence and a splendid example of persistent endurance of hardships and setbacks, strong enough, too, to resist the seductive temptations of Circe and the Sirens.[119] This association of particular qualities with particular characters in epic is illustrated by some of the notes of Servius on Aeneas and Turnus. He not infrequently pauses to observe that the *pietas* of Aeneas is shown by his reverence for the gods, his acceptance of the divine will, his respect for his father in great matters and in small, his loyal affection for his friends and his magnanimity towards his foes, and his conscientious observance of the last respects due to the dead.[120] When the Sibyl encourages Aeneas, Servius sees that she 'well teaches that the blows of Fortune are avoided, or lessened, by courage, and may be endured by patience'.[121] Again, he notes that the poet, in accord with Horace's precept, utters 'things helpful to life'; when, for example, the Sibyl shows how traitors are damned and patriots blessed, 'the poet teaches that sins must be avoided and virtues ardently pursued'.[122] Aeneas, says Servius, is also a man of courage, and so, too, is Turnus, but Turnus, though a great and proud warrior, is also a violent man; with

him courage is unsuccessful courage and becomes temerity.[123] Such
moral lessons must have been drawn from Virgil, upon occasion, long
before the time of Servius; though they were probably not as yet given so
much attention in Latin as with Homer and the tragedians in Greek. At
all times, however, much would have depended upon the personality and
interests of the teacher.

Finally, there was another, quite different, approach to the exposition
of poetry which was not at all concerned with philosophical moralizing,
but had much more in common with the study of rhetoric. This is why it
is so strongly recommended by Quintilian. He urges that teachers
'should particularly impress on boys' minds what are the good qualities
of arrangement, what appropriateness there is in the treatment of the
events described, how it was fitting for the characters to behave, what is
praiseworthy in thoughts and diction, where the elaboration and where
the restraint is commendable'.[124] One might say, truly, that it was not
necessary to be a rhetoric student to appreciate such merits, but the main
features concerned — structure, propriety of characterization, striking
thoughts, expansion and conciseness — were just those which would
prove most relevant when the pupils of the *grammaticus* came to
compose miniature speeches themselves. It was not until a later stage,
with the rhetorician, that Quintilian expected a more detailed rhetorical
analysis of both poets and prose-writers to be made, but the ancient
commentators themselves, both in published work and in teaching, came
more and more under the influence of rhetorical doctrine. Some
examples from them will show the kind of thing which Quintilian had in
mind at this point.

Arrangement (*oeconomia, dispositio*) was of primary importance, for
it was itself one of the five 'parts' rhetoric. Here the teacher would
consider first the overall structure of the poem or play. He would
certainly draw attention to the successful use of inverted chronological
order by Homer and Virgil, who plunge the reader into the midst of the
story at the outset, and then allow him to learn later what had happened
before.[125] But he would also bring out from time to time those more
subtle details by which the poet created added interest or suspense, or
foreshadowed some subsequent development.[126] The Homeric
scholiasts saw a very good example of skilful arrangement in the
movements of Patroclus. Towards the end of the eleventh book of the
Iliad, Patroclus was urged by Nestor to seek Achilles' permission to join
the fray, if Achilles would not come forth himself. Instead, he delayed to
care for the wounded Euryalus, and then does not appear again until the
end of book fifteen, where he tells Eurypylus that he must go at once and
summon Achilles. Thus Homer was enabled to describe in full the bitter
fighting around the wall and the ships in the intervening books, and this
made it even more urgent for Patroclus, shocked at the ghastly carnage,

to approach Achilles.[127] Without those books, the drama would have been much less intense. Again, in the eighteenth book, after the death of Patroclus, Polydamas advised the Trojans to retire to the city, lest Achilles should return, but Hector over-ruled him, and the Trojans applauded, 'for Pallas Athene had stolen away their wits'. Homer himself observed that Polydamas' plan was the wiser, but the scholiasts were quick to notice that, if it had been followed, the elders would never have allowed Hector to come forth again to combat with Achilles, and the climax of the story would have been lost.[128] Finally, an excellent example of arrangement was seen in Homer's treatment of Andromache and her receipt of the news of Hector's death. The scholiast observed that, if Andromache had been included by Homer among the Trojans who watched the final duel from a tower, her husband's death, though grievous, would have been less completely shattering that it actually was in the circumstances which Homer described. For Andromache was indoors, working at her loom, whilst her handmaids prepared a bath for Hector on his return, and had no suspicion of the imminent tragedy. Only when she heard the great wailing from the walls did she suddenly realize the terrible truth, and the quiet domestic scene was transformed into one of utter dismay.[129] How admirably Homer managed these things!

Many further observations on arrangement could be drawn from the scholia to Homer and the tragedians,[130] and from the commentaries of Servius on Virgil and, particularly, Donatus on Terence.[131] They serve to show how alert the *grammatici* were to the possibility that small points might have significance. The same closeness of observation was brought to the study of 'propriety' (*prepon, decor*), which Quintilian mentions next. Here, however, their remarks often do not show particular insight, but merely reflect the conventional ideas which were current in antiquity about the way in which gods and heroes ought to speak or behave. The Alexandrian critics, most notably Zenodotus, applied their own notions of propriety to the text of Homer, and were sometimes prepared not merely to query the genuineness of lines or passages, but to expunge them on the ground that they were not befitting to the character concerned.[132] Subsequent scholars did not necessarily agree, but, in any case, the criterion was a dangerously subjective one; though it is only fair to the Alexandrians to add that modern critics, too, have sometimes had their doubts. A few examples from the Homeric scholia will perhaps be of interest here.

When, at the beginning of the *Iliad*, Agamemnon angrily refused to give back the priest's daughter, Chryseis, he declared that she should return with him to Argos to be his handmaid, 'plying the loom and visiting my bed'. The verses were athetized because it was 'unbecoming' for a king to speak in this way.[133] Similarly, near the end of the poem,

Thetis, when consoling Achilles, and urging him to make the most of what little remained to him of life, said that it was 'a good thing to lie with a woman in sweet love'. Aristarchus deleted the line, because it was improper for a mother to speak thus to her son.[134] Here modern critics, too, have been uncertain whether Homer really wrote the line; Cobet accepted it, Leaf, with hesitation, allowed it to stand, and Bayfield discreetly dropped it. Quite apart from any question of morality, passages describing some small item of behaviour might be called into question. In the third book of the *Iliad*, Aphrodite is described as placing a chair for Helen. Zenodotus deleted and re-wrote the lines, because it was an unfitting action for a goddess, but Aristarchus defended them on the ground that she was here represented in the guise of an old woman.[135] Finally, in a passage of the eleventh book of the *Odyssey* (which some think interpolated from the *Iliad*), Odysseus said that the responsibility had been laid on him of opening and shutting the door of the Wooden Horse. The scholiast marked the line as 'unbecoming', as this was a janitor's duty![136]

Criticism of propriety, however, might be favourable rather than adverse, and in schools it was much more satisfactory to draw attention to examples where the poet was to be praised for his sense of appropriateness than to be on the look-out for shortcomings. Servius' commentary on the *Aeneid* well illustrates this approach. When, for example some critics said that Aeneas made a poor showing after the storm at sea, because Virgil said that his limbs were 'numbed with chilling fear', and claimed that Homer's description of Odysseus in a similar situation was 'more noble and in keeping with a heroic character', Servius was undeterred. 'Virgil preserved propriety', he stoutly maintained 'because he says Aeneas was the *last* to be afraid', though the text does not prove it at all![137] Later, when the Trojans reached a safe harbour, Virgil describes how the rest of them set about preparing a meal, whereas Aeneas climbed a rock and scanned the sea for signs of other survivors. 'Persons of reputable standing', observes Servius, 'should not take part in trivial occupations, and Virgil well observes this rule'.[138] When, in the third book, Virgil says that 'father Anchises' gave the order to sail, Servius noted the propriety, as the enterprise gained in importance from being invested with paternal authority.[139] The poet's sense of appropriateness is also praised from time to time when some small point seems to the commentator to be entirely in keeping with the courage or dignity of the person concerned. Similarly, the schoolmaster would use the opportunity, as it arose, to instil admiration for the nobility of epic character. But there was also a further important aspect of propriety, which concerned not so much what was actually done as what was said, and, especially, the way in which it was said. The teacher would show how the style of speaking reflected the character of the individual or the mood of the moment. In Homer, for instance, he would observe how well suited to an old and experienced counsellor was the sweetly persuasive speech of Nestor, and how Diomedes, after his valorous deeds addresses even Agamemnon with all the outspokenness of a young and doughty warrior.[140] Such comments on style and manner paved the way for rhetoric, and would soon prove useful, when boys began to compose 'speeches in character', as rhetorical exercises, themselves.

Propriety was also frequently the criterion used in the criticism of diction, for, as Cicero says,[141] the *grammatici* were especially concerned with this aspect of poetry. From Aristotle onwards, critics insisted that words and expressions should conform to the subject in hand, which might mean that they should suit a particular literary genre, or a particular episode or topic.[142] It was a doctrine which gave rise to many observations, whether favourable or unfavourable, sensible or pedantic, in ancient literary criticism. Critics of Terence, such as Probus and Asper, seem to have taken a hard line about the distinction between the diction of comedy and tragedy, claiming that this or that word or expression was 'too lofty' for the genre. Donatus, however, though he occasionally accepts such objections without demur, generally prefers to defend his author.[143] Epic diction was expected to have a certain grandeur about it, though it was recognized that much depended on the topic in hand. The *grammatici* were so conscious of the importance of maintaining epic dignity that they had a special term for anything which tended to lower it, and called it *tapeinosis*, or 'weakening'. But they also recognized that the opposite fault might occur when a minor matter was expressed in exaggerated language.[144] Servius gives praise to Virgil for substituting a more elevated term for what might have been, in ordinary language, too commonplace or trivial. When the poet said that Aeneas unloaded from his ship 'the implements of Ceres', meaning mortars, pestles and handmills, Servius noted that he did so deliberately to avoid such exceedingly humble words.[145] Similarly, he approves of Virgil's use of *lychni* for 'lamps', instead of the commonplace *lucernae*.[146] In addition to several such notes, he observes that sometimes an added epithet, such as 'huge' or 'vast' served to enhance the scene.[147] Quintilian well observed that 'some words are more distinguished, more sublime, more elegant, more attractive, more melodious than others', [148] and would have wished teachers to draw attention to examples where the choice of a particular word was commendable on one of these grounds. He noted, too, that sometimes archaic words, used with artistry and discretion, would cast upon the style a pleasant aura of antiquity, and selected for praise Virgil's use of *olli* for *illi*, *moerus* for *murus*, *pone* for *post*.[149]

In advising the teacher which aspects of poetry he should stress, Quintilian combines with the virtues of diction 'that which is praiseworthy in the thoughts', and here he would certainly have included thoughts which were conveyed in a succinct manner and, at the same time, embodied something memorable and valuable as a guide to life and conduct. He himself defined the *sententia* in general as that which might be 'praiseworthy quite apart from its immediate context'.[150] Just as the primary teacher had given his boys single-line maxims from the poets to write out and memorize, so the *grammaticus* drew attention to them as they arose in the text. So 'Plutarch' noted that there were many examples in Homer,[151] and the author of the hypothesis to the *Phoenissae* of Euripides observed that 'there are many excellent reflections to be found in this play'. Interest in the *sententiae* of the poets was universal. The philosophers adapted them to their own teaching, praising them when they were acceptable and disagreeing with them when they were not.[152] But they had a particularly close association with rhetoric. They had always been useful for orators to quote,[153] but they showed students how a single short sentence might enshrine 'what oft was thought but ne'er so well expressed'. That is why, at a later stage of study, Quintilian draws attention to them as one of the major features in many poets, from Homer and Hesiod to his own day.[154] In declamation, as we shall see, *sententiae*, whether of universal or only limited application, were all-pervasive.

Of equal interest to future students of rhetoric was Quintilian's final requirement, that the *grammaticus* should observe where abundance and where conciseness of expression deserve praise.[155] This is an aspect which often recurs both in the Homeric scholia and in Servius. Both qualities were admired according as they were deemed to suit the circumstances, whether in narrative (especially descriptions) or in speeches. Most famous of all examples of superbly effective brevity was Antilochus' announcement to Achilles of the death of Patroclus; praised by Quintilian and Tryphon, it is also admired by the scholiast because, in just two lines, it said quite simply all that needed to be said.[156] Elaboration, on the other hand, which was called *exergasia* or *epexergasia*, though often found excellent, especially by the rhetorically-minded, also sometimes presented problems, at any rate in Homer. For textual critics, it raised the question of possible interpolation, and the Alexandrians, including Aristarchus, would athetize lines or passages because they thought them 'redundant' or 'unnecessary', or 'the context requires brevity'.[157] Zenodotus, for example, rejected the whole description of the scenes on the shield of Achilles because of its 'elaboration', leaving only a few introductory lines; here Aristarchus did not agree.[158] Sometimes modern scholars are not sure whether the elaboration is Homer's or not. Early in the eleventh book of the *Iliad*, thirty lines are taken up with an account of the arming of Agamemnon. Some think there is extensive interpolation, but the scholiast noted that

Homer had made much of the arming in order to prepare the listener for Agamemnon's subsequent valorous deeds.[159] But, as a rule, the *grammaticus* would draw attention to both expansion and brevity in order to praise them. So Servius observes that Virgil 'prudently extends or compresses a speech according to the circumstances', and that 'descriptions are developed or cut short according to the nature of the events'.[160] He remarks on the admirable brevity in some of the more rapid narrative,[161] as in the fighting in Troy, but also notes that Virgil sometimes finds occasion to describe a little more fully something which he had described elsewhere more concisely, or introduces descriptions at different points (as of the armour of Turnus) which are complementary to each other.[162] All this teaching had its uses as well as its interest; for when boys came to write rhetorical compositions, one of the fundamental abilities which they had to acquire was that needed in expansion and contraction of their themes.

Such were the many and varied aspects of the teacher's commentary. There remains one final point, which can only be briefly mentioned here, namely, the extent to which textual criticism formed part of the 'grammarian's' work. This has often been considerably over-estimated, in view of the fact that Varro[163] names as the third and fourth 'duties' of the *grammaticus*, textual correction and criticism (*emendatio, iudicium*). This part of Varro's scheme (derived from earlier Greek sources) has led to the misapprehension that, after the reading and commentary, the 'grammarian' proceeded to discuss textual matters separately, as a further part of his course.[164] There is no evidence that this was true in the average school, and Quintilian's account, which says nothing about textual problems, cannot be made to fit Varro's scheme. What happened was that (as we see, for example, in Servius) the *grammaticus* simply mentioned variant readings, or alleged interpolations, occasionally in the course of his commentary. Beyond that he had no need to go, for his pupils did not need to become involved in such matters of scholarship. Their steps were being directed towards rhetoric, and, in the view of many, the sooner they could begin their rhetoric the better; so a start might be made in the 'grammar' school.

CHAPTER XVIII

Progress into rhetoric: preliminary exercises

Although the course of the *grammaticus* in language and literature could be both interesting and instructive, it was not originally designed to provide any opportunity for constructive work in prose, essential though this was for those whose ultimate objective was usually to become good public speakers. Traditionally, this was part of the province of rhetoric, and Greek rhetoricians, long before Quintilian's day, had evolved a whole series of exercises in composition, each based on a stereotyped framework of rules supplied by the teacher, which, adapting the language of physical education to intellectual studies, they termed *progymnasmata*, or 'preliminary training-exercises'.[1] When the series was fully developed there were about a dozen types in all, and much consideration was given to grading them in order of difficulty, for they ranged from fairly straightforward exercises based on the Fable, the Saying (*chreia*), and the mythological Narrative to much more difficult ones, such as the Speech in Character, the Thesis, and the Discussion of a Law. They were 'preliminary' in the sense that they were designed to lead up to the full-scale mock-deliberative and mock-legal speeches, called by the Greeks *hypotheses*, and by the Romans *suasoriae* and *controversiae*. Some of these exercises (e.g., the Thesis) were extremely old, and dated back to classical Greece, but the often-repeated statement that the set of *progymnasmata* goes back to the fourth century B.C. lacks any firm basis, for the occurrence of the word in the text of the *Rhetorica ad Alexandrum* in a general sense can hardly warrant this deduction. [2] Moreover, the practice of inventing mock-deliberative and mock-legal themes, for which these exercises afforded a preparation, was itself somewhat later, and was generally associated with the name of Demetrius of Phalerum.[3] It seems likely, therefore, that the formation of the standard set of preliminary exercises, known to us mainly from writers of the imperial period, was a gradual process, which took place during the Hellenistic Age. It must, however, have been fairly complete by the first century B.C., and maybe earlier, for already in the late Republic the set, or a good part of it, was being used by teachers of rhetoric in Latin,[4] who called them *exercitationes* or, later, *materiae*. It was not long, however, before the Latin rhetoricians began to hand some of them down to the *grammatici*, who, by Quintilian's time were dealing with the whole series. Greek teachers of rhetoric, on the other hand, did not go anything like so far as this, but themselves retained for centuries most of what had always been part of their standard rhetorical teaching.[5] The most detailed treatise for our period is that of Aelius Theon, who was probably a younger contemporary of Quintilian,[6] but mention may be made here of later Greek compilations, on which, in view of the remarkably faithful adherence to tradition, it would seem not unreasonable to draw from time to time for the better illustration of the subject. The short manual of Hermogenes,[7] dating from the late second century, shows how stereotyped the system had by then become; but it gives little beyond the bare rules. Although the grammarian Priscian later produced a Latin version of it,[8] far greater success attended the fourth-century work of Aphthonius, for this included worked-out examples of the various exercises.[9] This little manual exercised a quite extraordinarily protracted influence in education, for, long after it had been assiduously annotated and commented upon by Greek scholars,[10] it was reproduced in Latin form in the sixteenth century, with supplementary themes and notes by Reinhard Lorich,[11] and was widely used in schools in that and the following century. Thus the Latin Aphthonius has become very much within the purview of students of English literature, notably in works on Shakespeare[12] and Milton.[13] Very much less widely known has been the substantial collection of model versions in Greek, composed for the use of students by that indefatigable rhetorical expert, Libanius,[14] the teacher of Aphthonius. Nor is the fifth-century treatise of Nicolaus Sophista[15] much used, though he has some quite valuable observations on the reasons which lay behind the order of the exercises and the placing of each one.

In Latin, the material is far less rich, and, apart from certain references in the *Ad Herennium* and Cicero's rhetorical works, and a few important remarks in Suetonius, we rely mainly upon Quintilian. At Rome, it is clear that the use of preliminary exercises in Latin was at first the prerogative of rhetoric, and the order of exercises enumerated by Suetonius accords closely with Greek practice.[16] There is just one important addition — the practice of translation from Greek into Latin becomes a new exercise. But it so happened (as doubtless often in the Hellenistic period) that many of those who taught at Rome in the late Republic took classes in both 'grammar' and rhetoric.[17] Consequently, there was no reason, in principle, why a *grammaticus* should not pave the way, provided that he had the competence, for exercises which really belonged to the rhetorician. By the Augustan Age, with increasing specialization, the professions of 'grammarian' and rhetorician had become quite distinct,[18] but in the interest of pupils it was obviously desirable to do something towards integrating the two stages of study. In this connection it should be made clear that the attitude of the Greek teachers and that of the Latin teachers, in either subject, was by no means the same. The Greeks interlocked the two courses, and required students who joined the rhetoric class to continue to attend, for a time, the school of their *grammaticus*. This was still true in Quintilian's time,[19] and we shall see that, even in the textbook of the rhetorician Theon, there are some very simple forms of treatment of the early exercises which would in fact usually have been dealt with by a Greek 'grammarian'. But Latin teachers took a rather different view about the interlocking of their two disciplines. At first, the 'grammarians' were content to devise their own exercises, 'so that their boys should not be transferred to the rhetoricians with an entirely jejune and arid style'.[20] Suetonius mentions a few of these, which will be mentioned later; they are none of them listed separately in the standard Greek *progymnasmata*, but were intended to lead up to them. But circumstances in Latin rhetorical circles soon encouraged 'grammarians' to do very much more than this.

A great impetus was, under the Empire, given to the extension of rhetorical teaching in the Latin grammar school by the vast increase in the popularity of declamation of *suasoriae* and *controversiae*. Rhetoricians, both in and out of school, found this so tempting an avenue to fame that they became content to leave more and more of what should have been their preliminary work to the *grammatici*. The pressure of ambitious parents and pupils no doubt aided the process, but, although some 'grammarians' may have felt that teaching composition in prose was none of their business, the probability is that many were quite eager to embrace the opportunity, as the teaching of a subject which had traditionally belonged to the higher level would be felt to enhance their status. The result was that the course of the *grammatici* was prolonged (a development which they would welcome from an economic standpoint), and boys were rather older when they reached the rhetoric-school. But, as the 'grammarians' gradually extended their range to take over all the Latinized *progymnasmata*, their pupils, on entering the rhetoric-school, could tackle mock-deliberative and mock-legal themes at once. Quintilian regarded this development with the greatest disfavour, and considered it a dereliction of duty on the part of Roman teachers of rhetoric.[21] But even he could not stem the tide completely, and the most that he could do was to propose a compromise, which would bring the Latin and the Greek teaching into closer line. He urged that the *grammatici* should retain only a few of the preliminary exercises, from the earliest types in the list, and leave the rest to their rhetorical colleagues.[22] He probably had serious doubts about the ability of the average *grammaticus* to tackle properly the more advanced exercises, and in this he may well have been right. But it is also noteworthy that he does not encourage them to attempt to deal even with the early exercises in a full rhetorical manner, for he wished boys to proceed to the rhetoric-school as soon as possible, and merely to continue, at that time, to attend the grammar-school for a few lessons at certain hours during the period of transition. Compositions were written either in Greek or in Latin or in both, according to the teachers whom the boy attended.

The easiest exercises, which were always taught early in the course (though not necessarily in the same order), were those based on the instructive Saying (*chreia*), the Maxim (*sententia*), the Fable (*apologus, fabula*) and the mythological Narrative (*narratio*). Here there was the advantage that all of these had been used at the primary level simply for writing-practice, whether by copying or dictation, and for learning by heart. Now boys had to reproduce them in their own words, and explain and expand them in short essays. This was all that Quintilian expected the *grammaticus* to do, though he was fully aware that even with such simple forms more difficult exercises could be evolved, and a rhetorician like Theon could treat them much more elaborately. Theon made gradations of difficulty within the individual type, and elaborated half a dozen methods of making exercises out of each one; not satisfied merely with explanation and expansion, he required his pupils to proceed to a confirmation and refutation of the Saying, Fable or Narrative, and argue that it was sound and plausible, or the reverse.[23] After these initial exercises, the next step forward was to bring pupils more into the field of practical oratory by making them develop Commonplaces, themes involving Praise and Denunciation, and Comparisons, all of which involved amplification. These were followed by types which demanded use of the imagination, as well as range of expression. The Speech in Character was a particular favourite, in which it was necessary to impersonate some well-known character in myth or history, and to speak as he or she might have spoken in some dire crisis or dilemma. Here, for the first time, we see the rhetoric-teacher moving into subjects which required both psychological insight and portrayal of emotion (*ethos* and *pathos*). Next came the full-scale Description — always a valuable asset to an orator keen on showmanship. Finally, the power to argue a case both *pro* and *contra* was developed by the exercise of the Thesis, and, last of the stock series, the Discussion of a Law. These, as we shall see, led straight to the full-scale declamation, the *suasoria* and the *controversia*, of which any of these preliminary exercises might provide a useful component part.

Such was the preliminary course in outline. But, although the text-books present it in a very schematic form, teachers were at liberty to make what use of it they wished; the order was not immutable, and Suetonius remarks that Latin teachers did not all consistently follow the same programme.[24] But two important aspects, sometimes over-looked, should be noticed. First, although these were primarily written exercises, they were also expressed orally, and Theon makes special mention of delivery;[25] thus in this respect, too, they were an introduction to the practice of declamation on more specialized themes. Secondly, although they were clearly directed towards oratorical fluency, they were also regarded by their teachers as laying the foundations for a wider sphere of literary activity,[26] and they did, in fact, exert a considerable influence on the methods of composition of both prose-writers and poets. Classical authors of earlier days provided the background reading-material for the course, and students who became authors themselves were influenced in turn by the rules which they had learnt at school.

From early childhood, when their nurses had told them stories of the animal kingdom to keep them quiet, and from their primary school days, when they had laboriously copied out fables, boys had become familiar with the delightful world of Aesop, in which animals met and talked and behaved like human beings, and in which there was always a moral to adorn the tale. Now they had to try their hand at writing these fables for themselves, first telling the story orally, and then writing it down in their own words. Only a simple, natural style was needed, for periodic structure was quite alien to fable;[27] but more than mere reproduction was required. It was necessary to learn to expand the fable, to make more of it by developing the details. It was the most natural thing in the world that animals should hold conversations with one another, but the fox and the wolf did not think and speak like the sheep, or the lion like the lamb.[28] So the young writer was encouraged to build into the story little speeches,[29] in keeping with the characters and the circumstances, whilst still maintaining an easy conversational tone. There was the fable of the apes, who thought it would be a good idea to live in cities, like men, and held a public meeting to discuss the matter; some pointed out the advantages, but it was a wise old ape who dissuaded them, and drew attention to the dangers of allowing themselves to be enclosed.[30] There was the fable of the simple sheep, who were willing to leave the sheepdogs and make a peace-compact with the wolves, until a wise old ram showed them how stupidly they were rushing to their own destruction.[31] Such little speeches were the first steps towards the as yet far distant goal of deliberative oratory.[32] Then again, expansion could often be achieved by the introduction of descriptions, with circumstan-tial details. We may see how delightfully a master-hand like Horace does this if we compare his version of the fable of the Town Mouse and the Country Mouse with that of Babrius.[33] Whereas Babrius is content to refer briefly to the contents of the well-stocked larder which the mice raid together, Horace introduces the charmingly humorous description of the country mouse being invited to recline on purple coverlets, whilst his town-brother acts as waiter, serving course after course, and first tasting of everything he presents. Embellishment by description might well be introduced, as Theon suggests, in the fable of the dog and his reflection;[34] carrying a piece of meat, the dog was walking beside a river, when he thought he saw another dog beside him, also carrying a piece of meat; the temptation was too great, and in attempting to acquire two pieces of meat, he lost what he had, or in Theon's version, was drowned. Here was an opportunity to describe the placid stream, the brightness of a sunny day, and the clarity of the reflection in the water. All this encouraged the young to use their imaginations and at the same time developed their powers of expression. And it is interesting evidence of the careful way in which these exercises were integrated that both the Speech in Character and the Description were to become exercises in themselves later on in the course. The reverse process too, might be used; a fable might be presented in a long-winded form, with plenty of unnecessary detail, and the boys would have to make a *précis* of it, reducing it in length and retaining only the essentials.

The essence of the Fable, and in fact, its very *raison d'être*, was the moral, which might appear either at the beginning (*promythion*), or at the end (*epimythion*).[35] In Phaedrus, the fable of the dog is prefaced by the moral that 'he who covets what belongs to another deservedly loses his own'; in Babrius, it has been added (probably by a later hand) at the end. Schoolmasters naturally did not like to miss the chance of drawing a moral, so, using this instance, Theon recommends that the boys should find the moral for themselves, and add it at the end of their essay. It was also possible, though perhaps at a rather more advanced stage, to utilize Fable exercises in a wider context. Pupils might be given a fable, and told to illustrate it from some historical occurrence, or, conversely, be given a historical narrative and required to find a fable to suit it.[36] In fact, the Fable obviously had a close connection with the Narrative, an exercise which was soon to follow. Even in the oratory of real life, the Fable was not without its uses, as a source of wise moralizing, or more often, a means of amusing an audience;[37] at this elementary stage, it was an excellent exercise, for the subject-matter was so enjoyable, and, apart from its moral value, it encouraged the young to compose and to let their style develop without the restraint of close adherence to a copy.

Immediately after his precepts on the Fable, Quintilian[38] mentions an exercise which was long practised in the grammar-schools, that of the Paraphrase of passages of verse. Unfortunately, he does not make his transition very clear, and, as he speaks of recasting poetry in prose order, altering the diction, expanding here and shortening there, but always keeping the general sense of 'the poet', it has been widely thought that he was still speaking about the Fable, and that, consequently, the schools in his day must have used the versified fables of Phaedrus[39] or Babrius,[40] or both.[41] There is, however, a lack of supporting evidence for this interpretation, which has been strongly contested,[42] and there is much to commend the view that *versus* means not 'the verses' (of fable) but 'verses' in general. Moreover, although Quintilian shows elsewhere that he was well aware that one could find 'Aesopic fables' in verse (e.g., the Hawk and the Nightingale in Hesiod, the Lark and its Young in Ennius, the Fox and the Sick Lion in Lucilius, the Town and Country Mouse in Horace),[43] it is pretty clear that he thought of them as normally in prose form.[44] He is thinking here, then, of the poets usually read in grammar schools, such as Homer and Virgil, and when he remarks that paraphrase of poetry can be a quite difficult and exacting task, if it is to be done well, his point is made clear by his much fuller discussion of paraphrase in general at a later stage in his work.[45] Theon, too, discourses at length on the value of paraphrase,[46] which, whilst not listed as a *progymnasma* in itself by Greek theorists, was a basic feature in all these early exercises, though in the rhetoric school it was more often paraphrase from prose.

But, to return to the standard list of rhetorical *progymnasmata*, we have mentioned the Fable first because Quintilian gives it priority, and, after his day, it regularly came at the head of the list. It is so, too, in the transmitted text of Theon, but this has evidently been adjusted to bring it into line with later practice, for Theon's own remarks make it clear that he took the Saying first,[47] and, to judge from the order in Suetonius, the Saying has at least an equal claim to priority.[48] It is best taken in conjunction with the Maxim (which Theon mentions but does not treat separately), for there was a considerable similarity between the two. For instance, 'Money is the root of all evil' is a maxim (*sententia*), but 'Bion the sophist said that greed for money is the metropolis of all evil' is a saying (*chreia*).[49] The main difference is in the introduction of the author's name; though sometimes the meaning of the Saying was not quite so immediately obvious as that of the straightforward Maxim. It might, for instance, be couched in a metaphorical form, such as the favourite example: 'Isocrates said that the roots of education are bitter, but the fruits are sweet.'[50] Often it was presented as the answer to an inquiry, as: 'Pittacus of Mitylene, when asked if anyone doing evil escaped the gods' notice, replied that no one did, even when thinking evil.'[51] These were examples which merely reported a remark. But the same term, *chreia*, was extended to apply also to instructive incidents in which something was both done and said. For example, 'Diogenes, seeing a boy misbehave, beat his pedagogue' is an Act-*chreia*, whilst the addition of the words 'saying "Why did you educate him like this?"' could cause the example to be classed as 'Mixed'[52] — a somewhat academic distinction. The various types of Saying are rather elaborately classified by Theon; sometimes they are proverbial, sometimes paradoxical, and often they take the form of a witty observation or repartee. The sources used are sayings of the Seven Wise Men, of Socrates, and, most particularly, Diogenes and the Cynic school generally.[53] But, whatever the origin, the Saying, like the Maxim, was treated in a series of quite formalized exercises.

The simplest form of treatment, which was already in use under the Republic, and which reappears in Quintilian and Theon, was surprisingly elementary, and clearly associated with the grammar school, for it consisted merely in 'declension'. The saying was quoted in the first instance as a statement, in which the person responsible for the remark, or incident, naturally appeared in the nominative case. The pupil then had to present this in all the oblique cases, using certain stock introductory formulae. For example, the *chreia* beginning 'Isocrates said ...' had to be recast to become 'There is a story of Isocrates having said ...' (genitive), 'It occurred to Isocrates to remark ...' (dative), 'They say that Isocrates observed ...' (accusative), and even 'You once said, Isocrates ...' (vocative). This was all very well, even if quite mechanical, if it went no further.[54] But Greek teachers were not satisfied until the same example was written out in all cases in the dual and plural as well, with the rather ludicrous result that we get 'The two orators, Isocrates, said ...', or 'The orators, Isocrates, said ...'. A very interesting example of such a declension in full, written on a wooden tablet of the third century A.D., was acquired by the British Museum early in the present century.[55] Here the *chreia* is: 'The philosopher Pythagoras, having disembarked and begun teaching letters, counselled his disciples to abstain from meat', and it duly appears in all the cases and numbers until it becomes: 'O you philosophers, you Pythagorases, ... you counselled ...'. This certainly stems from a grammar school, for on the other side of the tablet is a full declension of all the forms of the optative of a Greek contracted verb. Quintilian, too, is perfectly willing to leave this kind of exercise to the grammarian. But what value could a rhetorician like Theon have found in it? Here we must remember that pupils apparently left primary school without having had any experience in composition whatever, and if they then went to a grammarian who did not teach composition, they might even arrive at the rhetoric school quite unprepared. In any case, the likelihood is that beginners tended to express everything in the simplest nominative forms, such as 'He said this ... then he said that ...'. The exercise made them vary their forms of expression, and when, as in the Pythagoras example, there were also participles in agreement with 'Pythagoras', these, too, had to be varied in case and in number. This provided a recapitulation of grammatical forms which was certainly sometimes necessary. So the schoolboy in question proceeded very nicely until he came to the dative plural of the participle 'teaching', which he then mistakenly wrote as διδακοντοις instead of διδασκουσιν. It is of interest, too, to notice that in another tablet, one of a series of eight which formed a schoolboy's book, the identical formulae for the use of the various cases recurs among a collection of grammatical notes (Fig. 23).[56]

At this point, mention may be made of a particular form of Saying, which appears in the context of teaching by *grammatici*, and which was called the aetiology (*aetiologia*).[57] The exact nature of the exercise is a matter for deduction, but the term clearly suggests that it was a statement to which a reason (*aitia*) was appended, and this is the definition of it in rhetorical sources when it is mentioned as a figure.[58] It was, as an exercise, attributed to particular persons, and could be either a saying or a quotation.[59] Now, in discussions of the Maxim, in Aristotle[60] and even earlier,[61] a distinction is made between a generally acceptable statement and one which is paradoxical or controversial, and this latter type, we are told, should have a brief 'explanation' subjoined, so that it becomes a sort of enthymeme. For example, the verse of Euripides, 'No man alive is there who's truly free' is followed by the explanation, 'for he's the slave of money or of chance'.[62] The Aetiology, therefore, must have been a paradoxical or controversial saying or quotation. A prose example, which Theon includes as a form of *chreia*,[63] would be the remark of Isocrates: 'Teachers should be honoured more than parents; for parents are responsible only for bringing children into life, teachers for bringing them to a good life.' Probably, then, this was an easy saying-exercise, which the pupil was merely required to paraphrase and 'decline'; for here the author himself supplied the 'explanation', which, in subsequent treatments, the boy might have to find for himself.[64]

From the rhetorician's point of view, however, much more valuable exercises than this could be devised, particularly those which aimed at the amplification of an anecdote or saying. Practice in any form of amplification was useful for the future orator, and it had the advantage that either a quite straightforward or a more complex and detailed development of the theme could be required. The simplest method was merely to expand the original into a short essay of a few sentences. Theon shows how this could be done. His example is as follows:[65] 'Epaminondas, dying without offspring, said to his friends: "I have left two daughters, the victory at Leuctra, and that at Mantinea".' When expanded, this becomes: 'Epaminondas, the Theban general, was, then, a good man even in time of peace, but when war broke out between his country and the Spartans, he performed many brilliant deeds of courage. When Boeotian leader at Leuctra, he defeated the enemy, but whilst campaigning and combating on his country's behalf, he died at Mantinea. But when, being wounded, he was at death's door, and his friends were particularly distressed that he would die childless, he smiled and said: ''Cease grieving, my friends, for I have left you two immortal daughters, two victories for my country against Sparta, the one at Leuctra, the older, and the younger, the one just born at Mantinea''.' The reverse process would be, as with the Fable, to present it in an expanded form, and then to require it to be reduced to a brief compass.

Much more thoroughgoing than this was the 'elaboration' (*ergasia, expolitio*) of the original according to a number of fixed headings, or topics. The details of this treatment must have been worked out quite early by Greek theorists, for we find them already applied in Latin to the development of a maxim in the *Rhetoric to Herennius*. [66] Theon preferred to put such forms of elaboration considerably later in the course, [67] but they are part of the standard teaching at this point from Hermogenes onwards. We may take, as the commonest example, the saying of Isocrates about the roots and the fruits of education. Hermogenes and Aphthonius both give the headings with brief development, [68] but more interesting is the full-scale model essay of Libanius, [69] which runs to some fifteen pages of text, and is so lucid and natural that, if one did not already know the pegs on which it was hung, one would not suspect it to be an artificial composition at all. The method was to begin with a few words in praise of the author — e.g. Isocrates said many wise things, but nothing wiser than this. Then the saying must be paraphrased — Isocrates meant that the early stages of learning were full of trouble, but the results later on were well worth it. Next, we must have an explanation, to show how true this was. Here we have an account of the trials and tribulations of schoolboys (which, incidentally, throw a vivid light on ancient discipline), the tyrannous demands of teachers, reproof, abuse, threats and blows if a boy gets things wrong, and the prospect of something more difficult if he gets them right; the harassing pressure of the ubiquitous pedagogue, always breathing down a boy's neck and keeping his nose to the grindstone; the unreasonableness of parents, always eager to test progress; nothing but work, work, from early morning till late at night. But the rewards, ah!, the rewards — to be respected as an educated man, to be introduced to the council and the assembly, to be heard by the people with attention, to represent one's city as an ambassador, to win fame as an advocate, and perhaps even, in old age, to be publicly honoured with a statue! As if the point of the saying were not yet clear enough, the writer must now proceed to argue it from contraries — those who have an easy start never get anywhere — and then he must give a parallel from a quite different sphere — the farmer, for instance, and the merchant in his ship, have a hard time at first, but they live to reap their rewards. Next, a specific example which clinches the argument — and what better example than the great Demosthenes himself? Finally, to cap it all, a quotation from the poets, those much-respected purveyors of succinct wisdom. Did not Hesiod say that the gods made sweat the precursor of Virtue, and that though the road was long and steep, and rough at first, it was nice and easy when you reached the top?[70] Of course, even a very promising young pupil could hardly have written as artfully and persuasively as a professional rhetorician; but these were the lines along which boys were encouraged to think and compose.

　　The purpose of these exercises in providing a preliminary training for the future orator becomes very clear in the next type of written composition, the Narrative; for, in rhetorical theory and often in advocacy, the narrative was an integral part of a speech. Boys were not expected, however, at this early stage, to write the sort of 'statement of the case' which an advocate would present in court. Rather, they were given narrative themes which were closely related to their own studies, but which, nevertheless, helped them to acquire the art of telling a story. The simplest form of material was the myth, and it was entirely appropriate that these 'stories made famous by the poets' should be written, as Quintilian suggests, whilst boys were studying the poets at the grammar school.[71] He does not expect young pupils to attempt any rhetorical embellishment as yet in writing out these stories, but merely that they should present them straightforwardly and become familiar with the subject-matter of each myth. In Greek, this kind of exercise was not thought beneath the attention of the rhetorician, and the models which they provide are quite short (a dozen lines or so) and are usually cast in a simple, unadorned style. Aphthonius gives as his example the story of Aphrodite and Adonis, telling how the jealous Ares, himself in love with the goddess, just as the goddess herself doted on the beauteous youth, sought to slay Adonis, but was prevented by Aphrodite, who in so doing lacerated her ankle on a rose-thorn — hence the colour of the red rose.[72] Many more models — some thirty of them — are given by Libanius,[73] and include many of the famous stories which we meet in Ovid, such as that of Apollo and Daphne, Procne and Philomela, Marsyas and the flute, Atalanta and the golden apple, Pasiphae and the bull, the Danaids, or in Greek Tragedy, such as the stories of Alcestis, Iphigeneia, Adrastus. Fragmentary examples of schoolboys' work in Greek[74] show evidence of the two last mentioned, and also of the stories of the Labours of Hercules, of Philoctetes, and of themes drawn from Homer. Hermogenes[75] selects as his model subject the story of Medea and the Golden Fleece; his approach, however, is more rhetorical, and he tries to show how, instead of mere sentence by sentence statements, the use of a series of rhetorical questions, or quick-moving asyndeton, can impart liveliness and vigour to the style. To quote him, 'what wicked thing did Medea not do? was she not enamoured of Jason? did she not betray the golden fleece? did she not murder her brother, Absyrtus?', or 'Medea, Aeetes' daughter, loved Jason, betrayed the golden fleece, slew her brother ...'. Most teachers, however were probably content if their pupils could write at this stage in a manner that was clear, succinct and convincing — the traditional virtues of the narrative style. Nearly all the evidence for the subjects of these mythical narratives is in Greek, but it is quite clear from Cicero's youthful treatise on rhetoric that Roman teachers drew on their native literature for their stories;[76] not only did Roman Tragedy provide many of the stock myths, but, as we may now see, Comedy was also pressed into service.

So far, we have dealt with stories which are far removed from reality and truth; but there was a second type, which, although it did not record what actually occurred, was closely modelled on the happenings of everyday life — that is, the subject-matter of Greek New Comedy. Roman teachers had an excellent model for this kind of fictitious, but realistic, narrative (*argumentum*) in the plays of Terence. It is interesting to find that Terence should have been utilized for rhetorical teaching as early as the time of Cicero's youth, and that the opening scene of the *Andria* in which Simo describes how he discovered that his son, Pamphilus, had fallen in love with Glycerium, should have been selected as a model narrative, which boys would have been required to recount in their own words.[77] The purity of the style and the clarity and natural development of the story made this an excellent example of the narrative art.

All such stories, being based on poetic sources, were quite legitimate material for the *grammaticus*, even though, in Greek, the rhetorician did not disdain them. But the next kind of narrative, the historical, was very much the rhetorician's concern, and it is at this point that Quintilian insists that the rhetorician should take over.[78] This again was perfectly reasonable, for the reading of historians was begun at the rhetoric school, whether privately by the boys themselves, or under the guidance of an assistant master.[79] Whilst this class of narrative was strictly supposed to record 'events which actually occurred', in practice the material would range, in Greek, from such stories as that of Arion and the dolphin, or Polycrates and his ring, in Herodotus, or Gyges and his ring in Plato, to serious historical accounts such as that of Thucydides of the Theban attack on Plataea.[80] In Latin, the legendary stories of early Rome provided a wide range of subjects, which fully made up in human interest what they sometimes lacked in veracity. For these, and for genuinely historical material, teachers could draw on Livy, an author considered particularly suitable for beginners in the rhetoric school. The briefly-told stories in Valerius Maximus, with their strong moral flavour, would also have made a very useful source-book, and the collection may well have been compiled for rhetorical purposes.

The first need was to ensure that each boy was familiar with the subject matter, and, as with the Fable, it seems that oral exposition preceded the writing out of the exercise, at least with beginners. Quintilian speaks of boys first repeating individually, at the master's desk '(or, in Roman conditions, 'lap'), what the teacher said. Then he would require the story to be repeated from different starting-points, either beginning in the middle, returning to what preceded, and then concluding, or even beginning at the end and then working back over the events which led to the conclusion.[81] All this was a test of memory, and was only possible if the pupil had a real grasp of the whole. There were good precedents in literature for this kind of treatment; Theon points to the examples of the *Odyssey*, where Odysseus is at first with Calypso, and only later are his previous adventures recounted,[82] and Thucydides, who starts at the beginning of the Peloponnesian War and later introduces his account of the previous fifty years. Herodotus, too, starts the story of Cambyses and then proceeds to relate what had previously happened. In Latin, the *Aeneid* was an obvious example. Not all critics approved of this kind of treatment in practice, but they would probably not have objected to it as a preliminary method of testing a boy's memory and ability to manipulate his subject-matter. When this was satisfactory, the writing of the exercise began, and now attention was paid in particular to style.

The standard virtues of narrative style were clarity, succinctness, and plausibility. Clarity, says Theon,[83] should be obtained by viewing the subject as a whole and not merely tacking together a series of episodes, by proper arrangement of topics, by avoiding repetition and long digressions. Care should be taken to avoid the use of poetic, archaic or unfamiliar words, and especially, expressions which could be ambiguous. In this last point, Stoic influence is noticeable, as elsewhere in Theon. Conciseness, he proceeds,[84] is obtained by keeping the mind firmly on the central issue and including only what contributes to that issue. Faults which militate against conciseness arise from inserting material which is not immediately germane, from mentioning what may safely be left to be understood, or from beginning at a point too distant in time. These precepts, like that of plunging *in medias res* above, are interestingly similar to those so admirably expressed in the *Ars Poetica* of Horace.[85] For conciseness of expression, says Theon,[86] doublets, circumlocutions, and the use of compound for simple words, should all be avoided; but care must be taken that the desire for succinctness does not lead to obscurity. Here again, we are reminded of Horace.[87] Finally, plausibility is obtained by envisaging the events from the point of view of the persons, the occasion, and the place concerned, and describing actions or reactions according to what seemed most *likely* to have happened. Even small details could sometimes be remarkably convincing and true to life.[88] As with the previous exercises, the rhetoricians had several varieties of treatment which could be applied to the narrative.[89] They might require it to be expanded or contracted, or to be cast in different sentence-forms, or to be rounded off at the end by an appropriate epigrammatic comment, a stylistic feature much appreciated in the Silver Age of Latin. But the most advanced treatment, which was sometimes put later in the course as a separate exercise, was what was known as Refutation and Confirmation (*anaskeue* and *kataskeue*);[90] that is, the writer had to examine a given story from the point of view of its general credibility, and then write an essay either arguing that it was lacking in likelihood, or supporting it as quite feasible. The material here was largely drawn from poetry, especially mythology. Favourite subjects were the stories of Apollo's love for Daphne, Medea's murder of her children, Arion's adventure and escape on the dolphin.[91] Homeric themes could also be used, as that of Chryses and his daughter at the beginning of the *Iliad*.[92] Theon also includes legends from prose sources. In each case, there were guide-lines laid down for procedure; after setting out the alleged facts, the pupil should ask himself, according as he wished to substantiate or refute, whether the account was clear or obscure, possible or impossible, seemly or unseemly, consistent or inconsistent, expedient or inexpedient. He should argue accordingly, bearing also in mind at each stage the person, the act, the place, the time, the manner, and the motive. Although boys were thus exercising their wits and critical faculties mainly in the realm of mythology, the search for arguments based on likelihood had a quite important application later; for in criminal cases, both in the rhetoric schools and in the courts, considerations of likelihood came very much to the fore when tangible evidence was limited or lacking.[93] It is also interesting to note that Quintilian wishes the early Roman legends to be examined critically in this way — can we believe the story of Valerius and the raven, Romulus and the she-wolf, Numa and Egeria?[94] The credibility of early Roman history, then, was a subject which does not entirely belong to modern times.

Even more closely allied to forensic practice was the next exercise, the Commonplace. This was a form of amplification which, if aptly applied, could be extremely effective in court. Most commonly, it was an exposure, both reasoned and emotional, of various types of evil-doer, though it also had its converse, dilation on the merits and services of various types of benefactor. All kinds of vice, as represented by an imagined, but not named, individual, are denounced. Cicero mentions commonplaces directed against an embezzler, a traitor, a parricide;[95] Quintilian instances commonplaces against an adulterer, a gambler, a profligate;[96] and Greek rhetoricians are very fond, in addition, of exercises directed against a tyrant, a murderer, a traitor, a temple-robber.[97] For the praise of virtue, typically Greek is the commonplace on behalf of the tyrant-slayer.[98] All these were classified as 'straightforward' themes, but they could be made more complex; the picture of vice might be blackened if, for instance, an attack is prepared against a doctor who is a poisoner,[99] or some palliative considerations might be introduced, as in the modified denunciation of an adulterer who was blind.[100] Generally speaking, the treatment of the commonplace was very similar to part of an advocate's speech in court, the main difference being that in the exercise no specific individual was attacked or defended. The exercise assumed that the case against, or on behalf of, the particular type of offender, or benefactor, had already been substantiated by argument, and the commonplace, therefore, was especially appropriate to the peroration of a speech,[101] in which it was customary to try to leave the audience emotionally roused and deeply impressed. In teaching boys to compose commonplaces, the rhetoricians, as in most of these exercises, realized that some guide-lines must be provided, and worked out a series of headings. The order of these became fairly standardized from the time of Hermogenes onwards.

The best way to open an attack on an evil-doer, said the theorists,[102] was, after a few words of introduction, to start from the opposite and recall the public honour and appreciation shown towards those whose lives were meritorious. Then a sharp contrast could be drawn with the scoundrel under consideration, and a reasonable call be made for dire punishment. Next a full statement of the enormity of his offence. After this, a comparison — if we punish lesser criminals, how much more so this one, whose offence is even worse? Then, a further blackening — a man who would stoop so low must have committed many other offences in his lifetime, of which this is the culmination. After this, a sententious summing up of the offender's way of life, followed by a strong demand that no mercy must be shown. To enforce this, a short, dramataic description of the offender actually committing the crime, which thus leaves the audience with a vivid picture, calculated suitably to horrify their minds and ensure a verdict of condemnation. It should be observed, however, that in legal practice the purpose of a commonplace was sometimes rather different and more subtle. The gravity of a crime could be emphasized not for condemnation but for defence; so Cicero amplifies the crime of parricide only to prove that a man such as Roscius of Ameria could not possibly have been guilty of it.[103]

Very similar in some respects to the commonplace was the next exercise, that of Encomium and Denunciation; indeed the general similarity was such that the order of treatment could easily be reversed. Quintilian[104] mentions the Encomium before the commonplace, but the general consensus of the Greek theorists was that they should be taken in the order which is followed here. Both exercises were concerned with either praise or blame, but whereas the commonplace dealt only with types, encomium and denunciation were concerned with specific historical (or legendary) persons. Again, just as the commonplace was useful because it could be introduced incidentally in an actual speech, so praise and vituperation were frequently necessary in both forensic and deliberative oratory.[105] But there was this difference: the commonplace was usually no more than an inserted passage, or section, in a practical speech, whereas an encomium or denunciation could take up an entire oration. In fact, so common was this, and so highly rated was this form of speech, especially by the Greeks, that panegyric became a major branch of oratory, parallel to the judicial and the deliberative, which, though generally termed 'epideictic', or 'show-oratory', was sometimes called the 'encomiastic' branch, because the speech of praise formed a major constituent part of it.[106] In the rhetorical schools, the preliminary exercises, with which we are here concerned, concentrated on the topics to be used when praising famous men, or denouncing evildoers.[107] The subjects were drawn from Greek and Roman history, though in the Greek schools the praise, or dispraise, of Homeric heroes was also much favoured.[108] The range of epideictic, as a major branch of oratory, was very much wider than this. Quintilian mentions praise of gods, of cities, of public monuments, of localities, and Libanius' examples include praise of justice and of agriculture, and denunciations of wealth, poverty, anger, wine. Quintilian refers to the praise of sleep, and young Marcus Aurelius wrote in dispraise of sleep for Fronto. Then there were paradoxical themes, such as praise of Thersites (mentioned by Polybius and included in Libanius), and denunciation of Penelope. There was the praise of the trivial, such as Lucian's encomium on a fly, or of the apparently unpraisable, such as young Marcus' sketches in praise of smoke and dust, and negligence. But these were the refinements of the trade. At this stage, boys would be dealing mainly with the praise and censure of individuals, the kind of material which survives in Cicero's praise of Pompey in *Pro Lege Manilia* and Pliny's panegyric of Trajan, and the rhetorical invectives against Sallust and Catiline.[109]

The topics of praise were legion, and it was recognized that not all were appropriate in every case; the student must make a selection to suit the subject concerned, but the general scheme which he was required to follow remained remarkably consistent throughout ancient theory. It was based on a threefold division, which goes back to Plato and Aristotle, according to which praiseworthy features of a person were classified as either physical qualities, qualities of mind and character, or extraneous accessions, whether inherited or acquired.[110] Students were advised to proceed chronologically,[111] considering first the origin and background of the person concerned; if of noble birth, he might be praised as having matched, or surpassed, the glory of his ancestors; if of humble origin, he might be praised for having risen in the world from a lowly beginning.[112] His country should similarly be introduced — Demosthenes added to the renown of the illustrious Athens, Odysseus brought fame to the little island of Ithaca. Any manifestations connected with his birth, such as an omen, a prophecy, an oracle, should be recalled.[113] As with his antecedents, so with his upbringing and education, anything to his credit, or, if denouncing, his discredit, should be mentioned. Next, his 'extraneous' circumstances — the resources which he acquired, such as wealth, power, influence, friendships; these should not simply be praised in themselves, but it should be shown that they were wisely and honourably used,[114] and did not lead to insolence, or injustice, or self-assertiveness. Philanthropy in prosperity, loyalty in friendships, creditable development of acquired resources, would all deserve praise. Next, a closer look at the man himself; it might be that his physical attributes,[115] such as stature, vigour, handsome appearance, were noteworthy, but even more important were his qualities of mind and character. Stress should particularly be laid on qualities which did not merely enhance the man himself, but were beneficial to the community. Praise, or dispraise, of character was best taken in conjunction with a review of the person's actions throughout his career. There were two ways of doing this. Either each action, or achievement, could be taken in due order and shown to exhibit some particular virtue (or vice), or, alternatively, the major virtues, such as fortitude, temperance, justice, could be made the basis of treatment, each being illustrated by acts done at different times.[116] Outstanding achievements should be mainly selected. Naturally, honours, offices held, official decrees, or public approval should be brought to the fore, but an achievement or action could redound to a person's credit for a whole variety of reasons. If, for instance, it was done without thought of payment or reward, or with difficulty or risk, or in time of personal adversity, or single-handed, or with little assistance, or as something which no one had previously succeeded in doing, or with great ease or speed, or contrary to what anyone had a right to expect — any of these facets might be turned to reflect new glory and win fresh admiration.[117] Comparison with accepted paragons of virtue might also add lustre.[118] The record of praise (or the reverse) might continue to death and beyond, as when the person was happy in the occasion of his dying (*felix opportunitate mortis*), or was gratefully remembered by posterity. In fact, there was very little of good or bad in human life that did not find its niche somewhere in the rhetorical panegyrics or vituperations of antiquity.

The writer of a commonplace, or a panegyric, or an invective, sees everything as either black or white; if he uses comparison as one of his topics, it merely serves to enhance his argument one way or the other.

But students also required practice in making a more balanced assessment, and this was done at the next stage, when they were given the names of a pair of individuals, whose merits or demerits appeared to have a certain similarity. They then had to produce a Comparison, which was worked out point by point in accordance with the scheme adopted for praise and denunciation.[119] The object was to prove one or the other superior, or less iniquitous; the more evenly balanced the selected characters were, the more care and judgment the exercise required, and the result might be that they were evenly matched. In the Greek schools, comparisons between Homeric heroes, such as Ajax and Odysseus, were popular.[120] Aphthonius takes together the lives of Achilles and Hector, and finds them equally meritorious.[121] Libanius, however, seeks to demonstrate the superiority of both Diomedes and Ajax over Achilles.[122] Historical figures, such as Demosthenes and Aeschines, might also be used for the comparison.[123] A fruitful source of such exercises would have been the kind of comparisons between famous Greeks and Romans which are appended to Plutarch's *Lives*, and, although evidence is lacking, it is quite possible that this was sometimes practised. Quite apart from persons, there was a wide range of possible subjects for exercises in comparison,[124] as with panegyrics and denunciations. Libanius gives models of two which must have been quite as popular in Roman schools as in Greek, namely comparisons of seafaring with agriculture, and of town life with country life, a subject which we shall also meet as a Thesis. It is also interesting to find that the Comparison, like others of these later exercises, could very easily be utilized as a subject for a *controversia*. Among the *Lesser Declamations* attributed to Quintilian, there is one in which three brothers, an orator, a doctor and a philosopher, dispute about the succession to their father's estate, which he had bequeathed to whichever of them proved his art most serviceable to the community; it is basically a comparison of the three professions, in which the superiority of medicine is eloquently expounded.[125]

So far, students would have learned from these exercises a good deal which would prove useful later in actual discourse; but they had not as yet quite put themselves into the position of a person making a speech. The first step in this direction was taken in the excellent exercise known as the Speech in Character, or Impersonation (*ethopoeia* or *prosopopoeia*). Here it was necessary to imagine oneself in the position of some mythological or historical personage, at some critical point in life, and to try to speak as he or she might have spoken under the circumstances. The form might vary from a soliloquy to an address,[126] according to the subject. Greek examples of this kind of exercise are very numerous — there are twenty-seven in Libanius alone. They were usually introduced by the formula: 'What kind of speech would so-and-so have made...?' —

for example, Priam to Achilles, Achilles over the body of Patroclus, Andromache over the body of Hector, Medea when about to slay her children, Ajax when deprived of the arms of Achilles, Achilles on being deprived of Briseis, Niobe over her dead children, Medea on Jason's marriage to Creusa.[127] There was no end to the possibilities here, and the most valuable feature of the exercise was that it required psychological insight and gave excellent scope for imaginative treatment and the expression of emotion. Sympathetic reading of epic and dramatic poetry could provide the ideas and the approach, and sometimes poetry itself, as in the *Heroidum Epistulae* of Ovid, was directly indebted to this kind of exercise. A translation of part of Libanius' example on Achilles and Patroclus will give a good idea of the kind of writing which was expected:[128]

> Woe for the disaster that is upon us! You have fallen, Patroclus. How different were the hopes with which you were sent forth from the fate which you have met! I hoped to welcome you back victorious, but now I mourn you in death. It was an evil chance that you ever assisted the Greeks; for I shall look upon you no longer, my dear companion, most treasured of all my friends. Would that I had had you stay within my tent; then we should have been spared all these lamentations. This was what I feared, this is what has come to pass. But rather will I remember the blessings of earlier days, of the time when you despised Agamemnon but loved me, when, instead of cherishing your father in his old age, you chose to make the expedition with me, and neither your mother nor anyone else could persuade you to stay behind. And what followed meant no less to me; for you were the one who loved those whom I loved, hated those whom I hated, taking pleasure in my ways rather than those of others, thinking well of me, taking counsel with me, paying me honour due, sharing my anger, you, to whom I entrusted all my armour when you wished to enter battle, when you rescued the Greeks and all their ships from fire. So it was then; but henceforth only tears, mourning, laments. Whom shall I find to take your place? ...

Libanius is here following traditional rhetorical doctrine, not only in faithfully representing the character of the speaker, but also in beginning with the circumstances of the immediate present and then taking the story back to happier days.[129]

The doctrine of the rhetoricians here, that the style must be appropriate to the speaker's character, time of life, and status, and to the particular circumstances, is again remarkably similar to that given by Horace in the *Ars Poetica* for composition in verse.[130] But the teaching and the practice at this point also linked up very effectively with the grammar-school teaching, in which, as we have seen, the virtue of propriety in style was often praised in the exposition of the poets. The 'grammarians', too, prepared their young pupils for such compositions by an exercise which they termed an *allocutio*, or 'address',[131] for which they drew upon existing speeches in the poets; they made their pupils paraphrase them, and attempted to recreate the appropriate style and feeling in prose. In Latin, Virgil came to be much used for this purpose. So St Augustine writes of his days at the grammar school, in rueful memory:

A task disturbing enough to my spirit was set before me, that, for a reward of praise and in dread of disgracing myself and being whipped, I should deliver the words of Juno in her anger and resentment because she could not deflect the Trojan King from Italy: I had heard that Juno never uttered such words, but we were constrained to ramble on, following the traces of poetic fictions, and to say in prose the sort of thing that the poet had said in verse; and the pupil won the greater praise according as he more faithfully represented the dignity of the character concerned, and more convincingly reflected her anger and resentment, clothing his ideas in a befitting style.[132]

It is clear from the last sentence that this was not a mere word for word paraphrase of Juno's speech in Virgil, but a fully-developed Speech in Character; and usually the pupil had something to work upon, and was not entirely thrown on his own resources for ideas. More precocious boys must have been very good at this kind of thing, and even produced their own impersonations extempore in verse. An inscription of the time of Domitian found near the Porta Salaria in Rome, records that Quintus Sulpicius Maximus, a boy of eleven and a half years of age, in a poetic contest with fifty-two competitors, won with improvised Greek verses representing Zeus upbraiding Helios for lending his sun-chariot to Phaethon.[133] In the rhetoric school, however, the subjects were not restricted to poetry and mythology; the speech required could be the kind of military harangue which some renowned leader might make at a critical juncture, and here the distinction between the Speech in Character and the more advanced protreptic speech (*suasoria*) might be very tenuous indeed.[134] Political subjects were also possible, and Quintilian mentions a character-speech of Sulla addressing the Roman people on laying down the dictatorship.[135] In practical oratory, Cicero makes very effective use of other recognized forms of *prosopopoeia*, when he introduces the Roman State, personified, to address a speech of recrimination to Catiline, and another of exhortation to himself, and in the *Pro Caelio*, recalls old Appius Claudius Caecus from the dead to make an eloquent denunciation of his descendant, Clodia, for disgracing the family name.[136] Thus the range of subject-matter of this exercise was wide; in Quintilian's opinion, it was also one of the most exacting, and this was why he postponed it to an advanced stage in the course, and treated it together with the *suasoria*, with which it had so much in common. He fully recognized its value, not only to the orator, but to the poet and the historian as well.[137]

No exercise had a wider applicability than the next type, the Description, for which poetry and history afforded much more scope than oratory, though there are some very good examples in Cicero in the form of digressions, most notably in the Verrines.[138] Declamation had so much favoured the introduction of descriptions that certain types became stock themes, developed as show-pieces, which had little bearing on the argument of a *suasoria* or *controversia*, but were accepted avidly enough by declamatory audiences.[139] Declaimers liked to be thought to have rivalled the poets (notably Virgil and Ovid) in their descriptive passages, and themselves influenced the taste for what Horace calls the 'purple patch'[140] in other poets, such as Lucan.[141] The sober judgment of Quintilian found little point in allowing young students to be caught up in the prevalent craze for descriptions,[142] and he does not include it in his list of exercises, though he mentioned it in connection with narratives and fully recognized the merits of a vivid portrayal which brought the events described before the very eyes of the listener.[143] All the Greek theorists include the exercise,[144] which might call for a description of a place, such as a meadow, a harbour, an island, a sea-shore, or of a season, such as spring or summer, or an occasion, such as a festive gathering; or yet again, of a happening, such as a storm, a famine, a plague, an earthquake, or a war-scene such as a land- or sea-battle; or it might be a description of a person, an animal, or some human activity such as the making of a shield (modelled on Homer) or the laying of fortifications (suggested by Thucydides). Boys were encouraged to describe in a clear and graphic manner, for ideally the description should almost enable one to see what was described; but they were warned against the temptation to enter into excessive detail and the production of an excessively lengthy account.[145] On the whole, there is every likelihood that schoolboys enjoyed writing this kind of descriptive essay, for which there was such a variety of subject-matter and so rich a store of literary models. If kept within reasonable bounds, it was a good means of encouraging imagination and observation, and, not least, it helped to develop power of expression.

The two final exercises in the standard course, the Thesis and the Discussion of a Law, were recognized to be of particular importance because they developed the pupil's ability to argue both sides of a debatable question.[146] Up to this point, he had only tried his hand at arguing both ways in the exercise of Refutation and Confirmation of legends. He now began to tackle subjects of much wider scope, such as the favourite theme 'Should one marry, or not?', or 'Should one have children, or not?', or 'Should one take to seafaring, or not?', or 'Should a wise man engage in politics, or not?'.[147] The general question could also take a comparative form, as recommended by Quintilian, when one took a stand on one side or the other on such subjects as 'Is country life or town life preferable?', or 'Does the soldier deserve more credit than the lawyer?',[148] a theme which Cicero introduced so effectively in the *Pro Murena.*[149] When equipped with a short proem and epilogue, these compositions, first written and then declaimed, came very close to the fully-developed speech. Their most immediate relationship was, as Quintilian pointed out, with the deliberative speech (*suasoria*).[150] Sometimes, the difference could be mainly one of form; the *thesis* 'Should a man marry' treated the matter as an open question, but the *suasoria* 'Cato deliberates whether or not to marry' required advice to a particular person in a particular situation. It was a feature of many preliminary exercises that they were generalized;[151] only when specific individuals, times, and places are introduced do matters become more complex, and we have the more advanced exercises of declamation proper. But, quite apart from the possible similarity to particular cases, there was obviously a very wide area indeed of 'general questions'. In the preliminary stages of rhetorical training, there seems to have been general agreement that subjects could be divided into two main groups, those which were purely speculative, such as 'Is the world governed by Providence, or not?', 'Do the gods care for humanity, or not?', and those which had a direct bearing on the daily life of the community, such as the debates on marriage and political ambition.[152] At this stage, most rhetoricians were content to use the 'practical' type, and to leave the 'theoretical' type to the philosophers, though Theon (being Stoic-influenced) wished his students to proceed from the one to the other. Roman teachers, according to Suetonius,[153] dealt with theses which 'showed that some practices were useful and necessary to everyday life, whilst others were harmful or superfluous'. But no such sharp dichotomy was possible at a later stage, for general questions of morality arose in oratory as well as philosophy, whether in a deliberative debate or in a forensic case.

Practice in theses had this advantage that the topics, or lines of argument, on which the treatment of the general question was based were very much the same as those required for dealing with any *suasoria*, or indeed any advisory speech in actual life, since they all belonged to the same field of deliberative oratory. The general lines of approach to a deliberative speech had been formulated as early as the fourth century B.C., the speaker being advised to urge that the proposed course of action was just, lawful, expedient, honourable, easy and, especially, necessary;[154] alternatively, if dissuading, he would use the reverse arguments. It was exactly on such lines that the student was expected to treat the thesis. Not every topic would be needed in every thesis, but there was a very wide selection. By the time of Theon, almost every aspect which could be brought into consideration was duly listed — is the course proposed possible?, natural?, easy?, befitting?, pious?, necessary?, reputable?, profitable?, and so on.[155] As to the very important connection of the thesis with forensic oratory, which has been referred to in our discussion of Cicero and other Republican orators[156] — that is, the general question which formed the core of the case (*krinomenon*), or arose in the course of it (*locus*) — this was a matter which which students could only be expected to familiarize themselves at a more advanced stage, when they had mastered the theory of the textbooks and had practised the declamation of *controversiae*.[157]

It only remains to consider the last, and most advanced, of the *progymnasmata*, which Quintilian calls the Praise and Denunciation of Laws.[158] This had close associations with both the *suasoria* and the *controversia*. The law selected might either be an imaginary piece of new legislation, the merits and demerits of which required discussion, or a law which was regarded as already established, the advantages and disadvantages of which could be argued.[159] In either case, the student was in the position of one offering reasoned advice, and so obtained further experience in applying the procedure of deliberative oratory, as with the *thesis*, but in a much more limited field of inquiry. Theon and Quintilian show us the lines on which a proposed law should be either confirmed or rejected. The first move was to examine it for any possible obscurity, which might arise, for example, from the use of words of uncertain meaning, or words capable of different meanings, or a number of synonymous words which could create confusion, or syntactical ambiguity, or redundancy, or inadequate definition.[160] After the wording, the student must consider whether the law showed any conflict within itself, whether it should be treated as retrospective, whether its provisions should be limited to certain persons. Next came the wider issues, which were of particular importance — was the law honourable and just, was it expedient, was it practicable, and was it necessary?[161] On the question of justice, the extent of the penalty, or reward, proposed might require discussion. All this was obviously very useful as an immediate preparation for the *suasoria*, in which the topics of justice, expedience, feasibility, and the rest played a prominent part. How close this connection with declamatory exercises was may best be seen from one of the *Lesser Declamations* attributed to Quintilian. The situation proposed is as follows: 'Two states were at war; many deserters crossed over from one to the other; someone proposes a law that they should not be received.' This type of declamation, says the author, 'comes very close to the *suasoria*, for advocacy of, and opposition to, a law, is part of the sphere of deliberative speeches'.[162] A very good example from Latin literature, selected by Lorich in illustration, may be seen in the two speeches for and against the repeal of the Oppian Law of 215 B.C. regarding the 'luxury' of women's apparel and equipment, as rhetorically developed by Livy.[163] But the exercise also had a connection with the *controversia*, since the examination of the wording and the meaning of law, or laws, on which the theme was based was an important feature in arguing the case.[164] At the preliminary stage, a law was examined *per se*, whereas at the more advanced level its interpretation and implications were considered in regard to a particular situation. Thus the model essay given by Aphthonius is a denunciation of the law concerning the slaying of an adulterer taken in the act, and in the *Controversiae* of the elder Seneca and elsewhere this is one of the commonest laws on which declamatory exercises are based.[165]

The discussion of these preliminary exercises in Theon and Quintilian tells us a great deal not only about their substance and the lines on which they were treated, but also about the kind of background material which the boys needed, and the manner in which the teacher dealt with them in class. Believing that nothing was better than to utilize standard authors as models for imitation, teachers selected passages from the prose-writers to illustrate each kind of exercise, and made their pupils learn them by heart. In Greek, Theon prefaces his work with a quite detailed reading-list, in which he draws his examples not only from the orators, but from Plato and Xenophon, and particularly from the historians, including not only Herodotus and Thucydides, but Ephorus, Theopompus, and Philistus.[166] In Latin, Quintilian advocates the same method, but gives only a few general directions. He does, however, make a distinction between those authors who are more suitable for beginners and those who are best reserved until the boys have acquired proficiency and a more mature judgment. For beginners, he strongly recommends the study of great prose-writers whose style is straightforward and easily understood, notably Cicero and Livy; his hope is that boys will soon learn to enjoy Cicero, and he agrees with Livy that, after Cicero, the best models are those whose style comes closest to his.[167] Quintilian is anxious that beginners should not be led astray by teachers who unduly admire such archaic writers as Cato and the Gracchi, lest their style become rough and arid, or by those who encourage imitation of the all too seductive embellishments of modern stylists. Only when good judgment is formed in matters of style would he recommend that students might benefit from the vigour of the 'ancients' and the more acceptable stylistic charms of the 'moderns'. Sallust, too, of whom he had a high opinion as a historian, wrote in too difficult a style for beginners, and would be most profitably studied later on.[168] But both

Theon and Quintilian make it clear that the master should also compose models himself for the boys to study and imitate, that is, the kind of *exempla* which Libanius later provided in such abundance. Quintilian makes the interesting observation that the boys appreciated this kind of personal demonstration, and learnt a good deal from it, at least in well-regulated schools.[169] Theon says that beginners should be made to repeat aloud such examples, so as to model themselves exactly upon the teacher.[170]

The next stage was for the boys themselves to try their hand at such compositions, and here the amount of preliminary assistance which they required from the master depended partly upon their own abilities and progress, and partly on the methods of individual teachers. Whereas beginners needed to have their work sketched out for them, those who were gaining confidence and proficiency merely required a few hints on what the main points and the order of their treatment should be. Teachers differed, however, and some gave a great deal of help beforehand, whereas others provided the barest guidance in the beginning, and reserved their detailed discussion until the boys had written and declaimed their own versions, whereupon they dealt with omissions, made criticisms, and elaborated particular passages with care.[171] Quintilian himself compromised, but noted that pupils should not be allowed to 'rely on someone else's efforts' for too long, lest they fail to use their own intiative; in a quite poetic simile, he compares the teacher to the mother bird feeding her young chicks, and then teaching them to flutter around the nest, until such time as they can fly freely and trust themselves to the open sky.[172] Elsewhere, in an equally charming comparison, he likens the good teacher to an adult who adapts his pace of walking to that of the child with whom he goes hand in hand.[173]

It is also in the context of preliminary exercises that both Theon and Quintilian stress the need to develop the individual capabilities of each pupil, for some are good in one way, some in another. Theon found that some were better in expressing emotion, others in depicting character, whilst some were inferior in both of these, but good at putting their points in a logical order.[174] Quintilian, too, who discusses the whole question quite fully, agreed exactly with Theon that no innate good quality should be neglected; rather, it should be enhanced, and any deficiency should be made good.[175] But, in doing this, it was important for the teacher to know how far to go in criticizing faults, and how to apportion praise and blame. Theon advised that teachers should not correct every single error from the beginning, but only the most glaring ones, so that the young boy might not become dispirited and lack confidence for future work; and the teacher should not only explain why what was written was wrong, but should show how it might be done correctly.[176] Many of Quintilian's remarks on this subject are made in his discussion on correcting narrative essays, and the fact that they correspond to, and complement, those of Theon shows that both must be reflecting the practice of the best teachers of their time. Quintilian, too, knew from experience that it was unwise, with beginners, to make too much of faults to be avoided, lest the apprehension of incorrectness should impede the imagination and the natural flow of the style.[177] He particularly deprecated the arid, pedantic methods of the purists, whose pupils produced a style which, though it might lack serious faults, also lacked any positive merits. He himself was in favour of setting subjects which would allow plenty of scope, and of encouraging boys to express their ideas, even if they did so extravagantly.[178] He was strongly against severity in correction, the manner of which should be tempered to the boy's age and the stage of his study. Using a simile of quite Virgilian tenderness, he noted that the young vine seems to 'shrink from the steel'[179] and that there would be time later on to prune this youthful exuberance, which was not in itself at all a bad sign. In correction, then, the teacher should be kindly, praise what is good, accept what is tolerable, make some changes, but explain why they are necessary, and improve by inserting something of his own. He himself, when teaching, used to say, if some expression was too daring or high-flown: 'I approve of that for the present, but the time will come when I shall not permit it.' But if a boy's work was thoroughly careless, he would go over the subject again and then make him do the whole exercise afresh.[180] Nor was it only adverse criticism which required care; there was also the question of how far to go in bestowing praise. Here, there was a danger in showing too much enthusiasm, for too much praise was forthcoming from parents and school-fellows, and it was fatally easy to breed complacency and self-esteem. This was why he disapproved of the practice of boys learning all their own compositions by heart for public declamation, and preferred to allow this privilege only occasionally, as a reward when they had done something particularly well.[181] He recognized, too, that, although some pupils were too self-confident, others were too passive, and that is why he urged that, throughout the course, the teacher should not only readily respond to those who asked him questions, but should also remember to put questions of his own to those who failed to ask.[182]

To conclude, surely it would be too unappreciative to criticize the teaching of these preliminary exercises on the ground that the lines laid down for their treatment were too conventional and stereotyped. Not only would boys have dealt with them far less effectively if the framework had not been supplied, but, even given the framework, they had to use their own inventiveness to fill it in with their own ideas in each particular case. From the emulation of classical models and from their teachers' suggestions, corrections and demonstrations, they must have learned a great deal in the matter of style and composition. There is some truth in the criticism that the same subjects recur over the centuries with monotonous regularity,[183] but in good hands, the *progymnasmata* were still, as discerning critics have seen,[184] one of the most valuable sections of the ancient academic course.

CHAPTER XIX

Declamations on historical themes

Ancient rhetorical teaching, at all stages, was based on a combination of theory and practice. From the beginning, for each type of exercise, boys had been told what the rules for treatment were, before they wrote out and read aloud their own versions of the subjects prescribed. As the preliminary exercises became more advanced, they had begun to approximate — as in the Impersonation and the Thesis — to miniature speeches in themselves. The rhetoric course proper, on which students now embarked, was concerned with full-scale speeches, in which there were often opportunities to incorporate such features as the maxim, the commonplace, and the description, which had been studied at an earlier stage. Here, too, there was both theory and practice; speeches were first written, but the delivery of them aloud, the real declamation, became all-important. The theory for the full-scale speech was systematically set out in the textbooks, or 'arts' (*technai*) of rhetoric, of which many, offering substantially the same doctrines, but differing in individual detail and emphasis, were in constant circulation. In Greek, the textbook of Hermagoras long survived, and was utilized as late as St Augustine; considerable fragments and references enable an outline reconstruction of it to be made.[1] In Latin, the *Rhetorica ad Herennium*, which, unlike Cicero's *De Inventione*, covers the whole field, is an excellent example from the Republican period,[2] and represents traditional teaching even better than the *Partitiones Oratoriae*, which Cicero composed for his son, for this is more philosophically-influenced, and reflects much of the teaching of rhetoric in the New Academy.[3] After Cicero's time, the long since lost Greek textbooks of Apollodorus of Pergamum, who taught Octavian, and Theodorus of Gadara, who taught Tiberius, had a considerable vogue;[4] that of Apollodorus was translated into Latin by Valgius, and that of Theodorus was still in use in Juvenal's day.[5] Among Latin rhetorical manuals of the first century known to Quintilian may be mentioned that of Cornelius Celsus, which formed part of his encyclopaedia,[6] and that of Verginius Flavus, who taught Persius; the latter was specifically designed for school use, and Quintilian thought well of it.[7] But in scope, breadth of outlook, and detail of treatment,

Quintilian's own work far surpassed these rather utilitarian productions of his predecessors.

The relative weight attached to theory and practice varied with different teachers and at different times. Under the Republic, a thorough grounding in theory was considered indispensable, and, to judge from the teaching of Cicero's son, the rules were presented as a whole in compact form, and had to be memorized. Under the Empire, however, the practical exercises of declamation, which were coming into favour in Latin at the end of the Republic, became so popular that some teachers thought that they could dispense with theory altogether.[8] Wise teachers, and most certainly Quintilian, did not agree. Although Quintilian states that students proceed to declamation immediately after the preliminary exercises,[9] and then, in the next chapter, begins the long discussion of theory, which occupies him for several books, theory and practice, in actual teaching, must have gone closely together, and the rules from the handbooks must have been introduced immediately before, and during the course of, the practical exercises in which they had to be applied.

Most of the textbooks dealt with all three branches of oratory, the judicial, the deliberative and the epideictic, but of these the last two required only a modest space, whereas the judicial branch, which was regarded as quite the most important (Apollodorus restricted his work to it), took up the main bulk of the rules on invention and arrangement. It was also generally acknowledged to be the most difficult.[10] Hence the younger students (*pueri*) began by declaiming on deliberative themes, which were easier, and the *controversia*, which was originally designed to reflect, and in the best hands continued to reflect, real-life advocacy, was reserved for the more advanced (*robustiores, adulescentuli*).[11] At the outset, then, they tackled the exercise called under the Republic a 'deliberation' or 'consultation', but which then became universally known as the *suasoria*. In this, the student was required in his speech to offer advice (*consilium dare*) to a famous historical (or, occasionally, legendary) personage, or to a body of people, in a critical situation, or dilemma. Usually the situation was one drawn from the distant past, so the boy had to know some history, and he had to imagine himself present, in these dramatic circumstances, attempting to sway the decision this way or that by his arguments. It should be noted, however, that teachers of declamation were not satisfied merely to utilize historical crises which had really given rise to debate at the time; ever fertile in the invention of new subjects, they readily modified or embellished history, and sometimes conjured up, for the enhancement of rhetoric, dramatic situations which had never existed in fact.

The Greek teachers, who brought these exercises to Rome, naturally prided themselves on declaiming on themes drawn from their own national history,[12] those based on the Persian Wars, or on Alexander the Great, being prime favourites. Some declaimed only in Greek,[13] but many declaimed as fluently in Latin as in their native language.[14] Thus *suasoriae* on Greek subjects were sometimes introduced in the Roman curriculum, and no less than five of the seven *suasoriae* from which the elder Seneca records copious extracts are drawn from Greek. Thus, Xerxes is at Thermopylae; three hundred Spartans debate whether to flee or stand their ground (II). Xerxes is imagined as threatening to return, unless the trophies erected to commemorate the victory over Persia are removed; the Athenians deliberate whether to remove them or not (V). The victorious Alexander stands at the confines of the known world, and debates whether to embark upon the Ocean, in the hope of finding new worlds to conquer (I), or Alexander is outside the city of Babylon, and debates whether to enter, though the auguries forbode peril (IV). Greek drama, too, provides a subject: Agamemnon deliberates whether to sacrifice Iphigeneia, when Calchas warns that he may not otherwise sail to Troy (III). *Suasoriae* on many other subjects were part of the stock-in-trade of Greek sophists, and a number are mentioned in Philostratus.[15] But it would be quite wrong to suppose that the themes used in Roman schools were mainly Greek. On the contrary, the subjects mentioned in Latin rhetorical treatises are almost entirely derived, as one would expect, from the history of Rome. Even before Seneca's day, rhetoricians who taught their subject in Latin had associated many of their themes with great national events, and military leaders in particular; subjects connected with the struggle against Carthage were a favourite field. The Senate deliberates whether or not to ransom prisoners after Cannae,[16] whether to send an army against Philip of Macedon, whether to destroy, or spare, the defeated Carthage.[17] Hannibal was a figure on whom boys still delighted to declaim even in Juvenal's day; Hannibal deliberates whether to attempt the crossing of the Alps,[18] and whether to attack Rome after Cannae.[19] Scipio, too, deliberates whether to cross to Africa.[20] Questions of military strategy might involve three possible alternatives, and create a more complex *suasoria*, such as the dilemma of Hannibal, when summoned back to Carthage, whether to remain in Italy, or return home, or seize Alexandria.[21] Similarly, in regard to the Civil War, which was also an abundant source of *suasoriae*, Pompey, after his defeat at Pharsalus, debates whether to make for Parthia, or Africa, or Egypt, and the speaker imagines himself one of his council at Syhedra.[22] The dilemma of a gallant garrison in critical circumstances provides a poignant setting, as when the inhabitants of Casilinum, cut off by Hannibal's troops and facing starvation, deliberate whether or not to surrender,[23] or, in the Civil War, a detachment of Caesar's troops from Opitergium, surrounded on their raft as darkness falls, deliberate whether to surrender or put each other to the sword.[24]

The contemplated suicide of a noble Roman was always a popular theme, and juvenile eloquence was never more frequently aroused than in the younger Cato's deliberation whether to take his own life rather than yield to Caesar.[25] Similarly, Cicero, in two of the Senecan *suasoriae*, debates whether to beg Antony for his life (VI), or (by what Seneca called a 'stupid fiction'[26]) whether to agree to burn his speeches as the price of his safety (VII). The careers of Caesar and Pompey afford further material: Caesar deliberates whether to invade Britain,[27] and whether to press forward into Germany, when his soldiers are making their wills,[28] the Egyptian council debates the advisability of assassinating Pompey,[29] and Caesar deliberates whether to avenge his rival's death.[30] Not all *suasoriae*, however, had so dramatic a setting; political and constitutional problems also played a part. The Senate deliberates whether to relax the laws so that Scipio may become consul before the proper age,[31] or whether or not to grant the citizenship to the Italian allies;[32] Sulla deliberates whether to resign his dictatorship,[33] and Caesar has to be advised whether or not he should accept the kingship.[34] Just as the Greeks seem rarely to have chosen subjects later than Alexander, so the Romans appear to have continued to draw nearly all their subjects from the Republic; but there were probably scores of them, of which only a fraction has survived.

The main problem was to find the most relevant and cogent arguments, and here boys had some hard thinking to do, though the teacher would give them some suggestions on which to work. They were already by no means unfamiliar with the technique of arguing for or against a general proposition, or, indeed, a particular enactment, in the latest of their preliminary exercises. Now they needed to apply their methods to build up arguments appropriate for the persuasion of particular people in particular situations. The textbooks varied in the emphasis which they placed on the different lines of argument,[35] called by the Greeks the 'final headings' and by Quintilian the 'parts of persuasion', the arrangement of which made up what was known as the 'division' of the case. It was generally agreed that two essential considerations were those of expediency (*utile*) and honour (*honestum*). Those who considered, like the author of *Ad Herennium*,[36] that expediency was the dominant aspect, subdivided it into considerations of safety (*tutum*) and honour (*honestum*), the latter being exemplified when the proposed course was urged to be in accord with one or more of the cardinal virtues of prudence, justice, courage and moderation, or, at least, to be in accord with what was generally considered praiseworthy (*laudabile*). This view, however, was evidently influenced by the high-minded Stoic concept that whatever was honourable must necessarily be expedient,[37] and most authorities recognized that honour and expediency were both major aspects. Some, however, added a third major heading, that of necessity (*necessarium*), and this was certainly a powerful argument if it could be substantiated. Quintilian did not include it, but preferred to make practicability his third major aspect,[38] and this again, in dubious or dangerous projects, might often be the dominant question.[39] But, in fact, the range of situations in the exercises, as in real life, was so wide that there were many other considerations which might be involved, whether one regarded them as logically subordinate to honour or expediency, or as deserving to be listed alongside them. One might have to urge that a course advocated was legal, or fair, or morally right, or in accord with piety, or clemency.[40] But, at least, all these possible headings were starting-points for thought, and often it was practicable to take two or three of them and to make them support one another in building up one's argument.

In exercises in which the choice lay between continuing a struggle against impossible odds and flight (as with the Spartans at Thermo-pylae), or surrender (as with the inhabitants of Casilinum, and the men of Opitergium), or between running a high risk and making an ignominious concession (as with the removal of the Greek trophies, and the deference of Cicero to Antony, or of Cato to Caesar), the alternatives were either to argue that honour must at all costs be kept unimpaired, or to urge that safety and survival must be the prime objective. In the latter case, one might stress that without safety there could be no further scope for valour and virtue, that a temporary loss of honour could be later retrieved, that Heaven helped those who helped themselves,[41] and, in the case of a Cicero or a Cato, that it was in the interest of the State that so valuable a life should be preserved.[42] But many declaimers found that the opposite argument was more attractive, since it gave much scope for the utterance of high and noble sentiments; only Gallio, says Seneca, argued that the Athenians should remove the trophies,[43] only a few urged Cicero to appeal to Antony,[44] and no one could bring himself to advocate that Cicero should destroy his works — for, as he drily remarks,[45] the declaimers were more concerned about Cicero's speeches than about Cicero himself! In the Senecan *suasoriae*, the stock key-words of deliberative theory sometimes provide the framework of the argument, as when Cestius urges that it is honourable (*honestum*), expedient (*utile*), and necessary (*necessarium*) for Cicero to die;[46] or he and Arellius Fuscus agree that it is not honourable for the Spartans to flee, but question whether it is safe (*tutum*) or necessary (*necesse*);[47] or Cestius argues that it is neither legally permissible (*licere*, i.e. *ius*) nor morally right (*fas*) to remove the trophies.[48] But frequently, these considerations proved too general and one had to come to close grips with the situation itself, and evolve arguments which would be cogent within the particular circumstances. The declaimers had a very effective way of building up their main arguments in steps and producing a climax, thus: (to Alexander) '*even if* the Ocean were navigable, it should not be sailed upon — but it is not navigable';[49] 'there are no lands on or beyond the Ocean — *even if* there were, they could not be reached — *even if* they could be reached, it is not worth while to sacrifice certain gain for uncertain advantage'.[50] Similarly, to Agamemnon: '*even if* he could not sail without sacrificing his daughter, he ought not so to act — murder involved more loss than possible gain, the life of Iphigeneia was too high a price for vengeance on Helen, parricide too much for the punishment of adultery — but, even if he did not sacrifice her, he would still sail, when the elements were calmed'.[51] Finally, in many *suasoriae*, as where military strategy was concerned, the question was not one of honour at all, but of expediency, and, as Quintilian observed, expediency could have many facets, even though it was agreed to be the dominant consideration. One might argue that a course was indeed expedient, in general, but not at this particular time, or place, not for these particular people, not under these particular circumstances, or did not warrant so drastic an action.[52] In other words, if one aimed at making a worthwhile advisory speech, one had to apply one's mind closely to the subject, and not be content merely to echo the textbook headings.

The lines of argument, however, though fundamentally important, provided only the bare bones of the speech, which had to take on a living form and be endowed with vigour and movement. Here, the experience gained in preliminary exercises was again of service, for the subjects of many *suasoriae* either naturally invited, or permitted, the introduction of a stirring description. Obviously, the young declaimer, who sought to deter Alexander from further ventures, could conjure up a picture of the menacing gloom which brooded over the limitless Ocean, the sudden storms and violent winds which bore down from all directions, the vain and endless quest for land amid a waste of waters, in the unfathomable depths of which lurked creatures of unbelievable size ...[53] The task of advising the Spartans to stand firm would invite an equally impressive description of the site of Thermopylae, a place designed by Nature herself for defence.[54] Such descriptions of natural settings were greatly favoured by declaimers like Arellius Fuscus and Fabianus, and one may well imagine how readily ardent young advisers would depict for Hannibal the dizzy heights, the numbing cold, the catastrophic avalanches of the Alps, or warn the too-confident Caesar of the hidden perils of German forests, or of the surging tides of a narrow sea, beyond which lived a wild race of painted warriors in a climate made foul by continuous rain and cloud ... Transported once more to Rome to advise Cicero, they would describe, with equal relish and due attention to detail, the horrible physical tortures which would be his lot if he entrusted himself to Antony.[55]

The danger of the description was that it might easily carry the speaker away into a purple passage, high-flown and poetical in style, which, if not entirely irrelevant, at least made only a limited contribution to the presentation of a convincing case.[56] More immediately related to the issue was the production of historical analogies, or *exempla*, which were drawn from times preceding the period of the exercise, and, being themselves well-known and recognized, might be expected to carry weight. But, as no two historical situations were ever exactly alike, these analogies were often hinged to a widely-accepted truth, or general proposition (*locus*), which was appropriate to the case in hand. For example, when urging the hitherto undefeated Alexander not to embark on the Ocean, one might utilize the favourite commonplace that Fortune was fickle and that it was dangerous to tempt her too far (*locus de varietate fortunae*); illustrative examples would then follow of great leaders who had fallen from high renown.[57] Sometimes it was sufficient merely to touch on the *locus*, which was easily adaptable to so many different circumstances, and, for instance, to hearten the Spartans, who might be deterred by Xerxes' previous achievements (the Hellespont, Athos), by reminding them that, by a reversal of fortune, even great empires may be doomed to fall;[58] on the other hand, when advising the Athenians to agree to take up the trophies, one might warn them that, despite their previous triumphs, fortune, next time, might change.[59] A historical background was always useful, even if, in the opposite case, one merely produced a list (*enumeratio*) of great Athenian victories.[60] Another much-used commonplace was that on despising death (*locus de contemnenda morte*); the Spartan detachment, or the men of Casilinum, or Cato, or Cicero, might be reminded that life is in any case uncertain, that death is inevitable anyway, that glory is immortal, and that, when the fragile body is destroyed, the imperishable soul survives.[61] Examples of those who had died nobly were not hard to find; let the spirit of Socrates be a guide to Cato, and to Cicero that of Cato himself. Both popular beliefs and philosophy might provide material for a *locus*; in cases where some supernatural warning had intervened, or the omens were unfavourable, the speaker might well present his views as to whether dreams or divination can be trusted, and whether, if there are any gods, they care to interest themselves in human affairs.[62] On a wide variety of topics an array of illustrative examples existed from the time of Tiberius in the nine books of Valerius Maximus' *Memorable Deeds and Sayings*. This is quite a little treasure-house of short stories from Greek and Roman history, illuminating very many aspects of human conduct, of which religion, superstition, ancient custom, discipline, courage, patience, friendship, generosity, gratitude and ingratitude, father-son relationships, luxury, cruelty, avarice and pride are only a few. So indispensable did it become that a fourth-century epitomator, Julius Paris, still regarded it as an essential aid to discourse and declamation alike.[63]

Moralizing is most concise when presented in the form of a maxim (*sententia*), as, for instance, when Alexander is advised that 'the sign of a great spirit is moderation in success'.[64] With this kind of aphorism, or gnomic *sententia*, boys had been familiar from primary-school days. But now they learnt, from listening to their teachers of declamation, that the most effective kind of *sententia* was not a general truth, but an apt and pithy comment on a particular situation. By far the most frequent and most admired *sententiae* quoted in the Senecan collection are of this type.[65] For example, Sparta, the unwalled city, prompts the reflection: 'there Sparta has her walls, where are her men'. Antithesis often sharpens the point, as in: 'we came for Sparta; let us stand firm for Greece', or 'it may not be ours to conquer; conquered we cannot be'.[66] Word-play may heighten the effect of brevity, as in: 'We are hand-picked, not derelict' (*electi sumus, non relicti*).[67] At gatherings of declaimers, there was keen competition in producing ever more original and striking *sententiae*, with the result that those who lacked sense and judgment over-stepped the mark, and were derided for their folly. Under the Empire, the craze for *sententiae* must often have done at least as much harm as good among immature students, who were all too easily tempted to try to be clever. Wise teachers, like Quintilian, protested against excessive addiction to epigram, and observed that, whilst a speech might gain from a few of these neat and apt comments, it was not improved by being littered with them.[68] Also, the placing of the *sententia* was important, and it was often at its best when it came at the end, rounding off a tirade or description.[69] But the *sententia* was not the only form of verbal artistry which was practised. Characteristic, too, of the declamatory style was the use of carefully balanced clauses (*parisosis*), sometimes three or four of them (*tricolon, tetracolon*), often with repetition of a leading or concluding word or phrase. This, too, was a favourite device in Asiatic oratory, used also by Cicero, but more particularly in his youth.[70] Here is an example from a *suasoria* of Cestius, addressing Cicero: 'If you think of the people's yearning for you, Cicero, whensoever you die, you have *lived too little*; if you think of your own achievements, you have *lived long enough*; if you think of Fortune's cruel blows and the state of the times, you have *lived too long*; if you think of men's memory of your works, you are to *live for ever*'.[71] Highly artificial and elaborate, of course, and only superficially attractive; but this was the kind of stylistic *tour de force* which elicited a round of applause in the schools.

In order to compose and deliver a *suasoria* successfully, a boy needed to exercise his imagination, for he was not supposed to be speaking in his own character, but impersonating an adviser. This meant that he had to adapt his arguments, his manner, his tone, to the type of person he was supposed to be, whether an ordinary citizen, or a soldier, or a senator, or a member of a military council, or a courtier, according to the circumstances of the debate. He had also to use the same discretion to suit the audience whom he was supposed to be addressing. Even experienced declaimers, as Cestius pointed out, sometimes made mistakes here, for it was not the same thing to speak under a monarch and in a democratic state. If one presumed to advise a king, one must first take note of his personality; one had to take care in counselling a proud monarch like Alexander, avoiding undue outspokenness, or excessive flattery, and proffering advice with polite compliments and great respect.[72] Similarly, Quintilian observed that one did not use the same approach in advising Marius as in advising Cato on a political theme, and in counselling Scipio on military strategy one would not take the same line as when addressing Fabius Maximus. When the audience was not an individual, but a group, it mattered a great deal whether it was the Senate, or the Roman people, or citizens of a provincial town, or foreigners.[73] The old Aristotelian precept of appropriateness to the subject, the audience, and the speaker, had always to be borne in mind.[74] But, although the schoolboy was thus playing a part, there was a difference between the *suasoria* and the *prosopopoeia*, for only in the latter did he seek to impersonate the main character concerned;[75] to advise Sulla whether or not to abdicate was a *suasoria*, but to represent the address of Sulla to the people, abrogating his dictatorial powers, was an impersonation,[76] and Quintilian thought that this was the more difficult exercise of the two.[77]

The reading of history was clearly an essential background for such exercises — in fact, the more history, the better. Here there was the great advantage that many historians were themselves trained in rhetoric, and were fond of composing rhetorical speeches. Polybius was rather exceptional in disapproving of the practice, for which he severely criticized Timaeus.[78] For Roman themes, Livy, whom Quintilian recommended as most suitable for boys,[79] must have been a prime source of information, and sometimes a direct model. Livy himself, for example, includes two speeches, for and against the ransom of prisoners after Cannae, which were *suasoriae* in themselves.[80] Many of the subjects propounded must have been derived by teachers from hints in Livy. For *suasoriae* concerning Cicero and Antony, Cicero's own speeches, especially the second Philippic, were an essential basis, and the Senecan excerpts are full of quotations and adaptations of Cicero. Nor must the interplay of rhetoric and historical epic be forgotten. Lucan, who probably used Livy, and Silius Italicus, who certainly did, were themselves highly trained in the schools of rhetoric.[81] Lucan is, in turn, highly recommended by Quintilian to students of rhetoric,[82] and so speeches which were themselves deeply indebted to the declamation schools, such as the speech of Vulteius to the men from Opitergium, of Pompey and of Lentulus to Pompey's military council, of Pothinus to the Egyptians on assassinating Pompey,[83] may well have been utilized by students of declamation, once his epic became established in the schools. Where students collected their material for Greek themes is much less certain; for the Persian Wars, one might expect that they would have consulted Herodotus, whilst among the many who had written about Alexander, Clitarchus and Timagenes (himself a declaimer) are mentioned by Quintilian.[84] But in Greek schools certainly, for the deliberative oratory of Greek politics, it was the speeches of Demosthenes against Philip of Macedon for which the highest praise was reserved.[85]

It is noteworthy that Quintilian, whose discussion of deliberative oratory is characteristically sensible and adapted to the needs of real life, considered that rhetorical speeches in the historians (as well as those actually delivered by orators) often provided a better model for students than the performances, and published notes (*commentarii*), of professional declaimers.[86] In fact, he specifically warns young readers of the faults which they will later have to eradicate,[87] and he very probably has in mind his own experience in having to re-teach those who came to him from inferior schools.[88] In the first place, there was the question of the exordium. It was generally agreed that, in deliberative speeches, an introduction, when required at all, need only be brief, though, as Aristotle and Quintilian remarked, it might be necessary to secure the goodwill of a prejudiced audience.[89] But many declaimers took matters to extremes, and sought to arrest attention by an abrupt start.[90] It is, for instance, not unlikely that some who urged Alexander not to embark on the Ocean, began with the dramatic words: 'How much farther, O unconquered one?' (*Quousque, invicte?*), which, in one version of the exercise, were supposed to have been uttered as a warning by a divine voice.[91] In this case, it could have been argued that Cicero was equally abrupt in the opening of his first speech against Catiline. Similarly, the remark of the declaimer, Argentarius: 'Hold back! your own world recalls you!' may well have come from the beginning of his speech.[92] Secondly, declaimers are criticized for cultivating an impetuous style, and using grandiloquent language. Here Quintilian observes that the very nature of school exercises, with their concentration on great personages, encourages a certain elevation of style, but straining after it produced something very different from the manner of real-life debates.[93] Finally, it was a common mistake to denounce the opposite point of view in a hostile and aggressive manner, and to speak as though they were reviling their audience instead of advising it.[94] All of which goes to show that everything depended on the quality and commonsense of the teacher to whom boys were entrusted.

The *suasoria*, however, despite the false emotion which it often engendered,[95] and the frequent remoteness of its subject-matter from the immediate questions of contemporary debate, had a certain value in stimulating the historical imagination, and developing power of argument and fluency of speech. Ovid, who was a pupil of Arellius Fuscus and an admirer of Porcius Latro's *sententiae*, enjoyed declaiming *suasoriae* much more than *controversiae*, which he rarely tackled.[96] This is not surprising, for the quasi-legal cases of the *controversiae* were generally much more intricate and difficult to argue. They could also, however, be concerned with historical personages, like the *suasoriae*, with the difference that, instead of being advised on a course of action, the main character was imagined as standing his trial on some major charge, and the speaker had to produce an accusation or defence. There are innumerable examples of such themes in Greek, and quite a number in Latin, as, for example, when Popillius is 'prosecuted' for the murder of Cicero, or Flamininus for treason.[97] Plenty of latitude was allowed in imagining possible accusations. But most of the surviving Latin *controversiae* dealt not with historical persons but, as we shall see, with certain types of stock character, who were not actually named. In the rhetorical handbooks, the rules for deliberative oratory took up relatively little space; but, in order to declaim a *controversia* effectively, as, indeed, any real court-case, a student needed to understand the much more extensive doctrine of the textbooks on forensic oratory. To a summary of this doctrine, then, we next direct our attention.

CHAPTER XX

Learning the art of the advocate

The main doctrines of the rhetorical handbooks on the subject of speech-construction, which were concerned with the basic component parts of introduction, statement of the case, arguments to strengthen one's position and refute that of an opponent, and peroration, and which gave detailed instructions on how to determine the central issue and to handle it, were quite obviously designed to be especially applicable to law-court cases. These precepts, which Greek rhetoricians had evolved from the accumulated experience of Greek pleading, and from careful study and analysis of the speeches of the great Greek orators, contained much that was of permanent value. They were, in due course, faithfully transmitted to Latin, and both the treatise *Ad Herennium* and, especially, Cicero's youthful *De Inventione*, though formal and redolent of school-instruction, are nevertheless remarkable for their thoroughness and patient attention to detail. Cicero came to realize later that the rules had their limitations in practice, and we may be sure that, in Greek, they were never more valuable than when they were transmitted by a man such as Molo of Rhodes, from whom Cicero learnt much, and whom he describes as eminent both as an advocate and as an instructor.[1] Cicero's own speeches show in innumerable ways how much he had learnt from rhetorical theory; but they also show how necessary he often found it to ignore, or modify, the rules and adapt them to the practical requirements of Roman pleading.[2] Many teachers of rhetoric, however, especially under the Empire, did not have this practical experience, but were content to transmit the precepts in stereotyped and compact form, and to make their students learn them by heart.[3] It is precisely because Quintilian was so very much better qualified than the average teacher of rhetoric that his own detailed discussion of theory and practice is of inestimable value. He had not only analysed the speeches of Cicero and other Roman orators, to see exactly how they obtained their effect, and then supplemented this study by listening to practising orators and learning much from Domitius Afer, but he had also been active himself as a pleader in the courts for many years before he became the most prominent teacher of rhetoric at Rome.[4] His own account constantly switches from theory to practice, from school to law court, and represents the best teaching which Roman students ever received on the subject of public speaking in general, and of advocacy in particular. It will always be useful, therefore, to see how far he accepts, supplements or rejects traditional doctrine and contemporary teaching methods.

The introduction (*exordium*, sometimes *ingressus*), with which, in modern terminology, the speaker 'opened the case', was recognized to be of primary importance, in that it must prepare the ground and win the audience over to one's side. The audience might be either a single judge or a panel of judges, the former in an ordinary civil case, the latter in civil cases brought to the centumviral court, and in the criminal *quaestiones*. The case for the prosecution, or plaintiff, came first, and was followed by that for the defence, and the rhetorical rules were sufficiently generalized to be applicable to both. By long-established tradition, it was taught that the introduction must have a threefold objective, to render the audience well-disposed (*benivolum*), attentive (*attentum*), and well-informed (*docilem*).[5] Of these, particular attention was paid to the means of securing goodwill (*captatio benevolentiae*), and here there was a fourfold analysis of possible approaches. Provided that his remarks were related to the case in hand, a speaker might win approval for himself by modestly drawing attention to the high sense of duty he had always shown in his public and private life; or he might excite sympathy by describing the troubles which had befallen him, and appeal to the court as his only means of securing justice. Again, he might seek to arouse in his listeners a feeling of loathing, or jealousy, or contempt towards his opponents by representing them as unscrupulous, treacherous, arrogant, or as a powerful clique using wealth, influence and connections to gain their ends, or as cowardly, indolent and dissipated. Then again, he might flatter the judges by reference to the acknowledged wisdom, courage, clemency of their previous decisions, and the high public expectation that their standards would be maintained. Finally, he might confidently assert that the facts were all in his favour, and that his opponents had no case. Such methods, though derived from Greece, were also applicable in Roman courts, but in Roman pleading, as Quintilian saw,[6] there was a further dimension which had to be introduced. The scheme outlined envisaged the litigant himself as the speaker, for in Greece, though advocates were sometimes used, a man commonly conducted his own case, even though his speech might be prepared by a professional speech-writer; but in Rome, although a man sometimes spoke on his own behalf, it was more usual for him to employ an advocate. Consequently, the advocate's personal standing came into the picture, and it was he who was enabled to claim that he had taken up the case out of a sense of public duty, or out of a sense of obligation to his client, whose merits he would thus be able more unreservedly to praise, and whose opponents he would denigrate. It was the trained advocate who carefully ascertained what was the character and general disposition of the judge — whether he was harsh or mild, cheerful or solemn, strict or easy-going — and what effect public opinion on the subject of the case might have upon him.[7] All this Quintilian knew both from his own experience and from his study of Cicero, and he advised his students accordingly.

Quintilian fully agreed with standard rhetorical theory that an attentive audience could often be secured by asserting at the outset that the case was important, or novel, or scandalous, or had serious political implications, and also by promising to be brief and stick to the point. One had also to see, therefore, that the listeners were properly informed, and it was necessary to tell them clearly and concisely what was the gist of the case.[8] The question was — how far should one go in anticipating points which would need to be made in the subsequent statement of the facts? Here Quintilian warned that one should not develop these at any length, but select just a few of the points which were most strongly in the speaker's favour, and impress these upon the court.[9] Quintilian is here in remarkably close agreement with modern authorities on advocacy, who recommend exactly this approach.[10]

Ancient rhetoricians were well aware, however, that it was not always feasible to adopt such clearly defined and straightforward methods. Much depended on what they called the 'shape' (*schema*) or 'look' (*frons*) of the case, which was assessed by the general opinion (*doxa*) held by people about it. The business which the advocate was concerned to defend might be thought disreputable, or the age, or standing, or weak condition of an accused man might make the task of an accuser invidious. Furthermore, when he appeared for the defence, he might find that the prosecutor, or opposing counsel, had had a powerful effect upon his listeners, and that he was faced with an uphill struggle in persuading them to change their minds. Alternatively, the audience might be simply tired and bored. In these cases, the rhetoricians realized that he must seek a 'remedy', and devised a separate type of introduction, called an *insinuatio*, to enable him to 'wriggle' into a better position by a cautious, tentative and ingratiating approach.[11] He must not waste time over what could not be denied, but palliate his client's actions and minimize the opponent's allegations, or shift the responsibility, or urge that an argument was irrelevant, or find some other means of damaging his opponent's case. If the audience was tired and difficult to arouse, an apt infusion of wit might work wonders. Such conditions tended to make the introduction longer, but otherwise the advocate must keep it to a very modest length.[12]

Above all, as the best authorities advised, the style and manner were most important in the introduction. It was wise to prepare it carefully beforehand, and have it committed to memory, but it was even better to begin from something said by an opponent and then, after refuting it, to proceed to prepared material. This gave an impression of spontaneity, which served to allay suspicion. The speaker should be deferential and not assertive and domineering; he should create an image of naturalness and good intention, but know that the greatest art was to conceal art. Diction should be restrained — the purple passages could come later and bold figures or high-flown or poetic words should be avoided.[13] Each introduction should be made to fit the case in hand, and the advocate must avoid those which were faulty (*vitiosa*) because they were commonplace and conventional, or could equally well be used by the other side, or were laboured or longwinded, or ill-connected with the case in hand.[14] Such was the substance of rhetorical teaching on the opening of one's case, doctrines which the critic Dionysius found most admirably exemplified in the speeches written by Lysias.[15]

After the introduction,[16] the rhetoricians proceeded to deal with what they called the 'narrative' (*narratio*), that is, the 'story' of what happened, or the statement of the facts, as each side wished them to be viewed. They were, however, too much inclined to insist that such an exposition was invariably necessary. Quintilian rightly saw that this was not so, for sometimes the facts were already fully known to the court.[17] This, we may observe, was particularly true when there was more than one advocate appearing on each side, as often in Cicero's day; later speakers did not need to re-traverse familiar ground. Then again, the defence might accept the opponent's statement as regards the facts, but concentrate on the interpretation of them; or the prosecution might make the essential allegations succinctly, as a 'proposition', without elaborating the matter, whereas the defence might have to explain the situation much more fully, to set it in the desired light. Sometimes, too, the whole question revolved round a point of law.[18] Quintilian, however, strongly disagreed with the view of Celsus, that in criminal cases where the defendant simply denied the charge, as in cases of murder, political bribery, and extortion, there was no need for a 'narrative.' He rightly saw that in such cases the prosecutor would normally develop his exposition of what happened, whilst the defence, too, would have to bring in material concerning the defendant's past record, the motives which lay behind the accusation of an innocent man, and considerations which would make the charge incredible.[19]

Wider controversy existed among rhetoricians on a second question, namely, whether, assuming that a statement of the case would be made, it should always immediately follow the introduction, once a favourable atmosphere was secured. Quintilian did not think so, for there might be times when the defence counsel would still feel that there were certain pre-existent factors about the case which were strongly prejudicial, and which needed to be cleared away before he could effectively present his statement.[20] There were two very good examples of this in Cicero. In the trial of Milo, as presented in Cicero's written, but not actually delivered, defence, there were three awkward 'prejudices': (1) as Milo admitted killing Clodius, there was a general assumption that he deserved to be condemned, and Cicero had to preface a strong exposition of the right to kill in self-defence; (2) there was an impression abroad that the Senate desired a condemnation, and this had to be dispelled, as did (3) the belief that Pompey had surrounded the court with armed guards because he, too, was hostile to Milo. Only when these three points were argued away[21] did Cicero venture to present his version of what happened — and so ingeniously, indeed, that, if the orator had only spoken as plausibly as he subsequently wrote, Milo might well have secured an acquittal. Similarly, in his defence of Caelius, Cicero had to go to rather surprising lengths to counter the existing prejudice against his young client's luxurious living, wantonness and immorality before he proceeded to deal with the allegation of attempted poisoning.[22] In fact, all this discussion in Quintilian shows how much there was, under the Empire, for rhetoricians to learn and teach from the example of Cicero, whereas in Cicero's youth there was so much less illustrative material available in Latin.

Traditional doctrine, much influenced by the Isocratean school, required that the statement of facts should have three qualities — it should be lucid, brief and plausible.[23] Quintilian agreed that these qualities, which were theoretically desirable throughout the speech, were particularly necessary at the point where the speaker was revealing his position for the first time to the judge, and were particularly applicable when the facts were on the speaker's side.[24] Lucidity was obtained by the use of a plain style, with correct and meaningful, but not vulgar, diction, and by clear indication of the facts, the persons concerned, the times, places, and motives.[25] Brevity was achieved by beginning at a point which was directly related to the issue, by avoiding irrelevancies, by sacrificing everything that did not immediately serve the case, and by succinct expression, without unnecessary verbiage or repetition. But compression must on no account create obscurity, and it was better to say rather too much than too little, especially if the judge happened to be a countryman and liable to miss the point. Any details which added to plausibility should be included.[26] Moreover, many cases were of so complex a nature that a long statement of facts was inevitable, and in that case it was best to indicate that one had to reserve, or omit, some points, and to divide into sections, indicating their content to begin with, and pointing the transition from one to the next, so that the listener was not bored, but gratified to have finished with one section, and prepared to hear something fresh.[27] Finally, plausibility was attained by considering beforehand what would be natural in the circumstances, by assigning the appropriate motives for each act alleged, by using denigration, or praise, of a defendant's character, so that it seemed in keeping for him to act as he did. In all this, an eye must be kept on questions of timing, locality, circumstances, and opportunity, and these might be lightly touched on here, and dealt with more fully in the proofs. Most valuable in their effect were those subtle, but apparently natural and artless touches which predisposed the listener to accept one's coming arguments,[28] as when Cicero, intent on proving that Milo could not have planned to ambush Clodius, described, with all the naturalness in the world, how he had returned home from the senate, changed his shoes and clothing, and 'as usually happens' (*ut fit*) 'waited around for a time whilst his wife got ready'.[29] What could have been less consistent with criminal intent than this leisurely and entirely typical domestic scene?

Most of the standard doctrine on the statement of the facts was reasonable enough if those facts were in the speaker's favour and he had, as we say, a 'good case'. But, as Quintilian knew only too well from experience, it was a very different matter when the facts did not favour the advocate, and the counsel for defence might often find himself in this position.[30] Moreover, he had to speak second, and, especially in criminal cases where the charge was denied, the prosecutor, or his advocate, would not only have stated what happened, but would have described events in the most disparaging language, would have excited prejudice, and then, having added his proofs, would have ended with stirring peroration which left his listeners with a feeling of strong indignation.[31] There was no sure prescription which the defence counsel could adopt; he must in Quintilian's medical metaphor, adapt his treatment to the case, mend the damage where he could, and apply a 'temporary bandage' to what he might hope to heal later.[32] Without necessarily confining himself to chronological order, he should select his points, and where his opponent's account had been merely tendentious and designed to create suspicion, he must take the force out of the implications, and set the matter to rights. Some things he would have to deny, some he would put differently, some it would be safer to gloss over or omit. Quintilian himself often won approval in the courts by his method of dividing the statement into sections and proving each point in turn.[33] In cases where the defence counsel did not deny the allegations against his client, but sought to mitigate the offence, he must attribute a less dishonourable motive, or give a different explanation, and use words which were more charitable than his opponent's derogatory expressions, presenting, for instance, 'luxurious extravagance' as 'generosity' and 'avarice' as 'thrift'. His expression, voice and manner should be such as to enlist favour, or elicit sympathy; finally, emotion might be aroused by a plea for mercy, for 'sometimes even confession may draw tears'.[34] But not all was honest pleading, for Quintilian admitted that sometimes an advocate had to produce a fabricated story.[35] In that case, it was well to remember the proverb that 'a liar should have a good memory', and see to it (as some failed to do) that what he said was entirely self-consistent. In putting the whole matter in a different light (or, as the Romans said, using a *color*), he must make it his primary care to see that his fabrication was within the bounds of possibility, that it fitted the person, the time, the place, and that the motives and sequence of events were believable. Where possible, it was useful to hinge a fabrication on to something accepted as true. Finally, if the facts were neither entirely against, nor entirely in favour of the speaker, he should weigh them up carefully first. If damaging facts predominated, it was best to take the favourable facts first, develop and substantiate them, and then apply 'treatment' to the rest. If favourable considerations predominated, it was best to take the matter as a whole, parading the good points, and creating the impression that the rest were merely part of an auxiliary force, on which one did not need to call.[36] But, whatever the merits of the case, there was no part of the advocate's speech to which the judge paid more careful attention than his statement of the facts.[37]

Theory next prescribed that, before the advocate entered on his 'proofs' (*argumenta*), which would normally constitute the main body of the speech, he should introduce a section known technically as the *partitio*, or 'division'.[38] This was an enumeration of the main arguments to come — Hortensius, rather to Cicero's amusement, used to count them out on his fingers.[39] Some authorities allowed each argument to be succinctly summarized (*expositio*) rather than merely listed (*enumeratio*); but, in a speech for the defence, it was agreed that it should above all be a clarification of (a) the points on which one agreed with the opposite side, and (b) the essential points in dispute. The purpose of this section (which some theorists required to be restricted to a maximum of three points, though Quintilian found this impracticable [40]) was not only to make the advocate draw up a succinct plan of campaign, but also to provide the judge, or judges, with a clear idea of the direction in which he proposed to proceed. Quintilian was, in general, quite in favour of the introduction of this section, though experience had taught him that it sometimes had its disadvantages. In the first place, it smacked rather too much of careful premeditation; certainly, it gave the judges a clear outline of what to expect, but they were apt to be suspicious of something previously manufactured (*domo adlata*), and an argument was sometimes much more effective if it appeared to be spontaneous, or was introduced as something which the speaker had almost forgotten to mention.[41] Secondly, in a row of arguments, there was usually one which was of fundamental importance (*potentissimum*), and if the judge saw that the proof of this was all that really mattered, he might (especially if pressed for time) pay scant attention to the rest of the arguments, for which the advocate had so kindly prepared him.[42] Quintilian observed that, usually, Cicero was very skilful (as in the *Pro Murena*, where he states three main points) in thus clarifying his arguments.[43] In the *Pro Milone*, too, his main point was that Milo did not set an ambush for Clodius; his second point was powerfully supplementary, namely, that, even if he had deliberately encompassed the death of a man so dangerous to the State, he would rightly have been acclaimed as a public hero.[44] Finally, said Quintilian, the 'division' could be dispensed with if one intended to treat the whole case on an emotional basis; but, if used, it should not be split up into minute and unnecessary subsections, and the plan proposed must be accurately followed out in the sequel.[45]

The most fundamental part of a forensic speech, indeed, the only part which could never be omitted, was that which dealt with the proofs. From Aristotle's time, these had been divided into two major categories, (1) those derived from sources beyond the advocate himself, such as the decisions of previous courts, the examination of relevant documents, and, most important, the evidence of witnesses, and (2) those created by the advocate from his own inventive mind, that is, his method of argument and his use of reasoning. The former were called 'non-technical' the latter 'technical', because the former could not, and the latter could be reduced to some kind of system.[46] In practice, of course, there was no such absolute dichotomy, but the area as a whole was so vast that most teachers of rhetoric did not attempt to give instruction on the 'non-technical' matters, even though they were often of vital importance in legal cases, beyond providing general common-places for and against witnesses, torture, use of precedents, documents and so on.[47] Otherwise, students had to learn for themselves later how to deal with such matters by attending the courts and associating with advocates. Quintilian supplied the fullest information on all kinds of proofs, but even he admitted in due course that skill in the examination of witnesses, which was not at all cultivated in the schools, was really the product of natural acumen and experience.[48] He himself gives some admirable advice on assessing the character of witnesses, on proper preparation by the advocate of those whom he called, on discrediting the opponent's witnesses, and on leading a witness from an apparently casual and irrelevant inquiry into more significant questions, which might trap him into a damaging admission.[49] All this, of course, could not have been taught practically unless the rhetoricians had been willing to set up full-scale mock trials, in the manner of modern law-schools. As it was, they did so only in so far as concerned the set speeches (*oratio perpetua*) of either side. They were therefore concerned with teaching students to develop their own arguments and apply them to the facts of the case. There were two ways of doing this, both of which were used.

The first, and the older,[50] method was to provide examples of logical, and of fallacious, reasoning, classifying types and providing illustrative examples. This came very near to the philosophical domain, and, if thoroughly carried out, would have approximated to a course in logic. But, although extremely valuable, this method did not give a student the specific guide-lines which he needed for treatment of particular kinds of legal case. It was Hermagoras who first supplied this need, with his classification of the major types of legal issue, (Greek *stasis*, Latin *constitutio* or *status*) and his development of the appropriate topics (*loci*) to be used in each.[51] All subsequent rhetoricians, however much they adapted and rearranged, worked by this kind of classification system, which at first grew up alongside, and eventually overshadowed, the older method of logical training. Quintilian dealt with both in great detail, but for the average rhetorician, and for the average student, it was the determination of the issue, and the lines of argument required, which were the main concern.

This was perhaps the most technical matter in the whole system of ancient rhetoric, and one of the most-discussed among professionals, but it is possible to simplify it, and for young students it had to be simplified. They were taught not to jump to the ultimate question in the case, but to reach it by stages. For example, one of the most commonly used illustrations in the textbooks was the Orestes-Clytaemnestra case.[52] It ran like this: (1) Prosecution: 'Orestes, you are charged with murdering your mother'; (2) Defence: 'I was justified in so doing'; (3) Primary Question: Was he justified? But it was impossible to decide this until the supporting reason of the defendant and the countering point of the prosecution were brought in. Thus we continue: (4) 'My mother had murdered my own father'; to which the reply is: (5) 'That was not sufficient reason for you to kill your mother.' We thus reach (6), which is the ultimate question (*summa quaestio*) or the point for adjudication, as Hermagoras called it; this could be treated as a matter of general principle, arguable both ways, and in that case it became a thesis: Is any son whose mother has murdered his father justified in killing her? The *Eumenides* of Aeschylus, from which the subject was ultimately derived, shows how equally opinion might have been divided in antiquity.

The first type of case taken was that in which the accused denied the act with which he was charged; the issue was one of fact (*an sit*); but the case did not admit of definitive proof, and had to be decided by inference (*coniectura*) and degree of probability.[53] In the textbooks, murder-charges particularly fell into this category, and we must first show how closely related they were to real life. The favourite Greek example, much used in the Roman schools, was that concerning Ulysses and Ajax. Ajax, realizing with shame what he had done in his madness, flung himself on his sword, and just as Ulysses, who then came on the scene, had drawn out the blood-stained weapon, Ajax's brother, Teucer, appeared, and, assuming enmity to be the motive, charged Ulysses with murder.[54] The example, therefore, was intended to prepare students to argue in cases where the circumstances were highly incriminating, and the question was — was it murder or suicide? Such cases were common in the courts, and one of Quintilian's earliest speeches — the only one which he published himself — concerned a certain Naevius of Arpinum, charged with the murder of his wife, the question being whether he had thrown her out of the window, or whether she had thrown herself![55] Another case, given fully in Cicero's early textbook, concerned a murder at an inn.[56] Briefly, two travellers, one of whom was carrying a good deal of money, joined company, dined together, and shared a room at an inn. In the night, the inn-keeper took the sword of the man who had not the money (the weapon lay by his side), killed the other man, stole the money, and replaced the sword in its sheath. Very early next morning, the surviving traveller called his companion more than once, but receiving no answer, decided that he must be sleeping heavily, packed his belongings, and left. The inn-keeper then raised a cry of 'murder', and brought him back to stand trial. This may well have been a genuine case, for there is a basically similar story, told as a recent occurrence by Cicero in his defence of Roscius of Ameria, who was charged with the murder of his father.[57] T. Caelius of Terracina had shared a room overnight at an inn with his two grown-up sons, and, at dawn, was found with his throat cut. The youths, who had slept beside him, declared that they had heard no sound, but as there was no other conceivable perpetrator, they were charged with parricide. In this case, the Roman jury decided to acquit the youths on very interesting grounds. It transpired that they were not only found asleep themselves, but that they had even left the door of the room open; and no juryman could persuade himself that any son could have so casually gone off to sleep after committing so terrible a crime.

How, then, should the student be prepared to tackle such cases, whether for the prosecution or for the defence? There were, he was told, two major considerations which must arise in the early stages, that of the reason for the act (*causa*), and that of the character, position and past record of the accused (*persona*); together, they helped to answer the question whether or not the accused would have wished to commit such a crime (*an voluerit*).[58] As to which of the two should come first, there was some division of opinion; Cicero preferred to begin from the reason, Quintilian from the person concerned.[59] The reason itself might be one of two kinds; either it was an impulse of the moment, or else it involved premeditation. If the former was alleged, the prosecutor must enlarge on the effects of violent emotions, cite similar examples, and proceed to align all this with the known character and record of the accused;[60] if premeditation was alleged, the prosecutor must expose the motive, whether it was to retain, increase or acquire some advantage, or to get rid of, or lessen, or avoid some loss. Whether the motive was vengeance, fear, acquisition of money or power, what mattered was not so much whether the accused actually secured his object, as whether he had thought he could secure it.[61] Defence counsel must deny the alleged impulse[62], or gain, or show that it was inadequate for the commission of such a crime.[63] As to the character and record, the prosecutor will seek out, and stress, any previous conviction for a grave offence, or any suspicion thereof; failing that, he will associate the defendant's action and motive with some other fault in his character and behaviour, provided always that he can make it relevant; if even this material is lacking, he will urge concentration on the facts themselves and argue that a clean record is of no consequence — it may merely indicate successful concealment in the past, and, in any case, there had to be a first time.[64] Defence counsel will make the very most of his client's good standing, record and general behaviour, and will rebut the charge with indignation; failing that, he will argue that the alleged offences or faults were not relevant, or not heinous, or excusable, or merely due to scandal-mongering. If even this is impracticable, he, too, will confine attention to the facts.[65] Here the question for both sides was — could the defendant have committed the crime (*an potuerit*)? could anyone else have done so? would he have chosen that particular time, or that particular place, or that particular method, or accomplice, and what hope would he have had of concealment?[66] Finally, in deciding innocence or guilt (*an fecerit*), attention must be directed to anything the accused may have actually, or allegedly, said or done before the event, and, especially, immediately after it.[67]

The second major rhetorical category was called that of definition (*definitio*), and was intended to cover cases in which the defendant admitted having done that with which he was charged, but denied that it was punishable (as we say) 'within the meaning of the act'. Such cases occurred when the law itself was loosely drawn, and the legal description of the offence was capable of being either sharply or broadly interpreted. An example commonly used in Roman handbooks was that of the law of treason, or, to use the phrase derived from Latin, lese-majesty (*laesa maiestas*). The law defined the crime simply as 'diminishing the sovereign majesty' (*maiestatem minuere*) of the Roman people.[68] How far could one go in interpreting this phrase? Was it applicable to one who laid violent hands on a representative of the Roman people? Even if he had justification, and a moral right? For example, the tribune Flaminius seditiously proposed an agrarian law to the people against the senate's wish, but his own father, exercising his private paternal right (*patria potestas*) to deal as he thought fit with his own son, dragged him from the rostrum. He was accused of lese-majesty, and Cicero gives the arguments and interpretations of both sides. Again, both Greeks and Romans found the law of sacrilege ill-defined. A man steals from a temple money deposited there by a private individual, or steals sacred vessels from a private house — is it sacrilege, or theft?[69] Similarly, even with adultery — a man caught in the act with another man's wife is chargeable — but suppose the act takes place in a brothel?[70] Similar questions of definition arose when, for instance, it was asked what exactly the law meant by *venenum* ('poison') — would a love-potion be thus classified?[71] Was a person enslaved and bonded (*addictus*) for repayment of debt, the same as a *servus*?[72] Particularly common was the problem of deciding what constituted 'madness' (*dementia*) — could it be deduced from a single act, or several acts, or only from consistent evidence of mental derangement?[73] Finally, there was the problem of interpreting the Roman legal phrase which referred to the defendant as having been 'the cause of death' (*causa mortis*) to another? Quintilian gives a fictitious case (*ficta controversia*) for the benefit of students ('my young men', as he calls them) as follows.[74] Some merry youths decided to dine out on the seashore, but one of their party failed to appear, and so, for a jest, they raised a tomb to him and inscribed his name thereon. Later, the youth's father, returning from overseas, happened to land near the spot, and, reading his son's name, in anguish, hung himself. The youths were charged with having been 'the cause of his death'. Quintilian gives the view of the prosecution, and, more fully, that of the defence; and, though the case itself might be thought far-fetched, the need for definition was there, and even Roman laws must sometimes have been drafted in such general terms that they led to conflicting arguments in court.

The third main category covered cases where the defendant admitted the charge, but urged that his action was either justifiable or, at least, excusable; here everything depended on the view one might take of the nature of the act, and the issue, therefore, was termed that of 'quality' (*qualitas*). The types of argument used by the defence could be learnt in a descending order of efficacy, from the strongest down to the weakest, according to the nature of the case. The most powerful form of defence, the 'defence absolute', was that in which it was claimed that the alleged offence was an entirely justifiable act, supported by natural law, or statute, or custom, or precedent, or equity, or the terms of an agreement.[75] The remaining forms were 'assumptive', in that they were supported by extraneous considerations. The advocate might feel that attack was the best form of defence, and maintain that the offence was justified as a retaliation for a crime committed or attempted against his client (*relatio criminis*). The favourite example in the textbooks was that of the 'indictment' of Orestes for the murder of his mother, Clytaemnestra; the defence was that he was justified because she had killed his father, Agamemnon.[76] Naturally, prosecuting counsel would point out that two wrongs do not make a right — what would happen if everyone thus took the law into their own hands? But the argument was most efficacious when it was used to condone killing in self-defence; Cicero defended Milo on this ground, and early in his speech, to mislead the jury, cited examples in which manslaughter was never publicly condemned.[77] But even when there was no question of personal aggression, the act might be defended as necessary in the public interest, or even in the defendant's own interest.[78] The next type was that known as 'comparison' (*comparatio*), where all other possible alternatives to the defendant's action were examined, and it was claimed that he had no option, or chose the wisest course. It could be used, for example, in the case of a military leader accused of treason for making an agreement with the enemy to surrender arms and equipment on condition of being allowed to withdraw and save the lives of his men.[79] Another form of defence, sometimes quite strong, was that of the 'shifting of blame' (*remotio criminis*) to some other person, or to the circumstances. A favourite example, Greek in origin, was that of ambassadors brought to trial for having failed to set out on the appointed day; their defence was that the expenses for such journeys were defrayed from public funds, and the treasurer had failed to provide payment beforehand.[80] Coming a little further down the defence scale, an advocate might have to agree that his client's action was reprehensible in itself, but would make it appear excusable (*concessio, excusatio*) on the grounds that he had acted in ignorance, or was the victim of an unfortunate chance, or had had to yield to necessity; his client's intentions, he would argue, had been of the best.[81] Lastly, the weakest defence was really no defence at all, as it consisted in a plea for pardon (*deprecatio*); but, said the textbooks, one should never be content to rest the case as a whole on this, but only make a partial and judicious use of it.[82] All these various types, with detailed points for both prosecution and defence, were dealt with in rhetorical theory. They provided a system of arguments on matters of fact.[83] But often the point on which the advocate took his stand was a matter not of fact, but of law. Consequently, a further classification of issues was taught, in which the meaning, intent and applicability of a statute, or the interpretation of a document, was the subject of debate. This category was very similar to that of 'definition' .(which was sometimes subsumed here), but was usually given separate treatment after the three main types of constitution.

Of these so-called 'legal issues', quite the most frequently debated, both in the courts and in the schools, was that which related to the 'letter' (*scriptum*) and the 'intent' (*voluntas* or *sententia*); for not only in the law itself, but in cases involving wills, agreements, contracts and any form of document, conflict might arise between those who demanded a strictly literal interpretation and those who stressed the intention of the originator.[84] The law, for example, might be obscurely or inadequately expressed: 'A thief must refund four times the amount stolen' — but, supposing there are two thieves, must they each refund four times, or pay the amount between them?[85] Alternatively, the law might be quite plainly worded, but the question arose — was it intended to admit of no exceptions whatever? Here, a favourite example in the schools concerned the law which punished with death any foreigner who scaled the city wall; but suppose the enemy had scaled the wall, and a foreigner ascended to drive them off — was he still punishable, even though he acted to save the city?[86] Another example, based on historical fact, and very much used in Greek schools, was that of the prosecution of Epaminondas for having failed to hand over his army on the required date to his legally-appointed successor, though as a result he was able, within a short time, to inflict a resounding defeat on the Spartans.[87] In such cases, discussion of the position would broaden out into general considerations of equity (*aequitas*).[88] In the forum, Cicero, defending Caecina in a dispute over property, strongly pressed for an equitable rather than a literal, interpretation of a praetorian interdict. The same principle of the letter and the intent often arose in cases concerning documents, especially wills. The classic example, often used as a model, was that of the *causa Curiana*, of 93 B.C., in which Crassus and Scaevola appeared as opposing advocates before the centumviral court. A testator, believing his wife to be with child, left all his property to his posthumous son, with the proviso that, if the son died before coming of age, the estate should pass to M. Curius. No son was in fact born, and Curius laid claim. But a relative of the deceased, M. Coponius, contested it on the ground that as the condition of the succession of Curius had not been fulfilled, the estate should revert to him as the nearest heir (*agnate*). Scaevola appeared for Coponius and argued on the literal terms of the will, but Crassus won the case for Curius on the grounds of equity, and what could be argued to have been the testator's wish, had he known.[89] In the rhetorical textbooks, the stock topics (*loci*) by which prosecution and defence counsel in such cases might weaken each other's position were fully set out, the former enlarging on the dangerous effects of departure from the stated text, and the latter denouncing such adhesion as mere pettifogging, and calling for a more liberal approach, in the interests of that fairness which it was the purpose of the law to secure.

There were also other forms of legal issue, such as that in which there was ambiguity in the text, and either of two interpretations was possible.[90] Sometimes an individual word, sometimes the syntax, sometimes the division of a compound into separate words, gave rise to different meanings. Here some of the textbook examples (resulting, doubtless, from Greek over-ingenuity) were such as would rarely occur in practice, such as the supposed doubt whether a testator left 'all his estate' (*panta*) to Leon, or his estate to Pantaleon.[91] But, in fact, ambiguity could be a very real problem, especially in wills and other documents, and it was sensible enough to teach students to be on the lookout for it. Other types of issue were that in which the juxtaposition of two statutes created a conflict (*contrariae leges*), so that anyone who faithfully observed the one might, in certain circumstances, transgress the other;[92] and that in which the applicability of a particular law to a given case, for which it did not expressly cater, could only be decided by a process of reasoning by analogy (*ratiocinatio*).[93] The cases in which one or other of these legal issues might arise were, as Quintilian knew, innumerable, and no two cases were exactly alike; the best that a teacher could do was to select a different example each day, and show how it could be argued. Here, too, Quintilian stressed the importance of teaching students to present their arguments in the most effective order, but recognized that, as there was no golden rule, they must also learn to rely on their own wits and commonsense.[94] Such, in bare outline, was the so-called doctrine of issues ('*status* doctrine'), which offered a constructive and useful approach to some of the main lines of advocacy in court.

The second method of teaching students to deal with the section of 'proofs' was that which concentrated on reasoning in the abstract, showed how individual arguments could be formulated, and illustrated what was logical and what was not. Although this tended to be treated as supplementary to the status doctrine, there was a good deal about it in the textbooks, and Quintilian devoted half of his fifth book to it.[95] It is far too detailed and close-knit to admit even of a summary here, and only a few pertinent points can be made. In brief, although the method of induction (as used in the Socratic dialogues) was recognized to be valuable in court in the cross-examination of witnesses[96], most stress was laid on the method of deduction. This was taught both positively and constructively, with a view to the strengthening of one's own arguments (*confirmatio*), and negatively and destructively, with a view to avoiding false conclusions from given premises, and, especially, to detecting logical fallacies in an opponent's arguments (*refutatio*). The positive deductive argument, the rhetorical syllogism, or 'enthymeme' (in more developed form the 'epicheireme') might consist of three basic parts only, a major premise, a minor premise and a conclusion, or be extended to four, or five, parts, according as the major, or minor, premise, or both, required to be supported by reasons.[97] The negative side was illustrated by giving a list of examples in which the deduction was not cogent, or not relevant.[98] Of all the forms of positive deduction, perhaps the most useful in actual practice was one which was much employed by Cicero, the 'dilemma'. Here either two propositions were offered, and the elimination of one was held to compel acceptance of the other, or several propositions were suggested, and all in turn were eliminated, except the one which was being upheld. In practice, of course, although two propositions might be mutually exclusive, judges might not always realize that they were based on a false assumption. Cicero argued that either (a) Milo set a trap for Clodius or (b) Clodius set a trap for Milo, and by demolishing (a) sought to compel acceptance of (b). But in fact, as we know from Asconius, the meeting of the two was fortuitous, and neither had set a trap for the other. Here the dilemma affected the whole argument, but it was frequently used simply to score a point in passing. Already in Cicero's youth it was explained and illustrated in the rhetoric schools, though students were warned that they must be careful lest it might be capable of conversion, or denial, and used against themselves.[99]

After the proofs came the last section of the speech, the peroration (*conclusio, peroratio*), which, as both theorists and legal practitioners well knew, was of very great importance, as it was the culmination of all that went before, and produced the final impression which the speaker would leave in the listeners' minds. It needed to have an element of recapitulation (*enumeratio*), but the rhetoricians rightly warned that the main arguments should only be succinctly summarized, and not allowed to develop into a second speech.[100] If law-court audiences had been guided by purely rational considerations, as philosophers might have wished, there would have been no need for more than this. But in fact they rarely were, and that is why, both in practice and in the theory which was born of observation of practice, the peroration was also very much concerned with a strong appeal to the feelings (*indignatio, conquestio*) [101] — provided, of course, that the subject allowed of it, for to attempt to arouse emotion in a trivial case was, said Quintilian, rather like equipping an infant with the mask and buskins of Hercules.[102] Major trials, however, gave great scope, and theory prescribed that the advocate should use a weighty and distinguished style, allowing the grandeur of his eloquence to sweep on to full flood.[103] He should dwell most of all on those aspects of the case which would arouse the listeners' feelings, whether of indignation and hostility, or of goodwill and — most powerful of all — of pity (*miseratio*). The accuser should amplify the wrong done by intensifying the guilt of the perpetrator, the sufferings of the victim, the shamefulness of the time, the place, and above all the manner of the infliction. He should seek, also to forestall any possible appeal for sympathy which the defence might use.[104] The defence counsel, in turn, might have first to dispel the emotions thus aroused before he sought to enlist sympathy for his client, but he, too, would amplify the defendant's good qualities, his personal worth, his laudable pursuits, his patriotism, his nobility, even the merits of his ancestors. In his appeal for pity, he might lament his undeserved plight, draw a mournful picture of the effects of a condemnation upon him, his aged parents, his children, his friends, and even introduce an imaginary speech (*prosopopoeia*) of some relevant and worthy person uttering a condolence.[105] The presence of a man's children in court, though sometimes effective, might not always prove an unmixed blessing, and the client himself needed to be warned to see to it that he looked as abject as his advocate made him out to be.[106] Above all, the appeal for compassion must not be made too long, for, in a famous phrase of the rhetorician Apollonius, 'nothing dries more quickly than a tear'.[107] Behaviour in Roman courts during perorations, however, must often have been surprisingly uninhibited, and it is small wonder that future advocates were carefully briefed in that part of a forensic speech in which Cicero, the greatest of Roman advocates, had particularly excelled.

In the teaching of the standard doctrine on speech-construction, the primary consideration was to ensure that boys knew the basic rules, which could be, and often were, set forth in textbooks of compact form, with the minimum of illustrative material. Once they had been expounded — often in rather dogmatic fashion — they had to be learnt by heart, and then considerable use was made of question and answer, to test the knowledge acquired. Even a distinguished orator like Antonius admitted that, with beginners, teachers had to be 'constantly hammering at the same anvil', or, by a different metaphor, 'feeding their pupils, a morsel at a time'.[108] This teaching and testing would be normally done in Latin, unless a boy happened to have chosen to attend a Greek rather than a Roman rhetorician. Cicero was probably exceptionally thorough in first teaching and testing his son in Greek, and then going over the same ground in Latin, this time allowing Marcus to put the questions, and providing the answers himself.[109] But even in a Latin school, pupils would probably be told the Greek equivalents of the relevant technical terms for the classifications and subdivisions, rather as we find them in the textbook of the late rhetorician, Chirius Fortunatianus, which is based throughout on question and answer, and where the query is regularly put: 'What do the Greeks call this?'[110] Once the rules were known, and had been illustrated by examples, students might be made to consider how far they had been applied in speeches of the great orators of the past.

After long experience in teaching, Quintilian came to realize that no method was more valuable than that of expounding and analysing speeches in class, and he asserted that young students could benefit more from this than from studying any of the standard textbooks.[111] Often, without doubt, the speech chosen would have been one of Cicero, and we may be fairly sure that one of those selected would have been the *Pro Milone*, which he described as 'a most noble speech',[112] and from which he frequently quotes. He would, he tells us, begin by giving a summary of the case, and would then make his boys stand up and read aloud in turn. As the reading proceeded, he analysed the speech rhetorically, showing how conciliatory was the proem, how clear, concise and convincing the narrative, how skilful the 'division', how clever and forcefully persistent the argument. He would draw attention to powerful or pleasing passages, noting the alternation of sharp invective with urbane humour, and the emotional appeal which had finally proved irresistible. Especially important, too, were observations on style. Here Quintilian would comment, now on the appropriateness, dignity, or elevation of some particular word, now on praiseworthy amplification or effective compression, now on a brilliant metaphor, now on a figure of speech, now on smooth and polished, yet none the less vigorous, composition.[113] In this last connection he would probably have introduced observations on word-order and particular prose rhythms, a subject which he expounds at some length in his ninth book.[114]

Quintilian also had the excellent, and original, idea of reading and commenting upon *bad* speeches in class, as a vivid method of showing students what they must at all costs avoid; and he would also often question them to see if they themselves could observe what was wrong.[115] Here, too, he was especially concerned with style. There was so much which was corrupt in contemporary oratory and, to make matters worse, standards were so false that the vices themselves were praised. Natural expression, says Quintilian, was thought incompatible with genius, and the more *recherché* the words seemed to be, the more fatuously were they admired. So he would pick out examples of unsuitable, obscure, bombastic, trivial, sordid or extravagant expression, and of the lilting and effeminate rhythms so characteristic of his day. He would also have drawn attention to passages in which there was much empty verbiage, or where brevity had been secured at the expense of clarity, or where the style was over-elaborate, incongruous or monotonous.[116]

To what extent the average rhetorician made use of this kind of critical analysis we do not know, but it is fairly certain that most teachers concentrated on listing, explaining and illustrating with examples the numerous figures of speech. Cicero, in both the *De Oratore* and the *Orator*, gives very succinct indications of the nature of each one of these (there were several dozens of them), and they are much more fully expounded in both the *Ad Herennium* and Quintilian.[117] The fact that they were frequently set out in separate treatises shows the importance generally attached to them. The term 'figures', representing the Greek *schemata*, covered an extremely wide variety of patterns into which expression — whether involving words, clauses, or sentences — could be shaped for greater effect. The teacher might draw his examples from the textbooks or from his own reading, but usually the most appropriate and abundant material was to be found in the orators, especially Demosthenes[118] and Cicero. The use of figures was, however, by no means confined to oratory; many of them could also be found in Homer and Virgil, and they illustrated almost every possible facet of what was termed 'embellishment' (*ornatus*) in style.

The standard classification into 'figures of language' and 'figures of thought' was not an altogether satisfactory one. Even though in a number of instances it was based on a valid distinction, it led to a good deal of fruitless controversy because often it could not be agreed whether the pattern was simply a verbal device or one which persuaded the listener, or reader, to a particular way of thinking or feeling. Various forms of word-repetition were classed as figures of language. A speaker might reiterate his opening word, or words, for emphasis (*conduplicatio*), or he might begin or end successive clauses or sentences with the same word or expression (*epanaphora, repetitio*).[119] Cato, for instance, defending himself, began five successive sentences with the word *numquam* — '*never* did I do this ...', '*never* did I do that ...'.[120] Such repetition might be simply the natural result of strong feeling, or it might be designed for effect. But with other figures in the group we move more definitely into the area of conscious artistry. When the clauses are nicely balanced or parallel (the Greek *parisosis*), or equal in length (*isokolon, compar*), or have similar-sounding endings (*homoeoteleuton, similiter desinens*),[121] or are based on word- or clause-contrast (*antithesis, contentio* or *contrarium*),[122] they reflect the kind of composition which dates back to Gorgias. Word-play, too (*paronomasia, adnominatio*), in its many forms, is a recurrent figure in this group,[123] as is the building up of a climax (*gradatio*).[124] These are all devices much sought after in Asianist oratory and the declamations of the imperial period.

Only a few of the numerous figures of thought mentioned by Quintilian (some of which earlier writers call figures of language) can here be selected for illustration. Sometimes they are a means of enforcing an argument or anticipating an objection, sometimes they are forms of pretence designed to mislead, or to present the speaker in a favourable light, sometimes they are devices calculated to arouse interest or emotion. Use of the rhetorical question (*interrogatio*), whether to stir or to elicit sympathy, was a very familiar device, but a speaker could put a number of points in the form of rhetorical questions, to each of which he provided succinct answers to suit his own case (*subiectio*).[125] He could make a pretence of dismissing, or not dwelling on, certain points in the very act of mentioning them ('I say nothing of ...', 'I do not need to mention ...'). This was called 'concealment' (*occultatio*) or 'omission' (*praeteritio*), and was a favourite device of Cicero.[126] It could serve merely to suggest that the speaker had a wealth of material to draw upon, or it could be a means of stating, and quickly skating away from, something which would not bear closer examination. The speaker could, again, affect to consult the audience and ask their opinion (*communicatio*), as when Cato said: 'Come now, if you had been in his place, what would you have done?'[127] Sometimes an orator could hesitate and pretend to be at a loss (*dubitatio*),[128] just in order to suggest genuine concern. One of the most powerful of all the figures at an orator's disposal was irony (*dissimulatio*), though much could also be done by innuendo (known as *emphasis*).[129] Finally, the speaker could introduce an exclamation now and again (like Cicero's *O tempora! O mores!*), or a dramatic apostrophe (*exclamatio*), or a vivid illustration (*evidentia*), or an impersonation (*prosopopoeia*),[130] as Cicero does so effectively when he invents a speech of old Appius Claudius rebuking his descendant Clodia, or of the fatherland rebuking Catiline.[131] Such were some of the many types of figures which were taught to students in rhetoric schools.

We come now to the rhetoricians' advice on the learning and the delivery of a speech. Obviously, with so many points to be borne in mind, the greatest blessing of all was that of memory. But this was a quality with which individuals were varyingly endowed. Some were phenomenally gifted, others had to work hard to plant the material in their minds. Systems of mnemonics had been invented and experimented with from the time of Simonides onwards, and orators and rhetoricians usually had their own ideas to communicate.[132] What was particularly needed was orderliness in the setting out of visual images, and in the textbooks much play was made with the notion of associating particular arguments or ideas with the various parts of a familiar and easily visualized locality, such as the rooms of a spacious house, from the forecourt onwards.[133] Such a method may seem to us highly artificial, but evidently there were those who found it practicable. It was certainly sensible to recommend that the advocate should visualize the series of actions involved in his case — e.g. the successive stages of an alleged crime[134] — but to suggest, as many theorists did, that symbols might be found for individual words and expressions was taking matters to rather absurd extremes. Typically sound was Quintilian's advice to the future advocate to memorize his script, a section at a time, and to read it over to himself aloud, thus utilizing the auditory memory as well. Clear division and subdivision of topics was most essential, but, whilst what had been written might remain clearly reflected in the mind, one should create the impression of speaking with artless ease.[135]

Last of all came a subject which Demosthenes and Cicero, and many others, orators and theorists alike, recognized to be of supreme importance, namely, that of delivery (*pronuntiatio, actio*). Here, however, the textbook writers would have acknowledged that, although they could classify and explain the various tones of voice and types of gestures, no written account could be satisfactory without the personal demonstration of the teacher.[136] Quite the most interesting exposition of the subject is that of Quintilian, for not only does it show how he taught, but it gives a vivid, and sometimes amusing, picture of the extravagances of contemporary advocates. After discussing the volume and the quality of the voice, and the contribution which professional trainers could make to its development (though he does not entirely subscribe to their methods), he recommends learning by heart and delivering practice passages of considerable variety, which may require either loud, or argumentative, or colloquial, or modulated utterance.[137] But he particularly stresses that the voice should not be over-strained in early youth.[138] Applying the Theophrastean classification of virtues of style to delivery, he urges that it must be correct, clear, appropriate and distinguished. Distinction is achieved by mastery of varying tones, and here he takes the opening of Cicero's *Pro Milone*, clause by clause, and shows exactly how the voice should be used at each point for maximum effect.[139] Among the faults which he criticizes are excessive volubility or slowness, running out of breath before the end of the sentence, and, above all, the utterly reprehensible habit of 'chanting'.[140] Turning to gesture he has many an illuminating remark to make about stance, position and movement of head, neck and shoulders, arrangement of the toga and movement of the arms, the eloquent use of the hands and fingers, and even the expression of the eyes. Facial expression, too, is important, but one should not become an actor — though occasional discreet use of mimicry could be very realistic.[141] We learn from Quintilian many of the undignified or distracting habits of contemporary orators, such as pacing up and down (like the rhetorician whom a rival wittily asked how many *miles* he had declaimed), or addressing the audience as if receiving a goblet, or using the right arm like a flail to deliver a rain of blows in the air, or bidding fair to lay low some unsuspecting by-stander by a sudden sideways sweep![142] All these things Quintilian would have told his students — surely to their enjoyment — when they came to the final stage of their course, the declamation of mock-legal themes.

CHAPTER XXI

Declamation as a preparation for the lawcourts

In teaching their pupils to distinguish the various types of issue which could arise in legal cases, the rhetoricians had, as we have seen, provided illustrative examples of each type, and had explained what the relevant topics were, for both accusation and defence. It was necessary, however, to supplement this doctrine with actual practice in speaking, and teachers therefore not only used the textbook examples, but invented many others of their own as practical exercises on which their pupils could declaim, either for or against, like advocates in court. After stating clearly the law, or laws, governing each particular exercise, they propounded a situation or 'theme' in which the protagonist, or one of the protagonists, was imagined as the accused, and his course of action was either denounced or upheld or excused. This form of declamatory exercise was called in Cicero's day simply a 'case' (*causa*), but soon came to be known as a 'disputation' or 'controversy' (*controversia*);[1] this word, originally applied to the basic issue of a conflict, was then extended as a general term for the exercise as a whole.[2] As, under the Empire, many of the situations imagined became more bizarre and artificially contrived, the exercise was especially associated with the *scholasticus* or 'school-man', and was called a 'scholastic theme' (*scholastica materia*, or simply *scholastica*),[3] to distinguish it from the genuine legal contests of the Forum. Nevertheless, the laws quoted at the head of the exercises, which used to be dismissed as fictitious, or as of Greek origin, have been shown to contain much that is either genuine, or adapted, sometimes loosely, from previous Roman legislation.[4] There is also considerable evidence of familiarity with Roman legal terminology,[5] and, despite the unlikelihood of many of the actual situations envisaged in the themes, the argumentation still provides some very interesting parallels to genuine advocacy, as a preparation for which the *controversia* was originally designed. As Quintilian repeatedly shows, the basic principle involved, and the lines of argument taken, were often the same in declamation and legal practice, and he was perfectly prepared to use school-themes himself, provided that they retained some link with reality.[6]

In Roman times, rhetoricians often published their own declamations, [7] and, even when they did not, excerpts and particular points were noted by their listeners, whether at school or in a public audience, and came into general circulation. The elder Seneca's collection, based on a phenomenal memory, represents what was said at public gatherings of professional declaimers, cleverly competing with each other on the standard themes, and is enriched by his own critical comments. Young students may well have been sometimes present on such occasions, but the treatment is not that of a teacher with his class. Much more germane to our present purpose is the collection of *Lesser Declamations* which have come down under the name of Quintilian.[8] Even though it is perhaps unlikely that they derive directly from his pen, they do contain some quite significant parallels with the *Institutio Oratoria* in doctrine, and general attitude to the subject, and may well have been drawn up by someone trained in his school.]9] The most important point is that they were certainly intended for teaching purposes, and frequently include the master's preliminary remarks (*sermo*) before the model declamation.

Many of the subjects of the declamations are concerned with criminal charges, among which cases of poisoning are typical themes.[10] There is ample evidence of the prevalence of poisoning at Rome[11] — quite a good deal of it derives even from the Republican period (notably, Cicero's *Pro Cluentio*), but much more from the Empire, in which period the numerous references in the historians, including the accounts of the deaths of Germanicus, Drusus, Claudius and Britannicus represent only the most notorious of many such crimes.[12] In the declamations, as often in real life, the murder, or the alleged attempt, takes place within the family itself; a son (especially a disowned son) is accused of poisoning his father, a wife (especially an adulterous wife)[13] her husband, a step-mother the child of a previous marriage. As in real life, the doctor, too, easily becomes suspect.[14] One of the exercises which must come fairly close to a genuine court-case runs as follows.[15]

Two brothers, who were joint-owners, quarrelled, and divided their property; one of them made a doctor his heir. Later, they became reconciled. The one whose heir was the doctor returned home after dining with his brother, and said that he suspected he had been poisoned. The doctor said he would give him a remedial drug, and did so, but after drinking it, the man died. The surviving brother and the doctor bring accusations of poisoning against each other.

Here we have a case of what the rhetoricians called 'mutual accusation' (*antikategoria*), in which the defendant has both to establish his own innocence and incriminate his opponent.[16] The teacher's model gives the case in favour of the brother. As there was no doubt about the fact of poisoning, and the only question was which of the two was the culprit, the arguments used are those of the 'conjectural' type of issue, and concentrate on likelihood. The speaker begins by dilating upon the strong natural bond of brotherly love, minimizes the quarrel, which, he says, merely served to enhance the affection, and proceeds to compare himself and the doctor as regards motive. He had no reason to wish to kill his brother, whereas the doctor stood to gain his inheritance at once — the point is emphasized by a brief diatribe on the effects of greed. Even more important was the question of place and time — would he have been likely to commit such an act in his own home, violating the sanctities of hospitality, and taking such a risk in the presence of servants? Would not an intending criminal have sought to ensure, above all things, that he would be in a position to deny any such charge? Would he not have feared that his brother might die instantaneously, or that the taste or smell of the food might make him suspicious? Contrast the doctor's opportunity, for 'no one is more easily poisoned than he who takes what he thinks to be medicine'. Finally, to arouse sympathy, a contrast between the satisfaction of the now wealthy doctor and his personal grief and sense of loss.

In poisoning cases, the question of the chances of detection could obviously be of relevance. In this declamation, the accused brother would have been in a stronger position if he had not himself been the host, and this may be illustrated by what Tacitus says about the trial of Cn. Calpurnius Piso in A.D. 20 for the murder of Germanicus. The only charge, he remarks, of which the defence disposed satisfactorily was that of poisoning. Even the prosecution could not sufficiently substantiate their allegation that Piso, when invited to dine with Germanicus, and when seated beside him, had tampered with his food; 'for it seemed absurd that he would have dared to do this in the company of another man's slaves, in the sight of so many by-standers, and in Germanicus' own presence'.[17] Usually, in fact, the preparations for poisoning were far more subtle, and of this the declaimers, who knew a good deal about the subject, were fully aware. They sometimes posit cases in which the symptoms were indeterminate (*ambigua signa*), and might point either to poison or to some natural disorder,[18] and, in real life, slow-acting drugs were often selected for this purpose. Sejanus, when plotting the murder of Drusus, 'chose a poison, the gradual working of which might be mistaken for a fortuitous illness'.[19] When such cases of 'ambiguous symptoms' were tried, forensic science being still in its infancy, the court could only consider, as Quintilian suggests,[20] the immediately previous disposition, behaviour and general condition of the deceased, and, particularly, his age, and medical background; sometimes, the decision had to depend on assessment of the character of the accused, and the likelihood of his innocence or guilt. Declaimers tended to concentrate on this last aspect, and invented cases which, although most unlikely in reality, contained balancing factors and gave opportunity for general argument on either side. For instance, Quintilian quotes, as an example 'familiar to students' the following.[21]

A son disowned by his father took to the study of medicine. When his father fell ill, and the other physicians despaired of his life, the son was called in, and said he would cure him, if he took the draught which he prescribed. The father, having drunk part of it, declared that he had been poisoned. The son drank the remainder of the draught,[22] but the father died, and the son was accused of parricide.

Generally the declamatory fictions on poisoning are of this 'conjectural' type, though sometimes the poison is not actually administered, but the accused person has been discovered preparing it, and the question is one of intent — had he murder in mind, or did he plan to take his own life? Here again, the circumstances in the theme are quite unrealistic, but they are merely designed to provide a situation in which one might plausibly argue either way. The son, accused of attempting to kill his father, is suspect because he has been 'thrice disowned',[23] or because he has twice been compelled by his father to go into battle, and has performed heroically, but is determined not to be sent a third time;[24] on the other hand, it could be argued that the son, in such a situation, had become completely dejected, and saw no way out except to take his own life. What mattered was the fundamental question for the student to debate in such cases, namely, that of the intentions of the accused man. Something similar could easily arise in the lawcourts, for there was a provision in the *Lex Pompeia de parricidiis* for the prosecution of a son 'who purchased poison in order to administer it to his father, *even though he was not able to administer it*'.[25]

There are very many declamatory exercises which are concerned with father-son relationships, but those in which the son is accused of any criminal act or intent form only a small minority. Far more commonly, the theme is one in which the son has been disowned (*abdicatus*) by the father, and then brings an 'action', contesting the justice of this measure. Here the basic issue is one of 'quality', in which there is no question as to whether an act was committed or not, but only argument and counter-argument on its justification. At first sight, it may appear difficult to relate such themes to any genuine legal proceedings. It used to be thought that these exercises, if at all relatable to legal action, were the reflection of a Greek public process on the repudiation of a son (*apokeryxis*). But more recent research has directed attention to the fact that the terms *abdicare, abdicatio*, are used in Roman historical references to the repudiation of a son, and that the effects in these cases and in declamatory exercises are much the same as those of the Roman *relegatio*, the extreme measure which any *paterfamilias* was entitled to take to debar an erring son or daughter from house and home.[26] This was a domestic affair, and the proceedings on such occasions were usually conducted in a family council, or 'domestic court' (*iudicium domesticum*), over which the father presided. But, although there are occasional allusions to this in the declamations,[27] it does not provide an entirely satisfactory parallel, for the exercises do not suit a *private* setting, in which the repudiation is carried out, but envisage a *public* legal process, in which *iudices* are addressed,[28] and in which the repudiation has already taken place, but is being contested. It is much better, therefore, to follow up Quintilian's observation that 'scholastic themes on the repudiation of children are parallel to cases in the Forum of children who have been disinherited by their parents, and who reclaim their property in the centumviral court'.[29] In the exercises, *abdicatio* may be tantamount to disinheritance, or the father may have previously taken the decision and then relented, so that we sometimes meet the 'thrice repudiated son'. In real life, disinheritance (*exheredatio*) had to be signified in proper legal form when the will was drawn up in the presence of witnesses, and it is to legal processes arising from wills that our investigation now leads. It will be seen that the main difference between declamatory arguments and those of real life is that in the exercises the father is still alive and presents his case, as does the son, whereas in legal disputes the father is dead, his will has been challenged, and the court has to decide on the justification of the disinheritance.[30] But the basic position remains the same.

There was in Roman law an action known as the 'complaint of undutiful will' (*querela inofficiosi testamenti*), which the jurists say led to frequent litigation.[31] Such cases came within the jurisdiction of the centumviral court, and a son who had been expressly disinherited could challenge the will, which the instituted heir(s) would then have to defend. If the court accepted the plaintiff's arguments, it could render the will null and void, the implication being that, in its view, the testator could not have been in his right mind (the so-called *color insaniae*) thus to have rejected the claims of natural feeling (*officium pietatis*[32]). Even if not entirely overlooked, a person entitled to bring the *querela* could do so if allotted less than a quarter of what he would have received on intestacy.[33] It should not, however, be supposed that it was an easy matter thus to upset a will; indeed, one case is recorded in which the *centumviri* refused to rescind the will of a man whose daily behaviour had shown him to be mentally unbalanced, on the ground that 'what was written in the tablets mattered more than who had written them'.[34] But changing social conditions, particularly the increased licentiousness of youth and reaction against parental control, must have rendered disinheritance more common, and it was worthwhile for the repudiated son, who could do nothing in the face of *patria potestas* whilst his father was alive, to attempt to have his will countermanded after his death.[35] Often, too, the children themselves had been badly treated. The jurist Gaius says that one of the commonest causes of unfair disinheritance was 'the beguilements and instigations of step-mothers',[36] and Pliny describes his own appearance before the centumviral court on behalf of a lady of rank, whose eighty-year-old father had disinherited her eleven days after bringing a step-mother into the house.[37] Thanks to Pliny, she won her case.

Clearly, what mattered in such cases was the reason for the disinheritance. When, on another occasion, a woman disinherited her son, and left Pliny himself and others as co-heirs, Pliny and his advisers discussed the matter privately with him, and remarked: 'We take the view that your mother had just cause to be angry with you'; but, by a generous personal offer, Pliny enabled the case to be settled out of court.[38] In Roman legislation, these 'just causes' seem to have remained scattered in various enactments until Justinian collected fourteen of them together, and classified them all under the heading of 'ingratitude' on the part of children.[39] They included, for example, physical assault on parents, attempted parricide, adultery with a step-mother, association with miscreants, and failure to hasten to ransom a parent captured by enemies. Also, in the case of a daughter (!), her preference to lead a life of luxury instead of accepting the offer of a husband and a dowry. Viewed in this light, declamatory exercises begin perhaps to seem not quite so fantastic after all.

In the repudiation exercises, the son would regularly begin by claiming, if he could, (1) that he had not been a voluptuary (*luxuriosus*), (2) that he had not squandered his father's possessions, and (3) that he had not been enamoured of a courtesan (*meretrix*).[40] In some exercises, however, an indulgent parent does not object to a *meretrix* (and may be associating with one himself).[41] Quintilian shows how often this matter of morality was brought into direct relationship with the courts when he posits the case of a son disinherited for such a love-relationship, and says that 'the whole question is whether the father ought to have forgiven such conduct, and *whether the centumviri should extend pardon*'[42] — that is, by rescinding the will. Similarly, the question of the son's expenditure would inevitably arise in court.

It was a favourite practice of teachers of declamation to invent situations in which the repudiation had been due to filial disobedience, for this enabled them to introduce the fundamental question as to what was a reasonable use of *patria potestas*;[43] by balancing a son's services to his father against the fact that he had flatly disobeyed him, they created an arguable case, in which the question was essentially one of moral justification. Here is one such theme.[44]

A man who had a son and a rich enemy was captured by pirates, and wrote to his son to effect a ransom. As the son had no money, and the rich man offered him his daughter's hand in marriage, he married the girl, and with her money ransomed his father. On his return, the father ordered him to divorce the girl, and when he refused, repudiated him.

It may well be that the father had a legal right to insist on a son's divorce,[45] but the question here was whether it had been reasonable to do so. Equally basic was the question regularly raised in such exercises, whether a father's command ought always to be obeyed. This had long been a favourite subject of debate (*thesis*), particularly among philosophers;[46] for the rhetoricians, it became an essential matter in this type of special case (*hypothesis*).[47] It was rightly argued that disobedience would be justifiable if the father's order affected the son's exercise of his duty as a citizen, as when giving evidence in court, or making decisions as a senator or magistrate. Likewise, an order which involved committing a public offence, such as setting fire to a temple, could clearly not be obeyed. Where, then, should one draw the line? In the exercise, the son claims (as, doubtless, many sons did in real life) that freedom of choice was nowhere more necessary than in the matter of matrimony.[48] Besides, the girl's character was irreproachable,[49] his own action in ransoming his father had been honourable, and gratitude should have overridden prejudice against a former enemy.

It was not only in matters of father-son relationships that family disputes came into declamatory exercises and also into court. Often, the basic issue concerns the relations of husband and wife, particularly in the matter of adultery and divorce, and, here again, the cases imagined not only reflected contemporary social conditions, but also had a legal connection. Sometimes the situation is dramatic, as in the exercise in which the husband, being long abroad, is believed dead, and the wife, having inherited under his will, marries again and provides her house as dowry. One night, the husband returns, and, finding the couple together, slays them both, and is then charged with murder.[50] At other times, the exercise revolves on the suspicion of the wife's adultery, in circumstances which are very compromising. For example, in the husband's absence abroad, a rich foreign merchant seeks repeatedly, but in vain, to seduce the wife; he then dies, but in his will praises her chastity and leaves her all his possessions. The husband returns, and accuses her of adultery.[51] In a similar case of unjustified suspicion, the wife brings a charge of maltreatment (*mala tractatio*) against the husband.[52] There was, in fact, no such action in Roman law, but Quintilian says that exercises based on this 'law' were parallel to legal proceedings instituted by a divorced wife for the recovery of her dowry (*actio rei uxoriae*), in which the judge had to decide whose fault had led to the divorce.[53] In fact, if adultery, or even some lesser offence against good morals, could be proved against the wife, the husband would be permitted to retain a portion of the dowry (*retentio propter mores*), just as he would be allowed to retain a portion for the maintenance of the children (*retentio propter liberos*).[54] The purpose of the *actio rei uxoriae* was to secure a settlement based on equity.[55] But in the declamations, it is more usual to find that the wife who has been unfairly repudiated brings not an 'action for maltreatment', but an 'action for unjustified divorce' (*actio iniusti repudii*),[56] or an 'action for ingratitude' (*actio ingrati*).[57] Again, neither of these so-called actions was available in law to the wife, but the arguments used concerning the services of the wife and the harshness of the husband's attitude (e.g., divorce on the ground of sterility) must again be fairly parallel to those used in actions for recovery of dowry. This kind of subject was only one of a whole series of themes based on family quarrels, which were grouped together as 'domestic disputes', or 'themes on duties',[58] and were designed to enable the future advocate to argue his case on the ground of equity.

One of the main objectives of teachers of declamation, from the Ciceronian period onwards, was to provide exercises in which both the literal wording of a document (*scriptum, verba*) and its meaning and intention (*sententia, voluntas*) required to be closely examined. This was of practical value, for Quintilian says that the question of the letter and the intent was a most frequent source of discussion among jurists, and that a large part of legal disputation arose therefrom; and, he adds, 'it is not surprising that such cases occur in the schools, where they are also invented of set purpose'.[59] Conflict of opinion often arose over the wording of a will and the intention of the testator. It is immediately after mentioning the famous *cause Curiana* that Cicero remarks that 'this is the kind of thing in which all boys are trained in the schools, where they are taught at one time to defend the letter, and at another to uphold the claims of equity'.[60] An interesting declamation on these lines is that of the man who made two wills.[61] Two laws are placed at the head of the exercise: (1) last wills are to be ratified, and (2) the property of those who die intestate without children may pass to the nearest of kin. The theme is that a man, in his first will, institutes a friend as his heir, and then, in a later will, a different friend. After his death, the second will is declared invalid (presumably on technical grounds). The heir in the original will and the deceased's male relatives contest the succession. The model declamation gives the case for the first named heir, who maintains that the second will may be treated as non-existent, and that the original will is the last will. He had a good case in law, for the rule, as stated by Gaius and Justinian, was that 'a previous will is broken by a subsequent one *which is executed according to law*'.[62] Even if the second will had been valid, the relatives would only have obtained the succession in the event that the named heir could not take (e.g. through death or disqualification).[63] On the other hand, the original heir had a bad case in equity, for, even though the second will was invalid, there was no disguising the fact that the testator had changed his mind, and that his last wish, which the law was normally concerned to uphold, would be completely disregarded, if the claim was accepted.[64]

Of the many declamatory exercises which deal, in one way or another, with the interpretation of law, few are more interesting and likely to reflect genuine disputes than those which deal with the subject of evasion of customs' duties. One of the *Lesser Declamations*,[65] which Suetonius cites independently as having been taken from real life,[66] is concerned with a slave-dealer, who, in order to avoid paying duty, dresses a recently-acquired young slave in the clothing of a free-born youth, and passes him through the customs. The device, however, is not entirely successful, for a claim is then put in on the slave's behalf for his freedom, on the ground that he has been treated as free by his master's wish.[67] The model declamation gives the case for the slave, and is based both on interpretation of the wording of the relevant regulation, and on considerations of equity. A second exercise[68] is introduced with the quite genuine provision that 'anything taken past the customs' officials without being declared may be confiscated', and the situation is evolved in which someone steals an article as he passes through, and does not declare it. The theft is discovered, and the customs' officials then have to argue the case with the original owner. They claim the article as confiscated property, but the owner maintains that it belongs to him by right. The extant declamation gives the case of the customs' officers, who stick to their law,[69] and argue that, if the owner wishes to recover the value, he should sue the thief. But it has been suggested that, on behalf of the owner, relevance might have been claimed for the provisions of the *Lex Atinia* (mid-second century B.C.), by which not only the thief but a third party was debarred from usucapion of stolen property.[70]

Lastly, we have an amusing case[71] which is based on four laws: (1) On all goods except travelling equipment, 2½% duty is payable to the customs' official; (2) The customs' official is empowered to conduct a search; (3) Anything not declared is to be forfeited; (4) It is not permitted to lay hands on a matron. A matron arrived at the customs' post with 400 pearls concealed in her bosom. When the official made inquiry, she offered to allow herself to be searched. He declined to do so, but, when she had passed through, seized the pearls and claimed possession. The teacher's advice to students declaiming the exercise is quite enlightening, though he merely puts the questions which they have to answer. 'Can pearls be regarded as travelling-equipment? Even though they cannot be so regarded, nevertheless, since they were acquired for the use and adornment of the matron, could they be liable to confiscation? Were they in fact acquired for her use? If they were, could they, if not displayed, be seized, when, if displayed, they would not have been taxable? Even though it is forbidden to search a matron, would it be permissible if the matron herself agreed? Is the offer to be searched tantamount to displaying the article? Can an article which has been passed then be requisitioned? Was this article passed? The customs' official says he passed over the argument, not the article concerned.' This exercise must come very close indeed to real life,[72] and the regulations quoted may well be those imposed by the censors, who controlled the allocation of revenue-collecting contracts to the companies of profiteering speculators, the *societates publicanorum*. Travelling equipment was certainly exempt from tax, but the term *instrumentum itineris* was intended to cover vehicles, baggage-animals, and such like,[73] and could not conceivably have been extended to jewellery. Otherwise, the percentage of value payable as tax varied at different times and places, but there is very frequent reference to the amount of 2½% (*quadragesima*).[74] Everything was supposed to be declared (*profiteri* is the term used), whether dutiable or not, under pain of confiscation (*commissum*). But all manner of attempts to defraud the customs' officials were perpetrated,[75] and they certainly used to the full their right to search; they were generally detested as prying busy-bodies,[76] and apparently could even open personal correspondence.[77] That pearls were on the list of dutiable articles is beyond question,[78] but the awkward problem was that certain concessions were legally allowed on objects acquired for personal use. The law distinguished, for example, between slaves acquired for 'domestic use' (*usualia*) and those intended for sale (*venalia*).[79] Even here, there was difficulty in defining what was 'domestic'.[80] How far the concession extended in law we do not know, but it is highly probable that it included the dress actually worn. In that case, it could have been a very contentious matter if the pearls were sewn on the dress itself. The exact details are not known, nor, apparently, the procedure regarding the search of women. But surely we have in this exercise an instance of the constant battle of wits between the ingenious traveller and the rapacious tax collector of ancient times.

The declamations of the imperial period include many other cases which may be related, with varying degrees of proximity, to genuine legal actions, such as those on recovery of deposit,[81] on pacts and agreements,[82] on partnership,[83] on inheritance by women (the *lex Voconia*),[84] on unlawful damage,[85] on injury,[86] and on claims laid by, or on account of, exposed children.[87] The probability is that, in the late Republic, when declamation in Latin began, there was a fairly high proportion of such themes, though even then some were taken over from Greek (notably, those involving tyrants and tyrant-slayers), and some were quite imaginary (*fictae*). But under the Empire, the search for new subjects, and the desire to make declamation more exciting, led frequently to the invention of situations which were very far-fetched, and too contrived for words. Certainly adultery, and probably rape, were common in real life, but there are far too many exercises in which the victim of rape exercises her option of the death of the perpetrator or marriage with him; and although adultery cases are sometimes settled by pecuniary compensation,[88] a quite disproportionate use is made of the old law (severely restricted by the *Lex Iulia*), which permitted the slaying of an adulterous couple taken in the act.[89] Rarely, if ever, for instance, would an advocate in the law courts have had to deal with a case in which a young man raped his brother's fiancée during his absence abroad, she opted for marriage at the father's entreaty, the man returned, killed the 'adulterous' brother, despite the father's plea, and was then disowned. [90] Similarly, there are too many military heroes and tyrannicides who are allowed to choose their own reward, and usually make an awkward option. The characters are nearly always drawn from stock, and fathers and sons, rich men, poor men, blind men, thieves, stepmothers, priests and priestesses, deserters and returning exiles, as well as adulterers, rapists, and war-heroes, find themselves tied up in a series of knotty and embarrassing situations, contrived with all manner of permutations and combinations. By Quintilian's time, the supernatural, too, had been introduced in the form of sorcerers practising magic incantations — an innovation probably introduced by declaimers of Asiatic Greek origin, and very popular with audiences in the Second Sophistic.[91] It is small wonder that there was a chorus of derisive critics, such as Petronius, Messalla in the *Dialogus*, and Juvenal.[92] Obviously, it would have been far better if this trend towards the sensational and the fantastic could have been severely checked, and if themes had been, as Quintilian advised, properly related to real life. He himself blamed the teachers for the degeneration of declamation, and held the licence and ignorance of declaimers responsible for the decline of Roman eloquence.[93] He was fully aware that it was vain to look for 'sorcerers, pestilences, oracular responses, stepmothers more cruel than those of tragedy, and even more fabulous themes, among guarantees and interdicts'.[94] Nevertheless, he was broad-minded enough to accept that even such imaginative inventions could be utilized to provide an outlet for the exuberance of youth, and to serve as 'richer fare' than some of the duller subjects of day-to-day litigation.[95] He himself cites a surprising number of purely scholastic themes, but even he, in his eminent position, could not possibly have reversed the current fashion. He therefore compromised, and sought to draw some useful legal lesson, or, at least, some practice in argument, from the most unlikely tale.

It would require a much closer study of the *Lesser Declamations* than is possible here to determine the varying degrees of practical utility inherent in the *controversiae* of the schools. Admittedly, the claim of the author that school-exercises 'embraced whatever can take place in the

Forum' must be an over-statement.[96] Yet it is not always wise to dismiss even a concocted theme as entirely devoid of value. For instance, there was an exercise in which a father repudiates his son for marrying a courtesan, when the son himself was born of the association of his father with a *meretrix*. This might seem pure invention, yet Quintilian says that such a case could quite possibly occur in the Forum.[97] Sometimes, the law on which an exercise is based does reflect a genuine legal process, but the theme itself is so improbable or trivial that the connection with actual legal cases must be tenuous. Quintilian remarks, for example, that exercises in which a father is accused of *dementia* are parallel to cases in which an application was made to the praetor for a *curator* to take charge of him.[98] But in the surviving exercises, any sort of ground seems good enough for an *actio dementiae*,[99] and Pollio had observed long before that the praetor would never grant a *curator* simply because a father was unfair or irresponsible, but only if he was a raving lunatic (*furiosus*). [100] The only residue of value here seems to be that in such exercises it sometimes became necessary to define what constituted 'madness' and what did not,[101] and the line here has never been easy to draw. It is this question of definition which commonly arises in other exercises, whether it is basic or incidental. In poisoning cases, the legal definition of poison as 'a harmful drug' was too vague; was a love-potion a 'poison'? (the jurists eventually decided that it was);[102] was a sleeping-draught poison?[103] Similar problems arose over the definition of treason. Even the definition of a 'wife' could need clarification. An absurd case is posited in which a man commits a rape, and, when the girl fails to opt for marriage, commits suicide; but just before he expires, she relents, decides for marriage, and then claims his property! At precisely what point, and with what necessary antecedents, does a woman become legally a 'wife'?[104] In an early fictitious case, quoted by Suetonius, some young men bargain with fishermen to pay a certain sum for the catch. They pay, but, when the nets are hauled in, there are no fish, but there is a sewn-up gold casket. Both parties claim it as theirs.[105] In fact legal sources do show that it was normal to strike such bargains beforehand, and that the purchaser had to pay the agreed sum even if no fish were hauled in.[106] But the jurists did not think it necessary to define what was meant by the 'catch'. In short, it is always worthwhile to look for positive points. The value of declamation depended a great deal on the commonsense and judgment of individual teachers, but the best of them would have agreed with Quintilian that 'of that which is naturally good, good use may be made'.[107]

For an understanding of the teaching-methods employed in dealing with these declamatory themes, the 'comment' (*sermo*), which is included in many of the *Lesser Declamations*, is extremely instructive. Sometimes the teacher would, after stating the theme, begin by reminding his pupils of the types of issue which they had previously studied. Thus, he might say:[108] 'I have often told you how to arrive most easily at the determination of the issue. You all know what the issues are. First, recall each of them in turn; then after removing those which it is certain do not apply here, let us examine what is left. The method of examination will be this: we must first see what the plaintiff puts forward, and what ... the accuser replies; from this, the question in dispute arises.' In other words, the student begins by a process of elimination, so that, for example, he may first test and dismiss 'conjecture', then 'definition', then 'quality', and decide that the case is one of 'interpretation of law' and 'equity'. As Juvenal observes,[109] 'they (the students) all want to know in what light to present the case, into what category it falls, what is the essential problem (*summa quaestio*), and what volleys to expect from the opposite side'. The teacher, therefore, provided an analysis (*divisio*) of the 'questions' (*quaestiones*) which arose, whether main or subsidiary, for these represented what he called 'the bones and muscles of the exercise', which were later to be clothed in the 'flesh' of eloquence.[110] These questions could also be classified in a different way, and divided into those which were recurrent (*communia*) in many cases of the same general type,[111] and those which were special (*propria*), and applicable only to the particular case in hand. An interesting point here is that the teacher often needed to repeat the 'recurrent' questions in treating the exercises because, at various points in his course, new boys, who had only just reached the stage of preparation required for *controversiae*, kept arriving from time to time in the class. So the teacher apologizes and says:[112] 'If there are points in the division of cases which are repeated by me several times, you must understand that this is primarily due to the arrival of new pupils, and, secondly, to the nature of divisions; for those who have not previously heard that which is relevant to several cases must learnt it.' Generally, the introductory comment was in one piece, and the teacher followed it up with a model declamation on one side or the other, sometimes indicating which side was the more amenable to treatment.[113] But he might decide to give the comment and the exemplification in sections, so that he would say:[114] 'This is the general argument' and give a few lines of illustration, then: 'This is a particular argument', and illustrate further. Or he might say:[115] 'Here are the points in favour of the wording of the law', and declaim part of the model, and then: 'Here are the points in favour of equity', and declaim the rest. Sometimes he would preface the exercise with a recapitulation of rhetorical doctrine on the parts of a speech (proem, narrative, etc.), and then apply it to the case in hand.[116]

Whilst giving a preliminary talk, the master would remain seated, as he would do when making his preliminary remarks at a public declamation, [117] and the boys wrote down his observations and studied them.[118]

To deliver a model speech, he would, as in public, rise to his feet. After this, the boys prepared their own declamations, on the same or a similar subject, in written form. It would appear from a passage of Juvenal (which is otherwise unconfirmed) that each boy in turn, whilst seated, would read out aloud what he had composed, and would then deliver it standing, with the appropriate intonation and gesture.[119] Juvenal's word *cantabit* seems intended to refer to the modulated, almost sing-song delivery which was so popular both in the schools and among advocates.[120] Thus there was not only a great deal of repetition, but, in a large class, a plethora of juvenile effusions on the same theme — which is why Juvenal sarcastically referred to the *crambe repetita*, which bored the master to death as effectively as if he had been the tyrant murdered in the exercise! When students became proficient in handling themes, they might dispense with a model, and all that they needed was a few preliminary hints from the master. Quintilian strongly believed in encouraging individual initiative.[121] As with preliminary exercises, the teacher criticized faults, filled in gaps and bestowed praise where it was deserved, and the boys would take down in their notebooks, for future imitation, anything of which he had signified his approval.[122] One of the difficulties which arose from the numbers in class was that, if the procedure was thoroughly carried out, it was very time-consuming; also, some teachers were prone to encourage showmanship rather than systematic analysis. The result was that their pupils were allowed to do 'selections' (*flosculi*), to prepare the most attractive pieces of various exercises, and introduce them at every possible opportunity. Many, under easy-going masters, developed, says Quintilian, 'an excessive loquacity', and, when dealing with a theme in full, expatiated 'not only on everything in the case, but on everything in heaven and earth'. He himself strongly urged that 'one thoroughly-treated case will be of more value than several which are merely sampled and nibbled at', and, when time pressed, he thought it better to make his students simply deliver the outline analysis of the case.[123]

As declamation was intended as a preparation for advocacy, it might have been expected that speakers would regularly use the third person, as would a lawyer representing his client. But, in fact, as the extant declamations show, declaimers normally preferred to use the first person, and to impersonate, rather than represent, the litigant. Some latitude of choice was allowed, but the teacher usually suggested whether it was wise to speak in the person of an advocate or not.[124] He would certainly advise it when the litigant was a person who would not normally conduct a case in reality, being, say, a woman, or a slave, or a person publicly disgraced (*ignominiosus*). But he might also advise it when, for instance, the litigant was an erring son, whose misdeeds were so flagrant that they would best be palliated by an advocate, or, in the opposite case, a son whose actions were so patently honourable that they could be more unrestrainedly praised by another person. But there were two reasons why the practice of impersonation was so much encouraged. In the first place, the declaimer always had in him something of the actor, and loved to take the part of the father, the son, the rich man, the poor man, the severe or indulgent parent, and all the varieties of character which might be met in comedy on the stage;[125] that is one reason why Menander's plays were recommended to students of declamation.[126] The second reason was that teachers and students loved emotional (or pseudo-emotional) passages, and found it easier to give free play to emotional expression when speaking in their own person.[127] At one point, the author of the *Lesser Declamations* draws a distinction between a quite short declamation, which was confined to the essential arguments, and a fuller treatment, with emotion-rousing commonplaces (*loci*), which his students evidently expected.[128] After giving a brief and compact declamation, he remarks: 'I do not wish anyone to blame me on the ground that I am not including the commonplaces. If you wish to amplify the declamation, and exercise your talents, you will be saying something which is of no concern to the case, though it may perhaps give pleasure to the ears.' He then shows (though the theme is absurd enough in itself) how such an expansion may be made.

But, although sensible use could be made of traditional themes, particularly if they had a legal bearing, there was no denying the fact that the practice of declamation had certain inherent disadvantages and inadequacies as a form of training for pleaders in a court of law. In the first place, declaimers and their students were liable to take too much for granted. As the theme was stated at the outset, they could assume that the facts of the case were known, and plan their exordium accordingly; but in real life, at least at first hearings, it was rash to suppose that the judge was already acquainted with the details, for he rarely looked at the case beforehand.[129] Similarly, some were far too fond of beginning by anticipating the opponent's argument and demolishing it.[130] Then again, provided that they did not actually contradict or disregard any of the facts as stated in the theme, they could readily assume that any aspect of the case which was not thus defined was in their own favour. For example, in poisoning cases, the defending declaimer would confidently ask, as though the questions were merely rhetorical, 'Where did I buy the poison? From whom? For how much? Through whose agency did I supply it?'; or, in an adultery-case, 'What witness is there? What informer?' — whereas, of course, this could be to invite disaster in a court-case, where opposing counsel might have some damaging material on any of these points.[131] Declaimers in school tended to forget that there was a judge, often taciturn and unimpressed, and an alert opponent, who might interrupt with an awkward objection at any time.

Moreover, the declaimer, though in theory he was supposed to uphold either side with equal ability, in fact preferred to select the side which appealed to him; also, he spoke as long as he wished, whereas in the courts the time for each case was strictly limited, and either an impatient judge or the running-out of the water-clock might stem the flood of his eloquence.[132] When the orator Albucius deserted the forum, where he had been made to look a fool by an opponent, for the schools, he remarked that he could now speak when he wished, as long as he wished, and for whom he wished, and use his favourite figures of speech without risk of being discomfited.[133]

A further argument against declamation, which its critics never failed to press home, was that the cloistered shade (*umbra*) of academic seclusion was a poor preparation for the glare (*sol*) and publicity of legal cases in the forum.[134] Stories of the failure of such leading declaimers as Albucius and Porcius Latro were long remembered, and lent force to the critics' case. Quintilian himself did not deny it, but admitted that those who had 'grown old in the schools' were living in a world of their own.[135] He would also have agreed with the views of Cassius Severus, Votienus Montanus, Petronius and Messalla, to the extent that the atmosphere of the schools, the laxity of the training, and the mutual applause of the immature, left much room for improvement. Whilst he firmly defended the practice of declamation as such, he considered that, in his day, students were spending too much time over it; after all, though useful to a degree, this was mere fencing, and a young man had to learn to handle real weapons in the contests of the legal arena. He therefore made some very sound suggestions, which were intended to apply, first, to the period whilst the youth was still attending the rhetoric school, and, secondly, immediately after he had left it. They formed a very sensible method of bridging an awkward gap.

First, he recommended that boys at school should make a particular study of celebrated cases of earlier days in which the speeches of great advocates both for the prosecution and for the defence were still extant.[136] In Greek, there were the opposing speeches of Demosthenes and Aeshines, in Latin, those of Servius Sulpicius and Messalla Corvinus in the Aufidia case, of Asinius Pollio and Cassius Severus in the poisoning-case of Nonius Asprenas, that of Tubero against Ligarius, and of Hortensius in defence of Verres, which should be studied along with Cicero's own speeches on the opposite side. Furthermore, there were cases in which more than one distinguished advocate had composed a speech on the same side. Calidius, as well as Cicero, spoke on the subject of Cicero's house; Brutus composed a defence of Milo as an exercise, in which he took a stronger line than Cicero dared to do; both Pollio and Messalla had appeared for the same defendants; and there were speeches of no less than three orators in one case, all of which were in high repute and in circulation in Quintilian's own boyhood. But the young student could do more than this; he could go along to the lawcourts and attend as many cases as possible himself. He should, as in the old days of the Republic, select an orator whom he could take as his model. Moreover, he could then try his own hand at cases which were currently being held, and actually write up speeches both for prosecution and defence.[137] This was much better, thought Quintilian, than the practice adopted in the early Empire by the celebrated Cestius Pius, of writing his own replies to the famous speeches of Cicero, such as the *Pro Milone*. Cestius' own students, who idolized him as a great orator, merely learnt up these speeches,[138] but Quintilian rightly saw that it was unsatisfactory to compose replies simply based on the knowledge of the case provided by one extant speech, when one had no longer access to the full facts available to the court.

But, useful as such methods of preparation were, when combined with experience in declamation, they only went part of the way towards providing the future advocate with a working knowledge of law. Even though the declamation of *controversiae* familiarized students with types of case, and a certain amount of legal knowledge could be acquired in this way, and increased by attendance at court cases, there was nothing systematic about it, and even a substantial amount of somewhat haphazard information was a poor substitute for a proper course in the subject. It was, indeed, possible to take such a course, for, under the Empire, legal studies had become much more organized.[139] The jurists themselves, who may now have been required to be licensed as such by the Emperor, enjoyed high prestige, and had their own auditoria at well-known spots in the city (particularly, near the great libraries), where they not only gave counsel, but taught publicly. Instruction became more systematic, and Masurius Sabinus, who was licensed under Tiberius, was the founder of what became one of the two most famous Roman law-schools. Nevertheless, it does seem that they catered mainly for those who intended to become professional jurists themselves, and that they were not frequented by most of those who proposed to become advocates. Consequently, the criticism was often voiced that advocates did not know sufficient law, and were too apt to rely, in time of need, on the services of the attorneys (*pragmatici*), who were usually to be found in court. Quintilian thought this an extremely dangerous procedure, and urged that law should be studied personally by the young man who had left the rhetoric school,[140] just as he should study philosophy and history, in the true Ciceronian tradition. It is noticeable, however, that Quintilian does not suggest attendance at a law-school. There was, as we saw earlier, a consciousness among orators and jurists that they belonged to different professions.[141]

The popularity of advocacy was increased by the fact that, in Roman times, there was no rule about 'silence in court'. Lawcourt audiences, who had little interest in points of law, would rapturously applaud a glowing description, an eloquently-turned commonplace, or a smart epigram, just as, in Cicero's defence of Roscius of Ameria, the listeners had applauded a highly artificial and pompous passage about parricide, which he himself subsequently deprecated.[142] In fact, the declamatory style and manner was taken over directly from the schools and invaded the courts of law.[143] Here again, it was Quintilian who, whilst realizing that tastes had changed, did his best to reinstate the old Ciceronian ideal, and no better illustration could be found of the value of sensible rhetorical training, and of its successful application in public life, than the oratorical career of the younger Pliny.

As a boy, Pliny not only had natural ability, but was in the fortunate position of being able to take advantage of the best education available in his day. His literary interests must have developed quite early, for, although we do not know who his *grammaticus* was, he was already composing a Greek tragedy at the age of fourteen.[144] He then took the rhetoric course in both languages, and attended the lectures of Nicetes in Greek and Quintilian in Latin.[145] He always looked back on his school-declamations with pleasure, and in later life remained on friendly terms with the rhetoric-teachers (*scholastici*), and appreciated their work.[146] He went to hear the declaimer Isaeus, and spoke highly of his argumentation and style. At the same time, he had himself found that, for an advocate, the best teacher of all was experience.[147] He began his forensic work at the early age of eighteen, and already, as a very young man, was pleading in the centumviral court, where those fresh from the schools generally made their debut.[148] He long remained very much in demand as an advocate for the civil cases which came before this court, and won so much acclaim there that he came to regard it as his particular 'arena'.[149] But he also took on criminal cases, and in one of those in which he was engaged as defence-counsel the allegations were of forgery of a will and of poisoning.[150] But he had always been ambitious to appear in trials of the highest public importance, and, once the tyrant Domitian was dead, he found opportunities rapidly coming his way.[151] He had already held the praetorship under Domitian, and in A.D. 100, at the age of about thirty-eight, he reached the consulship. Even before then he had begun what became a series of engagements as counsel in cases of extortion brought against various ex-governors by the provincials. He was counsel for the prosecution on behalf of the Baetici of southern Spain, against Baebius Massa (*c.*93), and against Caecilius Classicus (*c.*100), and on behalf of the Africans against Marius Priscus (also 100).[152] For the defence, he represented Iùlius Bassus[103] and Varenus (perhaps 106), ex-governors of Bithynia, and it was his appointment as imperial legate to this province which marked the culmination of his career. In both his literary and his legal skill, as well as in many qualities of his personal character, Pliny was as good an example as any of the results of a first-class education in his day.

Conclusion:
a few lessons from the past

In our own time, when education has become so vast an enterprise, and is a subject on which a multitude of voices can claim a hearing, it may well be the common opinion that there is little or nothing to be learnt any longer from the experience of two thousand years ago. But perhaps those who have followed the story of Roman education to this point will be disposed to agree that it still carries a few lessons for today. Obviously, there was much that was extremely unsatisfactory in Roman times, and we may take the deficiencies first. The Roman state neither created an educational system itself nor gave anything like adequate financial support to the system which developed of its own accord. Education was not made compulsory even at the primary stage, and the acquisition of literacy was haphazard. There was no provision for the training of teachers. There was no schools building programme, and most of the instruction was given in premises never designed for teaching purposes. It is true that some of the more enlightened rulers gave help and encouragement here and there, and the state eventually allowed municipalities to appoint and pay a certain number of teachers, granted exemptions from civic burdens, and gave a more permanent, though limited, patronage to the higher learning. But it left most of those who were engaged in education in our period to rely on such fees as they could obtain in competition with one another, with the result that they had no security of livelihood. Private tuition (which had both its advantages and its disadvantages) was far more extensively employed than it is today. There was, clearly, inequality of opportunity, and the children of the well-to-do classes benefited most. But it should not be forgotten in this connection that there were also poorer parents who were prepared to make sacrifices for their children's education. Also, by necessity, there was a great deal of self-help, and quite a number even of the teachers had experienced most adverse conditions in early life and yet had managed somehow to educate themselves. Despite the disadvantages, and the lack of any organized examination system, there was an extraordinary uniformity, and a good deal that was permanently sound, in both the substance and the methods of teaching, which, derived in large measure from the Greeks, still made their influence felt long after the Roman Empire had crumbled.

Whatever we may think of the limitations of a teaching programme which culminated for so many in our period in preparation for the needs of advocacy, we must surely admit that within its own field Roman education was extremely methodical and thorough. At the primary stage, the teaching of the alphabet and the orderly progression from letters to syllables, and from syllables to words, step by step from the monosyllabic to the polysyllabic, had basically much to commend it, and remained unchallenged for many centuries. For instance, precisely the same process of combining each consonant with each vowel in turn in the teaching of syllables, which is seen in school papyri from the third century B.C. onwards (cf. Fig. 18), was still being recommended in John Brinsley's *Ludus Literarius* of 1612, and, of course, remained in use long after his time. In Roman schools much importance was attached to oral repetition and memorizing, but children were none the worse for that. The teaching of writing was done equally conscientiously, despite the very considerable difficulty which pupils found at first in manipulating a stilus on a waxed surface without the firm base of a school desk. The use of 'copy-book maxims', each of which conveyed some general truth or sensible precept, was a rather charming way of combining writing practice with moral training. In the teaching of reading, the lack of division between words in ancient texts made the task far more formidable than it is for a modern child; even more help was required from the teacher, but progress, though slow, was steady, and patience and perseverance often produced good results. The use of fingers, pebbles and abaci ensured ability to count and reckon. We may, of course, think of many activities in the primary schoolroom — such as drawing, painting, modelling — which might well have been included because they are a form of creative work and give pleasure to children. But the Romans were not so much concerned to give children what they liked to do as what they knew to be essential for their adult life. Even so, in teaching the three Rs they had very limited resources — there were few visual aids and no blackboards. It could no doubt be said that they were insufficiently interested in experiment and innovation; they thought they had a good system and kept it. But the Romans, like the Greeks, merit praise for much that they did; they carefully grouped their pupils according to progress, encouraged them (as at all stages) by competition, and sometimes gave displays to show their achievements. Some teachers, however, were far too severe in their discipline. In general, although some time was allowed for games, primary education was regarded as a serious business; children were expected to be industrious, to improve themselves and to take a pride in their work. And in this view parents fully concurred.

Equally methodical was the teaching in the grammar school, which, again following the lines laid down by the Greeks, proceeded logically from letters to syllables and from syllables to words. Instruction in the phonetic values of the letters led on to the rules of syllabic quantity, which were necessary for the scansion of verse. Then pupils were expected to understand something about the structure of language, that is, the classification and characteristics of the various parts of speech, and to be able to recognize what part of speech a word was when they saw it. Next came the declensions and conjugations, of which the paradigms were written out. Syntax was taught by the indirect method of showing many possible types of error (solecisms), in which the rules were contravened. Parsing was a favourite exercise, and of this, and sentence analysis in general, more use might well be made today. Teachers in antiquity had no doubts whatsoever that a firm basis of systematically taught grammar was essential for all their future work. Particular attention was also paid to pronunciation and spelling — and who will deny that, in spelling especially, better standards are sadly needed today? It may well be that Roman teachers were over-meticulous in such matters, and that they were too analytical in their classifications of types of error. But at least they insisted on *Latinitas*, and sought to improve the quality of both writing and speaking in their day. Finally, linguistic study was one of the very few areas in which Roman teaching could claim a distinct advance as compared with Greek; for whereas the Greek schools which had preceded them taught no other language than Greek, the Roman schools taught both Greek and Latin. As a form of mental training, the study of a foreign language was an extremely valuable addition in itself. But beyond this it also enabled boys to read the best poetry and prose in two sister languages, and opened up the fruitful field of the comparative study of literature. The Romans were thus truly the pioneers of a full classical education.

In the teaching of literature, some of the best work of the 'grammarians' was done in showing boys how to read poetry aloud, with proper attention to pauses, variety of speed and tone, and the numerous modulations of the voice which were needed to suit the context and bring the words to life. Having first ensured that each passage was fully understood, the teacher would give a personal demonstration, and his pupils sought to emulate him in turn. The boys learnt by heart and recited much more than is usual in modern times. So too did the girls, though they were at this stage more usually taught by a tutor at home. In their continuous commentaries on poetic texts, schoolmasters probably varied a good deal according to their particular interests and quality of mind. Most of them carried their grammatical studies into literature, and had a keen eye for the words themselves, their form, their meaning, and their derivation. Most of them were also very well informed on mythology, and left no allusion unexplained. Tropes and figures were their stock-in-trade, and on metaphor and simile, for example, though inclined to push analysis too far, they usually had something worthwhile to say. Whilst not neglecting anything which was uplifting or instructive in the thought, they were sometimes prone to moralize, and applied their own curious notions of propriety to the interpretation of small episodes. Some of them gained from a more rhetorical approach, being interested in such matters as structure, characterization, literary embroidery and sententious expression, the shifting shades of style and the arrangement of words. The rhetoricians were accustomed to observing such features in both poetry and prose, and although they were too fond of treating all literature as grist to their own mill, it would probably be true to say that they were, on the whole, better literary critics than the 'grammarians' themselves.

There is much to be learnt from the standard preliminary exercises (*progymnasmata*) with which the study of rhetoric was introduced. Beginning with the treatment of fables, anecdotes, maxims and narratives of all kinds, then proceeding to commonplaces, panegyrics and invectives, speeches in character, descriptions and comparisons, and finally leading up to theses and assessments of laws, they formed a carefully graded series of essay themes which were a valuable form of constructive work. Taught in antiquity more properly by rhetoricians, but also not uncommonly anticipated by the 'grammarians', they were still being found of service by teachers in grammar schools in Elizabethan times and long afterwards. They accustomed boys to précis or to elaborate and expand, to tell a story vividly and convincingly, to use their imaginations, to improve their style and composition, and to argue for and against a proposition. The teachers were very conscientious not only in providing the framework (especially for beginners), but in supplying models of their own for guidance, and showing where other examples might be found in literature. The best teachers showed admirable good sense in the correction of errors, in encouraging promising features, and in adapting their criticisms to the needs of individuals. Though primarily directed to the acquisition of oratorical skill, these exercises were of a much wider educational value and well deserved their quite remarkable longevity.

We must accept that for the Romans of our period effective public speaking was the prime objective of the standard school curriculum. Under the Republic, oratory flourished in a society accustomed to freedom of expression, and was a living force in public life. It could be turned to advantage in political debate as well as in important criminal trials, and it was a valuable means of furthering a young man's career.

Under the Empire, its range of flight was restricted, yet it still ranked high in public esteem. Not only was the theory of speech-construction, as devised and elaborated by the Greeks and taken over by the Romans, long predominant in the advanced school curriculum, but it was also supplemented by constant practice in declamation. In antiquity, boys learnt to make their addresses in the classroom rather than in a separate debating society. Naturally, such over-emphasis on speech-making would not commend itself to us, but it remains true that in a modern democracy ability to present a case to an audience persuasively is still constantly needed in many walks of life. There is still something to be learnt from the ancient insistence on a carefully considered approach, clarity in arrangement and argument, the use of devices of style, and effective enunciation and delivery.

But although so much good work was done, we may, nevertheless, discern in our period two significant changes, both of them changes for the worse. One affected the balance of studies, the other the conditions of teaching. The first concerns the position of declamation. This was in itself an integral part of oratorical training, and Cicero used such practice-speeches and found value in them, as did other orators in his day. Under the Empire, the selected themes were more bizarre, but they still contained more elements of practical relevance than adverse critics have supposed. But even if the themes of declamation had remained far more closely adapted to the requirements of the law courts and deliberative assemblies, and had been given sober and sensible treatment, Cicero would never have wished the subject to stand in splendid isolation as the culminating point of the standard curriculum. He was a firm believer in combining professional oratorical training with a liberal education, including both literature and the mathematical disciplines, and leading on to philosophy, history and law. It was an ideal, but in his day it commanded considerable support, and later Quintilian and Tacitus still strongly believed in it. Under the Empire, however, when public declamation helped to fill the vacuum created by political change, and there was a larger element of showmanship in it, many parents were mainly impressed by fluency of speech. They could also see that this was the way in which advocates were trained. They therefore became less interested in a broad general education, and pressed the teachers to bring their boys on to declamation as soon as possible, even at the cost of curtailing the study of grammar and literature. Thus the breeze of ill-informed popular opinion helped to drive a good education off course.

The second change was even more fundamental, for it sprang from the conditions of home upbringing. Under the Republic, as a general rule, parents exercised a rather firm control over their children, and required them to conform to good standards of behaviour and to be diligent in their studies; but at the same time they usually took a keen interest in their progress. Under the Empire, there were still such well-regulated families, but there were also many more parents who delegated their responsibilities to nurses and 'pedagogues', who might, or might not, keep a proper check on their conduct. Other parents went to the opposite extreme, and spoilt their children by over-indulgence. Thus in the classroom the schoolmaster's task was made more difficult, for some of his pupils were idle and ill-behaved, and others were self-willed and conceited. To rectify matters, he acted according to his temperament, and either sought to correct them by meting out hard punishment, or took the line of least resistance and gave them what they liked, or found easiest, to do. Neither method succeeded, and the result was deterioration. But we hardly need the Romans to remind us that education cannot remain immune from the influences of contemporary society.

List of abbreviations

A.J.P.	*American Journal of Philology*
C.A.H.	*Cambridge Ancient History*
Carm. epigr.	*Carmina Latina Epigraphica*, in Buecheler's *Anthologia Latina*
Christ-Schmid	W. von Christ and W. Schmid, *Geschichte der griechische Literatur, Nachklassische Periode* (6th edn), Munich, 1919, rpd. 1959
C.G.L.	*Corpus Glossariorum Latinorum*
C.I.L.	*Corpus Inscriptionum Latinarum*
C.J.	*Classical Journal*
Cod. Iust.	*Codex Iustinianus* in *Corpus Iuris Civilis*
Cod. Theod.	*Codex Theodosianus*, ed. *Mommsen* (Berlin, 1905, rpd. 1962)
C.P.	*Classical Philology*
C.Q.	*Classical Quarterly*
C.R.	*Classical Review*
C.W.	*Classical Weekly*
Dar.-Sag.	*Dictionnaire des Antiquités grecques et romaines*, ed. C. Daremburg and E. Saglio (Paris, 1881-1919)
Decl. Min.	*Declamationes Minores*, ascribed to Quintilian, ed. C. Ritter (Leipzig, Teubner, 1884)
F.Gr.H.	*Fragmente der griechischer Historiker* (Jacoby)
G.L.	*Grammatici Latini*, ed. H. Keil, 7 vols (Leipzig, 1856-79)
G.R.F. (Funaioli)	*Grammaticae Romanae Fragmenta*, ed. G. Funaioli (Leipzig, 1907)
G.R.F. (Mazzarino)	*Grammaticae Romanae Fragmenta Aetatis Caesareae*, ed. A. Mazzarino (Turin, 1955)
I.L.S.	*Inscriptiones Latinae Selectae* (Dessau)
J.H.S.	*Journal of Hellenic Studies*
J.R.S.	*Journal of Roman Studies*

Jullien, *Les Professeurs*	E. Jullien, *Les Professeurs de Littérature dans l'ancienne Rome* (Paris, 1885)
Marrou, *Hist. Educ.*	H.-I. Marrou, *Histoire de l'Education dans l'Antiquité*, Paris, 1948, 7th edn 1977; English translation by G. Lamb, *A History of Education in Antiquity* (London, 1956)
N.J. klass. Alt.	*Neue Jahrbucher für klassische Altertum*
N.J. klass. Phil.	*Neue Jahrbucher für klassische Philologie*
O.C.D.[2]	*Oxford Classical Dictionary*, 2nd edn (Oxford, 1970)
O.L.D.	*Oxford Latin Dictionary* (Oxford, 1968- in progress)
O.R.F.	*Oratorum Romanorum Fragmenta*, ed. H. Malcovati (2nd edn, Turin, 1955)
Phil. Woch.	*Philologische Wochenschrift*
P. Oxy.	*The Oxyrhynchus Papyri* (London, 1898-)
Pap. Soc. Ital.	*Pubblicazioni della Societa Italiana per la ricerca dei papiri Greci e Latini in Egitto*
P.-W., *R.E.*	Pauly-Wissowa-Kroll, *Realencyclopädie der klassischen Altertumswissenschaft*
R. Phil.	*Revue de Philologie*
Rh.M.	*Rheinisches Museum*
Rhet. Graec. (*Sp.*)	*Rhetores Graeci*, ed. L. Spengel, 3 vols. (Leipzig, 1863)
Rom. Declam.	*Roman Declamation in the late Republic and early Empire*, by S.F. Bonner, (Liverpool University Press and California University Press, 1949, rpd., Liverpool, 1969)
Rom. Orat.	'Roman Oratory', by S.F. Bonner, in *Fifty Years of Classical Scholarship*, ed. M. Platnauer (Oxford, 1954), reissued Oxford, 1968, pp. 335-83
S.H.A.	*Scriptores Historiae Augustae*
Schanz-Hosius	M. Schanz and C. Hosius, *Geschichte der römischen Literatur* (4th edn) (Munich 1927-35, rpd. 1959)
Sitz. preuss. Akad.	*Sitzungsberichte der preussischen Akademie*
Sitz. Wien. Akad.	*Sitzungsberichte der Wiener Akademie*
T.A.Ph.A.	*Transactions of the American Philological Association*
Thes. Ling. Lat.	*Thesaurus Linguae Latinae*
Wien. Stud.	*Wiener Studien*
Woch. klass. Phil.	*Wochenschrift für klassische Philologie*
Z.S.S.	*Zeitschrift der Savigny-Stiftung für Rechtsgeschichte, Romanistische Abteilung*

Notes

PART ONE

Chapter I

1 E.T. Salmon in *O.C.D.*², s.v. 'Sabini'
2 Livy, *Epit.*, 11.
3 Strabo, V, 3, 1.
4 Horace, *Carm.*, III, 6, 33*ff*.
5 Seneca the elder, *Contr.*, I, 6, 4; II, 1, 8; Valerius Maximus, IV, 4, 4-11.
6 Valerius Maximus, IV, 3, 5; Pliny the elder, *N.H.*, XVIII, 4, 18.
7 Cicero, *Pro S. Rosc. Am.*, 27, 75; *Cato maior*, 16, 55-6; *Par. Stoic.*, 48; Valerius Maximus, loc. cit.; Lucan, X, 151-4.
8 Cato in Festus, p. 350, Lindsay.
9 Plutarch, *Cato*, 1, 5-6.
10 Ib., 13 and 14, 2-3.
11 Cicero, *In Vat.*, 15, 36; Livy, I, 18, 4; Horace, *Epp.*, II, 1, 25; Ovid, *Am.*, III, 8, 61.
12 Varro in Nonius, p. 155, Lindsay.
13 Cicero, *Pro Lig.*, 11, 32; Livy, I, 18, 4; Juvenal, X, 298-9.
14 Ovid, *Am.*, II, 4, 15; Martial, 11, 15, 1-2.
15 Columella, I, *Praef.* 19; XII, *Praef.* 10.
16 Id., XII, *Praef.* 7; cf. Horace, *Ep.* 2, 38*ff*.; Statius, *Silv.*, V, 1, 123-6.
17 Livy, II, 16, 4.
18 Cicero, *Cato Maior*, 11, 37.
19 Gaius, *Inst.*, I, 55; cf. Justinian, *Inst.*, I, 9, 2.
20 Dionysius, *Ant. Rom.*, II, 26, 4.
21 Livy, VIII, 7.
22 Dionysius, *Ant. Rom.*, VIII, 79; Valerius Maximus, V, 8, 2. (but see

Livy, II, 41, 10-11); Seneca, *De Clem.*, I, 15, 2.
23 Sallust, *Cat.*, 39, 5; Valerius Maximus, V, 8, 3.
24 See R. Düll in *Z.S.S.*, LXIII (1943), pp. 54*ff*.
25 Dionysius, *Ant. Rom.*, exc., XX, 13.
26 Cf. Seneca, *De Clem.*, I, 15, 1.
27 Dionysius, *Ant. Rom.*, II, 26.
28 See below, c. xxi.
29 Seneca, *De Ben.*, III, 38, 2.
30 Cicero, *De Inv.*, I, 30, 48; *De Sen.*, 18, 63; Tacitus, *Ann.*, III, 31; Juvenal, XIII, 53*ff*.
31 Valerius Maximus, II, 1, 9.
32 Ib.; Gellius, II, 15, 2.
33 Ovid, *Fasti*, V, 67-8; cf. Cicero, *De Rep.*, I, 12, 18.
34 Cf. Plutarch, *Cic.*, 2, 2 (mark of honour).
35 Cicero, *De Off.*, I, 34, 122-3; Valerius Maximus, II, 1, 9; cf. Plato, *Leg.*, V, p. 729 b.
36 Cf. *C.I.L.* I, pp. 280*ff*.
37 *Carm. Epigr.*, 52, 8; 63, 14; 237; 492, 16, *et al.*; cf. Livy. I, 57, 9; *Laudatio Turiae*, I, 30.
38 Pliny, *N.H.*, VIII, 74, 194; Plutarch, *Quaest. Rom.*, 31
39 Suetonius, *Aug.*, 64. 2.
40 Varro, in Nonius, p. 239 L.
41 Id., *R.R.*, II, 10, 1.
42 Horace, *Epp.*, II, 1, 139-44; Virgil, *Geo.*, II, 527 *ff*.
43 Cf. Fronto, *Ad M. Caes.*, IV, 6 (p. 63, van den Hout).
44 Tacitus, *Ann.*, XIII, 16, 1;

Corrigenda to Notes

c. III, n. 60	for '5, 5' read '15, 5'
c. IV, n. 4	for 'p. 28' read 'p. 6'
c. IV, n. 8	for 'XXIII' read 'XXXIII'
c. IV, n. 9	for '744*ff.*' read '734*ff.*'
c. IV, n. 14	for 'XL, 1, 13' read 'XL, 2, 13'
c. V, n. 2	for 'Paris, 1955' read 'Paris, 1960'
c. V, n. 9	for '35, 5' read '33, 5'
c. V, n. 25	for 'p. 121' read 'p. 21'
c. V, n. 40	for '14, 11' read '14, 9'
c. V, n. 47	for '*Phorm.* 38' read '*Phorm.* 86'
c. VI, n. 8	for 'I, 1, 4' read 'II, 1, 4'
c. VI, n. 9	read 'I, 4, 14'
c. VI, n. 58	for '48, 150' read '48, 180'
c. VII, n. 70	for '19, 305' read '89, 305'
	for '30, 309' read '90, 309'
c. VII, n. 118	for 'I, 23, 59' read 'II, 23, 59'
c. VIII, n. 48	add 'Suetonius, *Aug.*, 8, 2'
c. IX, n. 29	for 'LXVI, 15, 2' read 'LXV, 15, 2'
c. IX, n. 35	for '*Dial.*, 20' read '*Dial.*, 29'
c. IX, n. 53	for 'VII, 23' read 'VI, 23'
c. IX, nn. 57, 58	references should be transposed
c. IX, n. 63	for 'I, 5' read 'I, 4'
c. IX, n. 70	for 'IV, *praef.* 4' read 'IV, *praef.* 3'
c. X, n. 2	for 'Paris, 1955' read 'Paris, 1960'
c. X, n. 10	for '38, 3' read '38, 1'
c. X, n. 34	for '110–12' read '111–30'
c. X, n. 35	add 'Marrou, *Hist. Educ.*, p. 549, accepts.'
c. X, n. 36	add 'M. della Corte, *Case ed Abitanti*, pp. 110–12.'
c. X, n. 43	for 'XXXV, 10, 36' read 'XXXV, 36, 84'
c. X, n. 66	for 'II, 18' read 'III, 18'
c. XI, n. 20	for 'IV, 26, 11' read 'IV, 86, 11'
c. XI, n. 29	for 'VII, 5, 22' read 'VII, 5, 2'
c. XI, n. 49	add 'and 12, 8'
c. XI, n. 50	delete '13'
c. XII, n. 18	delete 'and 22'
c. XII, n. 21	for 'XXIV, 30' read 'XXXIV, 30'
	for 'II, 205' read 'III, 205'
c. XII, n. 69	for 'XXI' read 'XXXI'
c. XII, n. 133	add '*Id.,* VI, *Praef.*'
c. XIII, n. 114	for 'II, 2, 17–18' read 'II, 3, 17–18'
c. XIX, n. 24	for 'II, 8, 30' read 'III, 8, 30'
c. XIX, n. 81	for '184' read '284'
c. XIX, n. 83	for 'VII, 262*ff.*' read 'VIII, 262*ff.*'
c. XIX, n. 89	for 'II, 14, 12' read 'III, 14, 12'
c. XX, n. 117	read '134–9'
c. XXI, n. 145	for 'II, 14, 3' read 'II, 14, 9'
c. XXI, n. 146	for 'III, 3, 5–7' read 'II, 3, 5–7'
c. XXI, n. 149	read 'VI, 12, 2; cf. IV, 16'

Suetonius, *Aug.*, 64, 3; *Claud.*, 32.
45 Plutarch, *Aem.*, 5; Valerius
Maximus, IV, 4, 8.
46 Servius on Virgil, *Aen.*, I, 730.
47 Varro in Nonius, p. 229, L. s.v.
'puerae'.
48 Horace, *Serm.*, II, 2, 114 *ff.*;
Juvenal, XI, 77 *ff.*
49 Plutarch, *Cato maior*, 20, 5; cf.
Cicero, *De Off.*, I, 35, 129.
50 Juvenal, XIV, 47.
51 Lucretius, III, 894-6; Virgil, *Geo.*,
II, 523.

52 See Thomas Woody, *Life and
Education in Early Societies* (New
York, 1949), pp. 510-11.
53 Virgil, *Aen.*, VII, 162*ff.*; IX,
603*ff.*
54 Sallust, *Cat.*, 7, 4-7.
55 Polybius, VI, 39; 54, 4.
56 Ib., 53-4.
57 Sallust, *Iug.*, 4, 5-6.
58 *C.I.L.*, I, 15; cf. D.C. Earl, *The
Moral and Political Tradition of
Rome* (London, 1967), p. 27.

Chapter II

1 Plutarch, *Cato maior*, 20.
2 Ib., 1, 4-5; 3, 1-2; 15, 1-4.
3 Livy, XXXIX, 40; Pliny, *N.H.*,
VII, 27, 100.
4 Iulius Victor in *Rhet. Lat. Min.*,
p. 374, 17.
5 Plutarch, *Cato maior*, 7, 1.
6 Schanz-Hosius, I, 66.
7 Cf. Nepos, *Cato*, 3, 1; Quintilian,
XII, 11, 23.
8 Plutarch, *Cato maior*, 20, 6-8.
9 Schanz-Hosius, I, 79.
10 Cicero, *Brutus* 15, 61.
11 Valerius Maximus, II, 7, 6.
12 Livy, V, 18, 5.
13 Pliny, *Epp.*, VIII, 14, 4-6.
14 Plautus, *Most.*, 120-54.
15 Servius on Virgil, *Aen.*, V, 546.
16 Cicero, *Brutus*, 20, 79.
17 Id., *De Orat.*, III, 20, 74.
18 Ib., II, 1, 1.
19 Nepos, *Atticus*, I, 2-3.
20 Velleius Paterculus, II, 10, 2.
21 Pliny, *N.H.*, VII, 43, 139-40.
22 Ib., 44, 142; Cicero, *De Fin.*, V,
27, 82; Suetonius, *Aug.*, 89, 2.
23 Livy, XLII, 34, 2-5.
24 Tacitus, *Dial.*, 28.
25 Cf. Petronius, *Sat.*, 46 (painting);
Lucian, *Somn.*, 1 (modelling).
26 Plutarch, *T. Gracch.*, 1; Pliny,
N.H., VII, 13, 57.
27 Cicero, *Brutus*, 27, 104; 58, 211;
Quintilian, I, 1, 6.
28 Emporius in *Rhet. Lat. Min.*,
p. 568, 17; Plutarch, *Caes.*, 9.
29 Cf. below, p. 26.

30 Cf. below, p. 96
31 Plutarch, *Sert.*, 2.
32 Tacitus, *Agric.*, 4.
33 Suetonius, *Aug.*, 64, 2-3, accepting
the reading *notare*.
34 Id., *Vesp.*, 2.
35 Quintilian, VI, *praef.* 8.
36 Horace, *Serm.*, II, 3, 88; cf.
Persius, III, 96; Otto, *Die Sprich-
worter der Römer* (Leipzig, 1890,
rpd, 1965), s.v. *'patruus', 'tutor'*.
37 Cicero, *De Orat.*, II, 1, 2.
38 Id., *Ad Q.F.*, II, 14, 2; III, 1, 7;
Ad Att., VIII, 4, 1; *Part. Orat.*, 1,
1-2.
39 Plutarch, *Cato minor*, 1; Valerius
Maximus, III, 1, 2.
40 Tacitus, *Ann.*, IV, 8, 6.
41 Pliny, *Epp.*, II, 1, 8; IV, 19.
42 Suetonius, *Nero*, 6, 3.
43 Livy, XXXIX, 9, 2.
44 Cicero, *Pro Cluent.*, 9, 27.
45 Id., *Pro Planc.*, 24, 59.
46 Id., *De Rep.*, I, 22, 36.
47 Columella, XI, 1, 26; Seneca,
Epp., 94, 27; Plutarch, *Cato
maior*, 4; Gellius, XI, 2, 6; for
Cato 'the oracle', Seneca the elder,
Contr., I, *praef.* 9; Pliny, *N.H.*,
VII, 51, 171; XXIX, 8, 27.
48 Horace, *Epp.*, II, 1, 103-7.
49 Id., *Serm.*, I, 4, 105*ff.*
50 Plautus, *Trin.*, 295*ff.*
51 Terence, *Ad.*, 414*ff.*
52 Horace, *Serm.*, I, 4, 109-26.
53 Terence, *Hauton.*, 206-7.
54 Polybius, XXXI, 27, 10-11;

Cicero, *Pro Cael.* 16, 38.
55 Cf. G.E. Duckworth, *The Nature of Roman Comedy* (Princeton, 1952), pp. 286-7.
56 Dionysius, *Ant. Rom.*, XX, 13. Cf. in Elizabethan times William Cecil, Lord Burghley: 'And I am persuaded that the foolish cockering of some parents and the over-stern carriage of others causeth more men and women to take ill courses than their own vicious inclinations' (Lord David Cecil, *The Cecils* [London, 1973], p. 80).

Chapter III

1 Hieronymus, *Chronicon*, ad Ol. 148, 1-2 — 188/7 B.C.
2 Cicero, *Brutus*, 18, 72, and edd. ad loc.; Gellius, XVII, 21, 42-3. On the Livii Salinatores, F. Münzer in P-W., *R.E.*, x.v. 'Livius' 32 and 33; on Andronicus, Schanz-Hosius, §23; E. Fraenkel in *R.E.*, *Suppbd.*, V, 598-607; W. Beare in *C.Q.*, XXXIV (1940), pp. 12*ff.*; H. Mattingly in *C.Q.*, N.S., VII (1957), pp. 159*ff.*; E.H. Warmington, *Remains of Old Latin* (Loeb Library), II, pp. viii-xiv, accepts traditional dating.
3 Suetonius, *De Gramm.*, 1.
4 Warmington, op. cit., pp. 2-43.
5 Horace, *Epp.*, II, 1, 69-75.
6 Livy, XXVII, 37, Festus, p.446, s.v. 'scribae'; E.G. Sihler in *A.J.P.*, XXXVI (1905), pp. 1-21.
7 Gellius, XVII, 17, 1.
8 Nepos, *Cato*, 1, 4; Silius Italicus, XII, 393*ff.*
9 Cicero, *Pro Arch.*, 11, 27; *Tusc. Disp.*, I, 2, 3.
10 Id., *Brutus*, 20, 79.
11 Cicero, *Acad. Pr.*, II, 16, 51; Lucretius, I, 124*ff.*; Horace, *Epp.*, II, 1, 50*ff.*; Persius, VI, 10-11.
12 Cf. below, p. 223.
13 Suetonius, loc. cit.; *Thes. Ling. Lat.*, s.v. 'foris', col. 1041*ff.*
14 Petronius, *Sat.*, 46.
15 The painting is no longer extant, but is reproduced from an engraving by H. Roux Aîné, *Herculanum et Pompeii, Recueil Général des Peintures, Bronzes, Mosaiques* (Paris, 1861), Pl. 49; cf. the accompanying commentary of M.L. Barré and J. Bories (pp. 165-8).
16 *Cod. Theod.*, XIV, 9, 3.
17 Plutarch, *Aem. Paul.*, 5, 3.
18 Ib., 6, 5.
19 Pliny, *N.H.*, XXXV, 40, 135.
20 Plutarch, *Aem. Paul.*, 33, 3; 35, 1-2.
21 Ib., 6, 5.
22 Ib., 28, 6.
23 Polybius, XXXI, 23, 5.
24 Ib., 23, 4; 24, 6-12.
25 Suetonius, *De Gramm.*, 2.
26 Plutarch, *Cato maior*, 22.
27 Cicero, *De Orat.*, II, 37, 154; A.E. Astin, *Scipio Aemilianus* (Oxford, 1967), pp. 294*ff.*
28 Cicero, *Brutus*, 27, 104; Plutarch, *T. Gracch.*, 8, 4.
29 Suidas, s.v. 'Alexander Milesios'; Servius on Virgil, *Aen.*, X, 388; *G.R.F.* (Funaioli), pp. xii-xiii.
30 Suetonius, *De Gramm.*, 7; *G.R.F.* (Funaioli), pp. 97-100.
31 Suetonius, *J.C.*, 56; Fronto, p. 209, van den Hout.; G.L. Hendrickson in *C.P.*, I (1906) pp. 97-120; H. Dahlmann in *Rh. M.*, LXXXIV (1935), pp.365*ff.*
32 Suetonius, *De Gramm.*, 7.
33 Cf. below, p. 77.
34 Strabo, XIV, p. 650; Funaioli, op. cit., p. xv.
35 Plutarch, *Quaest. conv.*, IX, 1, 3.
36 Id., *Pomp.*, 55, 1-2.
37 Catullus, 35.
38 Tibullus, IV, 7-12.
39 Ovid, *A.A.*, III, 329*ff.*; cf. *Trist.*, II, 369.
40 Cicero, *Ad Q.F.*, II, 4, 2.
41 Suidas, *s.v.* 'Tyrannion' cf. Funaioli, op. cit., pp. xv*ff.*
42 Plutarch, *Lucull.*, 42.
43 Ib., 19.
44 Christ-Schmid, II, i, p. 429.

45 Cicero, *Ad Att.*, II, 6, 1; Strabo, XII, p. 548.
46 Cicero, *Ad Att.*, XII, 2, 2; 6, 2; [Sergius] *G.L.*, IV, 529.
47 Strabo, XIII, p. 608; Plutarch, *Sulla*, 26.
48 Cicero, *Ad Att.*, IV, 4a, 1.
49 Ib., 8, 2.
50 Id., *Ad Q.F.*, III, 4, 5; 6, 6.
51 Ib., 3, 4, cf. below, p. 103.
52 Id., *Ad Att.*, IV, 8, 2; 8a, 1; 11, 2; for his name, 15, 1.
53 Ib., 15, 10.
54 Ib., VI, 2, 3; VII, 3, 10.
55 Ib., VI, 1, 12.
56 Ib., VII, 4, 1; 7, 1.
57 Ib., 18, 3.
58 Ib., VIII, 4, 1.
59 Ib., 5, 1; 10.
60 Ib., IX, 12, 2; 5, 5.
61 Ib., X, 16, 1; XIII, 2, 3.
62 Dionysius, *De Ant. Orat., Praef.*
63 Id., *De Isoc.*, 5-8 (I, 61, 10*ff.*, U-R.).
64 Id., *De Comp. Verb.*, 1.
65 Suetonius, *De Gramm.*, 16.
66 Cf. below, p. 105.
67 Lucian, *De merc. cond.*, 10-23, 37-8.
68 Quintilian, I, 2, 11.
69 Symmachus, *Epp.*, I, 20, 2.
70 Cf. below, pp. 107*ff.*
71 Suetonius, *Titus*, 2, 1.
72 Ib., 3, 2.
73 Anthony Birley, *Marcus Aurelius* (London, 1966), pp. 34*ff.*; 75*ff.*, 86*ff.*

Chapter IV

1 Livy, III, 44, 6; Dionysius, *Ant. Rom.*, XI, 28, 3.
2 Livy, VI, 25, 9.
3 Plutarch, *Quaest. Rom.*, 59, where the word used is *grammatodidas-caleion*, 'school of letters'; on the divorce, cf. also ib., 14.
4 Ib., 54; cf. H.J. Rose's ed. (Oxford 1924), ad loc., and W.M. Lindsay, *The Latin Language* (Oxford, 1894), p. 28; *G.R.F.* (Funaioli), p. 3.
5 Plutarch, *Thes.-Rom.*, 6, 3; *Lycurg.-Num.*, 3, 7.
6 Dionysius, *Ant. Rom.*, II, 25, 7; Gellius, IV, 3; XVII, 21, 44. Valerius Maximus, II, 1, 4, dates as early as 604 B.C.; for other divorces, cf. VI, 3, 10-12.
7 Cicero, *Phil.* II, 28, 69; Valerius Maximus, II, 9, 2; date confirmed by Livy, IX, 43, 25.
8 P.E. Corbett, *The Roman Law of Marriage* (Oxford, 1930), pp. 218*ff.* and esp. Alan Watson in *Tijdschrift voor Rechtsgeschied-enis*, XXIII (1965), pp. 38-50.
9 Plautus, *Merc.*, 292*ff.*; 303*ff.*; *Truc.*, 744*ff.*; *Asin.*, 226*ff.*
10 Probably *erô*; cf. Menander, *Heros* 15.
11 Cf. Quintilian, V, 10, 67, on types of slave.
12 Juvenal, XIV, 166-71.
13 Horace, *Ep.* 2, 65-6; Tibullus, II, 1, 21-4; Martial, III, 58, 22.
14 Plutarch, *Cato maior*, 20, 3; Gaius, *Inst.*, I, 39; *Dig.* XL, 1, 13; *C.I.L.* XIV, 2413.
15 Horace, *Serm.*, II, 6, 63*ff.*; cf. Martial, II, 90, 9.
16 Seneca, *De Prov.*, I, 6; Petronius, *Sat.* 66; Martial, XIV, 54; [Quin-tilian], *Decl. Min.*, 316 (p.245, 29, Ritter).
17 Cf. Quintilian, I, 1, 7; Jerome, *Epp.*, 14, 3; R.H. Barrow, *Slavery in the Roman Empire* (London, 1928), p. 51.
18 Homer, *Odyssey*, XV, 363-5; see A.N. Sherwin-White, *The Letters of Pliny* (Oxford, 1966), pp. 650-51.
19 J. Heurgon, *Daily Life of the Etruscans* (trans. J. Kirkup, London, 1964), p. 66; cf. esp. E. Benveniste in *R.E.L.* X (1932), p. 437.
20 Diodorus Siculus, V, 40.
21 Cicero, *De Rep.*, II, 21, 37; Valerius Maximus, I, 6, 1; III, 4, 3.
22 A. Grenier, in *Mélanges d'Archéo-*

logie et d'Histoire XLI (1924), pp. 1-42.

23 Cf. Marrou, *Hist. Educ.*, pp. 339 and 541.

24 Livy, IX, 36, 2-4.

25 Horace, *Serm.*, I, 6, 78*ff.*; Juvenal X, 117.

26 See R. Boulogne, *De Plaats van de Paedagogus in de romeinse Cultuur* (Diss., Groningen, 1951).

27 Suetonius, *De Gramm.*, 23.

28 Horace, *Epp.* I, 20, 17-18; cf. S.F. Bonner in *A.J.P.*, XCIII (1972), pp. 509-28.

29 Plutarch, *Cato maior*, 21, 7.

30 Ib., 20, 3; cf. Livy, V, 27, 1.

31 Id., *Crass.*, 2, 6. See further C.A. Forbes in *T.A.Ph.A.*, LXXXVI (1955), pp. 321-60.

32 Nepos, *Att.*, 13, 3.

33 Suetonius, *De Gramm.*, 4 (from Orbilius).

34 Cf. Apuleius, *Flor.*, 20.

35 Horace, *Epp.*, II, 2, 1-8.

36 Plato, *Lysis*, 208c; *Symp.*, 183c; Xenophon, *Resp. Lac.*, 2, 1.

37 Plato, *Lysis*, 223a (brothers); Lysias, XXXII, 28 (brothers and sister).

38 Plato, *Protag.*, 325c, d.

39 Cf. Theon, *Rhet. Graec.* (Sp.), II, 98, 32; Quintilian, I, 9, 5, with F.H. Colson's note.

40 Plato, *Leg.* VII, p. 808d, e.

41 Xenophon, *Resp. Lac.*, 3, 1.

42 Cf. Euripides, *Ion*, 725*ff.*; *Electra*, 286-7; *Medea* and *Phoenissae, passim*.

43 Plato, *Alc.*, I, p. 122b.

44 Id., *Lysis*, 223a.

45 Illustrations in F. Winter, *Die antiken Terrakotten, III, Die Typen der figürlichen Terrakotten*, ii, (Berlin and Stuttgart, 1903), pp. 403*ff.*

46 See further P.-W., *R.E.*, s.v. 'Paidagogos' (Schuppe).

47 Cf. *e.g.*, the Plato passages in notes 38 and 40 above; [Plutarch], *De Lib. Educ.*, 16, p. 12a; Plutarch, *Aem.* 33, 3; Dio Cassius XLVI, 5, 1; Varro in Nonius, p. 718, L; Pliny, *Epp.*, V, 16, 3.

48 Plautus, *Bacch.*, 420*ff.*

49 Ib., 120*ff.*

50 Cf. Petronius, *Sat.*, 85.

51 Diogenes Laertius, VI, 30*ff.*

52 Plutarch, *Fab. Max.*, 5, 4.

53 Schuppe, loc. cit., col. 2379-80.

54 Cf. Boulogne, op. cit., p. 65.

55 *Rhet. ad. Herenn.*, IV, 52, 65.

56 Appian, *B.C.*, IV, 30.

57 Cicero, *De Am.*, 20, 74.

58 Cf. esp., *C.I.L.*, VI, 8012 and reff. in Boulogne, op. cit., p. 83, n.2.

59 Dio Cassius, XLVIII, 33, 1.

60 Cicero, *Ad Att.*, XII, 33, 3, (suspicion here dismissed).

61 Suetonius, *Aug.*, 67. 2.

62 Valerius Maximus, VI, 1, 3.

63 Martial, XI, 39, 1-2:

64 See *Thes. Ling. Lat.*, s.v. 'educator', 'educo'. Note Cicero, *Pro Planc.*, 33, 81.

65 Ib., s.v. 'educatrix'.

66 Juvenal, VI, 633, with Friedländer's note.

67 In large households, the *tropheus* might be a different person from the *paedagogus*; cf. Plutarch, *Alex.*, 5, 4-5; *Aem.*, 33, 3.

68 Cicero, *De Orat.*, II, 39, 162 (cf. our metaphor 'spoon-feeding'); Quintilian, X, i, 19.

69 Tacitus, *Ann.*, XIII, 15, 4.

70 Ib., XIV, 3, 5; Suetonius, *Nero*, 35, 2. For *educator*, cf. also Tacitus, *Ann.*, XI, 1, 2; XII, 41, 8.

71 Seneca the elder, *Contr.*, II, 1, 29.

72 Plato, *Rep.*, IV, 425a; Aristophanes, *Nub.*, 963-4, 993-4, 998.

73 Cf. Suetonius, *Nero*, 36, 2.

74 Plutarch, *Virt. doc. posse*, 2; *De Lib. Educ.*; 7; cf. Aristophanes, *Nub.*, 981*ff.*; Seneca, *Epp.* 94, 8.

75 Cf. Aristophanes, *Nub.*, 983.

76 Plutarch, loc. cit.; Lucian, *Am.*, 44.

77 *Rhet. ad Herenn.*, IV, 10, 14.

78 Dio Chrysostom, LXXII, 10.

79 Plutarch, *Cat. min.*, 1, 5.

80 Cicero, *De Orat.*, II, 24, 99; Seneca, *Epp.*, 89, 13; 94, 8-9, 72.

81 Valerius Maximus, III, 1, 2; Epictetus, III, 19, 5.

82 Suetonius, *Aug.*, 44, 2; cf. *C.I.L.*, VI, 1796.

83 Cf. Sir James Mountford, 'Music and the Romans', *Bulletin of the John Rylands Library*, XLVII (1964), pp. 198-211.

84 See esp. G. Wille, *Musica Romana. Die Bedeutung der Musik im Leben der Römer* (Amsterdam, 1967).

85 Cf. e.g. Cicero, *De Orat.*, III, 23, 87; Propertius, I, 2, 27-8; II, 1, 9-10; Statius, *Silv.*, III, 5, 64*ff.*; Juvenal, VII, 175-7.

86 Horace, *Serm.*, I, 10, 90-91; Columella, I, *Praef.* 3 and 5; Seneca, *Epp.*, 90, 19.

87 Nepos, *Epam.*, 1; Cicero, *Pro Mur.*, 6, 13; *In Pis.*, 10, 22; Sallust, *Cat.*, 25, 2.

88 Macrobius, III, 14, 6-7 (*O.R.F.*, p. 133).

89 Plautus, *Stich.*, 380-81; cf. Livy, XXXIX, 6, 8 (187 B.C.)

90 Cf. Wille, op. cit., pp. 212*ff*.

91 Terence, *Phorm.*, 85*ff*. and 144.

92 Horace, *A.P.*, 161-2; Martial, IX, 27, 10-11; XI, 39.

93 Juvenal, III, 61.

94 Quintilian, I, 1, 12-14.

95 Suetonius, *Claud.*, 2, 2.

96 Quintilian, I, 1, 8, with Colson's notes.

97 Plutarch, *Virt. doc. posse*, 2 (p. 439f) speaks of the 'fee' of pedagogues.

98 S.L. Mohler, in *T.A.Ph.A.*, LXXI (1940), pp. 262-80; C.A. Forbes, loc. cit., pp. 334-6; P.-W., *R.E.*, s.v. 'paedagogiani', 'paedagogium Palatini'.

99 Tacitus, *Ann.*, III, 66, 4, speaks of the 'obscura initia' of the senator Iunius Otho, once a primary schoolmaster; Florus, *Virg.*, 3, 2 'rem indignissimam'.

Chapter V

1 Cicero, *De Rep.*, IV, 3, 3.

2 E. Ziebarth, *Aus dem griechischen Schulwesen*² (Leipzig/Berlin, 1914); M.P. Nilsson, *Die hellenistische Schule* (Munich, 1955); A.H.M. Jones, *The Greek City* (Oxford, 1940), c. xiv; J. Delorme, *Gymnasion* (Paris, 1955), c.xi.

3 Suetonius, *Vit. Terent.*, 1.

4 Quintilian, I, 2, 9-10.

5 Plato, *Prot.*, 325e.

6 Xenophon, *Mem.*, IV, 2, 20.

7 R. Pfeiffer, *History of Classical Scholarship* (Oxford, 1968), pp. 85-233.

8 Ib., pp. 156-9. See esp. Suetonius, *De Gramm.*, 10 (Ateius Philologus). Cicero uses *philologus* (adj.) and *philologia*, of liberal studies, including philosophy; cf. *Ad Att.*, II, 17, 1; XIII, 12, 3; 52, 2; *Ad Fam.*, XVI, 21, 4; *Ad Q.F.*, II, 10, 3.

9 Polybius, XXXI, 35, 5 and XXXII, 2, 5, of the same person.

10 Sextus Empiricus, *Adv. Gramm.*, 79 and 248.

11 Gellius, XIV, 6, 3, P.-W. *R.E.*, s.v. 'Grammatikos'.

12 See below, c. xiv, n.1 (esp. Steinthal).

13 See below, c. xiv, n.1 (esp. Barwick).

14 Diogenes Laertius, VII, 56-9.

15 Text (Uhlig), Leipzig, 1883; Scholia (Hilgard), Leipzig, 1901.

16 Quintilian, I, 4, 20.

17 Charisius, p. 149, Barwick (Aristophanes); Varro, *De Ling. Lat.*, VIII and IX, *passim*, esp. IX, 1; Gellius, II, 25 (Crates and Aristarchus).

18 See Christ-Schmid, II, p. 430; B.A. Müller, *De Asclepiade Myrleano* (Leipzig, 1903).

19 Sextus Empiricus, *Adv. Gramm.*, 47.

20 Ib., esp. 91*ff*., compared with 252.

21 Schanz-Hosius, III, pp. 55*ff*.

22 Text by G. Brugnoli (Leipzig, Teubner, 1960); edns by R.P. Robinson (Paris, 1925); F. della Corte (Torino, 1968).

23 Cf. *G.R.F.* (Funaioli), pp. 327-9 (Varro fr. 320).

24 On Crates' Homeric studies, cf. W. Kroll in P.W., *R.E.*, s.v. 'Krates'; Pfeiffer, op. cit., pp. 238*ff*.

25 Fronto, p. 15, van den Hout.; *G.R.F.* (Funaioli), p. 121.
26 Athenaeus, IV, p. 184b.c.; Strabo, XIV, p. 675; Pfeiffer, op. cit., pp. 252*ff*.
27 Suetonius, *De Gramm.*, 3; *G.R.F.* (Funaioli), pp. 51*ff*.
28 Quintilian, X, 1, 99.
29 T. Bergk, *Opuscula* I, pp. 580*ff*. ('Anecdoton Parisinum'); *G.L.*, VII, 533*ff*.; S.F. Bonner in *Hermes* LXXXVIII (1960), pp. 354*ff*.
30 F. Marx, *Prolegomena* to his edn of *Rhet. ad Herenn.* (Leipzig, 1894), pp. 138*ff*.
31 Cicero, *Ad Fam.*, IX, 16, 4; *G.R.F.* (Funaioli), pp. 95*ff*.; Bonner, loc. cit., p. 359.
32 Gellius, III, 3, 1-3.
33 See M. Fuhrmann, *Das systematische Lehrbuch* (Göttingen, 1960).
34 Cicero, *De Orat.*, I, 42, 187.
35 *Rhet. ad Herenn.*, IV, 12, 17.
36 Cicero, *De Orat.*, III, 13, 48.
37 Juvenal, VI, 452; K. Barwick, *Remmius Palaemon und die römische Ars Grammatica* (Leipzig, 1922).
38 Seneca, *Epp.*, 88, 3.
39 Quintilian, I, 4, 2 ('brevissime'); 2, 14 (more expansive).
40 Suetonius, *De Gramm.*, 4, quoting Messala Corvinus, but missing the irony; Catullus, 14, 11, 'Sulla litterator' is uncertain, but Martianus Capella, III, 229, took the reference as primary; cf. Apuleius, *Flor.*, 20. See, however, E.W. Bower in *Hermes* LXXXIX (1961), pp. 46-77 (mostly late evidence).
41 See Bower, pp. 462*ff*.; but the term would apply to Livius Andronicus and Ennius.
42 Cicero, *Ad Fam.*, IX, 10, 1 (text crit.); Horace, *Epp.*, II, 1, 51 (lit. crit.)
43 Cf. Dar. Sag., s.v. 'Ludus, Ludimagister'; Jullien, *Les Professeurs*, pp. 113-14.
44 Aelius, fr. 59 (*G.R.F.*, p. 72, Funaioli); Quintilian, I, 6, 34.

45 Festus, p. 470, L., s.v. 'schola'.
46 Scott, *Kenilworth*, c. ix (p. 150 in Andrew Lang's edn).
47 Cf. Plautus, *Rud., Prol.* 43; Terence, *Phorm.*, 38 (music); Scipio fr. 30, in *O.R.F.* p.133 (acting, dancing).
48 Suetonius, *De Rhet.* 4; cf. 1; Cicero, *De Orat.*, II, 22, 94; 24, 100; III, 9, 35.
49 Virgil, *Aen.*, V, 552*ff*.; Suetonius, *Aug.*, 43.
50 Virgil, ib. 674; cf. Livy, VII, 33, 2 (*ludo militari*).
51 Cicero, *Div. in Caec.*, 14, 47.
52 Id., *De Orat.*, II, 80, 325; Virgil, *Georg.*, III, 234.
53 Seneca the elder, *Contr.*, III, *Praef.* 12; cf. IX, *Praef.* 4.
54 Quintilian, XII, 11, 20; Suetonius, *De Gramm.*, 4, *sub fin.*; *Dig.*, L, 13, 1 and 6.
55 *C.I.L.*, VI, 9453, 9454; II, 2236; III, 12702; X, 3961.
56 *C.I.L.*, II, 2892; III, 406; V, 3433, 5278; VI, 9455; IX, 5545.
57 *C.I.L.*, II, 3872, 5079; VI, 9444-52; IX, 1654.
58 *C.I.L.*, VI, 9454; P.-W. *R.E.*, s.v. 'Epaphroditos'.
59 Suetonius, *De Gramm.*, 3.
60 Quintilian, II, 1, 1.
61 Cicero, *De Div.*, I, 18, 34; *De Orat.* I, 42, 187.
62 Quintilian, I, 8, 5-8; cf. 4, 2.
63 Seneca the elder, *Contr.*, II, *Praef.*, 5; cf. Cicero, *De Off.*, I, 42, 151, and see further S. Treggiari, *Roman Freedmen during the late Republic* (Oxford, 1969), pp. 110*ff*.
64 Suetonius, *De Gramm.*, 9.
65 Ib., 11.
66 Ib., 21.
67 Ib., 19.
68 Ib., 20
69 Suidas, s.v. 'Epaphroditos', and n.58 above.
70 Suetonius, *De Gramm.*, 3.
71 Ib., esp. the words 'nam in provincias ...'
72 Ib., 13, with Pliny, *N.H.*, XXXV, 58, 199.

73 Cf. *G.R.F.* (Funaioli), pp. 106-7.
74 Fronto, p. 15, van den Hout.
75 Suetonius, *De Gramm.*, 15, with Pliny, *N.H.*, XXV, 3; *G.R.F.* (Funaioli), pp. 403-4.
76 Suetonius, *De Gramm.*, 18, 22, and 23.
77 Ib., 24. See further J. Aistermann, *De M. Valerii Probi Berytii vita et scriptis* (Bonn, 1909).
78 Ib., 6; Gellius, III, 3, 1.
79 Suetonius, *De Gramm.*, 8.
80 Ib., 14.
81 Ib., 11; R.P. Robinson in *T.A.Ph.A.*, LIV (1923), pp. 98-116.
82 Ib., 18; cf. Catullus, 95.
83 Horace, *Epp.*, I, 19, 39-40.

84 Cicero, *Ad. Fam.*, IX, 10, 1-2; Suetonius, *De Gramm.*, 14.
85 Ib., 10.
86 Ib., 16.
87 Ib., 20.
88 Ib., 21.
89 Suidas, s.v. 'Dionysios Alexandreus'; Christ-Schmid, II, p. 677.
90 Suetonius, *De Gramm.*, 10, 11, 18.
91 Cf. P. Petit, *Les Etudiants de Libanius* (Paris, 1956), p. 101.
92 Statius, *Silvae*, V, 3, 116*ff.* (family; 146*ff.* (Naples); 176*ff.* (Rome); 185*ff.* (pupils).
93 Cf. the *Professores* of Ausonius.
94 *S.H.A., Pertinax*, 1.

Chapter VI

1 Cicero, *Brutus*, 14, 53-57.
2 Plutarch, *Fab. Max.*, 1.
3 Cicero, *De Orat.*, I, 4, 14; Quintilian, X, 1, 43; XII, 10, 40.
4 Ennius, *Varia*, fr. 38, V.
5 Cicero, *Brutus*, 26, 100; 27, 104.
6 Suetonius, *De Rhet.*, 1.
7 Pliny the elder, *N.H.*, VII, 112-13; cf. Cicero, *De Rep.*, III, 6, 9; Quintilian, XII, 1, 35.
8 Cicero, *De Orat.*, I, 1, 4; II, 36, 153.
9 Ib., 4, 14.
10 Tacitus, *Dial.*, 38, 4.
11 Ib., 36-7.
12 Polybius, XXXI, 29, 8; 12.
13 Cicero, *Brutus*, 27, 106.
14 Cf. A.W. Lintott, *Violence in Republican Rome* (Oxford, 1968).
15 Tacitus, *Dial.* 34, 7; Cicero, *De Orat.*, III, 20, 74; *De Off.*, II, 13, 47 (Crassus); Plutarch, *Lucullus*, 1, 2 (Lucullus); Suetonius, *J.C.* 4, 1; 55, 1 (Caesar); ps. Asconius on Cicero, *Div. in Caec.*, 7, 24 (Appius Clodius Pulcher); Cicero, *Pro Cael.*, 30, 73 — 31, 74 (Caelius); St Jerome, *ad Euseb. Chron.* Ol. 189 (Atratinus).
16 Cicero, *De Off.*, II, 14, 49-51; cf. *De Orat.*, I, 8, 31, and *Div. in Caec.*, 19, 63, on defence.

17 Id., *De Orat.*, I, 5, 16.
18 Ib., II, 38, 160; *De Inv.*, II, 2, 6; *Brutus*, 12, 46; L. Radermacher, *Artium Scriptores* (Vienna, 1951).
19 Text by D. Matthes (Leipzig, Teubner, 1962); discussion in *Lustrum*, III (1958), pp. 58*ff.*
20 See below, c. xx.
21 Cicero, *Brutus*, 76, 263; 78, 271.
22 Id., *De Orat.*, I, 2, 5.
23 Ib., 32, 145; II, 18, 75; III, 19, 70.
24 Ib., II, 18, 75-6.
25 Ib., I, 31, 137-42, 145.
26 Ib., II, 38, 160.
27 Ib., 19, 79.
28 Ib., 19, 81; 76, 307-8.
29 Ib., 76, 306-9; 314-15.
30 Ib., 80, 326-81, 330.
31 Ib., I, 48, 208; *Brutus*, 44, 163; Quintilian, III, 1, 19; 6, 45.
32 Cicero, *De Orat.*, II, 27, 117; 30, 132; 31, 133; 32, 140. Note the repeated *isti*.
33 Ib., 77, 310-12.
34 Suetonius, *De Rhet.*, 2; Seneca the elder, *Contr.*, II, *Praef.* 5.
35 Cicero, *De Orat.*, III, 24, 93-4; cf. Tacitus, *Dial.*, 35.
36 F. Marx, *Prolegomena*, pp. 147*ff.*; A. Gwynn, *Roman Education from Cicero to Quintilian* (Oxford, 1926), pp. 60*ff.*; G. Perl in *Acta*

Antiqua Philippopolitana, Studia Historica et Philologica (Sofia, 1963), pp. 265-84, fully develops Marx's view.

37 Cicero, *Pro Archia*, 9, 20.

38 Cicero, *Prov. Cons.*, 8, 19 (*alienus*, i.e. 'estranged').

39 P.-W., *R.E.*, s.v. 'Marius' 15, col. 1812; cf. M. Gelzer, *Kleine Schriften*, I, (Wiesbaden, 1962), p. 214 and n.26.

40 Cicero, *De Orat.*, III, 24, 94.

41 Seneca the elder, *Contr.*, II, *Praef.* 5; cf. Cicero, *Orat.*, 42, 145.

42 Quintilian, II, 4, 41-2.

43 *Rhet. ad Herenn.*, III, 11, 20 and following chapters.

44 Galen, *De sanitate tuenda*, VI, 155 K.; Oribasius, VI, 8 and 9 (I, 159*ff.*, Raeder); Krumbacher, *Die Stimmbildung der Redner im Alterthum* (Paderborn, 1920), pp. 105*ff.*

45 *Rhet. ad Herenn.*, loc. cit.

46 Cf. Cicero, *De Orat.*, I, 59, 251 (actors) with Seneca the elder, *Contr.* I, *Praef.* 16 (declaimers).

47 Demosthenes, *De Corona*, 280; 308; *De Fals. Leg.*, 255; 336.

48 Quintilian, XI, 3, 143.

49 Varro, *Sat. Menipp.*, p. 157, Riese; cf. Greek *agroikizesthai*.

50 Suggested in *Rom. Declam.*, p. 20, n.3; confirmed by *C.G.L.*, III, 351, 65, *declamatio/anaphonesis*.

51 Cicero, *De Orat.*, II, 20, 85-6.

52 Ib., I, 33, 149.

53 Id., *Brutus.*, 95, 325; cf. Petronius, *Sat.* 2.

54 Id., *De Orat.*, I, 18, 83; 23, 105; Valerius Maximus, II, 2, 2; Juvenal, III, 74; Pliny, *Epp.*, V, 20, 4 (*impudentissimo*).

55 Cicero, *Brutus*, 90, 313; 91, 316.

56 Suetonius, *De Rhet.*, 2.

57 Varro, *Sat. Menipp.*, p. 186, Riese. Marx, *Prolegomena*, pp. 148-9, quite disguises the fact that *rabula*, like *bubulcitarat*, is intentionally sarcastic.

58 Cicero, *De Orat.*, I, 46, 202; *Orat.*, 15, 47; *Brutus*, 48, 150; 63, 226.

59 Suetonius, *De Rhet.*, 3; R.G. Lewis in *C.R.*, *N.S.*, XVI (1966), pp. 271-3; *contra*, S. Treggiari, *ib.*, XIX (1969), pp. 264-6.

60 Ib., 4.

61 *Vita Vergilii Bernensis*, p. 44.

62 Suetonius, *De Rhet.*, 5.

63 Cicero, *Phil.*, II, 17, 42-3.

64 Suidas, s.v. 'Timagenes'; Horace, *Epp.*, I, 19, 15; Seneca the elder, *Contr.* X, 5, 22; Seneca, *Epp.*, 91, 13.

65 Plutarch, *Ant.*, 2, 5.

66 Virgil, *Catalepton*, 5, (probably genuine), with Westendorp-Boerma's notes.

67 Suetonius, *Aug.*, 86. 3.

Chapter VII

1 Cicero, *Div. in Caec.*, 12, 39-40. For Cicero's oratorical ideals, see A. Gwynn, op. cit., pp. 118*ff.*, and esp. K. Barwick, *Das rednerische Bildungsideal Ciceros* (Berlin Academy, 1963); G.M.A. Grube in *Phoenix*, XI (1962), pp. 234-57.

2 Id., *Brutus*, 74, 258.

3 Ib., 58, 210*ff.* (the elder Curio); 59, 214; 74, 259 (Flamininus).

4 Ib., 28, 108 (Furius Philus); 82, 283 (Calvus).

5 Ib., 45, 167 (C. Titius).

6 As did C. Memmius (ib., 70, 247).

7 Ib., 30, 114 (P. Rutilius); 35, 131 (T. Albucius); 45, 168 (M. Gratidius); 47, 173 (L. Philippus); 67, 237 (C. Censorinus).

8 Ib., 28, 107 (D. Brutus, cos. 138); 46, 169 (Valerii Sorani); 47, 175 (D. Brutus, cos. 77); 56, 205 (Aelius Stilo).

9 Cicero, *Pro Archia*, 3, 4-6; Quintilian, X, 7, 19.

10 Plutarch, *Cicero*, 2, 3.

11 On Cicero's poems, cf. G.B. Townend in *Cicero* (*Studies in Latin Literature and its Influence*, London, 1964), pp. 109-34.

12 W. Zillinger, *Cicero und die altrö-mischer Dichter* (Würzburg, 1911).

13 F. Kühnert, *Allgemeinbildung und Fachbildung in der Antike* (Berlin, 1961); M.L. Clarke, *Higher Education in the Ancient World* (London, 1971), pp. 45*ff*. On the latter work, which is philosophy-orientated, see *J.R.S.*, LXIII (1973), pp. 268*ff*. (Bonner).

14 Quintilian, I, 12, 5-6.

15 *S.H.A.*, *Vit. M. Ant.*, 2 (music and geometry); cf. Clarke, op. cit., p. 49.

16 Cicero, *De Orat.*, III, 15, 58; *De Fin.*, I, 21, 72.

17 Id., *Acad. pr.*, II, 36, 115; *De Nat. Deor.*, I, 3, 6.

18 Id., *Ad Fam.*, XIII, 16, 4.

19 Id., *Tusc. Disp.*, V, 39, 113.

20 Id., *Brutus*, 90, 309.

21 Id., *De Nat. Deor.*, II, 41, 104; cf. G.B. Townend, op. cit., pp. 112*ff*.

22 Id., *Brutus.*, 47, 175; *De Off.*, I, 6. 19.

23 Id., *De Sen.*, 14, 49; cf. Pliny, *N.H.*, II, 53.

24 Cf. above, p. 27.

25 Suetonius, *Vit Verg.*, 15.

26 Vitruvius, I, 1, 3; IX, 1, 16; H. Weinhold, *Die Astronomie in der antiken Schule* (Munich, 1912), pp. 85*ff*.

27 Columella, I, *Praef.* 5.

28 O.A.W. Dilke, *The Roman Land Surveyors* (Newton Abbott, 1971), pp. 51*ff*.

29 Cicero, *Tusc. Disp.*, I, 2, 5; Seneca, *Epp.*, 88, 10-11.

30 Polybius, IX, 14, 5*ff*. (astronomy), 19, 5-20, 5 (mathematics) with Walbank's notes.

31 Cf. Quintilian, I, 10, 3*ff*.

32 Ib., 35-6.

33 Ib., 34; cf. Cicero, *De Rep.*, I, 18, 30; Isocrates, *Antid.*, 261, 266-7.

34 Cicero, *De Orat.*, III, 15, 58; *Part. Orat.*, 23, 80.

35 Cf. W.H. Stahl, *Martianus Capella and the Seven Liberal Arts*, I *The Quadrivium* (Columbia University Press, 1971), pp. 90*ff*.

36 Cicero, *De Orat.*, I, 6, 23.

37 Id., *Brutus*, 76, 263; 78, 271.

38 Cf. *Rom. Orat.*, pp. 343-6.

39 See now works listed in G. Calboli's edn of *Rhet. ad Herenn.* (Bologna, 1969), pp. 287*ff*.

40 *Rhet. ad Herenn.*, IV, 8-10; analysed by J. Marouzeau, *Traité de Stylistique latine* (Paris, 1954), pp. 194-5.

41 Cicero, *Orat.*, 21, 69.

42 Ib., 5, 20-9, 29; 23, 75-28, 99; S. Schlittenbauer, *Die Tendenz von Ciceros Orator* (Leipzig, 1903).

43 E. Norden, *Die antika Kunst-prosa*³ (Leipzig/Berlin, 1915), I, pp. 131-52; U. von Wilamowitz-Moellendorff in *Hermes*, XXXV (1900), pp. 1*ff*.

44 Cicero, *Orat.*, 29, 100-104.

45 Cf. Eric Laughton in *A.J.P.*, LXXXII (1961), pp. 27-49.

46 Cicero, *Orat.*, 8, 25 and 27; 17, 57; 67, 226.

47 Id., *Brutus*, 13, 51; 75, 325-6.

48 Dionysius, *De Ant. Orat.*, *Praef.*

49 Cicero, *Opt. Gen.*, 4, 13-5, 16.

50 Id., *Brutus*, 33, 126.

51 Ib., 127.

52 Ib., 44, 164.

53 Id., *De Orat.*, III, 10, 37; *Orat.*, 23, 79; J. Stroux, *De Theophrasti virtutibus dicendi* (Leipzig, 1912).

54 Diogenes Laertius, VII, 59.

55 W. Kroll on Cicero, *Orat.*, 39, 134; cf. Dionysius, *De Isoc.*, 3 (I, 58, 4, U.-R.).

56 *Rhet. ad Herenn.*, IV, 12, 18.

57 Cicero, *De Orat.*, III, 49, 188.

58 Ib., 52, 200*ff*.; *Orat.*, 29, 135*ff*.

59 Aristotle, *Rhet.*, III, 8 and 9. Cicero, *De Orat.*, III, 47, 182-4; *Orat.*, 51, 172; 57, 192 and 194; 63, 214; 64, 218; 68, 228.

60 Id., *Brutus*, 8, 32-4; *Orat.*, 13, 40; 52, 174.

61 Id., *Orat.*, 44, 151; Dionysius, *De Isoc.*, 2 (I, 57, 7, U.-R); Demetrius, *On style,* 68;

Quintilian, IX, 4, 35.

62 Cicero, *Orat.*, 49, 165-7; 52, 175-6.

63 E. Lindholm, *Stilistische Studien* (Lund, 1931), pp. 117*ff*.

64 Aristotle, *Rhet.*, III, 8, 3; Isocrates, fr. 6 (II, 275, Benseler-Blass).

65 See *Rom. Orat.*, pp. 358*ff*.; add W. Schmid, *Uber die klassische Theorie und Praxis des antiken Prosarhythmus* (Wiesbaden, 1959).

66 Cicero, *Orat.*, 61, 204*ff*.; 63, 212*ff*.

67 See esp., F. Solmsen in *C.P.*, XXXIII (1938), pp. 390-404.

68 Cicero, *De Orat.*, II, 54, 216-71, 289. See *Rom. Orat.*, pp. 352*ff*.; add A. Haury, *L'Ironie et l'Humeur chez Ciceron* (Leiden, 1955).

69 H.V. Canter in *A.J.P.*, LII (1931), pp. 351-61.

70 Cicero, *Brutus*, 19, 305; 30, 309-10.

71 Id., *Tusc. Disp.*, I, 4, 7.

72 Id., *Ad Q.F.*, III, 3, 4; cf. E.G. Sihler in *A.J.P.*, XXIII (1902), pp. 283-94.

73 Id., *De Orat.*, III, 27, 107-28, 109.

74 Id., *De Fin.*, V, 4, 10; *Tusc. Disp.*, II, 3, 9; *Orat.*, 14, 46; Quintilian, XII, 2, 25. For the history, see H. Throm, *Die Thesis; Ein Beitrag zu ihrer Entstehung und Geschichte* (Paderborn, 1931); cf. Barwick, op. cit., pp. 51-64.

75 Theon, *Rhet. Graec.* (Sp.), II, 69, 1.

76 H. von Arnim, *Dio von Prusa* (Berlin, 1898), pp. 92*ff*.; cf. Philodemus, *Rhet.*, I, 206, 17*ff*., Sudhaus.

77 Theon, II, 120, 15*ff*.; 121, 6*ff*.; 123, 6*ff*.; Quintilian, II, 4, 25; Suetonius, *De Rhet.*, 1 (Republican period). See below, pp. 271-2.

78 Cicero, *De Nat. Deor.*, II, 67, 168.

79 Id., *De Orat.*, 11, 27, 118.

80 Quintilian, II, 1, 11; 4, 27.

81 *Rhet. ad Herenn.*, II, 6, 9-8, 12.

82 Theon, II, 69, 4*ff*., Sp.

83 Apollodorus in Augustine, *Rhet. Lat. Min.*, p. 140, 6*ff*.; Quintilian, X, 5, 13.

84 Cf. Cicero, *De Orat.*, III, 28, 109; Theon, II, 61, 5*ff*., Sp.

85 Cicero's view that the *thesis was* an integral part of a case (*Part. Orat.*, 18, 61; *Top.*, 21, 80) was anticipated by Athenaeus, contemporary of Hermagoras (Quintilian, III, 5, 5). For Hermagoras, cf. Quintilian III, 6, 56 with VII, 4, 2.

86 Cicero, *Brutus*, 93, 322; *Orat.* 14, 45; 36, 126.

87 J. Marquardt-A. Mau, *Das Privatleben der Römer* (Leipzig, 1886), pp. 124*ff*.; H. Blümner, *Römische Privataltertümer* (Munich, 1911), pp. 335*ff*.; W. Warde Fowler, *Social Life at Rome in the Age of Cicero* (London, 1908), pp. 191*ff*.; Marrou, *Hist. Educ.*, pp. 318*ff*.; P.-W., *R.E.*, s.v. 'tirocinium fori'.

88 Marquardt-Mau, pp. 128*ff*.

89 Cf. Servius on Virgil, *Aen.*, V. 546.

90 Cicero, *Pro Cael.*, 5, 11.

91 Ib., 4, 9; Quintilian, XII, 11, 6.

92 Cicero, *De Amic.*, 1, 1; *Brutus*, 89, 306.

93 Tacitus, *Dial.*, 34; Quintilian, X, 5, 19.

94 Seneca the elder, *Contr.*, I, *Praef.* 6.

95 Cicero, *De Orat.*, II, 22, 90-92.

96 See n. 93.

97 Cicero, *Brutus*, 89, 305.

98 Cf. Quintilian, XII, *Praef.* 3.

99 Cicero, *Ad Fam.*, XIII, 1, 2; *De Fin.*, I, 5, 16; cf. A.E. Raubitschek, in *Hesperia*, XVIII (1949), pp. 96-103.

100 Id., *Brutus*, 89, 306.

101 Id., *De Orat.*, I, 22, 104; *Brutus*, 90, 310.

102 Ib., 91, 315-16.

103 See below, c. viii.
104 Ib., 97, 332.
105 Id., *Orat.*, 4, 16; *Tusc. Disp.*, V, 25, 72.
106 Id., *Orat.*, 32, 113.
107 Ib., 29, 102.
108 *Rhet. ad Herenn.*, II, 11, 16; Cicero, *Orat.*, 32, 114; 33, 117.
109 Cicero, *De Orat.*, II, 38, 157-9; *Brutus*, 31, 117-19.
110 Id., *Part. Orat.*, 40, 139.
111 Id., *Orat.*, 33, 118; *Part. Orat.*, 39, 140; cf. Quintilian, XII, 2, 15-20.
112 Cicero, *Orat.*, 34, 119; cf. Quintilian, XII, 2, 20-22.
113 Id., *Pro Mil.*, 31, 84-6.
114 Id., *De Nat. Deor.*, I, 3, 6; cf. *Rom. Orat.*, p. 347.
115 Id., *Orat.*, 3, 12.
116 Id., *Brutus*, 8, 32.
117 Ennius, fr. 433, Vahlen; Cicero, *De Orat.*, II, 37, 156; *Tusc. Disp.*, II, 1, 1; *De Rep.*, I, 18, 30; Gellius, V, 15, 9; 16, 5.
118 Cicero, *De Leg.*, I, 23, 59.

119 Id., *Brutus*, 56, 205-7.
120 Ib., 89, 306; *De Leg.*, I, 4, 13.
121 Id., *De Am.*, 1,1.
122 Gellius, I, 22, 7; Quintilian, XII, 3, 10.
123 Cicero, *Orat.*, 41, 141.
124 Id., *Brutus*, 39, 145; 41, 151.
125 Id., *Orat.*, 41, 142; *De Orat.*, I, 45, 200.
126 Id., *De Orat.*, I, 34, 159; 38, 175; *Orat.*, 34, 120; Quintilian, XII, 3, 1.
127 Id., *De Orat.*, I, 48, 208; 56, 238; 57, 242; 58, 248, 250.
128 Quintilian, XII, 3, 2*ff.*
129 Cicero, *Brutus*, 21, 81; 26, 98; 39, 145; 47, 175; 48, 178-9.
130 Id., *De Orat.*, I, 34, 159; 36, 165; 46, 201.
131 Id., *Orat.*, 34, 120.
132 Cf. *Rom. Orat.*, p. 348.
133 Id., *De Orat.*, II, 12, 51-14, 58; *Brutus*, 3, 14-4, 15; *De Leg.*, I, 2, 5-3, 10.
134 Id., *Brutus*, 43, 161.
135 Ib., 93, 322.

Chapter VIII

1 Cf. L.W. Daly in *A.J.P.*, LXXI (1950), pp. 41-58.
2 Cicero, *De Orat.*, I, 11, 45-7; II, 90, 365, III, 20, 75. Daly, p. 44, confuses the orator Crassus with the financier.
3 Ib., I, 18, 82-19, 85; II, 1, 3; 88, 360.
4 Suetonius, *J.C.*, 4, 1; Plutarch, *Caes.*, 3.
5 Dio Cassius, XLVII, 33, 4; Appian, IV, 67.
6 Cicero, *Brut.*, 97, 332; *Orat.*, 30, 105; *Acad.*, I, 3, 12; Plutarch, *Brut.*, 2, 2-3; 24, 1.
7 Horace, *Epp.*, II, 2, 43-5.
8 Ovid. *Trist.*, I, 2, 77.
9 Suetonius, *Vita Lucani*.
10 Strabo, IV, 1, 5; Cicero, *Pro Flacc.*, 26, 63.
11 Cicero, *Ad Att.*, XII, 32, 2.
12 Ib., X, 11.
13 Id., *De Off.*, II, 13, 45.

14 Id., *Ad Att.*, XII, 7.
15 Cf. D.R. Shackleton Bailey, *Cicero* (London, 1971), pp. 201*ff.*
16 Cicero, *Ad Att.*, XII, 32, 3. On Marcus at Athens, cf. also Tyrrell and Purser, *The Correspondence of Cicero*, V, pp. civ*ff.*; J. Stinchcomb in *C.J.*, XXVIII (1932/3), pp. 441*ff.*
17 Cicero, *Ad Att.*, XIII, 37, 1; XIV, 16, 4; XVI, 1, 5 (Xenon); XV, 15, 4; XV, 17, 1-2 (Eros).
18 Ib., XIII, 1, 1.
19 Ib., XIV, 7, 2; 16, 4.
20 Ib., XIII, 47, 2.
21 Ib., XIV, 7, 2; 11, 2.
22 Ib., XV, 15, 4; 17, 1.
23 Ib., XVI, 1, 5.
24 Ib., XIV, 16, 3.
25 Id., *Ad Fam.*, XII, 16, 1-2.
26 Id., *Ad Att.*, XV, 16; 17, 2.
27 Id., *Ad Fam.*, XVI, 21, 6, with Tyrrell and Purser's note.

28 Plutarch, *Cic.*, 24, 6-7.
29 Cicero, *Ad Fam.*, XVI, 21, 1-5 and 8 (quite illuminating).
30 Plutarch, *Brut.*, 24, 2.
31 Pliny the elder, *N.H.*, XIV, 28, 147; Dio Cassius, XLVI, 18, 5.
32 Seneca the elder, *Suas.*, VII, 13.
33 Cicero, *Ad Brut.*, 2, 6.
34 Appian, IV, 51.
35 Cicero, *De Off.*, II, 13, 45.
36 Cf. Tyrrell and Purser, op. cit., pp. cviii-cix.
37 By Fust and Schöffer at Mainz, and Sweynheim and Pannartz at Subiaco, both in 1465.
38 Cicero, *De Off.*, II, 13, 44.

39 Ib., 45.
40 Ib., III, 2, 6.
41 Ib., I, 32, 116.
42 Seneca the elder, *Contr.*, IV., *Praef.* 4.
43 Cicero, *De Off.*, II, 13, 46.
44 Ib., 14, 48.
45 Ib., I, 24, 122.
46 Id., *Pro Planc.* 12, 29; *Pro Mur.*, 26, 53.
47 Nicolaus of Damascus. *Vit. Caes.*, 3 and 13 (*F. Gr. H.* IIA, pp. 393, 396, Jacoby); cf. Dio Cassius, XLV, 2, 7-8; Enid R. Parker, *A.J.P.*, LXVII (1946), pp. 29*ff*.

Chapter IX

1 See L. Friedländer, *Roman Life and Manners* (Eng. trans. by Freese and Magnus, London, 1908), vol. I, c. 1.
2 Cf. Strabo, XIV, p. 675.
3 Pliny the elder, *N.H.,* VII, 115; XXXV, 9.
4 Suetonius, *J.C.*, 44.
5 Id., *Aug.*, 29; Propertius, II, 31; C.E. Boyd, *Public Libraries and Literary Culture in Ancient Rome* (Chicago, 1915).
6 Friedländer, op. cit., vol. II, c. 2; J.F.D'Alton, *Horace and his Age* (London, 1917), pp. 167*ff*; J. Griffin in *J.R.S.* LXVI (1976), pp. 87*ff*.
7 Tacitus, *Ann.*, XVI, 5, 1.
8 Ib., III, 55, 4; Suetonius, *Vesp.* 2.
9 Seneca the elder, *Contr.*, II, 1, 28.
10 Seneca, *Epp.*, 27, 5-7; Petronius, *Sat.* 48; Lucian, *De mercede conductis*; A.M. Duff, *Freedmen in the Early Roman Empire* (Oxford, 1928).
11 Petronius, *Sat.*, 58.
12 Martial, IX, 73, 7-10.
13 See esp. Hugh Last in *C.A.H.*, X, pp. 434-56.
14 P.E. Corbett, *The Roman Law of Marriage* (Oxford, 1930), pp.228*ff*.; H.F. Jolowicz and B. Nicholas, *Historical Introduction to the*

Study of Roman Law (Cambridge, 1972), pp. 235*ff*.
15 See A.N. Sherwin-White's commentary on the letters of Pliny (Oxford, 1966), p. 558.
16 Notably the *Laudatio Turiae* (edited in the Collection Budé by M. Durry).
17 Seneca the elder, *Contr.*, I, *Praef.*, 8; contrast 16.
18 Columella, I, *Praef.*, 13-17.
19 Quintilian, I, 6, 44; XII, 11, 18.
20 Strabo, V, 3, 8.
21 Horace, *A.P.*, 161-2.
22 Id., *Carm.* I, 8; III, 7, 25-8; 12, 7-9.
23 Cf. ib., III, 2, *init.*
24 Id., *Serm.* II, 2, 9*ff*.; *Epp.* I, 18, 44*ff*. On hunting and military training, Cicero, *N.D.* II, 64, 161; Columella, I, *Praef.* 17. Cf. Polybius XXXI, 29, 5-7 (the younger Scipio).
25 Horace, *Carm.*, III, 24, 51*ff*.
26 Dio Cassius, LII, 26, 1-2.
27 See S.L. Mohler in *T.A.Ph.A.*, LXVIII (1937), pp. 442-79; Marrou, *Hist. Educ.* pp. 299-301, 439-40.
28 Lily Ross Taylor in *J.R.S.*, XIV (1924), pp. 158-71; *O.C.D²*., s.v. 'Iuvenes' (Balsdon).
29 Suetonius, *Aug.*, 43; Dio Cassius,

LV, 10, 6-7; for *ludi iuvenales*, see
Tacitus, *Ann.*, XIV, 15; Suetonius,
Nero, 11, 1; Dio Cassius, LXVI,
15, 2; LXVII, 14, 3.

30 Livy, XXVI, 22, 15.

31 Quintilian, I, 2, 6-8.

32 Seneca, *De Ira*, II, 21; Pliny,
Epp., IV, 2.

33 Suetonius, *Nero*, 37.

34 Seneca, loc. cit; Quintilian, I, 1, 4
and 9; 3, 17.

35 Tacitus, *Dial.*, 20; [Plutarch] *De
lib. educ.*, 7.

36 Tacitus, *Dial*, loc. cit; Quintilian,
I, 2, 8; Juvenal, XIV, 31*ff.*

37 Petronius, *Sat.*, 46.

38 Seneca, *De Prov.*, II. 5.

39 Juvenal, XIV, 189*ff.*

40 [Plutarch], *De lib. educ.*, 13.

41 Martial, I, 17; II, 30; VIII, 17; cf.
Pliny, *Epp.*, V, 13, 6-7; Quintilian,
XII, 7, 11.

42 Tacitus, Dial., 38, *sub fin.*

43 Petronius, *Sat.*, 4.

44 Juvenal, X. 114*ff.*

45 See E. Patrick Parks, *The Roman
Rhetorical Schools as a preparation
for the courts under the early
Empire* (Baltimore, 1945).

46 Petronius, loc. cit.

47 Tacitus, *Dial.*, 30, *init*; cf. Petronius, *Sat.*, 5.

48 Quintilian, II, 1, 1-3.

49 Theon in *Rhet. Graec.* (Sp.), II,
59; Quintilian, I, 10. On Petronius,
loc. cit., see H.L.W. Nelson, *Ein
Unterrichtsprogramm aus Neronischer Zeit* (Netherlands Academy,
Amsterdam, 1956).

50 Seneca the elder, *Contr.*, I, *praef.*
11 and 12; Suetonius, *De Gramm.*,
7; cf. *Rom. Declam.*, p. 31.

51 Seneca the elder, *Contr.* IV, *Praef.*
2 (Pollio); X, *praef.* 4 (Labienus);
Rom. Declam., pp. 39-40. Cf. the
parallel development of *recitatio.*

52 Cicero, *Ad Q.F.*, III, 3, 4.

53 But see Tacitus, *Dial.*, 2; Quintilian, V, 7, 7; Pliny, *Epp.*, VII, 23;
VII, 24, 5.

54 Petronius, *Sat.*, 3; cf. Cicero, *Pro

Cael.*, 17, 41 for the phrase.

55 Tacitus, *Dial.*, 29.

56 Juvenal, VII, 160; Quintilian, X,
5, 21.

57 Quintilian, II, 6, 3.

58 Id., II, 2, 9-12.

59 Id., X, 5, 21; II, 4, 15-16. The last
context shows that parents were
present; M.L. Clarke, *Higher
Education in the Ancient World*
(London, 1971), p. 162, n.200,
omits the reference.

60 Id., II, 2, 3-5.

61 Seneca, *Epp.*, 88, 2; cf. Juvenal,
X, 224; Martial, VII, 62;
Suetonius, *De Gramm.*, 23.

62 Quintilian, I, 2, 4.

63 Marcus Aurelius, *Medit.*, I, 5.

64 Quintilian, I, 2, 9.

65 Ib., 4, 5.

66 Cicero, *Ad Att.*, VI, 1, 12.

67 *C.I.L.*, VI, 8012, *I.L.S.* 7763;
Pliny, *Epp.*, III, 3, 3.

68 Cf. Suetonius, *De Gramm.*, 16.

69 Quintilian, I, 2, 9-31.

70 Contrast, however, Seneca the
elder, *Contr.*, IV, *praef.* 4.

71 Pliny, *Epp.*, V, 16; on all Pliny
references, see the commentary of
A.N. Sherwin-White.

72 *I.L.S.*, 1030.

73 Pliny, *Epp.*, III, 3.

74 Quintilian, I, 2, 3.

75 Pliny, *Epp.*, II, 18.

76 Ib., VII, 24.

77 Ib., VIII, 23.

78 Cf. ib., II, 14.

79 Ib., IV. 13.

80 See further E. de Saint-Denis in
Revue Universitaire, 1946, pp.
9-21.

81 Cf. C. Martha, *Les Moralistes sous
l'Empire romain* (Paris, 1866), c.i.

82 Seneca, *Epp.*, 108, 13-14; Seneca
the elder, *Contr.*, II, 1, 10-13.

83 Persius, *Sat.*, V, 30*ff.*

84 Tacitus, *Agric.*, 4.

85 G. Pire, *Stoicisme et Pédagogie*
(Paris, 1958).

86 Text and translation in the Loeb
Library Plutarch, *Moralia*, vol.1.

PART TWO

Chapter X

1 See works cited in c.v. above, n. 2.

2 J. Delorme, *Gymnasion* (Paris, 1955), pp. 324-30.

3 Philostratus, *Vit. Soph.*, p. 618 (Smyrna); *C.I.G.* 3376 (Smyrna); Libanius, I, 72 (I, 118, 19, F., Nicomedia); *Epp.*, 88 (Antioch).

4 Libanius, I, 102 (I, 133, 5, F.); cf. A.F. Norman, *Libanius' Autobiography* (Oxford, 1965), p. 167 and esp. pp. 175-6.

5 This was itself, at Antioch, a temple; cf. Libanius, V, 42, 46, 52 (I, 317, 11; 318, 16; 320, 8, F.), and see J.W.H. Walden, *The Universities of Ancient Greece* (London/ New York, 1912), pp. 267*ff*.

6 The evidence from classical Greece is sparse and inconclusive; cf. F.A.G. Beck, *Greek Education* (London 1964), pp. 88-9.

7 See below, p. 161; but we do not know where even Quintilian taught.

8 *C.G.L.* II, 475, 16; cf. *Edict. Dioclet.*, VII, 66.

9 Dio Chrysostom, XX, 9.

10 Cicero, *De leg. agr.*, II, 96; Tacitus, *Ann.*, XV, 38; Juvenal, III, 236; VI, 78; Suetonius, *Nero*, 38, 3; cf. Platner-Ashby, *Topographical Dictionary of Ancient Rome* (Oxford, 1929), pp. 575-6.

11 Justinus, XXI, 5.

12 Quintilian, I, 4, 27.

13 Horace, *Epp.* I, 20, esp. 17*ff*.

14 Cf. article cited c. iv above, n. 28.

15 Cicero, *Pro Mur.*, 13; Horace, *Serm.*, I, 9, 59; *A.P.*, 244; *Epp.* I, 17, 58-9; Virgil, *Ecl.*, III, 26-7; Galen, IX, 823 K.

16 W. Helbig, *Wandgemälde Campaniens* (Leipzig, 1868), no. 1492; O. Jahn, in *Abhandlungen d. sachs. Gesellsch. d. Wiss.* V, 1870, pp. 288*ff*. and pl. I, no.3; Dar-Sag, *Dict. Ant.*, s.v. 'educatio', fig.2614. Mau-Kelsey, *Pompeii, its Life and Art* (New York, 1902), pp. 54-6.

17 M. della Corte, *Case ed Abitanti di Pompei* (Rome, 1954), p. 186.

18 Demosthenes, *De Corona*, 129; *De Fals. Leg.*, 249, 281.

19 Suetonius, *De Gramm.* 15

20 Helbig, op. cit., no. 1499; Dar. Sag., fig. 2610. I follow the interpretation of E. Pottier in Dar. Sag., p. 482, n. 313, rather than that of Helbig, and Jahn, p. 272.

21 Suetonius, *De Gramm.*, 7.

22 Cicero, *Brutus*, 56, 207; Gellius, XVI, 8, 2.

23 Suetonius, *De Gramm.*, 24.

24 Ib., 17.

25 Cicero, *De Nat. Deor.* I, 6, 15; *Ad Fam.*, VII, 23, 3.

26 Most notably, in the 'House of the Faun'.

27 'Si ti(bi) Cicero do(let), vapulabis'; other *graffiti* include the opening words of Virgil, *Aen.*, II. See M. della Corte, op. cit., p. 85.

28 Augustine, *Conf.*, V, 12, 1.

29 Libanius, I, 102 (I, 133, 2, F.). Grammar schools at Carthage were also in the Forum (Augustine, *Conf.*, I, 16).

30 Cf. Marrou, *Hist. Educ.*, p. 362 (primary), 370 (secondary).

31 Livy, III, 44, 6; Dionysius, *Ant. Rom.*, XI, 28.

32 Demosthenes, *De Corona*, 169; della Corte, op. cit., p. 186.

33 Note the *septem tabernae* of Livy, XXVI, 27, 2.

34 M. della Corte in *Bulletino della Commissione Archaeologica Comunale di Roma*, LXI (1933), pp. 110-12.

37 Suetonius, *De Gramm.*, 18.

38 *S.H.A., Saturn.*, 10, 'pergulas magistrales'.

39 Marquardt-Mau, *Das Privatleben der Römer* (Leipzig, 1886), French trans., p. 110, n. 5; Jullien, *Les Professeurs ...* pp.114-15; H. Blümner, *Römische Privat-Altertümer* (Munich, 1911), p. 316; A.S. Wilkins, *Roman Education* (Cam-

bridge, 1905), p. 44; Marrou, *Hist. Educ.*, p. 362.

40 Augustine, *Conf.*, I, 13.

41 Martial, VII, 61, with Friedländer's note.

42 Suetonius, *Aug.*, 94.

43 Lucilius, frag. 489 M. (*pergula pictorum*); Pliny, *N.H.*, XXXV, 10, 36.

44 *Dig.*, IX, 3, 5, 12.

45 Fronto, *Ad M. Caes.* IV, 12 (p. 67, van den Hout), *Dig.*, V, 1, 19, 2, 'tabernulam, pergulam'.

46 *C.I.L.* IV, 1136, 138.

47 A. Mau in *Römische Mittheilungen*, II (1887), pp. 214-20; Mau-Kelsey, *Pompeii*, pp. 276-7; 489-90; P.-W., *R.E.*, s.v. 'pergula', 2.

48 Mau (op. cit. pp. 216-7) suggests that the *pergula* was originally an external upper gallery.

49 Cited by Mayor on Juvenal, XI, 137.

50 Cf. Carcopino, *Daily Life in Ancient Rome* (London, 1941), p. 29, 'loggias (*pergulae*) resting on the porticos'. Tertullian, *Adv. Valent.*, 7, 'aliis atque aliis pergulis superstructis', shows that they could be built one above another.

51 Pliny, *N.H.*, XXI, 8.

52 Livy, I, 35, 10; corroborated by Dionysius, *Ant. Rom.*, III, 67, 4.

53 Livy, IX, 40; XXVI, 11, 7; 27, 2; XL, 51, 5. Cf. XLI, 27, 12 (elsewhere in Italy).

54 See Dar-Sag., x.v. 'maenianum,' fig. 4778, for a good illustration, and P.-W, *R.E.* s.v. 'maenianum.'

55 Paul ex Fest., p. 120, L.; Isidore, *Orig.*, XV, 3. They were often used as sun-rooms (*solaria*); cf. K. Sittl, in *Archiv für lateinische Lexicographie*, 1888, pp. 290-93. Note Suetonius, *Nero*, 16.

56 Cicero, *Acad, pr.*, II, 22, 70; cf. Varro in Pliny, *N.H.*, XXXV, 37, 113.

57 Vitrubius, V, 1, 2.

58 *Cod. Theod.*, XIII, 4, 4.

59 Tacitus, *Ann.*, III, 43, 1, and Furneaux ad loc.; cf. T.J. Haarhoff, *Schools of Gaul* (Johannesburg, 1958), p. 38; W. Brandes, *Arch. lat. Lex.*, 1888, p. 519.

60 Eumenius, *Pan. Lat.*, V, 20.

61 *C.G.L.*, III, 380, 49-54.

62 E. Ziebarth, op. cit., pp. 99*ff*.; J. Delorme, op. cit., pp. 326-7; G.E. Bean, *Aegean Turkey, an archaeological guide* (London, 1966), Pl. 54.

63 Cicero, *De Fin.*, V, 2, 4.

64 Vitruvius, V, 11, 2.

65 H.-I. Marrou, in *Mél. d'Arch. et d'Hist.*, XLIX (1932), pp. 93-110; cf. *Hist. Educ.*, p. 381.

66 Venantius Fortunatus, *Carm.*, II, 18, 7-8; VII, 8, 26.

67 *Cod. Theod.*, XIV, 9, 3; XV, 1, 53.

68 In two MSS of [Quintilian], *Decl. maior.*, X, the *subscriptio* reads: 'legi et emendavi ... in schola fori Traiani'; hence Marrou rejects the location of the *schola* in Trajan's Library, as this was not in the forum proper. The chief difficulty is that there does not appear to be any identification of a manuscript-room attached to the exedra.

69 Tacitus, *Dial.*, 9, 3; Juvenal, VII, 39-40, 45-7; Pliny, *Epp.*, VIII, 12, 2.

70 Seneca the elder, *Contr.*, VII, *Praef.* 8; Eunapius, *Vit. Soph.*, p. 483.

71 Vacca, *Vita Lucani*, 'in Pompeii theatro'; Petronius, 90; Gellius, XVIII, 5, 2.

72 F. Schemmel in *Woch. klass. Phil.*, 1919, 91-5, and *Phil. Woch.*, XLI (1921), 982-4.

73 Sidonius Apollinaris, *Epp.*, II, 9, 4; IX, 14, 2.

74 Philostratus, *Vit. Soph.*, p. 589 (declamation); *S.H.A.*, *Pertinax*, 11, 3 (recitation), *Gord.*, 3, 4 (declamation); *Sev. Alex.*, 35, 2 (declamation and recitation).

75 Aurelius Victor, *Caes.*, 14, 1-3.

Chapter XI

1 Cf. e.g. John Brinsley, *Ludus Literarius or The Grammar Schoole* (1612), ed. E.T. Campagnac (Liverpool/London, 1917), pp. 296-7; Nicholas Carlisle, *The Endowed Grammar Schools* (London, 1818), I, p. 515; E. de Selincourt on Wordsworth's *Prelude*, Book ii, 349*ff.* notes: 'The daily work in Hawkshead School began — by Archbishop Sandys' ordinance — at 6 a.m. in summer, and 7 a.m. in winter'.

2 Martial, XIV, 223.

3 *C.G.L.*, III, 380, 66*ff.*

4 Suetonius, *De Gramm.*, 4.

5 Augustine, *Conf.*, I, 16.

6 Suetonius, loc. cit., 9.

7 *C.G.L.*, III, 377, 9*ff.*

8 Cf. Horace, *Serm.*, I, 10, 91.

9 Ib., I, 6, 82.

10 Martial, X, 62, 5.

11 N. Carlisle, op. cit.

12 Juvenal, VII, 227, with commentators.

13 Schol. ad loc. (p. 134, Wessner).

14 So Friedländer in his edn (Leipzig, 1895); Marrou, *Hist. Educ.*, p.370.

15 Suetonius, *Cal.*, 34, 2; Porphyrio on Horace, *Serm.*, I, 4, 21-2.

16 Blümner, op. cit., p. 318. n.7.

17 Cf. Vitruvius, VII, 3, 4; 4, 4.

18 See further F.G. Kenyon, *Books and Readers in Ancient Greece and Rome* (Oxford, 1951); W. Schubart, *Das Buch bei den Griechen und Römern* (1921, re-issued Heidelberg, 1962); Th. Birt, *Das Antike Buchwesen* Berlin, 1882, rpd. 1959), and *Die Buchrolle in der Kunst* (Leipzig, Teubner, 1907); E.G. Turner, *Greek Papyri* (Oxford, 1968).

19 Horace, *Serm.*, I, 10, 72; Cicero, *In Verr.*, II, 2, 101.

20 Martial, IV, 26, 11.

21 Pliny, *N.H.*, XXVII, 28, 52.

22 Horace, *Serm.*, II, 3, 2; *A.P.*, 389; Birt, *Das Antike Buchwesen*, p. 59.

23 Quintilian, X, 3, 31*ff.*; cf. Martial, XIV, 5, 1.

24 F.G. Kenyon in *J.H.S.*, XXIX (1909), p. 39. *C.G.L.*, III, 382, 34 seems dubious evidence.

25 H. Stuart Jones, *The Sculptures of the Museo Capitolino* (Oxford, 1912), I, pp. 165*ff.*, and II, Pl.41; P.-W. *R.E.*, s.v. 'Tabula Iliaca'.

26 E.g. Jullien, op. cit., p. 120; Wilkins, op. cit., p. 45.

27 Cf. Blümner, op. cit., p. 328, n.8; Stuart Jones, p. 171, and Lippold in P.-W., *R.E.*, col. 1893, doubt any connection with the schools; Marrou, p. 522, disagrees.

28 Cf. Marquardt, op. cit., p. 130 (alternatively, he thinks, in temples).

29 Pliny the elder, *N.H.*, XXXV, 40, 144; Vitruvius, VII, 5, 22. Also in temples; cf. Virgil, *Aen.*, I, 456, with R.G. Austin's note.

30 Pliny the elder, *N.H.*, III, 2, 17; Dio Cassius, LV, 8, 4; Schanz-Hosius, §§332-3.

31 Eumenius, *Pro rest. schol.*, 20.

32 Propertius, IV, 3, 37.

33 Vegetius, III, 6; cf. J. Oliver Thomson, *History of Ancient Geography* (Cambridge, 1948); pp. 322*ff.*

34 Thomson, op. cit., pp. 379*ff.*

35 Suetonius, *Dom.*, 10; Florus, *Praef.* 3; cf. Plutarch, *Theseus*, 1.

36 Strabo, II, 5, 17; Vitruvius, VIII, 2, 6.

37 Lucan, I, 396-465 (Gallic tribes); II, 399-438 (Italian rivers).

38 Cf. L. Bourgery in *Rev. de Phil.*, 3rd ser., II (1928), pp. 25-40; C.W. Mendell in *Yale Class. Stud.*, VIII (1942) pp. 3-22.

39 Seneca, *N.Q.*, IVa, 1; Lucan, X, 188-331.

40 Martial, X, 60.

41 Diogenes Laertius, VI, 69; Athenaeus, VIII, 41, p. 348.

42 Libanius, XXXIV, 14 (III, 197, 20, F.).

43 Suetonius, *De Gramm.*, 16 and 24.

44 Quintilian, I, 2, 1, and 2, 9, 15, 16, 29.

45 Libanius, I, 37, and 102 (I, 102, and I, 133 F.)

46 Seneca the elder, *Contr.*, I, *Praef,* 2.

47 See below, p. 153.

48 *Dig.*, XVII, 2, 71.

49 *S.H.A.*, *Pert.*, 1.

50 Cicero, *Ad Fam.*, IX, 18, 4; Augustine, *Conf.*, VIII, 6, 13; Ausonius, *Prof.* 22.

51 Quintilian, II, 4, 3; for Libanius, F. Schemmel in *N.J.Kl.Alt.*, XX (1907), pp. 56*ff.*; P. Wolf, *Vom Schulwesen der Spätantike* (Baden-Baden, 1952), pp. 60*ff.*; P. Petit, *Les Etudiants de Libanius* (Paris, 1956) pp. 84*ff.*

52 Petronius, *Sat.*, 81; cf. Ausonius, *Prof.*, 6, 6-12.

53 Juvenal, VII, 151 and 240.

54 *C.G.L.*, III, 226, 2*ff.*; 382, 35-53.

55 Libanius, XXXVI, 10 (III, 231, 24*ff.*, F.); *Epp.* 139; Schemmel, loc. cit.

56 Quintilian, XII, 5, 6; Pliny, *Epp.*, II, 14, 10; Carcopino, op. cit., pp. 187*ff.*

57 *C.G.L.*, III, 382, 47*ff.*

58 Seneca the elder, *Contr.*, I, *Praef.* 24; Quintilian, I, 2, 23-4.

59 Suetonius, *De Gramm.*, 17.

60 Ziebarth, *Schulwesen*, pp. 18-19, 59, 121, 138*ff.*; A.H.M. Jones, op. cit., p. 352, n. 25; Nilsson, op. cit., p. 48.

61 Plutarch, *Sert.*, 14, 2-3.

62 Id., *Cic.*, 2, 2.

63 Nepos, *Att.*, 1, 3; cf. below, c.xvi.

64 Martial, IX, 68, 1-2; cf. Ausonius, *Epp.*, 22, 33-4.

65 See Jullien, *Les Professeurs ...*, pp. 147*ff.*

66 Ovid, *Trist.*, II, 369-70.

67 Martial, I, 35, 1-3; III, 69; and esp. VIII, 3, 13-16.

68 Quintilian, I, 8, 5*ff.*

69 Probus, *Vit. Pers.*

70 Jullien, op. cit., p. 138.

71 Quintilian, I, 1, 17-19; 4, 1.

72 Cf. below, p. 269.

73 Quintilian, I, 4, 1.

74 Cf. below, c. xviii *init.*

75 Probus, *Vit. Pers.*

76 Persius, V, 30*ff.*

77 Quintilian, II, 2, 3-4 and 14.

78 *Cod. Theod.*, XIV, 9, 1; for more mature students, cf. Walden, op. cit., pp. 292-3.

79 Philostratus, *Vit. Soph.*, p. 604; cf. Tacitus, *Dial.*, 35, 3.

80 Plutarch, *De rect. aud. rat.*, *init.*

81 Lucian, *Paras.*, 61; Apuleius, *Met.*, X, 5; *C.G.L.*, III, 377, 72.

82 [Lucian] *Am.*, 44-5.

83 Martial, IX, 29, 7; XII, 57, 5; Ausonius, *Epp.*, 22, 28; cf. Apuleius, loc. cit.

84 *C.G.L.*, III, 378, 8-21.

85 Pliny the elder, *N.H.*, IX, 8, 25.

86 Ausonius, *Epp.*, 13, 9-10.

87 Augustine, *Conf.*, VI, 11.

88 Libanius, *Orat.*, I, 108 (I, i, 135, F.); XLIII, 19 (III, 347, 17, F.); LI, 13 (IV, 12, 16, F.); LVIII, 9 (IV, 185, 14, F.); Walden, op cit., pp. 278-9.

89 Id., I, 104 (I, i, 134, 9, F.); XXXII, 9 (III, 153, 11, F.); XXXVII, 1 (III, 239, 1, F.); so Acacius, in *Epp.* 274; cf. A.F. Norman's edn of *Orat.* I, p. 177.

90 Strabo, XIV, p. 650; Suetonius, *De Gramm.*, 4.

91 Quintilian, I, 12, 13.

92 Libanius, *Progymn.*, 3 (VIII, 86, 5, F.); cf. below,.p. 259.

93 Nonius Marcellus, p. 316, 19*ff.* L. (from Varro); Festus, p. 177, L. L. Halkin in *Revue Belge de phil. et hist.*, 1932, pp. 121-30 argues that the primary schools only thus benefited.

94 Suetonius, *De Gramm.*, 7.

95 Martial, V, 84; Pliny, *Epp.*, VIII, 7.

96 Horace, *Epp.*, II, 2, 197; Juvenal, X, 114-15; Symmachus, *Epp.*, V, 85.

97 Martial, X, 62.

98 *Cod. Theod.*, II, 8, 19 (A.D. 389).

99 In the three weeks between the two festivals, the law-courts remained open, and St Augustine still taught rhetoric at that time; cf. *Conf.*, IX, 2.

100 Walden, op. cit., pp. 279-80.
101 Libanius, *Orat.*, XLIII, 14 (III, 344, 24, F.).
102 *C.G.L.*, III, 380, 29-38.
103 Ib., 377, 4-8; 380, 55-9, and 72-381, 19.
104 Quintilian, II, 9, 1-2.
105 Cicero, *Pro Planc.*, 32, 81; Seneca, *De Ben.*, VI, 15, 1-2.
106 Ib., III, 3, 4; VII, 28, 2.
107 *C.I.L.*, V. 7834; VI, 9449 (former pupils) VI, 9454; II, 3872 (freed-men); VI, 9450 (friend); VI, 9445-6; X, 3961 (wife).
108 Nepos, *Att.*, 1 and 10, 2-3; Ovid, *Ex Pont.*, IV, 12, 20; cf. *C.I.L.*, X, 6544 (schoolfellow).
109 Nicolaus of Damascus, *F.G.H.*, IIA, 393, 26*ff*.
110 Persius, III, 44*ff*. (not a reference to truancy).
111 Cf. F.G. Kenyon, in *J.H.S.*, XXIX (1909), p. 39.
112 Lucian, *Somn.*, 2.
113 Mau-Kelsey, op. cit., p. 549.
114 T. Woody, op. cit., p. 591.
115 G. Wissowa in *Römische Mittheilungen*, V (1890), pp. 3-11.
116 Cato, fr. 205 (*O.R.F.*, p. 83).
117 Martial, IX, 29, 5*ff*.; 68, 4; XII, 57, 4-5.
118 Quintilian, II, 5, 6; cf. Pliny, *Epp.*, II, 18.
119 *Anth. Lat.*, II, p. 268 (Burman).
120 Varro, p. 251, Riese; R. Müller, edn of Varro, *de liberis educandis*
(Leipzig, 1938), pp. 52-3.
121 Seneca the elder, *Contr.*, IV, *Praef.* 11; Juvenal, VII, 237*ff*.
122 Valerius Maximus, III, 1, 3.
123 Dio Cassius, XLI, 39, 4.
124 Juvenal, VII, 213-4; cf. Augustine, *Conf.*, V, 8 (Carthage).
125 Plutarch, *De rect. aud. rat.*, 13, p. 44d and 45d; 15, p. 46a; 17, p.47d; 18, p. 48a.
126 Cicero, *Rosc. Com.*, 11, 31.
127 Seneca, *Epp.*, 94, 9.
128 Ausonius, *Epp.*, 22, 2, 11, 14, 25.
129 Pliny the elder, *N.H.*, XIII, 42, 123.
130 Ovid, *Am.*, I, 13, 17-18; Augustine, *Solil.*, II, 20; Fulgentius, *Myth.*, I, p. 608.
131 Lucian, *Par.*, 13.
132 Juvenal, I, 15.
133 Martial, X, 62, 8-9; Ausonius, *Epp.*, 22, 30; *Anth. Pal.*, VI, 293.
134 Pliny the elder, *N.H.*, IX, 39, 77.
135 Cicero, *Ad Fam.*, VII, 25, 1.
136 Horace, *Epp.*, II, 1, 70; cf. Suetonius, *De Gramm.*, 9.
137 Varro, p. 250, Riese.
138 Seneca, *De Clem.*, I, 16.
139 Quintilian, I, 3, 14-17.
140 (Plutarch), *De lib. educ.*, 12.
141 Ausonius, *Epp.*, 22, 66-79.
142 Herondas, III.
143 F. Gladstone Bratton, *A History of Egyptian Archaeology* (London, 1967), p. 253.
144 Augustine, *Conf.*, I, 9 and 10.

Chapter XII

1 Aristotle, *Eth. Nic.*, IX, 1, 6-7.
2 Lucian, *Rhet. Praec.*, 9 *sub fin*,: Philostratus, *Vit. Soph.*, p. 604.
3 On the legal validity of 'stipulation', see J.A. Crook, *Law and Life of Rome* (London, 1967), pp. 207-8; for apprenticeship-contracts (e.g. to learn shorthand) in papyri, cf. ib., pp. 200-202, and C.A. Forbes in *T.A. Ph. A.* LXXXVI (1955), pp. 328-34.
4 Suetonius, *De Gramm.*, 7. Isocrates, *Against the Sophists*, 5
mentions deposit in advance with a third party.
5 Juvenal, VII, 158, with Mayor's note; add Libanius, XLIII, 6 (III, 340, 14, F.).
6 Suetonius, *De Gramm.*, 9.
7 Cf. Libanius, XXXI, 29-30 (III, 139, 1*ff*. F.).
8 Cf. id., III, 33 (I, 277, 9*ff*. F.).
9 Quintilian, XII, 11, 14.
10 Ovid, *Fasti*, III, 829.
11 Juvenal, VII, 203; R.P. Robinson in *C. W.* XV (1921/2), pp. 57-61.

12 Ulpian, *Dig.*, L. 13, 1, 1 and 6.
13 Juvenal, VII, 228-9.
14 H.F. Jolowicz and Barry Nicholas, op. cit., p. 330, n. 3 and p. 396, n. 5.
15 Juvenal, VII, 166*ff*.
16 Horace, *Serm*, I, 6, 75; Theophrastus, *Characters*, XXX (Greece), and Herondas, *Mimes*, III, 8-10 (Alexandria).
17 Lucian, *Hermotimus*, 80.
18 Augustine, *Conf.*, V, 12 and 22; Libanius, XLIII *passim*.
19 Stobaeus, *Ecl.* II, 31, 97 (II, 218, Wachsmuth).
20 Juvenal, VII, 218-9.
21 Libanius, XXIV, 30 (II, 205, 19 F); LVIII, 36 (IV, 198, 1); *Epp.* 405 (X, 400, 8).
22 Ovid, *Fasti*, III, 809*ff*.; Tertullian, *De Idol.*, 10.
23 Macrobius, I, 12, 7.
24 Varro, *De Re Rustica*, III, 2, 18.
25 Ib., II, 4, 17; Festus, p. 157, L.
26 *C.G.L.*, V. 605, 16; cf. G. Esau, *Glossae ad rem librariam et institutionem scholasticam pertinentes* (Diss., Marburg, 1914), p. 19.
27 *P. Giessen*, 80; Edgar and Hunt, *Select Papyri* (Loeb Library), I, no. 116. Cf. also Ziebarth, *Aus dem griechischen Schulwesen* (Berlin, 1914), pp. 114-15.
28 Tertullian, loc. cit; Juvenal, X, 116.
29 Diocletian, *Max.*, VII, 65*ff*.
30 See n. 16 above.
31 *C.I.L.*, X, 3969, 'testamenta scripsit cum fide'; cf. H. Nissen in *Hermes*, I (1866), pp. 147*ff*.; H.-I. Marrou, ΜΟΥΣΙΚΟΣ ΑΝΗΡ (Rome, 1964), pp. 46-7.
32 Juvenal, VII, 243.
33 Seyffert-Nettleship-Sandys, *Dict. Class. Ant.* (London, 1894), s.v. 'Coinage'.
34 *Schol. in Iuv. vetustiora*, ed. P. Wessner (rpd Stuttgart, 1967), p. 135; cf. *S.H.A., Vit. M. Ant.*, 11.
35 Cf. Martial, X, 74; Friedländer, op. cit., vol. 2, p. 24.
36 Juvenal, VII, 171.
37 Suetonius, *Claud.*, 21, 5.
38 Fronto, p. 17, van den Hout.
39 Cf. M.L. Clarke in *C.R., N.S.* XXIII (1973), p. 12.
40 Mommsen in *Ephemeris Epigraphica*, VII, pp. 388*ff*., esp. 413-4 (cited by E.G. Hardy in his note); Friedländer, op. cit., vol. 2, p. 53.
41 So Marrou, *Hist. Educ.*, p. 551, M.L. Clarke (n. 39 above), and others.
42 Philostratus, *Vit. Soph.*, p. 604.
43 *Anth. Pal.*, IX, 174, 9-10; cf. Alan Cameron in *C.R., N.S.* XV (1965), pp. 257-8.
44 Schol. on Juvenal, VII, 241 was first adduced in *Proc. Class. Assoc.*, XLVIII (1951), p. 30.
45 So, rightly, C. Barbagallo, *Lo Stato e l'istruzione pubblica nell' impero Romano* (Catania, 1911), p. 91, n.1.
46 Suetonius, *De Gramm.*, 7.
47 Ib., 9.
48 Ib., 8.
49 Ib., 11.
50 Ib., 3, sub fin.
51 Ib., 9; cf. Juvenal, III, 200*ff*.
52 Ib., 20.
53 Ib., 15.
54 Ib., 14, from Cicero, *Ad Att.*, XII, 26, 2.
55 Ib., 17.
56 Ib., 23.
57 Juvenal, VII, 220-24.
58 Pliny the elder, *N.H.*, XIV, 5, 48-52.
59 Suidas, s.v. 'Epaphroditos'.
60 Still in the Palazzo Altieri, Rome, though the Collection is now dispersed.
61 Juvenal, VII, 217.
62 Cicero, *Pro Flacco*, 46-7.
63 Philostratus, *Vit. Soph.*, p. 591.
64 Isocrates, *Against the Sophists,* 9.
65 Seneca the elder, *Contr.*, IX, 3, 14.
66 Juvenal, VII, 174-5.
67 Barbagallo, op. cit., p. 88.
68 See further Mommsen — Marquardt, *Manuel des Antiquités romaines* (Paris, 1888), X, pp. 160*ff*.

69 Libanius, XXI, 25 *ff*.
70 Id., III, 6 (I, 269, 20 F.).
71 Id., LI, 14-15 (IV, 13, 1*ff*. F.).
72 Suetonius, *De Rhet.*, 1.
73 Tacitus, *Ann.*, III, 66;
Bornecque, *Les Déclamations et les Déclamateurs d'après Sénèque le Père* (Lille, 1902), pp. 176-7.
74 Juvenal, VII, 197-8.
75 Pliny, *Epp.*, IV, 11, 1.
76 Juvenal, VII, 186*ff*.
77 Philostratus, *Vit. Soph*; see G.W. Bowersock, *Greek Sophists in the Roman Empire* (Oxford, 1969).
78 Juvenal, III, 74; Pliny, *Epp.*, II, 3; Philostratus, p. 513.
79 Philostratus, *Vit. Soph.*, p. 519 (Scopelian), 600 (Apollonius of Naucratis).
80 See E. Ziebarth, op. cit., n. 27 above: A.H.M. Jones, op. cit., pp. 220-26.
81 See esp., J. Delorme, op. cit., ch. xi (pp. 316-36).
82 See Ziebarth, p. 60, Delorme, p. 318.
83 Ziebarth, pp. 63*ff*.
84 Pliny, *Epp.*, IV, 13, 6.
85 Strabo, IV, 1, 5.
86 See below, n. 115.
87 Seneca the elder, *Contr.*, II, 5, 13 (cf. Porphyrio on Horace, *Epp.* I, 5, 9); X, *Praef.*, 10; II, 6, 12.
88 Tacitus, *Agricola*, 4, 2-3.
89 See Mayor's note on Juvenal, XV, 111.
90 Tacitus, *Ann.*, III, 43.
91 Suetonius, *De Rhet.*, sub fin. (p. 36, Brugnola).
92 Quintilian, X, 1, 118 (cf. Peterson's note on X, 1, 86); X, 3, 13.
93 Suetonius, *Calig.*, 20; cf. Juvenal, I, 44, with Mayor's note.
94 See Gudeman's edn (Berlin, 1914)), pp. 66*ff*.
95 Tacitus, *Agric.*, 21, 2.
96 Juvenal, XV, 112.
97 Cf. the series of articles by H. de la Ville de Mirmont in *Bulletin Hispanique*, XII (1910), XIV (1912), XV (1913).
98 Vacca, *Vita Lucani.*
99 *C.I.L.*, II, 2236 (*grammaticus*, Corduba); 1738 (*rhetor,* Cadiz); 3872 (*grammaticus,* Saguntum); 5079 (*grammaticus*, Asturica).
100 *C.I.L.*, II, 2892 (Tricio).
101 Pliny, *Epp.*, X, 60; *C.I.L.*, V, 3433 (*grammaticus*, Verona); 5278 (*grammaticus*, Como).
102 A.H.M. Jones, *The Later Roman Empire* (Oxford, 1964), II, pp. 757*ff*.
103 Libanius, XXXI *passim*.
104 *Cod. Iust.*, X, 52, 2.
105 Ib., 7; cf. Lucian, *Eun.*, 2-3, and J.W.H. Walden, op. cit., pp. 135*ff*.
106 *Cod. Theod.*, XIII, 3, 6; *Cod. Iust.*, X, 52, 7; so, for physicians, Ulpian, *Dig.*, L, 9, 1; cf. Pliny, *Epp.*, X, 58.
107 Cf. St Augustine, *Conf.*, V, 13.
108 Pliny, *Epp.*, IV, 13, 6.
109 *Cod. Iust.*, X, 52, 2; cf. Libanius, LXII, 6 (IV, 348, 13 F.).
110 Dio Cassius, LIII, 30, 3.
111 See John Scarborough, *Roman Medicine* (London, 1969), p. 132.
112 Suetonius, *J.C.*, 42, 1.
113 Id., *Aug.*, 42, 3.
114 Barbagallo op. cit., p. 46*ff*., considered that such exemptions probably dated back to Nero, but subsequent scholars deduce much less from *Dig.* L, 4, 18, 30.
115 See the full discussion by R. Herzog in *Sitz. preuss. Akad.*, 1935, pp. 967-1019.
116 *Dig.*, XXVII, 1, 6, 8-9. On Bowersock, op. cit., pp. 32-3, see Miriam Griffin's review in *J.R.S.* LXI (1971), pp. 279-80.
117 See further, Barbagallo, op. cit., pp. 50-55.
118 Pliny, *Epp.*, X, 58, 1.
119 Cf. *Dig.*, XXVII, 1, 6, 7; L, 5, 8, 4.
120 *Dig.*, XXVII, 1, 6, 1-4.
121 Ib., 10. But exemption was granted if they taught at Rome, *Dig.*, L. 5, 9.
122 *Dig.*, L. 4, 11, 4; L, 5, 2, 8.
123 *Eph. Epigr.* III, 170 (Hübner),

187-8 (Mommsen); Barbagallo, pp. 56*ff*.; J.S. Reid. *The Munici-palities of the Roman Empire* (Cambridge, 1913), pp. 323-4, 461.

124 Suetonius, *Aug,* 29 (Palatine); Dio Cassius XLIX, 43, 8 (Porticus Octaviae); Suetonius, *Tib.*, 74; Gellius, V, 21, 9 and XVI, 8, 2 (Templum Pacis); Suetonius, *Dom.* 20.

125 Suetonius, *Nero*, 12; Tacitus, *Ann.*, XIV, 20-21 (*Neronia*) Suetonius, *Dom.*, 4, 4 (*certamen Capitolinum*).

126 Suetonius, *De Gramm.*, 17; Tacitus, *Ann.*, XIV, 52*ff*.

127 Suetonius, *Vesp.*, 18. Zonaras, XI, 17c adds the limitation 'at Rome'; cf. Barbagallo, pp. 83-4.

128 See Barbagallo, pp. 89-90 for some examples.

129 Philostratus, *Vit. Soph.*, p. 589.

130 Jerome, *Chron.*, on the year A.D. 68.

131 Quintilian, I, init.

132 Id., IV, *praef.* On Quintilian's career, see Schanz-Hosius II, pp. 745-6; cf. below, c. xx, n.4.

134 Tacitus, *Agric.*, 2, 1 and 45, 1.

135 Suetonius, *Dom.*, 10, 3.

136 Dio Cassius, LIX, 20, 6; cf. Juvenal, VII, 203*ff*.

137 Dio Cassius, LXVII, 12, 5.

138 Pliny, *Paneg.*, 47.

139 Philostratus, *Vit. Soph.*, pp. 488 and 532.

140 *S.H.A., Hadr.*, 16, 8-10.

141 Philostratus, *Vit. Soph.*, p. 524 (Dionysius of Miletus); pp. 531, 533 (Polemo).

142 *S.H.A., Hadr.*, 16, 11.

143 Juvenal, VII, 1.

PART THREE

Chapter XIII

1 Dionysius, *De Dem.*, 52; *De Comp. Verb.*, 25; Manilius, II, 755*ff*., with Housman's notes.

2 Quintilian, I, 1, 21*ff*.; Jerome, *Epp.*, 107.

3 J.G. Milne in *J.H.S.*, XXVIII (1908), pp. 121-32; P. Beudel, *Quomodo Graeci liberos docuerint, papyris, ostracis, tabulis ... illustratur* (Münster, 1911); E. Ziebarth, *Aus der antiken Schule* (Bonn, 1913), in Lietzmann's *Kleine Texte*; P. Collart in *Chronique d'Egypte*, XI (1936), pp. 489-507; Marrou, *Hist. Educ.*, pp. 210*ff*.; G. Zalateo in *Aegyptus*, XLI (1961), pp. 160-248; R.A. Pack, *The Greek and Roman Literary Texts from Greco-Roman Egypt*, 2nd edn (Ann Arbor, 1967), pp. 137*ff*.

4 O. Guéraud et P. Jouget, *Un Livre d'Ecolier* (Cairo, 1938); Pack², no.2642; cf. Marrou, op. cit., p. 516.

5 Cicero, *De Leg.*, II, 23, 59; Augustine, *Conf.*, I, 13.

6 Athenaeus, X, p. 453d; F.A.G. Beck, op. cit., pp. 114-15.

7 Jerome, *Epp.*, 107, 4.

8 Columella, X, 251; Housman on Manilius, II, 756.

9 Xenophon, *Oecon.*, VIII, 14; *Mem.*, IV, 4, 7; Plato, *Polit.*, 275c.

10 Quintilian, I, 1, 24-5.

11 Horace, *A.P.*, 180.

12 Quintilian, I, 1, 26; Jerome, loc. cit.

13 Horace, *Serm.*, I, 1, 25-6; cf. *S.H.A., Tacitus*, 6, 5.

14 Quintilian, I, 1, 20.

15 Plato, *Protag.*, 326d; Maximus of Tyre, p. 20, 13.

16 Quintilian, V, 14, 31.

17 Seneca, *Epp.*, 94, 51.

18 Quintilian, I, 1, 27, Jerome, loc. cit.

19 C. Wessely, *Studien zur Palaeo-graphie und Papyruskunde*, II (1902), pp. LII*ff*.; Pack², no. 2735.

20 A.E.R. Boak in *C.P.* XVI (1921) p. 189; Pack², nos. 2708-9; Zalateo, p. 171.
21 J.G. Milne, loc. cit.; Ziebarth, no.1.
22 Petronius, *Sat.*, 58; Wessely, loc. cit., p. XLIII.
23 Fulgentius, *Myth.* III, 10.
24 Quintilian, I, 1, 30-31.
25 Athenaeus, X, p. 453cd; K. Freeman, *Schools of Hellas* (London, 1912), pp. 88-9.
26 U. Wilcken, *Urkunden der Ptolemäerzeit*, I (Berlin, 1927), no.147, p. 634.
27 Wessely, p. XLIX: cf. Ziebarth, no.3.
28 Ziebarth, no.5.
29 Wessely, p. XLVII.
30 Plato, *Polit.*, 278ab.
31 Guéraud-Jouget, op. cit., p. 6 of Commentary.
32 P. Collart, *Les Papyrus Bouriant* (Paris, 1926), pp. 17*ff*.; Ziebarth, no.46; Pack², no. 2643.
33 Cicero, *Ad. Fam.*, II, 10, 1; Terentius Scaurus, *G.L.*, VII, 13, 10.
34 Clement of Alexandria, *Strom.*, pp. 359-60, Stählin; Beudel, p. 14; cf. Quintilian, I, 1, 37.
35 Wessely, p. XLV, no.2.
36 Guéraud-Jouget, op. cit., pp. 8-10 of Commentary.
37 Zalateo, nos.73, 89, (Michigan ostraca).
38 Guéraud-Jouget, pp. 11-13 of Commentary.
39 Varro, *L.L.*, IX, 15.
40 *C.G.L.*, III, 348*ff*. cf. *P. Tebt.*, II, 278, (Zalateo, no.353).
41 Quintilian, I, 1, 35.
42 Guéraud-Jouget, p. 14 of Commentary.
43 Beudel, op. cit., p. 41.
44 Cf. Horace, *Epp.*, II, 1, 126.
45 Quintilian, I, 1, 32-4.
46 Cf. Petronius, *Sat.*, 75.
47 See H.-I. Marrou, op. cit. (c. xii, n.31 above), p. 34.
48 Aeschines, III, 135; Lucian, *Anach.*, 21.
49 *R.E.*, s.v. 'Gnome, Gnomendichtung, Gnomologien' (Horna).
50 I Corinthians, xv, 33; *P. Hibeh,* 1, 7, with Grenfell and Hunt's note.
51 S. Jaekel, *Menandri Sententiae* (Leipzig, Teubner, 1964), pp. 33*ff*.
52 Ib., pp. 5-6.
53 Quintilian, I, 1, 35; Porphyrio on Horace, *Epp.*, II, 1, 128.
54 Brit. Mus.*, Add. Ms.* 34186, part 1, Ziebarth, no. 11; Jaekel, p. 15. E.G. Turner in *Bulletin of the Institute of Classical Studies* (University of London), no.12 (1965), pp. 67-9.
55 Ziebarth, nos. 13, 15, 19.
56 Id., no.12; Pack², no.2736.
57 Seneca, *Epp.*, 33, 7; Phaedrus, III, *epil.*, 33.
58 Jaekel, op. cit., 2, 50, 811, 698, 111, 524, 705.
59 Ib., 162, 577, 370, 385, 412.
60 Ib., 849, 841, 710, 305, 678, 431.
61 Ib., 775, 348, 564, 572, 806, 759.
62 Ib., 779, 596, 65.
63 Ib., 827, 115, 865, 857, 852.
64 *Rhet. ad Herenn.*, IV, 4, 7; H.D. Jocelyn, *The Tragedies of Ennius* (Cambridge, 1967), pp. 54, 305-6.
65 Ennius, *Tragedies, frr.*10-12, 216, 416, Warmington.
66 Seneca the elder, *Contr.*, VII, 3, 8; Seneca, *Epp.*, 8, 8.
67 Quintilian, I, 1, 36.
68 U. von Wilamowitz-Moellendorff, *Griechisches Lesebuch* (Berlin, 1913), I, pp. 32-42.
69 Seneca, *Epp.*, 94, 9.
70 Ziebarth, no.46, p. 22.
71 Plutarch, *Cato maior*, 2, 4.
72 Cicero, *De Off.*, I, 29, 104.
73 *C.G.L.*, III, 381, 54-382, 8, with 381, 20-53.
74 E.G. Turner, *Greek Papyri, An Introduction* (Oxford, 1968), pp. 91-2.
75 H.R. Hall, in *C.R.*, XVIII (1904), pp. 2-5.
76 Horace, *Serm.*, I, 10, 74-5, and

Porphyrio ad loc.

77 Persius, I, 29-30.

78 Plato, *Euthyd.*, 276-7; Galen, V, 65, Kuhn; W.G. Rutherford, *A Chapter in the History of Annotation* (London, 1905), pp. 20, 32.

, 79 Horace, *Epp.*, I, 18, 12*ff.*

80 Quintilian, I, 1, 36.

81 *C.G.L.*, III, 39, 49*ff.*

82 T. Birt, *Die Buchrolle in der Kunst* (Leipzig, 1907), pp. 304*ff.*

83 Cf. Quintilian, I, 9, 2.

84 D.C. Hesseling in *J.H.S.*, XIII (1892/3), pp. 293-314; Ziebarth, no.30.

85 See below, p. 254.

86 See note 1 above.

87 Quintilian, I, 1, 12-14.

88 Id., I, 4, 27.

89 *C.G.L.*, III, 225-6 (*Hermeneumata Einsidlensia*), with Wilamowitz-Moellendorff's introduction, op. cit., (note 68 above), I, p. 400; cf. *C.G.L.*, III, 121-2.

90 Augustine, *Conf.*, I, 13.

91 Cf. Aristophanes, *Vesp.*, 656; Theophrastus, *Char.*, 14.

92 Plato, *Leg.*, 819b; Quintilian, I, 1, 20.

93 Guéraud-Jouget, 21-6 (Comm., p. 5); Wessely, op. cit., p. LVI.

94 Ziebarth, no.48 (pp. 30-31).

95 Ib., pp. 29 and 31.

96 Brit. Mus., *Add. Ms* 34186, part II.

97 Guéraud-Jouget, 216-34 (Comm., p. 44).

98 Petronius, *Sat.*, 46, 3.

99 Guéraud-Jouget, 235-42 (Comm., p. 45).

100 *Pap. Soc. Ital.*, VII, 763.

101 Horace, *A.P.*, 326-30.

102 Petronius, *Sat.*, 75.

103 Ib., 58, 7.

104 Horace, *A.P.*, 325-6, with Kiessling-Heinze ad loc.

105 H.S. Stuart Jones, *Sculptures of the Museo Capitolino* (Oxford, 1912), p. 138.

106 Martial, X, 62, 4-5; Marrou, *Hist. Educ.*, pp. 550-51.

107 Marquardt, *Privatleben*, II, pp. 101*ff.*; P.-W., *R.E.*, s.v. *abacus*

(Hultsch) and *Suppbd.*, III, col. 4-13 (Nagl); Dar. Sag., s.v. 'abacus'. See esp. A. Nagl in *Sitz. Wien. Akad.*, 177 (1914). Cf. J.M. Pullan, *The History of the Abacus* (London, 1966), pp. 19-20.

108 Pullan, pp. 26-7.

109 The British Museum model (on which Mr. Beresford Hutchinson kindly reported) is not accepted as of Roman date by the Department of Mediaeval and Later Antiquities or the Department of Greek and Roman Antiquities. It is considered of relatively recent manufacture. Scientific testing yields no evidence of date. An abacus of this type was in the possession of the sixteenth-century scholar Fulvius Ursinus, and illustrations were first published in the seventeenth century (Pignorius, *De Servis*, 1674; M. Welser, *Opera*, 1682). The type has been accepted as quite genuine by the authorities named in n.107, and others, mainly on the basis of the Continental examples. M.J.B. Giard of the Cabinet des Médailles, Paris, and Signor La Regina of the Museo Nazionale, Rome, have kindly notified me that their models are considered authentic, but of uncertain date. See also E. Babelon-J. Blanchet, *Catalogue des bronzes antiques de la Bibliothèque Nationale* (Paris, 1895), no. 1925. For the numerical symbols see J.E. Sandys, *Latin Epigraphy* (original edn, Cambridge, 1919), p. 55. Karl Menninger, *Zahlwort und Ziffer* (Göttingen, 1958), p. 112, has a good photograph.

110 D.H. Leavens in *American Math. Monthly*, XXVII (1920), pp. 180-84.

111 Mabel Lang in *Hesperia*, XXVI (1957), pp. 271-87, esp. p. 278.

112 E.A. Bechtel, in *C.P.* IV (1909), pp. 25-31; Marrou, *Hist. Educ.*,

pp. 517-18.

113 Quintilian, I, 10, 35, and Colson ad loc.

114 Ovid, *Ex Pont.*, II, 2, 17-18; cf. Cicero, *Ad Att.*, V, 21, 13.

115 Cicero, *De Off.*, III, 19, 77; 23, 90.

116 Juvenal, X, 249, and Mayor ad loc.

117 Marrou, *Hist. Educ.*, p. 216

118 E.F. Wüstermann in *Jahrb. f. Philol. und Pädagogik, Suppbd.*, XV (1849), from which fig. 17 is taken.

119 Firmicius Maternus, I, 4, 13.

120 Varro, p. 248, Riese; Müller's edn of fragments of *De Lib. Educ.*, pp. 54-7.

121 Vegetius, II, 19.

(Plate).

Chapter XIV

1 On the history of grammatical theory, see: H. Steinthal, *Geschichte der Sprachwissenschaft bei den Griechen und Römern* (2 vols., Berlin, 1890); R.H. Robins, *Ancient and Mediaeval Grammatical Theory in Europe* (London, 1951); K. Barwick, *Probleme der stoischen Sprachlehre und Rhetorik* (Berlin Academy, 1957); F. della Corte, *La Filologia latina delle origini a Varrone* (Turin, 1937); H. Dahlmann, *Varro und die hellenistische Sprachtheorie*, Berlin, 1932); J. Collart, *Varron Grammairien Latin* (Paris, 1954).

2 Quintilian, I, 4 and 5-8. with F.H. Colson's commentary (Cambridge, 1924), and papers in *C.Q.*, VIII (1914), pp. 33-47, X (1916), pp. 17-31; K. von Fritz in *A.J.P.* LXX, (1949), pp. 337-66; F. Pini, *M. Fabio Quintiliano, Capitoli Grammaticali* (Rome, 1966).

3 Dionysius Thrax, ed. G. Uhlig (Leipzig, 1883), with R.H. Robins in *T.A.Ph.A.* LXXXVIII (1957), pp. 67-106; Sextus Empiricus, *Adversus Grammaticos*, 97-168, with B. Heinecke, *De Quintiliani, Sexti, Asclepiadis arte grammatica* (Diss., Strasbourg, 1903).

4 Dionysius Thrax, pp. 9-14; Sextus Empiricus, *Adv. Gramm.*, 99-103.

5 Quintilian, I, 4, 10.

6 W.S. Allen, *Vox Graeca* (Cambridge, 1968), pp. 16*ff*.

7 F.G. Kenyon in *J.H.S.*, XXIX (1909), p. 36; Zalateo, no.358; Pack², no.2712.

8 Varro in *G.R.F.* (Funaioli), fr.241; Pompeius, *G.L.*, V, 101.

9 Cf. Quintilian, XII, 10, 28, with R.G. Austin's note.

10 Id., I, 4, 9; Varro, fr.240; Nigidius Figulus, fr.19; Terentius Scaurus, *G.L.* VII, 27, 1.

11 Quintilian, I, 4, 7-8 with Colson's notes; cf. Varro, fr. 270.

12 Id., I, 4, 12*ff*.

13 Id., IX, 4, 47.

14 Dionysius Thrax, pp. 17*ff*.

15 Id., p. 21; Pompeius, *G.L.*, V, 115, 26*ff*.

16 Cf. Quintilian, IX, 4, 51.

17 Pompeius, *G.L.*, V, 118, 6.

18 Cf. Quintilian, I, 4, 17 with 7, 9. Sextus Empiricus, *Adv. Gramm.*, 169.

19 H. Stuart Jones in *C.R.*, XV (1901), pp. 396-401; W. Dennison in *C.P.*, I (1906), pp. 47-68.

20 See W.M. Lindsay, *The Latin Language* (Oxford, 1894), pp. 124-6; for modern scansion, cf. J.P. Postgate, *Prosodia Latina* (Oxford, 1923), sections 23*ff*.

21 Sextus Empiricus, *Adv. Gramm.*, 173-4; Quintilian, I, 7, 9.

22 Varro, fr. 290, 291, 292; Caesius Bassus in *G.R.F.* (Mazzarino), pp. 147-8.

23 Horace, *A.P.*, 251*ff*.

24 Quintilian, I, 8, 13.

25 Quintilian, I, 4, 20.

26 Ib.; Juvenal, VI, 452.

27 *G.R.F.* (Mazzarino), p. 101; Steinthal, op. cit., II, p. 218; cf. Quintilian, I, 4, 19.

28 Dionysius Thrax, pp. 70*ff*.

29 *G.R.F.* (Mazzarino), pp. 84-93.
30 Ib., p. 75; K. Barwick, *Remmius Palaemon und die römische Ars Grammatica* (Leipzig, 1922) is more conjectural.
31 Varro, *L.L.*, IX, 31; X.17; VI, 36.
32 Diogenes Laertius, VII, 57-8; Priscian, *G.L.*, II, 54, 8; cf. Robins op. cit. (note 1), p. 27.
33 Cf. Robins, p. 33.
34 Id., p. 56.
35 Varro, *L.L.*, X, 62; cf. *G.R.F.* (Funaioli), fr.251.
36 Cf. Quintilian, I, 4, 26.
37 Ib., 23-4; Sextus Empiricus, *Adv. Gramm.*, 142-53.
38 See below, pp. 204*ff*.
39 Varro, fr. 247, 248; Quintilian, I, 6, 4 and 6.
40 Apollonius Dyscolus, *De Adv.*, p.

141, 25, Schneider.
41 Ziebarth, no.49.
42 Varro, *L.L.*, X, 62; Collart, p. 168.
43 Ib., 70; Quintilian, I, 5, 63; Aurelius Opillus, fr. 25 in *G.R.F.* (Funaioli).
44 Dionysius Thrax, pp. 53*ff*.
45 Ziebarth, nos. 22 and 47 (*J.H.S.*, XXIX, 1909, 30*ff*.)
46 Ziebarth, no. 23 (late papyrus).
47 Dionysius Thrax, pp. 125*ff*.
48 Varro, *L.L.*, IX, 108-9.
49 Id., fr. 261; Collart, pp. 184-5.
50 Id., *L.L.*, VIII, 6.
51 Ib., X, 22; cf. 44.
52 Ib., 48.
53 Ib., 33.
54 Quintilian, I, 4, 27.
55 Ib., 29.
56 Ib., 22.

Chapter XV

1 R. Pfeiffer, op. cit., pp. 37*ff*. E. Siebenborn, *Die Lehre von der Sprachrichtigkeit und ihre Kriterien: Studien zur antiken normativen Grammatik* (Amsterdam, 1975) is not yet accessible.
2 Aristotle, *Rhet.*, III, 5, 1; Cicero, *Orat.*, 23, 79, (Theophrastus); Diogenes Laertius, VII, 59.
3 Cf. Quintilian, I, 5, 29; Sextus Empiricus, *Adv. Gramm.*, 187.
4 *Rhet. ad Herenn.*, IV, 12, 17; Quintilian, I, 5, 6 and 34.
5 Diogenes Laertius, loc. cit.
6 *Rhet. ad Herenn.*, loc. cit., Cicero *De Orat.*, III, 13, 48.
7 Quintilian, I, 5, 8.
8 Cicero, *Brutus*, 46, 171.
9 Quintilian, I, 5, 57; cf. L.R. Palmer, *The Latin Language* (London, 1954), p. 53.
10 Catullus, 97, 6; Quintilian, I, 5, 8.
11 Quintilian, I, 5, 56; cf. Suetonius, *Vit. Verg.*, 43, on Virgil, *Ecl.* 3, 1.
12 Quintilian, I, 5, 7.
13 Ib., 6.
14 Cicero, *Brutus*, 58, 210; *De Orat.*, III, 12, 45.
15 Quintilian, I, 1, 4-5; 11.
16 Ib., 13.

17 Varro, fr. 278 in *G.R.F.* (Funaioli).
18 Cf. Charisius, pp. 350-51, Barwick.
19 Quintilian, I, 5, 18.
20 Ib., 22-4.
21 See W.M. Lindsay, op. cit. pp. 153-4; E.H. Sturtevant, *The Pronunciation of Greek and Latin* (Philadelphia, 1940), pp. 186-9.
22 Lindsay, pp. 150-52; W.S. Allen, *Vox Latina* (Cambridge, 1965), p. 84.
23 Quintilian, I, 5, 28; cf. Allen, p.90.
24 Augustine, *Conf.*, I, 18.
25 Allen, pp. 26-7; Sturtevant, pp. 156-60.
26 Quintilian, XII, 10, 57.
27 Cicero, *Orat.*, 48, 160.
28 Cf. Varro, fr. 280c in *G.R.F.* (Funaioli).
29 Quintilian, I, 5, 34*ff*.
30 Servius on *Aen.*, VIII, 168, cf. Quintilian, I, 7, 34.
31 Cicero, *Ad Att.*, VII, 3, 10.
32 Terence, *Eun.*, 115, 539.
33 Quintilian, I, 5, 38-9; contrast Suetonius, *Aug.*, 86.
34 Quintilian, I, 5, 42*ff*.
35 Ib., 50; cf. Lucilius, fr. 39 in *G.R.F.* (Funaioli).
36 Pompeius, *G.L.* V, 289, 6.

37 Lucian, *Soloecista*; Sextus Empiricus, *Adv. Gramm.*, 209*ff.*, 214*ff.*

38 Homer, *Il.*, II, 135; Sextus Empiricus, 206.

39 Schol. Homer, *Il.*, I, 129.

40 Quintilian, 1, 5, 52.

41 Id., I, 6; cf. F.H. Colson in *C.Q.*, XIII (1919), pp. 24-36.

42 Varro, *L.L.*, IX, 12; X, 68: Steinthal, op. cit., II, pp. 71*ff.*; Pfeiffer, op. cit., pp. 202-3.

43 Cf. Steinthal, II, pp. 160-61.

44 Charisius, p. 149, 26, Barwick; cf. Colson, loc. cit., p. 28.

45 Cf. Caesar, fr. 11 in *G.R.F.* (Funaioli).

46 Gellius, II, 25, 1-4.

47 Varro, *L.L.*, VIII, IX, X; Collart, op. tic., pp. 144-57.

48 Ib., VIII, 34; 68; IX, 91; Quintilian, I, 6, 12.

49 Quintilian, I, 6, 25.

50 Ib., 5; Charisius, pp. 55, 25-56, 5, Barwick.

51 Quintilian, I, 6, 27; cf. *G.R.F.* (Mazzarino), p. 267.

52 Ib., 16.

53 Varro, *L.L.*, X, 59.

54 Quintilian, I, 6, 22-4.

55 G.L. Hendrickson in *C.P.*, I (1906), pp. 97-120.

56 Quintilian, I, 6, 3.

57 Ib., 27.

58 *G.R.F.* (Mazzarino), pp. 219*ff.*; A. della Casa, *Il dubius sermo di Plinio* (Genoa, 1969).

59 Cf. Tacitus, *Dial*, 32, 3.

60 Cicero, *Brutus*, 75, 261.

61 Ib., 74, 259.

62 Quintilian, I, 6, 44-5.

63 Cicero, *Orat.*, 46, 155-6; cf. Varro, *L.L.*, VIII, 71.

64 Ib., 157; Quintilian, I, 6, 17 and 21.

65 Cf. Quintilian, IX, 4, 59.

66 Varro, fr. 268.

67 Suetonius, *Vit. Ter.*, sub fin.

68 Quintilian, I, 6, 39*ff.*

69 Sextus Empiricus, *Adv. Gramm.*, 98.

70 Gellius, XVII, 1.

71 Cicero, *Brutus*, 74, 258; Quintilian, I, 6, 42.

72 Id., I, 6, 10.

73 Varro, fr. 268.

74 Quintilian, I, 4, 25; 6, 31.

75 Varro, *L.L.*, V, 9; Collart, op. cit., pp. 251-301.

76 Ib., 6; Quintilian, I, 6, 32.

77 Ib., VI, 4 and 8; Quintilian I, 6, 30.

78 Gellius, I, 18, 2; Varro, *L.L.*, V, 101; Quintilian, 1, 6, 33.

79 Barwick, *Probleme ...*, c. iv.

80 Varro, *L.L.* V, 86, and fr. 265 (*G.R.F.*, p. 283, 174).

81 Id., fr. 280 (*G.R.F.*, p. 298, 16*ff.*); Quintilian, I, 4, 14.

82 P.-W., *R.E.*, s.v. 'Orthographia', col. 1456*ff.*; W. Brambach, *Die Neugestaltung der lateinischen Orthographie* (Leipzig, 1868).

83 Quintilian, I, 7, 2*ff.*

84 Lucilius, fr. 12, 13 in *G.R.F.* (Funaioli).

85 Id., in *G.R.F.*, pp.36-8; Quintilian, I, 7, 14-16; Allen, pp. 53-5; Sturtevant, pp. 114-5; R.G. Kent, *The Sounds of Latin* (Baltimore, 1945), p. 39.

86 W.M. Lindsay, op. cit., p. 10.

87 Varro, fr. 272; Collart, op. cit., pp. 120*ff.*

88 Varro, fr. 269; Quintilian, I, 7, 21; cf. Velius Longus, *G.L.* VII, 49; 67-8.

89 See Allen, op. cit., pp. 56-9.

90 Marius Victorinus, *G.L.*, VI, 9, 5; Suetonius, *Aug.*, 87.

91 Quintilian, I, 7, 22, 24.

92 Ib., 18; cf. I, 5, 17.

93 Ib., I, 7, 25.

94 Ib., 20.

95 Sextus Empiricus, *Adv. Gramm.*, 170.

96 But see Quintilian, I, 7, 28-9.

Chapter XVI

1 Quintilian, I, 8, 5 and 8.
2 Id., X, 1, 27 and 46*ff*.
3 W.A. Oldfather, *The Greek Literary Texts from Greco-Roman Egypt* (University of Wisconsin Studies in Social Sciences and History, ix, Madison, 1923); P. Collart in *R. Phil.*, VI (1932), 318*ff*.; VII (1933), 61*ff*.; XIII (1939), 289*ff*., XVI (1943) 5*ff*., and *Mélanges Desrousseaux*, (Paris, 1937), 69*ff*.; fullest detail in R.A. Pack, op. cit.
4 Horace, *Epp.*, II, 2, 41-4; Petronius, *Sat.*, 5; Quintilian, I, 8, 5; Pliny, *Epp.*, II, 14, 2.
5 Cf. W.J. Verdenius, *Homer, the Educator of the Greeks* (Netherlands Academy, 1970).
6 Quintilian, X, 1, 46.
7 Statius, *Silvae*, V, 3, 146*ff*.; II, 1, 117-19.
8 *Anth. Pal.*, IX, 168, 169, 173.
9 Cf. Oldfather, op. cit., 67.
10 Horace, *Epp.* II, 1, 69*ff*., and 53-4; Cicero, *Brutus*, 18, 71; 19, 75.
11 Cf. A. Vergeest, *Poetarum Enarratio: Leraren en School-auteurs te Rome* (Breda, 1950), 33*ff*.
12 Suetonius, *De Gramm.*, 16; Propertius, II, 34, 65-6.
13 Suetonius, *Vit. Verg.*, 43*ff*.; cf. Henry Nettleship in Conington-Nettleship's edn of Virgil, I (London, 1881), xxix *ff*.
14 Macrobius, *Sat.*, V and VI.
15 Juvenal, VI, 434*ff*.
16 Cf. above pp. 119-20.
17 Ovid, *Trist.*, II, 533-6.
18 Augustine, *Conf.*, I, 13.
19 Quintilian, I, 8, 6 and 8*ff*.
20 Cf. P. Collart in *R. Phil.*, XVI (1943), pp. 25*ff*.
21 Quintilian, X, 1, 67-8.
22 Cicero, *De Orat.*, III, 7, 27; Velleius Paterculus, II, 9, 3.
23 Horace, *Epp.*, II, 1, 55-6, with Porphyrio's note on 60; cf. H.D.

Jocelyn, *The Tragedies of Ennius* (Cambridge, 1967), p. 52.
24 Persius, I, 76-82; Tacitus, *Dial.*, 20, 8; 21, 13; Martial, XI, 90, 6.
25 Cicero, *Tusc. Disp.*, II, 11, 27.
26 Tacitus, *Dial.*, 12. 6; Quintilian, X, 1, 98.
27 Martial, VIII, 3, 13-16.
28 Statius, *Silvae*, II, 1, 115*ff*.; Ausonius, *Epp.* 22, 46-7.
29 Ovid, *Trist.*, II, 369-70.
30 Quintilian, I, 8, 7-8.
31 Id., I, 11, 12-13.
32 Id., X, 1, 69-72.
33 Volcacius Sedigitus in Gellius, XV, 24; Horace, *Epp.*, II, 1, 57-9; Velleius Paterculus, I, 17, 1.
34 Suetonius, *Vit. Terent.*, sub fin.; Varro, fr. 99, Funaioli.
35 Jerome, *Comm. in Eccles.*, 1; Augustine, *Conf.*, I, 16; Sidonius, *Epp.*, II, 2, 2.
36 Quintilian, I, 8, 6.
37 Statius, *Silvae*, V, 3, 151*ff*.
38 Horace, *Carm.*, IV, 2, 1; Quintilian, X, 1, 61.
39 Petronius, *Sat.*, 2.
40 Horace, *Carm.*, IV, 9, 5*ff*.; Ovid, *Trist.*, II, 363*ff*.; *A.A.*, III, 330-31; *et al.*
41 Seneca, *Epp.*, 27, 6.
42 Quintilian, X, 1, 96; Juvenal, VII, 226-7; Ausonius, *Epp.* 22, 56.
43 Pliny, *Epp.*, IV, 14.
44 Horace, *Epp.*, II, 2, 100; Quintilian, X, 1, 58; cf. Propertius, III, 1, 1.
45 Statius, *Silvae*, V, 3, 156-7; *Anth. Pal.*, IX, 175.
46 P.W., *R.E.*, s.v. 'Epaphroditos'.
47 Suetonius, *De Gramm.*, 11; 16; 18.
48 Ib., 16 (Domitius Marsus).
49 Tacitus, *Dial.* 20, 5.
50 Quintilian, X, 1, 90.
51 Suetonius, *Vit. Luc.*, sub fin. ('praelegi').
52 Statius, *Theb.*, XII, 815; Martial, VIII, 3, 13*ff*.
53 Quintilian, I, 2, 12.
54 Cicero, *Ad Fam.*, VI, 18, 6.

55 Sextus Empiricus, *Adv. Gramm.*, 57-8.
56 Ib., 270*ff*.
57 Quinitilian, II, 5, 1; Martial, V, 56, 3-5.
58 Cicero, *Ad Q.F.*, III, 1, 4.
59 See below, p. 251.
60 Theon, in *Rhet. Graec.*, II, 65, 26*ff*.; 70, 30*ff*., Sp.; Quintilian, II, 6, 5.
61 Quintilian II, 5, 18-20.
62 Ib., 3-4.
63 Cicero, *De Orat.*, I, 42, 187; Seneca, *Epp.*, 88, 3; Quintilian, I, 2, 14; 8, 18; Juvenal, VII, 231. See esp. L. Friedländer, *De historiarum enarratione in ludis grammaticis* (Königsberg, 1874).
64 D. van Berchem in *Mus. Helv.*, IX (1952), 79*ff*.
65 Servius, *praef.* (I, p. 4, Thilo-Hagen).
66 *C.I.L.*, VI, 9447.
67 Dionysius Thrax, *suppl.*, p. 114, Uhlig.
68 *G.L.*, V, 133, 12 (Pompeius), on Virgil, *Aen.*, VIII, 83.
69 W.G. Rutherford, *A Chapter in the History of Annotation* (London, 1905), p. 127.
70 See note 73.
71 Dionysius Thrax, pp. 7-8, Uhlig; Rutherford, pp. 168*ff*.; and esp. G. Flock, *De Graecorum interpunctionibus* (Greifswald, 1908), and Pfeiffer, op. cit., pp. 179-80.
72 On Latin texts, see Marrou, *Hist. Educ.*, p. 553.
73 *G.L.*, V, 133, 4*ff*.
74 W. Deecke, *Auswahl aus den Iliasscholien* (Bonn, 1912), pp. 44*ff*.; H. Erbse, *Scholia Graeca in Homeri Iliadem* (Berlin, 1969 — in progress).
75 Schol. A, 322; B 8; 56.
76 Schol. A, 401.
77 Ausonius, *Epp.* 22, 49-50; Schol. A. 349.
78 Schol. A 334; B 85 (co-ordinates); A 94; B 21; 77 (relative); A 509 (temporal); A 185 (final); A 526 (explanatory); A 178; 324 (conditional).
79 Schol. A 234 (parenthesis); A 99 (adjectives).
80 Cf. Schol. Dionysius Thrax, p. 6, 9.
81 Schol. A 106.
82 Schol. A, 225; B 235.
83 Quintilian, XI, 3, 36-8.
84 Cf. E.G. Turner, *Greek Papyri* (Oxford, 1968), pp. 90-91.
85 *G.R.F.*, p. 383 (Funaioli); R. Berndt in *B.Ph.W.*, XXX (1910) 508*ff*., 540*ff*.
86 Schol. Dionysius Thrax, p. 139, 27*ff*.
87 Ib., p. 6, 4*ff*.; 170, 33*ff*.
88 Quintilian, I, 8, 1.
89 Dionysius Thrax, p. 6, 8*ff*.
90 Horace, *A.P.* 89-98; cf. *Serm.* I, 4, 45*ff*.
91 Aristotle, *Rhet.*, III, 7, 2 (subject); 6 (character); 7, 3 (emotion); Horace, *A.P.*, 105*ff*.; 144*ff*.; 156*ff*.
92 Cf. G. Degenhardt, *De veterum grammaticorum scholis* (Münster, 1905), pp. 10-13; W. Kroll in *Philologus*, LXXV (1918), pp. 68*ff*.
93 Cicero, *De Orat.*, III, 57, 216-58, 219.
94 Euripides, *Medea*, 502*ff*.; Ennius in Cicero, loc. cit.; Cicero, *De Orat.*, III, 56, 214; Catullus, 64, 177*ff*.
95 Cicero, loc. cit 217, from Ennius, *Andromache*.
96 Id., *De Orat.*, III, 58, 218, from Accius, *Atreus*.
97 Ib., from Ennius, *Alcmeo*.
98 Quintilian, I, 11, 1*ff*.
99 Pliny, *Epp.*, V, 19, 3.
100 *Rhet. ad Herenn.*, III, 14, 24; Lucian, *Anach.*, 23.
101 Quintilian, II, 10, 13; XI, 3, 4.
102 Id., I, 8, 2: cf. XI, 3, 57.
103 Id., I, 11, 12.
104 Cf. Degenhardt, op. cit., pp. 11*ff*.
105 Quintilian, I, 11, 8.
106 Id., I, 8, 2; 11, 6; cf. Persius, I, 17-18; 32*ff*.
107 Nepos, *Att.*, 1.
108 Quintilian, VI, *praef.*, 11.

109 Id., I, 2, 15; Seneca the elder,
    Suas. II, 13; Macrobius, *Sat.*, I,
    24, 5.
110 Quintilian, II, 5, 3-5.

111 Id., I, 2, 12.
112 Cf. Degenhardt, op. cit., pp.
    82*ff.*
113 Cf. Quintilian, II, 5, 6 (rhetoric).

Chapter XVII

1 Varro, fr. 236 in *G.R.F.*
  (Funaioli); Dionysius Thrax, p. 5.
2 Quintilian, I, 8, 13.
3 Sextus Empiricus, *Adv. Gramm.*,
  159.
4 See esp. M. Glück, *Priscians
  Partitiones und ihre Stellung in
  der spätantiken Schule*
  (*Spudasmata* XII, Hildesheim,
  1967).
5 Quintilian, I, 8, 14.
6 Ib., 15.
7 Glück op. cit., pp. 40*ff.*
8 Quintilian, I, 8, 16.
9 Schanz-Hosius, sect. 835.
10 Servius on Virgil, *Aen.*, I, 41;
   451; 332.
11 Ib., 119.
12 Ib., 22; 292; 196.
13 Ib., 30; 359; 26; 249.
14 Quintilian, VIII, 5, 35.
15 Id., VIII, 6, 1-3; IX, 1, 1-9.
16 Cf. *G.L.* IV, 397, 5 (Donatus).
17 *Rhet. ad Herenn.*, IV, 31, 42-34,
   46.
18 *Rhet. Graec.*, III, 191*ff.*, Sp.;
   Rutherford, op. cit., pp. 183*ff.*;
   Degenhardt, op. cit., pp. 24*ff.*
19 J.L. Moore, in *A.J.P.*, XII
   (1891), pp. 157*ff.*
20 Quintilian, VIII, 6, 9*ff.*;
   Tryphon, III, 192, 11, Sp.;
   [Plutarch], *De vita et poesi
   Homeri*, 20.
21 Cf. Demetrius, *On Style*, 78.
22 Virgil, *Aen.*, VI, 1; XII, 499; V,
   662; *Geo.*, II, 364.
23 Aristotle, *Rhet.*, III, 11, 3, p.
   1411b; Demetrius, 81; Tryphon,
   loc. cit.
24 Virgil, *Aen.*, VIII, 728; Quintilian, VIII, 6, 11.
25 Quintilian, VIII, 6, 13.
26 Aristotle, *Rhet.*, III, 10, 7,
   p. 1411a; *Poetics*, 21, p. 1457b.

27 Id., *Poet.*, loc. cit.; Quintilian,
   VIII, 6, 13.
28 *Rhet. ad Herenn.*, IV, 34, 45;
   Cicero, *De Orat.*, III, 41, 163*ff.*;
   Quintilian, VIII, 6, 14*ff.*;
   Demetrius, *On Style*, 78-87. See
   also W.B. Stanford, *Greek Meta-
   phor* (Oxford 1936).
29 Quintilian, VIII, 6, 34*ff.*;
   Tryphon, III, 192, 20, Sp.
30 Barwick, op. cit., pp. 88*ff.*
   Rutherford, op. cit., pp. 209*ff.*
31 *Rhet. ad Herenn.*, IV, 32, 43;
   Cicero, *De Orat.*, III, 42, 167;
   Quintilian, VIII, 6, 23*ff.*;
   Tryphon, III, 195, 20, Sp.;
   [Plutarch] op. cit., 23.
32 Virgil, *Aen.*, II, 311; Quintilian,
   VIII, 6, 25.
33 *Rhet. ad Herenn.*, IV, 31, 42;
   Quintilian, VIII, 6, 29-30.
34 *Rhet. ad Herenn.*, IV, 33, 44-5;
   Cicero, *De Orat.*, III, 42, 168;
   Quintilian, VIII, 6, 19*ff.*:
   Tryphon, III, 195, 27, Sp.
35 Servius on Virgil, *Aen.*, I, 724.
36 Schol. Hom., *Il.* I, 477; Tryphon,
   III, 196, 1, Sp.
37 [Plutarch], op. cit., 16; Demetrius, *On Style*, 94; Quintilian,
   VIII, 6, 31*ff.* Contrast Tryphon,
   III, 196, 13.
38 Homer, *Il.*, II, 209-10; Dionysius,
   De Comp. Verb., 16 init.
39 Dion Chyrsostom, XII, 68.
40 Homer, *Il.*, IV, 504.
41 Ib., XVI, 161; Demetrius, *On
   Style*, 220.
42 Quintilian, I, 5, 72.
43 Homer, *Od.*, II, 1; *Il.*, VIII, 68.
44 Virgil, *Aen.*, IV, 6, with Austin's
   note; Servius, ad loc.
45 Ib., VI, 535, with Norden's note.
46 Ib., II, 268; Quintilian, VIII, 6,
   60.

47 Servius on Virgil, *Aen.*, XII, 170; IV, 254.

48 Tryphon, III, 197, 4, Sp.

49 Servius on Virgil, *Aen.*, I, 244; 310; III, 191, et saep.

50 Quintilian, VIII, 6, 62*ff.*; Tryphon, III, 197, 20, Sp.

51 Id., VIII, 2, 14 on Virgil, *Aen.*, I, 109; Charisius, p. 363, 3, Barwick.

52 *Rhet. ad Herenn.*, IV, 33, 44; Quintilian, VIII, 6, 67*ff.*; Tryphon, III, 198, 30, Sp.

53 Homer, *Od.*, IX, 481; Virgil, *Aen.*, X, 127-8; Seneca the elder, *Suas.*, I, 12; cf. Ovid, *Met.*, XIII, 882.

54 Homer, *Il.*, X, 436-7; Tryphon, loc. cit.; Demetrius, *On Style*, 125.

55 Quintilian, VIII, 6, 73.

56 *Rhet. ad Herenn.*, IV, 34, 46; Cicero, *De Orat.*, III, 41, 166; Quintilian, VIII, 6, 14 and 44*ff.*: Demetrius, *On Style*, 99*ff.*

57 Virgil, *Geo.*, II, 541-2; cf. Servius ad loc., 'allegorice'.

58 Horace, *Carm.*, I, 14; cf. also Porphyrio on II. 5.

59 Virgil, *Ecl.* IX, 7*ff.*; Quintilian, VIII, 6, 46-7.

60 Servius on Virgil, *Ecl.*, I, 1; V, 20.

61 Quintilian, VIII, 6, 54*ff.*; Charisius, p. 363, Barwick.

62 Exx. in Degenhardt, op. cit., pp. 42*ff.*

63 Quintilian, VIII, 3, 72*ff.*; Tryphon, III, 200-201; M.H. McCall, *Ancient Rhetorical Theories of Simile and Comparison* (Harvard, 1969).

64 Schol., Homer, *Il.*, XV, 381; XVII, 657.

65 [Plutarch] op. cit., 84-90.

66 Ib., 90; Homer, *Il.*, II, 394*ff.*

67 Schol., Homer, *Il.*, XII, 278.

68 Virgil, *Aen.*, I, 498*ff.*, with Austin's and R.D. Williams' notes; Gellius, IX, 9, 12*ff.*

69 Servius, ad loc.

70 Id., on *Aen.*, I, 430*ff.*

71 Macrobius, V, 11, 2-4.

72 Servius on *Aen.*, XII, 587*ff.*

73 Id., on *Aen.*, IV, 69*ff.*; IX, 25*ff.*

74 Id., on *Aen*, IV, 441*ff.* See Page, Austin, and Williams on 449.

75 Sextus Empiricus, *Adv. Gramm.*, 252-3; cf. Cicero, *De Inv.*, I, 19, 27.

76 Ib., 265.

77 Tertullian, *De Idol.*, 10.

78 Cicero, *In Verr.*, II, 1, 18, 47.

79 On Homeric illustration, K. Bulas in *Eos, Suppl.* III (1929).

80 See below, pp. 260-61.

81 Servius on *Aen.*, VI, 617.

82 Apollodorus, III, 10, 4, with Frazer's note.

83 Sextus Empiricus, *Adv. Gramm.*, 260-62.

84 Quintilian, I, 8, 18*ff.*

85 Epictetus, II, 19, 6-7.

86 *Pap. Soc. Ital.*, I, 19; cf. Marrou, *Hist. Educ.*, p. 233.

87 Sextus Empiricus, *Adv. Gramm.*, 253; cf. John Pinsent, *Greek Mythology* (London, 1969), pp. 53-4.

88 Schol. Homer, *Il.*, II, 212; Servius on *Aen.*, I, 284.

89 Schol. Homer, *Il.*, I, 39; see also Deecke, op. cit., pp. 67*ff.*

90 Servius on *Aen.*, I, 242; cf. 247; VIII, 9; Servius Danielis on *Aen.*, XI, 246.

91 Id., on *Aen.*, VII, 678.

92 Degenhardt, op. cit., pp. 61*ff.*; 68*ff.*

93 Schol. Homer, *Il.*, XXI, 196; Schol. Hesiod, *Theog.*, 4; Lucan, II, 403*ff.*

94 Servius on *Aen.*, I, 245; IX, 30.

95 Sextus Empiricus, *Adv. Gramm.*, 91-3.

96 Ausonius, *Prof.*, 21, 25.

97 Seneca, *Epp.*, 88, 3; Juvenal, VII, 230-31.

98 Quintilian, I, 2, 14.

99 Juvenal, VI, 450-51; Quintilian, I, 8, 18-21.

100 Seneca, *Epp.*, 88, 37 (Didymus); ib., 6-8, *Dial.*, X, 13, 2.

101 Charisius, p. 162, 6, Barwick; Servius on *Aen.*, V, 4; Servius Danielis on *Aen.*, IV, 682.

102 Suetonius, *Tib.*, 70, 3; *S.H.A. Hadrian*, 16, 8.
103 Virgil, *Aen.*, X, 388-9.
104 K. Lehrs, *De Aristarchi Studiis Homericis* (Leipzig, 1882), pp. 197*ff*.
105 Suetonius, *De Gramm.*, 11, sub fin.
106 Schol. Juvenal, VII, 234; Servius on *Aen.*, X, 388; Hyginus, *Fab.*, 96.
107 Seneca, *Epp.*, 108, 24-9.
108 Virgil, *Geo.*, III, 66*ff*. and 284.
109 Id., *Aen.*, VI, 275.
110 Seneca, loc. cit., 33-5.
111 W. Kroll, *Studien zum Verständnis der römischen Literatur* (Stuttgart, 1924), pp. 64*ff*.
112 Plutarch, *Moralia*, 15-18.
113 Exx. in Degenhardt, op. cit., pp. 95-6.
114 Lucian, *Menipp.*, 3.
115 Plutarch, *Moralia*, 19b; 26c-e.
116 Ib., 19d (Homer, *Od.*, VIII, 329; cf. W.B. Stanford on 266*ff*.).
117 Ib., 20b.
118 Ib., 20c-21d; 22c.
119 Horace, *Epp.*, I, 2, 1-26. See W.B. Stanford, *The Ulysses Theme* (Oxford, 1954), pp. 121*ff*.
120 Servius on *Aen.*, II, 428, 638; III, 713; VI, 176, XI, 169; XII, 465, 940.
121 Id., on *Aen.*, VI, 95.
122 Id., on *Aen.*, VI, 660.
123 Id., on *Aen.*, II, 726, VIII, 110; IX, 3, 57, 62, 121, 734; X, 454, 644; XII, 786.
124 Quintilian, I, 8, 17.
125 [Plutarch], *De vita et poesi Homeri*, 162; Schol. Homer, *Il.* XI, 690; *Od.*, III, 184; cf. Cicero, *Ad Att.*, I, 16, 1; Quintilian, VII, 10, 11; Pliny, *Epp.*, III, 9, 28; Servius, *praef.*, p. 4.
126 Cf. Kroll, op. cit., p. 135.
127 Schol., Homer, *Il.*, XI, 809, XV, 390.
128 Schol., Homer, *Il.*, XVIII, 312.
129 Schol., Homer, *Il.*, XXII, 437, 447.
130 Cf. Schol., Sophocles, *Elect.*, 1098.
131 Donatus on Terence, *And.*, 228, 399, 459, 481; *Ad.*, 78, *et al.*
132 C.G. Cobet, *Miscellanea Critica* (Leiden, 1876), pp. 225-39; D.M. Schenkeveld in *Mnemosyne*, XXIII (1970), pp. 162*ff*.
133 Schol. Homer, *Il.*, I, 29-31.
134 Ib., XXIV, 130-32.
135 Ib., III, 423-6.
136 Schol. Homer, *Od.*, XI, 525. See now R.R. Schlunk, *The Homeric Scholia and the Aeneid* (Ann Arbor, 1974), pp. 8*ff*.
137 Servius (with Servius Danielis), on *Aen.*, I, 92.
138 Id., on *Aen.*, I, 180.
139 Id., on *Aen.*, III, 9; cf. E. Thomas, *Essai sur Servius* (Paris, 1880), p. 240.
140 [Plutarch], *De vita et poesi Homeri*, 165-8; Schol. Homer, *Il.*, IX, 31.
141 Cicero, *Orat.*, 21, 72, with Kroll's note.
142 Aristotle, *Rhet.*, III, 7, 1-2; Demetrius, *On Style*, 120, 237; Theon, II, 116, 13, Sp.
143 Donatus on Terence, *And.*, 808, 832; *Eun.*, 590; *Ad.*, 111, 638, 731.
144 Quintilian, VIII, 3, 48.
145 Servius on *Aen.*, I, 177.
146 Ib., 726; *Geo.*, I, 391.
147 Id., on *Aen.*, I, 118; II, 482; III, 217, *et al.* Norden on *Aen.*, VI, p. 115,n.
148 Quintilian, VIII, 3, 16.
149 Id., 24-5.
150 Id., VIII, 5, 3.
151 [Plutarch], *De vita et poesi Homeri*, 152*ff*.; 186; Schol. Homer, *Il.*, XVII, 32.
152 Plutarch, *Moralia*, 35f; Sextus Empiricus, *Adv. Gramm.*, 277*ff*.
153 Quintilian, I, 8, 12.
154 Id., X, 1, 50, 52, 60, et saep.
155 [Plutarch], op. cit., 174.
156 Quintilian, X, 1, 49; Tryphon, III, 202, 7, Sp.; Schol., Homer, *Il.*, XVIII, 20.
157 Schenkeveld, op. cit., pp. 173-5.
158 Schol., Homer, *Il.*, XVIII, 483.
159 Ib., XI, 17; Schenkeveld, p. 171.

160 Servius on *Aen.*, I, 145; II, 268.
161 Id., on *Aen.*, II, 322; III, 291;
    Serv. Dan. on XI, 756; XII, 754.
162 Id., on *Aen.*, VIII, 607; XII, 90.
163 See note 1 above.

164 Jullien, op. cit., pp. 266*ff.*;
    Wilkins, op. cit., pp. 68*ff.*; H.I.
    Marrou, *Saint Augustin et la fin
    de la culture antique* (Paris, 1938),
    pp. 20*ff.*

Chapter XVIII

1 Jullien, *Les Professeurs* ..., c. viii;
  G. Reichel, *Quaestiones progymnasmaticae* (Leipzig, 1909); W.
  Kroll in P.-W., *R.E.*, Suppbd.
  VII, 'Rhetorik', col.1118-9; D.L.
  Clark, *Rhetoric in Greco-Roman
  Education* (New York, 1957), c. vi
  (scarcely using Theon, a major
  source); Marrou, *Hist. Educ.*,
  pp. 238*ff.* 273*ff.* (Greece), 379
  (Rome).
2 *Rhet. ad Alex.*, 28, p. 1436a
  25; *kata ta prostagmata*, i.e.
  'according to directions'
  previously given, was proposed
  by Usener.
3 Quintilian, II, 4, 41-2.
4 Suetonius, *De Rhet.*, 1.
5 Quintilian, I, 9, 6.
6 Text in Spengel, *Rhetores Graeci*
  (Leipzig, 1854), II, 59*ff.* Christ-
  Schmid, II, i, pp. 460-61, date
  him *c.* A.D. 100.
7 Text in *Rhet. Graec.* (Sp.), II,
  1*ff.*, and H. Rabe, *Hermogenis
  Opera* (Leipzig 1913); but Rabe
  doubts the authenticity.
8 Text in *Rhet. Lat. Min.*, pp.
  551*ff.*
9 Text in *Rhet. Graec.*, II, 21*ff.*,
  and H. Rabe, *Aphthonii Progymnasmata* (Leipzig, 1926). All
  references to Theon,
  Hermogenes, and Aphthonius are
  given, for convenience, to
  Spengel's pages.
10 Notably by Doxapater and
   Ioannes Sardianus.
11 *Aphthonii Progymnasmata, a
   Rodolpho Agricola partim, partim a Ioanne Maria Catanaeo
   Latinitate donata, cum scholiis
   R. Lorichii* (1542), often
   reprinted.

12 T.W. Baldwin, *William
   Shakespere's Small Latine and
   Lesse Greeke* (University of
   Illinois Press, Urbana, 1944), II,
   pp. 288*ff.*
13 D.L. Clark, *John Milton at St
   Paul's School* (New York, 1948),
   pp. 230*ff.*
14 Text in R. Foerster, *Libanii Opera*
   (Leipzig, Teubner, 1915), VIII.
15 Text in *Rhet. Graec.* (Sp.), III
   449*ff.*, and J. Felten (Leipzig,
   1913).
16 Suetonius, *De Rhet.*, 1.
17 Id., *De Gramm.*, 4.
18 Id., ib., 'iam discretis professioni-
   bus'; Quintilian, II, 1, 4.
19 Ib., 12-13.
20 Suetonius, loc. cit.
21 Quintilian, II, 1, 1*ff.*
22 Id., I, 9, 1*ff.* and esp. 6; II, 1, 8
   and 4, 1.
23 Theon, 76, 5*ff.* (fable); 93, 5*ff.*
   (narrative); 104, 15*ff.* (*chreia*).
24 Suetonius, *De Rhet.*, 1.
25 Theon, 72, 24.
26 Ib., 70, 24.
27 Quintilian, I, 9, 2; Theon, 74, 8;
   Hermogenes, 4, 12; Nicolaus
   Sophista, III, 454, 22*ff.*, Sp.
28 Nicolaus Sophista, III, 454, 3, Sp.
29 Theon, 75, 16.
30 Hermogenes, 3, 18.
31 Aesop, 268, 269; Babrius, 93;
   Libanius, VIII, 24, F.
32 Nicolaus Sophista, III, 452, 27.
33 Horace, *Serm.*, II, 6, 79*ff.*;
   Babrius, 108.
34 Theon, 75, 17*ff.*, Aesop, 339;
   Phaedrus, I, 4; Babrius, 79.
35 Theon, loc. cit.; Hermogenes, 4,
   14; Aphthonius, 21, 10.
36 Theon, 75, 9, and 31.
37 Aristotle, *Rhet.*, II, 20, 7; *Rhet.*

ad Herenn. I, 6, 10; Cicero, *De Orat.*, II, 66, 264; Quintilian VI, 3, 44.

38 Quintilian, I, 9, 2.

39 So J.P. Postgate in *C.R.*, XXXIII (1919), pp. 19-24.

40 So B.E. Perry, *Babrius and Phaedrus* (Loeb Library, 1965), *Introduction*, pp. 1-1i. He places Babrius in the second half of the 1st century A.D.

41 Quintilian is certainly not speaking of Greek alone; Perry's citation of I, 1, 12-13 refers to a much earlier stage.

42 See F.H. Colson's note on Quintilian, I, 9, 2, and in *C.R.*, XXXIII (1919), pp. 59*ff*.

43 Hesiod, *W.D.*, 202*ff.*; Gellius, II, 29; Lucilius, 988-9, M. and Porphyrio on Horace, *Epp.*, I, 1, 74; Horace, *Serm.*, II, 6, 79*ff*.

44 Quintilian, V, 11, 19-20 (not cited by Colson); note 'ne in poemate quidem', i.e. normally in prose.

45 Quintilian, X, 5, 4-8.

46 Theon, II, 62, 10*ff.*, Sp.; cf. 65, 23; Dio Chrysostom, XVIII, 19.

47 Id., 64, 29; 74, 9.

48 Suetonius, *De Rhet.*, 1.

49 Theon, 99, 17.

50 Hermogenes, 6, 21.

51 Theon, 97, 30.

52 Hermogenes, 6, 1; slightly varied in Theon, 98, 32 and Quintilian, I, 9, 5.

53 See G. von Wartensleben, *Begriff der griechischen Chreia und Beiträge zur Geschichte ihrer Form* (Heidelberg, 1901).

54 Quintilian, I, 9, 5, refers only to cases; Theon, 101, 8*ff.* to number as well.

55 British Museum *Add. MS.*37516, published by F.G. Kenyon in *J.H.S.*, XXIX (1909), pp. 29-31.

56 British Museum *Add. MS.*37533; Kenyon pp. 32*ff.* and esp. p. 38. See further, A Brinkmann in *Rh. M.*, LXV (1910), pp. 149-55.

57 Quintilian, I, 9, 3; Suetonius, *De Gramm.*, 4. The reading

aetiologiae has rightly replaced ethologiae in modern editions of both authors. See Colson, ad loc., and in *C.R.*, XXXV (1921), pp. 150*ff.*, and esp. R.P. Robinson in *C.P.*, XV (1920), pp. 370*ff*.

58 Rutilius Lupus, II, 10 (*Rhet. Lat. Min.*, p. 21, 8); Quintilian, IX, 3, 93.

59 Quintilian, I, 9, 3, 'personis continetur' (if the text is sound).

60 Aristotle, *Rhet.*, II, 21, 2-8.

61 *Rhet. ad Alex.*, p. 1430b.

62 Euripides, *Hecuba*, 864-5, quoted by Aristotle, loc. cit.

63 Theon, 99, 19*ff*.

64 Colson's contention that the *pupil* always supplied the reason is dubious; cf. Robinson, p. 378, and the frequent use of *subiecta ratio* in definitions, as *Rhet. ad Herenn.*, IV, 17, 24-5; Cicero, *De Orat.*, III, 54, 207; Quintilian, VIII, 5, 4; IX, 3, 93.

65 Theon, 103, 28.

66 *Rhet. ad Herenn.*, IV, 42, 54*ff*. The example is a *sententia*, not a *chreia*, as is often wrongly stated from Marx, *Proleg.*, p. 111, onwards.

67 Theon, 65, 23.

68 Hermogenes, 6, 19; Aphthonius, 23, 14.

69 Libanius, VIII, 82*ff*. F.

70 Hesiod, *W.D.*, 287*ff*.

71 Quintilian, I, 9, 6; cf. II, 4, 2.

72 Aphthonius, 22, 14.

73 Libanius, VIII, 29*ff.*, F.

74 J. Grafton Milne in *J.H.S.*, XXVIII (1908), pp. 128-30; E. Ziebarth, *Aus der antiken Schule*, Bonn, 1913), nos.17b and 40; Pack², nos. 2723, 2731, 2649.

75 Hermogenes, 5.

76 Cicero, *De Inv.*, I, 19, 27 (*exercitatione*).

77 Id., ib.; *Rhet. ad Herenn.*, I, 8, 12, *exerceri* and 13, in *exercendo*.

78 Quintilian, II, 4, 2.

79 Id., ib., 5, 1-3.

80 Theon, 66, 16 (Gyges); Libanius, VIII, 41 (Polycrates), 52 (Arion); Theon, 84, 26; 87, 21*ff.* (Plataea).

81 Quintilian, II, 4, 15; Theon, 86, 7.
82 Cf. above, p. 244, on the teaching of *oeconomia* by the *grammaticus*.
83 Theon, 80, 8*ff*.; 81, 8*ff*.
84 Id., 83, 14*ff*.
85 Horace, *A.P.*, 43-4.
86 Theon, 84, 5*ff*.
87 Horace, *A.P.*, 25-6.
88 Theon, 84, 18*ff*.
89 Id., 85, 28*ff*.; 87, 13*ff*.; 91, 11*ff*.
90 Id., 93, 4*ff*.; Hermogenes, 8, 29*ff*., and Aphthonius, 27, 25*ff*. and 30, 14*ff*., treat it separately.
91 Aphthonius, loc. cit. (Daphne); Theon, 93, 23, and 94, 17*ff*. (Medea); Hermogenes, 9, 8. (Arion); other exx. in Theon, 95, 6 and 96, 4*ff*.
92 Libanius, VIII, 123*ff*. F.
93 See below, pp. 296*ff*. on the 'conjectural' type of issue.
94 Quintilian, II, 4, 18-19.
95 Cicero, *De Orat.*, III, 27, 106.
96 Quintilian, II, 4, 22.
97 Theon, 106, 8*ff*.; Hermogenes, 9, 20; Aphthonius, 33, 6; Libanius VIII, 158*ff*.; 171*ff*. F.
98 Libanius, VIII, 203*ff*., F.
99 Ib., 182*ff*.
100 Quintilian, loc. cit.
101 Cf. ib., 'perorare'; Aphthonius, 32, 33.
102 Theon, 107, 19*ff*.; Hermogenes, 9, 24*ff*.; Aphthonius, 32, 27.
103 Cicero, *Pro Rosc. Am.*, 13, 37-8.
104 Quintilian, II, 4, 20.
105 *Rhet. ad Herenn.*, III, 8, 15.
106 Ib., III, 6, 10, with Caplan's note; Quintilian, III, 4, 12*ff*.
107 Suetonius, *De Rhet.*, I; Quintilian, II, 4, 20.
108 Libanius, VIII, 216*ff*., and 282*ff*., F.
109 Quintilian, III, 7, 7*ff*. and 26-8; Libanius, VIII, 257*ff*., 306*ff*.; Polybius, XII, 26b; Fronto, pp. 6 and 203, van den Hout. See esp. T.C. Burgess, *Epideictic Literature* (University of Chicago Press, 1902).
110 *Rhet. ad Herenn.*, III, 7, 13*ff*.; Cicero, *De Orat.*, II, 84, 342*ff*.;

Quintilian, III, 7, 12; Theon, 109, 28*ff*.
111 Quintilian, III, 7, 10-11.
112 Theon, 111, 23*ff*.
113 Quintilian, III, 7, 11.
114 Cicero, loc. cit.; Quintilian, III, 7, 13; Theon, 111, 15.
115 Quintilian, III, 7, 12.
116 Ib., 15; Cicero, *De Orat.*, II, 84, 345*ff*. and Theon, 112, 3*ff*. prefer treatment according to each quality.
117 Cicero, loc. cit., 346-7; Theon, 110, 21*ff*.
118 Cicero, loc. cit., 348; Theon, 111 1*ff*.
119 Quintilian, II, 4, 21; Theon, 112, 20*ff*.
120 Theon, loc cit.
121 Aphthonius, 43, 8*ff*.
122 Libanius, VIII, 334*ff*. F.
123 Ib., 342*ff*.
124 Theon, 113, 24*ff*. (topics) Libanius, VIII, 349*ff*., 353*ff*. F.
125 [Quintilian], *Decl. Min.*, 268.
126 Cf. Hermogenes, 15, 22.
127 Quintilian III, 8, 53; Hermogenes, 15, 34*ff*.; Libanius, VIII, 372*ff*. Aphthonius, 45, 21.
128 Libanius, VIII, 379*ff*.
129 Cf. Hermogenes, 16, 4.
130 Cf. Theon, 115, 22, and Hermogenes, 15, 29, with Horace, *A.P.*, 114*ff*.; C.O. Brink, *Horace on Poetry, The Ars Poetica* (Cambridge, 1971), pp. 190*ff*.
131 Suetonius, *De Gramm.*, 4; Priscian, *Rhet. Lat. Min.*, p. 557, 27, thus translates the Greek *prosopopoeia*.
132 Augustine, *Conf.*, I, 17.
133 Friedländer, op. cit., vol. 3, p. 45.
134 Theon treats the exercise entirely as an address, and includes the protreptic speech as one type.
135 Quintilian, III, 8, 53.
136 Cicero, *In Cat.*, 1, 7, 18; I, 11, 27-9; *Pro Caelio*, 14, 33, with R.G. Austin's note; this last form was called *eidolopoeia* (Hermogenes, 15, 14; Aphthonius, 44, 28).
137 Quintilian, III, 8, 49-54.

138 Cicero, *In Verrem*, II, 4, 107
(Henna); 117*ff*. (Syracuse);
Gellius, X, 3, 7*ff*. on *In Verrem*
II, 5, 161; Quintilian, IV, 3,
12*ff*.; XI, 3, 164.

139 See below, p. 282-3. and esp.
Seneca the elder, *Contr.*, II,
Praef. 1.

140 Horace, *A.P.*, 14*ff*., with Brink's
notes; *descriptio* was included
among the figures, as well as
being an exercise in itself.

141 Cf. S.F. Bonner, in *A.J.P.*,
LXXXVII (1966), pp. 278*ff*.

142 Quintilian, II, 4, 3; cf. Lucian's
warning to historians, *De conscr.
hist.*, 57.

143 Quintilian, VIII, 3, 61-71; IX, 2,
44.

144 Theon, 118, 11*ff*.; Hermogenes,
16, 10*ff*. Aphthonius, 46, 12*ff*.;
Libanius, VIII, 460*ff*. F.

145 Theon, 119, 27*ff*.

146 Ib., 65, 17.

147 Ib., 120, 12; Hermogenes, 17, 16;
Aphthonius, 49, 17 and 50, 5;
Libanius, VIII, 550*ff*., F.

148 Quintilian, II, 4, 24-5.

149 Cicero, *Pro Murena*, 9, 21*ff*.

150 Quintilian, loc. cit.

151 Id., II, 1, 9, 'citra complexum
rerum personarumque'; cf. II, 4,
36.

152 Theon, 121, 6*ff*.; Hermogenes,
17, 26*ff*.; Aphthonius, 49, 15,
cf. above, p. 83.

153 Suetonius, *de Rhet.*, 1.

154 *Rhet. ad Alex.*, 1421b.

155 Theon, 121, 18*ff*.; Hermogenes,

18, 7; Aphthonius, 50, 1.

156 See above, p. 83.

157 See below, p. 321.

158 Quintilian, II, 4, 33.

159 Theon, 128, 25.

160 It is at this point that the text of
Theon breaks off.

161 Quintilian, II, 4, 37*ff*.

162 [Quintilian], *Decl. Min.*, 255 (p.
44, Ritter).

163 Livy, XXXIV, 2-4 (Cato) and 5-7
(Valerius).

164 See below, pp. 301-2, 320.

165 Aphthonius, 54, 5; Seneca the
elder, *Contr.*, I, 4; IX, 1; [Quin-
tilian] *Decl. Min.*, 244, 284 et
saep.

166 Theon, 65, 29*ff*.

167 Quintilian, II, 5, 18-20.

168 Ib., 21-3.

169 Id., II, 2, 8.

170 Theon, 70, 30.

171 Quintilian, II, 6, 1-2.

172 Ib., 4-7.

173 Ib., II, 3, 7.

174 Theon, 72, 15.

175 Quintilian, II, 8, 6-10.

176 Theon, 72, 5.

177 Quintilian, II, 4, 10.

178 Ib., 4-9.

179 Ib., 11.

180 Ib., 12-14.

181 Id., II, 7, 1 and 5.

182 Id., II, 2, 6.

183 Jullien, *Les Professeurs*, pp.
323-4.

184 Cf. F.H. Colson's Introduction to
Quintilian I, p. xxxvi; D.L. Clark,
op. cit., p. 211.

Chapter XIX

1 See Part I, c. vi, no. 19.

2 In addition to the *Prolegomena* of
F. Marx, see H. Caplan, *Rhetorica
ad Herennium* (Loeb Library,
(1954), and the commentary of G.
Calboli, *Cornifici Rhetorica ad C.
Herennium* (Bologna, 1969).

3 Cicero, *Part. Orat.*, 40, 139.

4 Quintilian, III, 1, 17-18; cf. M.
Schanz in *Hermes*, XXV (1890),

pp. 36-54, and G.M.A. Grube in
A.J.P., LXXX (1959), pp. 337-65.

5 Quintilian, loc. cit., and Juvenal,
VII, 177.

6 F. Marx, *A Corneli Celsi quae
supersunt* (*Corp. Med. Lat.*, I,
pp. 409-21).

7 Quintilian, VII, 4, 40.

8 Id., II, 10, 2; 11, 1.

9 Id., II, 10, 1.

10 *Rhet. ad Herenn.*, II, 1, 1.
11 Tacitus, *Dial.*, 35; see esp. R. Kohl, *De scholasticarum declamationum argumentis ex historia petitis* (Paderborn, 1915).
12 Seneca the elder, *Suas.*, IV, 5. The *Suasoriae* were edited by W.A. Edward (Cambridge, 1928). H.J. Müller's text of *Suas.* and *Controv.* (Vienna, 1887) is reprinted (Hildesheim, 1963); brief notes in H. Bornecque's edn (Paris, 1932); see now text and trans. by M. Winterbottom (Loeb Library, 1974).
13 On the Greek declaimers (*Suas.*, I, 16), see italicized names in H. Bornecque, *Les déclamations et les déclamateurs* (Lille, 1902), pp. 143*ff*.
14 Id., *Contr.*, IX, 3, 13.
15 Listed by D.L. Clark, op. cit., p. 221.
16 *Rhet. ad Herenn.*, III, 2, 2; cf. *Rom. Declam.*, p. 23.
17 Cicero, *De Inv.*, I, 12, 17.
18 Schol., Juvenal, X, 167 (p. 172, Wessner).
19 Juvenal, VII, 162.
20 Quintilian, III, 8, 17. On this book of Q., see the commentary of J. Adamietz (Munich, 1966).
21 *Rhet. ad Herenn.*, loc. cit.
22 Quintilian, III, 8, 33.
23 *Rhet. ad Herenn.*, III, 4, 8; Cicero, *De Inv.*, II, 57, 171-2; Quintilian, III, 8, 23.
24 Quintilian, loc. cit., and II, 8, 30.
25 Martianus Capella, p. 221, 3, Dick (*Rhet. Lat. Min.*, p. 456, 30); for other Cato-themes, cf. *Rom. Declam.*, pp. 8-9.
26 Seneca the elder, *Suas.*, VI, 14-15.
27 Quintilian, VII, 4, 2.
28 Id., III, 8, 19.
29 Id., VII, 2, 6.
30 Id., III, 8, 55; cf. Seneca the elder, *Contr.*, II, 4, 8.
31 *Rhet. ad Herenn.*, III, 2, 2.
32 Ib.
33 Juvenal, I, 16.
34 Quintilian, III, 8, 47.
35 See now J. Martin, *Antike Rhetorik, Technik und Methode* (Munich, 1974), pp. 167-76.

36 *Rhet. ad Herenn.*, III, 2, 3; cf. Cicero, *Part. Orat.*, 24, 83.
37 Cf. Emporius in Halm, *Rhet. Lat. Min.* p. 571, 16*ff*.
38 Quintilian, III, 8, 22 and 25.
39 Id., III, 8, 16, where more recent themes, dating probably from Claudius or Nero, are also mentioned, viz., whether the Isthmus can be cut, whether the Pomptine Marshes can be drained, whether a harbour can be made at Ostia.
40 Id., III, 8, 26-7.
41 *Rhet. ad Herenn.*, III, 5, 8.
42 Seneca the elder, *Suas.*, VI, 13; Emporius, p. 571, 34.
43 Seneca the elder, *Suas.*, V, 8.
44 Id., VI, 12-13.
45 Id., VII, 10.
46 Id., VI, 10.
47 Id., II, 11.
48 Id., V, 4.
49 Id., I, 8 and 9.
50 Id., I, 10.
51 Id., III, 3,
52 Quintilian, III, 8, 35.
53 Seneca the elder, *Suas.*, I, 1, 4, and 13.
54 Id., II, 1, and 14.
55 Id., VI, 10.
56 Id., III, 4, 5, on Virgil-imitation; cf. *Contr.*, II, *Praef.* 1,; Quintilian, II, 4, 3; Pliny, *Epp.*, VII, 9, 8.
57 Seneca the elder, *Suas.*, I, 9.
58 Id., II, 3.
59 Id., V. 8.
60 Id., V, 1-2 (Marathon, Salamis), 5 ('enumeratio bellorum').
61 Id., II, 2; VI, 6; *Rhet. ad Herenn.*, III, 5, 9; Seneca, *Epp.* 24, 6-7.
62 Seneca the elder, *Suas.*, III, 3-4; IV, 4.
63 Valerius Maximus, p. 473, Kempf; cf. Norden, óp. cit., I, pp. 303-4.
64 Seneca the elder, *Suas.*, I, 3.
65 Cf. S.F. Bonner in *A.J.P.* LXXXVII (1966), pp. 260*ff*.
66 *Suas.*, II, 2, 3, and 7.
67 Ib., 4.
68 Quintilian, VIII, 5, esp. 26-30.
69 Ib., 2, 11, and 13-14; cf. *A.J.P.*, loc. cit., pp. 264*ff*.
70 Cf. Cicero, *Pro Rosc. Am.*, 26, 72,

and *Orator*, 107.

71 Seneca the elder, *Suas.*, VI, 4; cf. II, 5.

72 Id., *Suas.*, I, 5-6.

73 Quintilian, III, 8, 37.

74 Id., III, 8, 15.

75 D.L. Clark, op. cit., pp. 219, 222, 224, tends to confuse the two forms; cf. *Rom. Declam.*, p. 53.

76 Contrast Juvenal, I, 16, 'consilium dedimus Sullae', with Quintilian, III, 8, 53, 'verba ... Sullae'.

77 Ib., 49.

78 Polybius, XII, 25a and b.

79 Quintilian, II, 5, 19.

80 Livy, XXII, 59 and 60.

81 For Silius, R. Rebischke, *De Silii Italici Orationibus* (Diss., Königsberg, 1913); for Lucan, cf. *A.J.P.*, loc. cit., pp. 184-9.

82 Quintilian, X, 1, 90.

83 Lucan, IV, 476*ff.*; VII, 262*ff.*, 331*ff.*, 484*ff.*

84 Quintilian, X, 1, 74-5; he does not mention the markedly rhetorical

work of Curtius Rufus in Latin.

85 Dionysius, *De Demosthene*, 21 (I, 175, 20*ff.*, U.-R); Hermogenes, II, 401, 25*ff.*, Sp.

86 Quintilian, III, 8, 67-8.

87 Ib., 69-70.

88 Id., II, 3, 1-2.

89 Aristotle, *Rhet.*, II, 14, 12; Cicero, *Part Orat.*, 13; Quintilian, III, 8, 6-7.

90 Quintilian, III, 8, 58*ff.*

91 Seneca the elder, *Contr.*, VII, 7, 19; cf. Kohl, op. cit., p. 86.

92 Id., *Suas.*, I, 2; Bornecque, ad loc. compares Schol., Lucan, III, 233.

93 Quintilian, III, 8, 61-2.

94 Ib., 69-70.

95 On the importance of emotional appeal in real debates, cf. Quintilian, III, 8, 12.

96 Seneca the elder, *Contr.* II, 2, 8 and 12.

97 Ib., VII, 2 (Popillius); IX, 2 (Flamininus); cf. Exc. VI, 5 (Iphicrates); Exc. VIII, 2 (Phidias).

Chapter XX

1 Cicero, *Brutus*, 89, 307.

2 Cf. *Rom. Orat.*, pp. 343-6.

3 Quintilian, II, 13, 15.

4 Cf. M.L. Clarke in *Greece and Rome*, 2nd series, XIV (1967), pp. 24-37; G. Kennedy, *Quintilian* (New York, 1969), c.i.

5 *Rhet. ad Herenn.*, I, 5, 6*ff.*; Cicero, *De Inv.*, I, 15, 20*ff.*; *Part. Orat.* 28-30; Quintilian, IV, 1; Martin, op. cit., pp. 60*ff.*

6 Quintilian, IV, 1, 6-7.

7 Ib., 16-17; 20-21.

8 Ib., 33-4.

9 Ib., 23-6.

10 Cf. Richard Du Cann, *The Art of the Advocate* (London, 1964), ch. 4 ('Opening the Case'), esp. p. 67.

11 *Rhet. ad Herenn.*, I, 6, 9*ff.*; Cicero, *De Inv.*, I, 17, 23*ff.*; and esp. Quintilian, IV, 1, 40-49.

12 Quintilian, IV, 1, 62.

13 Ib., 54-60.

14 *Rhet. ad Herenn.*, I, 7, 11; Cicero, *De Inv.*, I, 18, 26; Quintilian, IV, 1, 71.

15 Dionysius, *De Lysia*, 17; for occasional omission of *exordium*, cf. Quintilian, IV, 1, 72.

16 For the transition to the *narratio*, cf. ib., 76*ff.*

17 Id., IV, 2, 4*ff.*

18 Ib., 8.

19 Ib., 9-23.

20 Ib., 24-7.

21 Cicero, *Pro Milone*, 3, 7-8, 23.

22 Id., *Pro Caelio*, 2, 3-20, 50; cf. R.G. Austin's edn, p. 45.

23 *Rhet. ad Alex.*, c.30; *Rhet. ad Herenn.*, I, 9, 14*ff.*; Cicero, *De Inv.*, I, 20, 28*ff.*; *Part. Orat.*, 31-2. Aristotle, *Rhet.*, III, 16, p.1416b, rejected the requirement of brevity. Cf. Martin, pp. 80*ff.*

24 Quintilian, IV, 2, 31*ff.*

25 Ib., 36*ff.*

26 Ib., 40-47.

27 Ib., 47-51.

28 Ib., 52-8.

29 Cicero, *Pro Milone*, 10, 28.

30 Quintilian, IV, 2, 66*ff.*

31 Ib., 75-6.

32 Ib., 84.
33 Ib., 86.
34 Ib., 76-7.
35 Ib., 88-91.
36 Ib., 101-2.
37 Ib., 119.
38 *Rhet. ad Herenn.*, I, 10, 17; Cicero, *De Inv.*, I, 22, 31-23, 33; Quintilian, IV, 5; Martin, pp. 92*ff*.
39 Cicero, *Div. in Caec.*, 14, 45; *Pro Quinctio*, 10, 35; *Brutus*, 88, 302; Quintilian, IV, 5, 24.
40 Quintilian, IV, 5, 3.
41 Ib., 4*ff*.
42 Ib., 8*ff*.
43 Ib., 12; cf. Cicero, *Pro Murena*, 5, 11.
44 Ib., 15; cf. Cicero, *Pro Milone*, 11, 30-31 (*partitio*) and 27, 72*ff*.
45 Ib., 6 and 25.
46 Aristotle, *Rhet.*, I, 2, p.1355b and 15, p.1375a; Cicero, *De Orat.* 11, 27, 116; Quintilian, V, 1, 1-2; Martin, pp. 95*ff*.
47 *Rhet. ad Herenn.*, II, 6, 9*ff*.; Cicero, *De Orat.*, II, 27, 118-19; Quintilian, V, 1, 2-3; 7, 3-5.
48 Quintilian, V, 7, 28.
49 Id., V, 7, *passim*.
50 Cf. D. Matthes, in *Lustrum* III, p. 120.
51 Id., *Hermagorae Fragmenta*, pp. 17-41.
52 *Rhet. ad Herenn.*, I, 10, 17; 15, 25; 16, 26; Cicero, *De Inv.*, I, 13, 18, Quintilian, III, 11, 4; Martin, pp. 28*ff*.
53 *Rhet. ad Herenn.*, II, 2, 3*ff*.; Cicero, *De Inv.*, I, 8, 10; II, 4, 14-16, 51; Quintilian, VII, 2, 7*ff*.
54 *Rhet. ad Herenn.*, I, 11, 18; Cicero, *De Inv.*, I, 8, 11 and 49, 92. Hermogenes has a similar example concerning a man discovered burying the body of someone recently slain, and charged with murder (pp. 30, 36, 49, 54, of Rabe's text).
55 Quintilian, VII, 2, 23-4.
56 Cicero, *De Inv.*, II, 4, 14-15.
57 Id., *Pro Rosc. Am.*, 23, 64-5.

58 *Rhet. ad Herenn.*, II, 2, 3-3, 5; Cicero, *De Inv.*, II, 5, 17 — 8, 28 (*causa*), 9, 28 — 11, 37 (*persona*); Quintilian, VII, 2, 27-35 (*persona*), 36-41 (*causa*).
59 Quintilian, VII, 2, 39.
60 Cicero, *De Inv.*, II, 5, 19; Quintilian, VII, 2, 35.
61 Cicero, loc. cit., 5, 18; 6, 20 -7, 23.
62 Ib., 8, 25.
63 Ib., 8, 26-8.
64 Ib., 10, 32-4.; Quintilian, loc. cit. 28; *Rhet. ad Herenn.*, II, 3, 5.
65 Cicero, loc. cit., 35-7; Quintilian, loc. cit., 29, 33.
66 Cicero, loc. cit., 40-45; Quintilian, loc. cit., 42-5; *Rhet. ad Herenn.*, II, 4, 6-7.
67 *Rhet. ad Herenn.*, loc. cit., 5, 8; Cicero, loc. cit., 13, 42; Quintilian, loc. cit., 46-50.
68 *Rhet. ad Herenn.*, II, 12, 17; Cicero, *De Inv.*, II, 17, 52*ff*.
69 Cicero, loc cit., 18, 55; Quintilian, VII, 3, 9-10 and 21*ff*. Greek in origin, and almost certainly in Hermagoras; cf. Matthes in *Lustrum* III, pp. 146-7.
70 Quintilian, loc. cit., 6 and 10.
71 Ib., 30.
72 Ib., 26; cf. [Quintilian], *Decl. min.*, 311, pp. 233-4, Ritter.
73 Quintilian, VII, 3, 2; 4, 25; cf. *Decl. min.*, 316, p. 243, Ritter.
74 Id., VII, 3, 30-34.
75 *Rhet. ad Herenn.*, II, 13, 19-20; Cicero, *De Inv.*, II, 23, 69-71; Quintilian, VII, 4, 4-6.
76 Cf. above, n.52. Also, the case of Horatius and his sister, Cicero, loc. cit., II, 26, 78; Quintilian, III, 6, 76; VII, 4, 8.
77 Cicero, *Pro Milone*, 3, 7 — 4, 11.
78 Quintilian, VII, 4, 9-10.
79 *Rhet. ad Herenn.*, II, 14, 21-2; Cicero, *De Inv.*, II, 24, 72-8; Quintilian, VII, 4, 12.
80 *Rhet. ad Herenn.*, II, 17, 26; Cicero, *De Inv.*, II, 29, 88 — 30, 94; Quintilian, VII, 4, 13-14.
81 *Rhet. ad Herenn.*, II, 16, 23-4;

Cicero, *De Inv.*, II, 31, 94 — 33, 103; Quintilian, VII, 4, 14-16.

82 *Rhet. ad Herenn.*, II, 17, 25-6; Cicero, *De Inv.*, II, 34, 104-36, 109; Quintilian, VII, 4, 17-20.

83 Sometimes the issue was not one of 'quality', but of 'quantity', as in disputes over the assessment of a reward; cf. Cicero, loc. cit., 37, 110*ff.*; Quintilian, loc. cit., 21*ff.*

84 *Rhet. ad Herenn.*, II, 9, 13 — 10, 14; Cicero, *De Inv.*, II, 42, 121 — 48, 143. Quintilian, VII, 6; Martin, pp. 44*ff.* See esp. J. Stroux, *Römische Rechtswissenschaft und Rhetorik* (Potsdam, 1949); J. Santa Cruz in *Z.S.S.* LXXV (1958), pp. 91-115.

85 Quintilian, VII, 6, 2.

86 Cicero, *De Orat.*, II, 24, 100; Quintilian, loc. cit., 6-7.

87 Nepos, *Epaminondas*, 7-8; Plutarch, *Pelopidas*, 25; Cicero, *De Inv.*, I, 33, 55-6.

88 G. Ciulei, *L'Equité chez Cicéron* (Amsterdam, 1972).

89 Cicero, *De Orat.*, I, 39, 180; *Brutus*, 39, 144*ff.*; 52, 194*ff.*; Quintilian, VII, 6, 9*ff.*, *et al.*

90 *Rhet. ad Herenn.*, II, 11, 16; Cicero, *De Inv.*, II, 40, 116 — 41, 121; Quintilian, VII, 9.

91 Quintilian, loc. cit., 6.

92 *Rhet. ad Herenn.*, II, 10, 15; Cicero, *De Inv.*, II, 49, 144-7; Quintilian, VII, 7.

93 *Rhet. ad Herenn.*, II, 12, 18; Cicero, *De Inv.*, II, 50, 148-53; Quintilian, VII, 8.

94 Quintilian, VII, 10, 8*ff.*

95 *Rhet. ad Herenn.*, II, 18, 27 — 19. 30; Cicero, *De Inv.*, I, 24, 34*ff.*; Quintilian, V, 8-14.

96 Cicero, *De Inv.*, I, 31, 51 — 33, 56; Quintilian, V, 11, 2-5.

97 Cicero, *De Inv.*, I, 34, 57-41, 77; Quintilian, V, 10, 1*ff.*

98 *Rhet. ad Herenn.*, II, 20, 31 — 29, 46; Cicero, *De Inv.*, I, 42, 78 — 51, 96; Quintilian, V, 13.

99 *Rhet. ad Herenn.*, II, 24, 38; Cicero, *De Inv.*, I, 45, 83; Quintilian, V, 10, 65-70.

100 *Rhet. ad Herenn.*, II, 30, 47; Cicero, *De Inv.*, I, 52, 98-100; Quintilian, VI, 1, 1-8; Martin, pp. 147*ff.*

101 *Rhet. ad Herenn.*, II, 30, 47 — 31, 50; Cicero, *De Inv.*, I, 53, 100 — 56, 109. Quintilian, VI, 1, 9-52.

102 Quintilian, loc. cit., 36.

103 Ib., 51-2.

104 Ib., 12-20.

105 Ib., 21-7.

106 Ib., 37*ff.*

107 *Rhet. ad Herenn.*, II, 31, 50; Cicero, *De Inv.*, I, 56, 109; Quintilian, loc. cit., 27-9; cf. G.D. Kellogg in *A.J.P.*, XXVIII (1907), pp. 301-10.

108 Cicero, *De Orat.*, II, 39, 162.

109 Id., *Part Orat.*, 1, 1-2.

110 *Rhet. Lat. Min.*, p. 81.

111 Quintilian, II, 5, 1-9 and 14.

112 Id., XI, 3, 47.

113 Id., II, 5, 9.

114 Id., IX, 4.

115 Id., II, 5, 10-13.

116 Id., VIII, 2, 17 and 19; 3, 14, 18, 52, 55.

117 Cicero, *De Orat.*, III, 52, 201-54, 208; *Orat.*, 39, 134-40, 139; *Rhet. ad Herenn.*, IV, 13, 18-55, 69; Quintilian, IX, 2 and 3; A.D. Leeman, *Orationis Ratio* (Amsterdam, 1963), pp. 33*ff.*; Martin, op. cit., pp. 270*ff.*

118 Cicero, *Brut.*, 37, 141; *Orat.*, 39, 136.

119 *Rhet. ad Herenn.*, IV, 13, 19; 28, 38; Quintilian, IX, 3, 28.

120 Cato, fr.173 in *O.R.F.*

121 *Rhet. ad Herenn.*, IV, 20, 27-8; Rutilius Lupus, *Rhet. Lat. Min.*, p. 19; Quintilian, IX, 3, 76-7.

122 *Rhet. ad Herenn.*, IV, 15, 21; Quintilian, IX, 3, 81*ff.*

123 *Rhet. ad Herenn.*, IV, 21, 29-22, 32; Quintilian, IX, 3, 66*ff.*

124 *Rhet. ad Herenn.*, IV, 25, 34; Quintilian, IX, 3, 54*ff.*

125 *Rhet. ad Herenn.*, IV, 23, 33-24, 34; Quintilian, IX, 2, 15; cf. Cicero, *Orat.*, 223.

126 *Rhet. ad Herenn.*, IV, 27, 37; cf. S. Usher in *A.J.P.*, LXXXVI

(1965), pp. 175*ff.*

127 Quintilian, IX, 2, 21.

128 *Rhet. ad Herenn.*, IV, 29, 40; Quintilian, IX, 2, 19.

129 Quintilian, IX, 2, 44*ff.*, 64*ff.*

130 Ib., 26, 29*ff.*, 38, 40.

131 Cicero, *Pro Cael.*, 14, 33-4; *In Cat.*, I, 18 and 27-9.

132 See Harry Caplan, *Of Eloquence: Studies in Ancient and Mediaeval Rhetoric*, ed. Anne King and Helen North (Cornell University Press, 1970), c. ix.

133 *Rhet. ad Herenn.*, III, 16, 29*ff.*; Cicero, *De Orat.*, II, 86, 351*ff.*; Quintilian, XI, 2, 17*ff.*

134 *Rhet. ad Herenn.*, III, 20, 33-4.

135 Quintilian, XI, 2, 33-7 and 45*ff.*

136 *Rhet. ad Herenn.*, III, 11, 19-15, 27.

137 Quintilian, XI, 3, 25.

138 Ib., 28-9.

139 Ib., 47-51.

140 Ib., 44*ff.*, 51-6.

141 Ib., 68*ff.*; 88*ff.*

142 Ib., 117-18; 126.

Chapter XXI

1 Seneca the elder, *Contr.*, I, *Praef.* 12.

2 Cf. *Rom. Declam.*, p. 22.

3 Cf. S.F. Bonner in *C.R.*, LXI (1947), p. 86.

4 *Rom. Declam.*, cc.v and vi (Senecan laws); F. Lanfranchi, *Il Diritto nei Retori Romani* (Milan, 1938) for later ones also.

5 Lanfranchi, op. cit., pp. 573-668 (full Index).

6 Quintilian, II, 10, 12; X, 5, 14 and 21. On declamation and advocacy, see E. Patrick Parks, op. cit. (above, Part I, c.ix, n. 45), with the author's review in *J.R.S.*, XL (1950), pp. 157-8.

7 Suetonius, *De Rhet.*, 1.

8 Text by Constantin Ritter (Leipzig, Teubner, 1884).

9 See C. Ritter, *Die quintilianischen Declamationen* (Freiburg and Tubingen, 1881), pp. 219-56; F. Leo in his *Ausgewählte kleine Schriften*, ed. Eduard Fraenkel (Rome, 1960), pp. 249-61; N. Deratani in *R. Phil.*, XLIX (1925), pp. 101-17; A. Gwynn, op. cit., pp. 210*ff.*

10 For Senecan cases, *Rom. Declam.*, pp. 35, 111-2; *Decl. Min.*, nos. 246, 307, 319, 321, 350, 354, 377, 381; cf. Juvenal, VII, 169.

11 See Mayor on Juvenal, I, 70.

12 Comparison of real with declamatory cases by C. Morawski in *Wien. Stud.*, IV (1882), pp. 166-8,

and N. Deratani in *R. Phil.*, LV (1929), pp. 184*ff.*

13 Cf. the 'Adultera Venefica' themes of Seneca the elder, *Contr.* VI, 6 and [Quintilian], *Decl. Min.*, 319, 354, with Quintilian V, 11, 39, and Tacitus, *Ann.*, III, 22 ('adulteria, venena').

14 On distrust of doctors, cf. Pliny the elder, *N.H.*, XXIX, 7 (from Cato), and 8, 18; on poisoning-complicity, cf. Tacitus, *Ann.*, IV, 3, 5 (Eudemus), and XII, 67, 2 (Xenophon).

15 [Quintilian], *Decl. Min.* 321.

16 Quintilian, VII, 2, 18*ff.*, 23, 25-6.

17 Tacitus, *Ann.* III, 14, 1-3.

18 Seneca the elder, *Contr.*, exc. VI, 6; [Quintilian], *Decl. Min.* 319, 381; Quintilian, VII, 2, 8 and 13.

19 Tacitus, *Ann.* IV, 8, 1.

20 Quintilian, VII, 2, 14*ff.*

21 Ib., 17-18.

22 Cf. Seneca the elder, *Contr. exc.* VI, 4, for the shared cup, fatal to one.

23 Id., *Contr.* VII, 3.

24 [Quintilian], *Decl. Min.* 377.

25 *Dig.* XLVIII, 9, 1.

26 R. Düll in *Z.S.S.*, LXIII (1943), pp.54-116, esp. 96*ff.* (citing, *inter alia*, Livy, *Epit.* 54; Valerius Maximus, V, 4, 3 and 8, 3; Seneca, *De Clem.* I, 15, 2*ff.*; Suetonius, *Aug.* 65).

27 [Quintilian], *Decl. Min.* 356 is instructive.

28 As, e.g. in *Decl. Min.* 257 (p.52,

6, R.).

29 Quintilian, VII, 4, 11.

30 Cf. *Rom. Declam.*, p. 102.

31 *Dig.* V, 2, 1, 'frequentes esse inofficiosi querelas'; ib. 3, 'quod plerumque accidit'. See W.W. Buckland, *Text-Book of Roman Law from Augustus to Justinian* (Cambridge, 1932), pp. 325*ff.*; H.F. Jolowicz and B. Nicholas, *Historical Introduction to the Study of Roman Law* (Cambridge, 1972), pp. 198-9, and esp. E. Renier, *Etude sur l'histoire de la 'querela inofficiosi' en droit romain* (Liège, N.D. (1942)) and L. di Lella, *Querela Inofficiosi Testamenti* (Naples, 1972).

32 *Dig.* V, 2, 2; Renier, op. cit., pp. 94*ff.*

33 Id., pp. 257*ff.*

34 Valerius Maximus, VII, 8, 1.

35 See J.A. Crook in *C.Q.*, *N.S.* XVII (1967), pp. 120-21, on the late Republic.

36 *Dig.* V, 2, 4.

37 Pliny, *Epp.*, VI, 33.

38 Id., ib., V, 1.

39 *Cod. Iust.*, III, 28, 19 and 23, and esp. *Nov.* 115, 3. Conversely, Quintilian VII, 4, 26, mentions as a legal consideration 'quot et quibus causis abdicare non liceat'.

40 [Quintilian], *Decl. Min.*, 279, (p. 136, 15, R.); 330 (p. 297, 4, R.).

41 As in *Decl. Min.*, 356; 330 (p. 299, 9*ff.*) refers to real-life deceptions.

42 Quintilina, VII, 4, 20.

43 Ib., 27, classifies as a group those 'in quibus abdicatur filius, quia non pareat patri'.

44 [Quintilian], *Decl. Min.*, 257; cf. Seneca the elder, *Contr.* I, 6.

45 In *Decl. Min.*, 257 (p. 50, 21), the son accepts that the father has this power.

46 Aristotle, *Nic. Eth.*, IX, 2, 1; Musonius, XVI; Gellius, II, 7, 1.

47 [Quintilian], *Decl. Min.* 271 (pp. 109-10, R.); cf. Seneca, *Contr.* II, 1, 20.

48 Cf. *Decl. Min.*, 376, p. 417, R.

49 Cf. Seneca the elder, *Contr.*, I, 6, 8, 'hic de meritis puellae et moribus'.

50 [Quintilian], *Decl. Min.*, 347.

51 Seneca the elder, *Contr.*, II, 7.

52 [Quintilian], *Decl. Min.* 363; cf. 383.

53 Quintilian, VII, 4, 11.

54 Jolowicz-Nicholas, op. cit., p. 237; more fully, P.F. Girard, *Manuel élémentaire de Droit Romain* (8th edn, Paris, 1929), pp. 1018-9; P.E. Corbett, op. cit., pp. 182*ff.*

55 Cicero, *Top.*, 17, 66; *De Off.*, III, 15, 61; *Dig.*, IV, 5, 8.

56 [Quintilian], *Decl. Min.*, 251; 262.

57 Ib., 368; Seneca the elder, *Contr.*, II, 5; Quintilian, VII, 4, 37-8. In law, the *actio ingrati* concerns proceedings of a former master against an ungrateful freedman; cf. *Rom. Declam.*, p. 87.

58 Quintilian, VII, 4, 24 and 31.

59 Ib., 6, 1.

60 Cicero, *De Orat.*, I, 57, 244.

61 [Quintilian], *Decl. Min.*, 308.

62 Gaius, II, 144; Justinian, *Inst.*, II, 17, 2.

63 Gaius, loc. cit.; Lanfranchi op. cit., pp. 360*ff.*

64 On the whole subject of *verba/voluntas*, see now B. Vonglis, *La Lettre et l'Esprit de la Loi dans la jurisprudence classique et la rhétorique* (Paris, 1968).

65 [Quintilian], *Decl. Min.*, 340.

66 Suetonius, *De Rhet.*, 1, 'ex veritate ac re'.

67 Analogous to cases in which the praetor would grant his protection (*tuitio*); cf. *Rom. Declam.*, p. 19, with reff.

68 [Quintilian], *Decl. Min.* 341; Lanfranchi, op. cit., pp. 392*ff.*

69 Supported by Ulpian, *Dig.*, XXXIX, 4, 14, 'quod commissum est statim desinit eius esse qui crimen contraxit, dominiumque rei vectigali adquiritur'.

70 Gaius, II, 45, 49; Paul, *Dig.*, XLI, 3, 4, 6; Gellius, XVII, 7, 1; Mommsen, *Römisches Strafrecht*,

p. 756.

71 [Quintilian], *Decl. Min.*, 359.

72 S.J. De Laet, in his *Portorium* (Bruges, 1949), pp. 425*ff.*, accepts this and the previous declamations as valid evidence; cf. also Dar. Sag., s.v. 'portorium' (Cagnat).

73 De Laet, op. cit., p. 428.

74 Id., pp. 273*ff.*

75 Id., pp. 437*ff.*

76 Plutarch, *De Curios.*, 7; cf. Cicero, *De leg. agr.*, II, 23, 61; *In Vat.*, 5, 12; *Ad Q.F.*, I, 1, 33.

77 Plautus, *Trin.* 794-5.

78 Marcian., *Dig.*, XXXIX, 4, 16, 7.

79 Ib., 3.

80 Alfenus Varus, *Dig.*, L, 16, 203.

81 [Quintilian], *Decl. Min.*, 245, 361; cf. Lanfranchi, op. cit., pp. 297*ff.*

82 Id., ib., 336; Seneca the elder, *Contr.*, IX, 3; cf. Lanfranchi, pp. 316*ff.*, *Rom. Declam.*, p. p. 125.

83 [Quintilian], *Decl. Min.*, 320; cf. Lanfranchi, pp. 310*ff.*

84 Id., ib., 264; cf. Lanfranchi, pp. 354*ff.*

85 Seneca the elder, *Contr.*, III, 6; V, 5; [Quintilian], *Decl. Maior.*, XIII (the rich man who poisoned his poor neighbour's bees); *Decl. Min.*, 385; cf. Lanfranchi, pp. 320*ff.*, *Rom. Declam.*, pp. 116*ff.*

86 See Lanfranchi, pp. 334*ff.*

87 Seneca the elder, *Contr.*, IX, 3; [Quintilian&, *Decl. Min.*, 278, 338; 376; cf. Lanfranchi, pp. 268*ff.*, *Rom. Declam.*, pp. 125*ff.*

88 Ib., 275, 279.

89 Seneca the elder, *Contr.*, I, 4; IX, 1; [Quintilian], *Decl. Min.*, 244; 277; 284; cf. Lanfranchi, pp. 439*ff.*; *Rom. Declam.*, pp. 119*ff.*

90 *Decl. Min.*, 286.

91 Philostratus, *Vit. Soph.*, pp. 590, 619; [Quintilian], *Decl. Maior.*, X.

92 Petronius, *Sat.*, 1; Tacitus, *Dial.*, 35, 8 (with Gudeman's notes, pp. 462-3) Juvenal, VII, 150-4; 168-70.

93 Quintilian, II, 10, 2-4; 20, 4; cf. *Rom. Declam.*, pp. 80*ff.*

94 Id., II, 10, 5.

95 Id., X, 5, 14.

96 [Quintilian]., *Decl. Min.*, 338 (p. 331, 15*ff.* R.).

97 Quintilian, XI, 1, 82.

98 Id., VII, 4, 11.

99 Seneca the elder, *Contr.*, exc. VI, 7; VII, 6; X, 3; [Quintilian], *Decl. Min.*, 290, 295, 316, 349; cf. *Rom. Declam.*, pp. 93-4.

100 Seneca the elder, *Contr.*, II, 3, 13.

101 [Quintilian], *Decl. Min.*, 316 (p. 243, 7, R.); 349 (p. 373, 15, R.); 367 (p.402, 6, R.).

102 *Dig.*, XLVIII, 8, 3, 2; 19, 38, 5; cf. Mommsen, *Strafrecht*, p. 637.

103 [Quintilian], *Decl. Min.*, 246; cf. 350 (p. 378, 7*ff.* R.).

104 Id., 247.

105 Suetonius, *De Rhet.*, 1.

106 *Dig.*, XIX, 1, 11, 18.

107 Quintilian, II, 10, 3.

108 [Quintilian], *Decl. Min.*, 320.

109 Juvenal, VII, 155-7.

110 [Quintilian], *Decl. Min.*, 270 (p.102, 10, R.).

111 Ib., 271; 316; 326.

112 Ib., 314 (p. 232, 13, R.).

113 Ib., 254 (p. 44, 9, R.).

114 Ib., 315.

115 Ib., 309 (p. 217, R.); cf. 308 (p. 213, R.), on *verba* and *voluntas*.

116 Ib., 338; cf. translation in D.A. Russell and M. Winterbottom, *Ancient Literary Criticism* (Oxford, 1972), pp. 344*ff.*

117 Cf. *Rom. Declam.*, pp. 51-2.

118 Cf. Quintilian, II, 6, 3.

119 Juvenal, VII, 152-3 (taking *classis*, i.e. each boy, as subject).

120 Cf. Seneca the elder, *Suas.*, II, 10.

121 Quintilian, II, 6, 5-6.

122 Id., II, 11, 7.

123 Id., X, 5, 21-3.

124 [Quintilian], *Decl. Min.*, 260 (pp.

61-2, R.); 313 (p. 228, 4, R.); cf. *Rom. Declam.*, p. 52.

125 Quintilian, III, 8, 51.

126 Id., X, 1, 71.

127 Id., IV, 1, 46-7.

128 [Quintilian], *Decl. Min.*, 316 (p. 244, 23, R.).

129 Quintilian, IV, 1, 3-4.

130 Ib., 50; cf. *Decl. Min.* 338 (p. 331, 24*ff*. R.).

131 Id., VII, 2, 54-5, but see Cicero, *Pro Caelio*, 23, 57-8.

132 Quintilian, XII, 6, 5; Tacitus, *Dial*, 34, 3-4; cf. Seneca the elder, *Contr.*, IX, *Praef.*, 2 and 5.

133 Suetonius, *De Rhet.*, 6; Seneca the elder, *Contr.*, VII, *Praef.*, 6-8.

134 Seneca the elder, *Contr.*, III, *Praef.*, 12-14; IX, *Praef.*, 4-5.

135 Id., ib., IX, *Praef.*, 3; Quintilian, X, 5, 17-18.

136 Id., X, 1, 22-3; cf. Theon, 70, 7*ff*.

137 Id., X, 5, 19-20.

138 Seneca the elder, *Contr.*, III, *Praef.* 15-16.

139 F.P. Bremer, *Die Rechtslehrer und Rechtsschulen im römischen Kaizerzeit* (Berlin, 1868); Clyde Pharr in *C.J.*, XXXIV (1939), pp. 257*ff*.; F. Schulz, *History of Roman Legal Science* (Oxford, 1946), pp. 119*ff*.; cf. Sherwin-White on Pliny, *Epp.*, VII, 24, 8.

140 Quintilian, XII, 3; cf. ib., *Praef.* 3, 'a dicendi magistris dimissus'.

141 Cf. above, p. 88.

142 Cicero, *Pro Rosc. Am.*, 26, 72; *Orat.*, 30, 107; Quintilian, XII, 8, 3.

143 Cf. Quintilian, IV, 3, 2; Pliny, *Epp.*, II, 14.

144 Pliny, *Epp.*, VII, 4, 2.

145 Ib., VI, 6, 3; II, 14, 3.

146 Ib., III, 3, 5-7.

147 Ib., VI, 29, 4. On Pliny as advocate, cf. W. Menzies in *Juridical Review*, XXXVI (1924), pp. 197-217; as orator, G. Kennedy, *The Art of Rhetoric in the Roman World* (Princeton, 1972), pp. 526*ff*.

148 Ib., V, 8, 8; I, 18, 3; II, 14, 2.

149 Ib., VI, 2, 2; cf. IV, 12, 2; 16, 2. VI, 33; IX, 23.

150 Ib., VII, 6, 8.

151 Ib., IX, 13, 2.

152 Ib., VI, 29, 8-9; VII, 33 (Massa); III, 4 (Classicus); II, 11 (Marius).

153 Ib., IV, 9 (Bassus); V. 20 (Varenus).

Bibliography

Note: The reader will find some further works, relevant to particular topics, but not listed here, included in the Notes.

1. Education in antiquity

Barclay, W. *Educational Ideals in the Ancient World*, London, 1959.
Bowen, J. *A History of Western Education, I: The Ancient World*, London, 1972.
Boyd, W. *The History of Western Education* (7th edn), London, 1964.
Castle, E.B. *Ancient Education and Today*, Harmondsworth, 1961.
Clarke, M.L. *Higher Education in the Ancient World*, London, 1971.
Cubberley, E.P. *The History of Education*, Boston, 1920.
Dobson, J.F. *Ancient Education and its meaning to us*, London, 1932.
Grasberger, L. *Erziehung und Unterricht im klassischen Altertum*, 3 vols, Würzburg, 1864-81.
Krause, J.H. *Geschichte der Erziehung, des Unterrichts, und der Bildung bei den Griechen, Etruskern, und Römern*, Halle, 1851.
Lechner, M. *Erziehung und Bildung in der griechisch-römischen Antike*, Munich, 1933.
Marrou, H.-I. *Histoire de l'Éducation dans l'Antiquité*, Paris, 1948 (7th edn 1977). English trans. by G. Lamb, *A History of Education in Antiquity*, London, 1956. (The standard modern work.)
Smith, W.A. *Ancient Education*, New York, 1969.
Stadelmann, F. *Erziehung und Unterricht bei den Griechen und Römern*, Trieste, 1891.
Woody, T. *Life and Education in Early Societies*, New York, 1949.

2. Greek education

Beck, F.A.G. *Greek Education 450-350 BC*, London, 1964.
Beck, F.A.G. *Album of Greek Education*, Sydney, 1975.
Bowersock, G.W. *Greek Sophists in the Roman Empire*, Oxford, 1969.
Delorme, J. *Gymnasion*, Paris, 1960.
Forbes, C.A. *Greek Physical Education*, New York, London, 1929.
Freeman, J.J. *Schools of Hellas* (3rd edn), London, 1932.
Girard, P. *L'Éducation Athénienne* (2nd edn), Paris, 1891.
Jaeger, W. *Paideia: the ideals of Greek culture*, trans. from German by G. Highet, 3 vols, Oxford, 1946.
Jones, A.H.M. *The Greek City from Alexander to Justinian*, Oxford, 1940, c.xiv, 'Education'.
Nilsson, M.P. *Die hellenistische Schule*, Munich, 1955.
Pélékidis, C. *Histoire de l'Ephébie attique des origines à 31 avant J.-C*, Paris, 1963.
Rostovtzeff, M. *Social and Economic History of the Hellenistic World*, 3 vols, Oxford, 1941, c.viii.

Westaway, Kate W. *The Educational Theory of Plutarch*, London, 1922.
Ziebarth, E. *Aus dem grieschischen Schulwesen* (2nd edn), Leipzig/Berlin, 1914.

3. *Roman education* (*surveys*)

Blümner, H. *Die römische Privataltertümer*, Munich, 1911, pp. 299-340.
Eyre, J.J. 'Roman Education in the late Republic and early Empire', *Greece and Rome*, 2nd series, X (1963), pp. 47-59.
Gwynn, A. *Roman Education from Cicero to Quintilian*, Oxford, 1926.
Hulsebos, G.A. *De Educatione et Institutione apud Romanos*, Utrecht, 1875.
Jullien, E. *Les Professeurs de Littérature dans l'ancienne Rome*, Paris, 1885.
Kidd, D.A. *Roman Attitudes to Education*, Christchurch Classical Association, New Zealand, 1958.
Marquardt, J. *Das Privatleben der Römer* (2nd edn), rev. A. Mau, Leipzig, 1886, pp. 80-126.
Pottier, E. Article 'Educatio' (Rome) in Daremberg and Saglio, *Dictionnaire des Antiquités grecques et romaines*, Paris, 1881-1919.
Wilkins, A.S. *Roman Education*, Cambridge, 1905.

4. *Education in later antiquity*

Bechtel, E.A. 'Finger-counting among the Romans in the fourth century', *C.P.*, IV (1909), pp. 25-31.
Boissier, G. *La fin du paganisme*, 2 vols, Paris, 1891, i, pp. 171-231.
Bonner, S.F. 'The Edict of Gratian on the remuneration of teachers', *A.J.P.*, LXXXVI (1965), pp. 113-37.
Glück, M. *Priscians Partitiones and ihre Stellung in der spätantike Schule*, *Spudasmata* XII, Hildesheim, 1967.
Haarhoff, T.J. *Schools of Gaul*, Oxford, 1920, 2nd edn, Witwatersrand University Press, 1958.
Jones, A.H.M. *The Later Roman Empire*, 3 vols, Oxford, 1964, c.xxiv.
Lambert, G. *La grammaire latine selon les grammairiens du IV et du V siècle*, Dijon, 1908.
Marrou, H.-I. *Saint Augustin et la fin de la culture antique*, Paris, 1938.
Petit, P. *Les Etudiants de Libanius*, Paris, 1956.
Rauschen, G. *Das griechisch-römische Schulwesen zur Zeit des ausgehenden antiken Heidentums*, Programm, Bonn, 1900.
Roger, M. *L'enseignement des lettres classiques d'Ausone à Alcuin*, Paris, 1905.
Schemmel, F. 'Der Sophist Libanius als Schüler und Lehrer', *N.J. klass. Alt*, XX (1907), pp. 52-69.
Sickle, C.E. van 'Eumenius and the Schools of Autun', *A.J.P.*, LV (1934), pp. 236-43.
Stahl, W.M. *Martianus Capella and the Seven Liberal Arts*, I, *The Quadrivium*, New York, 1971.
Walden, J.W.H. *The Universities of Ancient Greece*, New York/London, 1912.
Wolf, P. *Vom Schulwesen der Spätantike, Studien zu Libanius*, Baden-Baden, 1952.

5. *Roman social and cultural background*

André, J.M. *O'Otium dans la vie morale et intellectuelle romaine des origines à l'époque augustéenne*, Paris, 1966.

Balsdon, J.P.V.D. *Life and Leisure in Ancient Rome*, London, 1969.

Barrow, R.H. *Slavery in the Roman Empire,* London, 1928.

Bergmann, A.A. *Zur Geschichte der socialen Stellung der Elementarlehrer und Grammatiker bei den Römern*, Diss., Leipzig, 1877.

Boulogne, R. *De Plaats van der Paedagogus in de romeinse Cultuur*, Diss., Groningen, 1951.

Bowersock, G.W. *Augustus and the Greek World*, Oxford, 1965, c.iii.

Boyd, C.E. *Public Libraries and Literary Culture in Ancient Rome*, Chicago, 1915.

Carcopino, J. *Daily Life in Ancient Rome*, trans. from French by E.O. Lorimer, with bibliography and notes by H.T. Rowell, London, 1941.

D'Alton, J.F. *Horace and his Age*, London, 1917.

Dill, S. *Roman Society from Nero to Marcus Aurelius* (2nd edn), London, 1905.

Duff, A.M. *Freedmen in the early Roman Empire*, Oxford, 1928.

Forbes, C.A. 'The Education and Training of Slaves in Antiquity', *T.A.Ph.A.*, LXXXVI (1955), pp. 321-60.

Frank, Tenney (ed.) *An Economic Survey of Ancient Rome*, Baltimore, 1933-40.

Friedländer, L. *Roman Life and Manners under the Early Empire*, 4 vols, trans. from German by L.A. Magnus and J.H. Freese, London, 1907.

Guillemin, A.-M. *Le Public et la Vie littéraire à Rome*, Paris, 1937.

Kroll, W. *Die Kultur der ciceronischen Zeit*, 2 vols, Leipzig, 1933.

Last, H. 'The Social Policy of Augustus', *C.A.H.*, X, c.xiv.

Mohler, S.L. 'Slave Education in the Roman Empire', *T.A.Ph.A.*, LXXI (1940), pp. 262-80.

Rech, H. *Mos Maiorum: Wesen und Wirkung der Tradition in Rom*, Diss., Marburg, 1936.

Rostovtzeff, M. *Social and Economic History of the Roman Empire*, 2 vols, rev. P.M. Fraser, Oxford, 1937.

Toynbee, A.J. *Hannibal's Legacy. The Hannibalic War's Effects on Roman Life*, 2 vols, Oxford, 1965.

Treggiari, Susan *Roman Freedmen during the late Republic*, Oxford, 1969.

Warde Fowler, W. *Social Life at Rome in the age of Cicero*, London, 1908, esp. c.vi, 'The Education of the Upper Classes'.

6. *State, municipalities, and education*

Abbott, F.F. and Johnson, A.C. *Municipal Administration in the Roman Empire*, Princeton, 1926.

Barbagallo, C. 'Stato, scuola, e politica in Roma repubblicana', *Rivista di Filologia*, XXXVIII (1910), pp. 481-514.

Barbagallo, C. *Lo Stato e l'Istruzione pubblica nell' Impero Romano*, Catania, 1911.

Hahn, L. 'Ueber das Verhältnis von Staat und Schule in der römischen Kaiserzeit', *Philologus*, LXXVI (1920), pp. 176-91.

Herzog, R. 'Urkunden zur Hochschulpolitik der römischen Kaiser', *Sitz. preuss. Akad.*, 1935, pp. 967-1019.

Mohler, S.L. 'The Iuvenes and Roman Education', *T.A.Ph.A.*, LXVIII (1937), pp. 442-79.

Schemmel, F. 'Das Athenaeum in Rom', *Woch. klass. Phil.*, XXXVI (1919), col. 91-5.

Schemmel, F. 'Das Athenaeum in Rom, II', *Phil. Woch.*, XLI (1921), col. 982-4.

Woodside, M. St. A. 'Vespasian's Patronage of Education and the Arts', *T.A.Ph.A.*, LXXIII (1942), pp. 123-9.

7. *Archaeological aspects*

Corte, M. della *Case ed Abitanti di Pompeii* (2nd edn), Rome, 1954.

Corte, M. della 'Le Iscrizioni Graffite della 'Basilica degli Argentari' sul Foro di Giulio Cesare', *Bulletino della Commissione Archaeologica comunale di Roma*, LXI (1933), pp. 111-30.

Jahn, O. 'Über Darstellungen des Handwerks und Handelsverkehrs auf antiken Waldgemälden', *Abhandlungen der sächsischen Gesellschaft der Wissenschaften*, V (1870), pp. 265-318.

Marrou, H.-I. MOYCIKOC ANHP. *Études sur les scènes de la vie intellectuelle figurant sur les monuments funéraires romains,* Grenoble, 1938.

Marrou, H.-I. 'La vie intellectuelle au Forum de Trajan et au Forum d'Auguste', *Mélanges d'Archéologie et d'Histoire*, LXIX (1932), pp. 93-110.

Mau, A. 'Sul significato della parola *pergula* nell' architettura antica', *Römische Mittheilungen*, II (1887), pp. 214-20.

Mau, A. and Kelsey, F.W. *Pompeii, its Life and Art*, New York, 1902.

Nissen, H. 'Metrische Inschriften aus Campanion, I. Grabschrift eines Schulmeisters von Capua', *Hermes*, I (1866), pp. 147-51.

Platner, S.B. and Ashby, T. *A Topographical Dictionary of Ancient Rome*, Oxford, 1929.

Wernicke, K. 'Lebenslauf eines Kindes in Sarkophag-Darstellungen', *Archäologische Zeitung*, XLIII (1885), col. 209-22.

Winter, F. *Die Typen der figürlichen Terrakotten*, 2 vols, Berlin/Stuttgart, 1903, ii, pp. 403*ff.*

Wissowa, G. 'Parodia d'una scena di scuola', *Römische Mittheilungen*, V (1890), pp. 3-11.

8. *Ancient books and their form*

Birt, T. *Das antike Buchwesen*, Berlin, 1882.

Birt, T. *Die Buchrolle in der Kunst*, Leipzig, 1907.

Esau, G. *Glossae ad rem librariam et institutionem scholasticam pertinentes*, Diss., Marburg, 1914.

Kenyon, F.G. *Books and Readers in ancient Greece and Rome*, Oxford, 1932.

Roberts, C.H. 'The Codex', *Proc. Brit. Acad.*, XL (1954), pp. 169-204.

Schubart, W. *Das Buch bei den Griechen und Römern* (3rd edn), Heidelberg, 1962.

Turner, E.G. *Greek Papyri, An Introduction*, Oxford, 1968.

9. *Teachers of 'grammar' and rhetoric*

Aistermann, J. *De M. Valerii Probi Berytii vita et scriptis*, Diss., Bonn, 1909.

Berndt, R. 'Cicero und der Grammatiker Nikias', *Phil. Woch.*, XXXV (1915), col. 955-60.

Bonner, S.F. 'Anecdoton Parisinum', *Hermes*, LXXXVIII (1960), pp. 354-60.

Bower, E.W. 'Some technical terms in Roman Education', *Hermes*, LXXXIX (1961), pp. 462-77.

Bryant, D.C. (ed.) *Ancient Greek and Roman Rhetoricians. A Biographical Dictionary*, New York, 1968.

Clarke, M.L. 'Quintilian, a biographical sketch', *Greece and Rome*, 2nd series, XIV (1967), pp. 24-37.

Graff, H. 'De Ateio Philologo, nobili grammatico Latino', *Mélanges Greco-Romains tirés de l'Academie Imperiale des Sciences de St. Petersburg*, vol. II, St Petersburg, 1866, pp. 274-320.

Hillscher, A. 'Hominum litteratorum Graecorum ante Tiberii mortem in urbe Roma commoratorum historica critica', *N.J. klass. Phil.*, *Supp.*, XVIII (1892), pp. 355-444.

Lewis, R.G. 'Pompeius' Freedman Biographer: Suetonius, *De Gramm. et Rhet.* 27 (3) *C.R.*, *N.S.*, XVI (1966), pp. 271-3.

Mentz, F. 'De L. Aelio Stilone', *Commentationes philologicae Ienenses*, IV (1890).

Müller, B.A. *De Asclepiade Myrleano*, Diss., Leipzig, 1903.

Planer, H. *De Tyrannione Grammatico*, Berlin, 1852.

Robinson, R.P. 'Valerius Cato', *T.A.Ph.A..*, LIV (1923), pp. 98-116.

Treggiari, S. 'Pompeius' Freedman Biographer again', *C.R., N.S.*, XIX (1969), pp. 264-6.
    See also esp. Schanz-Hosius, I, pp. 239*ff.*, 578*ff.*, II, 361*ff.*, 728*ff.*, and individual notices in P.-W., *R.E.*

10. *Theory and practice of teaching*

Bianca, G.G. *La Pedagogia di Quintiliano*, Padua, 1963.

Bonner, S.F. 'The Street-Teacher: an educational scene in Horace', *A.J.P.*, XCIII (1972), pp. 509-28.

Cameron, A.D.E. 'Roman School Fees', *C.R.*, *N.S.*, XV (1965), pp. 257-8.

Clarke, M.L. 'Three Notes on Roman Education', *C.P.*, LXIII (1968), pp. 42-4, 295-6.

Daly, L.W. 'Roman Study Abroad', *A.J.P.*, LXXI (1950), pp. 42-58.

Fuhrmann, M. *Das systematische Lehrbuch*, Göttingen, 1960.

Halkin, L. 'Le congé des Nundines dans les écoles romaines', *Revue Belge*, 1932, pp. 121-3.

Halkin, L. 'Sexta quaque die', *Les Études Classiques*, I (1932), pp. 117-23.

Nelson, H.L.W. *Ein Unterrichtsprogramm aus Neronischer Zeit*, Netherlands Academy, 1956.

Nybakken, O.E. 'Progressive Education in the Roman Empire', *C.J.*, XXXIV (1938/9), pp. 38-42.

Overbeck, J. 'Die Entdeckung des Kindes im I Jahrhundert n.Chr.', *N.J. klass. Alt.*, LIV (1924), pp. 1-8.

Parker, Enid R. 'The Education of Heirs in the Julio-Claudian Family', *A.J.P.*, LXVII (1946), pp. 29-50.

Pire, G. *Stoicisme et Pédagogie, de Zenon à Marc-Aurèle, de Sénèque à Montaigne et à J.-J. Rousseau*, Paris, 1958.

Robinson, R.P. 'The Roman Schoolteacher and his Reward', *C.W.*, 1921, pp. 57-61.

Saint-Denis, E. de 'Pline le Jeune et l'Education de la Jeunesse', *Revue Universitaire*, LV (1946), pp. 9-21.

Stinchcomb, J. 'The Two Younger Tullii', *C.J.*, XXVIII (1932/3), pp. 441-8.

11. *School-work from Graeco-Roman Egypt*

Barns, J.W.B. 'Literary texts from the Fayum', *C.Q.*, XLIII (1949), pp. 1*ff*.

Barns, J.W.B. 'A new Gnomologium: with some remarks on Gnomic Anthologies', *C.Q.*, XLIV (1950), pp. 126-37.

Beudel, P. *Qua ratione Graeci liberos docuerint, papyris, ostracis, tabulis in Aegypto inventis illustratur*, Diss., Münster, 1911.

Boak, A.E.R. 'Greek and Coptic School-tablets at the University of Michigan', *C.P.*, XVI (1921), pp. 189-94.

Brinkmann, A. 'Aus dem antiken Schulunterricht', *Rhein. Mus.*, LXV (1910), pp. 149-55.

Collart, P. 'A l'École avec les petits Grecs d'Egypte', *Chronique d'Égypte*, XI (1936), pp. 489-507.

Collart, P. *Les Papyrus Bouriant:* 1. *Cahier d'Écolier grec d'Égypte*, Paris, 1926.

Crusius, O. 'Aus antiken Schulbuchern', *Philologus*, LXIV (1905), pp. 142-6.

Guéraud, O. and Jouget, P. *Un Livre d'Écolier du IIIe Siècle avant J.-C.*, Cairo, 1938.

Hall, H.R. 'Greek Ostraca in the British Museum, including a Ptolemaic fragment of the *Phoenissae'*, *C.R.*, XVIII (1904), pp. 2-5.

Hesseling, D.C. 'On Waxen Tablets with Fables of Babrius (Tabulae Ceratae Assendelftianae)', *J.H.S.* XIII (1892/3), pp. 293-314.

Kenyon, F.G. 'Two Greek School-Tablets', *J.H.S.*, XXIX, (1909), pp. 29-40.

Milne, J.G. 'Relics of Graeco-Egyptian Schools', *J.H.S.*, XXVIII (1908), pp. 121-32.

Oldfather, W.A. *The Greek Literary Texts from Greco-Roman Egypt*, Madison, 1923, c.ii.

Pack, R.A. *The Greek and Latin Literary Texts from Greco-Roman Egypt* (2nd edn), Michigan, 1965.

Painter, K. 'Greek and Roman Wooden Writing Tablets in the British Museum', *British Museum Quarterly*, XXXI (1966/7), pp. 103-10.

Parsons, P.J. 'A School-Book from the Sayce Collection', *Zeitschrift für Papyrologie und Eipgraphik*, VI (1970), pp. 133-49.

Préaux, C. 'Lettres privées grecques d'Égypte relatives a l'éducation', *Revue Belge de Philologie*, VIII (1929), pp. 757-800.

Wessely, C. 'Einige Reste griechischer Schulbücher', *Studien zur Paläographie und Papyruskunde*, II (1902), pp. XLII-LVIII.

Zalateo, G. 'Papiri Scholastici', *Aegyptus*, XLI (1961), pp. 161-248.

Ziebarth, E. *Aus der antiken Schule* (2nd edn), Bonn, 1913.

12. *General education*

Appel, B. *Das Bildungs- und Erziehungsideal Quintilians nach der Institutio Oratoria*, Donauworth, 1914.

Barwick, K. 'Das rednerische Bildungsideal Ciceros', *Abhandlungen der sächsischen Akademie der Wissenschaften zu Leipzig, phil. -hist. Klasse*, LIV, 3; Berlin Academy, 1963.

Colson, F.H. 'Philo on Education', *Journal of Theological Studies*, 1917, pp. 151-62

Kühnert, F. *Allgemeinbildung und Fachbildung in der Antike*, Berlin Academy, 1961.

Nagl. A. 'Die Rechentafel der Alten' *Sitz. Wien. Akad.*, CLXXVII (1914).

Peter, H. *Die geschichtliche Literatur über die römische Kaiserzeit*, Leipzig, 1897, c.i. 'Die Geschichte in der Jugendbildung'.

Pullan, J.M. *The History of the Abacus*, London, 1968.
Schulte, H.K. *Orator. Untersuchungen über das Ciceronische Bildungsideal*, Frankfurt, 1935.
Thomson, J.O. *History of Ancient Geography*, Cambridge, 1948.
Weinhold, H. *Die Astronomie in der antiken Schule*, Diss., Munich, 1912.
Wille, G. *Musica Romana. Die Bedeutung der Musik im Leben der Römer*, Amsterdam, 1967.

13. *The study of grammar*

(i) *Ancient sources*

T. = Text, *C.* = Commentary, *Tr.* = Translation)
Dionysius Thrax *T.* G. Uhlig, Leipzig, 1883 Scholia *T.* A. Hilgard, Leipzig, 1901.
Grammatici Latini *T.* H. Keil, Leipzig, 1857-70.
Grammaticae Romanae Fragmenta. *T.* H. Funaioli, Leipzig, 1907.
Grammaticae Romanae Fragmenta Aetatis Caesareae. *T.* A. Mazzarino, Turin, 1955.
Quintilian Book I, *T.* and *C.* F.H. Colson, Cambridge, 1924; partial *T.* and *C.* F. Pini, *Quintiliano, Capitoli Grammaticali*, Rome, 1966.
Varro *De Lingua Latina, T.* and *Tr.*, with notes, R.G. Kent, 2 vols, Loeb.

(ii) *Modern works*

Allen, W.S. *Vox Graeca: A Guide to the Pronunciation of Classical Greek*, Cambridge, 1968.
Allen, W.S. *Vox Latina: A Guide to the Pronunciation of Classical Latin*, Cambridge, 1965.
Barwick, K. *Remmius Palaemon und die römische Ars Grammatica*, Leipzig, 1922.
Barwick, K. *Probleme der Stoischen Sprachlehre und Rhetorik*, Berlin, 1957.
Brambach, W. *Die Neugestaltung der lateinischen Orthographie*, Leipzig, 1868.
Casa, A. della *Il Dubius Sermo di Plinio*, Genoa, 1969.
Collart, J. *Varron Grammairien Latin*, Paris, 1954.
Colson, F.H. 'The grammatical chapters in Quintilian, I, 4-8', *C.Q.*, VIII (1914), pp. 33-47.
Colson, F.H. 'Some problems in the grammatical chapters of Quintilian', *C.Q.*, X (1916), pp. 17-31.
Corte, F. della *La Filologia latina dalle origini a Varrone*, Turin, 1937.
Dahlmann, H. 'Caesars Schrift über die Analogie', *Rh.M.*, LXXXIV (1935), pp. 258-75.
Dahlmann, H. *Varro und die hellenistiche Sprachtheorie*, Berlin, 1932.
Flock, G. *De Graecorum Interpunctionibus*, Diss., Greifswald, 1908.
Fritz, K. von 'Ancient instruction in "Grammar" according to Quintilian', *A.J.P.*, LXX (1949), pp. 337-66.
Heinecke, B. *De Quintiliani Sextii Asclepiadis arte grammatica*, Diss., Strassburg, 1903.
Hendrickson, G.L. 'The *De Analogia* of Julius Caesar, its occasion, nature, and date', *C.P.*, I (1906), pp. 97-120.
Lindsay, W.M. *The Latin Language*, Oxford, 1894.
Palmer, L.R. *The Latin Language*, London, 1954.
Postgate, J.P. *A Short Guide to the Accentuation of Ancient Greek*, Liverpool, 1924.
Raven, D.S. *Greek Metre, An Introduction*, London, 1968.
Raven, D.S. *Latin Metre, An Introduction*, London, 1965.

Robins, R.H. *Ancient and Mediaeval Grammatical Theory in Europe*, London, 1951.

Robins, R.H. 'Dionysius Thrax and the Western Grammatical Tradition', *T.A.Ph.A.*, LXXXVIII, 1957, pp. 67-106.

Stanford, W.B. *The Sound of Greek*, Berkeley/Cambridge, 1967.

Siebenborn, E. *Die Lehre von der Sprachrichtigkeit und ihre Kriterien: Studien zur antiken normativen Grammatik*, Amsterdam, 1975.

Steinthal, H. *Geschichte der Sprachwissenschaft bei den Griechen und Römern* (2nd edn), 2 vols, Berlin, 1890.

Sturtevant, E.H. *The Pronunciation of Greek and Latin* (2nd edn), Philadelphia, 1940.

14. *The study of literature*

(i) *Ancient sources*

Demetrius, *On Style*. *T.*, *Tr.* and *C.* W. Rhys Roberts, Cambridge, 1902; G.M.A. Grube, Toronto, 1961. *T.* and *Tr.*, with notes, W. Rhys Roberts (Loeb).

Dionysius of Halicarnassus, *De Compositione Verborum*. *T.* H. Usener and L. Radermacher in *Opuscula*, vol. 2 (Teubner). *T.*, *Tr.* and *C.* W. Rhys Roberts, London, 1910.

Donatus, *Commentum Terenti*, *T.* P. Wessner (2 vols, Teubner); H.T. Karsten, 2 vols, Leiden, 1912.

Horace, *Ars Poetica*. *T.* and *C.* C.O. Brink, Cambridge, 1971.

Menander, *Sententiae*. *T.* S. Jaekel (Teubner).

Plutarch, *Quomodo adulescens poetas audire debeat*. *T.* and *Tr.* F.C. Babbitt (Loeb).

[Plutarch], *De vita et poesi Homeri*. *T.* G. Bernardakis (Teubner).

Priscian, *Partitiones XII Versuum Aeneidos*. *T.* H. Keil, *G.L.*, II, 404*ff*. See also 4 above, s.v. Glück, M.

Quintilian, Books VIII and IX. *T.* L. Radermacher (vol. 2, Teubner); M. Winterbottom (vol.2, O.C.T.). *T.* and *Tr.* H.E. Butler (vol. 3, Loeb).

Scholia Graeca in Homeri Iliadem. *T.* H. Erbse, Berlin 1969-; Selections: *T.* W. Deecke, *Auswahl aus den Iliasscholien*, Bonn, 1912.

Scholia Graeca in Homeri Odysseam. *T.* G. Dindorf, 2 vols, Oxford, 1855.

Scholia in Euripidem. *T.* E. Schwartz, 2 vols, Berlin, 1887-1901.

Servius, *In Vergilii Carmina Commentarii*. *T.* G. Thilo-H. Hagen, Leipzig, 1881.

Suetonius, *De Grammaticis et Rhetoribus*. *T.* G. Brugnoli (Teubner). *T.* and *C.* R.P. Robinson, Paris, 1925; F. della Corte (3rd edn), Turin, 1968.

(ii) *Modern works*

Bachmann, W. *Die ästhetischen Anschauungen Aristarchs in der Exegese und Kritik der homerischen Gedichte*, Diss., Nürnberg, 2 parts, 1902 and 1904.

Berchem, D. van 'Poètes et grammairiens. Recherche sur la tradition scolaire d'explication des auteurs', *Museum Helveticum*, IX (1952), pp. 75-87.

Collart, P. 'Les papyrus de l'Iliade et de l'Odyssée', *R. Phil.*, XIII (1939), pp.289-307.

Collart, P. 'Les fragments des tragiques grecs sur papyrus', *R. Phil.*, XVI (1943), pp. 5-36.

D'Alton, J.F. *Roman Literary Theory and Criticism*, London, 1931.

Degenhardt, C. *De veterum grammaticorum scholis*, Diss., Münster, 1905.

Dorn, M. *De veteribus grammaticis artis Terentianae iudicibus*, Diss., Halle, 1906.

Friedländer, L. *De historiarum enarratione in ludis grammaticis*, Index Lectionum, Königsberg, 1874.

Funke, H. 'Euripides', *Jahrbüch für das Antike und Christentum*, VIII/IX (1965/6), pp. 233*ff*.

Georgii, H. *Die antike Äneiskritik aus den Scholien und anderen Quellen*, Stuttgart, 1891.

Grube, G.M.A. *The Greek and Roman Critics*, London, 1965.

Kroll, W. *Studien zum Verständnis der römischen Literatur*, Stuttgart, 1924.

Kroll, W. ' Ἐν ἤθει ', *Philologus*, LXXV (1918), pp. 68-76.

Lehrs, K. *De Aristarchi studiis Homericis* (3rd edn), Leipzig, 1882.

Moore, J.L. 'Servius on the tropes and figures of Vergil', *A.J.P.*, XII (1891), pp. 157-92.

Pfeiffer, R. *History of Classical Scholarship from the Beginnings to the End of the Hellenistic Age*, Oxford, 1968.

Rutherford, W.G. *A Chapter in the History of Annotation, being Scholia Aristophanica Vol. III*, London, 1905.

Sandys, J.E. *History of Classical Scholarship*, 3 vols, Cambridge, 1908-21, vol. I.

Schenkeveld, D.M. 'Ariostarchus and "ΟΜΗΡΟΣ ΦΙΛΟΤΕΧΝΟΣ", *Mnemosyne*, XXXIII (1970), pp. 162-78.

Stanford, W.B. *Greek Metaphor*, Oxford, 1936.

Thomas, E. *Essai sur Servius et son Commentaire sur Virgile*, Paris, 1880.

Trooz, C. de 'La critique de Virgile dans les Commentaires de Servius', *Musée Belge*, XXXII (1929), pp. 229-61.

Verdenius, W.J. *Homer, the Educator of the Greeks*, Amsterdam, 1970.

Vergeest, A. *Poetarum Enarratio: Leraren en Schoolauteurs te Rome*, Diss., Breda, 1950.

15. *Ancient rhetoric and Roman oratory*

(i) *Ancient sources*

Aristotle, *Rhetoric*. *T*. A. Roemer (Teubner); W.D. Ross (O.C.T.). *T*. and *Tr*. J.H. Freese (Loeb). *T*. and *C*. L. Spengel, Leipzig, 1867; E.M. Cope — J.E. Sandys, 3 vols, Cambridge, 1877.

Cicero, *De Inventione, T*. E. Stroebel (Teubner). *T*. and *Tr*. H.M. Hubbell (Loeb). *De Oratore, T*. A.S. Wilkins (O.C.T.); K.F. Kumaniecki (Teubner). *T*. and *Tr*. E.W. Sutton — H. Rackham (Loeb); E. Courbaud — H. Bornecque (Budé). *T*. and *C*. K.W. Piderit-O. Harnecker (6th edn) Leipzig, 1886; A.S. Wilkins, Oxford 1892. *Brutus. T*. A.S. Wilkins (O.C.T.); H. Malcovati (Teubner). *T*. and *Tr*. G.L. Henrickson (Loeb); J. Martha (Budé). *T*. and *C*. O. Jahn — W. Kroll, 6th edn. by B. Kytzler, Berlin, 1962: A.E. Douglas, Oxford, 1966. *Orator. T*. A.S. Wilkins, (O.C.T.); *T*. and *Tr*. H.M. Hubbell (Loeb); H. Bornecque (Budé). *T*. and *C*. J.E. Sandys, Cambridge, 1885; W. Kroll, Berlin, 1913. *Partitiones Oratoriae* and *Topica*. *T*. A.S. Wilkins (O.C.T.). *T*. and *Tr*. H. Rackham (Loeb); H. Bornecque (Budé).

Dionysius of Halicarnassus. *Opuscula. T*. H. Usener — L. Radermacher (Teubner). *T*. and *Tr*. S. Usher (Loeb, in progress). *Literary Letters. T., Tr.* and *C*. W. Rhys Roberts, Cambridge, 1901. *De Thucydide. T., Tr.* and *C*. G. Pavano, Palermo, 1958; *Tr.* and *C*. W. Kenrick Pritchett, Berkeley, 1975. See also s.v. 14, i.

Hermagoras. *T.* D. Matthes (Teubner).

Hermogenes. *T.* H. Rabe (Teubner).

Libanius. *T.* R. Foerster (Teubner). *Selected Works. T.* and *Tr.* A.F. Norman (Loeb). *Oration* I. *T., Tr.* and *C.* A.F. Norman, Oxford, 1965.

Oratorum Romanorum Fragmenta. *T.* H. Malcovati (2nd edn), Turin 1955.

Philodemus, *Volumina Rhetorica. T.* S. Sudhaus (Teubner).

Quintilian. *T.* L. Radermacher (Teubner); M. Winterbottom (O.C.T.). *T.* and *Tr.* H.E. Butler (Loeb); J. Cousin (Budé) in progress). *T.* and *C.* Book III, J. Adamietz, Munich. 1966; Book X, W. Peterson, Oxford, 1891; Book XII, R.G. Austin, Oxford, 1948, rpd 1965. See also s.v. 13, i, and 14, i; *Selections. Tr.* W.M. Smail, Oxford 1938.

Rhetorica ad Alexandrum, *T.* L. Spentel — C. Hammer (Teubner). *T.* and *Tr.* H. Rackham (Loeb). *Tr.* E.S. Forster (Oxford *Tr.* of Aristotle, xi).

Rhetorica ad Herennium. *T.* F. Marx — W. Trillitzsch (Teubner). *T.* with Prolegomena and Index, F. Marx, Leipzig, 1894. *T.* and *Tr.* with notes, H. Caplan (Loeb). *T.* and *C.* G. Calboli, Bologna, 1969.

Rhetores Graeci. *T.* C. Walz, Tubingen, 1832-49; L. Spengel, Leipzig, 1853.

Rhetores Latini minores. *T.* C. Halm, Leipzig, 1863.

Rutilius Lupus. *T.* and *C.* E. Brooks Jr., *Mnemosyne, Supp.* XI, 1970.

Seneca the Elder. *T.* A. Kiessling (Teubner); H.J. Müller, Vienna, 1887. *T.* and *Tr.* with notes, M. Winterbottom (Loeb); H. Bornecque, Paris, 1932. *Suasoriae, T.* and *C.* W.A. Edward, Cambridge, 1928.

Tacitus, *Dialogus de Oratoribus. T.* W. Peterson, rev. M. Winterbottom (O.C.T.), *T.* and *Tr.* W. Peterson (Loeb); H. Goelzer — H. Bornecque (Budé). *T* and *C.* A. Gudeman (2nd edn), Leipzig/Berlin, 1914; A. Michel, Paris, 1962.

(ii) *Modern works*

Arnim, H. von *Leben und Werke des Dio von Prusa*, Berlin, 1898, c.i.

Boissier, G. 'Introduction de la rhétorique grecque à Rome', *Mélanges G. Perrot*, Paris, 1903, pp. 13-16.

Bonner, S.F. 'Roman Oratory' in *Fifty Years of Classical Scholarship*, ed. M. Platnauer, Oxford, 1954, pp. 335-83, rpd in *Fifty Years (and Twelve) of Classical Scholarship*, Oxford 1968.

Bonner, S.F. *Roman Declamation in the late Republic and early Empire*, Liverpool, 1949, rpd 1969.

Bonner, S.F. 'Lucan and the Declamation Schools', *A.J.P.*, LXXXVII (1966), pp. 257-89.

Bornecque, H. *Les Declamations at les Déclamateurs d'après Sénèque le Père*, Lille, 1902.

Burgess, T.C. *Epideictic Literature*. Chicago, 1902.

Caplan, H. *Of Eloquence, Studies in Ancient and Mediaeval Rhetoric*, Ithaca, N.Y. 1970.

Clark, D.L. *Rhetoric in Greco-Roman Education*, New Yori, 1957.

Clarke, M.L. *Rhetoric at Rome, A Historical Survey*, London, 1953.

Clarke, M.L. 'The thesis in the Roman rhetorical schools of the Republic', *C.Q.*, *N.S.* I (1951), pp. 159-66.

Colson, F.H. 'Quintilian, I, 9, and the Chria in ancient education', *C.R.*, XXXV (1921), pp. 150-54.

Cousin, J. *Études sur Quintilien*, 2 vols, Paris, 1935/6.

Cucheval, V. *Histoire de l'éloquence romaine depuis la mort de Cicéron*, 2 vols, Paris, 1893.

Deratani, N. 'De rhetorum Romanorum declamationibus', *R. Phil.*, LI (1923) pp. 101-17.

Deratani, N. 'Le réalisme dans les declamationes', *R. Phil.*, LV (1929), pp.184-9.
Dorey, T.A. (ed.) *Cicero (Studies in Latin Literature and its Influence)*, London, 1964.
Gelzer, M. 'Die angebliche politische Tendenz in der dem C. Herennius gewidmeten Rhetorik', *Kleine Schriften*, I, Wiesbaden, 1962, pp. 211-21.
Grube, G.M.A. 'Theodorus of Gadara', *A.J.P.*, LXXX (1959), pp. 337-65.
Grube, G.M.A. 'Educational, rhetorical, and literary theory in Cicero', *Phoenix*, XI (1962), pp. 234-57.
Haury, A. *L'Ironie et l'Humeur chez Cicéron*, Leiden, 1955.
Jenkinson, Edna M. 'Further studies in the curriculum of the Roman schools of rhetoric in the Republican period', *Symbolae Osloenses,* XXXI (1955), pp. 122-30.
Kennedy, G. *The Art of Persuasion in Greece*, London, 1963.
Kennedy, G. *The Art of Rhetoric in the Roman World*, Princeton, 1972.
Kennedy, G. *Quintilian,* New York, 1969.
Kohl, R. *De scholasticarum declamationum argumentis ex historia petitis*, Diss., Paderborn, 1915.
Kröhnert, R. *Die Anfänge der Rhetorik bei den Römern*, Programm, Memel, 1877.
Kroll, W. 'Cicero und Die Rhetorik', *N.J. klass. Alt.*, XI (1903), pp. 681-9.
Kroll, W. 'Rhetorica, VI, Die πραγματικὴ στάσις des Hermagoras', *Philologus*, XCI (1936), pp. 197-205.
Kroll, W. 'Rhetorik', P.-W., *R.E.*, Suppl. VII, col. 1089*ff*.
Krumbacher, A. *Die Stimmbildung der Redner im Altertum*, (*Rhetorische Studien*, 10), Paderborn, 1921.
Lana, I. *Quintiliano, il 'Sublime', e gli 'Esercizi Preparatori' de Elio Teone*, Turin, 1951.
Laughton, E. 'Cicero and the Greek Orators', *A.J.P.*, LXXXII (1961) pp. 27-49.
Laurand, L. *Études sur le style des discours de Cicéron*, Paris, 1928.
Lausberg, H. *Handbuch der literarischen Rhetorik* (2nd edn), Munich 1973.
Leeman, A.D. *Orationis Ratio*, 2 vols, Amsterdam, 1963.
Leo, F. 'Quintilians kleine Declamationen', *Ausgewählte Kleine Schriften*, ed. E. Fraenkel, Rome, 1960, I, pp. 249-61.
McCall, M.H. *Ancient Rhetorical Theories of Simile and Comparison,* Harvard, 1969.
Martin, J. *Antike Rhetorik, Technik und Methode*, in Iwan von Müller's *Handbucher der Altertumswissenschaft*, Munich, 1974.
Matthes, D. 'Hermogoras von Temnos, 1904-1955', *Lustrum*, III, Göttingen, 1959.
Michel, A. *Rhétorique et Philosophie chez Cicéron*, Paris, 1960.
Neuhauser, W. *Patronus und Orator*, Innsbruck, 1958.
Neumeister, C. *Grundsätze der forensischen Rhetorik gezeigt an Gerichtsreden Ciceros*, Munich, 1964.
Norden, E. *Die Antike Kunstprosa* (3rd edn), 2 vols, Berlin/Leipzig, 1915.
North, Helen 'The use of poetry in the training of the ancient orator', *Traditio*, VIII (1952), pp.1-33.
Perl, G. 'Die Stellung der Latini Rhetores innerhalb der römischen Rhetorik', *Acta Antiqua Philippopolitana, Studia Historica et Philologica*, Sofia, 1963.
Pichon, R. 'L'Affaire des Rhetores Latini', *Revue des Études Anciennes*, 1904, pp.37-41.
Reichel, G. *Quaestiones Progymnasmaticae*, Diss., Leipzig, 1909.
Ritter, G. *Die Quintilianischen Declamationem*, Freiburg i.B./Tubingen, 1881.

Robinson, R.P. '*Ethologia* or *Aetiologia* in Suetonius, *De Grammaticis* c.4 and Quintilian, I,9' *C.P.* XV (1920), pp. 370*ff*.

Schlittenbauer, S. *Die Tendenz von Cieros Orator*, Diss., Leipzig, 1903.

Schmid, W. *Über die klassische Theorie und Praxis des antiken Prosarhythmus*, Wiesbaden, 1959.

Schottlaender, R. 'Der römische Redner und sein Publikum', *Wiener Studien*, LXXX (1967), pp. 125-46.

Sihler, E.G. 'ΘΕΤΙΚΩΤΕΡΟΝ'. Cicero ad Quintum fratrem III, 3, 4', *A.J.P.*, XXIII (1902), pp. 283-94.

Solmsen, F. 'Aristotle and Cicero on the orator's playing upon the feelings', *C.P.*, XXXIII (1938), pp. 390-404.

Solmsen, F. 'The Aristotelian tradition in ancient rhetoric', *A.J.P.*, LXII (1941), pp. 35-50, 169-90.

Stroux, J. *De Theophrasti virtutibus dicendi*, Leipzig, 1912.

Sumner, G.V. *The Orators in Cicero's Brutus. Prosopography and Chronology*, Toronto, 1973.

Throm, H. *Die Thesis. Ein Beitrag zu ihrer Entstehung und Geschichte, Rhetorische Studien* 17, Paderborn, 1932.

Volkmann, R. *Die Rhetorik der Griechen und Römer* (2nd edn), Leipzig, 1885.

Wartensleben, G. von *Begriff der griechische Chreia und Beiträge zur Geschichte ihrer Form*, Heidelberg, 1901.

Weidner, R. *Ciceros Verhältnis zur griechisch-römischen Schulrhetorik seiner Zeit*, Diss., Erlangen, 1925.

Wilamowitz-Moellendorf, U. von 'Asianismus und Attizismus', *Hermes*, XXXV (1900), pp. 1-52.

Winterbottom, M. 'Quintilian and the *Vir Bonus*', *J.R.S.*, LIV (1964), pp. 90-97.

16. *Roman advocacy and law*

Bremer, F.P. *Die Rechtslehrer und Rechtsschulen im römischen Kaiserzeit*, Berlin, 1868.

Buckland, W.W. *Textbook of Roman Law from Augustus to Justinian*, Cambridge, 1932.

Ciulei, G. *L'Équité chez Cicéron*, Amsterdam, 1972.

Corbett, P.E. *The Roman Law of Marriage*, Oxford, 1930.

Crook, J.A. *Law and Life of Rome*, London, 1967.

Crook, J.A. '*Patria Potestas*', *C.Q.*, *N.S.* XVII (1967), pp. 113-22.

Düll, R. 'Iudicium domesticum, abdicatio und apokeryxis', *Z.S.S.*, LXIII (1943), pp. 54-116.

Girard, P.F. *Manuel élémentaire de droit romain* (8th edn), Paris, 1929.

Jolowicz, H.F. and Nicholas, B. *Historical Introduction to the study of Roman Law* (3rd edn), Cambridge, 1972.

Kelly, J.M., *Studies in the Civil Judicature of the Roman Republic* (Oxford, 1976).

Kennedy, G. 'The rhetoric advocacy in Greece and Rome', *A.J.P.*, LXXXIX (1968), pp. 419-36.

Lanfranchi, F. *Il diritto nei retori Romani*, Milan, 1938.

Menzes, W. 'Pliny and the Roman Bar under Trajan', *Juridical Review*, XXXVI (1924), pp. 197-217.

Mommsen, T. *Römisches Strafrecht*, Leipzig, 1899.

Parks, E.P. *The Roman Rhetorical Schools as a preparation for the Courts under the early Empire*, Baltimore, 1945.

Pharr, C. 'Roman Legal Education', *C.J.*, XXXIV (1939), pp. 257-70.

Renier, E. *Étude sur l'histoire de la Querela Inofficiosi en droit romain*, Liège, N.D. (1942).

Santa Cruz, J. 'Der Einfluss der rhetorische Theorie der Status auf die römische Jurisprudenz', *Z.S.S.*, LXXV (1958), pp. 91-115.

Schulz, F. *History of Roman Legal Science*, Oxford, 1946.

Stroux, J. *Römische Rechtswissenschaft und Rhetorik*, Potsdam, 1949.

Vonglis, B. *La lettre et l'esprit de la loi dans la jurisprudence classique et la rhétorique*, Paris, 1968.

Watson, W.A.J. 'The Divorce of Carvilius Ruga', *Tijdschrift voor Rechtsgeschiedenis*, XXXIII (1965), pp. 38-50.

Watson, W.A.J. *Roman Private Law around 200 B.C.*, Edinburgh University Press, 1971.

Index